3rd Edition

Technical Writing
for Success

Darlene Smith-Worthington
Sue Jefferson

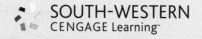
SOUTH-WESTERN
CENGAGE Learning

Australia • Brazil • Japan • Korea • Mexico • Singapore • Spain • United Kingdom • United States

SOUTH-WESTERN
CENGAGE Learning™

Annotated Instructor's Edition

Technical Writing for Success, 3e
Smith-Worthington/Jefferson

Vice President of Editorial, Business:
  Jack W. Calhoun

Vice President/Editor-in-Chief: Karen Schmohe

Senior Developmental Editor: Penny Shank

Consulting Editor: Marianne Miller

Editorial Assistant: Anne Kelly

Associate Marketing Manager: Linda Kuper

Content Project Management: PrePress PMG

Media Editor: Sally Nieman

Senior Manufacturing Coordinator: Kevin Kluck

Copyeditor: Daniel Nighting

Senior Art Director: Tippy McIntosh

Internal Designer: Joe Sherman

Cover Designer: Lou Ann Thesing

Cover Image: ©James Endicott/Stock
  Illustration Source

Photo Researcher: Darren Wright

For product information and technology assistance, contact us at
Cengage Learning Customer & Sales Support, 1-800-354-9706

For permission to use material from this text or product,
submit all requests online at **www.cengage.com/permissions**
Further permissions questions can be emailed to
permissionrequest@cengage.com

Exam*View*® is a registered trademark of eInstruction Corp. Windows is a registered trademark of the Microsoft Corporation used herein under license. Macintosh and Power Macintosh are registered trademarks of Apple Computer, Inc. used herein under license.

© 2008 Cengage Learning. All Rights Reserved.

Library of Congress Control Number: 2009944006

Student Edition ISBN-13: 978-0-538-45048-5

Student Edition ISBN-10: 0-538-45048-7

Annotated Instructor's Edition ISBN 13: 978-0-538-45057-7

Annotated Instructor's Edition ISBN 10: 0-538-45057-6

South-Western Cengage Learning
5191 Natorp Boulevard
Mason, OH 45040
USA

Cengage Learning products are represented in Canada by Nelson Education, Ltd.

For your course and learning solutions, visit **www.cengage.com/school**

Printed in the United States of America
1 2 3 4 5 6 7 13 12 11 10

Contents

An Applied Approach to Workplace Writing!

Welcome to *Technical Writing for Success 3e.* This text is lively and relevant for students and easy to use and effective for instructors. Using a learn-by-doing approach, skills are introduced and applied so that mastering technical writing is relevant and exciting.

GETTING STARTED

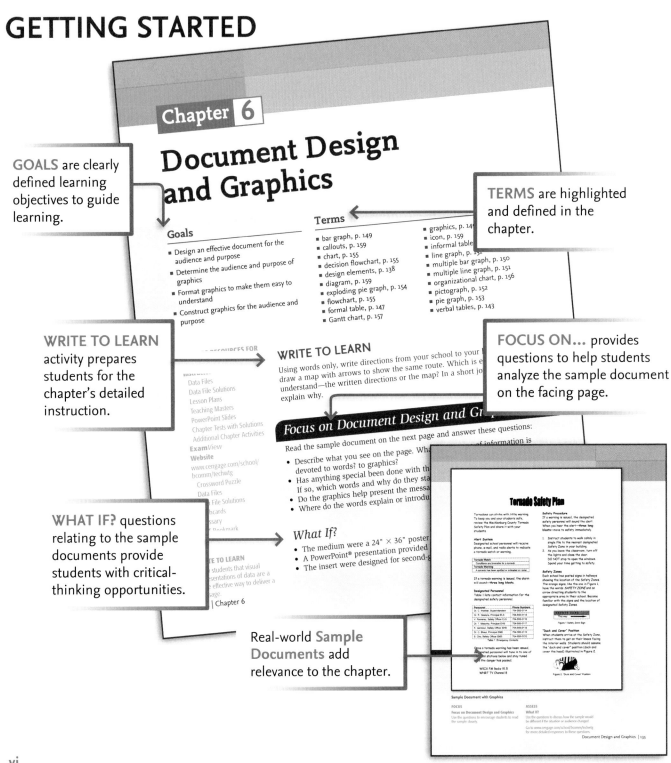

GOALS are clearly defined learning objectives to guide learning.

TERMS are highlighted and defined in the chapter.

WRITE TO LEARN activity prepares students for the chapter's detailed instruction.

FOCUS ON... provides questions to help students analyze the sample document on the facing page.

WHAT IF? questions relating to the sample documents provide students with critical-thinking opportunities.

Real-world **Sample Documents** add relevance to the chapter.

Chapter 6
Document Design and Graphics

Goals

- Design an effective document for the audience and purpose
- Determine the audience and purpose of graphics
- Format graphics to make them easy to understand
- Construct graphics for the audience and purpose

Terms

- bar graph, p. 149
- callouts, p. 159
- chart, p. 155
- decision flowchart, p. 155
- design elements, p. 138
- diagram, p. 159
- exploding pie graph, p. 154
- flowchart, p. 155
- formal table, p. 147
- Gantt chart, p. 157
- graphics, p. 14
- icon, p. 159
- informal table
- line graph, p. 15
- multiple bar graph, p. 150
- multiple line graph, p. 151
- organizational chart, p. 156
- pictograph, p. 152
- pie graph, p. 153
- verbal tables, p. 143

WRITE TO LEARN

Using words only, write directions from your school to your draw a map with arrows to show the same route. Which is e understand—the written directions or the map? In a short jo explain why.

Focus on Document Design and G

Read the sample document on the next page and answer these questions:

- Describe what you see on the page. Wh of information is devoted to words? to graphics?
- Has anything special been done with th If so, which words and why do they sta
- Do the graphics help present the messa
- Where do the words explain or introdu

What If?

- The medium were a 24" × 36" poster
- A PowerPoint® presentation provided
- The insert were designed for second-g

RESOURCES FOR

Data Files
Data File Solutions
Lesson Plans
Teaching Masters
PowerPoint Slides
Chapter Tests with Solutions
Additional Chapter Activities
*Exam*View
Website
www.cengage.com/school/
bcomm/techwtg
Crossword Puzzle
Data Files
File Solutions
hcards
ssary
Bookmark

RITE TO LEARN
students that visual
sentations of data are a
effective way to deliver a
age.
| Chapter 6

Tornado Safety Plan

Sample Document with Graphics

FOCUS
Focus on Document Design and Graphics
Use the questions to encourage students to read the sample closely.

ASSESS
What If?
Use the questions to discuss how the sample would be different if the situation or audience changed.

Go to www.cengage.com/school/bcomm/techwtg for more detailed responses to these questions.

Document Design and Graphics | 135

A LOOK INTO THE REAL WORLD OF TECHNICAL WRITING

The following are sample pages shown:

Writing@Work (page 136, Chapter 6)

Aidan Grey is a freelance graphic designer in Denver, Colorado, and former Director of Photography for Home&Abroad (H&A), a travel planning website. He has 13 years of graphics expertise, including contracting with photographers, publishing images in print and on the Web, and designing logos.

Aidan believes that a picture is worth a thousand words, but not necessarily in English. "There's a different kind of eloquence in graphics because we get to use many additional 'languages' simultaneously—color, texture, composition, line, light. Red is one 'word' and says one kind of thing, while blue is another and says other things." In other words, it's important to be sensitive to the "linguistics" and semiology (signs and symbols) of images.

The various constraints that Aidan considers when working with graphics include content, color, licensing and copyright, cost, lighting, size, and composition. He judges which constraints to prioritize on a project-by-project basis, but always gives credit when using others' work: "You're never going to get in trouble for crediting someone properly."

Knowing when images hurt your content is as important as knowing when they enhance it. "Images are not helpful when they are too busy and when they contradict the desired message," cautions Aidan. For example, "If your report is about why the company is not meeting goals, images of smiling, happy people can send a decidedly wrong message." Images should enhance and complement the message of the text they accompany.

Aidan's graphic design work requires him to use communication skills along with his graphics virtuosity. At H&A, for example, he wrote contracts, form letters, manuals, and e-mail messages and even translated documents into other languages for investors.

APPLY

Writing @ Work
Use this feature to show the importance of graphics in the workplace.

Think Critically
1. Answers may include color, shape, line, and light.
2. Answers can promote worthwhile discussion about the various messages graphics can convey.

Think Critically
1. With a partner, select a photograph in this book to analyze. Individually, jot down some notes about the "languages" the photo uses.
2. Compare notes with your partner. Does the photograph "say" more than you thought at first? Explain.

Printed with permission of Aidan Grey

136 | Chapter 6

WRITING @ WORK addresses the 16 Career Clusters and demonstrates various career options while showcasing people who use technical writing in their careers.

CAREER CLUSTERS

The U.S. Department of Education has grouped careers into 16 different clusters based on similar job characteristics.

The value:

- Allows students to explore a wide range of career opportunities from entry level through management and professional levels

- Provides an easy solution to implementing careers into any class

---

Writing@Work (page 78, Chapter 4)

Andrew Yoder has been a book production editor for Rowman & Littlefield Publishers in Lanham, Maryland, for nine years. He shepherds books through copyediting, proofreading, indexing, cover production, and finally manufacturing. Most of his technical communication involves e-mailing authors, freelancers, and in-house colleagues. He also is a book author and freelance writer and editor.

To begin a writing project, Andrew first gathers all of the resources he needs into one electronic file, organizes the contents of the file into smaller themed sections, and then finds the best section with which to start. "I'll occasionally read the quotes [in the file] and try to think about different angles and sections while doing mind-numbing tasks like mowing my yard."

Recently, Andrew talked with his fellow Rowman & Littlefield editors about how they approach writing. Each editor takes a different approach: "One colleague said she writes out a very detailed outline that serves as a draft replacement. Another coworker said that she doesn't draft; she just writes. That's me. Any revising that I do is more like copyediting than working from a draft."

Authors should not be afraid of the copy editor's red pen. After Andrew sends one of his own completed manuscripts to his copy editor, he hopes to receive a great many questions and corrections that will improve the book. "Some authors are offended when someone edits their work or asks questions, but I'd rather have a copy editor find mistakes in my work than have a reader find them." Furthermore, says Andrew, "The biggest enemy of revising or editing material is a large ego."

APPLY

Writing @ Work
Use this feature to illustrate the writing process for Andrew.

Think Critically
1. Answers will vary, but students must learn to correct their own work because school is preparation for the work world.
2. People are different—they think differently, their experiences are different, they process language differently, and they have different levels of education.

Think Critically
1. How would your instructors react if you had outside copy editors correct your work before you turned it in? Why is writing at school different from writing on the job?
2. Look at the section in this chapter "Writing Is Different for Everyone" on page 80. Why do different people use different approaches to writing assignments?

Printed with permission of Andrew Yoder

78 | Chapter 4

TWO NEW CHAPTERS

WRITING FOR THE WEB discusses blogs, FAQs, and home pages and provides information on organizing, designing, and writing web pages.

Chapter 7

Writing for the Web

Goals

- Plan web pages
- Organize and design web pages
- Write text for web pages
- Write text for special kinds of web pages

Terms

- animation, p. 172
- blog, p. 179
- demographics, p. 169
- discussion forum, p. 182
- FAQ, p. 180
- home page, p. 168
- hyperlink, p. 170
- interactive, p. 167
- Internet, p. 167
- keywords, p. 177
- RSS, p. 180
- scannable, p. 176
- usability, p. 172
- Web Accessibility Initiative (WAI), p. 173
- wiki, p. 181
- World Wide Web, p. 167

TEACHING RESOURCES FOR CHAPTER 7

Instructor's Resource CD
Data Files
Data File Solutions
Lesson Plans
Teaching Masters
PowerPoint Slides
Chapter Tests with Solutions
Additional Chapter Activities
Exam*View*
Website
www.cengage.com/school/
bcomm/techwtg
Crossword Puzzle
Data Files
Data File Solutions
Flashcards
Glossary
NET Bookmark
Sample Documents
Web Links
WRITE TO LEARN
Help students see how the Internet has changed the world. Compare the changes to the way the printing press, telegraph, telephone, radio,

WRITE TO LEARN

Think about all of the ways you use the Internet. Then try to imagine your life without the Internet. What would it be like? Write a short journal entry describing how your life would be different if there were no Internet.

Focus on Writing for the Web

Read the sample document on the next page and answer these questions:

- What is the reason for the site?
- Describe the color scheme. How does it make you feel?
- Does the page look balanced? Why or why not?
- What information is on the page? Is it easy to find? Explain.
- If you were a newcomer to the site, which part would you visit? If you had visited the site before, which part might you revisit?
- What combination of text and graphics do you see?

What If?

- The site provided FAFSA forms for different majors or different schools?
- The site provided a survey to determine eligibility for financial aid?
- An upcoming deadline was given for submission of FAFSA forms?
- The site highlighted college graduates who had used financial aid?
- The site hosted its own discussion forum?

Chapter 15

Ethics in the Workplace

Goals

- Explain what it means to act ethically
- Describe a culture of ethics
- Develop a plan for resolving an ethical dilemma
- Understand the barriers to ethical behavior

Terms

- code of ethics, p. 369
- corporate code of ethics, p. 369
- dignity, p. 375
- ethics, p. 365
- personal code of ethics, p. 370
- principles, p. 365
- rights, p. 375
- utility, p. 375
- values, p. 365
- whistle-blower, p. 377

TEACHING RESOURCES FOR CHAPTER 15

Instructor's Resource CD
Data Files
Data File Solutions
Lesson Plans
Teaching Masters
PowerPoint Slides
Chapter Tests with Solutions
Additional Chapter Activities
Exam*View*
Website
www.cengage.com/school/
bcomm/techwtg
Crossword Puzzle
Data Files
Data File Solutions
Flashcards
Glossary
NET Bookmark
Sample Documents
Web Links
WRITE TO LEARN
By thinking about a person they admire, students begin to identify the values and behavior they would like to emulate. Ask students to share their descriptions.

WRITE TO LEARN

Think of someone you admire and respect, someone you want to be like—a parent, friend, teacher, or political or entertainment figure. W particular, has this person done to earn your respect? If you were to person what values—for example, honesty, hard work, and courage important, what would he or she say? Write a journal entry describ person and naming some of his or her accomplishments. Summarize identifying which values are important to this individual.

Focus on the Ethics in the Workplace

Read the ethical principles on the next page and answer these questions:

- Why does the Society for Technical Communication (STC) list the six core values in this order?
- What are five things technical communicators can do to practice honesty?
- How can technical communicators maintain professionalism?
- Why do the principles include confidentiality?

What If?

- The principles were being explained to students considering a career as a technical communicator?
- Technical communicators needed STC guidelines for writing blogs and text for web pages?
- A banking or finance industry wanted to use similar principles?

ETHICS IN THE WORKPLACE includes information about ethical conduct, develops a plan for resolving an ethical dilemma, and discusses barriers to ethical behavior.

SPECIAL FEATURES ENHANCE LEARNING

Communication Dilemma

Marcus and Sophia are chemists conducting experiments for Wuxi Pharmaceuticals on how bacteria ward off viral invaders. They just left the lab to attend a retirement reception for the head of maintenance, a highly respected and well-liked man responsible for keeping the lab facilities running during power outages and holidays. Nearly everyone has come to wish him well. Marcus and Sophia are carrying on a lively conversation, excited about something that happened in the lab that day. They enter the reception area and settle into a corner with Uma, the public relations officer, and Drew, the new webmaster, who is looking uncomfortable in such a large group. During the presentation, Marcus and Sophia continue to talk quietly about the CRISPR-based immunity and RNA interference in higher organisms, ignoring everything that is taking place around them. Marcus sees Uma looking at him with a puzzled look.

Think Critically

Why do you think Uma [...] Marcus and Sophia?

COMMUNICATION DILEMMA provides real-world communication situations.

Focus on Ethics

Claudia is setting up a website for her floral business, Claudia's Creations. She is in a hurry to get the site up and running. She wants to show some of the sprays, wedding bouquets, and dish gardens she has created, but she cannot find the pictures she took of them. So she searches the Web and finds designs that she likes on two websites: Floral Fantasia and Flowers by Chenda. Claudia decides to use some of the designs from those sites on her own website until she finds her misplaced pictures or takes new ones.

Think Critically

What might happen if Claudia's customers discover that she used flower designs from other sites?

FOCUS ON ETHICS provides examples and scenarios of real-world ethical dilemmas for students to consider.

COMMUNICATION TECHNOLOGIES

An RSS (Rich Site Summary or Really Simple Syndication) is a feed or format that regularly updates web content. Just as a single [...] program is syndicated and sent to [...]wers, an RSS is syndicated, too, and [...] any readers. Subscribers receive [...] new content for the sites in their [...] example, a health feed on Google [...]vides a summary of current articles [...]alth. Search engines and news [...]nize RSS links by content area (for [...] Top Stories, Middle East, Business, and Entertainment).

Think Critically

What is the benefit of subscribing to an RSS?

COMMUNICATION TECHNOLOGIES contains helpful information about current workplace technologies.

⬢ STOP AND THINK

Discuss the importance of technical writing in the workplace. How can writing affect your chances for advancement?

STOP AND THINK allows students to check comprehension before moving to the next section.

NETBookmark

To find current articles about all aspects of technical communication, including web design and web writing, go to the NET Bookmark for Chapter 7.

Search the articles, looking for advice about blogging, FAQs, wikis, or discussion forums. Print one article, read it, and summarize it. Share your summary in an oral presentation to your classmates.

www.cengage.com/school/bcomm/techwtg

NET BOOKMARK provides chapter-related activities for students to complete using information found on the Internet.

Warm Up

How do you read a novel? How do you read a website? Do you read both in the same way, or do you read [...]tly? Explain.

WARM UP activities provide scenarios and questions to encourage students to start thinking ahead.

ABUNDANT END-OF-CHAPTER ASSESSMENT

The assessments found at the end of every chapter give students the opportunity to test their knowledge.

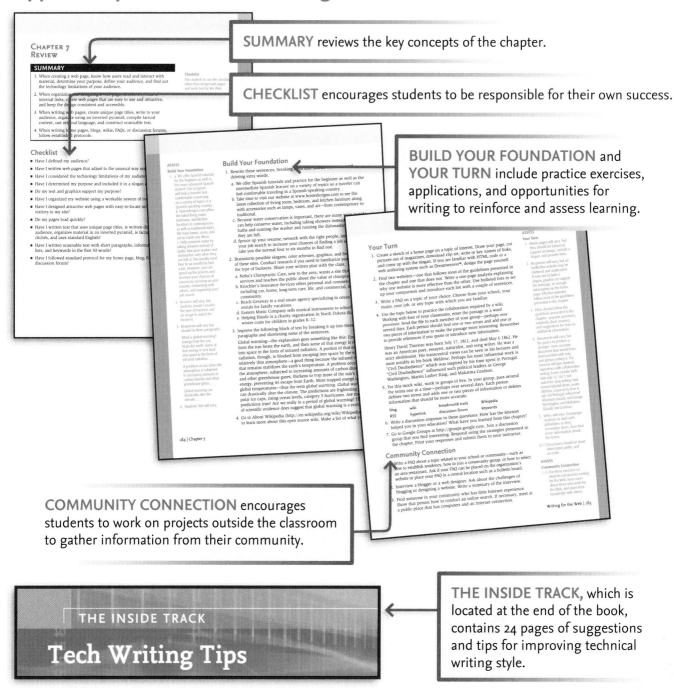

SUMMARY reviews the key concepts of the chapter.

CHECKLIST encourages students to be responsible for their own success.

BUILD YOUR FOUNDATION and YOUR TURN include practice exercises, applications, and opportunities for writing to reinforce and assess learning.

COMMUNITY CONNECTION encourages students to work on projects outside the classroom to gather information from their community.

THE INSIDE TRACK, which is located at the end of the book, contains 24 pages of suggestions and tips for improving technical writing style.

THE INSIDE TRACK

Tech Writing Tips

VISIT WWW.CENGAGE.COM/SCHOOL/BCOMM/TECHWTG
This interactive site provides an array of teaching and learning tools to assist you in getting the most from your course.

About the Authors

Darlene Smith-Worthington and Sue Jefferson are full-time teachers who are enthusiastic and earnest supporters of education that prepares people for the world of work. Darlene Smith-Worthington is a community college instructor who also has experience editing a weekly newspaper; directing public relations for a junior college; and managing small businesses, including a farming operation. Sue Jefferson's business experience includes managing a restaurant and editing copy for a weekly magazine. Early in her teaching career, she taught grades 7–12. Currently, she chairs the English and Humanities Department at Pitt Community College, where she teaches mythology, critical thinking, and technical writing classes.

Both authors have taught technical communication for more than 25 years. Using their business backgrounds and their combined 50 years' teaching experience, the authors present real-world-based reporting materials and sensible, useful teaching suggestions.

REVIEWERS

Sara A. Baker
Career and Technology Instructor
Anna High School
Anna, Texas

Sheri Carder
Marketing and Management
   Professor
Lake City Community College
Lake City, Florida

Hilary Hall
English and Humanities
   Adjunct Instructor
Central Carolina Community
   College
Sanford, North Carolina

Mark Hall
Humanities Instructor
Central Carolina Community
   College
Sanford, North Carolina

Linda Hoff
Curriculum Supervisor
Century Career Center
Logansport, Indiana

Amy Jauman
Field Training and
   Development Manager
Regis Corporation
Minneapolis, Minnesota

Becky Kammeyer
Business and Marketing
   Teacher and Coordinator
Mississinewa High School
Gas City, Indiana

Amy J. Major, NBCT
Department Chair and
   English Teacher
Roanoke Rapids High School
Roanoke Rapids, North Carolina

Linda O'Connor
Communication Specialist
Las Vegas, Nevada

Phyllis Porche
Instructor
Fox College
Bedford Park, Illinois

Christine Sandusky
English Teacher
Elk River High School
Elk River, Minnesota

Candace Schiffer, M.A.
Business, Computer,
   Information, and Technology
   Administrator and Lecturer
Mercyhurst College
Erie, Pennsylvania

Kevin Weeks
Business Education Teacher
   and Department Chair
Battle Ground High School
Battle Ground, Washington

Mary Whited
English and Business Education
   Teacher
Anacortes High School
Anacortes, Washington

Chapter 1

What Is Technical Writing?

Goals

- Define technical writing and its importance in the workplace
- Identify the characteristics of technical writing
- Compare and contrast technical writing to other types of writing

Terms

- academic writing, p. 15
- ambiguous, p. 16
- expository writing, p. 11
- expressive writing, p. 11
- field research, p. 11
- imaginative writing, p. 16
- inferences, p. 16
- jargon, p. 12
- persuasive writing, p. 15
- style, p. 12
- technical communication, p. 7
- technical writing, p. 7
- tone, p. 13

TEACHING RESOURCES FOR CHAPTER 1

Instructor's Resource CD
Data Files
Data File Solutions
Lesson Plans
Teaching Masters
PowerPoint Slides
Chapter Tests with Solutions
Additional Chapter Activities

Exam*View*

Website
www.cengage.com/school/bcomm/techwtg
Crossword Puzzle
Data Files
Data File Solutions
Flashcards
Glossary
NET Bookmark
Sample Documents
Web Links

WRITE TO LEARN
Help students realize that they are most comfortable with the kinds of writing that are most familiar to them, such as academic writing and writing for self-expression. Some students may realize that they already have experience with technical communication (e.g., computer manuals and directions for a science lab), but many students may not be able to verbalize an accurate definition of *technical communication.*

WRITE TO LEARN

Think about the many types of writing you do—for example, writing for school, on your job, in a diary or journal for self-expression, or to family and friends. With what kind of writing are you most comfortable? What kind of writing do you find most difficult or most uncomfortable? Of the writing you do, which would you consider to be technical writing? How would you define the term *technical communication?*

Focus on Technical Writing

Read the sample writing excerpts on pages 3–5 and answer these questions about each document:

- What is the subject?
- For whom was the document written?
- How is the document organized?
- How would you describe the writer's (or writers') style?
- What is the tone of the document?
- Does the document include any special features (for example, boldfacing, numbering, bulleted lists, visual aids, headings, or subheadings)?

Mitral Valve Prolapse: What You Should Know

What is the mitral valve?

The mitral valve controls the flow of blood between 2 chambers (or "rooms") of your heart called the left atrium and the left ventricle. Normally, blood flows in one direction only, from the atrium to the ventricle. When the heart relaxes in between beats, the 2 flaps of the mitral valve swing open to let blood flow from the atrium to the ventricle. The flaps normally open only one way. (See Figure 1 and 2 below.)

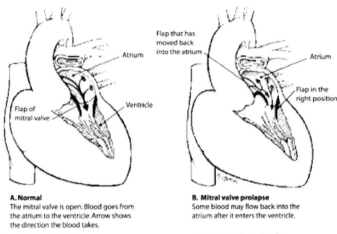

A. Normal
The mitral valve is open. Blood goes from the atrium to the ventricle. Arrow shows the direction the blood takes.

Figure 1. Normal Valve

B. Mitral valve prolapse
Some blood may flow back into the atrium after it enters the ventricle.

Figure 2. Prolapsed Valve

How do I know that I have mitral valve prolapse?

Here are some of the possible symptoms of mitral valve prolapse:

Racing heart rate   Skipped heart beats
Chest pain that comes and goes   Shortness of breath
Dizziness   Anxiety or panic

Your doctor can find mitral valve prolapse during a regular exam. When listening to your heart with a stethoscope, your doctor may hear a clicking sound. The flap makes the click. If blood is flowing back into the atrium, your doctor will hear a "whooshing" sound. This sound is called a murmur.

Sample Technical Document Excerpt

FOCUS

Focus on Technical Writing
Use the questions to encourage students to read the sample closely.

ASSESS

What If?
Use the questions to discuss how the sample would be different if the situation or audience changed.

Go to www.cengage.com/bcomm/school/techwtg for more detailed responses to these questions.

Jackie K. Bloomberg

Professor Kellogg

HSC 2132

December 3, 20—

Advantages of Porcine Valves in Heart Valve Replacement Surgery

Surgical techniques and materials for heart valve replacement surgery, pioneered in the 1950s, have constantly improved since then. One of the improvements for some patients involves the use of porcine, or pig, valves, rather than mechanical or man-made valves. While mechanical valves are long-lasting, patients who receive them must forever take anti-coagulant medications to prevent clots forming on the mechanical valve; such a clot could cause a heart attack or stroke (Gillinov). In addition, patients on anti-coagulants must be closely monitored by their physicians. For people living in remote areas or areas with limited physician coverage, close monitoring may be impossible. Furthermore, women with plans of childbearing should not be treated with anti-coagulants ("Valve Surgery Options"). Thus, the use of porcine valves in mitral valve replacement is best for many patients.

Porcine valves offer one important advantage over mechanical valves, a decreased threat of blood clots. Regardless of their exact characteristics, bioprostheses or live tissue replacement parts are unlikely to lead to the formation of blood clots after they have been in place for more than a few months. The body tends to cover these valves with a thin layer of its own cells, effectively walling off the prosthetic valve from the body's blood-clotting cells. As a result, most patients with a bioprosthesis can stop using blood thinners a few months after surgery ("Living").

Works Cited

Gillinov, Marc A., et al. "Valve Surgery—Past, Present, and Future." *Cleveland Clinic Miller Family Heart & Vascular Institute.* Web. 18 Mar. 2009.

"Living with an Artificial Valve." *Harvard Heart Letter.* 4.11 (July 1994): 4+. *MasterFILE Premier.* Web. 8 Apr. 2009.

"Valve Surgery Options." Women's Heart Foundation. Web. 6 Apr. 2009.

Sample Research Paper Excerpt

My Broken Heart

By Jessica S. Stuart

My big brother Danny was my hero. He was the one I rant to with skinned knees, the one I talked to about boys, and the only person I would let call me Nellie. I looked up to him. But the night of my Senior Sports Banquet, things changed. My hero fell.

Danny didn't show up for the banquet. He had promised to be there, to share my "moment." After all, he had taught me how to throw the knuckle ball that had helped our team win the Regional Softball Championship. I kept looking for him. He must be held up in traffic, I told my friends, or maybe he had a flat tire. I picked up several awards that night—including Most Valuable Player—but I would have preferred to have seen my brother walk through the door. Instead, Danny never showed up.

In fact, Danny hadn't shown up for much of anything my senior year—holidays, birthdays, anniversaries. He spent most of his time getting high—marijuana at first, then other drugs. When we did see him, he was incoherent or mean, hounding my mom for money or stealing it out of her purse.

I held tight to my trophy and fought back the tears—until I got home. Staring at the pictures of us on my nightstand, I cried all night for my big brother Danny, an addict. Today I'm sorry for him, but I'm sorry for me too. There's a big hole in my heart where Danny, my hero, used to be.

Sample Personal Essay Excerpt

Writing@Work

Courtesy of Mark Overbay

Mark Overbay manages marketing and communications for Counter Culture Coffee, a Durham, North Carolina–based specialty coffee organization. His many responsibilities include producing product copy, white papers, advertisements, packaging copy, online content, thematic signage, and tradeshow displays.

Agriculture, Food & Natural Resources

"Marketing is a form of storytelling," says Mark, who believes that marketing copy must be "short and sweet." "You only have a few words or phrases to 'hook' your readers, whether they are journalists reading a press release or grocery shoppers glancing at the coffee bags on a shelf. Good marketing copy must tell an interesting, sometimes even romantic story, but it should never be long-winded."

Mark's biggest technical writing challenge involves presentation and style: "Developing a Counter Culture Coffee 'voice' that authentically represents our company and all that we do is the most difficult aspect of my professional writing. When I write for our online news section or blog, I can write as Mark Overbay; but most of my professional writing is in the voice of Counter Culture Coffee, which represents not just me, but more than 40 staff members and hundreds of partnering coffee farmers."

Mark relies heavily on e-mail. "E-mail, for all its limitations and sterility, is invaluable in my professional life. Not only does it allow for structured written communication and instant delivery, but it also provides a permanent record of every e-conversation."

Mark advises aspiring technical writers to hone three skills in particular: (1) work ethic to constantly improve their writing; (2) preparation and care for each assignment because ". . . every word and detail matters. Successful communicators take the time to research their subjects thoroughly"; and (3) clarity because "successful communicators keep things simple—not dumbed down—and to the point. Be clear, concise, and confident in your message."

Think Critically

1. Search for the Counter Culture Coffee website and sample some of the writing. Does the writing tell stories, as Mark claims? Do you hear a distinctive "voice" in the writing? Explain.

2. What is a white paper? Research the origin of this term. What are some topics about which Mark might write papers?

Printed with permission of Mark Overbay

YOU ARE A TECHNICAL WRITER!

Have you ever given someone written directions or drawn a map to your home? Have you ever written brief instructions for how to use a fax machine at work? Have you ever told someone how to make French toast? If you answered yes to any of those questions or have had similar experiences, you have already engaged in technical writing or technical communication.

Definition of Technical Writing

Candace, an award-winning saxophonist, began teaching saxophone lessons to sixth graders. For the first lesson, she drew a diagram of an alto sax and created a step-by-step guide explaining how to take the instrument apart and reassemble it. When she saw how easily students could follow her instructions, she was pleased that her words were helping them learn to do something she enjoyed.

Candace might have been surprised to learn that she was using technical communication. **Technical communication** is communication done in the workplace. The message usually involves a technical subject with a specific purpose and audience. The approach is straightforward. Candace was giving practical information to a specific audience—information that would enable her audience to take action. When she referred to the diagram and explained the procedure aloud to her students, she was using technical communication. When she wrote the instructions to accompany her diagram, she was using technical writing. **Technical writing** is writing done in the workplace, although the workplace may be an office, a construction site, or a kitchen table. The subject is usually technical, written carefully for a specific audience. The organization is predictable and apparent, the style is concise, and the tone is objective and businesslike. Special features may include visual elements to enhance the message.

Warm Up

Think about a profession in which you are interested. What kinds of documents would you write in this profession?

FOCUS

Warm Up

Use the Warm Up to help students view themselves as writers on the job, to show how relevant technical writing is to their future, and to create enthusiasm for technical writing.

Use the *You Are a Technical Writer* worksheet as a guide to brainstorm the types of technical writing you already know. Go to www.cengage.com/school/bcomm/techwtg. Click the link for Chapter 1; then click Data Files.

TEACH

Use this section to reduce the apprehension some students may feel about technical writing. Technical writing can be fun and challenging because it covers a variety of subjects.

ksalt/iStockphoto.com

Technical documents can range from a half-page memo announcing the winner of a sales competition to a 500-page research grant proposal requesting money to test a new drug for treating obesity. The term *technical writing* describes documents produced in areas such as business, science, social science, engineering, and education. Sales catalogs, business letters, financial reports, standard operating procedures, medical research studies, lab reports—all of these and more are examples of technical writing.

Technical Writing Is Essential in the Workplace

Written communication is essential in the workplace for many reasons. It allows readers to read and study at their convenience, easily pass along information to others, and keep a permanent record for future reference.

Regardless of the career you choose, you will write in the workplace. According to Paul V. Anderson in *Technical Communication: A Reader-Centered Approach,* conservative estimates suggest that you will spend at least 20 percent of your time writing in a technical or business occupation. Professionals in engineering and technology careers spend as much as 40 percent of their time writing.

In today's business environment, employees can easily be overwhelmed by information overload, with information competing for their attention from every direction—television, radio, newspapers, magazines, books, e-mail, the Internet, CD-ROMs, and DVDs. Because of information overload, you must be able to read documents quickly and efficiently, understand them the first time you read them, and know that the information is accurate. Up-to-date information provides companies with a competitive edge, speeding critical decision making and allowing job specialization.

Good writers understand that they will not always know who is reading their writing (especially e-mail) or how their writing will be used.

TEACH

Demonstrate the importance of technical writing in the workplace by having students think of professions that may *not* use writing. Then have students work in groups to brainstorm ways these professions *do* use technical writing. Use this activity to show that nearly all professions require communication skills, even if most of the writing involves forms or graphics.

ENRICH

To identify how people use technical writing on the job, invite several people from business and industry to visit and describe the writing they do at work. Invite representatives from a variety of professions. Before your guests arrive, ask students to prepare questions specifically about communication that they can ask the guests.

jhorrocks/iStockphoto.com

Technical writers who help companies manage the information overload are vital resources. They understand that their readers must be able to skim or skip text and find important information quickly. As a professional in great demand, the technical writer faces a challenging, exciting, and rewarding future.

Different careers generate different kinds of reports: Nurses chart a patient's medical condition so that the next shift's nurses can continue patient care. Police accident reports record facts for later use in court. Chemists and engineers document procedures to comply with government regulations. Accountants prepare annual client reports. Sales representatives write sales proposals. Professors write grant proposals. Park rangers write safety precautions. Insurance claims adjusters write incident reports. Travel agents design brochures. Public relations officers write news releases, letters, and speeches.

When you write, you demonstrate your ability to analyze, solve problems, and understand technical processes. For example, Matheus Cardoso, personnel director for Osgood Textile Industries, impresses his supervisor and earns his colleagues' respect when his proposal for tax-deferred retirement plans is approved. On the other hand, the drafting crew at Stillman Manufacturing is frustrated with Jeff Danelli's instructions for installing wireless computing at the industrial site. The crew must redraft plans because Jeff's instructions are vague and incomplete. When writing is not clear, the thinking behind the writing may not be clear either.

All careers rely on technical communication to get the job done. Technical writing is the great connector—the written link—connecting technology to user, professional to client, colleague to colleague, supervisor to employee, and individual to community. No matter what career you choose, you can expect to read and compose e-mail, send accompanying attachments, give and receive phone messages, and explain procedures.

©Borodaev, 2009/Used under license from Shutterstock.com

TEACH

Have students review the types of technical communication that Sergeant Hardy uses. Then ask students to collaborate on additional items that could appear on the list or have them compile a list of their own uses of technical communication.

ONGOING ASSESSMENT

Stop and Think

Bring in examples of ineffective writing that you have saved from students in a previous class (delete names and identifying information) or that you find on the Internet. Ask students whether they would hire the person who wrote each document. Ask students whether they would like to work collaboratively on a project with these writers. Discuss students' reasons.

Tell students that the quality of their writing affects their chances for advancement because when they write, they demonstrate their ability to analyze, solve problems, respond to an audience's needs, and understand technical processes.

ftwitty/iStockphoto.com

In addition to work-related writing, the responsibilities of being a community and family member require technical communication. The following list shows how Sergeant Thomas Hardy of the Palmer City Police Department, father of two and concerned citizen, uses technical communication on the job and at home.

- **Colleagues:** e-mail, collaborative incident reports
- **Boy Scout den parents:** fund-raiser announcements, directions to jamboree
- **Victims:** incident reports, investigative reports
- **Legislators:** letter and e-mail in favor of clean-air regulations
- **Lawyers, court officials:** depositions, testimonies, statements (possibly televised)
- **State FBI office:** letter of application and resume to advance career
- **Community members:** safety presentation at the local high school
- **Supervisees:** employee regulations, letters of reference, training procedures
- **Local newspaper editor:** letter thanking community for its help with jamboree, press release announcing purchase of state-of-the-art police car

 STOP AND THINK

Discuss the importance of technical writing in the workplace. How can writing affect your chances for advancement?

CHARACTERISTICS OF TECHNICAL WRITING

While technical writing shares some characteristics with other kinds of writing, it is also significantly different. From the factual treatment of the subject to audience considerations, technical writing is unique. Subject, audience, organization, style, tone, and special features all contribute to the description of writing that is appropriate for the workplace.

Subject

The subject of each model at the beginning of this chapter is hearts, but the approach is different in each document. The personal essay expresses a young person's disappointment and frustration at the behavior of a sibling, an experience with which you might be able to identify. **Expressive writing** is created to convey personal observations or feelings. It relies on personal experience for research. Expressive writing is likely to be the type with which you are most familiar.

sjlocke/iStockphoto.com

The purpose of the research paper is not to relate personal experience, but to explain facts gained from research. Writing to explain or inform is **expository writing.** Like expressive writing, your academic career has probably required that you do some research writing. The excerpt from the research paper at the beginning of the chapter involves the pros and cons of using tissue from pigs for heart valve replacement in humans. While most academic research papers are factual papers written on topics that are interesting to the reader, the technical research document is written to fulfill a need.

In technical writing, often the need is to share information or to have someone perform an action. For example, a person may need to have heart surgery. Therefore, the technical document fulfills the special needs of a specific reader. The writer of the technical document on page 4 targets cardiac patients and explains the disease and its diagnosis. Technical writing may require library research, scientific observation, or **field research** (research done in the field, especially through surveys and interviews). Whether to inform or persuade, technical writing relies on data presented with precision and accuracy.

Warm Up

Review the three documents at the beginning of the chapter (pages 3–5). Have you written or read similar types of documents? If so, why? What was the situation? Which of the documents would you use to make a decision or to perform an action? Which type of document would you prefer to write? Why?

FOCUS

Warm Up

Use the Warm Up as a discovery learning activity to help students analyze the differences in various writing environments and to build on what they learned in the introductory section of this chapter. Provide students with the *Comparing Writing Environments* worksheet available as a supplemental activity on the IRCD.

TEACH

Have students bring in examples of their favorite type of writing to share with the class. Ask them how they use that type of writing and why the author chose to write it that particular way.

Ask students to compare examples of technical writing with their examples, focusing specifically on subject and audience.

COMMUNICATION TECHNOLOGIES

Technical writers must be familiar with desktop publishing software. Using programs such as Microsoft® Word, Adobe® PageMaker®, and QuarkXPress®, technical writers can apply special features (for example, boldfaced type, bulleted lists, and tables) to their documents. In addition, they can add visual aids such as diagrams, charts, and graphs to enhance the message.

To practice applying special features, complete the *Communication Technologies* worksheet available at www.cengage.com/school/bcomm/techwtg. Click the link for Chapter 1; then click Data Files.

Think Critically

Does your composing process change when you lack knowledge of software? For example, if you do not know how to insert tables or bulleted lists in a document, do you approach the writing differently? Explain.

Audience

The writer of the personal essay expects some understanding from his or her readers as they share experiences. The writer also expresses his or her point of view. The writer of the research paper may be interested in the subject and hopes that a reader will read the research paper for its facts.

The technical writer, however, expects more from a very specific reader—one needing information about mitral valve replacement and possessing some knowledge of the topic and its specialized vocabulary. The technical writer not only expects the reader to understand the writing, but also wants the reader to do something after reading—decide on surgical options. When you want something specific from a reader, you must work hard as a writer to meet the reader's needs.

In technical writing, the needs of the reader dictate every decision the writer makes. In the Sample Technical Document Excerpt on page 3, the writer worked hard to present the information the reader needs in a format that is easy to read. The headings, boldfaced type, visual aids, and no-frills language show that the writer is conscious of the reader.

Organization

The personal essay and research paper make standard use of a topic sentence and transitional expressions, but you still need to read far into each document before the main point and the organization become apparent.

However, the Sample Technical Document Excerpt uses headings to help you perceive the organization at a single glance. Questions in the headings draw your attention to the information this document provides even before you read it. Also, headings give you an opportunity to read only what you want or need to read. When a person who has not been diagnosed wants to learn about symptoms, the heading "How do I know that I have mitral valve prolapse?" allows his or her eye to travel quickly to the information needed.

Style

The **style** of a document, the way an author uses words and sentences, usually gives the audience an idea of the type of document they are reading. For example, the personal essay is casual, almost conversational, and predictable for an essay. The writer uses examples and some description. The style of the research paper also is predictable for a research paper—formal and more distant than the personal essay, with a thesis to clarify the purpose of the paper and documentation to enhance credibility.

The technical document uses a simple, concise, straightforward style that is easily understood. The long sentences are simply lists. The other sentences are short, and the sentence order is predictable. There are no surprises for the reader. **Jargon,** the highly specialized language of a particular discipline or technical field, is used.

Communication Dilemma

Isabel was recently assigned as Lead Technical Communicator on a team that is developing a high-profile software known as SpeedQuest. She is responsible for coordinating communication between the programming team and the marketing team. Because this position is likely to result in a promotion and career advancement, Isabel is eager to do a good job.

One evening Isabel overhears the lead computer programmer tell the project manager that SpeedQuest is not as advanced as advertised in the company's marketing materials. The programmer recommends delaying the launch date, but the project manager ignores the suggestion, deciding to issue a second release after the product is complete.

The next day in the meeting to discuss the marketing materials, Isabel struggles to decide whether she should list in the brochures the SpeedQuest features that do not work yet. She knows that the features would help sales of SpeedQuest. On the other hand, she knows that if she tells the truth and decides not to publish information about the features, she may not get the promotion she is counting on. What should Isabel do?

Think Critically

What resources might Isabel use to better understand and resolve this situation?

COMMUNICATION DILEMMA

Point out that Isabel's dilemma is common in the workplace. Discuss Isabel's options and the pros and cons of each option. Students should look at the dilemma from different perspectives—for example, those of loyal corporate citizen, project manager, marketing writer, and general public.

Think Critically

Isabel could rely on experts or experienced professionals in her organization, perhaps her mentor, to provide advice. For example, if the organization's legal counsel outlined the liability of false advertising, Isabel's decision might be clear. She might find other resources in company records that tell her how similar situations were handled in the past.

TEACH

Have students attend a poetry or book reading or a literary discussion. Ask them to write a report analyzing the differences between the types of writing at the event and technical communication, focusing on audience, organization, style, tone, and special features.

Tone

Tone refers to emotional overtones—the way the words make a person feel. It describes the emotional character of a document. The tone of a document also hints at the kind of document the audience is reading.

The tone of the personal essay is casual, dejected, and agonized. The tone of the research paper is generally objective. The tone in technical writing is best described as objective or businesslike.

The expressive nature of a personal essay can display a range of emotions—sadness, excitement, irony, humor. The aim of research papers and technical documents is not to convey emotion. In fact, emotion can get in the way of a technical document.

Readers of technical documents read for information, not for entertainment. They read to learn something or to take action. Some people say that technical writing is boring because of its lack of emotion. However, for the person needing or wanting that information, the targeted audience, the topic is not boring.

Special Features

The Sample Technical Document Excerpt is the only document of the samples on pages 3–5 to use special features. Technical writers use special features such as boldface, italics, capital letters, columns, underlining, and bulleted lists to draw readers' attention to certain words and to help important information stand out. Also, the use of graphics such as tables, graphs, pictures, and diagrams helps the audience grasp complex information quickly.

FOCUS ON ETHICS
Use the Focus on Ethics to generate discussion about what is "right" and "good" and what is not.

Think Critically
The Think Critically question should help students see the difference between legality and morality. Sometimes actions and decisions that are legal are not ethical.

TEACH
Bring several copies of a professional journal from a technical, medical, or scientific field to class. Ask students to examine at least two articles. Then have them list all of the special features they find. Also ask students to describe the function or effect of several examples of special features from the articles.

Focus on Ethics

Technical communicators can face thorny issues when they provide a service for a company or an organization that may expect results that the technical writer finds questionable or problematic. For instance, a technical writer working for Energy Battery Company may be asked to write a press release announcing the plant's unexpected two-week shutdown, but is told not to include information about the chemical spill that could have leaked into the local estuary. The technical writer may be torn between meeting management's expectations (and moving up the corporate ladder) and serving the public good. Writers need to be thoroughly aware of their ethics and explore all possible actions and outcomes in such situations.

Think Critically
How do an ethical dilemma and a legal dilemma differ?

More than the research paper or personal essay, the technical document relies on special features. Technical documents require more visual effort if they are to grab and hold the readers' attention. Writers use some of the following special features to make their documents more effective for the audience:

- Font size and style—what size is readable for the targeted audience? how many styles are appropriate?

- Numbered and/or bulleted lists—what kind of bullets?

- Columns—one, two, three, or more?

- Color—which colors? how much color?

- Graphs and tables—one-, two-, or three-dimensional? horizontal or vertical? number of columns? color or no color?

- Letterhead and logo—size? location? middle, upper left or right, or side?

- Photos and drawings—subject? style? black and white or color?

- Sidebars—what information to highlight? where to place?

- Clip art—what purpose? to add humor, to set a tone, or to celebrate a season?

Technical writers face a double challenge. They not only must write with clear, accurate, and specific words, but also must design the document to look inviting and attractive. Therefore, technical writers are production artists—writing with precision to locate the best word and sentence structure for the message and designing pages that combine a professional image with a user-friendly approach. To do so, technical writers use a tool of their trade: desktop publishing software. The software allows technical writers to craft documents that meet their readers' needs.

⬤ **STOP AND THINK**

Drawing from the activities in this section's Warm Up, write your own definition of *technical writing*. Make sure you incorporate concepts from this section, such as subject, organization, audience, style, tone, and special features.

HOW TECHNICAL WRITING COMPARES TO OTHER WRITING

Technical writing has much in common with the academic writing you have experienced in school. Technical writing also shares aspects of the literature you have read. The differences, however, set technical writing apart from other writing that is familiar to you.

Technical Writing and Academic Writing

Academic writing (for example, personal essays, research papers, analyses, and arguments) is the expository and **persuasive writing** (writing to convince others) done in academic circles. It must be unified, coherent, and well organized. Technical writing also must be unified, coherent, and well organized. Style and standard usage (the spoken and written English expected in business communication) are important in academic and technical writing. Both types of writing rely on a process of thinking and writing that takes place over a few hours, a few days, or several weeks. The purpose is often the same—to inform or persuade.

The difference between academic writing and technical writing is in the presentation, audience, and approach. Academic writing includes paragraphs—usually an introductory paragraph, paragraphs that develop a thesis (a statement of purpose), and a concluding paragraph. Academic writing is written for an academic audience—an instructor, classmates, or a group of interested scholars.

The purpose of academic writing is to expand on an idea or make observations about human experience. For example, Francis Bacon's essay entitled "On Reading" elaborates on the benefits of reading. In "Two Views of the Mississippi," Mark Twain observes that while a close study of the river is necessary to reveal its dangers, that study also takes away the river's mystery.

Technical writing also includes paragraphs. It, too, often begins with an introduction and closes with a conclusion. But technical writing (with its headings, itemized lists, boldfaced type, and graphics) looks different from academic writing. Technical writing is written for a specific audience. The subject is generally technical, business-related, or scientifically oriented. Generally, there is less flexibility in the subject matter, style, and tone. Often the intent is to clarify and consolidate rather than expand.

ONGOING ASSESSMENT

Stop and Think

Encourage students to incorporate the concepts about technical writing from this chapter in their definition: subject, organization, audience, style, tone, and special features. Have them compare and contrast their definitions with those of other students.

Warm Up

From your experience with writing, what characteristics does good writing share? In other words, how would you describe good writing?

FOCUS

Warm Up

Discuss the characteristics of all good writing, such as unity, coherence, effective organization, use of standard English, and appropriate style. Tell students that technical writing also requires those characteristics.

TEACH

Remind students that technical writing is not new to them. It shares characteristics with all effective academic writing, and they can build on many writing skills they already use.

REVIEW

Make sure students understand the differences between technical writing and other writing they know: differences in presentation, subject matter, and audience considerations.

Technical Writing and Imaginative Writing

Imaginative writing also adheres to principles of unity, coherence, and standard usage. Imaginative writers let their ideas emerge and develop over time. However, compared to technical and academic writing, imaginative writing is less academic and more artistic and creative.

Imaginative writing includes novels, short stories, drama, and poetry whose situations grow out of fantasy or imagination. Events and people are fictional, although the themes may reveal universal truths. Imaginative writing is often **ambiguous,** meaning that more than one interpretation is possible and describing writing that means different things to different people. Imaginative writing also requires the reader to draw **inferences,** which are judgments about the reading that the writer does not make for the reader.

Technical writing should be unambiguous and direct. A work of literature may be rich because it means different things to different readers. A reader might ponder the different meanings of the old man's voyage in Hemingway's *The Old Man and the Sea,* but W. Earl Britton says "that the primary, though not the sole, characteristic of technical and scientific writing lies in the effort of the author to convey one and only one meaning in what he says" (114).

The meaning of a sentence in technical writing must be clear. "Turn there," Mr. Ybarra said, and his daughter turned left when he meant for her to turn right. The word *there* can have different meanings to different people. However, "Turn right at Nottingham Road, the next paved road," has only one meaning.

Imaginative writing such as Emily Dickinson's "Because I could not stop for Death—He kindly stopped for me" often requires you to make inferences. You do not expect to make inferences about technical writing. If the poet's doctor gave the following instructions to a nurse, what would happen? *Because I couldn't remember the name of Ms. Dickinson's medication, would you kindly call the pharmacy and ask for the bottle that holds the blue and red pills?* Poor Ms. Dickinson. She'd find more comfort in the words of her poem than in the advice of her doctor.

 STOP AND THINK

Write a paragraph comparing technical writing to academic and imaginative writing.

CHAPTER 1 REVIEW

SUMMARY

1. You have probably used technical writing if you have given someone directions, written a recipe, explained closing procedures at work, or done many other everyday activities.

2. Technical communication, whether a written document or an oral presentation, presents technical information with a specific purpose and audience and a clear, straightforward approach.

3. Required in all professions, technical writing is critical in the workplace.

4. Technical writing exhibits the following characteristics:

   - Subject: technical, factual
   - Audience: carefully considered, targeted
   - Organization: predictable, apparent
   - Style: concise, direct, specialized vocabulary
   - Tone: objective, businesslike
   - Special features: visual elements

5. Technical writing differs from academic writing in its presentation, approach to subject matter, and audience and from imaginative writing in its "one-meaning-and-one-meaning-only" presentation.

Checklist

- Can I define technical writing?
- Can I list the characteristics of technical writing?
- Can I give examples of technical writing in the workplace?
- Can I explain how technical writing differs from academic and imaginative writing?
- Can I identify ways in which technical writing is similar to academic writing?

CLOSE

Summary

Use the chapter summary to review key points of class discussion. Then ask students if they disagree with or are unclear about any of the summary items. Ask students to write a brief document summarizing the points they thought were most important. Have them use headings and special features.

CLOSE

Checklist

Use the checklist to continue the chapter review or to quiz for a chapter test.

Divide the class into two groups. Ask each group to work together to answer the questions in the checklist. Give each group 5–10 minutes. When the time is up, designate two students from each group to write the answers on the board or to publish them online in a computerized classroom.

REVIEW

For a review of the key terms in the chapter, provide students with the *Key Terms* worksheet available as a supplemental activity on the IRCD.

1. All writing follows principles of unity, coherence, standard usage, and correct grammar and mechanics.
2. **Technical:** electric circuits and a computer screen
Academic: a sunset, homelessness, a first car, graduation, a wedding, a close friend, and flowers

Provide students with the "Build Your Foundation" worksheet available as a supplemental activity on the IRCD.

3. **Technical:** b. (RAM); c. (Z52 calipers); f. (output stage, voltage amplification, cathode-ray tube, blanking signals)
Imaginative: a. (memory, music); d. (mist, peeked); e. (once upon a time, princess)

4. Encourage students to include not just writing, but all forms of communication used in the role they have held. In deciding whether their communication was technical, students will review and use the definition of *technical communication.*

5. Use this activity to point out characteristics of effective and ineffective writing.

6. a. dental assistant; b. dental patient; c. parents; d. international travelers (who read English); e. elementary school-aged children

7. Answers will vary but should refer to the characteristics of technical communication discussed in the chapter.

Build Your Foundation

1. What characteristics does technical writing share with other types of writing?

2. Which of these subjects would most likely be written about in a technical style? Which of these subjects would most likely be written about in an academic style?

a sunset	homelessness	a first car
electric circuits	graduation	a wedding
a computer screen	a close friend	flowers

3. Which of the following statements would you expect to come from a technical writing document? Which would come from imaginative literature? How can you tell? What are your clues?

   a. My memory of her will never fade. She brought music into my life.
   b. There are two types of computer random-access memory (RAM): static RAM and dynamic RAM.
   c. Most intriguing is the adaptation of Corvette Z52 calipers to the car.
   d. The mist peeked over the marshland.
   e. Once upon a time there was a princess who ruled a vast country.
   f. The video output stage simply provides the voltage amplification and driving power for the cathode-ray tube and accepts the vertical and horizontal blanking signals.

4. In a role you have held, such as chairperson of an organization or a committee, employee, or team member, describe the kinds of communication required of you in that role. Would you describe the communication you did as technical communication? Why or why not?

5. Find a piece of technical writing (or another kind of writing) that you think is ineffective. Write a brief analysis of the writing, focusing on the characteristics that make it ineffective. Then analyze a piece of writing that you believe is effective. Compare the two pieces of writing for subject, audience, organization, style, tone, and special features.

6. Read each statement and identify the audience you think the writer is targeting.

   a. As instructed by the dentist, oxygenate the patient 5 minutes for every 15 minutes of nitrous oxide exposure to prevent diffusion hypoxia.
   b. Here at the office when nitrous oxide is used, the oxygen administered with it prevents headaches, grogginess, nausea, and that "hung-over" feeling.
   c. Make no bones about it—*City Dogs* is a gentle, funny movie that your entire family will enjoy!
   d. When booking train reservations in Spain, be aware that INTERCITY is the standard daytime service, while TALGOS offers more amenities and is more expensive.
   e. Come and see Big Bear at Ayden Centre on Saturday morning. Have your picture taken with him and take home one of the balloon animals he makes for you.

7. Examine the information found on a box or can of your favorite packaged food or beverage. In particular, notice the nutrition information. Write an explanation of why the information on the package is considered technical communication.

Your Turn

8. What skills do you need to improve your technical writing? How can you acquire those skills?

9. Conduct an Internet search for the keywords *technical writing, technical editing,* and *technical communication.* Write a summary of your findings and share your summary with the class.

10. Find an article in a professional journal, either in print or online. Read the article to understand the organizational strategy used. Because obvious organization is one of the characteristics of technical communication, analyze the article to determine whether its organization is obvious and is easy for readers to follow. Write a report of your findings and attach a copy of the article.

11. Collect brochures or pamphlets from a local government agency such as the health department or parks and recreation office. Use the headings and subheadings to create an outline. Then compare the outline you have created to the overall message of the document. Write a brief description of how effectively (or ineffectively) the system of headings and subheadings provides emphasis for important information in the document.

12. Read an article in your favorite magazine or textbook. Choose special features of technical writing. How do those features make the writing easy to read?

13. Write a short report describing the writing skills required in three of the following careers. You may need to research some of the job titles so you know the kinds of writing the jobs require. Or choose three careers that interest you and write a short report describing the writing skills that those careers require.

physical therapist	computer network administrator	medical assistant
audiologist	agricultural extension agent	veterinary care aide
research scientist	food service manager	electrical technician
real estate broker	construction project manager	reference librarian

14. Search the Internet for an example of technical writing written by someone who holds a job you might like to have someday. Explain the purpose of the example and the way the author used technical writing characteristics to achieve the purpose.

15. Visit the websites of two competing organizations, such as PepsiCo and The Coca-Cola Company or AT&T and Verizon. Can you determine the audience that each site targets? Why or why not? Is the site designed to reach consumers or shareholders or both? How effectively does each site use the principles of technical communication?

Community Connection

16. Interview a businessperson about his or her technical writing on the job. What types of documents does this person write most often? Ask if you may bring a sample of the writing to class.

17. Ask a technician or scientist about his or her technical writing on the job. Ask what mistake may have been made as a result of imprecise reporting.

ASSESS

Your Turn

8. Answers will vary but should relate to the characteristics of technical communication.

9. Answers will vary.

10. Explain that professional journals, typically holding high standards and communicating technical information, use headings and subheadings, visual aids, and other elements to communicate effectively.

11. Most pamphlets and brochures will likely be brief and well-written, with major ideas and concepts highlighted using headings and minor ideas and supporting details and examples highlighted using subheadings.

12. Through this activity, students should see how the special features used in technical communication, such as bulleted lists and headings, can be used to make any type of writing easy to read.

13. Use this activity to illustrate that all professions rely on technical writing in some way.

14. Answers will vary.

15. Reinforce the importance of audience analysis in this activity. Remind students that if a business does not successfully target its audience, it is likely to go out of business.

ASSESS

Community Connection

16–17. Use the *Community Connection* worksheet to guide students through the questions. Students can share their findings and their writing samples.

For interview questions, use the *Community Connection* worksheet available at www.cengage.com/school/bcomm/techwtg. Click the link for Chapter 1; then click Data Files.

Audience and Purpose

Goals

- Determine how to meet the needs of a specific audience and a multiple audience
- Plan a document's purpose, scope, and medium

Terms

- accommodate, p. 26
- culture, p. 27
- demographics, p. 25
- format, p. 37
- jargon, p. 26
- medium, p. 35
- multiple audience, p. 25
- primary audience, p. 30
- purpose, p. 33
- role, p. 27
- scope, p. 34
- secondary audience, p. 30
- specific audience, p. 25
- target audience, p. 25

TEACHING RESOURCES FOR CHAPTER 2

Instructor's Resource CD

Data Files

Data File Solutions

Lesson Plans

Teaching Masters

PowerPoint Slides

Chapter Tests with Solutions

Additional Chapter Activities

Exam_View_

Website

www.cengage.com/school/bcomm/techwtg

Crossword Puzzle

Data Files

Data File Solutions

Flashcards

Glossary

NET Bookmark

Sample Documents

Web Links

WRITE TO LEARN

Help students see that they already accommodate their readers' needs in their conversations. Accommodating readers in written communication is similar.

WRITE TO LEARN

Think of something you did recently about which you told a number of people. Consider how your description of the incident changed depending on whom you talked to. In one page, explain how you described this incident to (1) authority figures (for example, parents, instructors, or employers) and (2) close friends (who may include sisters and brothers). Did the purpose of your conversation change when you switched audiences? If so, how? How did each audience affect your tone, your body language, your choice of words, and the information you chose to include or omit?

Focus on Audience and Purpose

Read the sample document on the next page and answer these questions:

- Who is the audience for this web page?
- Who is the writer, and what does the writer want the reader to do?
- What has the writer done to show an understanding of this reader?
- What kind of information has the writer provided to convince the reader to give blood? Do you think the writer has done a good job? Explain.

What If?

- The reader did not have access to the Internet?
- The reader is a regular donor, but he does not have transportation to the Blood Mobile site?
- The reader is a willing first-time donor but wonders if it is all right to give blood on her way home after lifting weights at the gym?
- The reader might be willing to donate but is legally blind?

Top 10 reasons people don't give blood

1. **I don't like needles / I am scared of needles / I am afraid to give blood**
   Nearly everyone feels that way at first. However, most donors will tell you that you feel only a slight initial pinch, and 7–10 minutes later, you are finished and headed for the canteen. If you take the time (and courage) to make one donation, you'll wonder why you ever hesitated.

2. **I am too busy**
   The entire process takes about an hour, and the actual blood donation time is only 7–10 minutes. If you stop to think that an hour of your time could mean a lifetime for a premature baby, someone with cancer undergoing chemotherapy, or someone who's had an accident, you might decide that you can make the time to give the gift of life.

3. **No-one ever asked me . . . I didn't realize my blood was needed**
   Consider yourself asked! There is simply no other way to supply the blood needs of hospital patients but for the generous donations of people like you. Every two seconds someone in America needs blood. More than 38,000 donations are needed every day in communities across the U.S.

4. **I already gave this year**
   You can give every 56 days. Many donors give 5 times a year!

5. **I am afraid I'll get AIDS**
   It is not possible to get AIDS by donating blood to the American Red Cross. A new sterile needle is used for each donor and discarded afterwards.

6. **My blood isn't the right type**
   Every type of blood is needed daily to meet patient needs. If you have a common blood type, there are many patients who need it, so it is in high demand. If you have a less common blood type, there are fewer donors available to give it, so it is in short supply.

7. **I don't have any blood to spare**
   The average adult body has 10–12 pints of blood. Doctors say that healthy adults may give regularly because the body quickly replaces the blood you donate.

8. **I don't want to feel weak afterward**
   Donating blood should not affect adversely a healthy adult because your body has plenty of blood. You will donate less than one pint, and your body, which constantly makes new blood, will replace the donated volume within 24 hours. Most people continue their usual activities after donating.

9. **They won't want my blood (I am too old / I've had an illness)**
   If you have doubts, check with your physician. The qualified staff on duty at a blood drive or donor center will also review your medical history with you. There is no upper age limit to donate blood with the American Red Cross, and a great many medical conditions do not prevent you from donating blood, or may have done so only temporarily in the past.

10. **I have a rare blood type, so I'll wait until there is a special need**
    Blood that is rare or special is almost always in short supply. There is a constant need for these blood types in order to avoid having to recruit specific blood types in a crisis.

Sample Document Written for a Specific Audience
Source: www.givelife.org/donor/top10excuses.asp

FOCUS

Focus on Audience and Purpose
Use the questions to encourage students to read the sample closely.

ASSESS

What If?
Use the questions to discuss how the sample would be different if the situation or audience changed.

Go to www.cengage.com/school/bcomm/techwtg for more detailed responses to these questions.

Courtesy of Christopher Blackwell

Writing@Work

Dr. Christopher Blackwell is Assistant Professor at the University of Central Florida's College of Nursing. He teaches graduate-level nursing courses, serves on several faculty committees, and researches health and social disparities in vulnerable patient populations.

When Christopher needs to persuade fellow faculty members to make a change to their graduate program, he knows that he has to do more than simply speak up: He must produce documented evidence to support his case. "Verbally, I am able to communicate my opinion to my colleagues, but when I present effectively written documentation based on research, my points of view are validated by others."

Christopher's gift for speaking comes in handy in the classroom, where he has a different audience: nursing students. "To help students remember essential information," he says, "I use real clinical scenarios that I have experienced and also tell jokes. Students appreciate these types of communication." In addition to instructive anecdotes and humor, Christopher believes that body language, or nonverbal cues, are important to effective classroom communication.

While he teaches for a student audience, he researches and publishes writing for a professional scholarly audience. Christopher strongly believes that "the one thing that is most essential when preparing formal writing is *focus*." To focus his writing for an academic audience, Christopher writes an article's abstract—or a summary of the article—first and then uses this synopsis as an outline for the longer piece.

Think Critically

1. The profile describes three types of communication in which Christopher engages. What are they? How are they different? How are they similar? How does Christopher prepare to communicate effectively in each situation?

2. Are you surprised to read that a nursing professor tells jokes in class? Why does Christopher use humor?

Printed with permission of Dr. Christopher Blackwell

MEETING THE AUDIENCE'S NEEDS

Warm Up

Suppose your younger brother or sister did something that made you unhappy. How would you talk to your brother or sister about the problem? Now suppose the person who offended you was a coworker. How would your audience affect what you say?

Audience and *reader* are nearly interchangeable terms. As technical communication expands to include multimedia presentations, audience has a broader meaning. Sometimes the audience is not a reader, but a listener or an observer. On the Web, the reader also is an active participant. In any case, technical writers must know who the members of their audience are and what those readers need or want to know.

In the sample document on page 21, the writer knows who the audience is—potential blood donors. The focus is on the reader, and the writing shows an understanding of the reader's point of view. The Red Cross knows this reader well, obviously having heard these reasons many times. After identifying this audience, the writer systematically counters any objections with objective, precise, factual information.

Technical writing is written for both internal and external audiences. When Roweena, a dispatcher, writes a memo announcing pay increases to the police officers in her district, she is writing to the members of her organization—an internal audience. The author of "Top 10 reasons people don't give blood" is writing for an external audience—people outside the organization.

© Jeff Greenberg/ The Image Works

FOCUS

Warm Up

Use the Warm Up to illustrate how audience might affect language. Discussing a problem with a sibling does not require much prior thought. Talking to a coworker, however, requires some planning, tact, and consideration of the consequences.

TEACH

Invite a businessperson who creates marketing materials to speak to the class about planning for purpose and audience.

Make sure students know what it means for the writer to be transparent—focusing on the reader.

In technical writing, the writer is transparent. A technical writer is like a member of a stage crew, a behind-the-scenes operator, whose primary obligation is to satisfy the audience's need for information. In a good play, the audience is barely aware of the crew at work who is moving sets and producing sound on cue, but without the crew, the show would not go on. Similarly, good writers produce work without drawing attention to their role.

Types of Audiences

You may write a poem or short story without the intention of sharing it with anyone. However, technical writing implies an audience, often a very specific audience, but sometimes a more varied audience. Your readers may be customers, coworkers, managers, subordinates, or the general public. Usually, your relationship to your readers determines how you write your document—the tone you use, the formality of the language, and its medium.

COMMUNICATION TECHNOLOGIES

The BBC, the British Broadcasting Corporation, has two versions of the news on its website, a UK (United Kingdom) version and an international version. Users logging on are automatically taken to the broadcast deemed most relevant based on their geographic locations. Thus, a person from the Middle East will see news from the Middle East; a person from South Asia will see news from South Asia. Other news websites including VOA, Voice of America, and Google News offer news in similar formats. As you can see, these organizations have designed websites to reach out to many different audiences.

Think Critically

How might news about an event reported by India be different from the news about the same event reported by the United States?

A memo to the chief executive officer (CEO), for example, would be more formal than a memo to a coworker.

As you are planning your document, consider whether your readers fall into one of these categories:

■ **Lay reader:** a general reader without expert knowledge but with an interest in a subject. Readers of newspapers and magazines such as *Psychology Today* and *Popular Science* are lay readers.

■ **Technician:** a person with skilled knowledge in an area who implements the ideas or plans of the expert. Technicians, like lathe operators and network administrators, operate equipment, repair machinery, and train others. They read manuals, schematics, blueprints, and technical reports.

■ **Expert:** an authority in a particular field who is highly skilled and professional, perhaps with an advanced degree. Experts design equipment, conduct research, and create new products. Experts such as medical doctors and engineers contribute to professional journals such as the *Journal of the American Medical Association* and the *Journal of Applied Physics*, respectively, and they read professional journals.

■ **Manager:** a person who organizes personnel and is responsible for the day-to-day operations as well as long-range planning. Upper-level managers are leaders responsible for creating a vision and moving the organization forward. Depending on their level of expert knowledge, managers may read feasibility reports, research reports, financial reports, or professional articles.

A reader can fall into more than one category. Thinking through the categories will help you make decisions about how best to communicate with your audience.

Meeting the Needs of a Specific Audience

Do you understand the message below? It is written in Morse code—letters as a series of dots and dashes transmitted as sounds, lights, or electrical pulses. Many people have no need to know Morse code. They are not the target audience. Therefore, the message fails to communicate.

−.−   −.   −−−   .−−

−.−−   −−−   ..−   .−.

.−   ..−   −..   ..   .   −.   −.−.   .

A Navy radio operator during World War I would have understood this code. The operator's audience shared a common mission: to receive important military messages over long distances. In short, the Navy radio operator used Morse code to meet the highly specific needs of a particular audience.

The Navy operator is the **target audience,** the audience for which the message is written, the audience to which the writer is writing by using language this reader will understand.

To communicate successfully, you must speak the "language" of your audience. Failure to speak in terms that your reader expects creates a barrier that prevents communication, much the same way the Morse code keeps you from understanding its message. But to speak the language, you must know who the audience is. Your audience may be a **specific audience** (a single person or a group whose point of view is the same), or your audience may be a **multiple audience** (readers whose points of view differ). Once you know your audience, you can plan ways to appeal to your reader(s).

To help you target the needs of a specific group, gather information about the **demographics** of the group—information such as the age, sex, income, and educational level of your group. If you are planning to advertise a new day care center, for example, your target audience would be working parents with young children. You might look at census data to find out where to advertise your new center. If you are designing a website for retirees, look into what retirees are interested in—for example, health care, recreational activities, and travel.

Digital Vision/Getty Images

TEACH

Ask students who have performed in front of a live audience to share what they had to do to accommodate the audience. They may mention, for example, rehearsing, applying makeup, and smiling. Try to get students to focus on feelings they had as a result of accommodating different audiences.

As a writer, the relationship with your readers is also important. Are they customers, managers, peers, or subordinates? Your relationship will determine how you write your document—the tone you use, the formality of your document, and its medium.

The reader's needs determine what kind of information the writer supplies. When your manager needs to know the cost of hiring an administrative assistant, you provide cost. When the maintenance crew wants an e-mail that provides information about mosquito repellent, you research repellents and send the crew members an e-mail with your information. When the audience is unsure of its needs, the writer helps the audience think through the communication situation.

In technical writing, one rule dominates: *The needs and wants of your audience dictate every decision you make as a writer.* The writer uses a skill to provide a valuable service. Think of it this way: The writer is the server, and the audience is the person ordering from the menu. If the person ordering requests a salad with no tomatoes and Italian dressing on the side, the server obliges!

Audience and Purpose | 25

Analyze Your Target Audience

Sometimes your audience is a specific person or group with a common interest. After you identify the readers in your target audience, consider how their knowledge level, roles, interests, cultural background, and personalities may influence what you write and how you write it. Age, experience, attitude, organizational distance, income, and politics may affect the language you choose to communicate successfully. Targeting the special needs of a specific audience requires a writer to consider several factors at once. Understanding your audience's knowledge level, role, interests, cultural background, and personality is the first step to successful communication.

Attending to the needs and wants of your audience is much like attending to a special guest in your home. You are aware of this person's presence, and you make every effort to make this person feel welcomed. For example, a Spanish-speaking exchange student from Chile spoke English moderately well and enjoyed playing the guitar. His American host family attended to his needs and wants by defining unfamiliar words and borrowing a guitar for him to play. Just as the host family gave special consideration to the Chilean student, you should consider your audience by making every effort to **accommodate** (adjust to, make concessions for) your audience's needs and wants.

NET Bookmark

Cyborlink is a website that provides tips on how to conduct business in 122 countries according to each culture's norms. Included in this site is information on what to wear; how to greet people; when and how to present gifts; and how, in general, people should mind their manners when conducting business overseas.

Go to the NET Bookmark for Chapter 2 and find Hofstede's Dimension of Culture Scales. How does the United States rank on the scale? Compare your finding for the United States to those of two other countries. Bring your findings to class for a discussion of the similarities and differences.

www.cengage.com/school/bcomm/techwtg

Knowledge Level

What people know and how well they know it varies widely from one person to the next. As such, knowledge level can be high, low, or moderate. It can be technical or nontechnical. Ask yourself what your readers know or do not know about your subject. If you tell them what they already know, you risk wasting their time (not to mention yours). Yet if you omit something they need to know, you have not done your job.

For example, the knowledge level of Josh's parents prevented them from understanding a medical report. After 2-year-old Josh fell down a flight of stairs at home, his distraught parents took him to the emergency room. Josh's emergency room report read as follows: "The child suffered from contusions and lacerations." *Contusions* and *lacerations* are familiar terms to doctors and nurses. For Josh's parents, however, the medical **jargon** (the highly specialized language of a discipline or technical field) did not communicate as effectively as these everyday terms that are familiar to most parents: *The child suffered from cuts and bruises.* The medical jargon was confusing, and it made Josh's fall seem worse than it really was.

Experience, age, and expertise can affect how much someone knows. Josh's parents lacked the experience and background of a doctor or nurse. And because of his age, Josh did not understand medical terms. The technician who X-rayed Josh's finger knew how to position it to get the best picture but lacked the expert knowledge of the engineer who designed the machine.

Role

Consider your reader's **role** or his or her area of responsibility before you begin writing. A role is the function or job that someone performs at work. Role or job title affects not only knowledge level, but also the information your reader thinks is important.

Understand your reader's role and accommodate it. An accountant is concerned about her company's finances. If you write a memo to the accounting office about a planned purchase, you should accommodate the accountant's role by including information about cost. The technician who reads the same memo may be more interested in how to operate equipment being purchased, having little concern about the cost. For the technician, you should include sufficient information about the technical aspects of the equipment.

© Yuri Arcurs, 2009/Used under license from Shutterstock.com

Interest

When your readers are interested in your subject, they read with greater enthusiasm. Where you find common interest, take advantage of it. Where there is none, try to create it. Some readers, however, will never be interested in your subject. Accept those readers' lack of interest and focus on giving them the information they need.

Interest can be affected by age, experience, cultural background, and role. Your interests now are different from what they were ten years ago because you have a wider range of experiences. The camping and fishing trips you enjoyed as a child may have been replaced by long motor trips and concerts as a young adult. If everyone in your family enjoys eating black beans and rice, you may have a taste for those foods because of your background. Right now your role is to be a student. When you join the workforce, your interests will be determined in part by your professional role.

Cultural Background

Culture—the special beliefs, customs, and values specific to a particular group of people or to a particular region—affects what an audience considers to be proper behavior. Many beliefs regarding human relations are affected by an individual's cultural background. By failing to consider someone's cultural background, you risk offending your reader and creating barriers in the communication process. Your goal is to open the lines of communication and reach out to all of your readers.

In the United States, regional cultural differences affect communication. In the South, many parents insist that their children say, "Yes, ma'am," "No, ma'am," "Yes, sir," and "No, sir" to their elders as a sign of respect and proper etiquette. Other regions of the country do not rely as heavily on these endearments. While "Yes, ma'am" and "Yes, sir" are expected as polite gestures in one region of the country, the expressions may sound out of place—even offensive—in another region. Some people begin a telephone conversation with small talk, asking how the person or his or her family is, as a prelude to conducting business. Yet other people consider such small talk to be too personal or a waste of time.

U.S. businesses are becoming increasingly global. American-based businesses have interests abroad in countries such as Mexico, Argentina, Turkey, and India. Many documents are read by audiences outside the United States whose cultural differences affect communication. Where American business personnel perceive directness as a sign of open and honest business dealings, other cultures consider this approach brash and insensitive. Where American business relies heavily on written agreements ("put it in writing" and "read the fine print"), other cultures trust oral communication. Understanding these differences is imperative to accommodating your audience's cultural background.

Personality

Personality can be affected by culture, heredity, age, experience, and role. Also, someone's personality can shape his or her work habits. A legal researcher who prefers to work alone may appreciate receiving instructions via e-mail and therefore enjoys reading her e-mail. Someone who prefers working in a group may want to receive oral instructions in a meeting so he can share his reaction with others. For him, e-mail may be a nuisance. When communicating, you may not know your readers well enough to make judgments about their personalities. But if you do, you can tailor your communication style appropriately.

Mayur is a successful manager. Part of his success comes from analyzing the personalities of his subordinates and supervisors. He knows that his supervisor likes to make decisions based on facts. When Mayur talks to her, he is direct and presents only the facts. When Mayur writes to her, his tone is objective and he includes ample statistical data. In fact, the company's new medical plan is the result of Mayur's detailed proposal. Mayur's line manager, on the other hand, is laid-back and wants to know only the bottom line. Memos to him are short, infrequent, and friendly. The line manager is not interested in details, prefers a visit to a memo, and is hurt if the tone is too formal. Mayur has a good relationship with this line manager, who might otherwise be suspicious of a supervisor.

Before you begin to write a technical document, analyze your audience to determine their special needs. Use the questions in Table 2.1 to help you decide what is important to remember about your reader(s). When you have answered the questions, consider the single most important thing to remember about your audience. Then follow the suggestions in the second column for adjusting to your audience's needs.

ASK THESE QUESTIONS	MAKE THESE ACCOMMODATIONS
Knowledge Level	
What does my reader already know about the topic? Is my reader an expert, a technician, or a lay reader? What does my reader need to know? What does my reader want to know?	Add particular knowledge that your audience does not have. Leave out or quickly summarize knowledge your audience already has. Decide how much technical language to include. Use informal definitions or a glossary if necessary. Present complex information visually.
Interests	
How strong is my reader's interest in my topic? Are my reader's priorities different from mine or the same as mine? Is my reader likely to agree with my point of view?	Appeal to known interests or try to create interest. Express agreement with and understanding of a point of view when possible. Provide evidence to help sway others to your point of view.
Role	
Is my reader's role -to make decisions or implement a plan? -to operate equipment, encode data, train others? -to create or design or invent? Is my communication going to management, to a peer, or to a supervisee?	Include knowledge the role requires— planning parameters for managers, technical details for technicians. Write different sections for different roles. Be diplomatic with management, courteous yet straightforward with a peer, and respectful and direct with someone you supervise.
Cultural Background	
What is my reader's cultural background? What are my reader's beliefs? Are my reader's beliefs different from mine or the same as mine?	Understand how culture affects someone's beliefs and decisions. Learn about the cultural background of your audience and adhere to the cultural norms of that audience as much as possible.
Personality	
What kind of personality does my reader have? Is my reader analytical, quiet, or outgoing? Does my reader prefer having details or seeing the big picture?	Adjust tone and medium to personality. Provide facts, order, and evidence for the analytically minded; a personal touch for facilitators; and ideas and the overall picture for creative thinkers.

Table 2.1

After studying Table 2.1, complete the *Accommodating Your Audience's Needs* worksheet available at www.cengage.com/school/ bcomm/techwtg. Click the link for Chapter 2; then click Data Files.

Meeting the Needs of a Multiple Audience

Shakespeare was arguably the greatest writer who ever lived. His success depended on his wit, knowledge of theater, and understanding of his audience. As a businessperson, Shakespeare knew that he had to please England's royal family as well as the peasants who came to see his plays. He had to appeal to young and old, to men and women, to the educated and the uneducated. In the sixteenth century, Shakespeare wrote successfully to a multiple audience, an audience made up of multiple interests, with members whose needs and wants sometimes conflicted with one another.

TYPICAL READER

A person or group of people who want or need specific information.

WRITER'S FOCUS

Analyzing the audience's needs and providing information in the best possible way for the audience to understand.

Today technical writers face a similar challenge writing to an audience that can include executives, managers, and administrative assistants. In his day, Shakespeare was clever—he wrote different parts of the same play for different people. Today his "different parts for different folks" strategy is used by technical writers too. But technical writers go one step further. They "label" the parts with headings, short titles preceding sections of the document to alert readers to the information written for them.

Another strategy for meeting the diverse needs of a multiple audience is to determine who comes first—whose needs are most important. To decide what data to focus on as you write, divide your audience into two groups: **primary audience** and **secondary audience.** Think of the primary audience as readers or listeners to whom you are responsible first and the secondary audience as readers or listeners to whom you are responsible after having met the needs of the primary audience. Both audiences are important, but as a writer, you must organize your tasks according to some kind of priority.

TEACH

Because most students are familiar with the story of Romeo and Juliet, you can discuss how scenes in that play appeal to different audiences. Remind students of how the groundlings (peasants who stood on the ground to view plays presented at The Globe) would have enjoyed the street brawls between the Capulets and the Montagues. The court would have enjoyed the Capulets' masquerade ball and the prince's declarations. Shakespeare even changed the language to appeal to his varied audience. He wrote some of his play in rhymed verse for the upper class and other parts in prose for the lower class.

Point out that while the primary audience is the focus of attention, writers should not ignore their secondary audiences.

Walsh Plastics is considering building a plant in Thailand. Suppose you are the writer of the feasibility report analyzing the move for the company. Walsh's executives and the company lawyer must decide whether to open a factory in a foreign country. They constitute the primary audience. The architect who will design the new plant, the sales representatives who will move, and the managers who will train new workers make up the secondary audience. How will you address each audience's needs and wants?

The following criteria may help you determine who the primary and secondary audiences are for your writing projects.

PRIMARY AUDIENCE	SECONDARY AUDIENCE
■ Asked for or authorized the writing of the document	■ Will be affected by the document in some way
■ Will make decisions based on the information in the document	■ Is interested in the decisions made or the information in the document
■ Will request or take action based on information in the document	■ May use some information for a purpose different from the document's purpose
■ Will likely read the entire document	■ May read selected portions

Magdalena, a computer programmer, faced the challenging task of writing a proposal for the inventory management program of a local school system. The primary audience, the director, contracted services with Magdalena, specified what the program needed to do, and decided who would be trained to use the program. The secondary audience included assistants who would key data, the programmer who would modify the program, and the superintendent who would confirm that the programmer had fulfilled his or her contract terms.

Magdalena's audience ranged from readers with little knowledge of programming to readers with extensive knowledge of programming. To accommodate all of their needs, she wrote different parts of the report for different people. Table 2.2 on the next page reveals the adjustments Magdalena made to accommodate the needs of the multiple audience. Chapter 13 will cover long reports with different headings that are written to accommodate a multiple audience.

Sometimes, though, when a document is short, you can simply revise it for each audience and send it separately. For example, an e-mail from the director of information systems to the network administrators telling them to bring down the network Friday afternoon for routine maintenance specified what the network staff should do. The director reminded the network administrators that users would be notified to log off by noon.

Focus on Ethics

As a writer, to avoid biased language, you must be aware of stereotypes in your writing. Sometimes the stereotype is so engrained in the culture that you do not realize you are using biased language. You probably know that you should avoid sexist language in your writing (referring to men and women differently), but stereotypes include more than gender. People also can be stereotyped because of race, sexual orientation, age, physical or mental abilities, religion, ethnicity, and weight.

In your writing, strive to present everyone as being equal. There are several ways to do this. First, avoid sexist language by referring to men and women the same way. For example, do not assume that all doctors are men and that all nurses are women. Avoid using examples that reinforce stereotypes.

Do not mention a person's physical characteristics if they are not relevant. If you would not say, "Our new software developer is Max, a smart white man without disabilities," then do not say, "Our new software developer is Sandra, a smart white woman with physical disabilities."

Sometimes you are not aware of the biased language. If you are not sure whether you have used stereotypes in your writing, ask another person to look over the document.

Think Critically
What are the possible consequences of stereotyping people?

ENRICH

Bring in several newspapers or old phone books. Ask students to work in groups to describe how the newspaper and/or phone book appeals to different needs. Students should notice use of headings, graphics, and sections.

Ask a newspaper editor to visit the classroom to talk about audience analysis.

TEACH

Ask students to give examples of primary and secondary audiences. Ask them to suggest primary and secondary audiences in this example: The school board writes a policy for school uniforms. (Students and parents—primary audience. Stores that sell the uniforms— secondary audience).

RETEACH

Review Magdalena's writing challenge. Students should see that appealing to different readers is not that difficult if they think about using different report sections for different readers.

FOCUS ON ETHICS

Have students comment on stereotypes in TV shows, movies, magazines, and books. If they cannot think of anything, discuss the fact that stereotypes do exist. Have students view a TV show for a week to focus on stereotypes such as sex, race, sexual orientation, age, ethnicity, religion, and weight. Ask them to share their findings with the class. Share personal experiences of how unfair and inaccurate stereotypes are, showing that stereotypes create ill will, demean a person's individual worth, and ostracize people who would otherwise contribute to the group. In the extreme, stereotyping can lead to violence.

FOCUS

Table 2.2

Use the table to show how Magdalena accommodated the needs and wants of each member of her audience.

READER'S ROLES AND NEEDS	MAGDALENA'S ADJUSTMENT TO READER
As the *approver*, the **superintendent** needs to know whether the money spent on the programmer's services was responsibly invested and whether the terms of the contract have been completed.	Magdalena writes a **cover memo** briefly summarizing the report, describing the program, and outlining advantages to the school system. She uses little or no technical language, carefully defining any technical terms.
As the *decision maker* and *manager*, the **director** needs an overview of the program to see whether the specifications agreed upon have been met and to receive a demonstration of the product.	Magdalena writes the **Executive Summary**, which presents the most important information in the report. She includes some technical language and gives a formal demonstration of the program.
Despite *varied roles*, **all of the readers** need to understand the purpose of the manual and those parts that will help each of them.	In the **Introduction**, Magdalena explains the purpose of the proposal and its organization. She uses little or no technical language.
As the *technician*, the **programmer** needs to understand the program structure, to know how best to extend the functionality of the program, and to know how users interface with the program.	Magdalena documents her programming with UML diagrams and places this information in the **Appendix**. She invites the programmer to the training session for assistants.
As end users, the **administrative assistants** need to understand how to key, manipulate, and find data as quickly as possible.	Magdalena writes **Procedures** that explain how to use the program. She uses short commands, occasional explanations, and screen shots. She then follows up with a training session on how to use the program.

Table 2.2

Before the director sent the e-mail to users, she revised the message. Instead of specifying the work to be done, she asked users to log off by noon, announced that the maintenance was routine, and thanked them for their cooperation and patience. The reminder of the network outage in the bimonthly newsletter was even briefer. By the time she finished, she had revised her message for three different audiences.

Writing to a multiple audience, then, requires careful analysis of each possible audience member followed by a workable plan. Writing "different parts for different folks," focusing on the needs of the primary audience, and rewriting short documents are all strategies available to the technical writer. Remember, too, that an audience that you did not consider could read your document. Therefore, you must anticipate every possible audience member and write accordingly.

STOP AND THINK

Think of an issue about which you feel passionate—your candidate for Student Government Association president, pet adoptions, a political issue, or something else that is important to you. Suppose you had to convince the entire student body to agree with you. What kinds of adjustments would you make to appeal to your multiple audiences?

PLANNING YOUR DOCUMENT'S PURPOSE, SCOPE, AND MEDIUM

Understanding who your audience is and what they need and want is an important part of your job as a writer. However, you have other decisions to make before you are ready to write. Early in the writing process, determine the purpose of your document, its scope, and the medium you will use.

Purpose

Purpose is defined as a specific end or outcome to be obtained. It is what a writer wants a reader to do after reading a document. In technical writing, the purpose is to inform or persuade. Quite often the purpose is both. Because much technical writing is intended to persuade, you need to consider your topic from the readers' points of view. How will your readers react to the information you provide? For them, is the information good or bad news? With whom or what are you competing for your readers' attention? Is there a time limit for responding? Are your readers required to read your document? In other words, how hard must you work to get and keep your readers' attention? You should address these and other concerns as you think about the purpose of your document.

To determine the specific purpose of your writing assignment, ask yourself a couple of basic questions:

- What do I want to inform my readers about?
- What do I want to persuade or convince them of?
- What do I want to happen as a result of this document?

To determine the purpose of your writing, ask additional questions to figure out what you want to happen as a result of the document. What do you want your readers to do? What do you want them to know, to buy, to believe, to give? What would you like them to learn to do or change their minds about? Would you like them to stop doing something or start doing something? When you answer those questions, you will know the purpose of your document.

A statement of purpose may be to inform citizens of the latest employment trends or to convince the public to purchase smoke alarms. The persuasive purpose also implies providing information. Thus, a purpose to persuade becomes a purpose to inform, too. To convince bank customers to invest their money in money market accounts, you also must inform them about the advantages of such accounts. To convince the public to purchase smoke alarms requires evidence that smoke alarms save lives.

A statement of purpose on the same topic can vary for each audience. Consider the new employee evaluation system at Fabre Perfume Industries. Every employee is evaluated. Therefore, the purpose of the new Employee Evaluation Manual is to describe the procedure so that all employees understand how they will be evaluated.

However, because supervisors must conduct the evaluations, they receive the new Employee Evaluation Manual and the Evaluation Procedures Manual. The purpose of these manuals is to inform supervisors about the new procedure for conducting evaluations—how to download forms, where to file them, and what the deadlines are. The topic—new evaluations—is the same, but supervisors need additional information.

Scope

Once you have a clear, stated purpose, you must decide the following: How thorough will my coverage be? What information do I include and omit? Here you use your audience analysis and statement of purpose to make

© Vuk Vukmirovic, 2009/Used under license from Shutterstock.com

decisions about the **scope** of your writing—the extent of treatment, activity, or influence, that is, what is and is not included.

Suppose you are writing instructions telling car owners how to change a tire. You have settled on this statement of purpose: The user should be able to change a tire after reading my instructions. If you wonder whether to include information about how to select a dependable tire or how often to rotate tires, you could review your statement of purpose and say to yourself, No, my purpose is to explain how to change a tire, not to sell tires or inform users about proper tire maintenance. If you are wondering whether to tell your reader that changing a tire is not difficult and that it is an important survival skill, you can ask yourself this question: Will this information help me achieve my purpose with this audience? In other words, will it help my drivers change a tire? The answer is yes. You want to include anything that motivates your reader to perform your process.

Medium

Finally, you need to choose a medium for delivering your message. Today technology gives you many options.

The **medium** is a means by which information is conveyed (for example, a television commercial). What kind of document will you produce? Will it be printed? What medium will accomplish your purpose and appeal to your audience?

Do you need detailed instructions or a quick reference sheet? PowerPoint® slides or a memo? Do you need to post your document on the Web or send it as an e-mail attachment? Do you pay to print 20 copies of an 85-page formal proposal and then mail it, or is it more cost-effective to send 20 CDs that include an interactive menu, a video of the president, and photographs?

As you are making your decision, ask yourself three questions:

1. Is the medium appropriate for my audience, message, and purpose?

2. Is the time and money required to produce the medium worth the possible outcome?

3. What media are available to me?

Using the interactive CD complete with video for your 85-page proposal certainly takes advantage of the features made possible by technology. But is it appropriate for your audience? Such a presentation could generate more interest than the printed page. The CD is compact, is easy to produce and mail, provides many options for retrieval, and may appeal to an audience's fascination with technology. Once the CD is loaded, users have more choices. They can print some or all of the content.

kemie/iStockphoto.com

COMMUNICATION
DILEMMA

Use the dilemma to point out
the importance of adapting to
the communication needs of
others—whether the context is
academic or social.

Think Critically

Uma does not understand the
conversation about the lab
research and may wonder why
Marcus and Sophia do not
acknowledge her and introduce
themselves to Drew, the new
employee. Advice: Socialize
with the other employees.
Sometimes it is easy to "talk
shop" in a mixed group, but
such conversation can alienate
others. Also, it is important
to form relationships with all
coworkers.

TEACH

Help students see that the
medium is the vehicle for the
message. You might compare
it to an artist's medium—paint,
charcoal, clay—and the way that
affects the kind of art produced
and the way the art is produced.

Ask students whether they have
seen a commercial that had so
much action and moving scenes
that it overwhelmed them to
the point of switching channels.
Relate their experiences to
the concept of a medium
overwhelming the audience.

RETEACH

Emphasize the three things
to consider when selecting a
medium: (1) appropriateness
for the audience, (2) time and
cost versus possible outcome,
and (3) availability of the media.

Communication Dilemma

Marcus and Sophia are chemists conducting experiments for Wuxi Pharmaceuticals on how bacteria ward off viral invaders. They just left the lab to attend a retirement reception for the head of maintenance, a highly respected and well-liked man responsible for keeping the lab facilities running during power outages and holidays. Nearly everyone has come to wish him well. Marcus and Sophia are carrying on a lively conversation, excited about something that happened in the lab that day. They enter the reception area and settle into a corner with Uma, the public relations officer, and Drew, the new webmaster, who is looking uncomfortable in such a large group. During the presentation, Marcus and Sophia continue to talk quietly about the CRISPR-based immunity and RNA interference in higher organisms, ignoring everything that is taking place around them. Marcus sees Uma looking at him with a puzzled look.

Think Critically

Why do you think Uma looks puzzled? What advice would you give to Marcus and Sophia?

However, for someone who just wants to read a document, the CD may seem too complicated. If the reader is having a problem with his or her computer's internal hardware, the video of the president will not matter. Producing the CD may take extra time and greater skill, perhaps requiring the help of colleagues. You must ask yourself whether the possible outcome of this project is worth the extra effort. The extra time and effort may be worthwhile if you are hoping to land a major account using a media display. But if your audience is not the financial player you need, perhaps you are better off with the 85 printed pages or carefully chosen excerpts.

To help you decide what medium is appropriate, find out what kind of media are typically used in your organization. Your local department of social services may use e-mail for routine communication and interoffice mail for important memos and intake reports. The state agency, however, may expect e-mail attachments for monthly participation reports. Work at the national level may best be presented on a website from which PowerPoint® presentations and brochures can be downloaded and printed.

While many businesses have state-of-the-art computer equipment and fast Internet connections, some small businesses, such as Air Care's home heating and air-conditioning business, may have only a computer, a printer, and a minimum amount of accounting and word processing software. You, like Ramon, the owner of Air Care, may find yourself in a field for which you are well prepared professionally but not as adept with desktop publishing. So CD-ROMs and web pages are not yet options for everyone. Perhaps well-designed sales proposals, invoices, and interoffice memos meet the needs of this environment.

RETEACH

Tell students that finding out what medium is typically used can help them decide what medium is appropriate.

Remind students that formatting concerns are important to consider. Many organizations use formats that have been standardized over the years.

The **format** of your medium deals with the details of the document's arrangement: the type of document, its length, the preferred style manual, and its organization. Just as your English instructor may prefer that your essays be written a particular way, your employer also may prefer that your document be written a certain way. Your English instructor may require papers to be keyed and double-spaced using the guidelines from the *MLA Handbook for Writers of Research Papers.* Your business or psychology instructor may require another style guide, such as *The Chicago Manual of Style* or the *Publication Manual of the American Psychological Association.*

An employer may expect you to follow a company style sheet (with suggested headings and a specified way to present data) and include the company letterhead (with the logo, address, and slogan). Traditionally, correspondence outside an organization uses a business letter and correspondence inside an organization uses a memo. Furthermore, the level of formality may depend on the subject matter, the audience, and company standards.

Today electronic formats consisting of e-mail, CD-ROM, online help, and web-based information are changing traditional ways of communicating. E-mail is an informal and quick (although not always reliable) way to communicate and can be used for inside and outside correspondence. Forms and procedures can be posted on a company's intranet web server where templates set up for page layouts ensure design consistency.

Technical writers have many avenues with which to convey information. Writers' many choices provide them with creative and innovative solutions to any communication challenge. On the following page, Table 2.3 shows some of the choices for a medium once the purpose and scope have been determined.

FOCUS

Table 2.3

Use Table 2.3 to show how purpose and audience affect scope and medium. Also point out the variety of options available.

Provide students with the *Purpose, Scope, and Medium* worksheet available as a supplemental activity on the IRCD.

ONGOING ASSESSMENT

Stop and Think

Have students bring in assignments from other classes. Generally, the purpose will involve understanding and learning to do something; the scope will include the information in the assignment and the information that was left out; and the medium might be a handout, the board, or oral instructions.

PURPOSE	SCOPE		MEDIUM
To convince reader(s) to . . .	Includes . . .	Does *not* include . . .	Possible choices
Prepare for hurricane (residents of North Carolina)	Emergency supplies, hurricane routes, shelters, procedures	Routes/shelters for states other than North Carolina	Brochure, newspaper insert
Operate Brand X scanner	Information for scanning photos and texts	Information for any brand other than X; instructions for how to repair	Short user's manual, online help
Stop smoking with nicotine patch (smoker of ten years)	Information about the nicotine patch	Information about other methods such as gum, will power, and hypnosis	Pharmaceutical insert for nicotine patch
Eat nutritious meals (teens)	Simple, quick recipes to meet basic nutritious needs; foods teens typically like	Recipes for heart patients, diabetics, or aging population	Spiral-bound cookbook with CD
Book a vacation (middle-class families)	Vacation spots with group activities and fun parks; reduced rates	Vacation spots with long flights or honeymoon plans	Magazine article, brochure, website
Seek information about financial aid (high school seniors)	Information about parental income and college plans	Opinions about fairness of financial aid	Letter

Table 2.3

 STOP AND THINK

Analyze an assignment that one of your instructors has given you. What are the purpose, scope, and medium of the assignment?

CHAPTER 2 REVIEW

SUMMARY

1. The audience's needs and wants should dictate every decision a writer makes.

2. A specific audience is a single reader or a group of readers with a common purpose. Knowledge level, roles, interests, cultural background, and personality affect communication with a specific audience.

3. A multiple audience is made up of readers with different points of view. Analyzing knowledge level, roles, interests, cultural background, personality, and format are still important when communicating with a multiple audience.

4. A writer must analyze his or her audience, then decide how to accommodate the readers' needs and wants.

5. Early in the writing process, a writer must determine the purpose, scope, and medium.

Checklist

- Is my audience a specific audience or a multiple audience?

- Have I analyzed the knowledge level, roles, interests, cultural background, and personality of my audience?

- If I am dealing with a multiple audience, have I selected a strategy for accommodating their needs and wants?

- Have I put into words the purpose of my writing assignment?

- Have I determined the scope of my writing assignment by deciding what it should and should not include?

- Have I found an appropriate medium for the writing assignment?

- Did I match the audience to the medium?

- Have I weighed the costs and time of producing the medium?

- Have I considered other available media?

- Have I selected an appropriate format for the audience and purpose of the writing assignment?

- Have I checked for stereotypes in my writing?

Build Your Foundation

1. To make you more aware of audience, answer the following questions: Who might be the target audience for these TV shows, networks, or stations? To what groups of people might they appeal? Why?

Grey's Anatomy	Monday Night Football	Country Music Television
60 Minutes	Jeopardy	Nick at Nite
American Idol	Lost	The History Channel

2. Consider the following terms. If any are unfamiliar to you, look them up in a dictionary or ask your family or friends what they mean. Which audience(s) would understand these terms?

blitz	RAM	curl	sauté
goalie	billabong	dunk	arabesque
rap	compost	angioplasty	starboard

3. Look through the comic section of the Sunday newspaper. Which comic strips appeal to which audiences? How do you know? For each comic strip, list the target audience and features that help you identify the audience.

4. Bring several issues of your favorite magazine to class or visit a library. Spend 15–20 minutes looking at the table of contents and browsing through the articles and advertisements. After considering the following questions, write a few paragraphs analyzing one magazine for audience and purpose.

   a. What is the purpose of the magazine? Who is the intended audience?
   b. What are four things the editors of the magazine have done to accommodate their readers' needs and wants? In other words, how have the editors appealed to their readers?
   c. Do you like the way the magazine has tried to appeal to its readers? Why do you believe the appeal is or is not successful?
   d. What suggestions do you have for improving the appeal of the magazine?
   e. Do you notice stereotypes in the magazine, particularly in the advertisements? If so, what are they?

5. Suggest an appropriate audience and medium for the following situations:

   a. Nadia wants members of her scuba diving club to know the latest diving news.
   b. Thaddeus is responsible for selling manufactured homes in his territory.
   c. The County Health Department wants to tell the public how to prevent the flu.

6. Who are the primary and secondary audiences in the following situations?

   a. Aruna Amin, an advertising consultant, has been hired to write a series of ads to educate young people about the danger of using cell phones while driving.
   b. Lu-yin Chang, a professional technical writer, is working on a catalog for Pickernel Camping, a national outfitter of camping supplies.

Your Turn

7. Divide into teams of three or four students. Use the following scenario to answer items a and b.

   Sam, Kaito, and Meg have just started publishing *TV Highlights*, a weekly magazine. Sam sells the advertising. Kaito, a graphic designer, is responsible for the artwork. Kaito's uncle is the owner. He makes most of the decisions but often defers to Kaito's opinions. Meg is the accountant.

   Think about the role each person performs in this small company. How do each person's responsibilities affect decisions? How does each person's role affect how he or she communicates with the other people in the company? Also, who is the target audience for *TV Highlights*?

   a. Kaito wants a four-color cover for the first issue because he thinks the first issue should look impressive. Meg, on the other hand, believes that a four-color cover is too expensive. Sam says that the advertisers do not care how many colors are on the cover. They want only the local high school's blue and red colors to be represented. Meg decides to write a report to Kaito's uncle, recommending a two-color cover for the first few issues. Who is Meg's audience for the report? What should she remember about her audience? What kind of information might she include to convince Kaito's uncle (and Kaito)? Should she include information about Sam's concerns? Why or why not?

   b. Franz Bohm, a freelance writer, has written to Kaito, asking what topics interest the magazine's readers. The magazine is written for a rural audience in New England. The average reader is a teen-aged girl. In what types of articles do you think the readers of *TV Highlights* are interested?

8. Write a letter to your employer requesting time off for a special event, such as homecoming or a family vacation. Then switch roles. Write a letter from the employer to you denying the time off. How are your letters different?

9. Write a letter to the President of the United States about a particular policy you like (or do not like). Tell a friend what you like (or do not like) about the same policy. How does your language change?

Community Connection

10. Interview the editor or a news reporter for a local news agency— newspaper, radio, or television. What are the demographics—the specific breakdown of the members of the audience—by such identifiers as age, sex, income, and race? How do the demographics affect the news reported? How does the writer appeal to this multiple audience? How does the medium affect the message? Ask about one broadcast or column in particular. Who is the specific audience? What is the purpose, scope, or medium? Write a one-page Question and Answer (Q&A) of the interview.

11. Interview someone in your area who is from another country or from another part of the United States. Ask about differences in the culture, such as food, celebrations, customs, and manners. Research the person's culture. Write a list of suggestions that would help an area business communicate more effectively with this person. For example, what would a real estate broker need to know to work well with this person?

ASSESS

Your Turn

7. Use these communication dilemmas to point out how each person's responsibilities affect his or her decisions and how each person's role affects how he or she communicates. Additional answers are on the IRCD.

8. The letter to the employer would be carefully and tactfully worded. Explanation of why the employee should be given time off (the employee has worked hard, has not been late, deserves the time) along with the name of someone who could work during this time would be helpful. The letter to the employee should make the employee feel appreciated, include a reasonable explanation as to why the request is denied, and offer alternatives (perhaps a day off at a more convenient time).

9. A letter to the President would be respectful, formal in tone, and carefully thought out. A conversation with a friend would be casual and spontaneous.

ASSESS

Community Connection

10–11. Use these activities to apply audience and purpose analyses to real-world scenarios.

Chapter 3

Technical Research

Goals

- Distinguish the difference between researching at school and at work
- Identify and locate secondary sources
- Document secondary sources
- Evaluate sources
- Take notes from sources
- Collect primary data

Terms

- archives, p. 47
- citations, p. 55
- close-ended questions, p. 67
- direct quotation, p. 63
- documentation, p. 52
- open-ended questions, p. 67
- paraphrase, p. 62
- periodicals, p. 48
- plagiarism, p. 52
- population, p. 64
- primary sources, p. 46
- reliable data, p. 72
- respondents, p. 64
- sample, p. 64
- secondary sources, p. 46
- summarize, p. 62
- valid data, p. 72

WRITE TO LEARN

Think about a time you researched a topic. What was the reason for your research? What did researching the topic involve? In other words, how did you conduct the research? Did your research include a survey, an experiment, or an interview? What did you learn from your research activities?

Focus on Technical Research

Read the sample document on the next page and answer these questions:

- Notice that all lines after the first line of each bibliographic entry are indented. Why?
- How is the last entry different from all of the others?
- Of the sources listed, which ones did the researchers find online? in print?
- Which source is most recent?

What If?

- The researchers were planning to publish their work (1) in a newsletter for the science department at the university or (2) in a medical journal?
- If the audience was interested only in the most recent findings on the topic?

WORKING BIBLIOGRAPHY

Ben-Barak, Idan. "Radiation-proof Microbe Uses Its Powers for Good." *Sydney Morning Herald* 6 Nov.

    2008, first ed.: A24. *Newspaper Source Plus.* Web. 10 Oct. 2009.

Galhardo, Rodrigo S. and Susan M. Rosenberg. "Extreme Genome Repair." *Cell* 136.6 (2009): 998–1000.

    Print.

GuanJun, Gao, et al. "Engineering *Deinococcus Radiodurans* into Biosensor to Monitor Radioactivity and

    Genotoxicity in Environment." *Chinese Science Bulletin* 53.11 (2008): 1675–81. *Academic Search*

    Premier. Web. 21 Nov. 2009.

Fialka, John J. "Position Available: Indestructible Bugs To Eat Nuclear Waste: Scientists Envision New

    Role for Sturdy Bacteria Breed: Creating 'Super Conan.' " *Wall Street Journal* 16 Nov. 2004,

    eastern ed.: A1. Print.

Impey, Chris. *The Living Cosmos: Our Search for Life in the Universe*. New York: Random, 2007. Print.

"Tough Bug Reveals Key to Radiation Resistance." *New Scientist* 193.2596 (24 Mar. 2007): 21.

    MasterFILE Premier. Web. 11 Oct. 2009.

Sample Working Bibliography

FOCUS

Focus on Technical Research
Use the questions to encourage students to read the sample closely.

ASSESS

What If?
Use the questions to discuss how the sample would be different if the situation or audience changed.

Go to www.cengage.com/school/bcomm/techwtg for more detailed responses to these questions.

Courtesy of Sonya Parrish

Writing@Work

Education & Training

Sonya Parrish is a teaching associate and doctoral student in literature at Miami University in Oxford, Ohio. She has taught first-year college composition courses for three years. She researches primary and secondary sources regularly for her roles as graduate student and English teacher and incorporates technical writing in the syllabus for her composition courses.

Sonya's scholarly research includes hunting through digital archives, essays, and books by other scholars and through the literature in her field. "I rely heavily on using print sources in which I can write notes, underline important points or quotes, and make comments in the margins. I also compile notes from texts into Word documents that present the information in a more unified and organized manner."

Sonya teaches her students to evaluate sources using five criteria: authorship, objectivity, knowledge, accuracy, and relevance. When evaluating websites, Sonya helps her students see the way in which information on the Web is authored and constructed. Different kinds of sites—such as .org and .edu sites—deliver different kinds of information to different audiences in different ways.

When scholarly research responds thoughtfully to other scholars' work, it creates a dialogue that requires proper documentation. "Writers should acknowledge others who have provided them with information on a given topic," according to Sonya. "They should also think about their audience's expectations of accuracy and honesty in writing." She uses GPS navigation instructions as a metaphor for what proper citations should do: show the reader what "path" the author took in constructing his or her argument and prove that the path is credible. Another scholar or teacher, like Sonya, can then pick up the hunt for information using the bibliographical trail left by other authors.

Think Critically

1. If Sonya were getting an advanced degree in biology or architecture, would she rely as heavily on printed source material? Why or why not?

2. Suppose Sonya is teaching a section about Maya Angelou's poetry. Give an example of a primary source and a secondary source that Sonya might use.

Printed with permission of Sonya Parrish

CONDUCTING TECHNICAL RESEARCH

Information is everywhere: on the television; on the radio; in your textbook; in your home; on CDs and DVDs; on the Web; in magazines and newsletters; and on the lips of doctors, professors, parents, and friends. You drive to the library where there is a building full of information. If you want to know something, you only have to look in the right place.

The problem that technical researchers face is not a scarcity of information. The problem is in understanding what information they need, where it is, how it is stored, how to retrieve it, and what to do with it after they find it. The process of conducting research can be delineated as a series of steps, but like other parts of the writing process, in practice, the process is fluid, unfolding as you go.

RESEARCHING AT WORK

Employees rely on the information they collect to solve problems, to make decisions, to answer questions, and to perform many other functions at work. On the job, research is usually involved in all of the following situations (and more):

- Developing a new product
- Handling a production problem
- Purchasing equipment or services
- Establishing safety procedures
- Selecting employee benefits
- Planning an advertising campaign

Unlike writing for school, writing on the job provides information to help the business operate effectively. Its purpose is not to show the writer's knowledge of the topic.

For example, if a nurse writes a fact sheet explaining how patients should manage their diabetes, the nurse is not writing to show how much he knows about the subject, but to teach patients how to stay healthy. If a chef creates standard operating procedures, she does not write the document to impress readers with how much she learned in school, but rather to ensure food safety. All of the information that writers and researchers gather and present is used for effective job performance. Useful information that is presented effectively can determine whether an enterprise is successful or unsuccessful.

Before you can write at work, you may need to conduct research. In fact, many decisions and actions at work require more information than you have at hand. You probably begin by determining what you already know. Then considering your audience, purpose, and scope, you gather and evaluate new information and likely form conclusions about the material you read. Before you conduct the research, you must make sure you know who, what, where, when, why, and how. For example, who is involved and who will use your research? What do these people need to know? Where will you search for information—within or outside your organization or both? Why are you

To view an annotated bibliography, a list of sources with descriptive notes about each source, go to www.cengage.com/school/bcomm/techwtg. Click the link for Chapter 3; then click Sample Documents.

ENRICH

Ask professionals involved in research to share their experiences and insights with students. The professionals may include people in R&D departments, public relations workers, grant writers, and personnel officers.

Take students to the library and show them the almost limitless possibilities of electronic data collection.

TEACH

Have students view the annotated bibliography on the website. Tell them that annotated bibliographies are used by many professionals to stay current with changes and developments on particular topics. In addition, an annotated bibliography is an excellent way for a person to share knowledge and interest with another individual, such as an employee he or she is mentoring.

ENRICH

Ask the school librarian to pull a sample collection of primary source materials to share with your class.

researching this topic? How will you collect information, and how will it be used? You also need a strategy for:

- Finding and evaluating the right material and the best sources.

- Conducting the research and reading efficiently.

- Carefully and accurately recording the information you find so that you do not accidentally plagiarize or violate the owner's copyright.

- Documenting where you found the information so that you or someone else can find it again.

Researchers may find some data easily, such as production figures that are readily available on the corporate network. Sometimes, though, researchers must search extensively for information.

Employees have two basic sources of information: secondary sources and primary sources. **Secondary sources** are indirect or secondhand reports of

information, such as the description of an event the writer or speaker did not witness. When a newspaper reporter describes what executives of a closing textile plant said, that description is a secondary source. **Primary sources,** on the other hand, are direct or firsthand reports of facts or observations, such as an eyewitness account or a diary. The writer or speaker is the one who witnessed the event or developed the idea.

For example, hearing a company president rather than a reporter give reasons for a plant's closing is primary information. Likewise, a journal is a firsthand account of the writer's experiences and is, therefore, a primary source. However, if you use ideas from another person's journal in a report on healthy lifestyles, the borrowed ideas become secondary data in your report because you did not experience or observe them yourself.

Researchers generally start with secondary sources because they often give general overviews and offer useful background information. Secondary sources are usually easier and less expensive to consult than primary sources. The overviews these sources can give help researchers understand what is already known about the topic. A problem solver may even learn that someone has already discovered a solution.

STOP AND THINK

How is researching at work different from researching at school? Why do professionals conduct research?

ONGOING ASSESSMENT
Stop and Think
Use these questions to review differences between academic and work-related research and reasons professionals search for information.

FINDING SECONDARY DATA

To solve most problems, your first step is to explore the available secondary data. After all, you do not want to "reinvent the wheel." If the answer already exists, you do not need to spend time, effort, and money to rediscover it.

For work-related research, you will probably use one or more of the following sources of secondary data: your organization's correspondence and report **archives** (collections or repositories of documents), a library catalog, periodicals, and general reference materials. While these secondary data sources may be available in print (sometimes called *hard copy*), most will be available in print and electronic files.

Correspondence and Report Archives

A logical place to begin looking for an answer to a problem is in the organization where the problem exists. Most organizations keep archives of all correspondence and reports. Especially in large organizations, archives are generally maintained locally or remotely in an electronic format on the organization's intranet so that people who need the information have access but the files are not available to the public. On the other hand, some highly regulated organizations such as pharmaceutical companies may be required to keep print as well as electronic copies of essential information.

Employees may use archived documents to learn about the history of the problem or topic. They may find letters, memos, or reports explaining when problems were first noted, what kinds of investigation were conducted, and whether a solution was successful.

When the research topic does not have a history, relevant facts and statistics may be found in a variety of sources within the organization's records.

Library Catalog

The researcher's next stop is the company's library or a public or academic library. Some large businesses have an in-house or corporate library that contains specialized materials relating to the business it serves. In addition to company-produced reports such as production figures, accident reports, and personnel information, these internal libraries typically hold materials that employees need in order to stay current in the field in which they work. A software company's library may contain books and journals specializing in software development and marketing. Because these company libraries focus specifically on the needs of employees, they do not compete with public or other libraries by carrying all types of reading and research materials. They often contain more electronic than paper resources. If no in-house library is

Warm Up

As a new sales representative, you are going to Japan to meet your first prospective customer. If you know little about Japanese people and customs, where can you find out whether you should take the customer a gift and what is a good choice if you do take a gift? List several things you need to know and where you can find the information.

FOCUS
Warm Up
Use the Warm Up to explore what students already know about research. Students probably will begin by saying that they would ask a Japanese friend or a person who is well-traveled to explain customs, etiquette, and business practices. Beyond asking someone, students should be aware that what they are seeking is general knowledge that they can find online or in a library.

To view *Ways to Avoid Common Research Pitfalls,* go to www.cengage .com/school/bcomm/ techwtg. Click the link for Chapter 3; then click Data Files.

COMMUNICATION TECHNOLOGIES

When you visit a library, besides the physical library, you also have access to thousands of other libraries throughout the world. WorldCat, an Online Computer Library Center, Inc. (OCLC) product, links you to the collections of more than 71,000 (and growing) member libraries of OCLC, giving you access to more than 135 million records for books, manuscript collections, audiovisual materials, and computer files in a variety of languages.

Think Critically

Does access to so much information in many different media present problems for researchers? Explain.

available to the company's problem solvers, they must go to an academic, research, municipal, or regional library.

Whether in a corporate, public, or research library, employees looking for secondary data may start locating materials through the library catalog. The library catalog helps researchers find books, pamphlets, periodicals, audiovisual materials, and other holdings. In fact, it is now common practice for libraries also to catalog certain websites and other electronic sources such as e-books. Most libraries have computerized catalogs that are searchable by subject, title, and author and sometimes by other categories such as date or keyword. Most catalog systems also send requested entries to a printer for printing the records. Generally, libraries have integrated systems so that the online catalog can tell where a book is located and whether it has been checked out.

After the user keys the author's name, a title, or a subject, the online catalog displays a list of sources and their locations. Because materials are often cataloged using authorized subject headings from the Library of Congress Subject Headings, using keywords found in this reference can make a search more effective. If a search yields one book with useful information, a new search help the keywords found in that book's entry will likely produce other helpful sources.

If a researcher finds that a particular book is not in the library, the researcher may request that the book be ordered from another library through an interlibrary loan. The book also may be found online through a service such as NetLibrary, a subscription database that offers online access to full-text books.

Most online library catalogs are user-friendly, but you should not hesitate to ask a librarian for help. Librarians can explain how to use the equipment, what the standard subject headings are, and how to search so you find what you need quickly and efficiently. Remember that the catalog will lead you to sources for background and in-depth information. For more recent data, use periodicals or Internet sources.

Periodicals

Magazines, journals, newsletters, and newspapers are called **periodicals** because they are published at specified intervals of time. (Journals are magazines that are published for a scholarly or academic audience.) When you need current information, periodicals—whether online or in print—are one type of source you should seek. Periodicals are more current than books, but newspapers, especially daily papers, generally provide even more current information than periodicals. In addition, many periodicals, such as *Newsweek* and *The New York Times,* are now published on the Internet and in print.

The next question is how to find the articles you need in the periodicals. Library catalogs tell you what print periodicals the library holds in different subject areas, but to find specific articles, you need to search an index or a database.

In the past, indexes, printed on paper and bound as books or magazines, were time-consuming to use. Today most periodical searches are conducted electronically. Many web-based databases, available to libraries by subscription, index periodical content. Gale, EBSCOhost, ProQuest, and Elsevier are some of the best-known database providers. In addition, many of these databases are no longer just indexes; they now provide a large amount of full-text content from periodical articles, books, encyclopedias, and more. Some of the databases, such as LexisNexis and Academic Search Premier, are general; others are subject-specific, such as SIRS, which includes publications dealing with the social sciences. In addition, some databases, such as America's Newspapers and Newspaper Source Plus, specialize in newspapers, and these two databases index and include actual articles.

You can access other indexes through a service provider such as OCLC (Online Computer Library Center, Inc.). For example, WorldCat is an OCLC index of physical holdings (recordings, tapes, books, papers, and dissertations). WorldCat users might locate materials at other libraries to place an interlibrary loan request.

General Reference Materials

General reference materials such as encyclopedias, dictionaries, handbooks, almanacs, and fact books are quick ways to get information. Many users rely on easy access to general reference sources for background information. They may first check those that are available online, such as *Grolier Online Encyclopedia* or *Merriam-Webster Online.* However, a library usually offers more comprehensive resources either in the print reference collection or online in subscription databases.

Some websites even offer access to reference tools. For example, the *Encyclopedia Britannica* website provides an encyclopedia, a dictionary, and an atlas. Also, Bartleby.com gives users access to several reference tools, including dictionaries, thesauruses, fact books, and books of quotations. Some materials continue to be available on CD-ROM, such as *World Book Multimedia Encyclopedia*®, but the easy access to Internet materials is lessening the need for CD and DVD materials.

Reference materials come in general interest versions. Some examples include *World Book Encyclopedia, Encyclopedia Britannica,* and *Webster's Dictionary.* Others are special interest versions, such as *Encyclopedia of Information Ethics and Security* (2008) and *The American Heritage Stedman's Medical Dictionary* (2008). In addition, *The Encyclopedia of Educational Technology,* a website created and maintained by San Diego State University, covers performance, training, and instructional design and technology.

Electronic Resources

In addition to periodical databases, indexes, and online general reference materials such as encyclopedias and dictionaries, computers connected to the Internet provide a wealth of information on countless topics. Because the Internet is a worldwide collection of computer networks, it is an information

ENRICH

To convince students that libraries can be fun and exciting places to spend time, develop a scavenger hunt for specific information. Select facts, statistics, quotations, and graphics relating to students' potential career fields or other topics. For example, you might use your school, its history, famous graduates, and film clips from important school events.

To visit the San Diego State University site for *The Encyclopedia of Educational Technology,* go to www.cengage.com/school/bcomm/techwtg. Click the link for Chapter 3; then click Web Links.

tacojim/iStockphoto.com

highway connecting government, military, educational, and commercial organizations and private citizens to a range of services and resources. Therefore, you can get information from a huge variety of sources over the Internet. The World Wide Web (*WWW* or *the Web*) is one system for accessing information via the Internet. The Web uses http, a language for transmitting data, and browsers such as Internet Explorer® and Firefox® to locate web documents called *web pages* that may be linked to each other with hyperlinks. Web documents often contain graphics, sounds, text, and video.

Users with access to the Internet may participate in bulletin boards, e-mail, LISTSERVs, social networking, blogs (websites to which people regularly contribute content, including text, graphics, video, and sound, as well as links to other websites such as online journals and news/commentary sites), wikis (a collection of web pages to which any user may add or delete content), and other means of exchanging information. If, for example, someone had problems with his or her car and was not able to resolve the issue with the car dealer, the car owner could retrieve consumer information from the manufacturer, advocacy groups, legal professionals, and other consumers online.

Finding Electronic Information

As a researcher, how do you get to the tremendous amount of information on the Internet? You can search the Web using a search engine such as Yahoo, Google, or Clusty in much the same way you search a database using keywords and topics.

However, search engines do not look through all information on the World Wide Web. Each engine searches only a portion of all of the sites. Even metasearch engines such as mamma.com, surfwax.com, and dogpile.com do not cover the entire Web.

While search engines cover only a portion of the Web, a researcher's concern often is how to filter through so much information to find what is useful. Search engines use "spiders" to go out periodically and view web pages and links on sites; an "index" that catalogs words, Internet addresses, and other information about the pages the spider finds; and software to filter through all of the pages in the index to find matches when a search is requested. Because the "spider" goes out every few days or weeks, it detects changes made to web pages. However, until the information has been indexed, it is not available for researchers.

Because each search engine visits and indexes different sites and is updated at different times, you should routinely use at least three search engines. Then you can compare the results of your searches to determine which search engines are most effective.

Even after you have used three search engines, some Web information may evade your search. For example, *Invisible Web* or *deep Web* refers to sites that are not registered or typically searched by search engines. To get to this huge inventory of information, searchers may find Librarians' Internet Index (http://lii.org) and Infomine (http://infomine.ucr.edu) helpful in locating data in the deep Web. The wealth of information to be found in government documents also requires special search strategies. Use tools such as the Catalog of U.S. Government Publications (http://catalog.gpo.gov) and FedStats (www.fedstats.gov) or consult a government documents librarian.

TEACH
Remind students that all search engines do not follow the same process. For example, using the guides presented here on some search engines will give different results from those presented.

Searching with Keywords

Choose specific, precise keywords; then consider using the advanced or custom (terms may vary with search engines) search procedures to refine your search. The guidelines in the custom search or the Help section of the search engine should explain how to use logic or keyword connectors to limit or expand your search. While the following connectors are typical, check the guidelines for each search engine you use.

Use these strategies TO LIMIT A SEARCH:

When you connect keywords with **AND,** the search yields both keywords. Using + **(the plus sign)** gets the same results.

Ex: juvenile AND diabetes	Yields: Sites that deal with juvenile
Ex: juvenile + diabetes	diabetes only

When you connect keywords with **NOT**, the search yields the first keyword, not the second. Using − **(the minus sign)** gets the same results.

Ex: diabetes NOT juvenile	Yields: Sites that deal with any type of
Ex: diabetes – juvenile	diabetes except juvenile

When you surround keywords with quotation marks ("keyword keyword"), the search yields the same keywords in the same order beside each other.

Ex: "capital punishment"	Yields: Sites that include the same
	term, *capital punishment*, but not
	capital alone or *punishment* alone

ONGOING ASSESSMENT

Stop and Think

Use this feature to check comprehension. If students understand the definition of *secondary sources,* they should be able to identify the secondary sources in their own list.

FOCUS

Warm Up

Assign small groups to explore the questions relating to the cost of poor documentation. Ask the groups to share their work orally or ask for written notes.

Answers may include lawsuits for copyright violations, job dismissal, lost time in repeating work and research already performed, lost confidence in researchers who are sloppy or dishonest, and lost knowledge.

Use these strategies TO EXPAND A SEARCH:

When you connect keywords with **OR**, the search yields either keyword.

Ex: diabetes OR juvenile   Yields: Sites that contain *diabetes* and/or *juvenile* as the topic

When you place an asterisk (*) after the word, the search yields words that contain the base or root word.

Ex: biblio*   Yields: Sites that include *bibliography, bibliographer, bibliophile, bibliotheca,* and so on

Remember that you can get the same data in many different ways. One researcher may find an article by skimming a journal from the library shelf. Another researcher may do an online search in the library or on his or her home or office computer. Still another researcher may find a link to an online journal in a discussion group. Explore the many tools available to you for research.

 STOP AND THINK

Using the list you drafted in the Warm Up on page 47, underline the information that would come from secondary sources. For those underlined items, add any other sources or methods you can think of for accessing information.

Warm Up

DOCUMENTING SECONDARY SOURCES

Documentation is a system of giving credit to another person (writer or speaker) for his or her work. It is using a citation system to note whose ideas or words the writer is using and where he or she found them. Responsible writers document ideas and materials they borrow or use.

Plagiarism is the act of using another person's words and/or ideas without properly documenting or giving credit. While plagiarism is a serious academic offense, sometimes causing students to fail a course or to be expelled from school, it is even more serious in the workplace. Theft of another person's work often results in lost jobs, lawsuits, and ruined reputations.

For instance, Doris Kearns Goodwin, a respected historian who won the Pulitzer Prize for History in 1995, taught and served on the Board of Overseers at Harvard, assisted President Lyndon Johnson with his memoirs, and won many awards, admitted to plagiarism in a book she wrote in 1987.

Despite a long career with many achievements and honors, this admission caused Goodwin to be ridiculed in public, scorned by her peers, and subjected to significant financial loss. The University of Delaware withdrew its invitation for her to speak at graduation; PBS placed her on indefinite leave from the Jim Lehrer news show; she had to defend the credibility of

Communication Dilemma

You and your good friend Armando work for a desktop publishing company that creates marketing materials for bands performing in your area. Your job is to contact the bands, design the posters and other marketing materials, and publish and distribute the materials. You recently learned that you and Armando know the band members who are coming to town to give a concert. In fact, you know the band members so well that you have copies of some unpublished songs they shared with you before they became famous.

Armando is in charge of creating the marketing materials for this band. When you look over the finished products, you notice he included parts of the unpublished songs as a way to lure fans to the concert. You feel uneasy about publishing these songs, but you know that you cannot reach the band members in time to ask permission before the copy must be delivered to the printer.

Think Critically

How can you find out whether you and Armando are breaking copyright laws if you decide to publish the songs?

COMMUNICATION DILEMMA

Explain to students that all writing is copyrighted as soon as it is drafted, even if the writer has not gone through the legal process of copyrighting and even if the document does not include a copyright notation or the copyright symbol.

Explain *public domain.* Works created by or for the U.S. government and works with expired copyrights are examples of materials in the public domain.

Think Critically

Students could research copyright laws by asking an expert such as an attorney. Or they could search for websites such as www.copyright.gov. Publishing the songs would be an infringement of copyright.

her other books; and her publisher had to pay Lynne McTaggart, the author of the book from which Goodwin had extensively plagiarized. As you can see, plagiarism, intentional or accidental, can be damaging.

You may ask, "What exactly do I document?" You document anything you use from another person's work. Remember, if you do not document, you are no longer borrowing; you are stealing and will be treated as a thief of intellectual property. Therefore, to keep your credibility, reputation, and job, document borrowed phrases, sentences, or ideas in the form of summaries, paraphrases, and direct quotations. For instance, if you reported on the environmental impact of a new soy ink for your company's publications division, you would document researched facts, contradictory statements, and others' unique ideas.

On the other hand, you do not need to document common knowledge or information that your audience typically knows. However, common knowledge may differ for each audience, particularly expert audiences. For instance, the fact that Bill Gates is chief executive officer of Microsoft Corporation is certainly common knowledge for an audience of computer engineers. However, Gates's management philosophy might be common knowledge for business school graduates. If information is common knowledge for your target audience, you do not need to document it. The same information directed to a different audience may not be common knowledge and, therefore, would need to be documented.

The writer's field determines the documentation format. For example, Modern Language Association (MLA) format, which is most likely taught in your English class, is the documentation system used in the humanities.

For tips on avoiding plagiarism, see *How Do I Safeguard Against Plagiarism?* at www.cengage.com/school/bcomm/techwtg. Click the link for Chapter 3; then click Data Files.

For a review of what information should and should not be documented, see *Information to Cite and Not to Cite* at www.cengage.com/school/bcomm/techwtg. Click the link for Chapter 3; then click Data Files.

For more information on *Plagiarism—What It Looks Like and How to Prevent It,* go to www.cengage.com/ school/bcomm/techwtg. Click the link for Chapter 3; then click Data Files.

NET Bookmark

Although the University of Chicago Press online edition does not replace the book edition of *The Chicago Manual of Style,* you can still get information on how to cite books, electronic resources, journals, and newspapers.

The website of the Modern Language Association (MLA) provides the history of MLA along with many book titles about the English language and archives of MLA radio programs.

Go to the NET Bookmark for Chapter 3 and refer to the MLA Handbook FAQ. (1) In your research writing, should you use underlining or italics for titles of books, magazines, journals, and other publications? (2) How do you create the indention used in an MLA bibliographic entry and in a works cited list?

www.cengage.com/school/bcomm/techwtg

Other documentation systems include the American Psychological Association (APA) system for social sciences and the Council of Science Editors (CSE) system for biological sciences.

In addition, most fields have a style manual. A style manual is a book of rules for developing a document, including formatting and documentation. *The Chicago Manual of Style,* the stylebook of The University of Chicago Press, is the preferred style manual for many technical fields, including anthropology.

Because each documentation system has a particular format, consult your instructor (or employer) for the appropriate style manual. For example, if as a human resources officer you investigate the effectiveness of a test used to screen job applicants (a psychology-related topic), you probably will use American Psychological Association (APA) style. However, a report outlining the water quality of a prospective site for a trout farm (a biology-related topic) may require that you use Council of Science Editors (CSE) style guidelines.

All documentation systems explain how to identify each source. However, the emphasis, order, and punctuation may be different. For example, the APA and CBE emphasize publication dates in citations because dates are critical in the sciences. The MLA emphasizes the author and location in the text. This book uses the MLA system.

Documentation comes in two parts: (1) the Works Cited (or bibliography), a list of sources at the end of the document, and (2) the internal citations. The documentation process begins with a working bibliography.

Bibliography and Works Cited

A bibliography (also called *Works Cited* in MLA) is a list of sources used in researching a topic. While collecting data, researchers develop a working bibliography. They continue to locate and add new sources to the list during the research process. Sometimes they delete a source from the list when they find one that is more recent or more reliable.

When the research is finished, writers use the list's final form to prepare a bibliography. A bibliography has three purposes: (1) It establishes credibility by showing readers what sources you consulted; (2) it allows others to find your information path so they can continue or evaluate the study; and (3) it gives credit to other people's thoughts, words, and sentences that you used.

As you look at secondary sources, you develop a paper or an electronic working bibliography. You can enter publication information for each source on a 3" × 5" index card. Cards allow you to arrange entries easily for the final source list. However, many writers prefer to maintain bibliographic data electronically. Like the cards, computers allow you to add, delete, or

sdominick/iStockphoto.com

move sources easily. In addition, software is available that automatically puts source information into MLA form. Hypertext programs show images of cards where users key bibliographic information.

After you complete the research and draft the document, you remove the sources that you did not use. You place sources you did use in order. For MLA, use alphabetical order by the first author's last name or by the word that appears at the beginning of the entry (often a title) if the author is not given. Other systems arrange sources differently. You will use the arranged cards to compose the Works Cited page, as shown in the sample working bibliography on page 43. This page is placed at the end of the document or report.

Internal Citations

People will assume that ideas are yours unless they see a citation in the text. **Citations** are written indications of the source of borrowed materials. Enter internal documentation immediately after each summary, paraphrase, and direct quotation to tell your reader where you found the information. Internal citations in MLA consist of the author's last name (or a shortened form of the title if no author is named) and the page number. When the author's name is mentioned in the introductory sentence, only the page numbers are included in the citation. Readers then use the author's name or the title to find the full bibliographic entry in the alphabetical listing of works cited. Place the citation at the end of the sentence (or group of sentences) containing the source material in your document. Enclose the citation in parentheses and place the period after the ending parenthesis, as shown in Figure 3.1 on the next page.

Figure 3.1

Show the connection between in-text documentation and bibliographic entries in the works cited at the end of the document. For example, the parenthetical documentation for John J. Fialka's article in *The Wall Street Journal* tells readers the page on which the borrowed idea appears in the source.

For additional examples, refer to the Internal Citation and Works Cited Teaching Master and the Numbered Reference System Teaching Master on the IRCD.

Scientists who first found *Deinococcus radiodurans* in an irradiated can of meat in 1956 were surprised. Irradiating food, they thought, would preserve it, yet this pink bacteria was creating a nasty bulge in the can. Then in 1996, scientists working around a nuclear waste tank in Savannah River, South Carolina, found the same tough bacteria (which came to be known as Conan the Bacterium), growing on a rod in the tank. Because this bacterium can not only survive, but thrive in "some of Earth's most inhospitable environments," the United States Department of Energy believes it may be used as a solution to the potential $260 billion cleanup of nuclear waste sites across the country (Fialka A1).

Researchers are just beginning to understand how *Deinococcus radiodurans* survives radiation and what other uses it may have. According to Chris Impey's *The Living Cosmos,* this bacterium can repair damage to its DNA quickly, typically in 24 hours, by storing five or more copies of its genome ready to be replicated (107). One scientist for the Uniformed Services University suggests that, if people and animals can develop repair systems similar to *Deinococcus radiodurans,* they too can withstand higher doses of radiation. Avoiding radiation sickness would be helpful, for example, in cancer treatment and space travel ("Tough Bug"). Another use was found by a group of researchers in China who have genetically modified *Deinococcus radiodurans* with a green florescence protein to create a biosensor that glows when "biological hazards of radioactive and toxic pollutants" are present (GuanJun et al.).

Excerpt from Research Document

GuanJun, Gao, Fan Lu, and Hua YueJin. "Engineering *Deinococcus Radiodurans*

into Biosensor to Monitor Radioactivity and Genotoxicity in Environment."

Chinese Science Bulletin 53.11 (2008): 1675–81. *Academic Search Premier.*

Web. 21 Nov. 2009.

Fialka, John J. "Position Available: Indestructible Bugs To Eat Nuclear Waste:

Scientists Envision New Role for Sturdy Bacteria Breed: Creating 'Super Conan.'"

Wall Street Journal 16 Nov. 2004, eastern ed.: A1. Print.

Impey, Chris. *The Living Cosmos: Our Search for Life in the Universe.* New York:

Random, 2007. Print.

"Tough Bug Reveals Key to Radiation Resistance." *New Scientist* 193.2596 (24 Mar.

2007): 21. MasterFILE Premier. Web. 11 Oct. 2009.

Excerpt from Works Cited

Figure 3.1 Internal Citation and Works Cited

STOP AND THINK

What happens when writers incorrectly or incompletely cite sources? What are the costs to businesses? to professionals?

EVALUATING SOURCES

As you have discovered, not everything that appears in print (or on your computer, radio, or TV) is true. In fact, many mistakes, untruths, and half-truths that you would not want to repeat are published. For instance, a financial planner who uses information from an unreliable source to make faulty investments for her clients will not stay in business very long. So when you conduct research, choose your data sources critically and carefully.

These guidelines for evaluating sources will help you get started.

Publication Date

When you want to know the most recent discoveries and happenings in a particular area, you need up-to-date information. Therefore, you must check publication dates. The data in a book may be even older than the copyright date indicates because some books take two or more years to be published. Likewise, websites without dates may not have been checked or revised in several years.

Author's Credentials

An author's reputation is an important element in determining the value of a potential source. An author or authors with a strong and positive reputation can lend credibility to your writing. Furthermore, the methods and resources used by an author or editor have the ability to help or harm your writing.

Reputation

Often the preface or introduction of a book outlines the education and experience of the writers or editors. Likewise, magazine and journal articles sometimes include brief biographies. Check websites, particularly the beginning and ending pages, for an author's biography and credentials. If the publication gives no information about the author or editor, consider factors such as the reputation of the journal, publisher, or associated business or organization.

You also can check an author's reputation in reference sources such as *Who's Who in America, Contemporary Authors, Who's Who in Science,* and *Who's Who in Small Business and Entrepreneurship Worldwide.* Some of these references, such as *Contemporary Authors,* are found online.

Based on what you learn about the author's credentials, determine whether he or she qualifies as an expert in the field. If you have two sources on the same topic, you might find one author to be more credible than the other.

FOCUS ON ETHICS

When discussing this feature, generate a list of people in various work and academic situations whom students might consult.

Think Critically

If the use of the cartoon falls under the "one-time educational use" rule, it may be included without permission. However, if the report is to have widespread publication or is to be reproduced for profit, the writer needs permission.

APPLY

Help students use the discussion on evaluating sources to develop their own checklist. It might include questions such as these for each source:

Is it up to date?
Is it authoritative?
Is it accurate?
Is it reliable?
Is it complete?
Is the evidence compelling?
Is it unbiased?

Focus on Ethics

Another aspect of borrowing or using others' words and ideas involves copyright. Copyright legally protects the rights of writers and gives them a way to control how their work is used. Copyright applies only to tangible and original expression, not to oral presentations.

Using copyrighted work requires special considerations. If the way you plan to use someone's words or ideas fits the definition of fair use, you may use the work without paying for it or getting permission. Yet you still must give credit to the creator. Fair use guidelines are special exceptions that allow others to use a portion of a writer's work in a limited way. Fair use evaluates the purpose and nature of the new use, the character of the copyrighted work, the percentage of the work being used, and the effect of the use on the original's marketability. Ultimately, fair use requires that the new user not damage the original or profit from its use.

When you are uncertain about whether to request copyright permission or to document a source, consult other writers, your supervisor or mentor at work, or others with experience in the field. If you are still in doubt, it is better to request permission and to document. No writer or professional has ruined his or her reputation or career by overdocumenting, but many have by not documenting.

Think Critically

If you find a cartoon in the Sunday newspaper, should you document or request permission before using it to introduce a concept or highlight a point in a report you are writing?

Methods and Resources

Usually, in the introduction of a book or in the opening paragraphs of an article, the author or editor will explain the methods used to reach the conclusions. If you believe those methods are flawed, the book or article loses credibility as a potential source. Likewise, you may evaluate a potential source by the resources its author uses. Resources may be mentioned in the text and listed in the works cited or bibliography.

Depth and Coverage

Determine whether the source covers the topic in a way that is appropriate for your and your audience's needs. Does the text explore the topic deeply enough and in enough detail to be useful? Is it too technical, or does it provide only a surface treatment? Is the source a popular or commercial publication or a scholarly publication? Scholarly sources such as peer-reviewed journals and university press or academic publications generally offer more thorough and reliable information.

In addition, you should look critically at the tone and presentation of source material. Favor those sources that present all sides (opposing views) of an issue in an objective tone. Obvious biases, lack of logical reasoning, little or weak evidence, or unbalanced treatment are all reasons to look for other sources.

Special Considerations for Electronic Sources

These guidelines pertain to many sources, but the increasing availability of electronic materials means that researchers are spending more time and effort searching online. Therefore, you should give special consideration to evaluating electronic sources. Because its materials are not screened in any way, the Internet contains more trash than treasure. Remember that anyone, from the bored 10-year-old next door to the busy physics professor, can post a website.

You will find the following guidelines to be useful in evaluating electronic information:

- **Is an author or sponsoring group listed?** Are credentials or experiences noted to show that the author is an expert on the subject covered? Is the author or sponsor mentioned in other sources? If no author or sponsor is given, a critical reader might wonder why. For instance, an animal rights supporter could post an anonymous site exaggerating abusive aspects of corporate farming methods. Without knowing the author and his or her agenda, readers might not recognize the bias of the site.

- **What is the electronic address?** The abbreviation in the web address should show where the source originates. Several examples follow.

Educational institution	.edu
Nonprofit organization	.org
Government organization	.gov
Military	.mil
For-profit or commercial organization	.com

Sites sponsored by schools are usually academic and objective, providing reliable information. Government-sponsored sites—whether local, state, national, or international—typically present reliable information, such as U.S. census data. However, these sites may be biased. For example, the President controls the press secretary's message and the focus of a given story.

Likewise, many nonprofit organizations such as the American Lung Association maintain trustworthy sites, but some may be biased by the organization's agenda. For example, the website of the National Rifle Association is unlikely to provide statistics on the number of children killed by guns in their homes, but is more likely to show how many burglaries are stopped by homeowners with guns. However, commercial sites are almost always biased. After all, readers cannot expect a web page sponsored by Gerber® to explain to parents why they should not feed Gerber® baby food to their children.

ENRICH
Bring in several sources—some reliable, such as reputable scholarly journals, and some not as reliable, such as tabloids. Allow students to examine the sources and discuss their ability or inability to justify using the sources in a research paper or project.

Use the Guidelines for Evaluating Sources Teaching Master on the IRCD.

ENRICH
Ask students to locate one online source they consider trustworthy and one they do not. Ask them to explain their reasons for each.

ONGOING ASSESSMENT

Stop and Think

Form small groups to discuss this feature. Answers will vary for each group, but at the end of the discussion, point out that if Colleen's entire research project is based on one discredited or invalid study, her study is likely to suffer the same criticism. As an extension of this activity, discuss a responsible and ethical response for Colleen to take.

twohumans/iStockphoto.com

- **What are the references and/or links?** Does the website include a list of sources used in preparing the page that readers can check? Are links to other reputable, reliable sites included? Are the links to scholarly sites or to commercial or obviously biased sites?

- **Is there balance and a clear purpose?** Does the site present the subject fairly? Does it include opposing viewpoints? Is the design clear and careful to aid the reader's understanding, or does the design encourage strong reactions or confusion? Offensive images and cluttered, irrelevant information may be intended to create a particular response from users. For instance, viewers are more likely to have an emotional reaction than a logical response to an image of caged animals in a medical research facility. Understanding a site's purpose—to sell ideas, products, or services; to share knowledge; or to incite strong reactions—can help determine how reliable the information is.

- **What do design and presentation suggest?** If the site is well-designed and effective, the data it contains is more likely to have been treated with the same care and effort. Similarly, a site that demonstrates effective communication skills—free of grammar and spelling errors—is more likely to gain a reader's trust.

🛑 STOP AND THINK

Read this case and consider possible outcomes: Colleen received time and money to study the effects of a particular veterinary medicine on humans. Her report requesting permission for this project was based primarily on one study published in an animal science journal. Over the last year, this study was largely discredited in animal and human medical journals.

TAKING NOTES FROM SOURCES

Employees doing research note information they collect, just as you do when writing a paper in school. When you discover data you believe will be helpful, write complete, careful notes. Some researchers prefer to use 4" × 6" note cards because they are easy to arrange and carry. At the same time, laptop and handheld computers encourage researchers to take notes electronically. The computer user can transfer notes to the first draft of the report without having to rekey them. Also, researchers reading a document online can copy and paste material they want to quote directly into the draft document.

You should read your source material carefully before making any notes. Understanding your sources thoroughly is an important part of being a successful researcher.

Read the excerpt in Figure 3.2 from an article describing a genetically engineered bacterium developed from *Deinococcus radiodurans.* John J. Fialka wrote the article "Position Available: Indestructible Bugs To Eat Nuclear Waste" for *The Wall Street Journal.* You will find the complete bibliographic entry on page 43 in the sample working bibliography. This passage will be used to discuss note taking.

On each card or with note-taking software, include (1) the information you want to use—only one idea per card, (2) the topic, and (3) the source and page number(s) from which you took the data. Figures 3.3 and 3.4 illustrate the way some researchers use note cards.

You can use borrowed information in your notes three ways:

1. Summary
2. Paraphrase
3. Direct quotation

The original Conan proved to be a wimp among extremophiles. It could handle radiation but not the solvent toluene and other chemicals normally found in bomb makers' wastes. So in 1997, the Energy Department started work on a genetically manipulated bug that researchers called Super Conan.

Super Conan now lives in a petri dish at the Uniformed Services University of the Health Sciences, a U.S. military research facility in Bethesda, MD. It can handle nasty chemicals as well as radiation, but the researcher who developed it, Michael J. Daly, says that the government is afraid to let it out.

"We're at a point where we could do some field trials," he says, adding that his sponsors at the Energy Department doubt that the public is ready for the release of the laboratory-engineered bug into the environment. It might eat nuclear wastes, but they worry about what else it might do, he says.

Figure 3.2 Excerpt from a Published Article

Examine the notes you take during class. About what percentage of the notes are written in the instructor's or the speaker's exact words? About what percentage is written in your own words—your interpretation of the instructor's or speaker's comments? How many notes are your ideas or perhaps conclusions you came to as a result of something someone else said?

FOCUS

Warm Up

Use the Warm Up to remind students that note taking is a skill they already practice. Thus, they are building on what they already know. Students will probably say that most of their notes are written in their own words, while only a small portion are written exactly as the instructor or textbook stated. Also, most students will say that they add their own insights and conclusions to notes.

TEACH

Tell students that when they take notes, they should distinguish their own ideas by writing them in a different color, highlighting them, or enclosing them in brackets.

TEACH

Tell students that summaries may vary greatly. A writer may summarize a 500-page book in one sentence or summarize two paragraphs in two or three sentences.

Ask students to compare the summary with the original material from Fialka's article. Does the summary accurately reflect Fialka's intended meaning? Does the summary include only the most important information? Are the wording and sentence structure dramatically different from Fialka's?

FOCUS

Figure 3.3

Ask students to note the following: The source tag in the upper right corner has a section and page number because the material came from a newspaper source. The topic tag in the upper left corner summarizes as specifically as possible the note's one idea.

If the borrowed material had come from an electronic source without page numbers (as many websites do not have page numbers), the source tag would have shown the author's name or the site title when no author is named.

ENRICH

If you have access to note-taking software or if it is available in your library or computer lab, give students a demonstration. Compare the software to the use of index cards. Explain that the software was developed using the same principles researchers use with index cards.

RETEACH

Remind students to work carefully when taking notes. They are responsible for others' words and ideas.

> Fear of environmental damage from Super Conan Fialka A1
>
> To be able to deal with some of the defense industry's wastes, the Energy Department used the radiation-resistant Conan and genetically engineered the bacterium to handle hazardous chemicals left from bomb making. But now the government is unwilling to release this Super Conan for field testing for fear of unknown environmental effects.

Figure 3.3 Summary Note Card

Summary

To **summarize** is to condense longer material, keeping essential or main ideas and omitting unnecessary parts such as examples and illustrations. Be consistent with the source's idea, but use your words. When conducting job-related research, you might summarize a journal article or a chapter of a book that is helpful at supporting evidence in a report. The original material might be an entire book, but your summary could be a few paragraphs or one sentence. The note in Figure 3.3 summarizes the original material you read in the article about bacterium.

Paraphrase

To **paraphrase** is to present someone else's idea in one's own words, phrases, and sentence structure. While a summary should be shorter than the original material, a paraphrase generally is about the same length or even a bit longer than the original. A writer paraphrases when the material supports a point but is not unique or dramatic enough to be quoted. Most of the materials that writers use from other sources are paraphrased. Paraphrasing allows writers to include other people's thinking while putting the borrowed ideas into their own words and sentences. As you practice paraphrasing, you may find the following process helpful.

1. Read the original carefully.
2. Put it aside.
3. Write the idea in your own way.
4. Compare your version with the original.
5. Make certain you have used your own words and sentence structure and have accurately conveyed the author's idea. (Borrowing three or more words in a row is quoting and requires quotation marks.)

Figure 3.4 contains a paraphrase of the last two sentences from the excerpt on bacterium. Notice that the wording and sentence structure are significantly different. Changing or moving a word or two is not effective paraphrasing. Avoid plagiarism by stating the borrowed idea in your own way, choosing words and sentence structure you would normally use, and properly crediting the author of the source.

No field trials for Super Conan	Fialka A1
According to Michael J. Daly, the developer of Super Conan, the Energy Department refuses to field-test the bacterium for fear that it might eat not only the nuclear waste it was designed to eat, but also some things it was not intended to destroy.	

Figure 3.4 Paraphrase Note Card

Direct Quotation

Direct quotation, the third way writers incorporate material into their documents, is the use of borrowed ideas, words, phrases, and sentences exactly as they appear in the original document. However, you do not want to overuse quotations. Avoid a cut-and-paste patchwork style by making less than 20 percent of your document direct quotations. Copy phrases and sentences directly only when you cannot present the idea as well in your own words. For instance, if the original writer or speaker chose unusual words or composed unique or dramatic sentences, you may want your reader to get the flavor of the original by quoting directly. Another reason for using direct quotation is to enhance your credibility by using the words of a well-known authority. Figure 3.5 is a model of a note card using direct quotation.

Description of *D. radiodurans*	Fialka A1
One reporter describes *Deinococcus radiodurans* as "a wimp among extremophiles."	

Figure 3.5 Direct Quotation Note Card

Introduce Quotations

Writers introduce quotations to make the writing smooth. Do not let quoted sentences stand alone. You can integrate quotations into your text with words such as *according to one expert* and *Greg Markham claims* or with complete sentences such as the following:

Benjamin Franklin gave this advice in *Poor Richard's Almanac:* "Early to bed, early to rise, makes a man healthy, wealthy, and wise."

Indicate Added or Omitted Material

When you need to add to or edit a direct quotation for clarity or conciseness, use brackets to set your changes apart from the quoted words, as in the sentences below.

Original: "After the board meeting in which a 2 percent fine was approved, she signed her resignation letter."

Addition for clarity: "After the board meeting in which a 2 percent fine was approved, [Maureen O'Keefe] signed her resignation letter."

TEACH
Remind students that extended direct quotations are treated differently than brief ones in some style manuals. For example, MLA quotations of more than four keyed lines are begun on a separate line from the rest of the text, indented 1" from the left margin, presented without quotation marks (because the quotation is marked by its indention), and double-spaced.

TEACH
Explain that ellipses and brackets are used only in direct quotations.

ENRICH
For additional examples, show the Summary, Paraphrase, and Direct Quotation Note Cards Teaching Master on the IRCD.

Complete the activity *Working with Direct Quotations* available at www.cengage.com/school/bcomm/techwtg. Click the link for Chapter 3; then click Data Files.

ONGOING ASSESSMENT

Stop and Think

Assign this feature to check reading comprehension.

Tell students that a direct quotation is used when an idea is worded in such a unique way that the writer cannot express it as well in his or her own words or when the writer wants to enhance his or her credibility.

An ellipsis is used to indicate that the writer omitted part of a quoted sentence.

Warm Up

What could you do in the following situation? You stained your new sweater with a chemical from the chemistry lab. You do not know the name of the chemical, but you remember the experiment and probably would recognize the bottle containing the chemical. You want to have the sweater cleaned, but you are afraid to do so without knowing what chemical caused the spot.

FOCUS

Warm Up

Use this feature as a discovery exercise. The lists of what could be done should give students an inventory of the types of research, especially primary research, someone might do to solve a problem or answer a question. Entries may include questioning the chemistry instructor, reading the sweater's care instructions, talking to a professional cleaner, reading the chemical container's label, and testing water or a cleaning solution on the stain. Each answer represents a type of research. For example, questioning the instructor or the professional cleaner is surveying and testing a cleaning agent is experimentation.

You may need to quote only part of a sentence. In that case, use an ellipsis—three spaced dots—to show where you omitted words from the original. However, if you include a paraphrase of the idea (rather than omit it), you do not need an ellipsis. If the reason for O'Keefe's resignation is not important to your work, you might quote the source this way:

Omission: "After the board meeting . . . , [Maureen O'Keefe] signed her resignation letter."

The ellipsis shows that the clause "in which a 2 percent fine was approved" was left out of the quotation.

 STOP AND THINK

When should a writer use direct quotation? Would you use an ellipsis or brackets to indicate that you left out part of a quoted sentence?

COLLECTING PRIMARY DATA

Many job-related problems or questions are too unique or too current for secondary sources to answer. A commercial fisher may learn more about a new net's effectiveness by talking to other users and experimenting than by reading the literature on nets. To solve some work-related concerns, primary data may be more help. Primary data is gathered through field research: surveys, interviews, observation, and experimentation. Some field research is conducted in person, some by telephone, and some online.

Surveys

Surveys gather facts, beliefs, attitudes, and opinions from people. Many businesses rely on surveys to collect information for decision making. One example is a questionnaire accompanying a product registration form for small appliances such as hair dryers. The manufacturer uses the data to determine who is buying the product, how the buyer learned of the product (what advertising method worked), and how satisfied the buyer is.

A survey works only when you know what you want to learn before you begin. For example, if your goal is to learn students' preferences for cafeteria food, you may not want to ask for their favorite food. If you do, their responses may not be appropriate for a school cafeteria, such as flaming kabobs and baked Alaska. Once you decide what you want to learn, you should (1) carefully select your audience or **respondents** (people chosen to answer question), (2) decide how you will administer your survey, and (3) carefully plan your questions.

When you choose an audience, you must select a sample broad enough to represent that audience. A **population** is the target group from which a person wants to gather data. The owner of a garden center who wants to know whether customers will use a repotting service would have a population of all of the business's customers. If the owner cannot question all customers due to expense, time, or distance, she may choose a sample to provide representative answers. A **sample** is a subgroup with the same characteristics as the entire population. Keep in mind that the sample must

be small enough for you to tabulate and analyze the results but large enough to provide meaningful results. In some situations, companies hire specially trained people to design and conduct surveys.

Once you know your audience, the next step is to decide how to administer the survey. You can administer questionnaires in person, by mail, by telephone, or by e-mail. (Today many businesses survey by e-mail.) This decision is based on the kind of data you seek, how much time you have, and what your budget is. If you are asking personal or controversial questions, you should use a confidential mailed survey to ensure a higher return rate. Also, although many people believe their e-mail is private, it is far from secure. In fact, in the workplace, employers have the right to access information on company computers, which means that your e-mail is subject to scrutiny. If time is a concern, telephone, e-mail, and in-person surveys provide faster responses than mail surveys. Also remember that all survey methods can be costly.

Carefully planned, effective survey instruments increase the rate of responses received. Thus, it is important to consider the following suggestions as you prepare surveys:

- **Explain why you need the information and how it will be used.** Because you are asking respondents to share data, they have the right to know what you plan to do with the information. In a cover letter or an opening paragraph, explain what prompted the survey. Then describe the benefits. Estimate the time required to complete the survey. Many surveys also offer to send results of the study to respondents or tell respondents where they can find the published results.

- **Convince your audience to participate.** After all, you are requesting their time and thoughts. They may wonder what you are giving them in return. You might offer an incentive such as coupons, free merchandise or services, improved or additional services, or discounts.

Technical Research | 65

ENRICH

Invite an expert on data analysis to share insights with your class. For example, many colleges, universities, and government agencies have institutional researchers who can describe their jobs and ways their organizations collect and use information. For instance, many large nonprofit organizations have an institutional effectiveness office whose job is to collect data on how well (or poorly) organizations perform. The professionals working in these departments are experts in collecting, analyzing, and interpreting data.

- **Logically order questions beginning with easy-to-answer items.** If respondents have difficulty with the first questions, they are not likely to continue. The initial questions should ask for information that is easy to recall and not too personal. Also arrange questions in logical groupings to aid respondents' memory, as in the questions below.

  - In what county do you live?

  - How long have you lived there?

- **Ask only necessary questions.** If you do not need the answer, do not ask the question. For example, do not ask about income if income is not relevant to the data you seek. People will not respond if they believe you are wasting their time.

- **Write clear and nonleading questions.** For responses to be useful, questions must be clear and precise. Compare the following two questions:

  - Do you shop by mail often?

  - Do you shop by mail once a month?

With the first question, the respondent will answer based on his or her definition of *often.* That answer may not be useful. Likewise, questions should not lead respondents to particular answers. Consider the following questions as an illustration:

  - Don't you believe that the cost of class rings is outrageous?

  - Why don't you buy your lunch in the school cafeteria?

The wording suggests a particular answer. Consider changing it as follows:

  - Do you believe the cost of class rings is reasonable or unreasonable?

  - Is cost a factor in your decision not to purchase lunch in the school cafeteria?

- **Make the purpose of the question clear.** If the survey is to learn about consumers' reactions to your newspaper's new type style, do not ask general questions such as "Why did you purchase this newspaper?" Answers to that general question may vary tremendously from "It was the cheapest one on the newsstand" to "It is the one my father reads." Such responses will not help you find what you want to know—whether people like the new type style.

- **Prefer facts to opinions.** When designing questions, seek facts whenever possible. Facts provide stronger, more credible evidence. For example, ask "Do you purchase from a mail-order catalog at least once a month?" rather than "Do you like mail-order shopping?" However, sometimes opinions provide useful information, as in a satisfaction survey.

- **Stick to one topic per question.** While you might be tempted to include several issues in one question, the answers will be useless if you do not know to which topic the person is responding. Suppose respondents say yes to the question "Are you ever concerned for your safety as you walk through the parking deck and up the stairs into the Sollenberger Building at night?" You do not know what concerns the respondents—the deck, the stairs, the building, or the darkness.

- **Plan for tabulation.** Remember that once responses come in, you need to evaluate and interpret them. Your job will be easier if you design questions whose answers are stated as numbers. When you already know the range of possible answers, **close-ended questions** (questions that restrict the number of possible answers) such as those in Figure 3.6 allow for a limited number of responses and are easy to tabulate.

1. Do you live within five miles of one of our stores?

   Yes_____   No_____

2. Please indicate your level of satisfaction with your purchase.

   a. Extremely Satisfied < >

   b. Satisfied < >

   c. Somewhat Satisfied < >

   d. Somewhat Dissatisfied < >

   e. Dissatisfied < >

   f. Extremely Dissatisfied < >

Figure 3.6 Close-Ended Questions

Although more difficult to tabulate, **open-ended questions** encourage the respondent to provide any answer he or she likes; the question gives no suggested answers. These questions are sometimes necessary to discover respondents' thoughts and feelings. Unexpected attitudes or information may be uncovered this way.

Open-ended questions ask respondents to supply words, sentences, or short essays, as in the following examples:

- How do you think RFG's board should respond to the new regulations?

- What could Apgard do to improve service to you and your organization?

Leave adequate space for answers when asking open-ended questions.

On the next page, Figure 3.7 gives examples of different types of questions.

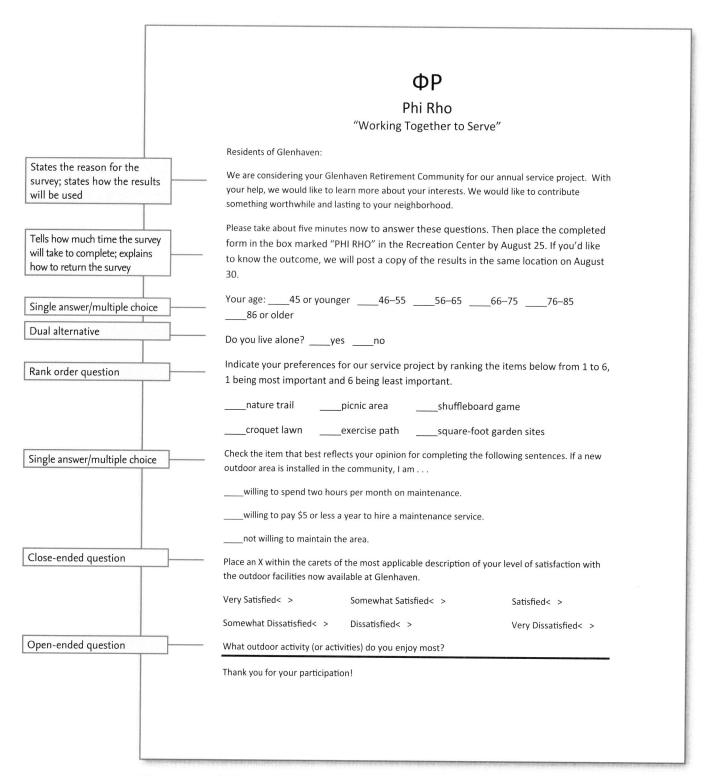

States the reason for the survey; states how the results will be used

Tells how much time the survey will take to complete; explains how to return the survey

Single answer/multiple choice

Dual alternative

Rank order question

Single answer/multiple choice

Close-ended question

Open-ended question

ΦΡ

Phi Rho

"Working Together to Serve"

Residents of Glenhaven:

We are considering your Glenhaven Retirement Community for our annual service project. With your help, we would like to learn more about your interests. We would like to contribute something worthwhile and lasting to your neighborhood.

Please take about five minutes now to answer these questions. Then place the completed form in the box marked "PHI RHO" in the Recreation Center by August 25. If you'd like to know the outcome, we will post a copy of the results in the same location on August 30.

Your age: ____45 or younger ____46–55 ____56–65 ____66–75 ____76–85 ____86 or older

Do you live alone? ____yes ____no

Indicate your preferences for our service project by ranking the items below from 1 to 6, 1 being most important and 6 being least important.

____nature trail ____picnic area ____shuffleboard game

____croquet lawn ____exercise path ____square-foot garden sites

Check the item that best reflects your opinion for completing the following sentences. If a new outdoor area is installed in the community, I am . . .

____willing to spend two hours per month on maintenance.

____willing to pay $5 or less a year to hire a maintenance service.

____not willing to maintain the area.

Place an X within the carets of the most applicable description of your level of satisfaction with the outdoor facilities now available at Glenhaven.

Very Satisfied< >   Somewhat Satisfied< >   Satisfied< >

Somewhat Dissatisfied< >   Dissatisfied< >   Very Dissatisfied< >

What outdoor activity (or activities) do you enjoy most?

Thank you for your participation!

Figure 3.7 Mailed Survey

Interviews

Interviews, like surveys, are an excellent source of primary data. Interviews give you access to experts' facts, opinions, and attitudes that you might not find any other way. However, interviewing can be time-consuming and costly. To make the process as successful as possible, use the following guidelines:

- **Define your purpose.** Know what information you want from each interviewee. Write down the purpose and review it before talking to the interviewee.

- **Make an appointment.** Telephone, write, or e-mail the respondent to describe the topic and to request an interview. Whether you will be interviewing someone by telephone, by mail, by e-mail, or in person, ask the respondent in advance for a convenient time to conduct the interview. If the interview will be in person, offer to visit the respondent or to arrange a suitable place to conduct the interview. If the interview will be via mail or e-mail, agree on a time frame for sending questions and receiving answers. For interviews by instant messaging, set an appointed time. Make certain that the respondent understands the topic and that you have allowed reasonable preparation time. Moreover, be professional in your appearance, writing, and speaking.

© Stephen Coburn, 2009/Used under license from Shutterstock.com

- **Do your homework.** Do not expect the respondent to make all of the effort. Learn as much as possible about the topic before you conduct the interview.

- **Plan and write your questions.** Prepare questions to draw out specific detailed information. Avoid vague questions such as "How do you feel about responding to emergency calls involving hazardous materials?" Instead, ask clear, specific questions such as "What training has prepared you for emergencies involving toxic gases?" In addition, avoid questions that require a yes or no response because they do not encourage the speaker to elaborate. Also avoid questions that reflect an opinion or bias, such as "Isn't it true that management overemphasizes shop safety?" Instead, ask for the respondent's views: "In regard to shop safety, does management underemphasize, overemphasize, or adequately emphasize?"

Many interviewers develop questions on a laptop or handheld computer. This method lets them read the questions from the machine and record answers on it as the interview takes place. Some interviewers write questions on one sheet of paper and record answers on another. Other interviewers prefer to write each question and its answer on a note card. An audio recorder may be helpful, but ask permission to record the interview before you begin. Choose the system that works best for you.

RETEACH
Show the Tips for Interviewing Teaching Master on the IRCD.

ENRICH
One of the most difficult factors in observing people is recording external actions rather than motivations. Have teams of students practice recording observations somewhere on campus, perhaps in the cafeteria or student commons. For example, assign an observation of students' eating habits—eating food from the school food service, bringing lunch from home, purchasing food from vending machines, or skipping lunch. Then discuss and review students' recorded observations.

■ **Conduct the interview in a competent and courteous manner.** Remember, you are in control and the success of the session depends on you, not the respondent. Make sure you do the following:

- Arrive on time.

- Introduce yourself.

- Explain the purpose of the interview.

- Stay on track; stick to the topic.

- If interviewee speaks off topic, be prepared to pursue unexpected and interesting topics by asking follow-up questions.

- Take notes, but not excessively.

- Listen attentively.

- Ask for clarification or more complete details if needed.

- Dress appropriately.

- Speak in a clear, distinct voice.

- Be assertive but not arrogant.

- Avoid small talk.

- Thank the respondent for his or her time.

- Offer a handshake as you leave.

- Add a more complete summary to your notes as soon as you leave.

Observation

In addition to surveying and interviewing, observing is another method of collecting primary data. Professionals frequently rely on observation to solve problems in their jobs. Medical professionals observe patients to diagnose illnesses. Crop scientists observe the numbers and types of weeds and insects in a field to decide whether the crop should be sprayed. Highway departments count vehicles to decide where to place traffic signals. However, you need to be careful when gathering data by observation. Observers may be biased, or subjects may act differently if they know they are being studied. Further, you should strive to interpret data objectively. Do not begin with preconceived ideas. To collect credible data by observation, use the following guidelines:

■ **Train observers in what to look for, what to record, and how to record.** If you wanted to know about traffic at a certain intersection, you would train people to count vehicles; in addition, you would need to tell the observers the rules. For example, how would they count enclosed-bed trucks such as moving vans? If one observer counted these trucks with passenger vehicles, another counted the trucks with commercial vehicles, and the third did not count the trucks at all, the data would be flawed. Also make sure that all observers are using terms the same way. For example, what is "peak period"? If you tell observers that the peak period is from 11 A.M. until 2:30 P.M., their counts for peak period will be useful data because each observer counted during the same time frame.

- **Make systematic observations.** For instance, if the observers counting vehicles work only from 7 A.M. to 9 A.M. and from 4 P.M. to 6 P.M., will you get an accurate picture? Because many people are commuting to work and school during these times, you are likely to get inflated numbers.

- **Observe only external actions.** You cannot project internal actions or reasoning. For example, you may observe that 24 percent more people displayed flags this Independence Day than last, but you cannot say that more people are flying flags because they feel more patriotic. Report only actions or events you can see.

- **Quantify findings whenever possible.** Being able to assign statistics adds credibility, showing that an action or event was consistent.

- **Support your observations.** If you cannot quantify, support generalizations with details, examples, and illustrations. You might even make drawings or take photographs.

While observation can be a valuable source of primary data, consider the time, equipment, and cost. For instance, hiring and training people to count vehicles can be time-consuming and expensive. Even if you decide to place a mechanical device across the highway to count vehicles, it must be paid for and it will not describe the vehicles.

Experimentation

Experimentation is the act of causing an event so that an observer can test an assumption or a hypothesis (a statement of what the tester believes will happen). Experiments test whether a change in one factor will cause another factor to change. For example, if the owner of a car-cleaning business wants to know whether his current car wax or a new product gives the longest-lasting shine, he might polish half a car with the current wax and the other half with the new wax. He then would check the car periodically for shine.

Employees frequently use experiments in the workplace. Manufacturers often test new products in limited markets to see whether the products will be successful. Managers may compare a current operating plan in one plant with a new plan in another plant. Researchers may gather samples of air, water, soil, food, medicines, body tissues, or even construction materials for testing.

As with observation, experimenters must be careful to avoid elements that will make the experiment and its results invalid. Sometimes other factors or variables can affect the results of an experiment. For instance, using different cleaners on the two halves of the car would affect the results of the wax study. Using adults for conducting clinical trials of a drug meant for children would not provide meaningful information about how the drug will work on pediatric patients. Therefore, when you design an experiment, try to eliminate as many outside factors as you can.

Objectivity is very important in experimentation as well. Interpret data collected objectively. Do not start with preconceived ideas of the

ONGOING ASSESSMENT

Stop and Think

Assign this feature to check students' reading comprehension.

The methods of collecting primary data are surveying, interviewing, observing, and experimenting. (Students must name three.)

Observations must be planned so that observers can be trained in what to look for and when to look, what terminology to use, and how to avoid projecting internal actions or reasoning.

experiment's outcome. And remember to use passive voice when writing about experiments; passive voice keeps the focus on the experiment rather than the person conducting the experiment.

Surveys, interviews, observation, and experimentation all serve as useful tools for acquiring information, and many researchers use a combination of those methods. Remember the stain on the wool sweater in the Warm Up at the beginning of this section? Even an everyday problem such as how best to clean a favorite garment may require you to interview, observe, and experiment to find a solution.

Validity and Reliability

To maintain credibility, primary researchers look for valid and reliable data. **Valid data** are data that provide an accurate measurement of what an individual intends to measure.

For example, a clothing store owner wanted to know whether her business would attract as many customers as it did on weekdays if it were open on Sunday. She devised a test to collect data. The Sunday she chose was during a weekend when two big football games were being played in town and visitors filled area hotels. Comparing the number of customers on that Sunday with the number of weekday customers would not generate valid data. The large number of visitors in town on that particular Sunday would influence the results.

Reliable data are data that provide results that can be duplicated under similar circumstances. If you explain that mixing two liquid chemicals will create a solid, then other people can try the same test. If they follow your procedures, the mixed liquids should solidify. Being able to repeat the test with the same results represents reliable data.

 STOP AND THINK

What are three methods of collecting primary data? Why should you plan observations?

CHAPTER 3
REVIEW

SUMMARY

1. Researching at work involves finding information to help people solve problems, make informed decisions, answer questions, and perform many other functions.

2. Secondary data, or reports of information from someone other than the witness or the person directly involved, are usually found in a business, school, or public library through print or electronic means.

3. Writers must give credit for borrowed material by documenting the source. Failure to credit others for their words and ideas means risking reputation, employment, legal action, and financial reward.

4. Writers should evaluate sources by checking publication dates, the author's credentials, and the author's methods and resources.

5. As researchers find useful material, they take notes using one method or a combination of three methods—summary, paraphrase, and direct quotation—on note cards or a computer.

6. Primary data, or information direct from the person involved, may be collected by surveys, interviews, observation, and experimentation.

Checklist

- Have I defined the problem or need for information?

- Have I considered what information I already have?

- Have I reviewed information available in my organization's archives relating to my problem or need?

- Have I viewed the library catalog, online when accessible or in the library when not accessible online?

- Have I searched periodical indexes and databases for more recent secondary sources?

- Have I relied on general reference materials, electronic or in print, for quick background information and for references to other sources?

- Have I searched the Web using strategies to filter for useful information? Have I found the most current information?

- Have I given credit, using an appropriate style system, for borrowed words and ideas unless the information is considered common knowledge or is material in the public domain?

- Have I evaluated all sources of information before using the data?

- Have I taken notes using summary, paraphrase, and direct quotation?

- Have I considered collecting primary data using surveys, interviews, observations, and/or experimentation to find information not available through other sources? Have I planned for validity and reliability?

CLOSE

Summary
Use the chapter summary for a review of essential information. Another option is to have students complete a five-minute writing of the "Most Important Thing I Learned" from the chapter.

CLOSE

Checklist
Have students use the checklist as a reference guide when doing research.

REVIEW
For a review of the key terms in the chapter, provide students with the *Key Terms* worksheet available as a supplemental activity on the IRCD.

ASSESS

Build Your Foundation

1. a. left corner: Distance Legislation; right corner: Rademacher and Schwartz 14; body: "Hog Farmers and Homeowners: Zoning Solutions" states that governments, municipal and regional, are legislating distance between farms' waste lagoons and residential areas. b. left corner: Key to Disease Management; right corner: Nuez 259; body: Diseases can be managed with "[c]areful record keeping and close observation."

2. a. According to the Center of Marine Conservation, volunteers on the beaches and inland waterways picked up over 7 million pieces of trash, everything from cigarette butts to syringes. b. The Highway Department says that vehicles will soon be on an 8.5-mile stretch of road between Henderson and Mount Clemmons. One part of the new road will be used to test asphalt created to combat hydroplaning, and another part will test asphalt created from crumbled tire rubber. c. In an article for *Photography Solutions,* Dee Kay recommends that amateur and professional photographers establish "backup to be redundant and automatic. Store photos in at least three ways, with one of those being off premises" (209).

3. Have students work in teams to check bibliographic entries.

4. Discuss what the purpose of the interview is; whether it will be tape-recorded; and when, where, and how long to meet.

5. Point out the need for information before being interviewed for a job.

Build Your Foundation

1. Compose a note card for each item.

   a. On page 14 of the magazine *Farm Review,* Edward F. Rademacher's and Janet Schwartz's article "Hog Farmers and Homeowners: Zoning Solutions" notes that municipal and regional governments are "legislating distance" between the farms' waste lagoons and residential areas. The article appears in the November 2009 issue of the magazine.

   b. In her 2008 book *Swine Herd Disease Management,* Dr. Iyana P. Nuez writes, "Careful record keeping and close observation are the key to disease management." The book is 463 pages long, and this statement appears on page 259. The book was published by Delmar, a publisher located in New York.

2. Paraphrase items a and b. Write a direct quotation for item c. Remember to include documentation and an introduction or integration so that readers will know the context from which the information came.

   a. "The Center for Marine Conservation reported that volunteers scouring ocean beaches and inland shorelines cleaned up more than 7 million pieces of trash, including cigarette butts, bottles, cans, lightbulbs, syringes, and plastic bags." Found in a magazine article by Cindianne Jernigan, "Cleaning Up," *Natural State,* Volume 8, Issue 43, page 105.

   b. "Yesterday the Highway Department reported approval of a plan to open an 8.5-mile corridor between Henderson and Mount Clemmons. However, the new road may be a little bumpy because two sections of experimental asphalt, one designed to combat hydroplaning and the other made of crumbled tire rubber, are being used." Found in a newspaper article by Bill Rogers, *The Hartford Daily Trumpet* (Hartford, Illinois), August 29, 2008, page B2.

   c. "Storage is so cheap now that photographers have no excuse for not backing up their images. Arrange backup to be redundant and automatic. Store photos in at least three ways, with one of those being off premises." Found in a magazine article by Dee Kay, "Preserving Your Best Photos," *Photography Solutions,* Volume 10, Issue 12, June 2009, page 209.

3. Choose a technical or scientific topic (for example, taxation of Internet sales, irradiation of food supply, or cosmetic use of Botox®). Find five sources, print and electronic, on the topic. Develop a working bibliography with each source listed in correct MLA bibliographic form or the style your instructor wants you to use.

4. You are calling Sanford Weiss to set up an interview about a new type of home security system he invented. What arrangements should you discuss with him? List three things you should cover in the phone call to set up the interview.

5. Identify a company where you might like to work and gather information that would help you apply for a job there. For instance, learn about products, services, and activities. Research the way the company is organized, its business philosophy, and its niche in the marketplace. Write a report that would be helpful to other students who might be interested in seeking employment there.

Your Turn

6. Think of a subject or hobby about which you know a great deal. In a brief essay, describe how you acquired your knowledge.

7. Find three specialized reference sources (for example, a medical dictionary or an aerospace encyclopedia) relating to your future career field or a topic of interest. (At least one of these reference sources should be online.) List the reference sources and a description of what each one offers.

8. Collect questionnaires for class analysis. Determine effective techniques as well as weaknesses in the surveys' strategies.

9. Watch a televised or video-recorded interview. Note the strategies the interviewer uses to make the interview effective.

10. Using the same keyword, use three Internet search engines. Bring to class the first ten listings that each search showed and compare the results.

11. Go to the Help section of any Internet search engine. Learn how this particular system works. Share what you learn with your classmates.

12. Using a full-text database available in your school or community library, find and print an article relating to your career field or to a term project. Write a summary of the article and bring the summary and the article to class. Explain to your peers how the information in the article impacts your professional or academic plans.

13. Choose a topic relating to your career field. Search for secondary information to provide basic background information. Write an essay summarizing your findings and prepare a bibliography.

14. Prepare questions and interview someone in your field of interest. From that person, collect information about a particular research project he or she undertook. Ask about methods, difficulties, and the outcome of the research. Record your findings on your sheet of prepared questions.

15. In a small group, identify an issue at your school.
    a. Develop a survey to collect facts and opinions about the issue.
    b. Establish your audience and administer the survey in person.
    c. Tabulate the survey results.

Community Connection

16. Choose a product that your school or a community organization uses and compare it to a similar product. Keeping that product in mind, design an experiment to test the question. Write a report on the experiment design, the findings of the experiment, or both. Make sure you collect valid and reliable data.

17. Identify a problem at school, in your community, or at work.

    Examples:

    Compared to the 55 mph speed limit, how does the 60 mph limit affect gas mileage?

    How can a person use leftovers to lower his or her food costs?

    How can students help their school lower electricity consumption?

    a. Decide what information you need to solve the problem.
    b. Determine how and where to find the information.
    c. Conduct the necessary research.

Chapter 4

Writing Process

Goals

- Identify a writing process that suits your writing style
- Plan your document
- Draft and revise your document
- Edit and publish your document
- Collaborate constructively with others

Terms

- collaborative writing, p. 79
- copyediting, p. 90
- draft, p. 86
- drafting, p. 86
- freewriting, p. 81
- groupthink, p. 94
- planning, p. 81
- publishing, p. 90
- recursive, p. 80
- revising, p. 87
- shaping, p. 83
- tentative outline, p. 84
- writing process, p. 79

TEACHING RESOURCES FOR CHAPTER 4

Instructor's Resource CD
  Data Files
  Data File Solutions
  Lesson Plans
  Teaching Masters
  PowerPoint Slides
  Chapter Tests with Solutions
  Additional Chapter Activities
*Exam*View
Website
www.cengage.com/school/bcomm/techwtg
  Crossword Puzzle
  Data Files
  Data File Solutions
  Flashcards
  Glossary
  NET Bookmark
  Sample Documents
  Web Links
WRITE TO LEARN
Encourage students to think about other processes with which they are familiar. Use the discussion as a springboard to introduce another process, the writing process.

WRITE TO LEARN

Think of a process with which you are familiar that involves several steps and some time to complete. The process could be anything from making a craft or troubleshooting a computer to painting a room or learning a football play. In one page, answer these questions about your process: What steps do you follow? Must you retrace your steps? Are some steps more important or enjoyable than others? How did you learn this process? Does the process get easier the more you do it? Explain.

Focus on Writing Process

Read the sample document on the next page and answer these questions:

- Can you identify this document as an early draft? Explain.
- For whom are the editing notes and questions?
- What kinds of problems do the editing notes address?
- Do you see any problems that the editing notes do not cover? Explain.
- Do your early drafts resemble this draft?

What If?

- The model represented an earlier or later draft?
- The draft were handwritten?
- The draft included comments from several readers?
- The model were in the note-taking stage?

need a title

Our brains begin as a single cell shortly after conception, and then begin dividing in a process we call meiosis. From this process *What process? Elaborate.* comes a brain that has much in common with other human brains, but is also different. Some brains are able to think visually. Others' have musical or linguistic talent. And others' have athletic ability. *Develop first paragraph. Use examples. Show that brain is remarkabale! Tone—sense of wonder?*

Their is still much we do not know about the brian, but scientists are learning more about it all the time. The brain has over trillion nerve cells of two types: glial and nerve cells. The adult human brain is a wet, fragile, pink mass—feels like play dough. It can seem to stop time by recapturing a memory. It has enough energy to power a lightbulb. *good info here* It weigh a little over three pounds, is shaped like a walnut, and fits into the palm of your hand. It works constantly. Represents 2% of body weight and consumes 20% of our calories and 25 % of our oxygen. It works unceasingly. When it "thinks" harder, it uses more fuel. It physically changes as it adapts to its enviroment. *sent are choppy—fix later* It has moreconnections, between cells. It forms more dendrites, between the neurons. It needs oxygen, glucose, and water to operate. ~~The basic structure of the brain is pretty common knowledge. Its is divided into 3 parts, the forebrain, the midbrain, and hindbrain.~~ *Do I need this?*

Purpose of paper missing—no thesis

Some spell/punc/sent errors. Fix later.

Sample First Draft of an Introduction in a Report

FOCUS

Focus on Writing Process
Use the questions to encourage students to read the sample closely.

ASSESS

What If?
Use the questions to discuss how the sample would be different if the situation or audience changed.

Go to www.cengage.com/school/bcomm/techwtg for more detailed responses to these questions.

kertlis/iStockphoto.com

Writing@Work

Andrew Yoder has been a book production editor for Rowman & Littlefield Publishers in Lanham, Maryland, for nine years. He shepherds books through copyediting, proofreading, indexing, cover production, and finally manufacturing. Most of his technical communication involves e-mailing authors, freelancers, and in-house colleagues. He also is a book author and freelance writer and editor.

To begin a writing project, Andrew first gathers all of the resources he needs into one electronic file, organizes the contents of the file into smaller themed sections, and then finds the best section with which to start. "I'll occasionally read the quotes [in the file] and try to think about different angles and sections while doing mind-numbing tasks like mowing my yard."

Recently, Andrew talked with his fellow Rowman & Littlefield editors about how they approach writing. Each editor takes a different approach: "One colleague said she writes out a very detailed outline that serves as a draft replacement. Another coworker said that she doesn't draft; she just writes. That's me. Any revising that I do is more like copyediting than working from a draft."

Authors should not be afraid of the copy editor's red pen. After Andrew sends one of his own completed manuscripts to his copy editor, he hopes to receive a great many questions and corrections that will improve the book. "Some authors are offended when someone edits their work or asks questions, but I'd rather have a copy editor find mistakes in my work than have a reader find them." Furthermore, says Andrew, "The biggest enemy of revising or editing material is a large ego."

Think Critically

1. How would your instructors react if you had outside copy editors correct your work before you turned it in? Why is writing at school different from writing on the job?
2. Look at the section in this chapter "Writing Is Different for Everyone" on page 80. Why do different people use different approaches to writing assignments?

Printed with permission of Andrew Yoder

APPLY

Writing @ Work

Use this feature to illustrate the writing process for Andrew.

Think Critically

1. Answers will vary, but students must learn to correct their own work because school is preparation for the work world.
2. People are different—they think differently, their experiences are different, they process language differently, and they have different levels of education.

A PROCESS FOR TECHNICAL WRITING

So far, you've learned why people write at work; how to plan for audience, purpose, scope, and medium; and how to conduct research. Now that you are ready to write, how do you begin? Where will the words come from to fill the pages of your document? They will come from completing the stages of writing your document—the **writing process.** This process includes planning, drafting and revising, and copyediting.

The writing process used by technical writers has much in common with the writing process used by any writer—an essayist, a novelist, a journalist, or a songwriter. However, each genre brings its own challenges. Along with considering audience, purpose, and medium, technical writers must spend the early stages carefully planning their writing. Working with technical data requires thinking not only about words, but also about graphics and page design. Furthermore, technical writers often work collaboratively. Sophisticated software becomes an integral part of the process too. In practice, the technical writing process builds on the writing process with which you are already familiar.

To learn about the technical writing process, you will follow the decisions Jenna makes as she participates in a collaborative writing project for educators in her state. (**Collaborative writing** is writing with others in a group.) Jenna, a middle school science teacher, is the team leader for a group of instructors given the task of researching new teaching methods for science teachers. The team will publish its findings in a journal and present them at a statewide conference.

This chapter follows Jenna through each stage of the process, from coming up with her idea in the planning stage to polishing the final paper in the publishing stage. The sample document on page 77 shows an early draft of the introduction to the paper. Other models in the chapter illustrate changes Jenna made to this draft as she worked through the writing process.

Warm Up

Think about the last writing assignment you completed. Maybe it was a letter or a report for a class. What process did you follow? What did you do first, second, third, and so on?

FOCUS

Warm Up

Use the Warm Up to encourage students to think about their writing processes.

To read two Letters to Students on the nature of the writing process, go to www.cengage.com/school/bcomm/techwtg. Click the link for Chapter 4; then click Data Files. These letters show that writing is different for different people. Which description do you relate to most?

Comstock Images/Getty Images

Tell students that Jenna's writing process will be illustrated throughout the chapter.

Thoroughly explain the recursive nature of the process. Compare the recursive nature to decorating a room, for example, or to rehearsing for a play. In decorating, a person may revisit the arrangement of furniture or the way items are placed on a bookcase. In rehearsing for a play, the actors may go back to the first act and try different methods of staging or different ways of saying their lines.

Point out that students must allow time for the process.

Caution students not to feel inadequate if their writing process is not like their classmate's. Instead, encourage each student to explore his or her process and to feel good about discovering what works best. Being different, as in having a different writing process, is expected.

ONGOING ASSESSMENT

Stop and Think

The recursive nature means that the thinking process sometimes circles back to earlier stages. Writing takes time because ideas need time to "cook" or "incubate" and because different stages have their own activities. The writing process is different for everyone because people are different; their thinking processes and learning styles vary.

To manage the stages of the technical writing process effectively, you should understand three characteristics of the process: It moves back and forth between predictable stages, it requires sufficient time to complete, and it varies from one person to the next. If you understand how the process works, you can customize each stage to fit your personality and thinking style.

Writing Is Recursive

Writing is an act of creativity, and often it does not move forward smoothly from one step to the next. Although the overall process does progress logically from planning to writing the finished product, it is a backward-and-forward process between predictable stages; that is, it is **recursive,** or circular, in nature.

For example, you plan an article about new city bus routes and begin to write. Then you discover that you overlooked the route in your own neighborhood. You go back to the research stage and gather more information. Next, you hear about some citizens who are not happy with the proposed routes. You circle back and change your purpose to reflect their discontent. After interviewing a few concerned citizens, you revise the article again.

Documents change depending on which stage of the process the writer is in. In some stages, writers expand documents, generating ideas and words without judging their usefulness. During other stages, writers make judgments, cutting some words and keeping others.

Writing Takes Time

Writing takes time. Most writers need a certain amount of time to let ideas "cook" in their heads. The process can be compared to baking bread. You gather ingredients, mix them, knead the dough, and place the dough in a warm place to rise. However, you cannot make the dough rise; it rises in its own time because you set the process in motion. Like the bread, your ideas need time to incubate. The other stages take time too. It may take you two weeks to conduct research and only one day to write a rough draft, but the revising may take another week. When you write, you must allow time for the process.

Writing Is Different for Everyone

While the writing process does have stages, what people do in each stage differs from one person to the next. How people feel about the stages differs too. Some people enjoy the prewriting and planning and dislike the revising. Others enjoy the revising but are frustrated by the planning. Some people let the ideas grow in their heads and write slowly with little revision. Others write many words quickly, using many drafts.

⬢ **STOP AND THINK**

Explain the recursive nature of the writing process. Why does the process take time? Why is the process different for everyone?

PLANNING

Like other tasks, writing is easier when you have a plan. **Planning** is the first stage of the writing process, when a writer thinks of an idea and prepares to develop and research it.

Choosing a Topic

Your first task is to choose a topic. Sometimes your employer or instructor will give you a topic with some guidelines. For example, a trainer in the home office of Pajoli's Pizza franchise is asked to write an operating manual for the entire chain. The manual includes the home office specifications (for example, how to open and close the restaurant, how to order, how to prepare each dish, and how to calculate food costs). Therefore, the research plan is straightforward—interview managers, observe them in action, and write the procedures step-by-step.

When the topic is given to you, learn as much as possible about the assignment. Ask about audience, purpose, scope, and medium. Note any gaps in the analysis, ask questions, and make changes based on new information. For example, the writer for Pajoli's manual notes that some restaurant owners are Hispanic. Based on this information, the writer provides a Spanish translation.

Working with someone else's idea can simplify the planning stage. Sometimes your writing assignment is not so specific. Your employer or instructor may give you general guidelines and expect you to come up with ideas and a plan.

Freewriting, mapping, and journaling are strategies that can help you choose a topic. For example, your assignment could be like Jenna's. When Jenna was given her task, she was not given a specific topic. Therefore, Jenna used freewriting and journaling to help her choose one.

Freewriting

Freewriting is writing freely to discover an idea. You write what comes to mind without judging what you have written or worrying about grammar or sentence structure. Three variations of freewriting are open freewriting, focused freewriting, and looping.

With open freewriting, you write about anything and see where your writing takes you. Jenna's open freewriting finally brings her to a possible topic in the last few sentences shown in Figure 4.1.

> What am I interested in? Today, not much today. Let's see. Okay, let's find a topic for the research. Could write about problem solving. Hmmm. Also saw on Discovery Channel a segment about the brain and learning disabilities. Hmmm. I have a learning disability. Maybe I could research that. Yeah—why do I have a learning disability, and what instruction works best for me? That would help instructors in the classroom.

Figure 4.1 Jenna's Open Freewriting

Warm Up

Everybody makes plans. People plan how to spend an afternoon or what to wear. They plan major events—weddings, graduations, the future. What are the benefits of having a plan? Are there drawbacks to having a plan? If so, what are they?

FOCUS

Warm Up

Use the Warm Up to show the benefits of planning (provides direction, is necessary when working with others, helps get things done on time) and the drawbacks of planning (the reluctance to consider a new but good idea because the plan is already set). The best plans allow for some flexibility.

FOCUS

Figure 4.1

Use the figure to illustrate the "free" and "anything goes" nature of freewriting.

FOCUS

Figures 4.2, 4.3, 4.4

Use each figure to illustrate different strategies for coming up with topics. Remind students that freewriting, mapping, and journaling are designed to help them discover ideas. Talk about writing as a discovery process— that something almost magical happens when they write. They uncover or discover ideas they did not know they had.

TEACH

Students should understand that different assignments can have different starting techniques.

ENRICH

Ask students to give examples of when freewriting techniques worked for them. As an instructor, share times when freewriting worked for you.

On the board or overhead, model open freewriting, focused freewriting, and looping so your students can see what happens as you work.

Tell students not to judge ideas at the freewriting stage. All ideas at this stage are welcomed— even those that seem silly— because you never know when an idea that seems silly may, in fact, be a good idea.

With focused freewriting, you choose a topic and freely associate ideas with that topic. This exercise, too, helps Jenna discover an idea. An example of Jenna's focused freewriting is shown in Figure 4.2.

TOPIC: Learning: How do students learn best—with good instructors when the students are motivated? What makes a good instructor? One who has enthusiasm, one who knows the subject, one who knows how students learn, knows students' learning styles. Who was my best instructor? Mr. Kohl. But what made him good? Why do students not learn? What happens in the brain when someone learns? Do we know the answer to that question? Maybe if we knew how the brain learns, instructors could do something to improve that process.

Figure 4.2 Jenna's Focused Freewriting

With the looping technique, you write for five minutes, stop, and summarize in a sentence what you have written. Staying focused on the summary sentence, you write again for five minutes, stop, and summarize. Then you repeat the process until ideas appear, as they do in Figure 4.3.

First Loop (write for 5 minutes): Tired, sleepy, head hurts, had a hard time paying attention to the stock market seminar—too much math. I wish I had gone to the counseling workshop—more my style. My sister would like this though; she is good with math—a math whiz. Why is that? Why do some people learn some things more easily than others? (Stop and wait a few minutes.)

Second Loop (write for 5 minutes): Why do some people learn some things more easily than others? Who else? Renee is good at karate; Jon is good with cars but dislikes English. Why? Was Einstein's brain different from everybody else's? If I knew, would it help me and others learn math? What would help me with my learning problems in math? (Stop and wait a few minutes.)

Third Loop: Jenna could summarize the last idea and begin freewriting again to start another loop.

Figure 4.3 Jenna's Looping Technique

Journaling

Another way to find an idea is to write in a journal regularly. Figure 4.4 shows a journal entry that Jenna wrote one morning.

I had this strange dream last night that I was late to class. Everyone was taking the exam, and I had only 10 minutes to finish it. I panicked, but then I saw three students get up and act out one of the problems. I saw more students writing on the board. In the back, I saw students talking in a group. Suddenly, the class became three classes— you know how weird dreams can be. Somehow I knew these students were learning. What does that mean? Maybe that people learn in different ways. There must be some kind of brain research on it.

Figure 4.4 Jenna's Writing Journal

Jenna notes that in several of her entries, she has come back to the question of what happens in the brain when people learn. Because she does not know much about brain research, she decides that she would like to know more about it. At this point, she selects brain-based teaching as a possible topic.

Shaping an Idea

After you choose a topic, you begin **shaping** the topic by giving it some direction. When you are shaping an idea, you must answer several questions: Is the idea narrowed or focused enough? How can I develop this idea? What are the subtopics or parts of the idea? How can I organize these subtopics?

Questioning, reading, mapping, and outlining will help you focus your idea and figure out subtopics.

Questioning

Jenna uses questioning to shape her idea. Who will benefit from learning about this topic? Clearly, instructors can benefit, but what do they need to know? When and where can they use this information? Why does learning take place? How can instructors improve classroom learning? After asking these questions, Jenna decided that the "why" and "how" answers were important for shaping her idea. She also approaches her colleagues to get their points of view.

Reading

Jenna found some direction from the reading journal she kept as she read about her topic. She tagged some pages with sticky notes when she found information that would help her shape her topic. An example is shown in Figure 4.5.

> "Improving Our Classrooms" article: Talks about how windows of opportunity for learning open and close in the growing brain. Example: The neurons for learning language are active until about age 10. After that, neurons not used die out.
>
> *How the Brain Learns* by Sousa: Sousa stresses how the brain constantly adjusts to its environment. Gives many teaching suggestions for the classroom.

Figure 4.5 Additional Research Notes from Jenna's Reading Journal

Mapping

Jenna used cluster mapping to shape her ideas. She began with her topic in the middle and allowed ideas to radiate from the center, drawing lines to connect related topics. As she listed topics, her list grew into other clusters and generated more ideas for topics. Jenna could then see at a glance the major ideas, their subtopics, and the relationship of the subtopics to the major ideas. For example, she could see that the amount of sleep that students get and the instructor's method of delivery affect retention. She also could see the need to clarify the differences between retention and learning.

TEACH
Remind students that many ideas come from others' ideas. Perhaps you can provide an example as an instructor.

ENRICH
Ask students to share an idea they have for writing or to share a different idea (an invention, a dance step, a football play). How did they choose the idea? How did they know it was good?

Take students to the library to browse magazines or to search online. Ask them to list ideas that interest them. Have them look for ideas about a subject and generate a classroom list.

Ask students to enter a subject into different search engines. Have them write as many ideas (possible topics) as they can by looking at the description of the first ten items that appear from their search.

Ask students to interview neighbors, businesspeople, and members of organizations about the importance of a variety of topics (e.g., city management or parks and recreation). Are ideas the same? Is one different? Does one idea appeal to students more than the other ideas?

Tell students that they should discuss their writing assignment with someone who will give them constructive feedback. This feedback can stimulate their thinking as they respond to the discussion.

FOCUS

Figure 4.5
Use the figure to illustrate how reading helps Jenna come up with more ideas.

You can view Jenna's cluster map at www.cengage.com/school/bcomm/techwtg. Click the link for Chapter 4; then click Sample Documents.

View the formal and informal outlines at www.cengage. com/school/bcomm/ techwtg. Click the link for Chapter 4; then click Sample Documents.

After looking closely at the cluster, Jenna knew she had to narrow her choices and decide which subtopics to include and which to omit. Not all of the ideas were relevant to her purpose, that is, to facilitate learning in a middle school classroom. She decided not to include learning disabilities because most schools have disability support programs where readers can get information on that topic. She also decided to leave out early brain development.

Outlining

From the cluster map, Jenna used a **tentative outline.** This outline is an informal, changeable plan for organizing topics and subtopics. Notice that the outline in Figure 4.6 is not a formal one, yet it gives Jenna a focus for her paper's topics and subtopics.

Introduction—some interesting facts about the brain—to get students' attention

–Basic Brain Anatomy—explain basic parts of the brain and what each part does

–How neurons work—how a neuron fires and passes information from one to another

–Relate basic brain anatomy and neurons' firing to how the brain learns (Show the actual changes in brain anatomy)

–Retention—what factors affect retention?

+Amount of sleep

+Timing of information presented

+Rehearsal

–Type of rehearsal

–Length of rehearsal

Figure 4.6 Jenna's Tentative Outline

As you outline topics, consider how to organize them. The document type may dictate the organizational pattern. You can use these organizational patterns to suit the document's purposes. Consider the following organizational patterns:

- **Chronological order** for things that must progress from first to last, as in the development of a product or the history of an event
- **Spatial order** for arranging items in space, as in a description of an office, a factory, a landscape design, or a home
- **Cause-to-effect order** (or effect-to-cause order), as in a presentation of reasons for an event or the consequences of an action
- **Comparing and contrasting,** as in the recommendation of one product or action over another
- **Classifying** or breaking something down into parts, as in an analysis of venture feasibility or product usefulness
- **Problem and solution,** as in a definition or an analysis of a problem followed by a workable solution

Other ways to organize data include strategies that meet your readers' needs as well as your purpose for writing. These strategies include the following:

- **General to specific** (or specific to general). Does your audience need the big picture or the details first?

- **Background before new information.** Do the members of your audience need to know how something happens or happened before they accept new information?

- **Familiar to less familiar.** Are you presenting your readers with new information following something familiar that will be easier for them to understand?

- **Simplest to most complex** (or most complex to simplest). Do your readers already understand the complex ideas, or do they need to be led to them logically?

- **Most important to least important** (or least important to most important). Will your audience benefit from reading the most important idea first or last?

Often using one organizational strategy is not enough. Longer, more complex documents may require one section to be organized differently from another section. In such cases, a combination of methods works best. Jenna considers using a combination of methods for her document, as follows:

- **Problem and solution:** Jenna presents the problem of lower science achievement and offers brain-based teaching as a solution.

- **Cause-to-effect order:** Jenna plans to develop her argument with the reasons instructors should change lesson plans and the effects those changes may have on student learning.

- **Background before new information:** Jenna believes that instructors need to understand the newest research about the brain before she presents the teaching strategies based on that research.

- **Simplest to most complex:** Because instructors are busy, Jenna plans to introduce simpler ideas first, which can be incorporated quickly into lesson plans, before moving on to strategies that require more time to implement.

Consider what headings (short titles in a document that identify a topic) you will use and what the final document will look like. A heading is appropriate when you have several paragraphs that relate to a single topic and that will likely come from the outline you wrote. The document type—a report, a resume, a brochure—also will dictate your headings. After reviewing her tentative outline, Jenna converts her topics to a parallel structure and plans to use the headings shown in Figure 4.7 on the following page.

ENRICH

Practice asking questions about a topic (e.g., trees in your area) to generate a list of things you might want to know. Write the questions on the board or overhead. What kinds of trees are in the area? What type are they? Are they endangered? Do animals live in them? If so, what kind? Do children climb the trees? Do they build tree houses in them? Are the trees used commercially?

Try another variation of the questioning exercise by completing this statement about snakes: I want to know ____ (what snakes are poisonous, what to do if I get bitten, if anyone has them as pets, if snakes are useful to the environment).

List the statements on the board or overhead. Divide students into groups to find the answers. Send one group to do research at the library, other groups to surf the Internet, others to ask family and friends what they know, and others to use their own knowledge. Did any method produce better results? Did students prefer one method over another?

FOCUS

Figure 4.7
Use the figure to show the relationship between Jenna's headings and her outline.

ONGOING ASSESSMENT

Stop and Think
Find out what students know about freewriting and shaping. Allow students to share what works best for them as individuals.

FOCUS

Warm Up
Use students' responses to remind them that the writing process is different for everyone.

How the Brain Is Structured (first-level heading)

How Neurons Create Memories (first-level heading)

How Brain Structure and Activity Affect Learning (first-level heading)

How to Aid Retention (first-level heading)

    Amount of Sleep (second-level heading)

    Timing of Information Presented (second-level heading)

    Amount and Type of Rehearsal (second-level heading)

Figure 4.7 Jenna's Tentative List of Headings

 STOP AND THINK

What strategies for freewriting and shaping have you used in the past? Which ones work best for you? Does this chapter present some methods you have not tried? If so, which ones?

Warm Up

Do you have difficulty writing the first words in a draft, or do the words come fairly quickly? How long does it take you to write a two-page first draft on a familiar topic?

TEACH

Emphasize that the best way to start writing is just to begin. Students will find writing easier the more they write because the act of writing helps ideas flow.

Ask students how many of them compose on the computer. Ask them to describe their writing process when they use the computer and any shortcuts they use. Tell them that research shows that students who compose on a computer have more developed, correct, and polished papers than students who do not because of the ease with which students can change the document and the professional pride they take in the way the printed document looks.

DRAFTING AND REVISING

Now that you have a plan and information about your topic, you are ready to write. This part of the writing process is called the drafting and revising stage. Review your audience analysis and purpose for writing. Keep your audience and purpose in the back of your mind as you draft and revise.

Drafting

Drafting is the second stage of the writing process. When drafting, you write the first, second, and third (or more) versions of your document. As soon as you begin to write, you are writing a first **draft**—an early version of a document that is subject to change. Do not put off writing because you are waiting for that perfect first sentence to come to mind. Just start writing. The order in which you write does not matter. What does matter is the order in which the reader reads. Force a few words until they start to flow. Drafting is like trying new paint: you do not know whether you like the color until you see it on the wall.

The Introduction

While the introduction might not be the first part you write, it is the first part your readers will see. It sets the tone and determines how receptive your readers are to the information you present. Use the introduction to:

- **Relate to your readers.** Discuss a situation that you and your readers have in common.

- **Hold your readers' attention.** Give startling statistics or an eye-opening quotation.

- **Forecast** the topics and information you will cover.

- **Identify questions** that are answered in the document. List the questions.

- **Identify the problem to be solved.** Define the problem.

- **Give the background of the situation.** Present events that lead to the need for the document or research.

- **Give a research overview.** Give the major headings. Explain where and how the research was conducted.

The Body

As you write, you decide how to support your subtopics in the body of your paper. When thinking about ways to elaborate, explain, or prove your points, ask yourself what your readers need. Do they need:

- Long or short examples—specific occurrences that happened or could happen?

- Testimonials—real-life stories from people who can attest to or support a view?

- Quotations—statements from people who are often authorities on a topic?

- Statistics—numerical data, percentages, and/or test results to support a view?

- Historical facts—verifiable information researched by credible scholars?

- Financial facts or estimates—financial reports, trends, and/or economic news?

The Conclusion

Use your conclusion to do what the document type requires. Proposals may need a reminder of the solution; sales letters may need a call to action; a recommendation may need a summary of key points and a possible decision; a research paper may answer questions posed earlier in the document.

Revising

When you finish drafting, you revise your document. When **revising**, you read your document and make changes to content, organization, and word choice. Use your audience analysis and purpose statement to guide you. Because the content affects the other revision strategies, start with the general content and move to the details.

After you print a first draft, put it aside for a while. Come back to the draft at a later time and read it again to decide what does and does not work. Make notes on the draft. Draw arrows when you see, for example, that paragraph 3 should be next to paragraph 6 and that the example in paragraph 2 should be in paragraph 5. Cross out phrases, sentences, and paragraphs that can be deleted.

Writing can be an untidy process, as Figure 4.8 on the next page illustrates. This document is the second draft of Jenna's introduction.

ENRICH

Ask students to describe the introductions—to chapters or to sections—in this textbook.

Ask students to browse a magazine in print or online, reading introductions, skimming the article, and reading conclusions. How would they describe the introductions and conclusions? Ask them to bring in a particularly effective introduction or conclusion.

Using the same articles, have students tell how writers developed their ideas. Did the writers follow the suggestions given here? Ask students to bring in several examples to share.

Have students listen to their favorite talk radio show (e.g., *Car Talk*) or to a speech (perhaps by the President). How do the speakers develop ideas?

Ask students to say words aloud while keying. How does talking affect their writing process?

Tell students to take a short walk before they write or when they get stuck.

Have students practice composing into a tape recorder. Then have them play back their words and physically write or key them. How does this affect their writing process?

Show the Ways to Get Over Writer's Block Teaching Master on the IRCD.

FOCUS

Figure 4.8

Use the draft to show the changes from the first to the second draft and to illustrate Jenna's content changes. Relate her changes to the "big-to-little" concept.

Th How the Brain Processes Information *good title*

Three to four weeks after the sperm and egg unite, one of the cell layers of the embryo thickens and develops into a flat neural plate. From this place comes a thinking mechanism that has much in common with other human brains, but that also differs in remarkable ways. Some brains are wired to envision and build bridges, skyscrapers, and superhighways. Others' create the songs of our youth, the art we hang on our walls, and the motion pictures that define our age. Still others' manage the linguistic marvels of a best-selling novel or the complex motor skills of an ice skater. *Much better! ¶ has good examples. Tone shows sense of wonder.*

Add transition Their is still much we do not know about the brian. *topic sent weak* The adult human brain is a wet, fragile, pink mass. It can seem to stop time by recapturing a memory. It has enough energy to power a lightbulb. It weigh a little over three pounds, is shaped like a walnut, and fits into the palm of your hand. It works constantly. Represents 2% of body weight and consumes 20% of our calories and 25 % of our oxygen. ~~It works unceasingly.~~ *choppy sent. Need variety. Use sent comb* When it "thinks" harder, it uses more fuel. It physically changes as it adapts to its enviroment. It has more connections, between cells. It forms more dendrites, between neurons. It needs oxygen, glucose, and water to operate. *This ¶ lacks unity—has 2 ideas: physical description and how brain works.*

Need to lead up to thesis If we understand how the brain learns, we can improve our methods of teaching.

Several errors, typos—fix later. Revise one step at a time.

Figure 4.8 Jenna's Second Draft of the Introduction

Figure 4.9 provides a hierarchy of questions to ask yourself while you revise. Notice that the questions begin with the general content and move to the details.

CONTENT QUESTIONS FOR REVISION

Do I have enough or too much information for my reader? Do I need to conduct more research or delete something?

Is my information clear? Do I need to revise for clarity?

Is my introduction effective? Do I need to revise to attract my readers' attention?

Is my purpose clear? Do I need to add a sentence that explains the purpose?

Do my details logically support my purpose?

ORGANIZATIONAL QUESTIONS FOR REVISION

Is the information in the best logical order for my reader? Do I need to move paragraphs or sections? Are my paragraphs and sections unified? Do I need to remove sentences that do not fit the purpose?

Do sections and paragraphs have topic sentences? Do I need to add topic sentences?

Are transitions clear between sections and paragraphs? Do I need to add transition sentences or phrases?

Does my conclusion logically end the document?

READABILITY QUESTIONS FOR ANALYSIS

Does my writing flow from one sentence and paragraph to the next?

Are sentences varied by length and type? Would my sentences be more interesting if I combined them?

Have I selected the best words? Do I need to replace overused words? Do I need to define words?

Figure 4.9 Hierarchy of Questions for Revision

FOCUS

Figure 4.9

Use the figure to show the hierarchy of revision decisions. Reiterate to students why the big changes must take place before the little ones. Tell students they may add questions of their own to this list.

Show students the Questions to Aid Revision with Jenna's Analysis Teaching Master on the IRCD.

Review Jenna's third revision at www.cengage.com/school/bcomm/techwtg. Click the link for Chapter 4; then click Sample Documents.

ONGOING ASSESSMENT

Stop and Think

Use these questions to summarize key points in the section "Drafting and Revising."

⬣ **STOP AND THINK**

What did you find to be the three most helpful pieces of advice in this section? Why do you find them so helpful?

COPYEDITING AND PUBLISHING

FOCUS

Warm Up

Errors are often interpreted as a sign of incompetence. In reality, they do not mean someone is incompetent. A welder may be an expert welder but still misspell words on a letter of application. An employer might not know the person is a good welder if the employer sees errors and decides not to hire him or her.

RETEACH

Make sure students understand the importance of copyediting and publishing. Just because students are near the end of the writing process does not mean they are finished. A professional-looking and correct document creates a positive impression.

FOCUS

Figure 4.10

Tell students that this stage is the time to look at little things. Encourage students to use these copyediting questions when they revise a document.

ENRICH

Provide students with the *Surgical Center Letter with Errors* worksheet available as a supplemental activity on the IRCD.

How important is an error-free document? In business, a professional image indicates a professional, responsible institution behind the image. In the absence of a person, the document represents a company. The document becomes the face of the company. If the face has smudges and errors, the impression is negative. If the face is clean and attractive, the impression is positive. Therefore, after you have planned, drafted, and revised your document, you must take care of the finishing touches by copyediting and publishing your writing. **Copyediting** means proofreading a document for correctness in spelling, grammar, and mechanics. **Publishing** means sending your document to the person or people who need or requested it.

Copyediting

After you have revised for content, organization, and word choice, it is time for copyediting, one of the final stages of the writing process. In this stage, you carefully proofread your document and polish it.

Figure 4.10 lists copyediting questions to ask yourself as you correct a document.

Use several aids when proofreading for errors. To help catch errors that you may not notice as you read silently, read your draft aloud to catch fragments, grammatical errors, and awkward sentences. You also can read the draft backward, starting with the last sentence of the paper and moving toward the beginning. In addition, if you know a good grammarian and speller, ask that person to help you copyedit. You may be surprised at what he or she catches!

Today you can use electronic aids for copyediting. Most word processing programs underline misspelled words as you key, alerting you to errors. You can check the spelling and correct it as you key, or you can wait until you finish the document to run the spell-checker. The checker will locate misspelled words, flag instances to correct, and provide a list of possible corrections.

Do I have any sentence problems—fragments, run-ons, or comma splices?

Is the punctuation correct?

Have I used words correctly? Have I double-checked frequently misused words?

Have I spelled the words correctly?

Is the documentation of sources accurate?

Does the document look professional?

Is the page design balanced and attractive?

Is the formatting consistent?

Figure 4.10 Copyediting Questions for Analysis

However, the spell-checker does not select the best word for you. For example, it does not flag an improper use of *their* or *there* if the word is spelled correctly but used incorrectly. Also, technology creates new uses for existing words for which spell-checkers cannot check.

The grammar checker operates the same way. It flags sentences that may have problems, but you must understand grammar to know whether to change the wording. You can look up grammar and mechanics questions in a current English handbook.

Other electronic aids include a dictionary (for parts of speech or meanings of words) and a thesaurus. A thesaurus is handy when you know that a better word exists for the one you have used or when you have overused a word and need a synonym. However, words have subtle differences in meaning. *Roget's Thesaurus* lists *steal* as a synonym for *borrow,* but you cannot use the two words interchangeably. When using a word from a thesaurus, look up its use in a dictionary. Otherwise, your use may be awkward or inaccurate.

Publishing

When you have finished copyediting your document, you are ready to publish. In this final stage, make sure the document looks professional, is ready on time, is presented in the form your reader needs, and uses sources correctly.

Print the document on good paper, using a high-quality printer and print cartridge or toner. To meet your deadline, have the document ready several days ahead of time to allow for mishaps—the printer not working, the cartridge running out of ink, or the power going out. If you are sending a document to a print shop, know how much time the printer needs. Include any accompanying letters and make sure appropriate people receive copies. For documents that require signatures of others in your organization, as many proposals do, allow adequate time for meeting with and requesting signatures of these busy people.

Document your sources using the proper style manual for the discipline. Separate style guides have been developed for fields such as the humanities, the social sciences, the legal sciences, medicine, and engineering. Electronic publications, web pages, and government publications have their own publishing preferences. Style guides also vary by country, with different publication guidelines for Australian English and Canadian English, for example. Do not risk plagiarizing your document. When in doubt, check a source.

Figure 4.11 on the next page shows the final draft of Jenna's introduction. Compare this version with the sample document on page 77 to see the changes Jenna made throughout the writing process.

At the Merriam-Webster online dictionary, you can quickly look up words and find definitions, parts of speech, and correct spelling. This website also has a thesaurus to help you find synonyms.

Choose five boldfaced terms from the chapter. Then go to the NET Bookmark for Chapter 4. Use the thesaurus to find one or two synonyms for each term you chose. Do the synonyms help you remember the definitions of the terms? Explain.

www.cengage.com/school/bcomm/techwtg

NET BOOKMARK
Each synonym should reflect the meaning of the term used in the context of this chapter.

TEACH
Tell students not to copyedit a draft while they are still revising unless it is to catch a misspelling. By the time they finish revising, they may have deleted those words anyway. Tell them to wait until the end of the process to make corrections.

TYPICAL READER
A person or people needing specific information presented in a well-organized, coherent document.

WRITER'S FOCUS
Working toward a well-organized, coherent document beginning with the idea and planning stages through the drafting, revising, and publishing stages.

How the Brain Processes Information

Three to five weeks after the sperm and egg unite, one of the cell layers of the embryo thickens and develops into a flat neural plate. From this plate comes a thinking mechanism that has much in common with other human brains but that also differs in remarkable ways. Some brains are wired to envision and build bridges, skyscrapers, and superhighways. Other brains create the songs of our youth, the art on our walls, and the motion pictures in our theaters. Still others manage the linguistic marvels of a best-selling novel or the complex motors skills of an ice skater.

Despite its obvious importance to our lives, there is still much we do not know about the brain. What we do know, however, is fascinating. We know it can reverse time by reliving a memory. We know it has enough energy to power a lightbulb. A wet, fragile, pink mass, the brain is shaped like a walnut and can fit into the palm of your hand. Weighing a little over 3 pounds, it comprises only 2 percent of your body weight but consumes 20 percent of your calories and oxygen. When it "thinks" harder, it actually uses more fuel.

Working around the clock, the brain constantly reshapes itself as a result of experience. It physically changes as it adapts to its environment—most noticeably in the number of connections, called dendrites, that it forms between its cells, called neurons. So when learning takes place, the brain is physically altered forever. Because the brain is where learning begins and ends, an understanding of this process can help us become better instructors and learners.

Figure 4.11 Jenna's Final Draft of the Introduction

 STOP AND THINK

What kinds of mistakes do you tend to miss when you copyedit your writing? Make a list of those mistakes and practice looking for them in a draft.

WRITING COLLABORATIVELY

Warm Up

Describe an experience when you worked as part of a group or team. What role did you and the others play? What was the final outcome? Could you have accomplished the final outcome by yourself? Explain.

Many writing projects are done collaboratively—newsletters, proposals, research projects, brochures, and web pages. The more complex and longer your project, the more likely you will work with others. Often writing produced collaboratively is better than anything anyone could have written individually. Interdependence is necessary in today's work environment. You are stronger when you use others' strengths along with your own.

The topic of your writing project may require the input of people from several disciplines. Each person brings a special area of expertise to the project—whether it is medical, technical, political, or socioeconomic—or the ability to write and design graphics. Applying for a grant to aid a hospital in a rural community might involve the following people:

Chief Surgeon Dr. Emily Coltrain	to address medical needs and equipment
Hospital administrator Ray Guevara	to address hospital and equipment costs
Two members of the hospital's board of trustees (an educator and a prominent business leader)	to represent community concerns
City council member Julia McNeil	to represent city and local business concerns
Senator Colin Elkins	to foster political support
Architect Holden Wacamau	to design the hospital trauma center requested in the grant
Professional grant writer Paula Solinski	to gather data from different areas to write, revise, edit, and publish the grant

A collaborative effort may be required not only for a long document, but also for a short piece of writing. A monthly departmental newsletter, for example, may include short articles from different employees with one editor putting the newsletter together—much the same way a newspaper editor collects articles from reporters.

Advantages of Collaboration

Employees pool their resources because collaboration works. Why? Collaboration works because it does the following:

- **Brings together different knowledge.** In this age of specialization, no one person has all of the answers. The more knowledge you can tap, the more credible your final project will be.

- **Brings together different talents.** Some people can depict information graphically; others are better at interviewing to get information; others write well. Members can offer the team what they do best.

FOCUS

Warm Up

Help students recall what it was like to work with others. Stress the benefits. If you hear of problems students experienced working in groups, tell them that this section may help them prevent those problems in the future.

TEACH

Before discussing the benefits and pitfalls of writing collaboratively, see how many examples students can come up with on their own.

Complete the *Observe a Group* worksheet available at www.cengage.com/school/bcomm/techwtg. Click the link for Chapter 4; then click Data Files.

Offer students extra credit for reading *The 7 Habits of Highly Effective People.* Have them present a report about working collaboratively.

To show how groups have more to offer than individuals do, divide students into groups of four or five. Ask each person to reveal two or three things he or she does well, listing the items as a group. Have each group share the results with the class to show that diverse talents contribute to a group's strength.

In groups, have students brainstorm a list of things that could be done with a brick, a bobby pin, or a wire coat hanger. Then ask each group to classify its list into subgroups, such as practical ideas, decorative ideas, silly ideas, impractical ideas, and common ideas. Share the categories and ideas with the class. This activity shows that groups come up with more ideas than individuals do.

- **Allows different perspectives and viewpoints.** Different perspectives can offer wisdom and balance.

- **Improves work relationships.** During a work project, people form friendships, empathize with each other's work problems, and may be able to help with solutions.

- **Is enjoyable.** People who get along in a group and successfully produce results have fun working with each other.

- **Keeps one person from being responsible for the entire project.** Often the work seems less stressful because the responsibility is shared.

Disadvantages of Collaboration

The rewards of collaboration are numerous, but not all group work produces good results. Working in a group can have pitfalls. For instance, collaboration:

- **Can be a dreaded event.** While most people enjoy working in a group, someone who does not get along with a group member may dread the experience. Some people prefer to work by themselves, and group interaction is frustrating for them.

- **Can include conflict.** However, some disagreements over content or procedure can be productive because they encourage more talking and thinking to reach the best outcome. Groups that learn to manage conflicts can work through them without creating ill will.

- **Can take longer than people working alone.** Group communication requires more time. More time is needed to talk over solutions in a group, collect data from different people, read drafts, and work through conflict.

- **Can take away personal motivation.** If someone has only a small interest in the group project, he or she may not care about the outcome and thus will not be productive.

- **Can encourage groupthink. Groupthink** is the tendency of group members to conform to the group's preferences without thinking through an issue individually. The danger of groupthink is that members may be lulled into believing that they are producing a superior product when, in reality, their unwillingness to confront tough issues produces a mediocre product. Groupthink results when people do not care enough about the project to risk confrontation or when people do not know how to manage conflict and therefore avoid it.

- **Can lead to unequal workloads.** Some task-oriented personalities will jump in to get the job done. Illness may keep someone else from working on the project. Sometimes members know more about certain areas of the project and assume more responsibility because of their specialized knowledge. In some instances, members do not "pull their weight." Inequity in workloads may lead to resentment.

- **Can produce fragmented writing.** If different parts of a document are written by different people with little agreement on how the writing should be organized or without a designated editor, coherence and readability may suffer.

Despite the pitfalls, collaboration is necessary in the workplace. People who learn to work collaboratively show their managers and teammates that they know how to accomplish a task with others. Many job descriptions ask for individuals with people skills, and job interviews include questions about the applicant's ability to work with others. Being a team player is one of the most important skills you can have at work.

Organizing Collaborative Projects

How do five or six people write one document? A collaborative writing project can be organized in one or more of the following ways.

- **Different people write different parts and use one editor.** Jenna's team eventually selected topics for the white paper required by the grant that funded the project. Each person wrote between 15 and 20 pages on his or her topic, as listed below.

Brian	Methodology and evaluation
Jenna	Brain research
Ray	Multiple intelligences
Mercedes	Teaching and learning styles
Sudomo	Technology in the classroom
Jenna	Final editor

Because Jenna agreed to be the final editor, team members sent her their sections in a Microsoft® Word document. Jenna cut and pasted their work into a longer document and made changes to promote consistency in tone, documentation, and formatting. She sent segments back to members asking them to rewrite a section or to clarify their data. She received responses and incorporated them into a single document. Then she sent the final version to everyone on the team so that each writer could make last-minute changes. This system works well when topics can be distributed and when people agree ahead of time on matters of style, length, purpose, scope, and medium.

- **Different people submit data to a central person who compiles the information.** For example, the grant writer for the rural hospital could collect information from notes, charts, spreadsheets, interview results, and rough drafts. She might need a letter written by the grant committee chair, but she would write most of the draft. After writing the final draft, she would send it to committee members for their feedback.

This system works well when the writing is specialized, as in writing grants. As a specialist in the grant-writing field, Paula is a paid consultant who knows the parameters of this grant, has experience pulling usable data from different sources, and understands how politics affect the awarding of grants.

COMMUNICATION TECHNOLOGIES

Follow these tips when using a word processing program. (1) Save your writing often. Power surges and outages can threaten the work you have completed thus far. (2) Save important documents in two places. When you have a backup, your work is safe. (3) Save multiple drafts as Paper1 and Paper2. You never know when you will need that first draft again. (4) Make use of the Undo feature.

Think Critically

Why might some people not follow these suggestions?

FOCUS ON ETHICS

Discuss the importance of ethics in a group. Collaborative projects include an all-for-one-and-one-for-all mentality. All get the same grade, same raise, or same commendation when working in a group. When other people are depending on you, you do not want to let them down. It also is important to present a unified voice to the reader.

Think Critically

The guidelines can conflict. You can feel so much loyalty to a person that you hesitate to be honest if the news is not what the person wants to hear.

ENRICH

Before discussing this section, ask students how they might organize a group writing task.

Focus on Ethics

Trust within a group is one of the most important factors in its success. Work to create trust by following these ethical guidelines:

Be responsible. Keep your word; do what you say you are going to do.

Be loyal. Avoid talking about others in the group to other group members or to people outside the group.

Be honest. Make sure that any research you bring to the group is properly documented. If you do not provide a source, your entire group could get into trouble for plagiarism.

Be respectful. Keep an open mind when individuals express opinions that are different from yours. Practice common courtesy. Show concern for others, say *please* and *thank you*, and apologize when necessary.

Be fair. Complete a reasonable share of work. Do not expect someone else to do more than a fair and reasonable share and do not take credit for another group member's work.

Think Critically

Is it possible for these guidelines to conflict with one another? For example, is it possible for loyalty to conflict with honesty? Explain your answer.

Complete the *Active Listening* worksheet available at www.cengage.com/school/bcomm/techwtg. Click the link for Chapter 4; then click Data Files.

- **Different people write different stages.** Writer 1 brainstorms ideas, organizes subtopics, and determines research questions. Writer 1 then passes this information to Writer 2, who collects the research. Writer 2 passes the plans for the document to Writer 3, who writes the first draft. Writer 3 passes the draft to Writer 4, who revises it. Writer 4 then gives the draft to Writer 5 for final editing and publishing.

A textbook chapter could be written this way, with the editor suggesting topics, a research assistant collecting data, the author writing the chapter, and the editor copyediting and publishing. This system works well with a team whose members are in the same field, who get along well, and who understand the writing process.

- **Groups divide research tasks and come together to write.** A committee of four team members divided research investigating an institution's compliance with financial regulations. They brought their research to one employee's office and composed their report aloud as a group. One team member suggested a sentence and another changed a word in that sentence while yet another team member keyed the sentence. Everyone gave suggestions, including the person keying the information. In two hours, their report was written and sent to a copy editor. This system works well for projects with a predetermined format and for people with outgoing personalities who do not waste time haggling over word choice.

When writing a longer document, a group may need to meet regularly. To organize tasks for a longer document, use the first meeting (or the first several meetings) to do the following:

- Create a vision
- Clarify the group's purpose
- Analyze the audience
- Determine the scope
- Select the medium and style guide
- Set meeting times and place
- Decide on the research plan
- Set up goals and tasks
- Assign responsibilities
- Set the timeline for work

A leader or chairperson can set the meeting agendas, write minutes, keep the group on task, and act as a spokesperson. A good leader will make sure that everyone has a say as to what the goals should be and how the meetings should be run. When people help make decisions, they are more likely to support those decisions.

Using Positive Work Habits

Once meetings get under way, your leader and your teammates will count on your participation. To be a productive group member, you need to have good work habits and communication skills to show others that they can count on you. To apply good work habits and contribute to the group effort, you must do the following:

- **Complete your share of the work.** Do whatever tasks are necessary to help the group, whether it is making phone calls, taking notes, looking up information, or creating graphics.

- **Come prepared to each meeting.** Review the agenda and come with suggestions, a notebook, a pen, or a laptop to show that you have done your homework and know what will happen at the meeting.

- **Be interested in the project.** Give positive feedback. Show that you care about the final outcome.

- **Be on time to meetings.** If you cannot be on time, let your leader or a group member know beforehand. If you are habitually late to meetings, your group members might think you do not care about the project.

- **Do not take criticism personally.** Remember that your goal is to produce a good product. When someone questions your suggestions, see the questions as a way to improve the final outcome, not as a criticism of you. If you show that you can handle constructive criticism, you will have an easier time offering it.

Good work habits are important to building group relationships, but communication skills are important too. Your teammates cannot read your mind, but they can hear words and read body language. To contribute to the success of your team, be honest and respectful in your communication.

The number one requirement for a group to work well together is trust. The second requirement is a shared group vision and enthusiasm for the outcome. Being a responsible group member and a good communicator will help build trust between you and your group members.

TEACH

Tell students that strategies for freewriting and shaping can be used with some variation for group freewriting. A leader can use a white board or chalkboard for freewriting or mapping and then eliminate and organize ideas. Once decisions have been made about topics and subtopics, people can work on their own. When drafts must be revised and edited, each person can read and make comments. Members can come together to discuss differences in opinion.

Show the Movement of Group Work Teaching Master on the IRCD.

Provide students with the *Teamwork* worksheet available as a supplemental activity on the IRCD.

Communication Dilemma

Brian is a new teacher in Jenna's research group. While the group has been holding meetings to discuss the project, Jenna has noticed that Brian does not seem all that interested in the project. Brian has not been doing his share of the work when the other members ask him to make telephone calls and look up information. He is not prepared for the meetings. In fact, when other people talk, he doodles or stares out the window. Sometimes he skips meetings altogether without telling anyone beforehand. His comments, when he gives them, are negative.

Jenna thinks that Brian's poor attitude is getting in the way of progress. She also believes that he is frustrating the other team members, who are working hard to make the project a success. She has already overheard some of the members talking about what a poor team player Brian is.

Jenna is worried. She does not want Brian's work habits to affect the final outcome of the team.

Think Critically
What should Jenna do?

Now that you understand the writing process, adaptations for collaborative writing, and some of the strategies for effective collaboration, you are ready to work on any writing project by yourself or with others. The more you practice the writing process, the more adept you will become at using it to accomplish your objectives. You also will experience the camaraderie that comes from working with others to achieve a common goal.

 STOP AND THINK

Using the suggestions for good work habits, take a personal inventory of your own work habits. Which ones produce positive results? Which ones need improvement?

CHAPTER 4
REVIEW

SUMMARY

1. The writing process is a creative act that moves back and forth between predictable stages, requires sufficient time to complete, and varies from one person to the next.

2. The first stage of the writing process, planning, begins with freewriting to generate ideas and moves to shaping to narrow a topic and organize the ideas.

3. Shaping strategies include questioning, reading, mapping, and outlining.

4. The second stage of the writing process is drafting and revising. The process involves writing a draft, analyzing its strengths and weaknesses, and revising the draft. The drafting and revising stage may be repeated two, three, four, or more times.

5. Writers revise drafts in a hierarchy from big to little to make changes that affect the content and organization first before they make changes that affect sentences, words, spelling, and grammar.

6. Copyediting includes reading carefully for errors and correcting them. Publishing presents the reader with the final version, a professional-looking document complete with sources in the form the reader has specified.

7. In today's workplace, many writing projects are done collaboratively.

Checklist

- Do I understand the writing process?

- Have I considered how to adjust the writing process to meet my personality and thinking style?

- Have I identified the planning strategies that work for me?

- Have I used shaping strategies to narrow my topic, generate subtopics, and organize them?

- Have I read and analyzed the first draft according to "big to little"—from content, organization, and sentences to words and mechanics?

- Have I revised my first draft?

- Have I written as many drafts as I need to create a well-written document that meets the needs and wants of my audience?

- Have I copyedited my document to find all errors?

- Have I published my document so that it is error-free and professional?

CLOSE

Summary

Use the summary to review major ideas in the chapter. Ask students to form pairs and elaborate on each statement, explaining what they remember from the chapter.

CLOSE

Checklist

Ask students if any item in the checklist is confusing. If so, review the concept.

REVIEW

For a review of the key terms in the chapter, provide students with the *Key Terms* worksheet available as a supplemental activity on the IRCD.

Build Your Foundation

1. Students should see that all processes require time, patience, and recursive thinking.

2. As an instructor, share your own ranking. Discuss the differences to familiarize students with other processes.

3–5. Practice will help students become familiar with their own writing process.

6. Encourage students to share their writing processes. Note similar responses and praise good ideas.

7. Circumstance—situation; excellence—perfection; describe—narrate; run—dash; communicate—talk; pleasant—fun; shirt—blouse; document—essay; fuel—energy; end—finish; building—apartment; employment—work.

8. Luis has been offered two jobs and must decide which one to accept. One job is at the movie theater; the other is at the golf course. If he accepts the job at the movie theater, he would work at the concession stand, selling popcorn, beverages, and candy. If he accepts the job at the golf course, he would work at the pro shop, selling golf balls, tees, and golfing supplies. Luis would earn more per hour at the golf course, but he would be 10 miles from home. At the movie theater, Luis would earn less per hour, but he would be a block from home. Luis decides to accept the job at the movie theater because it is closer to his home.

Build Your Foundation

1. How is writing like one of these processes: climbing a mountain, growing a plant, training a dog, or learning a song?

2. Listed below are the steps of the writing process. Rank them from easiest to most difficult for you, with 1 being easiest and 8 being most difficult. Rank them again for the time each one takes, with 1 taking the least time and 8 taking the most time. Which stage is most important? Why?

Prewriting	Researching	Revising 1	Copyediting
Shaping	Drafting	Revising 2	Publishing

3. Keep a writing journal each day for five days. Write in it for 15 minutes at a time. At the end of five days, underline topics about which you might consider writing. Choose one topic and practice mapping to come up with subtopics.

4. Use open freewriting, focused freewriting, or looping to come up with a topic for research. Then practice focused freewriting on your topic to help shape the idea. Another option is to practice focused freewriting on one of these topics: the environment, sports, music, or health.

5. Map your own writing process. Compare your process to a neighbor's, an instructor's, or a family member's.

6. Answer these questions about your writing process.

   a. Where and when do you prefer to write?
   b. Does the computer help or hinder your writing process? Explain.
   c. How do you prepare to write? Consider such tasks as playing music, gathering materials, making a sandwich, getting a beverage, or organizing your desk.
   d. What is the best piece of writing you ever wrote? Describe your process. How did you know the writing was good?
   e. How do you know you have finished revising and are ready to publish?

7. Think of as many synonyms as you can for the following words. When you are finished coming up with synonyms on your own, consult a thesaurus for additional synonyms.

circumstance	run	shirt	end
excellence	communicate	document	building
describe	pleasant	fuel	employment

8. Use a variety of ways to combine the following short sentences into longer ones to add variety to the sentence structure. Then add a suitable topic sentence, a concluding sentence, and an appropriate transition to create a smoother flow of ideas.

Luis has been offered two jobs. One job is at the movie theater. The other job is at the golf course. He might take the job at the movie theater. He would work at the concession stand. He would sell popcorn, beverages, and candy. He could take the job at the golf course. He would work at the golf pro shop. He would sell golf balls, tees, and other golfing supplies. One job pays more per hour. The golf course pays more per hour. The golf course is ten miles from Luis's home. The job at the movie theater pays $0.50 less per hour. It is a block from Luis's house.

Your Turn

9. Write two paragraphs, one discussing what you like about writing and the other discussing what you do not like about writing. Write one paragraph by hand on notebook paper and the other using a word processor. How does your writing process change?

10. Write a paragraph describing your favorite place by dictating your words to someone else. How does speaking aloud affect your writing process?

11. Write an essay or a paragraph on a topic of your choice. After you complete one draft, exchange papers with at least two of your classmates. Ask them to make comments using the list of questions for copyediting in this chapter.

12. Select one of the following topics and write a one-page essay: why people should exercise regularly, why people should stay informed about news events, or why people should recycle. Then practice writing collaboratively by dividing the topic into stages. Writer 1 will prewrite and organize three subtopics and pass the prewriting to Writer 2. Writer 2 will write the first draft and pass the draft to Writer 3. Writer 3 will revise and pass the revision to Writer 4, who will edit the revision, make changes, and submit the final draft.

13. In small groups, write a letter to the editor of your local newspaper, expressing your views on a current event (for example, a choice of a political candidate, the way your tax dollars are spent, or a community concern). Individually, brainstorm ideas, organize your ideas, and take notes. In one session, write the letter as a group. Ask one person to copyedit the final version, bringing it back to class for the group to see.

14. Think of the last time you worked on a group project with other people. What kind of experience did you have? What were the benefits of working with this group? What were the drawbacks? What could you do differently the next time you are part of a group to make sure you have a positive experience? Write a one- to two-page analysis.

Community Connection

15. Interview a writer in your area (a reporter, technical writer, local novelist, or public relations expert) about his or her writing process. Does the writer come up with topics, or does someone else provide them? What advice, if any, does the writer have for your classmates? Summarize the writer's process and share your findings with the class. If possible, bring to class something the writer has written. Better yet, invite the writer to class to talk about the writing process.

16. Help another person with all or part of the writing process for a writing project. You might help a family member or a member of Big Brothers Big Sisters or AmeriCorp. Coach the person through the stages of the writing process. Write a description of your experience.

17. Interview employees in your area, asking how often they work collaboratively, what kinds of projects they complete collaboratively, and how they organize tasks.

Brief Correspondence

Goals

- Identify brief correspondence
- Analyze and target the audience for brief correspondence
- Prewrite for brief correspondence
- Prepare for and determine how to format text messages, e-mails, memorandums (memos), and letters
- Understand and use strategies for composing good news, bad news, and persuasive messages

Terms

- block letter style, p. 121
- buffer, p. 124
- external audience, p. 110
- goodwill, p. 106
- hierarchical order, p. 117
- hooks, p. 127
- internal audience, p. 109
- modified block letter style, p. 121
- testimonials, p. 128

WRITE TO LEARN

Consider information you share with others in any work situation, whether a collaborative paper or class project, a task you manage at home, or paid employment. For example, do you need to schedule a team meeting or set a deadline? Is time a factor in the communication method? Is a record of your communication important? Is your communication usually face-to-face, over the phone, in notes or letters, by e-mail, or through other means? With one task in mind, write a few paragraphs about what and how you communicate.

Focus on Brief Correspondence

Read the sample writing excerpts on pages 103–104 and answer these questions about each document:

- Where is the main idea in the memo? in the letter?
- How is the message organized in the memo? in the letter?

What If?

- The memo writer needed a more immediate response from the reader?
- The letter writer were declining the student's scholarship application?

Kendall Developers, LLC

TO: Billy Franklin

FROM: Ellen Anderson   *EA*

DATE: May 7, 20—

SUBJECT: Changes in Deverville Site Plans Required by New City Regulations

After a conversation with Arden Sorbak, Deverville Planning Director, today, I think we should review our site plans for the new discount mall. Please examine the newly adopted city guidelines, make the necessary adjustments to our plans and delivery copies to me and Sorbak. We'll need those new plans in three weeks, no later than Friday, May 29, 20—, in order to present them for approval at the next meeting of the Planning and Zoning Commission. That time frame will allow us to request a time slot on the agenda for the upcoming meeting.

1. We had planned for 238 parking spaces with 24 handicapped spaces. The new city guidelines require that we provide 5 percent more overall parking.

2. The setback lines on the north side of the site allow 80 feet from the property line to the building. However, according to Sorbak, we need to allow 105 feet because of the drainage embankment.

3. The city planning and zoning committee also has some questions about the landscaping plans. In particular, committee members want to be certain that trees on the street side of the building do not create debris or hazards for drivers and that the trees are aesthetically consistent with the city plantings along the streets in that area.

We'll all be happy to see these plans recorded with a stamp of approval and this project under construction!

cah

Sample Memo

FOCUS	ASSESS
Focus on Brief Correspondence	**What If?**
Use the questions to encourage students to read the samples closely.	Use the questions to discuss how the samples would be different if the situation or audience changed.
	Go to www.cengage.com/school/bcomm/techwtg for more detailed responses to these questions.

Landover Community College

Office of the Dean of Students

Telephone (252) 555-0143

Fax (252) 555-0140

October 26, 20—

Ms. Regina Williams
P.O. Box 2453
Taylor, NC 28590-1237

Dear Ms. Williams:

I am pleased to award you an $800 Student Government Association Scholarship to attend Landover Community College for the 2010–2011 academic year. The selection committee recognizes your achievements and your need for assistance in reaching your academic goals.

The funds will be disbursed during the upcoming academic year. These monies will be available for you to use during preregistration and registration for tuition and fees, as designated in the scholarship. Any remaining funds may be used to purchase books, supplies, and other school-related items in the Landover bookstore. Remaining funds will be given to you approximately four to eight weeks after registration.

I warmly congratulate you and wish you every success. We look forward to having you as a student at Landover. If you have any questions, feel free to contact Mr. Rudy Conway in Room 345 of our scholarship office in the Thomas Hannam Building or call (295) 555-0164.

Sincerely,

Sylvia Sanchez

Dr. Sylvia Sanchez
Dean of Students

SMS/ta

P.O. Drawer 2877 • Farmville • North Carolina • 27828-2877
An Equal Opportunity/Affirmative Action Institution

Sample Letter: Positive Message

ENRICH

Using the questions and responses from the Write to Learn, have students consider this question: What advantages and disadvantages have you found with the types of communication you use? In two columns, list the advantages and disadvantages of each form of communication.

Writing@Work

Courtesy of Stephen Freas

Saren Erdmann is an Information Technology Project Manager for US Bank. Saren's primary responsibilities include managing software installations and enhancements for US Bank's branch locations. She identifies project stakeholders, coordinates and runs all project-related meetings and communications, documents each project, and assesses risks and solutions that keep initiatives running as smoothly as possible.

Because most of Saren's stakeholders are located in remote offices, she must coordinate with them via phone calls, e-mails, or instant messaging. Saren is quick to note the dangers of miscommunication when exchanging notes with colleagues in short digital texts. "Since the written word can be interpreted in so many ways, it is very important to be clear," she advises.

To write with clarity, Saren recommends keeping messages short and to the point and using a professional tone. Her rule of thumb is that "no matter how well you know someone, you must always maintain a level of professionalism when sending written communication at work." However, a little humor carefully delivered to a friendly audience won't hurt: "If I have been working with someone for a long time and we have a personal relationship, my work-related communications to them are slightly more relaxed, but still business-appropriate."

Project managers like Saren are agile at juggling correspondence. They multitask, prioritize which items need an immediate response, and have a strategy for managing items on the back burner. "I am bombarded with so much correspondence on a daily basis that it is difficult to absorb everything I receive right away. I am careful to archive all project documentation and correspondence in a central location. If I need to refresh my memory or read an original communication I missed, I can find the information in my files."

Think Critically

1. Research the word *stakeholder*. What is the original meaning? How is it used in this profile?

2. Why is clear writing so important to Saren? How does she keep her writing clear?

Printed with permission of Saren Erdmann

TYPICAL READER

A busy employee needing accurate, complete information delivered quickly in an easy-to-read document so that he or she can perform a job and contribute to the organization.

WRITER'S FOCUS

Responding quickly to convey pertinent and accurate information that adds to the work flow and builds goodwill.

FOCUS

Warm Up

Use the Warm Up to help students see the importance of written communication. They should understand that while talking might be more direct, records of ideas are valuable. Sharing written ideas gives people who work in different locations a means to think through a concept carefully and a way to respond efficiently. Certainly, science would not have advanced as far as it has without written communication.

TEACH

Discuss the format and organization of the Sample Letter: Positive Message. Remind students that the organization reflects what the audience would most want to know or read.

INTRODUCTION TO TEXT MESSAGES, E-MAILS, MEMOS, AND LETTERS

Communication is essential for being able to act and make decisions in the business world. People must be able to share information. Although some communication can take place face-to-face, a great deal of communication is conducted through text messages, e-mails, memos, and letters. All four of these may be used for brief correspondence. However, each one has its own distinguishing characteristics. For instance, text messaging and e-mail are the fastest and most efficient means of written communication. A writer can compose a message, send it electronically around the world, and receive an answer almost immediately.

Unlike electronic correspondence, memos and letters take more time. Of the two, memos are more efficient than letters, primarily because memos have fewer formal parts and because they are usually directed to an audience in the same organization as the sender. Memos also invite a speedy response. In some situations, receivers write a response on the memo they have received and send it back to the writers. In contrast, letters may have many parts and may be sent by postal service or a commercial carrier to readers outside the organization.

All brief correspondence seeks the **goodwill** of readers. Goodwill is the value of doing things that create mutual admiration and respect. It is the feeling of friendship. In addition, writers of brief correspondence practice the principles of effective communication.

Goodwill

Goodwill is the act of making and keeping a friend. Goodwill is a feeling of good intentions. Effective business correspondence fosters goodwill through its word choice and message. You can create goodwill in writing the same way you create the bonds of a friendship.

Goodwill, like friendship, is created by being honest and polite. It is fostered by doing what you say you will do when you say you will do it. Business friendships grow in an atmosphere of mutual respect and trust. You also foster goodwill by attending to correspondence as quickly as you can. In short, you generate goodwill by treating your reader the same way you would like to be treated.

Principles of Effective Communication

In addition to generating goodwill, brief correspondence should be helpful to readers. Table 5.1 suggests some of the characteristics of effective brief correspondence as well as traits to avoid in text messages, e-mails, memos, and letters.

COMMUNICATE EFFECTIVELY AND DEVELOP GOODWILL WITH ...	HINDER GOODWILL AND COMMUNICATE INEFFECTIVELY WITH ...
Concise language	*Fuzzy, unnecessary words* that take up readers' time with details they do not need
Accuracy and completeness	*Inaccurate, incomplete information,* creating misunderstandings and problems to be solved later
Professional appearance	*Sloppy appearance,* making you and your organization appear incompetent and careless
Conventional format	*Unfamiliar format* that confuses the reader and makes your intent unclear
Logical organization	*Illogical organization,* frustrating readers' efforts to follow your thinking
Standard English usage	*Grammatical and punctuation errors and misspelled words,* causing you and your organization to appear uneducated and/or careless

Table 5.1

Following conventional format and using standard English help make a positive impression on your reader. To ensure that the information in your correspondence is well organized, complete, and free of errors, reread the document before you send it. If you are unsure whether your message is clear and easy to understand, ask a colleague to read your correspondence and to provide feedback.

Text messages, e-mails, memos, and letters not only help get the job done, but also serve as a way to evaluate the writer's performance. Managers and administrators can tell from an employee's correspondence whether that employee is solving or creating problems, communicating with or confusing readers, building or ruining relationships, and getting the job done or making no progress.

Use of Suitable Tone and Humor

Brief correspondence usually has a conversational, informal tone. In fact, in this type of correspondence, it is appropriate to use *I*, the first-person pronoun. "You're busy, so I'll be brief" is the opening sentence of an effective sales letter for a magazine. Note the focus on the reader, the use of first person, and the casual tone. Readers are more likely to cooperate when the message sounds as if a person, rather than a machine, wrote it. This informal writing style is similar to a conversation you might have with a friend if that conversation were polished slightly.

TEACH

Introduce the following points about goodwill: goodwill in business is promoted by practicing good ethics, using proper manners, respecting others, accepting others as equals, being generous when possible, and providing high-quality service and products.

Provide students with the *Sample Correspondence* worksheet available as a supplemental activity on the IRCD.

TEACH

What destroys a good friendship? Many of the same things that destroy a friendship also destroy goodwill between business correspondents.

Students may be interested to know that goodwill can be bought and sold. When a business with an established name and reputation is sold, the company's goodwill increases its value.

Principles of good communication include being accurate, complete, and concise. Answering correspondence quickly in a professional-looking document without errors is also following good communication principles. Good communication promotes goodwill.

For an entertaining memo showing effective use of humor, see *Giving Up Your Blood* at www.cengage.com/school/bcomm/techwtg. Click the link for Chapter 5; then click Data Files.

ONGOING ASSESSMENT

Stop and Think

Goodwill is a positive feeling of trust and friendship. A person creates goodwill by behaving ethically and providing quality products and services. Effective communication promotes goodwill.

Writers should analyze their audience. If formality is expected and acceptable, writers should meet those expectations. However, brief correspondence usually uses an informal but slightly polished tone.

Warm Up

Imagine writing an e-mail or a note filled with private jokes, insider stories, or juicy gossip to your closest friend. Now imagine that message being misdirected to your parent, guardian, or instructor.

FOCUS

Warm Up

Use the Warm Up to tune in to your students' experiences and dramatically show how important targeting an audience is. Discuss the consequences of sending misdirected messages or failing to know your audience.

Ask students what they think about spamming, the indiscriminate sending of electronic messages. If they respond negatively, they should understand how readers on the job will respond to e-mails that do not meet their needs.

Use humor to create goodwill in difficult situations or with uncooperative audiences. For example, a club leader at school might use humor to convince students to volunteer to donate blood even if they have not donated before or are afraid to do so.

However, writers should be cautious about using humor. As useful as it can be, humor used carelessly may be harmful. For example, a manager whose daughter died in a work-related accident is not likely to laugh when her quality assurance officer writes that the government safety inspectors "are going to kill us." Consider audience, situation, and character of the relationship before deciding whether to use humor.

⬣ **STOP AND THINK**

What is goodwill? Why is it important? Is a formal tone ever appropriate for brief correspondence? Explain.

AUDIENCE

The readers of text messages, e-mails, memos, and letters have similar characteristics. All of them expect the communication to be brief, to target a specific reader or readers, to have a specific purpose, and to follow standard format.

Some correspondence is sent to a multiple audience, and some is written with a specific audience in mind. If the reader is only one person, meet the needs of that person. Use language and information that he or she will understand and answer questions that this reader would ask if he or she were present. If an audience is made up of a group of readers, consider the needs of all of them.

Regardless of how well you know your readers, use the table on page 29 in Chapter 2 to help you focus on your audience. If you know little about your audience, learn as much as you can. Ask others what they know about your audience or read correspondence your audience has written. If you cannot learn much about your audience, assume a serious or neutral tone.

Keep your language moderately simple and natural. Work especially hard to build goodwill.

Audience for Text Messages

Text messages are becoming more acceptable as a form of business communication, primarily because of the speed with which senders and receivers can deal with information. Because readers may be internal or external to the writer's organization, the writer may know a great deal, a little bit, or almost nothing about the reader. Therefore, senders must anticipate expectations of the audience, particularly the readers' expectations as to how formal the message should be. An employee may send a text message with incomplete sentences and extensive abbreviations (for example, B4 for "before" or NRN for "No reply necessary") to a supervisor. If that supervisor does not approve of such informality and does not understand the message, the communication is likely to be strained and create a poor impression. Even though text messages may be very brief and informal, they need to be clear and to provide the reader with the information he or she needs.

Because text messages are gaining in popularity, they are becoming not only a personal communication tool, but also an important business avenue. For example, Barack Obama's presidential campaign successfully used text messaging to "get out the vote" and to mobilize volunteers. Some advertisers use text messages to send coupon codes and discount notices to consumers. Used carefully, with perhaps one to three contacts per month rather than daily, this type of marketing campaign can be effective and inexpensive.

Also remember that your audience may not be available when you send your text. Wait a reasonable time for a response before sending another message. In addition, keep messages brief. If you have a long, complex message, send it as an attachment via e-mail or through some other medium.

Audience for E-mails

For personal as well as professional correspondence, e-mail has become a common way to communicate. Readers may be inside or outside the writer's organization. Thus, writers know some readers well and others not at all. Because readers often receive a great deal of e-mail in a day, they expect writers to focus on a point and to keep the message brief without omitting essential information. Readers expect messages to be relevant and clear. They will not waste their time with messages that are incomplete, confusing, or unclear.

Audience for Memos

Memos are used to correspond inside an organization. Therefore, the reader will be a receiver inside the writer's organization—an **internal audience.**

In an organization, everyone is likely to receive and read memos. For example, an employee might receive a memo from a coworker explaining a procedural change. A memo outlining the facts—implementation time, date, actions, and checklist—provides a written record so that the person receiving the notice does not become confused about the details of what is expected.

Even though memos are addressed to people inside a company, the writer must consider his or her audience carefully. The audience may consist of people with a variety of outlooks, backgrounds, opinions, interests, roles, and levels in the organization. Sometimes the writer will know the readers and sometimes not.

Remember that the internal audience of an international company may have members in Los Angeles and Moscow, for example. Once a writer identifies the audience, he or she must study the audience thoroughly to ensure that its needs are met.

ONGOING ASSESSMENT

Stop and Think

Text messages and e-mails may be sent to internal or external readers, memos typically target an internal audience, and letters generally address an external audience. However, in special circumstances when formality is needed, such as for a promotion, dismissal, or recommendation, letters may be sent to people inside an organization.

FOCUS

Warm Up

Use the Warm Up to stress the importance of prewriting and planning.

Warm Up

Think about the planning involved in hosting a party or preparing a meal. What kind of party or meal might result if you do not plan? Likewise, how effective can your correspondence be if you do not plan?

Audience for Letters

While memos are for readers inside an organization (internal communication), letters are generally for readers outside an organization (external communication). Although you may know a great deal about members inside your organization, you may know very little about readers outside your company, called an **external audience.**

A letter is an extension of your organization. The letter will be in the presence of your reader when you are not. If the letter is well written, you will make a good impression and inspire confidence in yourself and your organization.

⬢ **STOP AND THINK**

What are the primary differences among audiences for text messages, e-mails, memos, and letters?

PREWRITING

Effective text messages, e-mails, memos, and letters depend on planning. After analyzing your audience, you need to make decisions based on what you have learned. Ask yourself these questions before you write:

- What do I want the receiver to do or think after he or she reads this correspondence?

- What do I want to accomplish with this message?

- What is the main point?

- Does my reader need background information? If so, how much?

- Do I need to make the message simpler for this audience? What definitions or explanations will the audience need?

- Is this reader familiar with the subject matter? Does the reader have previous experience with this idea?

- What questions should my correspondence answer?

In addition to answering the questions above, you should take notes on the details you need for your correspondence. Gather the facts, such as situation background, events that occurred, problems created, order/part numbers, accurate descriptions, or questions to ask. Find out the name, title, and correct spelling and address of the person to whom you are writing. Double-check to make sure the information you have gathered is accurate and complete.

Using the answers to these questions, put your ideas on paper. Some writers prefer a list, such as the kind a person makes for grocery shopping. Other writers like to use freewriting. Remember that freewriting is writing down everything that comes to mind. Because this is the creative part of writing, you should not be critical of your ideas. Get all of the ideas, brilliant or otherwise, on paper.

Whichever technique you use will generate a collection of ideas you want to cover in the message or body. With all of the ideas before you, you can start to be critical. Cut the ones that are unnecessary and change those that do not communicate exactly what you want to say. Prewriting also is the time to rank ideas. Consider your purpose and the organization that will best help you achieve it. Decide what you will place first, second, third, and so on.

Planning Text Messages and E-mails

Prewriting for text messages and e-mails involves planning to communicate with readers who have diverse needs and expectations. First, remember that busy professionals may receive a great volume of correspondence. Thus, your subject line must be specific and descriptive. It should show readers how the topic relates to them. If your subject line is poorly written, chances are the receiver will delete your message without reading it.

Second, consider the reader's expectations for formality and length. If you are sending a text message or an e-mail to people in your company or organization, you are likely to know the formality they expect by referring to other e-mails. For instance, the corporate climate may be formal, in which case readers might expect complete sentences, correct punctuation, and few or no abbreviations. Likewise, review other text messages and e-mails to determine the appropriate length of your messages.

However, others with whom you communicate electronically may be more comfortable with informal messages—incomplete sentences; little punctuation; and the many abbreviations writers have developed to make online exchanges fast, such as BTW for "by the way" and HAND for "Have a nice day."

To see commonly used text and e-mail abbreviations, go to www.cengage.com/school/bcomm/techwtg. Click the link for Chapter 5; then click Data Files.

©Alex Hind, 2009/Used under license from Shutterstock.com

In addition to level of formality, plan the length of your messages to meet readers' needs and expectations. Most cellular carriers such as AT&T and Verizon limit the number of characters that may be used in a text message. When planning, keep that limitation in mind as well as the frustration your receiver would experience in trying to read a long message on a phone. Likewise, because people generally read e-mail from a computer screen rather than printing hard copies, keep your messages as brief as possible so that people can read the text without scrolling through several pages. Short messages also allow for easier response. If you have a long, involved message, send it as several different text messages or e-mails. Another option is to create a document with a word processor and send the document as an attachment.

Third, plan for differences in e-mail software. Avoid complex formatting such as bulleted lists, tables, italics, or underlining unless you know that the recipient's software can read them.

Fourth, clearly explain the context of your message so that all readers will understand. For example, when you respond to a question, make sure readers realize which question you are answering.

Also consider privacy and security, especially when planning text messages and e-mails. Little electronic communication is truly private. Employees using company computers to send e-mail should keep in mind that the e-mail belongs to (and represents) the company. Even people e-mailing from their homes may not have the privacy they expect because of hackers, worms, and viruses. In addition, people who use Forward, Reply All, and Blind Copy with e-mail should be particularly sensitive to the privacy of others with whom they correspond. For example, Dale sends a message that he thought was private to Jin-ho, but Jin-ho forwards the message to Neva. As a result, Dale's privacy was compromised because Neva now knows something Dale did not want her to see.

Communication Dilemma

You are sitting at your desk at Phoenix Fabrication when you receive an e-mail from an old friend, your former college dorm mate. He wants to know how you have been and whether you plan to attend the upcoming class reunion. Because you have not seen him in a couple of years, you want to make plans to meet at the reunion.

Just when you are about to tap "Reply," you remember that your boss cautioned you about using company time to conduct personal business. You think that perhaps this one quick personal e-mail will not be a problem, and you do not want your college friend to think you are ignoring him. (He did contact you at work first.) After all, how will anyone know you sent the e-mail?

Think Critically
How should you reply to your friend? Explain.

In addition, plan for handling emotions effectively. Do not flame. (When writers are harshly criticizing each other, they are flaming.) Avoid e-mailing when you are angry. Wait until you can handle the issue logically rather than emotionally. Using all capital letters generally equates to shouting, so use this style only when you intend to shout. For emphasis, you can surround a word or phrase with asterisks or white space.

Another way to convey feelings is through the use of emoticons, symbols created on the keyboard to convey emotions, such as :-), the smiley face. Yet writers must carefully consider how readers will react to the feelings expressed in an e-mail because feelings can be misinterpreted or misunderstood.

Finally, learn about good manners and etiquette in cyberspace, also known as *netiquette.* Keep in mind, though, that rules of etiquette may vary from one media to another. For example, abbreviations may be approved for some business uses of instant messaging but discouraged for use in other media. Table 5.2 lists some of the rules of netiquette.

ENRICH

Ask students what they already know about netiquette. Then have them conduct research and share their findings with the class. Or have students interview a professional, asking for examples of communication that break rules of netiquette and the consequences.

DO	DON'T
Read and respond to e-mail promptly. If you need time to reply, respond to say that you received the message and tell when you will reply.	Write long, complex messages; readers expect e-mail to be brief.
Represent yourself and others well and fairly.	Write anything that you would not say in front of any person, including those people discussed in the e-mail.
Communicate as clearly and rationally as possible. Remember that readers will not have your tone of voice or body language to help them interpret your meaning.	Include offensive, obscene, or illegal content.
Keep the correspondence thread when replying so that readers will be able to follow the line of discussion.	Quote large blocks of irrelevant text.
Develop a descriptive, precise subject line so that readers can predict the message, file the correspondence, and find it later.	Key in all capital letters (seen as shouting) or in all lowercase letters (perceived as lazy).
Keep your virus protection current so you do not to forward problems to others.	Believe or forward every urban legend and cybermyth that comes your way.
Respect others' bandwidth and download times.	Forward jokes and chain messages without being certain that the recipient wants them.

Table 5.2

Planning Memos

As with planning text messages and e-mails, prewriting memos requires writers to consider the audience's expectations. Readers usually expect memos to be brief and to cover one topic. However, the need to be brief should not override substance. Make sure the memo explains the topic fully—whether it offers a solution to a problem, outlines a change in procedures or policies, or deals with other business concerns.

Furthermore, writers sometimes choose to write memos as documentation (proof) of discussions, decisions, or actions. Perhaps you or your company would like something more substantial or concrete than e-mails to back up an offer that was made during a meeting with a vendor or an action that was taken following a safety review. Memos would serve that purpose.

You should plan to include all of the specific details—for example, names, dates, times, and locations—that your audience may need.

Planning Letters

Memos as internal correspondence may, in some circumstances, be informal. In other circumstances, memos may be formal. Letters, on the other hand, are usually formal. Because letters typically address external audiences, letter writers should inform the reader of all relevant information.

For instance, the reader may not be as aware of history and background as other readers inside the organization are. The reader is not likely to know insider language, or jargon. The reader may not be aware of corporate policies, organizational culture, chain of command, or other elements that are important in understanding the issues being discussed. In addition, when a writer is communicating with an unfamiliar audience, the writer should "put his or her best foot forward" by carefully choosing words, gauging tone, and focusing on the purpose of the correspondence.

When letters are used internally for special circumstances such as promotions, dismissals, recommendations, or disciplinary matters, writers should plan for a higher level of formality because of the importance of the subject and the legal implications. In general, formal documents do not use the following:

- Contractions
- Clichés
- Personal or emotional commentary
- Conversational speech
- Abbreviations
- Short, simple sentences

 STOP AND THINK

Why are e-mail privacy and security issues important to consider when prewriting?

FORMATTING

In much the same way fancy type identifies a formal invitation, the formatting features of text messages, e-mails, memos, and letters help readers recognize the type of correspondence they are viewing. Specific elements are unique to each type. For example, text messages, because they are viewed on a phone screen, are usually brief and simple blocks of text. E-mails may look like memos, but they typically include e-mail addresses for the sender and receiver. Memos are recognizable by their headings (To, From, Date, and Subject). Likewise, the mark of a letter is the inside and return addresses, salutation, and complimentary close—features that are familiar to audiences.

Formatting Text Messages and E-mails

Writers usually do not need to be concerned about formatting decisions when they create text messages and e-mails because the cellular and e-mail software providers have already made most of the decisions. Most programs, such as Microsoft® Outlook Express®, simply ask the writer to click a light-colored line or a blank box and key the intended receiver or subject line. Most programs automatically insert the sender's name or address and date.

Formatting Memos

A draft of a memo begins with a standard format of headings followed by the body, or message. Like the addresses and salutation in a letter (Dear Mr. Najafi), headings make a document recognizable as a memo. Four elements appear at the top of a memo, as shown in Figure 5.1.

However, in some cases, headings may not appear in that order. When you begin work, your new employer may give you a style manual that shows you a different format the company prefers.

Memo templates are included in most word processing software. Microsoft® Word 2007, for instance, provides several memo templates and a wizard to help writers create memos. The advantages of working with memo templates are that they are simple to use (even for writers with no experience), are easily modified, and provide attractive document design.

At the same time, these familiar templates have a number of shortcomings, such as overused design (readers will likely recognize the template) and

TO:

FROM:

DATE:

SUBJECT:

Figure 5.1 Memo Headings

Think about the information readers want to know when they receive messages. What are their questions? Compare that answer to the elements of formatting for e-mails, memos, and letters.

FOCUS

Warm Up

Use the Warm Up to show that formatting elements answer questions receivers ask. For instance, the receiver usually wants to know (1) who sent the message, (2) who the intended receiver is, (3) when the message was sent, and (4) what the message is about.

decisions made without the writer's input or consideration. Because writers do not need to think about design or headings, sometimes these "plug-and-play" templates encourage writers not to think about other decisions related to their message. Ineffective communication may be the result.

TO Line

In the TO section, you name your audience. You may name one person, such as Joanna Tschiegg, or you may name a group, such as the Employee Benefits Committee or the Sterile Manufacturing Division. On occasion, you may need to name several readers who are not connected by a unit or committee. In this case, you may simply list their names.

The list of receivers' names may be presented a couple of ways. When you are sending a memo to more than one person, key all names on one line, connecting them with commas, or key the names in a list, as shown in Figure 5.2.

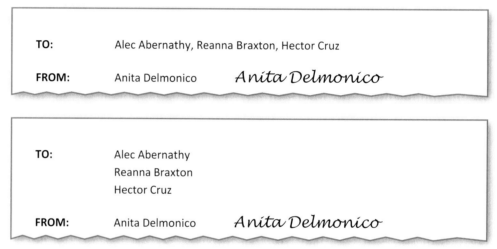

Figure 5.2 Formats of TO Line

When you are sending a memo to a large number of people, use a distribution list. This format is shown in Figure 5.3.

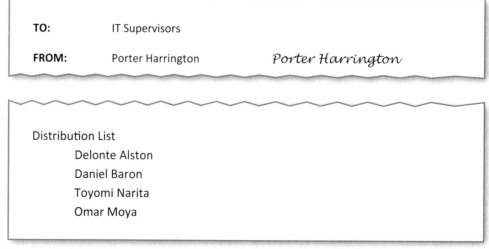

Figure 5.3 Format of TO Line with Distribution List

When you list several people's names, enter them in alphabetical order or **hierarchical order,** from the top to the bottom of the organizational chart. In hierarchical order, the people of greatest recognition and responsibility in the organization, such as the president and vice president, are listed first. Other employees are listed in decreasing order of rank within the organization. Remember, however, if the hierarchal list contains two employees of the same rank, such as two directors, you should place their names in alphabetical order so as not to offend either person.

FROM Line

After the FROM heading, you list the name or names of the sender of the message. If you are the only person responsible for the message, your name appears. If the memo comes from a group, the group or unit name is listed, such as FROM: Wooster Jazz Band.

Some memos are from several people who are not part of a group. In this case, list the names of each sender in a line joined by commas or in columns, again in alphabetical or hierarchical order. Remember to write your initials or sign your full name after the keyed name in the FROM section, as shown in Figure 5.3.

Initialing or signing memos is especially important when they deal with important legal or organizational matters. Memos become legal documents that can be used in a court of law when they are signed and dated. Your initials or signature also tells the reader that you have reviewed the memo and accept responsibility for the message, particularly if someone else keyed it.

Dateline

The dateline usually appears after TO and FROM and before the subject line. You can choose between two styles for writing the date: international (also called military in the United States) or traditional.

International date style is becoming increasingly popular in technical documents because of economy. International style requires no commas. In this style, the

deepblue4you/iStockphoto.com

writer gives the day first, the month next, and the year last, as in 12 May 2012. Another reason for its increasing popularity is that it is more clearly understood by readers outside the United States, most of whom use this style.

The traditional month-day-year style used in the United States, as in June 4, 1955, and April 1, 2011, gives the month, the date, a comma, and the year.

Subject Line

In most memos, the subject line logically appears as the last of the headings. It announces the point of the memo immediately before you develop that point. You may see terms such as *Reference, Regarding,* or *Re* (which comes from the Latin *res,* meaning "thing" or "matter") used the same way as the word *subject.* However, some readers consider those terms archaic. In addition to helping the reader predict the topic, the subject line distinguishes one message from another and focuses the writer on one main idea.

Predict   The subject line should allow readers to predict what the memo will say. In other words, it reflects the main idea discussed in the body. Be as specific as you can when composing the subject line. A subject line that reads "Insurance" does little to help the reader predict what the memo will cover. That subject line is too general to provide insight. "Dental Insurance Open Enrollment Period Set for June 20–27, 2010" is precise enough to tell readers what to expect and to encourage them to read the message. Make the wording as specific as possible, as in the following examples:

Use *Minutes of Strategic Planning Meeting*	instead of	*Minutes or Meeting*
Use *Questions about Requisitions*	instead of	*Questions or Requisitions*
Use *Incident in the Carpentry Shop on May 4*	instead of	*Incident in Carpentry Shop*

The subject line should not be a complete sentence, but a phrase or a clause—more like a newspaper headline.

Distinguish   In addition to helping the reader predict the subject of the memo, the subject line should clarify the difference between one memo and many others. For instance, servers at a restaurant may read many memos during the year that deal with menu items. Therefore, if the subject line says only "Menu Changes," the server reading it will not immediately know that this message is different from last week's memo. Instead, specific subject lines such as "Italian Items Added to Menu for June" or "Lobster Price Increase" or "Salmon Unavailable Until April 20" tell the server exactly what to expect the message to cover.

Focus   The subject line also aids the writer. Writing a subject line forces the writer to focus on the most important idea. Furthermore, it allows the writer to check the message of the memo against the subject line. The message should cover the same idea the subject line announces.

A memo should cover only one main point. Writers who have two messages for the same audience should write two memos for the following reasons. First, if a memo has more than one message, the reader cannot determine what is truly important. Second, the busy reader may find the first idea, assume that it is the only important information, and stop reading. Third, the memo might be so long that it intimidates readers. Readers generally expect memos to be one to four paragraphs long. Finally, some messages are inappropriate to combine, as Figure 5.4 illustrates.

TO:	X-ray Department
FROM:	Hannah Smith, Personnel Officer
DATE:	June 10, 20—
SUBJECT:	1. Vacation and Sick Leave Slips
	2. Death of Mr. Martin's Mother-in-law

1. Please ensure that all vacation and sick leave slips for this fiscal year (July 1, 20— through June 30, 20—) are turned in to Tammy by June 27, 20—.

2. Dan Martin's mother-in-law and Selma Hale's grandmother, Mrs. Sadie Harper, passed away on Sunday, June 9, 20—. Funeral arrangements are being handled by Belvedere's Funeral Home at 2 p.m. on Tuesday, June 11. You may send expressions of sympathy to

Dan at:	811 E. Cooper Street	Selma at:	Route 1, Box 32
	Aberdeen, SD 57401		Aberdeen, SD 57401

js

Distribution List
    Dr. Mendoza
    Dr. Joyner
    Mr. Umezaki
    Ms. Shankowski

Figure 5.4 *Ineffective* Memo with Two Main Ideas

Formatting Letters

All letters share a similar format. They are constructed using basic parts and may be written in one of several styles.

Letter Parts

On the next page, Figure 5.5 illustrates and describes the basic parts of a letter: heading, dateline, inside address, salutation, body, complimentary closing, signature, and reference initials.

Jefferson Gas and Appliance
HWY 17 South
P.O. Box 11
Washington, NC 27889-1107
13 July 20—

Ms. Rhea Tankard
Manager
Malloy's Manufacturing
1023 West Main Street
Washington, NC 27889-5043

Dear Ms. Tankard

Subject: Contract for . . .

Xx xxxxx xxxxxxxxx xxx
Xxxxxxx xxxxxxx xxxx
Xxxxxxxxxxx xx xxxxxx x
xxxxxx xxx Xx xxx xxxxx
xxxxxxxx xx xxx xxxx

X xxxx xxxxxxxx xxxxxx Xxx
xxxx xxxxxxx xxxx Xxxxxx xxx
xxxxxxxxxx Xxxxx xxxxxx x
xxxxxx x

Xxxxx xxxxxxxx xxx xxx Xx
xxxxx xxxxxxx xxxx Xxx
xxxxxx x xxxxxxx Xxxxx xx

Sincerely yours

W. B. (Jeff) Jefferson
President

WBJ/pjm

Enclosures (3)

c: Sofia Arellano
     Jay Reardon

INSIDE ADDRESS: Complete address of the sender as a return address (personal business letter). A letterhead (company/ organization letter) includes the company name, logo, address, and other optional information such and telephone and fax numbers.

DATELINE: Date the letter was written.

LETTER ADDRESS: Professional (for example, Dr., Rev., Capt.) or courtesy title (Mr., Miss, Ms., or Mrs.), correct name (first name/first initial and last name), title, and address of the person to whom you are writing (no abbreviations). Name here should match the name used in the salutation.

SALUTATION: Name of the person you want to read your letter. Typically uses professional (for example, Rev., Capt., Chief) or courtesy title (Mr., Miss, Ms., or Mrs.) and last name.
SUBJECT LINE (optional): Focuses on the topic of the letter.

BODY: Usually two to five paragraphs long but can be several pages and may use headings similar to reports. The letter should look balanced on the page.

The body of most letters is single-spaced with a double space (one blank line) between paragraphs. Organization depends on the type of letter you are writing.

In block letter style, all lines begin at the left margin. In modified block letter style, all lines generally begin at the left margin except the date and the closing lines, which begin at the center of the page.

CLOSING: Friendly but businesslike ending. Common closings include Sincerely, Yours truly, and Cordially (never Thank you).
SIGNATURE LINE: Keyed name and title with space for handwritten signature above.
REFERENCE INITIALS: Initials (in uppercase) of the person who dictated the letter followed by the initials (in lowercase) of the person who keyed the letter. The two sets of initials may be separated with a slash or a colon. Sometimes only the lowercase initials are used.
ENCLOSURE NOTATION: Indicates additional documents in the envelope. Often the word Enclosure is followed by a colon and the titles of the enclosed documents are listed.
COPY NOTATION: Indicates that a copy has been sent to another person or to other people.

Figure 5.5 Letter Parts

FOCUS

Figure 5.5

Explain to students what information is contained in each part of a letter.

Show the Parts of Letters Teaching Master on the IRCD.

ENRICH

Share a collection of letters for students to review. Engage the class in a discussion of style choices and the resulting impressions they make.

Assign students to create personal letterheads to use in their writing assignments.

Letter Styles

Letter styles vary. Business letters are usually written on letterhead stationery in block or modified block letter style. Personal letters include return addresses instead of letterheads and may be written in block or modified block letter style.

Block letter style aligns the return address, dateline, and closing at the left margin. Paragraphs are not indented. It is easy to key but may look off-balance. In **modified block letter style,** the dateline and closing begin at the horizontal center of the page. Paragraphs begin at the left margin. This style may be more difficult to key, but it looks more symmetrical on the page. Figure 5.6 illustrates basic differences in block and modified block letter style.

Two punctuation styles are used in business letters: open and mixed. Open punctuation means that no punctuation marks are used after the salutation and the complimentary close. Open punctuation is considered a time-saving style and is used with block letter style. Mixed punctuation may be used with modified block letter style, in which case the salutation and complimentary close are followed by punctuation marks. The proper punctuation with this style is a comma after the complimentary close and a colon (for business letters) or a comma (for personal letters) after the salutation.

TEACH
Compare the block and modified block letter styles to see what advantages one has over the other. For instance, students will probably note that block letter style is easier to key because it involves no indentions or spacing issues.

Block with No Indention, Open Punctuation

Letterhead

Dateline

Inside Address

Dear Mr. Torres

Xxxx xxxxx xxxxxx xxxxx xxxxxx xxx x xxxxx xx xxx xx xx xxx xxxxxxxx xxxxx x xxx xx xxxxx

Sincerely

Jerrod Mauer

JM/dsw

Modified Block with No Indention, Open Punctuation

Letterhead

Dateline

Inside Address

Dear Mr. Torres

Xxxx xxxxx xxxxxx xxxxx xxxxxx xxx x xxxxx xx xxx xx xx xxx xxxxxxxx xxxxx x xxx xx xxxxx

Sincerely

Darian Webster

Enclosure: Deed of Transfer

Figure 5.6 Letter Styles

Stop and Think

To avoid offending anyone, names should be listed alphabetically or according to the hierarchy of the organization.

Warm Up

Consider this opening line: *Dear Arnie, You're fired.* Does this message work? Will it build goodwill? Could the idea be presented more effectively? Explain.

No. Customary, acceptable complimentary closings include *Sincerely, Yours truly,* and *Cordially.*

FOCUS

Warm Up

Use the Warm Up to show students that one composition plan does not fit all messages. Other possible uses for the Warm Up include role playing, an essay describing how Arnie might feel or react, or a discussion about how to improve the delivery.

TEACH

Suggest that students test the organization of their good news messages by imagining that the reader has time to read only the first sentence before leaving the building due to a fire alarm. Does that one sentence provide the reader with the essential information? Is it the most important sentence in the document for the reader? If not, students should consider reorganizing.

Show the Illustrations of the Organizational Strategies Teaching Master on the IRCD.

⬣ **STOP AND THINK**

In what order should the names of recipients be listed in e-mails and memos? Should a writer use *Thank you* as a complimentary close in a letter? Explain.

COMPOSING THE MESSAGE

Because all e-mails, memos, and letters begin with a specific purpose, writers must keep that purpose in mind when composing a message.

Although formatting the document is important, the headings are only a means for conveying the ideas you want to share. The message, or the body, is the heart of the document.

The message section of correspondence should be organized for the reader, not for the writer. Because employees are busy and cannot waste time, correspondence should be organized accordingly. Imagine a busy decision maker opening an e-mail that she expects to be one page, only to discover that the message is more than four pages long. The receiver may decide not to spend time scrolling through and reading the four pages, especially when she expects an e-mail to be brief. Writers who frustrate their readers or who fail to meet their readers' expectations are not likely to be successful in achieving goals.

Organize ideas to suit the message. Some messages are best presented in a straightforward manner. Others, when presented bluntly and directly, are likely to offend readers. And still others, such as persuasive messages, require more motivation than a direct approach provides. The strategies for informative and good news messages, negative or bad news messages, and persuasive messages are useful in writing text messages, e-mails, memos, and letters.

Informative and Good News Messages

Brief correspondence usually gives the audience information that is pleasant—or at least acceptable. Pronouncements of good news, routine letters of inquiry, responses to letters of inquiry, and letters of appreciation all use a similar positive organizational structure.

You can expect the readers of a good news message to be in a receptive mood as they read your correspondence. Because your news is responsible for their pleasant mood, these readers are easy to approach. Therefore, the strategy is direct: Present the main idea first. Explanations, background information, and supplementary ideas follow the main idea.

The sample letter on page 104 and the e-mail from the production manager at Gene-Tech Laboratories in Figure 5.7 are examples of the direct approach to organizing informative and good news messages. The sample letter conveys good news to Regina Williams, the recipient of an $800 scholarship to a local community college. In that letter, the tone is enthusiastic, while the tone of the following memo is more neutral or matter-of-fact.

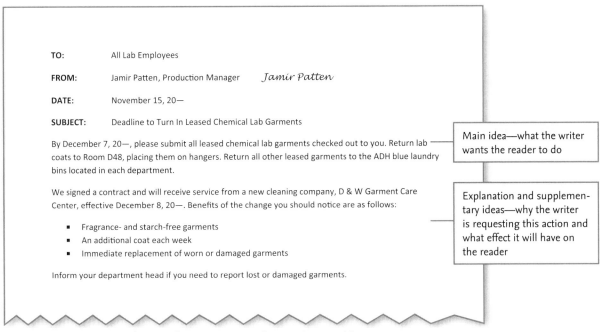

TO:	All Lab Employees
FROM:	Jamir Patten, Production Manager *Jamir Patten*
DATE:	November 15, 20—
SUBJECT:	Deadline to Turn In Leased Chemical Lab Garments

By December 7, 20—, please submit all leased chemical lab garments checked out to you. Return lab coats to Room D48, placing them on hangers. Return all other leased garments to the ADH blue laundry bins located in each department.

We signed a contract and will receive service from a new cleaning company, D & W Garment Care Center, effective December 8, 20—. Benefits of the change you should notice are as follows:

- Fragrance- and starch-free garments
- An additional coat each week
- Immediate replacement of worn or damaged garments

Inform your department head if you need to report lost or damaged garments.

Main idea—what the writer wants the reader to do

Explanation and supplementary ideas—why the writer is requesting this action and what effect it will have on the reader

Figure 5.7 Memo Using the Good News Strategy (Direct Approach)

Figure 5.8 shows the body of an e-mail of inquiry. Correspondence of inquiry, while employing a more neutral tone, still represents a positive message because it shows an interest in a concept, product, or service.

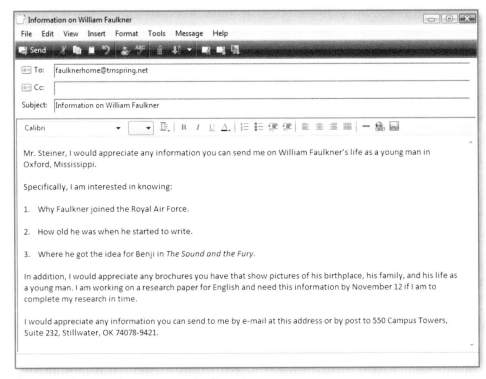

Information on William Faulkner

File   Edit   View   Insert   Format   Tools   Message   Help

Send

To: faulknerhome@trnspring.net

Cc:

Subject: Information on William Faulkner

Calibri

Mr. Steiner, I would appreciate any information you can send me on William Faulkner's life as a young man in Oxford, Mississippi.

Specifically, I am interested in knowing:

1.   Why Faulkner joined the Royal Air Force.

2.   How old he was when he started to write.

3.   Where he got the idea for Benji in *The Sound and the Fury*.

In addition, I would appreciate any brochures you have that show pictures of his birthplace, his family, and his life as a young man. I am working on a research paper for English and need this information by November 12 if I am to complete my research in time.

I would appreciate any information you can send to me by e-mail at this address or by post to 550 Campus Towers, Suite 232, Stillwater, OK 74078-9421.

Figure 5.8 Positive Message: E-mail of Inquiry

FOCUS

Figures 5.7 and 5.8

Review the strategy for good news messages and review formatting.

TEACH

Make students aware of current postal regulations regarding state abbreviations. See the Two-Letter Postal Abbreviations Teaching Master on the IRCD.

Introduce characteristics of positive messages by comparing them to how people give and receive good news in general. Point out that positive news is given quickly and is received well in good faith. Details usually follow the basic good news. Tone can vary from upbeat to enthusiastic.

Point out that the structure of each of the positive messages is essentially the same—general good news, necessary details, and a friendly close. Make sure students see this basic structure in all of the documents.

Bad News Messages

Occasionally, the purpose of a text message, an e-mail, a memo, or a letter is to share negative news—information readers will not be pleased to get, such as employee layoffs or unpopular policy changes. Negative messages can range from serious to mildly disappointing. A letter with a negative message may refuse a request, delay an order, or register a complaint.

ebstock / iStockphoto.com

Readers usually are not expecting bad news, and in this case, the direct approach is not the best choice. If readers see the bad news immediately, the disappointment may be so great that they miss the explanation entirely. A bad news message must relay the bad news and still try to maintain the reader's goodwill.

Therefore, the strategy of bad news messages is indirect. You can soften bad news by surrounding it with pleasant ideas in the following ways:

1. Open with a positive statement, or **buffer.** A buffer is something positive written to soften bad news. Sometimes a buffer states a point upon which the writer and reader agree. For example, a letter declining a businessperson's invitation to speak to the local Chamber of Commerce might mention the excellent work the Chamber does or the importance of the organization in developing relationships between the business community and citizens.

2. In the next section of the message, clearly announce the bad news, but place it in the middle or at the end of the section, not at the beginning. Writers may choose to explain the reason for the bad news. However, sometimes the explanation may be unnecessary or is counterproductive.

In some bad news messages, writers choose to imply the bad news rather than state it directly. For example, a writer rejecting placement of her product in a store might write, "Our contract specifies that Dura's Hair Magic will be displayed on the top shelf or end cap," rather than stating, "I cannot allow Dura's Hair Magic to be placed on the bottom shelf in your store."

3. Close the message on a pleasant note by offering an alternative solution or a different perspective, making a constructive suggestion, or looking positively to the future.

The memo in Figure 5.9, written by the owner of Precision Cuts Hair Studio, shows how the bad news in the middle is buffered by pleasant ideas in the opening and closing.

the explanation is given before the bad news. People generally try to console the receiver in some way after giving the bad news. Perhaps students can tell you of instances when bad news was given well, with the bearer of the bad news showing compassion and concern for the receiver.

TEACH

Conclusions in complaint letters ask for something to rectify the situation or to satisfy the person who complained.

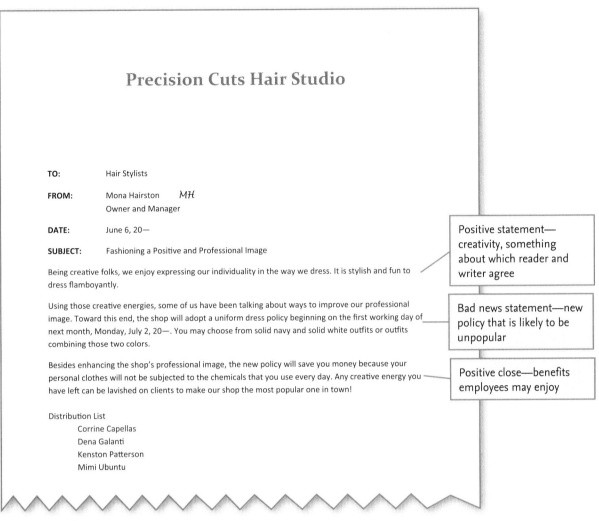

Precision Cuts Hair Studio

TO: Hair Stylists

FROM: Mona Hairston *MH*
Owner and Manager

DATE: June 6, 20—

SUBJECT: Fashioning a Positive and Professional Image

Being creative folks, we enjoy expressing our individuality in the way we dress. It is stylish and fun to dress flamboyantly.

Using those creative energies, some of us have been talking about ways to improve our professional image. Toward this end, the shop will adopt a uniform dress policy beginning on the first working day of next month, Monday, July 2, 20—. You may choose from solid navy and solid white outfits or outfits combining those two colors.

Besides enhancing the shop's professional image, the new policy will save you money because your personal clothes will not be subjected to the chemicals that you use every day. Any creative energy you have left can be lavished on clients to make our shop the most popular one in town!

Distribution List
Corrine Capellas
Dena Galanti
Kenston Patterson
Mimi Ubuntu

> Positive statement—creativity, something about which reader and writer agree

> Bad news statement—new policy that is likely to be unpopular

> Positive close—benefits employees may enjoy

Figure 5.9 Bad News Memo

The opening buffer protects the reader from the bad news; a positive closing ends on a friendly note; and the bad news is strategically sandwiched between the two, where it is least likely to become the reader's focus.

Figure 5.10 on the next page shows a negative news e-mail. Abraham Bizmark of Bizmark Gold Studio writes to La'Neice Jackson, president of D'Oro Jewelry Stores.

Letters of complaint also are examples of correspondence containing negative news. When an individual has a legitimate complaint, the challenge is to present the complaint without alienating the reader. Most complaint letters also include a request to make things right, sometimes a refund, an exchange, extra service, or at least an assurance that the problem will not recur.

Persuasive Messages

A persuasive message is any correspondence in which the sender attempts to convince the receiver to agree with the writer. Persuasive messages are often used to sell products or services. Persuasive messages also include requests for assistance, support, or participation, such as a request for an employment recommendation or an invitation to participate in a charity's telethon.

FOCUS

Figure 5.9

Note that the bad news occupies the least amount of space of any part of a bad news message. Likewise, writers should not dwell on the negative part of the message.

TEACH

Help students see that each negative news message uses a variation of the indirect approach.

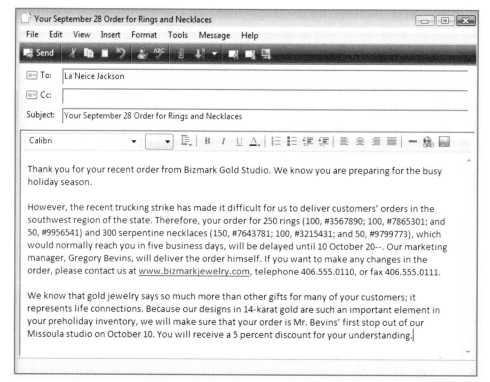

Figure 5.10 Bad News E-mail

Sometimes readers are receptive to the message—for example, the homeowner who wants to replace her leaky, rattling windows will eagerly listen to the salesperson who is telling her about the advantages of replacement windows. However, some audiences are not at all receptive to the persuasive message. Perhaps a previous experience or a lack of interest causes the audience to be hostile. In either case, the strategy of the persuasive message must not only gain the audience's attention, but also convince the audience to agree with the message. The memo in Figure 5.11, written by a sales director, shows a persuasive strategy at work. Notice how the opening paragraph, the "hook," grabs the readers' attention by using questions and humor. The second paragraph, the "convince," gives details and persuades the readers by making it easy to respond to the request. The third paragraph, the "motivate," tries to close the deal by calling the readers to action, telling them what to do and when to do it.

Organizing and Composing Persuasive Messages

Persuasion means that you make your idea, plan, product, or service look appealing. Presenting false information is unethical, but it is considered good business sense to present the strengths of an idea or a product in a persuasive letter or a sales letter. To make your idea, plan, product, or service seem appealing, write sales messages according to the following organizational plan:

- **Hook** your reader's attention.

- **Convince** your audience of the advantages or benefits.

- **Motivate** your reader to action!

FOCUS

Figure 5.11
Review the strategy for writing persuasive messages.

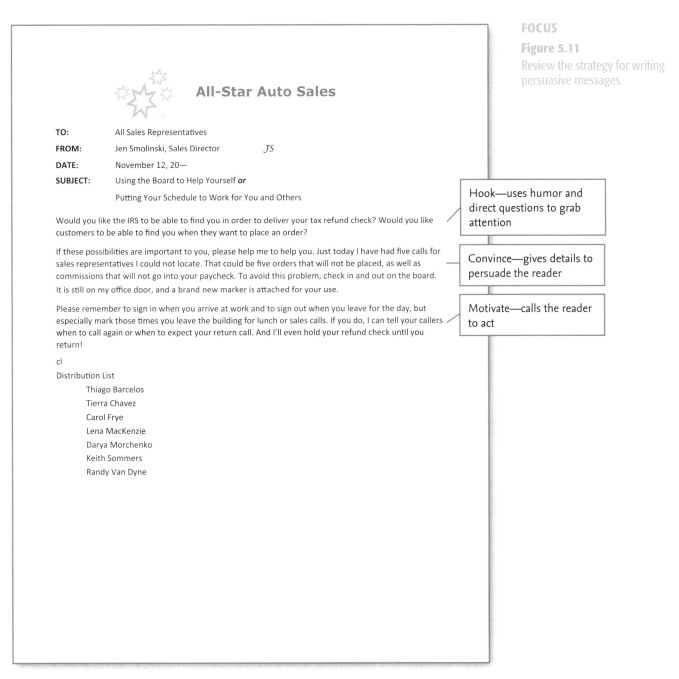

All-Star Auto Sales

TO: All Sales Representatives

FROM: Jen Smolinski, Sales Director   *JS*

DATE: November 12, 20—

SUBJECT: Using the Board to Help Yourself *or*

Putting Your Schedule to Work for You and Others

Would you like the IRS to be able to find you in order to deliver your tax refund check? Would you like customers to be able to find you when they want to place an order?

If these possibilities are important to you, please help me to help you. Just today I have had five calls for sales representatives I could not locate. That could be five orders that will not be placed, as well as commissions that will not go into your paycheck. To avoid this problem, check in and out on the board. It is still on my office door, and a brand new marker is attached for your use.

Please remember to sign in when you arrive at work and to sign out when you leave for the day, but especially mark those times you leave the building for lunch or sales calls. If you do, I can tell your callers when to call again or when to expect your return call. And I'll even hold your refund check until you return!

cl

Distribution List

    Thiago Barcelos

    Tierra Chavez

    Carol Frye

    Lena MacKenzie

    Darya Morchenko

    Keith Sommers

    Randy Van Dyne

Hook—uses humor and direct questions to grab attention

Convince—gives details to persuade the reader

Motivate—calls the reader to act

Figure 5.11 Persuasive Memo

HOOK Your Reader's Attention **Hooks** are attention-getters. That is, they are words designed to engage the reader. Hooks are designed to make the reader open the message and begin to read. Hooks may even start on the envelope of a sales letter (for example, an envelope that reads "Pay to the order of" in front of the recipient's name or "Free Gift Inside"). The hook may continue after the reader opens the letter.

Sometimes an announcement written in boldface precedes the message. The first line of the body sounds exciting. Throughout the letter, the writer "pulls out all the stops." Some information is boldfaced, underlined, bulleted, shadowed with color, or set apart from the text. Some persuasive messages use headings and different fonts. Some have borders, pictures, or graphics—anything to capture the readers' attention. Figure 5.12 illustrates some familiar attention-getters.

COMMUNICATION TECHNOLOGIES

You are in the midst of a worldwide intelligent network. Communication tools are wireless and increasingly smaller. Handheld computers allow you to fax, call, e-mail, and surf the Internet as well as send graphics, videos, and instant messages anywhere in the world. The use of devices such as Research in Motion's Blackberry™ handheld computer and Palm's™ TREO™ 800W or PRO allows you to conduct business and communicate with people anywhere at any time.

Think Critically
Describe some benefits and challenges of being constantly connected to people and your job.

COMMUNICATION TECHNOLOGIES

Generate a discussion about how today's communication devices are changing not only the way business is conducted, but also the way personal lives are led. What do students see as the future for communication in their business and personal lives?

Think Critically

Benefits of being constantly connected include always being able to collect information (for example, driving directions) and to receive aid (for example, getting a tow truck when needed). Challenges include difficulty having personal time when one is truly off work.

The appeals of the attention-getters vary. Some appeal to the desire to get something for nothing. Some appeal to the reader's sense of compassion, need for security, or desire for prestige. Some appeal to the reader's curiosity.

CONVINCE Your Reader This section, generally the longest part of the correspondence, usually begins with facts because decisions are most often based on facts—solid evidence. But the persuading does not end with the facts.

Advertisers describe their product (sometimes including visuals) to help readers understand, but also to provide a favorable impression of the product. It is unethical (and illegal) for an advertiser to lie, but the words are usually written to sell—to create a favorable impression and a desire for the product or service. Likewise, persuasive writers who want to sell an idea or a concept must explain the idea clearly so that readers will see its worthiness.

A persuasive message should offer convincing evidence of the merits of the idea, product, or service. Facts, figures, and statistics can provide objective proof. **Testimonials** are personal stories or people's statements (often famous people) that a concept, product, or service worked for them. Sometimes advertisers try to compel readers to try their product free for a limited time. The advertisers hope the product will convince readers to keep the product and pay for it. Often enclosures such as brochures with pictures, order forms, or more testimonials are included. Sometimes a sales message is not just a letter or memo; it is a whole packet of materials.

Figure 5.12 Hooks in Sales Messages

MOTIVATE Your Reader to Act Finally, the writer must try to motivate the reader to do something—go to the phone and dial a number, say yes to a requisition, get in his or her car and drive to the store, send an e-mail of approval, write a check, or fill in a credit card number. To move the reader to action, persuasive message writers make this part as convenient as they can. You have probably heard motivators similar to these:

- An operator is waiting to take your call.

- Buy now and save 15 % off the cover price.

- Send your tax-deductible contribution and help a homeless person find shelter from the cold.

Figure 5.13 on the next page is a persuasive letter from *Easy Home Cooking* magazine trying to convince Phoebe Nelson to subscribe. Using testimonials, a strong focus on Phoebe's needs and interests, and facts, the letter is persuasive. In addition, the use of an enclosed reply card makes it easy for Phoebe to say yes.

FOCUS ON ETHICS

Unless other legal arrangements have been made, intellectual property developed at work usually belongs to the employer.

Think Critically

If the new project involves information that a competitor could use, then telling a friend about it is a breach of trust that could place you and your organization at risk.

Focus on Ethics

Sending a personal e-mail that reveals proprietary information (ideas the company owns) might cost you your good standing with your colleagues or even your job. It might subject you to legal action as well. Do not say anything in an e-mail that you would not say directly to a person and do not write anything that might embarrass you or your organization, regardless of who reads it. E-mail can be deleted, but it never really disappears and may be forwarded anywhere to anyone. Most networks (the sender's and the receiver's) archive and back up all e-mail.

In addition, some people might think that a simple e-mail reply to a friend outside the company is not so bad. If so, then you might ask, "Where do we draw the line?" and "Who draws the line?" If using the office computer to answer personal messages is fine, then is it all right to use the company car to pick up your dry cleaning or to use the corporate credit card to pay for that dry cleaning? Can you use the office copy machine to photocopy brochures for your weekend real estate business? Can you use time you have at work to go online to order a gift for your brother's birthday or to pay your personal water bill? What about using the company phone to make a couple of calls to your grandparents who live in South Africa?

Using company time and equipment to conduct personal business is unwise. It could get your company in trouble legally, and you could be fired.

Think Critically

What is the harm in telling a friend about a new project at work that your supervisor has assigned to you?

Figure 5.13

Point out the two testimonials. Ask students to locate the "hook, convince, motivate" elements in this persuasive message.

Provide students with the three *Persuasive Writing* worksheets available as supplemental activities on the IRCD.

ONGOING ASSESSMENT

Stop and Think

Because the direct approach would begin with the main idea—the bad news—readers would be overwhelmed by the negative information. Such bluntness would not help to build and maintain goodwill. Imagine how many customers a store would lose if it offended everyone it had to refuse for special orders, for products out of stock, for credit applications, for employment, and for donations.

A call to action appears at the end of persuasive messages, in the "motivate" section. In a call to action, the writer tells the reader exactly what the reader should do.

Fine Dining at Home
224 North Leming Road · Richmond, Virginia 23231-8336
Phone 804-555-0171 · FAX 804-555-0190

April 17, 20—

Phoebe L. Nelson
764 Lord Fulford Drive
Somersworth, NH 03878-7873

Dear Ms. Nelson:

As a preferred customer in the Reader's Digest Association, we know that you like to prepare healthy, economical meals for your family and that you are busy and don't have time to waste. Also realizing that you're creative and enjoy fine food, we thought you would be interested in **Fine Dining at Home,** one of America's most progressive magazines for the young home chef.

Here is what others are saying about us:

"*Fine Dining at Home* is creating a buzz among the young professional set."
—*NYC Gourmet*

"The design is impressive. . . . The "culinary school" features rank number one."
—*Shireen Braddock, American Culinary Institute*

Fine Dining at Home offers 433 recipes; 52 weekly meal planners; 50 culinary school workshop features, each explaining a basic skill; and 70 tips. Pages, which are laminated to handle spills and splatters, come in an attractive binder. All of the materials are easy to read, and color photographs show serving ideas.

With our easy payment plans, don't miss the opportunity to spice up your time in the kitchen. **Fine Dining at Home** can be delivered to you each month for less than you spend on a cappuccino at your favorite coffee shop!

Want to learn more? Return the enclosed card so we can start your subscription immediately. Find out why **Fine Dining at Home** is the right choice for you.

Sincerely,

Marilyn L. Zavala

Marilyn L. Zavala
Editor-in-Chief

Enclosure

Figure 5.13 Sales Letter

 STOP AND THINK

The Warm Up contained the following statement: "Dear Arnie: You're fired." Why is the direct approach not effective for bad news messages? What is a call to action in persuasive messages?

CHAPTER 5
REVIEW

SUMMARY

1. Four types of brief correspondence—text messages, e-mails, memos, and letters—are essential tools in the business world.

2. Writers must analyze and appropriately address the audience in all brief correspondence by maintaining goodwill, following principles of effective communication, using a suitable tone, and using humor effectively

3. Considering audience needs and expectations, determining goals, thinking about technology and the situation, and freewriting are prewriting steps that ensure successful writing of brief correspondence.

4. Each type of brief correspondence uses specific formatting that distinguishes it from other correspondence.

5. To organize the body, writers must consider the type of message and the reader's needs. Writers use a direct approach in good news messages, an indirect approach to buffer unpleasant news in bad news messages, and a "hook, convince, motivate" strategy for persuasive messages.

CLOSE

Summary

Use the summary to review main ideas covered in this chapter. Ask students to identify one or two points they learned that they can use immediately.

Ask students to write a composition in which they explain how they might apply what they learned in this chapter to their future careers.

CLOSE

Checklist

Advise students to use the checklist as they plan, compose, edit, and revise brief correspondence.

REVIEW

For a review of the key terms in the chapter, provide students with the *Key Terms* worksheet available as a supplemental activity on the IRCD.

Checklist

- Have I identified and analyzed my audience? If I am addressing a multilevel audience, have I planned to meet the needs of each group or type of reader?

- Did I establish my purpose or goal in this correspondence?

- Did I use freewriting to generate the information I want to share with the audience?

- Did I develop an organizational plan? Does it take into account a good news, bad news, or persuasive message?

- Does my correspondence follow the correct format and use consistent style? Does it contain correct parts?

- Is the tone and level of formality appropriate to the audience?

- Have I asked a respected peer to read my correspondence and give specific feedback on the impact and effectiveness of my message?

- Did I proofread the headings for completeness and accuracy?

- Did I proofread the message for errors in spelling, keying, grammar, and punctuation?

- When the correspondence was acceptable, did I sign my name or, if appropriate, write my initials to the right of my keyed name?

ASSESS
Build Your Foundation

1. Here is one effective
   version: h, b, e, g, f, d, a, c.
2. Answers may vary.
   a. To: Robin Lytle, Coach;
   Diego Alvarez and Carey
   Johansen, Assistant
   Managers; From: Student's
   Name; Date: Month 1, 20—;
   Subject: Packing Duties for
   May 9 Game in Midland.
   b. Date: September 6, 20—;
   To: All Employees; From:
   Connie Famosa, Manager;
   Subject: Invitation to
   Company Picnic
   October 1, 20—.
3. Lists will vary depending
   on the circumstances the
   students make up. You
   could have students work
   on the lists in groups. Refer
   students to the checklist at
   the end of the chapter.
4. Make sure students use the
   checklist at the end of the
   chapter.

ASSESS
Your Turn

5–7. Allow students to
   compare their memos.
   One version of each memo
   is available as a teaching
   master on the IRCD. Using
   them, you may further
   compare choices that
   different writers made. Also
   discuss the effect those
   choices are likely to have
   on readers.

Build Your Foundation

1. Here are eight parts to a good news letter announcing that Tessa Heilig has won a cruise to the Caribbean. However, the parts are mixed up. Rewrite the letter, putting the sentences in proper order. Several combinations may be possible.

   a. To claim your prize, you must call 1-800-CRUISES before April 18 and provide the operators with proof of identity.
   b. You have just won an all-expenses-paid cruise to the Caribbean!
   c. Congratulations, Tessa. We look forward to helping you arrange the vacation of your life!
   d. Enjoy a variety of on-board recreational activities, delectable meals, and superb entertainment at our expense.
   e. Your name, Tessa Heilig, was drawn out of 456,897 entries to be our top-prize winner in the Colombo Publishers Sweepstakes.
   f. Colombo has reserved four nights and five days for you and a guest.
   g. You must schedule your trip between June 1 and September 21, 20—.
   h. Pack your bags, Tessa, and don't forget the sunscreen!

2. Read the following writing situations. Select the details you need; then write the headings for each memo.

   a. You are the manager for your school's soccer team. Normally, you coordinate the packing of equipment and supplies for traveling to away games. However, for the next conference game to be played at Midland on May 9, you will be out of state attending your cousin's wedding. So you are writing a memo to Coach Robin Lytle and your two assistant managers, Diego Alvarez and Carey Johansen, to remind them of what needs to be done in your absence.
   b. You are Connie Famosa, manager of A Helping Hand, a residential cleaning service in San Alto, New Mexico. Six full-time and fifteen part-time employees are under your supervision. To thank the entire staff for their service, you plan to hold a picnic in your backyard. The event will take place on October 1, 20—, from 5 P.M. to 8 P.M. You are writing a memo today to invite all employees and their families to the picnic.

3. Marcus Robiskie of the ABC Detective Agency has just located Akilah Massaquoi's car, stolen three months ago from a shopping mall. List information you would include in a letter to Akilah from Marcus announcing the good news. Make up the addresses. Before making your list, use your imagination to answer these questions: How can Akilah get her car back? When can she get her car back? How did the detective find the car? How does Akilah feel?

4. Compose and send an e-mail or a letter of inquiry to request some information. Consider a research project for another class, a question about a product you own, or a question about a place you want to visit. Share the correspondence and response with the class.

Your Turn

5. Write a memo from Christa Brinkdopke, Chief of Installation Services for Fox Cablevision, to Eric Monroe, an employee under her supervision. Eric has just completed 25 years of service with Fox Cablevision, and

Christa wants to show her support for his work. Eric has had perfect attendance for the last three years, and his customer evaluations are consistently positive.

6. As assistant to your Quality Assurance Team at World Wide Insurance, you are in charge of scheduling meetings. The chair, Ruben Flores, has asked you to call a meeting for Monday afternoon, April 24, 20—. He wants the group to discuss a recent employee concern regarding unsafe exercise equipment in the Employee Wellness Center. Ruben would like the Quality Assurance Team to gather in Room 124-C at 4:15. He expects the meeting to end at 5 p.m. Write a memo announcing the meeting.

7. You are Chief Food Scientist for Lehigh Bakery in Anderson, Wisconsin. Duane Carlson, president of the Logan Dairy Cooperative, a farmer-owned and farmer-operated sales organization under contract to sell its entire production to your company, has invited you to speak to his members regarding the effect of certain veterinary medicines on the taste of dairy products. On the date the Cooperative requested, Thursday, January 18, 20—, you are already scheduled to attend a meeting of the American Association of Bakers. Write a memo declining the invitation to speak to the Cooperative.

8. Plan and draft two e-mails that announce a new flextime program at Bauman Industries. The program will allow workers to share the responsibilities of one position among two or three people. Print the e-mails to give to your instructor or to share with your classmates or team.

   a. One e-mail should target and address the managerial staff of the company. Before composing the e-mail, consider the needs, concerns, questions, and biases of this audience.
   b. The second e-mail should target and address all employees of the company. Remember that you will need to meet the needs and answer the questions of all readers without offending anyone.

Community Connection

9. Ask an administrator or organization in your school if you can help edit and revise one piece of brief correspondence.

   a. After receiving the document, interview the writer or writers. Make sure you ask about the target audience and the purpose of the correspondence.
   b. Edit and revise the document. Then share it with a group of classmates or your entire class. Collect feedback from your peers.
   c. Edit and revise using the comments from your peers. Then submit the revised draft to the administrator or organization.
   d. Again collect feedback regarding the changes you made.

10. Contact a nonprofit organization or local government agency.

   a. Using a form letter or an e-mail from the agency, such as requests for contributions or welcome messages to new members or volunteers, analyze the target audience and the strategy used in the message.
   b. Offer to write a letter, a memo, or an e-mail, such as a message encouraging people to volunteer or to donate yard sale items.

8. a. Managers will be concerned about coordinating several people responsible for doing one job and determining who will be responsible for that coordination. Some managers may have experience with this type of program. Others may worry that supervising three people for one position will take more time and paperwork.
b. Employees who hope to use the program are likely to be pleased, while those opposed to it may need to be convinced or reassured.

ASSESS

Community Connection

9–10. These assignments allow students to face the real-life challenges of writing in the workplace. Because the writing is authentic, students are more likely to realize the importance of understanding the document's purpose as well as analyzing the audience. Some students may become frustrated with editing and revising.

Document Design and Graphics

Goals

- Design an effective document for the audience and purpose
- Determine the audience and purpose of graphics
- Format graphics to make them easy to understand
- Construct graphics for the audience and purpose

Terms

- bar graph, p. 149
- callouts, p. 159
- chart, p. 155
- decision flowchart, p. 155
- design elements, p. 138
- diagram, p. 159
- exploding pie graph, p. 154
- flowchart, p. 155
- formal table, p. 147
- Gantt chart, p. 157
- graphics, p. 140
- icon, p. 159
- informal table, p. 146
- line graph, p. 151
- multiple bar graph, p. 150
- multiple line graph, p. 151
- organizational chart, p. 156
- pictograph, p. 152
- pie graph, p. 153
- verbal tables, p. 143

WRITE TO LEARN

Using words only, write directions from your school to your home. Then draw a map with arrows to show the same route. Which is easier to understand—the written directions or the map? In a short journal entry, explain why.

Focus on Document Design and Graphics

Read the sample document on the next page and answer these questions:

- Describe what you see on the page. What percentage of information is devoted to words? to graphics?
- Has anything special been done with the words to make them stand out? If so, which words and why do they stand out?
- Do the graphics help present the message? Explain.
- Where do the words explain or introduce the graphics?

What If?

- The medium were a 24" × 36" poster or trifold brochure?
- A PowerPoint® presentation provided this information?
- The insert were designed for second-graders?

Tornado Safety Plan

Tornadoes can strike with little warning. To keep you and your students safe, review the Mecklenburg County Tornado Safety Plan and share it with your students.

Alert System
Designated school personnel will receive phone, e-mail, and radio alerts to indicate a tornado watch or warning.

Tornado Watch
Conditions are favorable for a tornado.
Tornado Warning
A tornado has been spotted or indicated on radar.

If a tornado warning is issued, the alarm will sound—**three long blasts**.

Designated Personnel
Table 1 lists contact information for the designated safety personnel.

Personnel	Phone Numbers
Dr. C. Webber, Superintendent	704-555-0114
Dr. R. Gaskins, Principal ELS	704-555-0115
V. Romerez, Safety Officer ELS	704-555-0116
Dr. T. Mazurka, Principal EHS	704-555-0117
K. Isenhour, Safety Officer EHS	704-555-0118
Dr. C. Shaut, Principal EMS	704-555-0119
S. Cho, Safety Officer EMS	704-555-0120

Table 1. Emergency Contacts

Once a tornado warning has been issued, designated personnel will tune in to one of the local stations below and stay tuned until the danger has passed.

WKIX FM Radio 91.5
WNRT TV Channel 8

Safety Procedure
If a warning is issued, the designated safety personnel will sound the alert. When you hear the alert—**three long blasts**—move to safety immediately.

1. Instruct students to walk calmly in single file to the nearest designated Safety Zone in your building.
2. As you leave the classroom, turn off the lights and close the door. DO NOT stop to open the windows. Spend your time getting to safety.

Safety Zones
Each school has posted signs in hallways showing the location of the Safety Zones. The orange signs, like the one in Figure 1, have the words *SAFETY ZONE* and an arrow directing students to the appropriate area in their school. Become familiar with the signs and the location of designated Safety Zones.

Figure 1 Safety Zone Sign

"Duck and Cover" Position
When students arrive at the Safety Zone, instruct them to get on their knees facing the interior walls. Students should assume the "duck and cover" position (duck and cover the head) illustrated in Figure 2.

Figure 2. "Duck and Cover" Position

Sample Document with Graphics

Courtesy of Aidan Grey

Arts, A/V Technology & Communications

Aidan Grey is a freelance graphic designer in Denver, Colorado, and former Director of Photography for Home&Abroad (H&A), a travel planning website. He has 13 years of graphics expertise, including contracting with photographers, publishing images in print and on the Web, and designing logos.

Aidan believes that a picture is worth a thousand words, but not necessarily in English. "There's a different kind of eloquence in graphics because we get to use many additional 'languages' simultaneously—color, texture, composition, line, light. Red is one 'word' and says one kind of thing, while blue is another and says other things." In other words, it's important to be sensitive to the "linguistics" and semiology (signs and symbols) of images.

The various constraints that Aidan considers when working with graphics include content, color, licensing and copyright, cost, lighting, size, and composition. He judges which constraints to prioritize on a project-by-project basis, but always gives credit when using others' work: "You're never going to get in trouble for crediting someone properly."

Knowing when images hurt your content is as important as knowing when they enhance it. "Images are *not* helpful when they are too busy and when they contradict the desired message," cautions Aidan. For example, "If your report is about why the company is not meeting goals, images of smiling, happy people can send a decidedly wrong message." Images should enhance and complement the message of the text they accompany.

Aidan's graphic design work requires him to use communication skills along with his graphics virtuosity. At H&A, for example, he wrote contracts, form letters, manuals, and e-mail messages and even translated documents into other languages for investors.

Think Critically

1. With a partner, select a photograph in this book to analyze. Individually, jot down some notes about the "languages" the photo uses.

2. Compare notes with your partner. Does the photograph "say" more than you thought at first? Explain.

Printed with permission of Aidan Grey

APPLY

Writing @ Work

Use this feature to show the importance of graphics in the workplace.

Think Critically

1. Answers may include color, shape, line, and light.

2. Answers can promote worthwhile discussion about the various messages graphics can convey.

DESIGNING THE DOCUMENT

A cluttered room with poorly designed lighting can make it difficult for people to find what they are looking for. A cluttered document with poorly designed elements can put readers in the same predicament. The readers may be discouraged if they cannot find the information they need quickly and easily.

When you write, you make many decisions—what to write, how to organize, which words to use, and so on. Indeed, words are important to any writer, but in technical writing, *how the words look on the page is just as important as what the words say*. If they want readers to stay focused, good technical writers must learn to design pages that are visually friendly.

For example, the 1" × 3" plastic tab inserted into Lorenzo's potted rosebush included six steps for planting and 57 tiny words squeezed onto the tab. Lorenzo could not read the tiny words, so he threw away the tab and dug a hole deep enough to plant the root-ball of the bush several inches below the ground. Stephanie, Lorenzo's next-door neighbor, showed him the 2" × 3" set of instructions that came tied around a branch of her new rosebush. With a couple of illustrations and print big enough for Lorenzo to see, he read the caution against burying the root-ball too deeply and adjusted the hole he had dug. In a few months, both neighbors had beautiful roses, thanks to Stephanie's better-designed instructions.

Figure 6.1 shows the two sets of instructions—one poorly designed and the other designed with the reader's needs in mind. The writer of instructions for commercial potting plants must consider the reading capabilities of home gardeners, many of whom find themselves squinting when trying to read small print.

Warm Up

Compare the newspaper *USA Today* with a newspaper that has a more traditional look (for example, *The Wall Street Journal* or *The New York Times*). Describe the front page of each newspaper. How is *USA Today* different from the other newspaper? Which paper is more appealing to you? Why?

FOCUS

Warm Up

Use the Warm Up to emphasize how document design affects reactions to the words that people see. *USA Today* may look more inviting and more interesting, while *The Wall Street Journal* and *The New York Times* look more serious. Point out how elements such as font size, illustrations, white space, and color affect the reader's psychological reactions to a document.

FOCUS

Figure 6.1

Use the two sets of instructions to illustrate how the larger one is user-friendly and the smaller one is not.

TEACH

Use the Cluttered Page Layout Teaching Master on the IRCD to reinforce how proper page design makes a document easier to read.

Tea Rose

Find an area that receives full sun. Use rich, well-drained soil that contains organic matter. Dig a hole slightly wider than the root-ball. Plant the bush so that the top of the root-ball is exposed. Do not cover the root-ball. Water the area thoroughly and fertilize twice a year: in spring and in late summer.

Tea Rose

1. Find an area that receives full sun.
2. Use rich, well-drained soil that contains organic matter.
3. Dig a hole slightly wider than the root-ball.
4. Plant the bush so that the top of the root-ball is exposed. *Do not* cover the root-ball.
5. Water the area thoroughly
6. Fertilize twice a year: in spring and in late summer.

Figure 6.1 Examples of Poorly Designed and Well-Designed Instructions

Design Elements

In addition to words, writers can use **design elements** to aid the reader's comprehension and keep the reader's interest. Design elements are considerations in the writing of a document that affect page layout. Elements to consider when designing a document are white space, text, headings, graphics, and medium.

White Space

White space is space that is blank. It rests the eyes, separates chunks of information, and makes a document look inviting. Writers can create white space in margins, between paragraphs, before itemized lists, between columns, and around graphics.

Text

Text refers to the words printed on the page. Readers read text more quickly if it is left-justified with ragged-right edges, meaning that the text is flush with the left margin of the page and uneven along the right margin. This page is set up with left justification and ragged-right edges. Figure 6.2 shows differences in page justification.

Type fonts, the design and shape of letters, are divided into serif and sans serif. (*Sans* is French for "without.") Serif refers to letters with distinguishing lines or "tails" (like this sentence), making it easy to see the differences between one letter and another. Sans serif refers to letters with few distinguishing lines and no "tails" (like this sentence). It is appropriate for something short, such as a title or heading. The major headings in this text use a sans serif font.

Size is measured in points, with a large point number (14 or 16) used for a larger letter. Text in 10 or 12 points can be seen easily. For paragraphs, use a 10- to 12-point serif font that mixes capital and lowercase letters. Do not write an entire document in all capital letters. They are difficult to read and should be used only for emphasis and for use in a title or major heading. Figure 6.3 on the next page shows a variety of serif and sans serif fonts.

Left Justification
Ragged Right

Left and Right Justification

Right Justification
Ragged Left

Center
Justification

Figure 6.2 Different Page Justifications

Sans Serif Fonts	Point Size	Serif Fonts	Point Size
Arial	**14 point**	Book Antiqua	14 point
Calibri	12 point	Times New Roman	12 point
Century Gothic	10 point	Courier	10 point
Tahoma	8 point	Goody Old Syle	8 point

Figure 6.3 Sans Serif and Serif Fonts in Different Sizes

FOCUS

Figure 6.2
Point out the differences in line justification.

Use the Examples of Line Justification Teaching Master on the IRCD to show the differences in left, right, aligned, and centered justifications.

Highlighting features are print styles such as **boldface,** underline, *italics,* and CAPITAL LETTERS that draw attention to words and phrases. Use these highlighting features sparingly. Overuse clutters the page and distracts the reader, drawing attention away from the text instead of to the text.

Another tool for focusing the reader's attention is an itemized list. To itemize a list, set up a list separate from the text. The list may be indented from the left margin. Bullets (• ■) or numbers often precede each item in the list. How do you determine whether to use a numbered list or a bulleted list? Use a numbered list when the sequence of items is important. Otherwise, use a bulleted list.

For example, in Figure 6.4, Mr. Gorham writes his students a letter, giving them last-minute instructions for their trip to France. He boldfaces the word *double-check* and sets up a bulleted list to draw attention to the five items the students must pack.

The following items are essential for a smooth, trouble-free trip. Check and double-check to make sure you have packed these items:

- Your passport—you will not be allowed on the plane without it
- Your money—credit card, traveler's checks, and some currency
- Your medical insurance card
- Any medication you routinely take
- Your driver's license

Figure 6.4 Use of Boldface and Bullets in a Letter

Headings

Headings are short titles that introduce the main idea of a selected portion of text. Like a formal outline, headings help your reader see the organization of a document in one glance. Instead of Roman numerals, capital letters, and Arabic numerals to show subdivisions, the size and placement of headings show the organization. Most reports use a system of two headings (first-degree headings and second-degree headings), but they can use more. For example, this textbook uses a system of four headings for chapters.

Complete the *Practice System of Headings* worksheet available at www.cengage.com/school/bcomm/techwtg. Click the link for Chapter 6; then click Data Files.

TEACH

Use the Three Levels of Headings Teaching Master on the IRCD to illustrate systems of headings.

Use the Four Popular Fonts Teaching Master on the IRCD to illustrate the difference between serif and sans serif fonts and the different sizes.

Help students see that a system of headings is like an outline. Instead of Roman numerals, capital letters, and Arabic numerals, the size and placement of headings show the organization and subdivisions.

Ask students to turn the headings in this chapter into a formal outline.

Use the Document Design Guidelines Teaching Master on the IRCD to review the guidelines.

ONGOING ASSESSMENT

Stop and Think

White space makes text easier to read because the extra space relaxes the eye. Ragged-right edges make the text end naturally along the right margin. Because the words are evenly spaced, ragged right is easier on the eye. Serif font is easier to read because the "tails" on the letters make them more noticeable. Headings make the organization more apparent.

Highlighting features draw attention to particular words, phrases, or lists by making them stand out in the text.

Graphics

Graphics are visual representations of information. They include many familiar visual aids such as tables, line graphs, pie graphs, and diagrams. But they also include more sophisticated and less familiar aids such as schematics, pictographs, decision charts, and Internet graphics.

Graphics are used in technical writing whenever information can be expressed better in a visual form than in words alone. Sometimes a graphic is used by itself, as in the traffic signs you see on your way to work or school. For technical writers, a graphic is often used along with text to fully convey meaning.

Whether you use graphics alone or with text, considerations of purpose and audience guide your decision and influence which graphic is appropriate for your document. The last section of this chapter introduces you to some of the more familiar and easy-to-design graphics.

Medium

In addition to considering white space, headings, and graphics, writers choose the best medium to use for their document. Possible choices include paper media (for example, heavy stock, 8 1/2" × 11", or a trifold brochure) or electronic media (for example, e-mail, CD-ROM, or web pages). Again, purpose and audience determine which medium you choose. In turn, the medium also influences the design.

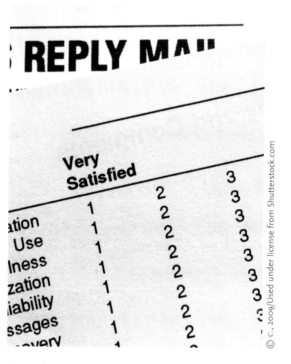

© c., 2009/Used under license from Shutterstock.com

For example, Washington Research Associates sent a one-page marketing survey to photography enthusiasts to determine potential customers for a photography supply store. Readers were sent one sheet of heavy-stock paper with the survey on one side and the return address with prepaid postage on the back. After completing the survey, readers could simply refold the document, use the enclosed sticker to seal the "envelope," and drop it in the mail. The purpose (receiving completed surveys quickly) influenced the medium (the envelope design). Likewise, the envelope design determined placement of the survey, address, prepaid postage, and sticker.

⬢ STOP AND THINK

Why do white space, ragged-right edges, serif font, and headings make text easy to read? What is the purpose of highlighting features?

WHO READS GRAPHICS?

A picture is indeed worth a thousand words. Graphics can clarify information quickly. At one glance, your readers can perceive more information than they would with words alone. Most complex technical material can be simplified with a graphic: a table, a drawing, a diagram, or a graph. Where academic readers rely heavily on words to understand meaning, technical readers often rely on words *and* graphics to convey meaning.

Audience

Technical subjects such as engineering, marketing, and medicine rely heavily on data that is presented visually. Therefore, readers of technical documents expect to see graphic aids in their reading. However, readers vary in their ability to understand graphics. As with decisions about text, decisions about graphics depend on what your readers can understand and what they already know.

Generally, the more data in a graphic, the more difficult it is to read. When deciding which graphic your audience will best understand, you should ask yourself these questions about your reader(s):

- How much does my reader know about the subject?

- How interested is my reader in the subject?

- Do my readers include a technical audience? In other words, do my readers need or expect technical information or figures?

- Will my audience be confused by technical information or figures?

- Does my audience's reading level tend to be higher (tenth grade or higher) or lower (ninth grade or lower)?

Purpose and Objectives

Audience is only one consideration in deciding what kind of graphic to use. You also must consider the purpose of your graphic as well as how much and what kind of information you want to convey.

To choose graphics that convey your meaning most effectively, ask yourself these two questions: What is the purpose of the writing? How can graphics help achieve that purpose? Then choose the graphic that best meets your needs.

To help you decide which graphic to use, look at the Purpose column in Table 6.1 on the following page and decide what you want to accomplish. Maybe you want your reader to operate a digital camera. To achieve that purpose, you want your reader to see what the camera looks like and where each button is. Drawing the mechanism of the camera with clearly labeled parts would help achieve that purpose. Do you need to show numbers to your readers in an easy-to-read format? If so, a formal table would serve your purpose.

Warm Up

What is being described here?
A circle that is 3″ in diameter contains three items. At the bottom of the figure, approximately 3/4″ from the bottom, is a single line approximately 2″ long that is curved in the shape of the bottom half of a small circle. At the top of the 3″ circle, approximately 1/2″ from the top and 1″ apart, are two small circles 1/4″ in diameter. At the top of the 3″ circle, a perfect square encloses the 3″ circle, the four sides of the square barely touching four points of the circle.

FOCUS

Warm Up

Ask students to draw the graphic. Then ask them which is easier to understand, the instructions for the graphic or the graphic itself. See the Who Reads Graphics? Warm Up Teaching Master on the IRCD for a drawing of the graphic.

TYPICAL READER

A person requiring visual representations of technical data to aid comprehension.

WRITER'S FOCUS

Presenting complex information visually, using page design to enhance readability and matching graphics to audience and purpose.

RETEACH

Remind students that audience and purpose still guide decisions about technical communication.

TEACH

Today communicators have many media from which to choose.

FOCUS

Table 6.1

Show how to match the writer's purpose and objectives to a graphic. Ask students to turn the purpose statements into questions to help them decide which graphic to use. For example, a writer may ask: "Do I want to show my readers how their tax dollars are spent (on education, Medicare, defense, national disasters, etc.)?" A pie graph would help readers understand how tax revenue is divided among different programs.

TEACH

Help students see that the more information a graphic contains, the harder it is to read. An experienced reader with a strong background and interest in the subject will read graphics more easily than a less experienced reader. Show the Visual Scale of Difficulty Teaching Master on the IRCD.

ONGOING ASSESSMENT

Stop and Think

Ask what the audience knows and does not know about the subject. What are the audience's expectations?

Students will mention a variety of graphics but may see tables, pictures, and diagrams most often. Review the purpose of the graphics students mention by referring to Table 6.1.

PURPOSE	GRAPHIC
To present a small amount of numerical data	informal table
To present numbers in easy-to-read rows and columns	formal table
To explain an idea using words set up in rows and columns	verbal table
To contrast data and focus on differences	bar graph or pictograph
To contrast several sets of data and focus on the differences	double or multiple bar graph
To follow a trend over time	line graph
To compare several trends and show how data is related	double or multiple line graph
To show how the whole is divided into parts or how the parts relate to the whole	pie graph
To present a process	flowchart
To tell how to make a decision	decision flowchart
To present the structure of an organization	organizational flowchart
To show a schedule of tasks	Gantt chart
To present an idea using a symbol	icon
To show representative details of an object or a mechanism	diagram or line drawing
To show how something actually looks	photo

Table 6.1

 STOP AND THINK

What are some questions to ask about your audience to help you select an appropriate graphic? Using Table 6.1, identify three graphics you frequently see in textbooks. What is the purpose of each graphic?

DESIGNING GRAPHICS

Graphics add critical information to your text and become part of the overall appearance of a document. Good writers create a flow between words and graphics that unifies a document, allowing readers to move along without interruption. To help your reader interpret graphics quickly and easily, you should keep graphics simple and neat, integrate graphics with text, give credit for borrowed graphics, and use color effectively.

Keep Graphics Neat and Simple

The quality of a graphic is a factor in how carefully it is read. A neat, clean graphic is easy to read and interpret. Leave enough white space so that the graphic looks uncluttered and make the graphic large enough so that the reader can see all parts clearly. Align decimals when they are presented in columns, as shown in the numbers below.

```
 8.3
 0.525
98.6
27.0
```

In general, a graphic should have one main point. Using two uncluttered, simple graphics to illustrate two concepts is better than using one cluttered graphic to illustrate too many concepts.

Integrate Graphics with Text

Clearly refer to each graphic in the text *before* you place it on the page. Refer to the graphic when you think your reader will look at it for the first time. Use the word *Figure* to refer to any graphic that is not a formal table. Use the word *Table* to refer to a formal table (a table with rules and titles). Number figures consecutively throughout. Number tables consecutively but separately from figures throughout. Call your reader's attention to figures or tables by incorporating references into your text, using parentheses, or creating stand-alone sentences as follows:

- Table 1/Figure 1 shows the amount of rainfall in Idaho over the past three years.

- The rainfall in Idaho over six years varied substantially. (See Table 1/ Figure 1.)

- The rainfall in Idaho over six years varied substantially (Table 1/Figure 1).

- The rainfall in Idaho over six years varied substantially. See Table 1/ Figure 1.

Choose one method and refer to all of your figures and tables the same way. Informal tables need not be referred to as a table or a figure. **Verbal tables** use words instead of numbers, and the information is given in rows and columns. They are not always referred to as tables or figures but are often integrated into the text with an appropriate introduction.

Warm Up

Take a close look at the graphics in the following sections of this chapter. What do you notice about each one? What do the graphics have in common? Notice some of the differences. In which graphics do the differences occur?

FOCUS

Warm Up

Help students see what the graphics have in common: they are neat and uncluttered; have short intros and referral statements; and are aids to comprehension. Some graphics look different—line graphs, pie graphs, and diagrams, for example.

TEACH

Remind students that the most important factor affecting whether a graphic is read is how it looks on the page. Graphics must be neat and uncluttered.

Tell students to refer to this section when they design their own graphics.

Show the Guidelines for Formatting Graphics Teaching Master on the IRCD.

Use the Cluttered Graphic Teaching Master on the IRCD to illustrate how difficult it is to read.

Ask students to look closely at the four ways to refer to graphics. Which way do they prefer? Why? Some may think that incorporating the reference in the text makes the reference less obtrusive and effectively directs the reader's attention. Others may prefer the use of parentheses because that style seems less obtrusive. Still other students may prefer the stand-alone sentence because it seems more direct.

COMMUNICATION TECHNOLOGIES

You can get thousands of free images from a variety of sources to add to your documents. Many websites have images, graphics, and photographs that are free and do not require permission to use. You also can purchase CDs that store thousands of images. These CDs organize the images by categories, such as business, wildlife, and travel. Once you purchase the CD, you may use the images without worrying about copyright permissions.

Think Critically

Why is it important to make sure you do not need permission before you use an image?

Place each graphic in a convenient place for the reader to see. If the graphic is small enough (1/5 to 1/2 page), try to place it on the same page as its reference. If the graphic is large (3/4 to 1 page), you may need to place it on the page immediately following your reference. In reports with complex graphics, the graphics are sometimes placed in an appendix—especially if the graphics interrupt the flow of the report.

For graphics used in reports, explain the significance of the graphic in the report as you introduce the graphic. For example, point out parts of a diagram, trends in a line graph, or important numbers in a table. You need not discuss every part of the graphic, but do point out what is important for the reader to know. Generally, explanations are presented in the introduction preceding the graphic. More complex graphics may require discussion before and after placement of the graphic.

Provide a title for every graphic—except for informal tables that are simply indented from the margin. Table titles and figure titles are often centered below the figure. However, placement may vary. Choose a placement and be consistent throughout the document. Use titles that are specific so the readers understand what they will learn from the graphic. For example, use

Salary Distribution for 1955–1956   *not just* Salaries
Regal Powerboat Model OTY-453   *not just* Powerboat

Give credit for a graphic if you do not compile it yourself or if you compile it using borrowed data. Place the word *Source* below your figure. Include the bibliographical reference for the source as you would a footnote or an endnote.

Use Color Effectively

Color often draws a reader's attention before the reader pays attention to the words. Color is a powerful design tool that can be used to:

Brand X Pictures/Getty Images

- **Indicate a document's organization.** By using the same color for major headings, you give your readers visual cues to the overall organization of a document and help them scan quickly for information.
- **Emphasize or clarify an important point.** When using a color for a key word, a phrase, an idea, or part of a graphic, you draw your reader's

attention to important information. You also can use color to signify a change or to guide readers through a process.

- **Support your text's meaning.** By using certain colors consistently to convey specific information, your reader begins to associate the color with the meaning (red with danger, for example) and therefore understands the text more quickly.

- **Make your document attractive.** By using colors to break up black and white text, your page will be more appealing.

With a click of the mouse, you can change color from blue to green or green to red, for example. But be careful. Like any technical writing tool, color can be misused. To use color effectively:

- **Avoid overusing color.** More than three or four colors (including black and white as two colors) can overwhelm a reader, and using one color (other than black) too often can be distracting.

- **Apply color consistently to elements throughout a document.** For example, if you set major headings in red and set key words in black boldface, do not suddenly switch a major heading to blue or a key word to red boldface.

- **Remain sensitive to cultural identifications with colors.** International audiences associate colors differently from American audiences. For instance, Americans associate green with go (traffic lights) and red with danger (fire trucks and stop signs). However, green is a holy color to a Muslim and red is a sign of mourning to a South African.

- **Avoid unusual combinations of colors.** Some colors, such as purple on a blue background and orange on red, are difficult to read.

Communication Dilemma

You work as a wedding planner for I Do Wedding Consulting. Your manager, Rachel, is proud of the way you communicate with clients to find out and provide exactly what they want for their wedding day. The company has recently expanded to include international clients, and Rachel has put you in charge of marketing the company's services to Chinese couples who want a "Westernized" wedding.

You decide to create a brochure that shows pictures of weddings you have planned. Personally, you believe that the most beautiful weddings are "all white." So on the cover of the brochure, you include pictures that show arrangements of white roses and other white flowers. Several weeks after the brochures are distributed, Rachel calls you to her office. She is upset because not a single Chinese couple has called to make an appointment.

Think Critically

Why was the brochure not effective for the target audience? You may need to research color associations in other countries to learn why the brochure was not an effective marketing tool.

COMMUNICATION DILEMMA

Ask students to use the Internet to research what psychological meanings are associated with certain colors or how different cultures associate meanings with colors. Students should learn that white is associated with death and mourning in China, so the color white was not a good choice for this audience.

ENRICH

Ask an art instructor to visit your class to talk about color associations.

● STOP AND THINK

Why should graphics be neat and simple? Identify three ways to refer to graphics in your text. How can colors be misused in a document?

Warm Up

When you look at a page with text and a graphic, which do you read first—the text or the graphic? Do you ever read the text without looking at the graphic? Do you ever look at the graphic without reading the text? Explain your answer.

FOCUS

Warm Up

Use the Warm Up to make students aware of their attitudes about reading graphics. Visual learners probably look at graphics before they look at text. Verbal learners probably look at text first. Some students tend to skip the text or graphics altogether. Note that such reading habits mean that writers must put forth extra effort to plan, create, and integrate graphics.

RETEACH

Thoroughly explain Theresa's writing assignment and make sure students understand the differences in the audiences for whom she is writing. The *Fitness* readers are younger, less capable, and less interested readers. The *Mind and Body* readers are older, more knowledgeable, and more capable readers, and they are more motivated. Theresa's other assignments involve different age groups, interests, and purposes. This ongoing scenario will help illustrate why different graphics are chosen.

CONSTRUCTING GRAPHICS

As a technical writer selecting graphics for a document, you have many options from which to choose. You make those choices by considering which graphics are most appropriate for different audiences and purposes. This section shows you how one writer selected graphics for different audiences in a series of articles promoting good health practices.

Theresa, a nutritionist and freelance writer, is working on several different writing and promotional assignments. One is an article for *Mind and Body*, a magazine for college students majoring in physical education. These readers have a solid background in physical education, a keen interest in the subject, a college reading level, and experience interpreting graphics. The second article will appear in *Fitness*, a magazine for junior high students. These readers have less knowledge about good health practices and may not be as motivated to make healthy lifestyle choices. As younger readers, their reading level is lower than that of the college students and their experience reading graphics is limited. Theresa's other assignments include writing a monthly newsletter for her clients, giving a speech at a middle school, creating a website, and organizing a health fair event. Theresa sometimes uses her clients' stories in her publications—with their permission, of course.

This section will take you step-by-step through Theresa's decision-making process as she decides how to disseminate information to her different audiences.

Constructing Tables

Tables are used to present words or numbers that can be organized into categories of columns and rows. Tables, one of the most popular graphic aids, can be informal or formal. A verbal table, often called a chart, is a variation of the formal table, categorizing words instead of numbers into columns and rows.

Informal Table

An **informal table** is a graphic that uses rows and columns drawn without rules (lines) or stubs (column headings). In an informal table, the information flows with the text. The explanation of the graphic is a brief summary of the information presented in the graphic.

Theresa wants to motivate the younger readers of *Fitness* to begin a fitness program. Theresa thinks that beginners could benefit from seeing how quickly she saw results. To present her own progress after two months on a workout regimen, Theresa uses an informal table. The informal table is a good choice because the information is simple (only three items to consider) and is appropriate for her younger audience. Figure 6.5 shows the informal table and its written introduction.

> Over the next two months, Theresa lost a total of 4.2 pounds. For every pound of fat she lost, she gained approximately 3/4 pound of muscle.
>
> Fat lost   14.0 lb
> Muscle gained   9.8 lb
> Total pounds lost   4.2 lb

Figure 6.5 Model of Informal Table

Formal Table

A **formal table** is an arrangement of information in rows and columns with rules (lines drawn). It is typically used to organize numbers, words, or other data in a consistent format.

Theresa wants the readers of *Mind and Body* to know at what rate they should exercise to burn fat. She uses part of a table from a published book. The older and more knowledgeable audience of *Mind and Body* will understand the detailed numerical data. They also will be motivated to find their heart rate and will appreciate the information given in the footnotes. Figure 6.6 is part of the formal table Theresa reproduced from *Exercise and You,* along with her brief introduction.

Table 1 shows the recommended heart rates by age during exercise. The athlete's training rate is for only the most fit athletes. The average training rate is recommended for a healthy person beginning a fitness program.

Table 1. Recommended Heart Rates During Aerobic Exercise

TRAINING RATES[a]			
Age	Maximum Heart Rate	Athlete, 85%[b]	Average, 80%
20	200	170	160
22	198	168	158
24	196	167	157
26	194	165	155
28	192	163	154

[a]Based on average heart rates of 72 beats per minute for males and 80 beats per minute for females

[b]Percentages represent percents of maximum heart rates in Column 2

Source: Alan Grayson and Suzanne Brazinski, *Exercise and You,* Clearview, ND: Mountain Press, 1994, 72.

Figure 6.6 Model of Formal Table and Introduction

Formal table is labeled Table

Superscript letters refer to footnotes

Stubs

Vertical rules

Footnotes explain parts of the table

Source provides bibliographic data

A formal table is appropriate here because the many numbers make the information more difficult to read. By presenting numbers in columns, the formal table helps to classify the information.

Theresa decides to use only a few rules because more would clutter the graphic. The columns are named with stubs. Notice the "a" and "b" super-scripts next to the column titles. They direct the reader's attention to the footnotes that give additional information about the table. Underneath the graphic, the word *Source* appears with a footnoted bibliographic entry. Notice that the introduction tells what kind of information is included in the table, but it does not explain every item. The table, with a short introduction, is self-explanatory.

Verbal Table

As already stated, a verbal table, also known as a chart, is similar to a formal table with its rows and columns. Like a formal table, it uses stubs and may include footnotes and bibliographic information if taken from another source. It is different, though, in the kinds of data included. Formal tables use numerals; verbal tables use words. Some writers refer to a verbal table as simply a table and number it. Other writers are less formal, referring to a chart, for example, without numbering it.

Theresa wants to emphasize to her younger audience the dangers of poor eating habits. She could write this information in a paragraph, but she decides that a chart presents the information more efficiently. So Theresa constructs this chart, the simple verbal table shown in Figure 6.7, and writes a short introduction. Note that she stays away from longer medical terms such as *hypertension, atherosclerosis,* and *gastroenterological disease.*

The following chart shows that some diseases have possible causes in poor eating habits.

DISEASE	DIET
Heart disease, stroke	High in saturated fat
High blood pressure	High in salt
Cancer	Low in fiber, fruits, and vegetables
Diabetes	High in sugar, low in fiber

Source: Raul Amaral, *Nutrition,* New York: Medical Press, 1992, 12.

Figure 6.7 Model of a Verbal Table with Introduction

Constructing Graphs

A graph is a visual aid that shows the relationships among numerical data. Five types of graphs are bar graphs, pictographs, Gantt charts, line graphs, and pie graphs.

To apply the concepts in this *section,* complete the *Formal Table Activity* worksheet available at www.cengage.com/school/bcomm/techwtg. Click the link for Chapter 6; then click Data Files.

TEACH

Tell students that usage differs with regard to identifying a verbal table (or chart) as a table (e.g., Table 1). Many writers introduce a verbal table with "The information below" or "The chart below," for example.

FOCUS

Figure 6.7

Compare the verbal table to the formal table to show similarity in design.

TEACH

Ask students to think of information that could be placed in a verbal table. Troubleshooting tables, parts guides, and job titles and responsibilities might use a verbal table. Verbal tables could contain more information than this one does and could be several pages long.

All of the graphics presented in the chapter are on the IRCD as teaching masters. Use them to point out specific features as you discuss the graphics.

Bar Graph

The **bar graph** is a graph that uses a horizontal axis and a vertical axis to compare numerical data presented in rectangular bars.

Theresa wants to show the readers of *Fitness* how much fat she lost each week for the first two months. She has already given these readers the total amount of fat she lost and wants to follow that information with more specific data. Because the bar graph is relatively easy to read, it is appropriate for the *Fitness* readers. Figure 6.8 shows the bar graph Theresa designed, along with the introduction that tells her readers which numbers to pay attention to.

Figure 1 shows the progression of fat loss per week for eight weeks. Notice that the greatest amount of fat loss occurred during weeks 1 (3.6 pounds lost) and 2 (2.7 pounds lost). Weeks 3 (1.5 pounds lost) and 4 (1.1 pounds lost) show the least amount of fat loss.

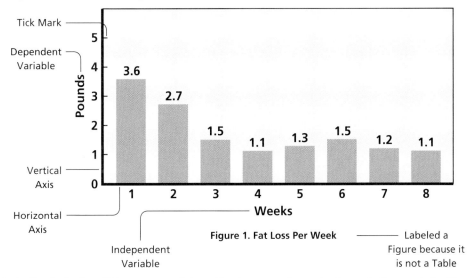

Typically, the body will lose more weight at first because of sustained metabolism and significant water loss. Several weeks into the weight-loss program, a person's metabolism slows down the amount of loss to protect the body from harm. Notice also that after seven weeks on the program, Theresa's weight loss stabilized at a little more than a pound a week.

Figure 6.8 Model of Bar Graph with Introduction

In her bar graph, Theresa uses the vertical axis for the dependent variable (the number of pounds lost) and the horizontal axis for the independent variable (the number of weeks). The dependent variable changes depending on, or relative to, the independent variable. Here the pounds lost depends on the number of weeks Theresa stays with her fitness routine. Typically, a vertical axis represents the dependent variable and a horizontal axis represents the independent variable. Often the horizontal axis depicts time or distance.

Theresa is careful to label both axes for the reader. She also added the specific number of pounds atop each bar for easy reference. To do so is not necessary, but is helpful. In fact, Theresa could have omitted the numbers next to the tick marks because the actual numbers were placed atop the bars.

TEACH

Help students see that graphs are mathematical. Point out the difference between a horizontal axis and a vertical axis.

ENRICH

Invite a math instructor to talk to your class about the importance of graphs, to explain the relationship of the horizontal and vertical axes, and to bring examples of different graphs.

FOCUS

Figures 6.8

Note how easy the bar graph is to read.

TEACH

Ask students to describe their first impression when they look at a bar graph. They will likely say that they notice differences in the height of the bars. Tell them that this perception is the strength of the bar graph—it is ideal for pointing out differences.

Make sure students understand the different variations of the bar graph—to use specific numbers atop the bars or to omit them; to create more tick marks or fewer. Each decision depends on what the purpose of the graphic is and what the writer wants the reader to pay attention to.

FOCUS

Figure 6.9

Note how easy the double bar graph is to interpret. Draw attention to the key, which is necessary in a multiple line graph to identify the data that each bar represents.

TEACH

Note that multiple bar graphs can include three or four bars. More than four bars makes the graphic difficult to read. Note that some bar graphs use horizontal instead of vertical bars.

ENRICH

Students can create a "human" bar graph" by lining up in rows to depict class data. You may ask all fall birthdays, all winter birthdays, all spring birthdays, and all summer birthdays to line up. You can choose other class data (e.g., career interests, miles students live from school, or hobbies).

The decision to add specific numbers depends on who your readers are and how much detail they need. Additional tick marks between pounds to mark individual ounces or half pounds were not added because the graph was understandable without them and Theresa wanted to avoid cluttering the graph. Notice that the bars are the same width and that the space between the bars is one-half the bar width.

Also notice how Theresa introduces the graphic before she places it in her article and continues her explanation after the graphic. Dividing the discussion this way breaks up her lengthy explanation.

Multiple Bar Graph

To compare how much fat she lost to how much muscle she gained, Theresa uses the **multiple bar graph,** a bar graph with more than one bar for each measurement, shown in Figure 6.9. With just two bars, this double bar graph is easy for both audiences to read. However, Theresa decides to use the multiple bar graph just for the *Fitness* readers because she wants to emphasize the difference in fat loss and muscle gain in the first weeks.

Figure 2 compares the amount of fat lost to the number of pounds gained. Notice that the amount of muscle gained is small compared to the amount of fat lost during the first weeks. However, as the fat loss stabilized during weeks 7 and 8, the amount of muscle gain is slightly higher. Muscle is denser than fat. As the body converts more fat to muscle, the net effect is to gain weight while still losing fat.

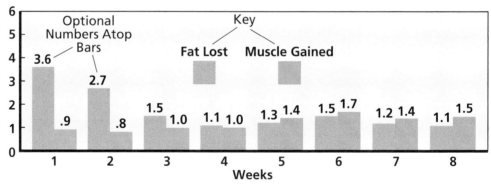

Figure 2. Fat Compared to Muscle Gain, in Pounds (for 8 weeks)

Figure 6.9 Model of a Double Bar Graph with Introduction

The double bar graph uses two sets of bars on a horizontal and vertical axis to compare several sets of numerical data. With some bars taller than others, the bar graph depicts differences dramatically. Again, the introduction points out what is most important to the reader.

The bars for fat lost are shaded differently from the bars for muscle gained. A key is provided to explain the shading. Also, Theresa adds the specific pounds atop each bar as she did in the single bar graph. This way her readers can see the specific amount easily. However, she could have omitted the numbers to give just a close approximation of the data.

Line Graph

The line graph is similar to a bar graph in that it uses a horizontal axis and a vertical axis to compare numerical data. Instead of bars, however, this graph uses a line that depicts a trend.

Theresa can use a **line graph** to show the same data she used in the bar graph. A line graph uses a horizontal axis and a vertical axis to show a trend or relationship among numbers. Theresa must decide which graph is more appropriate for her readers. To experiment with a different graph, she plotted the same eight-week fat-loss data on a line graph. Figure 6.10 shows the same data in a line graph that Figure 6.8 shows in a bar graph.

FOCUS

Figure 6.10

Compare the data in Figure 6.10 with the data in Figure 6.8. Continue to point out the brief introductions to each graphic.

Figure 3 shows how the fat loss peaked in the earlier weeks, dropped remarkably during the middle weeks, and plateaued during the last four weeks.

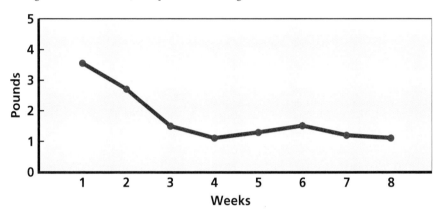

Figure 3. Fat Loss (8 weeks)

Figure 6.10 Model of Line Graph with Introduction

Theresa's line graph illustrates the fat loss over a period of time. Even though it shows the same data shown in Figure 6.8, it plays up the general trend, not the individual numbers. Therefore, the introduction focuses on the trend—the fat loss "dropped remarkably" and "plateaued"—playing up the relationships in the data instead of the differences.

This graph would be appropriate for either audience because the trend is easily interpreted, but Theresa decides not to use this line graph for either article. She believes that the bar graph is more appropriate for the inexperienced readers of *Fitness* because she wants to highlight differences in the fat lost. Instead, for her *Fitness* audience, Theresa considers using the multiple line graph shown in Figure 6.11 on the following page.

Multiple Line Graph

Theresa's Figure 6.11 puts the same information from the double bar graph in Figure 6.9 into a **multiple line graph.** A multiple line graph uses more than one line to compare data. You do not want to use too many lines, though. Otherwise, the graph may look cluttered and be difficult to read. Multiple lines are usually presented in different colors or line schemes— dotted, hyphenated, or straight. Theresa's double line graph compares two sets of data.

Figure 6.11

Compare the data in Figure 6.11 with the data in Figures 6.8 and 6.9. Discuss the difference in how the data is perceived. The bar graphs show differences in data; the line graphs emphasize the trend and the relationship between the sets of data. Also note that in showing the trend, the writer gives up the ability to show the details of the specific numbers written atop the bars.

TEACH

Ask students to explain Theresa's decision to use two bar graphs for the *Fitness* readers and one double line graph for the *Mind and Body* readers. The younger audience is better able to handle the data in two different sets; the older audience can handle the two sets of data in one graph.

Using the Models of Bar Graphs Teaching Master and the Models of Line Graphs Teaching Master on the IRCD, place one transparency over the other to show students the similarity of the data. Where the bars show differences, the lines show a trend. Furthermore, the double line graph shows how the two sets of data interact with each other. It shows what happens to fat loss as muscle gain increases. A multiple line graph can show the interactive relationships of two sets of data.

Point out that the double line graph needs a key to identify each line.

Figure 4 illustrates that the relationship between fat loss and muscle gain is more evenly matched after the first weeks of the physical fitness program. During the first two weeks, the amount of muscle gain is minimal and fat loss is at its maximum. As the fat loss plateaus, the muscle gain stabilizes, surpassing fat loss by a few ounces.

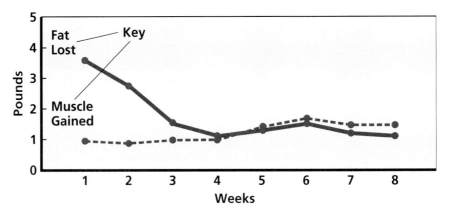

Figure 4. Fat Loss (8 weeks)

Figure 6.11 Model of Double Line Graph with Introduction

Theresa decides that the physical education majors would be interested in seeing how the two sets of data interact with each other and would have the educational background to understand how muscle gain affects fat loss. While she will provide her *Fitness* readers with the same information in two bar graphs, she will provide the information to her *Mind and Body* readers in one multiple line graph. Theresa always chooses her graphics by considering the needs of her audience as well as her own purpose for writing.

Notice how the double line graph illustrates the *relationship* between fat loss and muscle gain rather than the *differences* between fat loss and muscle gain. Again, the introduction emphasizes this relationship and provides Theresa the opportunity to make the relationship clear to her readers. Remember that writers use introductions to graphics to direct their readers' attention to certain parts of the figure.

Pictograph

A **pictograph** is a special kind of bar graph that uses pictures instead of bars to represent data. Like bar graphs, pictographs show differences in related data. In addition, pictographs add color and interest, are easy to read, and are especially appropriate for nonnative speakers of English. To be clear, the pictures or icons must be easily recognized and distinguishable from one another.

Employees of Grow Organic Consortium competed with other businesses in their area to see which company's employees could come closest to eating eight servings of fruits and vegetables every day for a month. Several weeks into the competition, Theresa presents the results in the pictograph shown in Figure 6.12. She decides to use the pictograph in her monthly newsletter to spur other companies to step up the pace.

Figure 5 shows the average number of servings of fruits and vegetables that the employees of Grow Organic Consortium ate for a month. The teamwork and friendly competition motivated them to meet the goal of eight servings during most weeks.

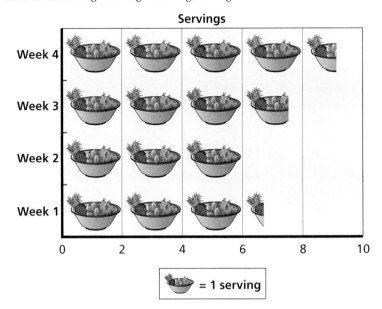

Servings

Figure 5. Average Number of Servings Consumed in One Month

Figure 6.12 Average Consumption of Fruits and Vegetables for Four Weeks at Grow Organic Consortium—Model of Pictograph with Introduction

FOCUS

Figure 6.12
Compare the pictograph to the single bar graph. The pictograph is a more "fun" representation of data, but it is not as precise.

TEACH
Ask students to think of icons to use on graphs that depict the school's library expenses or expenses of sporting events, increased enrollment at school, the number of sunny and rainy days, the growth of clubs, the decline in traffic accidents, the number of students ill with the flu, and honor roll students with a 3.5 GPA or higher.

Like the bar and line graphs, the pictograph uses horizontal and vertical axes to present data. The colorful fruits and vegetables will appeal to Theresa's general audience. The approximate numbers are rounded to the nearest quarter serving. However, if precision is important, a pictograph would not be the best choice. In the figure above, Theresa turns the graph to present the data horizontally so that her audience can read the data like a calendar.

Pie Graph

To represent what percentage of total daily food intake should consist of fat, protein, and carbohydrates, Theresa draws a pie graph, shown in Figure 6.13 on the following page. A **pie graph** is a circular graphic that shows how parts relate to the whole.

The whole totals 100 percent, with each piece of the pie representing a percentage of the whole. Notice that the pieces of the pie move clockwise from the twelve o'clock position from largest to smallest. A pie graph should contain no more than seven sections.

The introduction repeats the actual percentages in the pie and points out the significance of those numbers. The readers of *Mind and Body* already know these percentages and do not need to be reminded of them. So Theresa decides not to use the pie graph for this more knowledgeable audience but does include it for her *Fitness* readers.

Complete the *Pie Graph Activity* worksheet available at www.cengage.com/school/bcomm/techwtg. Click the link for Chapter 6; then click Data Files.

Tell students that the purpose of the pie graph is to show how parts relate to the whole. The pie graph is just what its name implies: a whole pie divided into different-sized pieces. The pie represents 100 percent. The pieces of the pie represent various percentages that total 100 percent.

Compare and contrast the two pie graphs on this page. Both of them are easy to read. One graph draws attention to a specific wedge, the amount of soft drinks consumed.

TEACH

Tell students that a pie graph divided into more than seven parts has too many pieces. Rather than using this many divisions, students should combine smaller pieces into one category.

Explain the importance of labeling pieces of the pie graph. Smaller pieces may require callouts instead of labels directly on the "pie."

Figure 6 shows the amount of protein, carbohydrates, and fat a person on a fitness plan needs in one day. Surprisingly, the human body needs more carbohydrates (65%) than protein and much less fat than previously thought.

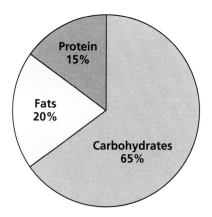

Figure 6. Daily Recommendations of Protein, Carbohydrates, and Fat

Figure 6.13 Model of Pie Graph with Introduction

Theresa creates an **exploding pie graph** for the readers of *Fitness* and *Mind and Body*. An exploding pie graph separates, or "explodes," one wedge from the circle, thus drawing attention to this piece of the pie. Theresa thinks that the younger readers need a reality check about consumption of soft drinks and that the *Mind and Body* readers should be alert to consumers' growing dependency on soft drinks.

Figure 7 shows the percentages of carbohydrates from different sources consumed in one week by Samir, a teen at risk for type 2 diabetes. Half the carbohydrates consumed come from unhealthy simple sugars. Note that more than 1/5 of his weekly intake comes from soft drinks alone.

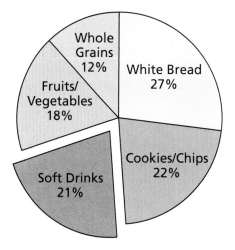

Figure 7. Types of Carbohydrates Consumed

Figure 6.14 Model of Exploding Pie Graph with Introduction

Theresa explodes the soft drinks wedge by separating it from the rest of the pie and shading it orange to signal a dangerous overconsumption. Even with a few extra pieces and a separated part, any audience will be able to understand the pie relatively easily.

Constructing Charts, Diagrams, and Pictures

A **chart** is a drawing with boxes, words, and lines to show a process or an organizational structure. Three popular charts include the flowchart, decision flowchart, and organizational chart. A diagram or drawing shows how something looks or how it operates.

Flowchart

Theresa wants a quick way to show the complex process of converting glucose to fat. She knows that the readers of *Mind and Body* already understand what happens to food the body does not use, but the readers of *Fitness* are unaware of this process. She chooses a **flowchart,** shown in Figure 6.15, to illustrate this process to her less knowledgeable readers. In a flowchart, the lines and arrows show a process or series of steps. Theresa's introduction summarizes the process.

Figure 8 shows what happens when sugars and starches are digested to glucose. The glucose that is not used by the brain or muscles is converted to fat.

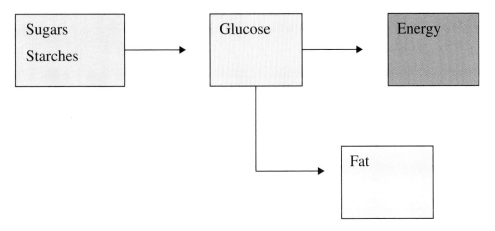

Figure 8. Result When Sugars and Starches Are Digested

Figure 6.15 Model of Flowchart with Introduction

Decision Flowchart

Theresa wants to help her *Mind and Body* readers stay within their target heart rate while exercising. So she creates the **decision flowchart** shown in Figure 6.16 on the next page to illustrate how to adjust heart rates. A decision flowchart is a special flowchart that uses symbols to indicate critical parts of making a decision. Flowcharts should cover only the major steps. You want to save the details of the process to include in your explanation in the text. Also, you should be careful not to confuse your reader with too many symbols and to provide a key for the symbols if necessary.

FOCUS

Figure 6.15

The flowchart depicts a process. Use the figure to explain construction of a flowchart. Point out that the direction of the flow is reflected in the direction of the arrows. In each box, short names describe stages in the process.

ENRICH

In groups, ask students to create a flowchart of a process they know well (e.g., the writing process, the drop/add procedure at school, the school's process for electing class representatives, or the procedure for completing a simple task).

FOCUS

Figure 6.16

The decision flowchart uses additional symbols—the oval (beginning and end), rectangle (steps), and diamond (decisions). Ask students to write this process in words to see the difference in perceiving the information in a graphic and in words only.

Use the process in Figure 9 to adjust your heart rate during exercise.

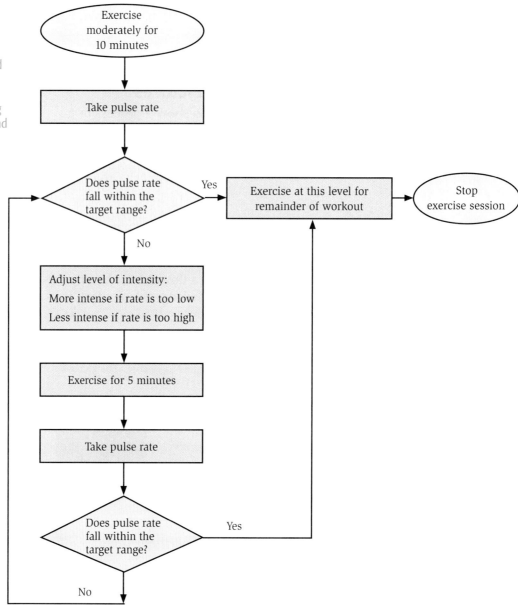

Figure 9. Process for Adjusting Your Training Rate

Figure 6.16 Model of Decision Flowchart with Introduction

Theresa uses standard symbols to indicate parts of the decision-making process: Ovals indicate where the process starts and ends, rectangles or squares indicate activities, diamonds indicate places to make decisions, and arrows direct the flow of the process. Colors applied consistently signal critical parts of the process, but readers could understand the chart without color. The flow of information moves up and down and from left to right.

Organizational Chart

Theresa was asked to speak to a student body during an assembly. To make students aware of the school's Wellness Center, she creates an **organizational chart.** An organizational chart is a drawing with boxes, words, and lines to show how an organization is structured. Theresa's chart, in Figure 6.17, shows the hierarchy of the Wellness Center's employees.

The following chart shows the organization of the school's Wellness Center.

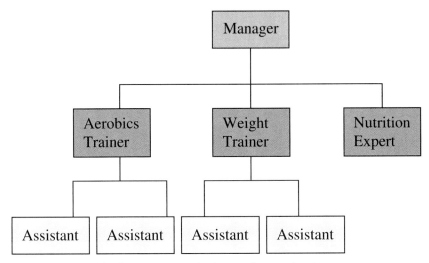

Figure 6.17 Model of Organizational Chart with Introduction

The blocks contain the job titles. The highest position is at the top of the chart. The lines show who reports to whom. The introduction describes information in the chart.

Gantt Chart

A **Gantt chart** is a bar graph used to schedule the major tasks of a complex project. Named for Henry Gantt, who developed it, the chart uses bars to depict the length of time needed to complete each task.

Theresa has been asked to chair a committee to organize a health fair for the retirees of her community. The team will meet in July to plan the fair, which will take place on September 23 and 24. At the second meeting, Theresa passes out the Gantt chart shown in Figure 6.18 on the following page. Theresa's chart provides the schedule for completing the tasks. To make sure the committee will have everything accomplished by September 23, Theresa completed the schedule by working backwards—from the date of the fair back through time to the July planning meetings. Her chronological list shows that some later tasks are dependent on the completion of earlier tasks.

© Helder Almeida, 2009/Used under license from Shutterstock.com

FOCUS

Figure 6.18

Ask questions about due dates to make sure students understand the Gantt chart. Point out that the dates represent a plan that may have to be adjusted if some parts of the project take more or less time than others.

TEACH

Point out the similarities between a Gantt chart and the bar graphs covered earlier. This chart is a good way to plan a large project to make sure all tasks are completed on time. It also shows how tasks build on one another.

ENRICH

Ask students to create a Gantt chart for a major school project.

FOCUS ON ETHICS

Use this feature to discuss the responsibilities of writers to represent data accurately with no distortions. Ask students to describe their perceptions of each figure.

Think Critically

The first graph exaggerates the trend. The second one minimizes the trend. A correctly drawn graph would fall between the extremes of these two graphs.

Planning Schedule for Health Fair September 23 and 24

Task	July			August			September		
Plan Events	████	████							
Arrange Venue			██						
Contact Vendors		████	████	██					
Arrange Security				██					
Sign Vendor Agreements				████	██				
Advertise Event						████	████	████	
Set Up Booths/Tents								█	
Hold Health Fair									█

Figure 6.18 Health Fair Planning Schedule—Model of Gantt Chart

A Gantt chart can include subtasks that fall under the major tasks, extra lines to indicate milestones reached, color coding to indicate areas of responsibility, and specific dates to indicate completion of tasks. The chart also helps group members assign the tasks necessary to complete the project on time.

Theresa keeps her chart simple. She presents it as a tentative schedule, realizing that the timeline may change. Also, because the schedule is not part of a written report but is simply distributed to the committee members for consideration, it has no figure title or number.

Focus on Ethics

Writers have a responsibility to present data accurately without creating distortions that may be misleading. When constructing graphs drawn on horizontal and vertical axes, make sure you begin the quantitative scale at zero and keep horizontal and vertical axes proportional. Study these two graphs of approval ratings for a political candidate.

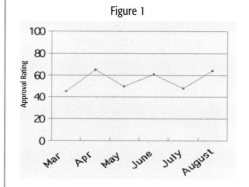

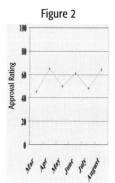

Thinking Critically

Which graph minimizes the trend? Which graph exaggerates the trend? How would you draw the graph to present the data in a fair and balanced way?

Diagram

For her *Mind and Body* article, Theresa uses a **diagram**—a line drawing—shown in Figure 6.19, from *Good Health* to show how triglycerides (fat) look in the bloodstream. She believes that her *Mind and Body* readers have the background for this information and hopes the diagram will reinforce the dangers of a diet that is high in fat.

Notice the use of **callouts,** names of specific parts of a diagram that are connected to the diagram or drawing with lines. The drawing represents a simplified version of the blood arteriole and capillaries. Adding other particles in the bloodstream would complicate the graphic. Here Theresa drew only what was needed to make her point.

Figure 10 shows how the blood cells clump together abnormally after a dinner high in triglycerides (fat). Notice that when the triglycerides create sludging, blood flow to the capillaries is impeded.

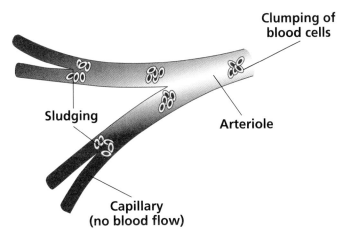

Figure 10. Effect of High Triglycerides on Blood Cells

Figure 6.19 Model of a Diagram with Introduction

Icon

An **icon** is a simple picture or drawing that represents an idea or a concept. Often the rendering uses clip art, drawings available for free or at a nominal cost. In all cases, the icon is an easily recognizable symbol of an idea. Such symbols can be used as signs. For example, most people are familiar with the no-smoking sign—a red circle around a picture of a cigarette with a red diagonal line drawn through the cigarette. The symbols also can signal a recurring idea in a newsletter, in a brochure, or on a website.

In her newsletter, Theresa uses the icons shown in the margin. These icons will alert readers to the exercise tips and recipes. Using the icons, readers can turn to them immediately without reading the text to find the tips and recipes. Once readers get used to seeing the icons, they will know what to expect when they come across them in the newsletter. Because the icons are simple symbols used to direct readers to text, they do not require figure numbers, captions, or titles.

FOCUS

Figure 6.19

Use the figure to explain the construction of a diagram. Point out that diagrams are simple depictions or representations of what something looks like but that they are not as realistic as a photo. Draw attention to the use of callouts. Remind students that the introduction refers to the graphic.

TEACH

Discuss icons and ask students to think of common ones (e.g., on a BlackBerry®, an iPhone®, or a computer screen).

FOCUS

Figure 6.20

Use Figure 6.20 to point out how photos differ from other graphics. Photos are realistic and can capture a mood, but unless they are of good quality, they may have too many details.

ONGOING ASSESSMENT

Stop and Think

Flowchart; organizational chart; diagram, drawing, or photograph

The advantage of a photograph is its realism and attention to detail. Its disadvantage is that it may show too many details without focusing on a central idea. If the photo is of poor quality, it is not a good choice for a graphic.

Photograph

A photograph can be inserted into a document when it is important to show what something looks like. Photographs include a great deal of detail, however, and are not always an appropriate graphic aid. To be effective, the photo should be clear and should focus on a particular idea or message.

Theresa decides to set up a web page to promote a healthy lifestyle. Because she believes exercising with others encourages people to continue their exercise plan, she decides to post a photograph of coworkers taking a walk after work. Her photo also helps create the mood she is after, that is, depicting fitness in a fun and positive way. Figure 6.20 shows the photo she chose.

Some workers at Sampsun Marine Industries, shown in Figure 6.2, get together every day for a walk through the park.

© Tyler Olson, 2009/Used under license from Shutterstock.com

Figure 6.20 Photograph of Employee Walk with Introduction

● STOP AND THINK

Which chart shows a process? an organizational hierarchy? the way something looks? What are the advantages and disadvantages of using a photograph?

Chapter 6
Review

SUMMARY

1. To create effective document design, (a) use adequate white space, (b) use left justification with ragged-right edges, (c) use a 10- to 12-point serif font that mixes capital and lowercase letters, (d) determine a workable system of headings, (e) use highlighting techniques to draw attention to important information, and (f) consider appropriate media.

2. Graphics should be neat and placed in a convenient location for the reader (usually after they are first mentioned in the text). Graphics require an introduction, appropriate figure and table captions and numbers, a citation for the source when necessary, aligned decimals, and effective use of color. Graphics presented by themselves (as in a poster or a sign) do not require labels and numbers.

3. Each type of graphic has a purpose that can be matched to writing objectives and audience needs.

4. Effective graphics include informal, formal, and verbal tables; bar graphs, line graphs, pictographs, and pie graphs; flowcharts, organizational charts, and Gantt charts; diagrams; icons; and photographs.

CLOSE

Summary
Divide students into groups and ask them to create a group quiz based on the summary. Duplicate the quizzes and distribute them to other groups to see whether they, as a group, can answer the questions. You could grade the quizzes or give prizes to the groups with the best score.

CLOSE

Checklist
Ask students to use the checklist when they design reports and construct graphics. See the Guidelines for Formatting Graphics Teaching Master on the IRCD for additional guidelines.

REVIEW
For a review of the key terms in the chapter, provide students with the *Key Terms* worksheet available as a supplemental activity on the IRCD.

Checklist

- Have I determined my writing objectives and found a graphic to match?

- Have I designed my page with adequate white space, left justification and ragged-right edges, a 10- to 12-point serif font, capital and lowercase letters, a workable system of headings, and appropriate highlighting features?

- Have I selected appropriate graphics?

- Have I selected an appropriate medium for my writing objectives?

- Have I constructed the graphic neatly?

- Have I referred to the graphic properly as a table or figure?

- Have I placed the graphic in a convenient place for the reader?

- Have I provided a specific title for each graph, chart, and formal table?

- Have I numbered the graphics consecutively?

- Have I given credit for the graphic found in an outside source?

- Have I explained the significance of the graphic?

- Have I kept the graphic as simple as possible?

- Have I used color effectively?

- Have I constructed each graphic according to the required criteria?

ASSESS

Build Your Foundation

1. Encourage students to think about the differences in page design.

2. Use this exercise to make students aware of the variety of graphics.

3. a. Informal table; Lamar should use a few sentences to introduce it. b. Bar graph or line graph; Thanh could even devise a double bar graph or double line graph and label different bars or lines "School Week" and "Vacation Week." c. Pie graph. d. Flowchart and/or decision flowchart. e. Diagram. f. Photo. g. Pictograph (using a picture of a fish) and icons. h. Gantt chart.

ASSESS

Your Turn

4. This exercise gives students an opportunity to use a graphic with a familiar topic.

5. Students are invited to make up details, but the percentages and associated expenditures should be the same as those in the solution on the IRCD.

Build Your Foundation

1. Examine several of your textbooks for design features. Describe each design. Which book has the best design? Why?

2. Create a scrapbook of graphics from newspapers, magazines, and the Web. Using your checklist, decide whether the graphics present the data effectively. Note the difference in the graphics that is not specifically covered in this chapter. Into which category of graphics do they fall?

3. Suggest the best graphic to use for presenting the situations below. In addition, try to construct the graphic.

   a. Lamar wrote to his father and listed his latest test scores in calculus: Chapter 1, 83; Chapter 2, 79; Chapter 3, 92.

   b. Using a pedometer, Thanh compared the miles she walked during a school week to the miles she walked during her vacation. School: May 25, 1.3; May 26, 1.9; May 27, 2.7; May 28, 1.6; May 29, 2.5. Vacation: June 1, 0.6; June 2, 1.2; June 3, 0.9; June 4, 1.4; June 5, 2.0.

   c. Gahiji wrote his parents to tell them how he spent the $1,250 they gave him for his first month of college: $850, books and educational supplies; $65, snacks and pizza; $210, dorm accessories (rug, poster, bedding); $46, entertainment; $40, parking fine; $39, unspent funds.

   d. Crystal, head cashier for a grocery store, must show her coworkers the procedure for gaining approval for a customer check over $300: Inform the customer about store policy, verify the identity of the customer with a photo ID, ensure that the information on the check is correct, get two phone numbers from the customer, write your initials on the check, and call the manager to approve the check.

   e. Alessandra must show her physics instructor the structure of a hydrogen atom and the location of protons, neutrons, and electrons.

   f. Patrick is designing a travel brochure for future Peace Corps volunteers. He wants to show how eager students were to learn English in a Philippine village last summer.

   g. Sasha is giving a PowerPoint® presentation on the growth of fish farms in her state. Five years ago there were 120 farms; four years ago, 200 farms; three years ago, 250 farms; two years ago, 350 farms; and now, 560 farms. She needs an attractive opening slide.

   h. In July, Zach is collaborating with three other researchers to write an article for an academic journal. To be published in the December issue, the article must be accepted by October 10. To meet this deadline, Zach plans these tasks: review of literature conducted, draft written, draft sent to editor, draft sent to reviewers, draft revised, article resubmitted, and article published.

Your Turn

4. Write a brief article explaining the significance of a special photo. Incorporate the photo correctly into your article.

5. Convert the following survey information into a pie graph: Out of 450 clients of Iron Works Gym, 175 want more weight-lifting equipment, 50 want child care services, 75 want a sauna, 50 want more personal trainers, and 100 want a juice bar.

6. Use the information from the table below to generate graphics. For each graph, write a brief introduction. Title and number each graphic properly.

Table 1. Beverage Consumption, 1970–2005

Beverage	1970	1975	1980	1985	1990	1995	2000	2005
Whole Milk	25	21	17	14	11	9	8	7
Other Milk	6	8	11	12	15	15	14	14
Tea	7	8	7	7	7	8	8	8
Coffee	33	31	26	27	27	20	26	24
Bottled Water	NA	NA	3	5	9	12	17	26
Diet Soft Drinks	NA	NA	NA	10	14	14	14	15
Regular Soft Drinks	NA	NA	NA	31	33	37	39	36

All numbers rounded to the nearest gallon per capita.

Source: Adapted from USDA/Economics Research Service. "Food Availability: Spread-sheets." February 27, 2009.

- A pie graph of the bottled water, diet soft drinks, and regular soft drinks consumed in 2005. Total the gallons of water and soft drinks and compute the percentages

- A table citing the use of caffeinated beverages—including tea, coffee, diet carbonated, and regular carbonated—since 1980

- An informal table with the whole milk, other milk, and total milk consumed in 1970

- A bar graph showing the total number of carbonated beverages consumed from 1980 to 2005

- A double bar graph showing the consumption of tea and coffee since 1970

- A pictograph showing water consumption from 1990 to 2005

- A line graph showing the amount of bottled water consumed since 1980

- A double line graph showing the consumption for whole milk and other milk since 1970. Do you notice a trend? Explain.

- A multiple line graph showing the consumption of bottled water, diet carbonated drinks, and regular carbonated drinks consumed from 1985 to 2005. Do you see a relationship among this data? Explain.

Community Connection

7. Create a poster, flyer, or brochure to advertise an area event, to educate people on a topic, or to alert them to some danger in your area. The document should follow principles of document design and use graphics to convey meaning and to support your message. Suggestions include an upcoming rabies clinic, free pound puppies, evacuation routes, allergen warnings, boating safety, a musical event, or a charity event. Ask permission to post your document in appropriate places.

6. Make sure students follow the guidelines for constructing graphs.

ASSESS

Community Connection

7. Give students some flexibility in choosing a project. Students should follow the guidelines for document design and graphics presented in the chapter.

Writing for the Web

Goals

- Plan web pages
- Organize and design web pages
- Write text for web pages
- Write text for special kinds of web pages

Terms

- animation, p. 172
- blog, p. 179
- demographics, p. 169
- discussion forum, p. 182
- FAQ, p. 180
- home page, p. 168
- hyperlink, p. 170
- interactive, p. 167
- Internet, p. 167
- keywords, p. 177
- RSS, p. 180
- scannable, p. 176
- usability, p. 172
- Web Accessibility Initiative (WAI), p. 173
- wiki, p. 181
- World Wide Web, p. 167

TEACHING RESOURCES FOR CHAPTER 7

Instructor's Resource CD
Data Files
Data File Solutions
Lesson Plans
Teaching Masters
PowerPoint Slides
Chapter Tests with Solutions
Additional Chapter Activities

ExamView

Website
www.cengage.com/school/
bcomm/techwtg
Crossword Puzzle
Data Files
Data File Solutions
Flashcards
Glossary
NET Bookmark
Sample Documents
Web Links

WRITE TO LEARN
Help students see how the
Internet has changed the
world. Compare the changes
to the way the printing press,
telegraph, telephone, radio,
and TV have changed
people's lives.

WRITE TO LEARN

Think about all of the ways you use the Internet. Then try to imagine your life without the Internet. What would it be like? Write a short journal entry describing how your life would be different if there were no Internet.

Focus on Writing for the Web

Read the sample document on the next page and answer these questions:

- What is the reason for the site?
- Describe the color scheme. How does it make you feel?
- Does the page look balanced? Why or why not?
- What information is on the page? Is it easy to find? Explain.
- If you were a newcomer to the site, which part would you visit? If you had visited the site before, which part might you revisit?
- What combination of text and graphics do you see?

What If?

- The site provided FAFSA forms for different majors or different schools?
- The site provided a survey to determine eligibility for financial aid?
- An upcoming deadline was given for submission of FAFSA forms?
- The site highlighted college graduates who had used financial aid?
- The site hosted its own discussion forum?

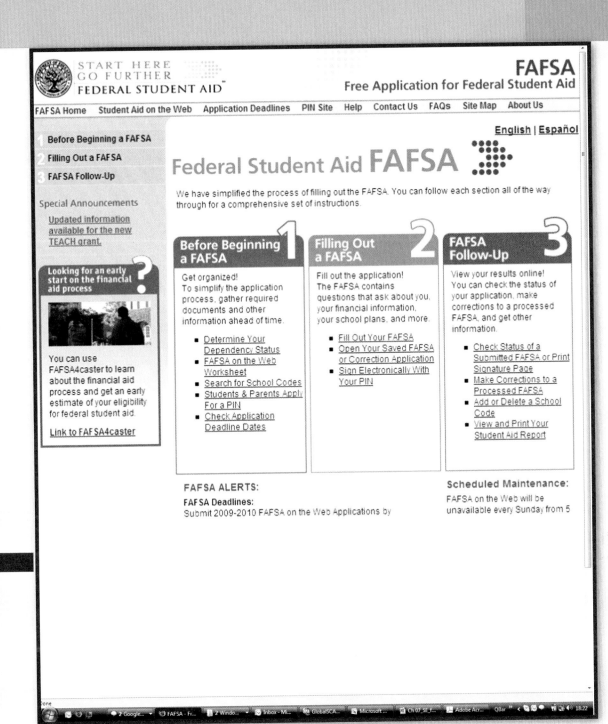

Sample Web Page

FOCUS

Focus on Technical Writing

Use the questions to encourage students to read the sample closely.

ASSESS

What If?

Use the questions to discuss how the sample would be different if the situation or audience changed.

Go to www.cengage.com/school/bcomm/techwtg for more detailed responses to these questions.

Writing@Work

Hospitality & Tourism

Michael Luongo is an experienced and prolific freelance travel writer based in New York City. For ten years, he has been publishing his work in magazines, in newspapers, in books, and on the Web. He works with all kinds of publishers, from prestigious ones such as *The New York Times* to specialized and small ethnic publishers.

© Ingrid Breyer

A versatile writer like Michael knows how important it is to adjust one's writing style and format for publication on the Web. His rule of thumb is that if you have to print something out to read it, it's too long to be readable on a screen. In addition, paragraphs in web articles must be shorter than they usually are in print.

"Think of ways to divide your work into pithy bits that are full of information and catchy," suggests Michael, "such as top tens and other 'listy' ways of writing." Michael also believes that avoiding the wordiness and punctuation of complete sentences increases readability and highlights the important content.

Web copy also must be interactive and clickable—full of words and images that contain links to other related material. According to Michael, "You want to make your work so clickable that a reader will lose all sense of time with it."

Michael's advice to those who want to publish on the Web is to start publishing on the Web. "Create your own website or blog first—since you can control it—and use your name or your specialty as a part of the website or blog name. You should always reserve yourname.com as soon as you can." For example, Michael's website is www.michaelluongo.com. "It's your calling card; your portfolio; and, in my case, part of my dream work as a travel writer."

Think Critically

1. Do you agree with Michael about the length of writing on web pages? Explain.

2. Starting with Michael's advice in this feature, create a "top ten" list of rules and tips for writing on the Web.

Printed with permission of Michael Luongo

GETTING STARTED ON WEB PAGES

WebMD, HowStuffWorks, eBay, Facebook, and Flickr are now household terms. The expression *to google,* which might have been mistaken for kiddy babble ten years ago, shows how quickly the search engine Google has infiltrated not only our homes, but also our lexicon. Over 1.6 billion people worldwide, or nearly 24 percent of the world's population, use the Internet (Miniwatts). Knowing how to write for these users will give you a critical advantage in the workplace.

Although the terms *the Web* (for **World Wide Web,** a collection of online resources) and the **Internet** are often used interchangeably, they are not synonymous. The Internet, a global system of networks, is the infrastructure on which the World Wide Web as well as other protocols, including e-mail and instant messaging, travel. Think of the Internet as the train track and the Web as one of the trains running on the track.

Reading Web Pages

Brand X Pictures/Getty Images

Because of the **interactive** nature of the Internet, with pages that respond to user input, users read online material differently from the way they read printed text. Where people read books and magazines in a linear fashion from one page to the next, web readers scan pages from the top center, then down from left to right, looking for keywords. Instead of turning pages, readers follow links, jumping from one page to another and one site to another, wherever their interests take them. In this way, readers control the flow of information, and no two readers read a website the same way.

On the FAFSA home page illustrated on page 165, users needing to apply for a PIN click "Students & Parents Apply for a PIN." If users already have a PIN, they move to the part of the site that meets their needs at the moment—perhaps "Make Corrections to a Processed FAFSA." The interaction is more like a conversation as the web page communicates with different users in different ways.

Online readers want speed and convenience. Most people find that just ten seconds is too long to wait for a page to load. If the site glitters with animation but does not give viewers the information they seek, they are not likely to return. Furthermore, readers prefer not to scroll horizontally (to the right) or vertically (down) to find information.

Warm Up

How do you read a novel? How do you read a website? Do you read both in the same way, or do you read them differently? Explain.

FOCUS

Warm Up

Use the discussion to show that reading web material is different from reading printed text such as a book or magazine.

ENRICH

In a CNN interview on *Fareed Sakaria GPS,* David Miliband (British politician, Secretary of State in 2009) said, "Technology breaks down borders and barriers. . . . Thanks to the Internet, nationalism is international." (July 5, 2009). Discuss with your students the implications of this statement.

In the early nineties, Bill Gates said, "The Internet is becoming the town square for the global village of tomorrow." Ask students to react to Gates's vision. Has his statement become true?

TEACH

From approximately 370 million users in December 2000 to over 1.6 billion users in March 2009, the Web has seen nearly a 350 percent growth in the last ten years alone. Furthermore, CISCO Systems estimates that Internet usage will double every two years at least through 2012.

TEACH

Ask students if they have difficulty reading a screen. Some say that reading a screen is harder on the eyes than reading a book. Book pages remain still and are usually black text on white or off-white paper. Screens are filled with bright colors and images that move, and the contrast ratio is lower than with paper.

Because of their desire to navigate quickly, readers pick up clues from one page to help them understand the next page. As a web writer, you must be familiar with these clues and adjust your writing to this different way of reading and accessing data.

Planning Web Pages

To write text for the Web, you need to think through the basics of planning a document: What is your purpose? Who is your audience? Your challenge is to achieve your purpose and meet the needs of your audience.

What Is Your Purpose?

In Chapter 2, you learned to determine the purpose of your writing early in the process and to use your purpose to guide you as you made decisions about your document. Here, too, determining your purpose is important. What do you want to happen as a result of this document? In other words, why does your website or web page exist? What is the reason for your post or discussion?

The purpose of most technical writing is to inform or persuade. In web writing, the purpose might expand to include other goals, such as offering a service, defining an image, soliciting opinions, creating a community, or entertaining people. One site informs customers about cell phone plans, provides a service by recording minutes used, and persuades customers to purchase a smartphone. Your bank's website projects an image of a responsible, conservative institution. MySpace brings people together, and YouTube entertains as well as informs.

Effective sites make their purpose clear on the **home page** (the first page of a website)—often as a slogan in the heading across the top of the page. Figure 7.1 shows Overton's home page. The slogan makes it clear that the company sells products for boating and water sports. The dark blue colors remind viewers of water, and the photo of canoes packed with gear support the image of family fun.

Figure 7.1 Website with a Clear Purpose

Who Are Your Readers?

Online readers come from all over the world, with English, Chinese, Spanish, and Japanese as the four most popular languages. The audience may include many readers looking for news headlines on MSN.com or a single stock broker looking for Exxon Mobil's performance in the S&P 500.

Defining the audience for your web-based project will help you get started on your writing. Who is your target audience? Describe this audience as specifically as you can. What are the **demographics**, or defining characteristics, of your audience? In other words, where do they live; how old are they; what is their income; are they male, female, married, or single?

After you have defined your target audience, consider how you can best appeal to your audience. Ask yourself these questions:

- What information does my audience need, expect, and want?
- What will my audience do with this information?

Some members of your audience will have the latest technology; others will not. When planning your site, consider monitor settings, Internet connection speeds, special requirements of hand-held devices, and browsers used by your target audience. Plan for a variety of technology setups and test your page in different browsers (for example, Internet Explorer® and Mozilla Firefox®).

Keep in mind that anyone anywhere in the world can read whatever you put on a web page. You may think that you are selling hand tools to the residents of East Texas, but do not be surprised to receive orders from China or Northern Ireland. Remember, the Internet is always open to anyone with a computer and an Internet connection.

 STOP AND THINK

How do visitors read a page on the Web? What issues should a web designer be concerned about when planning a web page?

ORGANIZING AND DESIGNING WEB PAGES

Now that you have a clear purpose and a good understanding of your target audience, it is time to organize your material and design your page.

Organizing Web Pages

To begin organizing your website, use sticky notes or index cards to list everything you want to include—no more than one item per note or card. Group your items into similar categories, considering the importance of each idea to your users. Place your notes on a white board or bulletin board so you can move them around until you have an outline that works—with topics and subtopics. Common ways to organize information on a website are by category, task, product, date/time, or department.

TEACH

Ask students which sites they visit and who the target audience is. Practice determining the audience's needs/wants and how the sites appeal to their audience.

ONGOING ASSESSMENT

Stop and Think

Visitors interact with web pages and control the flow of information by scanning and clicking, stopping to read interesting information.

A designer should determine the audience, the demographics of the audience, the information readers need or want, and readers' technology limitations.

FOCUS

Warm Up

Discuss what a typical web page looks like, what students expect to find, and what looks useful and attractive. Most students want to find information quickly using few clicks, find too much "noise" to be a distraction, lose patience with pages that load slowly, and become annoyed when they have to scroll too much or read too much text. Some pages look cluttered and unattractive, while others are organized and easy to follow.

Warm Up

What is your favorite website? What features make the site stand out? Describe the page—the kind of information, the colors, the graphics. Is the page easy to read? Do you have an easy time finding information on this site? Why or why not?

Once you have an outline, you can decide how to structure your website. A simple site may move forward in a linear fashion from one page to the next, similar to a flowchart. Other sites organize pages in a hierarchy, similar to an organizational chart. In the hierarchy, information flows progressively from "top" to "bottom" from the home page to a second or third tier in increasing levels of detail. Web design software such as Adobe® Dreamweaver® and Microsoft® Expression® Web 3 provides tools for setting up the structure for a website.

However you organize your pages, you will need to plan for a system of hyperlinks. **Hyperlinks,** also called *links*, are a word, phrase, or graphic used to link, or join, pages within a site or to an external site, allowing viewers to move easily from page to page. Depending on the browser settings, hyperlinks can be a different color, underlined, or graphical. They are activated by scrolling over a word and/or clicking. The goal is to make information accessible in three or four mouse clicks.

External links can enrich a subject with information from another site and reduce content on a page. However, if you plan to use external links, you will want to inform your readers that they are leaving your site and moving to another one. If you use an external link, make sure the link works. It is frustrating for viewers to click on a dead link that does not take them to the page you intended. There is no copyright infringement for providing links to other sites. However, it is illegal to provide a link to a site representing any form of illegal activity.

Not every site makes use of external links, but every site should include a clear system of links to take viewers to pages within the site. Without clear navigation, readers can get lost, wondering how to get back to a page they found interesting. Table 7.1 explains some common ways to provide internal links.

Focus on Ethics

Claudia is setting up a website for her floral business, Claudia's Creations. She is in a hurry to get the site up and running. She wants to show some of the sprays, wedding bouquets, and dish gardens she has created, but she cannot find the pictures she took of them. So she searches the Web and finds designs that she likes on two websites: Floral Fantasia and Flowers by Chenda. Claudia decides to use some of the designs from those sites on her own website until she finds her misplaced pictures or takes new ones.

Think Critically

What might happen if Claudia's customers discover that she used flower designs from other sites?

Home Page Link	A hyperlink back to the first page of a site. A home page link should be on every page of a site.
Previous Page/Next Page	A hyperlink to help readers go back one screen and forward to the next screen.
Breadcrumb Trails	Hyperlinks in a row near the top of the page that show visitors the links between the page being viewed and the home page. The viewer can click any link in the trail to move back quickly in the hierarchy. A good visual clue about linking relationships, it should be used in addition to other navigation tools.
Site Map	Hyperlinks that show a hierarchal list (word, phrase, or graphic) of information on the site—similar to a table of contents. Users can click a link to view a specific page quickly without having to go through multiple levels of pages.
Navigation Bar	A list of links—words, tabs, or pictures—that span the top, sides, or bottom of a page and direct users to other pages.
Drop-Down Menu	A word or phrase, usually at the top of a page, with options that open, or "drop down," when a user clicks the word or the arrow. Drop-down menus are useful because the navigation does not clutter the page, yet the options are still available.
Search	A feature that allows the user to enter keywords and search for pages in the site.

Table 7.1

FOCUS

Table 7.1

Discuss the pros and cons of each type of link. Ask students which internal links they like to use and why.

Ask students to pay attention to the descriptive names of the links (e.g., breadcrumb trails—like Hansel and Gretel finding their way back home).

FOCUS

Figure 7.2

Use this single page to point out all of the links from navigation bars, drop-down menus, text links, and search features.

Figure 7.2 illustrates links—including navigation bars, drop-down menus, and search features—on the home page of Georgia's official state website.

Figure 7.2 System of Links on a Home Page

ENRICH

Remind students of other search engines, including Dogpile, Excite, Lycos, AltaVista, and Bing. Other countries use Baidu (China), Ansearch (Australia, UK/US/NZ), Garuji.com (India), Onkosh (Middle East), Rambler (Russia), and Walla (Israel). Ask students to look at web pages using search engines from other countries. Even though students do not know the language, they can guess at what kind of information is included because placement is similar to that used in Google and Yahoo!.

TEACH

Reinforce the idea that usability is the top design principle. Attractiveness is second.

RETEACH

Remind students that some of the design principles given here are similar to those presented in Chapter 6—use of white space, lists, shorter paragraphs, and graphics that support the message.

Designing Web Pages

If users do not have a good experience the first time they access a site, they may not return. Consider **usability**—the ease with which an audience can access and use a site—as the top design principle. In addition to ease of use, web pages should look attractive—uncluttered, symmetrical, and inviting. Use the principles discussed next when designing your website.

Header

Create a header, the banner spanning the top of a web page, to set the appropriate image and tone for your site. A site advertising scented candles may use a photo of lit candles, pastel colors, and a simple script font to create a relaxing scene. A site advertising sports cars, on the other hand, might use bright colors, a photo of a red Corvette, and a bold font to evoke excitement.

Page Layout

To help readers scan for relevant information, organize information under relevant headings. If your page is too long, divide the information into multiple shorter pages with corresponding links to those pages. If you cannot break up the long pages, place the most important information—the title, purpose, key navigational elements, and search features—near the top so readers see it before scrolling vertically. Do not set up pages so visitors have to scroll horizontally.

Line Length

A shorter line length reduces eye movement needed to scan the text. The ideal line length is approximately half the width of the screen, or between 50 and 70 characters (or 10 to 12 words) per line.

Graphics

Graphics break up the text, attract the reader's attention, and offer instant identification with the purpose of the website. Use graphics to provide visual relief, to support your content and image, and to make the site attractive. A site focusing on the fun and challenge of a rock climbing club would not use a photo of a woman on the side of a wall panicked at the prospect of rappelling back down.

Graphics take time to load, and too many graphics may discourage people from investigating a site. To speed up the download time of graphics, use one of the following formats for compressing files: GIF (Graphics Interchange Format), JPEG (Joint Photographic Experts Group), or PNG (Portable Network Graphics). Use smaller logos as opposed to larger background logos. If more detail is needed, enable users to click the picture to see the full size.

Multimedia

Many pages use **animation** (text or graphics that move), audio, and video to make a page more interesting. Although the movement and audio may look and sound good, use them sparingly to support your message. Too much movement may annoy the reader, and if the extra graphics result in the page taking a long time to load, you may lose visitors.

Tables

Use tables to organize text and graphics. Tables give the page a uniform, clean, professional appearance. Data can go inside cells, and one table can be nested inside another. Invisible tables form the skeleton that holds the site together.

Borders

Use borders around the page to draw boundaries between sections or omit borders for a more seamless look.

Fonts

Font sizes and styles affect screen legibility. Sans serif fonts are usually recommended for online text because they look more distinct on a screen. Avoid all capital letters and boldfaced blocks of text because these styles slow down the reader and are the equivalent of YELLING.

As with printed text, you can emphasize important words or phrases with boldface or italics as long as you do not go overboard. Be wary of using underlining. Most viewers associate it with links and expect to be able to click to access another page.

Colors

Use colors to help create an inviting site. As you know, colors evoke a variety of emotional responses. Color should reflect the site's purpose and take into account the target audience's cultural associations with color. For example, red, often associated with the devil in the United States, is the color of wealth and good luck in China.

Consider, too, the color wheel and use colors that complement one another—for example, yellow and purple, and blue and orange. You want to keep colors to a minimum and use a neutral, white, or very dark background color with contrasting colors for the text. Use accent colors to direct visitors to important content.

Consistency

You teach the user how to read your site by repeating certain patterns. Repetition allows readers to anticipate the site's structure. To achieve consistency, make sure your pages look similar and use the same design features positioned in the same place on every page. A company name and logo that appears in the top left corner of one page, for example, should appear in the top left corner of every page. If the text is dark blue on a light blue background, do not experiment, for example, by changing the scheme on another page to dark blue text on a white background.

Accessibility

Whenever possible, follow Web Content Accessibility Guidelines (WCAG) 2.0. These guidelines are part of the **Web Accessibility Initiative (WAI).** Its goal is to make web content available to users with a wide range of disabilities, including visual and hearing impairments, learning disabilities, cognitive and movement limitations, speech disabilities, and combinations of disabilities.

TEACH
Stress the importance of being consistent—that lack of consistency can cause confusion.

Tell students that advertising banners do not command people's attention the way advertisers thought they would. In fact, banners tend to annoy and distract users. Most users prefer to locate information through keywords and links.

ENRICH
The Web Accessibility Initiative website at www.w3.org/WAI explains how technology can assist people with disabilities, including color blindness, deafness, dyslexia, repetitive injuries, and cognitive decline. Ask students to visit the website, search on *people with disabilities,* and read the article "How People with Disabilities Use the Web." Have students share with the class some bit of information they learned.

ONGOING ASSESSMENT

Stop and Think

Broader principles include usability and attractiveness. Specific goals include an attractive header to support the site's purpose, page layout with shorter paragraphs under headings, shorter line length, graphics that support the message but do not take long to load, limited multimedia, tables used to organize material, attractive borders or none at all, font size and type that is easy to read (usually sans serif), colors that support the purpose and are attractive without being

The MyPyramid home page shown in Figure 7.3 uses three vertical panels. The middle panel uses a white background with black sans serif text of 1 through 11 words per line. The left and right panels use blues and greens, colors that depict calmness and good health. The pyramid logo represents the colors of the various food groups and reminds the reader of the government-sponsored food pyramid. Each page in the site uses the same header across the top, the same top and left navigation bars, the same search feature, and the same three-panel design. The site's statement about accessibility (not shown in the figure) can be found by clicking the link at the bottom of the web page.

⬢ **STOP AND THINK**

List at least five design principles for the Web. How should color be used? What are some technology considerations?

Warm Up

How do you read a book? How do you read a web page? Do you read them the same way? Explain.

noisy, consistency used to teach people how to read the site, and accessibility for those with disabilities.

FOCUS

Warm Up

Help students see differences in the way they read a book compared to the way they read a web page. They turn pages in a book but click to go to another part of a website. They probably read word for word from a book, but scan until they find what they want on a web page. Reading from a screen may be harder on their eyes.

FOCUS

Figure 7.3

Discuss whether students think the figure follows the principles of design. Point out the three vertical columns with contrasting colors associated with the color of fruits and vegetables.

WRITING TEXT FOR THE WEB

In many ways, writing for the Web is similar to writing text for any other technical document. But remember, a web page is viewed on a screen, not on an 8½" × 11" sheet of paper. The screen influences all pages in important ways. Writing scannable text will help your readers find what they need.

Strategies for All Pages

Use the strategies beginning on the next page to keep your pages organized and focused on your audience.

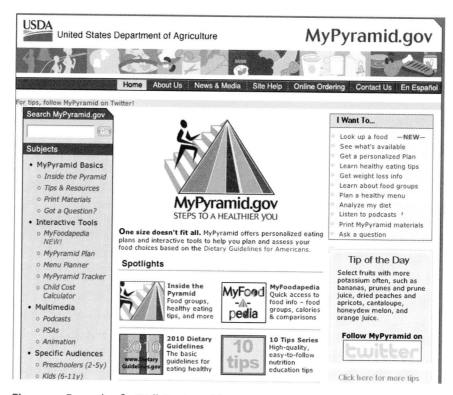

Figure 7.3 Example of a Well-Designed Page

Page Title

Give each page its own short, descriptive title—something visitors can read quickly in a browser title bar or history list. On the Federal Emergency Management (FEMA) website, for example, each page has a unique title, such as "Plan Ahead," "Disaster Information," and "Apply for Assistance." If you visit these pages, they will be listed in the order in which they were viewed under "History" in the browser window. FEMA and its logo appear in the upper left corner of each page, though, to tell readers they are still on the FEMA website. If readers bookmark a page (or save to Favorites), the page title is stored. Some search tools use page titles in their search results.

Audience

Know your target audience and write to that audience. Compare these two sentences from a job hunting website for displaced workers:

Original: The JDW site has been set up to help displaced workers find jobs in their immediate geographical areas whether their expertise is in construction, sales, or engineering.

Revision: If you have lost your job, we can help—no matter what your area of expertise or where you live.

The original example talks about the website. The revised example talks directly to the reader.

Also avoid jargon unless you know your reader will understand it.

Inverted Pyramid

State important points before you provide any detailed supporting information. At the website of the Salt Plains National Wildlife Refuge, the home page begins with what the Salt Plains Wildlife Refuge is and why it exists. Then readers learn about the size of the salt flat, two related habitats, and upcoming events—all in order of importance. The inverted pyramid allows viewers to see the most important content before they scroll down the page.

Facts, Not Hype

To keep your web page as informative as possible, state the facts and avoid the hype of an overdone sales appeal. People want information they can use.

Original: Are you sitting at home wondering when you'll meet Prince Charming? Skin Rejuvenation promises to restore skin scarred from acne or sun damage. Order your jar today and see how your life changes.

Revision: Skin Rejuvenation moisturizer is easily absorbed, thereby reducing winter chafing by 15%.

Original Phrases

Avoid the web cliché—the "Click here" or "Check out this site." A link can be easily made a seamless part of a sentence, as the following examples show:

Original: Click <u>here</u> to learn how variations in temperature affect the success of gel coat application.

Revision: Variations in <u>temperature</u> affect the success of gel coat application.

Standard English

Use standard English and follow rules of correct punctuation and usage. Nothing ruins the credibility of a web page more than errors.

Scannable Text

Except when the site posts an article or a resume, say as much as you can in as few words as possible. Your goal is to create **scannable** text to enable readers to locate important words and phrases—or keywords—quickly and effortlessly. To reduce words and make your text scannable, follow the suggestions discussed next.

Short Paragraphs

Use short paragraphs that stand out and can be quickly scanned and absorbed, usually six to eight lines. A single, well-worded sentence can stand alone as a paragraph. See the visual relief in the thumbnail sketch in Figure 7.4 where one longer paragraph is separated into three.

Short Sentences

While sentences can vary in length, aim for an average of 20 to 25 words per sentence. The revised sentence below is much clearer and easier to read when it is written as two shorter sentences.

Original: Set in the rustic Craghill Mountains near the small town of Wilcox, Tennessee, Spring Village, conveniently located close to a transportation center, medical center, and cultural alcove, is a caring community for seniors.

Revision: Set in the rustic Craghill Mountains near the small town of Wilcox, Tennessee, Spring Village is a caring community for seniors. It is conveniently located close to a transportation center, medical center, and cultural alcove.

Headings

Use short but informative headings to help readers identify topics and decide at a glance what they want to read. Headings also provide transitions to the next topic, alerting the reader to shift from one idea to another. For example, to help

Figure 7.4 Long Versus Short Paragraphs

readers locate information in its web page, the Community Orchestra provides three headings: Upcoming Performances, How to Join, and Director's Notes.

Paragraphs to Lists

Use bulleted lists to break up paragraphs, reduce the amount of text, and emphasize important content. The following list of e-mail "don'ts" is easier to scan than the paragraph with the same information.

Original: Respect your e-mail recipient's privacy and time by not sending chain e-mails. They are hoaxes and waste your reader's time. It is presumptuous to send attachments or other people's e-mail addresses unless you have permission to do so. Sending multiple postings to people who are not interested wastes time and takes up storage space. Finally, do not "Reply to All" unless it is necessary.

Revision: DON'T

- Send chain e-mails.

- Send attachments or other people's e-mail addresses unless you have permission to do so.

- Send multiple postings to people who are not interested.

- "Reply to All" unless it is necessary.

Keywords

To help search engines and your audience find your website, in approximately the first 50 words of your text, use **keywords,** important words that indicate subject areas. To find useful information, readers scan text looking for keywords and phrases. Keywords for a mythology website include *Joseph Campbell, The Hero with a Thousand Faces, myths, hero, Departure, Initiation, Return, Call to Adventure,* and *Healing and Reconciliation.* Which of the following versions does a better job of including more keywords in the first 50 words?

Original: Joseph Campbell compared myths of the hero from all over the world. He found similarities in the myths and identified 12 stages of the hero's journey. Below are Campbell's stages with a short explanation. The explanations and stages are typical of the journey but may not be found in all [50 words] myths. The stories and their plots are similar, but the characters and circumstances differ. Campbell's work is compelling. For more information, see his landmark book, [75 words] *The Hero with a Thousand Faces.*

Revision: In his book *The Hero with a Thousand Faces,* Joseph Campbell identifies 12 stages in myths of the hero's journey. The journey takes place in three parts: hero's Departure, Initiation into the journey, and Return to improve society. From the Call to Adventure through Healing and Reconciliation, the hero receives [50 words] Supernatural Aid, passes into the Darkness of the Realm of Night. . . .

In the original version, Campbell's book is not even mentioned until after 75 words into the passage. The second passage is more concise, relaying significant information in every sentence.

All of these suggestions have one goal—to make information useful and accessible.

TEACH

Compare and contrast these strategies to strategies used in technical writing. Documents have a single title compared to a title for every page of a website. Both media appeal to a target audience, use the inverted pyramid organizational strategy, present facts, avoid clichés, and use standard English.

Complete the *Paragraphs to Lists* worksheet available at www.cengage.com/school/bcomm/techwtg. Click the link for Chapter 7; then click Data Files.

ONGOING ASSESSMENT

Stop and Think

Answers may include using page
titles, writing to the audience,
organizing with the inverted
pyramid, sticking to the facts,
and using standard English. Text

 STOP AND THINK

Explain three overall writing strategies for web pages. Explain five ways to write
scannable text.

SPECIAL WEB PAGES

The Web offers a new medium for established ways of communicating. The
type of writing is not altogether new, but when the audience and medium
change, good writers adapt. The result? New avenues of writing for existing
genres. Five of these adaptations are outlined next: home page, blog, FAQ,
wiki, and discussion forum.

Home Page

Think of your website as a theme park. Your park may have many areas—
rides, a petting zoo, edutainment, restaurants, and more—or a single
nature trail. The home page of your website is like the entrance to the park.
Because you want many visitors, you design an inviting entrance, one that
reflects the theme and offers basic information to help people navigate
the site. Like a home page, there may be several ways to get from one area
to the next inside the park. Use the following tips when writing text for
a home page:

■ **Get your reader's attention and announce your purpose.** Use a catchy
phrase and meaningful slogan. For example, a website devoted to
transferring photos and videos to DVDs might replace its title and slogan
with something more appealing, as follows:

Original: title "Photo Transfer"; slogan "We turn photos into DVDs."

Revision: title "Keepsake Photos"; slogan "Keeping your memories
safe."

■ **Write a short introduction and conclusion.** The introduction
explains the purpose of your website. The conclusion brings the
page to a close. Consider the introduction and conclusion on the
Keepsake Photos site.

Introduction: "We transfer photos, 8mm film, and video into quality
DVDs."

Conclusion: "We'd like to help you preserve your special memories."
(after explaining about the company, its guarantee, and its contact
information)

■ **Consider links to short online articles.** You may want to include
Frequently Asked Questions (FAQs) and Tips on your website. On the
Keepsake Photos site, the FAQ might answer questions about how to mail
the photos or videos and Tips might tell readers how to safeguard their
photos and videos.

- **Include essential information.** A home page should include the following information:
  - Contact information telling readers how to contact the owner of the site—e-mail, phone number, and/or street address
  - A logo or graphic that helps "brand" the site, creating product and company recognition at a glance
  - An About section describing the organization and providing some of its history
  - A system of navigation to help readers find their way around the site
  - A date (usually at the bottom) showing the last time the site was updated
  - Any disclaimers or privacy/security statements—what kind of information may be collected by the site and what monitoring systems may be in use to track information

Figure 7.5 shows the home page of Hold Fast Custom Builders, a small construction business. The page has the characteristics of an effective home page: a logo, a slogan, and essential information.

Blogs

Similar to a journal or diary, a **blog** (short for *weblog*) is a website with periodic commentary or news posted in reverse chronological order. A blogger is usually an individual with special knowledge or passion about a topic. Because viewers can respond, a blog is not only a source of information, but also an online community. In addition, a blog may include links and graphics.

There are as many blogs as there are content areas. A doctor posts her administrative struggles, a news reporter posts commentaries about the day's events, and a businessperson posts progress on the development of a new product. The writing style used on a blog is informal. As with any web material, blogs should be read with a critical eye. Some blog "conversations" provide current, credible, and insightful news. Others merely vent and ramble.

Complete the *Critiquing a Web Page* worksheet available at www.cengage.com/school/bcomm/techwtg. Click the link for Chapter 7; then click Data Files.

FOCUS

Figure 7.5

Contrast this simpler home page of a small business with the more complex home pages of larger organizations. This page may be simple, but it achieves its purpose.

TEACH

The home page may include links to a blog, FAQ, wiki, or discussion forum. Through these links, the home page becomes a collaborative tool.

Ask students how a blog is like a journal. In both, entries are made periodically. Entries are personal viewpoints, are informal, and are in reverse chronological order.

ENRICH

Remind students that journals and diaries formed one of the first forms of literature for the United States: *Diary of Samuel Sewall* (1652–1730), *Journal of John Winthrop* (1588–1649), and *Secret Diary of William Byrd of Westover* (1674–1744).

Figure 7.5 Example of a Home Page

Many sites host blogs, including Livejournal.com, blogger.com, and Techcrunch.com, along with major search engines such as MSN and Yahoo!.

To post a credible blog,

- Write blogs on topics you know about or about which you are passionate.
- Post regularly so that you build up a following, but do not overwhelm readers with too many posts.
- Create a short name that is easy to remember.
- Communicate with people on other blogs.
- Post meaningful, accurate blogs.
- Make your blog site attractive and interesting.
- Let your personality come through.
- Use **RSS** (Really Simple Syndication), standardized web feed formats to send the content of your blog directly to your readers. By using RSS, your readers will not have to visit your website to get updates.

FAQ

FAQ, pronounced *fak* or *f-a-q*, is an acronym for *Frequently Asked Question* (and *Frequently Answered Question*). A FAQ is what its name implies—questions asked often enough to warrant publishing so that other people can benefit from the answers. The assumption is that if a sufficient number of people have asked these questions, the questions must be common enough that others will have the questions too. FAQs are found all over the Internet. There is even an archive of FAQs at www.faqs.org/faqs.

Communication Dilemma

Julian Mills, a local politician and long-standing member of the Sandhills community, is on the Board of Trustees for Hope Center Hospital. He maintains a blog on his political initiatives, including the construction of the hospital's new cardiac wing. So far, he has expressed concern over the cost of the wing, the many delays, and some decisions about equipment. Overall, though, he supports the construction and is proud to have played a role in such a state-of-the art facility. A local reporter, Sabrina Klein, also keeps a blog about area events. Her husband happens to be an architect for the company contracted to build the cardiac wing. In her blog, Sabrina criticizes Julian, saying, "Mr. Mills . . . nitpicks about decisions and micromanages the day-to-day operations of the board. He knows nothing about construction and is clearly pushing a political agenda. He should step down from the board." Julian, understandably angered by the remarks, wonders what, if anything, he should do about the remarks.

Think Critically

What factors should Mr. Mills consider before he decides whether to respond?

You may want to use a FAQ for a website. Or you can post a FAQ on Yahoo! Answers, a site that hosts a variety of FAQs maintained periodically by authorities in various fields. If you routinely respond to customer service calls, written FAQs can help you answer questions about your product.

To compile a FAQ,

- Determine the most frequently asked questions. What do your readers ask? What do your customers ask? What do they want to know?

- Ask the question the way your readers will ask the question. Use the readers' terms—the readers' vocabulary.

- Set up a consistent format to set questions apart from the answers— perhaps boldfacing questions and providing adequate white space between questions and answers.

- Keep the answers relatively short. One or two sentences is preferable, but no more than a couple of paragraphs. Embed links to other pages on your site or to external sites for more detailed information.

- Update your FAQ periodically to keep the information current.

- Organize questions in order of importance or in chronological order for your reader.

- Proofread for clarity and correctness to keep your FAQ professional.

- On a website, place the FAQ where your readers can easily find it—in links on the side, at the bottom, near Help items, or close to information about which readers may be curious.

©PricelessPhotos, 2009/Used under license from Shutterstock.com

Wikis

A **wiki** uses special software that allows a number of users to collaboratively author web pages, usually according to a set of guidelines. Some wikis, such as Wikipedia and BookShelved, provide open access to anyone. Other wikis are closed, and only people granted access can contribute. Medpedia, for example, is a medical wiki that allows only professionals to edit content. A wiki can foster creative collaboration for a process, such as programming code. Writers use wikis, too, to post articles and allow other writers to edit them.

If you are interested in participating in a wiki,

- Read several articles so you know how the text is written and edited.

- Become familiar with the process for editing articles in the wiki.

- Keep your tone polite and civil—even when you disagree.

- Keep the tone neutral and the information factual.

- Work toward consensus as you edit.

- Include references for information from other sources.

Discussion Forums

Operating like an electronic bulletin board, a **discussion forum** is a place where users can discuss items of interest or get specific questions answered. On the Apple website, for example, a discussion forum attempts to answer questions about Apple products and applications. A person who is having difficulty downloading iTunes might post a question and receive responses through this forum. Online discussion forums exist for nearly every topic imaginable—the stock market, art, architecture, business, family, science, and more. The major news networks post online discussion forums. In addition, forums can be found on Google Groups and are an integral part of online classes. Look for a discussion forum that meets your needs.

To interact with a discussion forum,

- Read other posts to see how people generally respond.

- Provide as much information as possible when posting a concern.

- Provide accurate information when responding to a concern.

- Think critically about others' responses. Not every response is credible.

- Be concise.

Whatever kind of text you write for the Web, keep in mind two guiding principles—the needs of your readers and the limited space on the screen. To keep readers engaged, design attractive sites that support your message and deliver valuable information. To help readers find the information they need, write text that can be scanned quickly. The tips below are sound advice for any technical document, but they are imperative for the web writer. Strive for a successful technical style by using:

- Concise wording.

- Short paragraphs.

- An inverted pyramid (main idea first).

- Meaningful headings and titles.

- Bulleted lists.

- Standard English.

⬤ STOP AND THINK

Name five types of writing assignments adapted especially for the Web. Choose two and describe them in detail.

CHAPTER 7
REVIEW

SUMMARY

1. When creating a web page, know how users read and interact with material, determine your purpose, define your audience, and find out the technology limitations of your audience.

2. When organizing and designing a web page, choose a system of internal links, create web pages that are easy to use and attractive, and keep the design consistent and accessible.

3. When writing web pages, create unique page titles, write to your audience, organize using an inverted pyramid, compile factual content, use original language, and construct scannable text.

4. When writing home pages, blogs, wikis, FAQs, or discussion forums, follow established protocols.

Checklist

- Have I defined my audience?

- Have I written web pages that adjust to the unusual way readers read them?

- Have I considered the technology limitations of my audience?

- Have I determined my purpose and included it in a slogan on the website?

- Do my text and graphics support my purpose?

- Have I organized my website using a workable system of internal links?

- Have I designed attractive web pages with easy-to-locate information for visitors to my site?

- Do my pages load quickly?

- Have I written text that uses unique page titles, is written directly to my audience, organizes material in an inverted pyramid, is factual, avoids clichés, and uses standard English?

- Have I written scannable text with short paragraphs, informative headings, lists, and keywords in the first 50 words?

- Have I followed standard protocol for my home page, blog, FAQ, wiki, and discussion forum?

CLOSE

Summary

Ask students to compile a FAQ for this chapter as a review.

CLOSE

Checklist

Ask students to use the checklist when they design web pages and write text for the Web.

REVIEW

For a review of the key terms in the chapter, provide students with the *Key Terms* worksheet available as a supplemental activity on the IRCD.

ASSESS

Build Your Foundation

1. a. We offer Spanish tutorials for the beginner as well as the more advanced Spanish student. Our program will help a traveler feel comfortable conversing on a variety of topics in a Spanish-speaking country. b. Homedezigns.com offers the latest living room, bedroom, and kitchen furniture in contemporary as well as traditional styles. We have lamps, vases, and art to match any décor. c. Help conserve water by taking showers instead of baths. Run your washer and dishwasher only when they are full. d. You usually need four to six months to find a job. However, you can speed up the process and increase your chances of success by sprucing up your resume, networking with others, and organizing your job search.

2. Answers will vary, but students should consider the type of business and an image to match the business.

3. Responses will vary but should be three paragraphs.

What is global warming? Energy from the sun heats the earth. Some of that energy is sent back into space in the form of infrared radiation. . . .

A problem occurs when the atmosphere is subjected to increasing amounts of carbon dioxide and other greenhouse gases. . . .

Global warming can drastically alter the climate. . . .

4. Students' lists will vary.

Build Your Foundation

1. Rewrite these sentences, breaking them into shorter sentences and deleting extra words.

   a. We offer Spanish tutorials and practice for the beginner as well as the intermediate Spanish learner on a variety of topics so a traveler can feel comfortable traveling in a Spanish-speaking country.

   b. Take time to visit our website at www.homedezigns.com to see the latest collection of living room, bedroom, and kitchen furniture along with accessories such as lamps, vases, and art—from contemporary to traditional.

   c. Because water conservation is important, there are many ways people can help conserve water, including taking showers instead of taking baths and running the washer and running the dishwasher only when they are full.

   d. Spruce up your resume, network with the right people, and organize your job search to increase your chances of finding a job so it does not take you the normal four to six months to find one.

2. Brainstorm possible slogans, color schemes, graphics, and links for one of these sites. Conduct research if you need to familiarize yourself with the type of business. Share your written plan with the class.

   a. Nehu's Chiropractic Care, new to the area, wants a site that describes services and teaches the public about the value of chiropractic care.

   b. Krischler's Insurance Services offers personal and commercial policies, including car, home, long-term care, life, and commercial, for a small community.

   c. Beach Getaway is a real estate agency specializing in ocean view rentals for family vacations.

   d. Eastern Music Company sells musical instruments to school bands.

   e. Helping Handz is a charity organization in North Dakota that collects winter coats for children in grades K–12.

3. Improve the following block of text by breaking it up into three paragraphs and shortening some of the sentences.

   Global warming—the explanation goes something like this: Energy from the sun heats the earth, and then some of that energy is sent back into space in the form of infrared radiation. A portion of that outgoing radiation, though, is blocked from escaping into space by the earth's relatively thin atmosphere—a good thing because the infrared radiation that remains stabilizes the earth's temperature. A problem occurs when the atmosphere, subjected to increasing amounts of carbon dioxide and other greenhouse gases, thickens to trap more of the sun's infrared energy, preventing its escape from Earth. More trapped energy raises global temperatures—thus the term *global warming.* Global warming can drastically alter the climate. The predictions are frightening: melting polar ice caps, rising ocean levels, category 5 hurricanes. Are these dire predictions true? Are we really in a period of global warming? The body of scientific evidence does suggest that global warming is a reality.

4. Go to About Wikipedia (http://en.wikipedia.org/wiki/Wikipedia:About) to learn more about this open source wiki. Make a list of what you learn.

Your Turn

1. Create a sketch of a home page on a topic of interest. Draw your page, cut pictures out of magazines, download clip art, write or key names of links, and come up with the slogan. If you are familiar with HTML code or a web authoring system such as Dreamweaver®, design the page yourself.

2. Find two websites—one that follows most of the guidelines presented in the chapter and one that does not. Write a one-page analysis explaining why one website is more effective than the other. Use bulleted lists to set up your comparison and introduce each list with a couple of sentences.

3. Write a FAQ on a topic of your choice. Choose from your school, your major, your job, or any topic with which you are familiar.

4. Use the topic below to practice the collaboration required by a wiki. Working with four of your classmates, enter the passage in a word processor. Send the file to each member of your group—perhaps over several days. Each person should find one or two errors and add one or two pieces of information to make the passage more interesting. Remember to provide references if you quote or introduce new information.

   Henry David Thoreau was born July 17, 1812, and died May 6 1862. He was an American poet, essayist, naturalist, and song writer. He was a strict abolitionist. His transcentral views can be seen in his lectures and most notably in his book *Weldene*. Perhaps his most influential work is "Civil Disobedience" which was inspired by his time spent in Portugal. "Civil Disobedience" influenced such political leaders as George Washington, Martin Luther King, and Mahatma Gradson.

5. For this mock wiki, work in groups of five. In your group, pass around the terms one at a time—perhaps over several days. Each person defines two terms and adds one or two pieces of information or deletes information that should be more accurate.

   | blog | wiki | breadcrumb trails | Wikipedia |
   | RSS | hyperlink | discussion forum | keywords |

6. Write a discussion response to these questions: How has the Internet helped you in your education? What have you learned from this chapter?

7. Go to Google Groups at http://groups.google.com. Join a discussion group that you find interesting. Respond using the strategies presented in the chapter. Print your responses and submit them to your instructor.

Community Connection

1. Write a FAQ about a topic related to your school or community—such as how to establish residency, how to join a community group, or how to select an area restaurant. Ask if your FAQ can be placed on the organization's website or place your FAQ in a central location such as a bulletin board.

2. Interview a blogger or a web designer. Ask about the challenges of blogging or designing a website. Write a summary of the interview.

3. Find someone in your community who has little Internet experience. Show that person how to conduct an online search. If necessary, meet at a public place that has computers and an Internet connection.

ASSESS

Your Turn

1. Home pages will vary, but they should be balanced, support an image, include a slogan, and provide links.

2. Responses will vary, but an ineffective website may be cluttered and unattractive. It may not include a slogan, graphics to support the message, or enough information on the home page. Effective websites follow most of the guidelines presented in the chapter.

3. FAQs should follow the guidelines presented in the chapter—popular questions, relatively short answers, and suggestions for links to additional information.

4. Documents will vary, but the goal is to produce a stronger, more accurate document than would have been possible with only one person writing it. The exercise will give students experience with collaborative writing. Errors include birth date July 12, 1817; not noted for song writing; had transcendental views; wrote *Walden;* inspired by time in jail, not Portugal; influenced Abraham Lincoln, not George Washington, and Mahatma Ghandi, not Gradson.

5. Wikis will vary. Encourage students to start with definitions as they remember them, then find more information about the terms.

6–7. Discussions should be short, informative, polite, and accurate.

ASSESS

Community Connection

1–3. Use these exercises so students can practice writing for the Web, learn more about those who write for the Web, and share their knowledge with others.

Informative Reports

Goals

- Write two types of summaries and an abstract
- Create a mechanism description with a visual
- Write a periodic report, a progress report, and a news release

Terms

- abstracts, p. 189
- dateline, p. 206
- embargo, p. 205
- fiscal year, p. 195
- hook, p. 203
- mechanism description, p. 192
- media, p. 201
- periodic reports, p. 195
- progress reports, p. 198
- PSAs, p. 201
- public relations, p. 201
- reporting period, p. 198
- spatial order, p. 193
- summary, p. 189

WRITE TO LEARN

Think about where you are on the path of your educational goals. Perhaps your career will require a two-year associate or a four-year bachelor's degree—or a master's or doctorate degree. Write several paragraphs answering these questions: What have you achieved toward reaching your educational goals? What do you still need to do to reach those goals? When will you reach your goals? What problems are you experiencing? Your audience can be your parents or guardians, a scholarship committee, or other people who have supported your educational career.

Focus on Informative Reports

Read the sample informative report on the next page and answer these questions:

- What is its purpose? Does the writer ask the reader to do anything?
- Can you determine the audience for whom this report was intended?
- What would make this report more useful and easier to read?
- In what fields might a report of this nature be needed?

What If?

- The readers were lacking in a basic science background?
- The subject of the technical description were an object, not a process?
- The process description were more complex and longer?
- The report were written in the future, when people no longer use or have access to incandescent bulbs?

Technical Process Description: How an Incandescent Lightbulb Works

When objects get very hot, they glow. This phenomenon, known as incandescence, is utilized in the lightbulb to convert electrical energy into light. An electric current passes from one contact to the other through a thin wire of tungsten in the bulb, called the filament. The current consists of electrons that move from the positive contact to the negative contact. As the electrons hit the atoms in the tungsten filament, they cause the atoms to vibrate and heat up. The filament heats to over 2500°C (over 4500°F), well below tungsten's melting point of 3410°C (6170°F). Because of this extreme temperature, the filament glows. The filament produces a broad spectrum of light with a peak wavelength around 1000 nanometers, which is in the infrared (meaning "below red") range of the electromagnetic spectrum. Infrared light cannot be seen, but it can be felt as heat. However, the broad emission spectrum of the bulb also extends into the visible range—to the reds, oranges, and yellows, which is the light that people see. An incandescent bulb appears more red-orange because the emission tapers off toward the shorter wavelengths of the visible range (i.e., green, blue, and violet). Because the peak of the emission is in the infrared range (and thus not visible), incandescent bulbs are not very efficient when compared to fluorescent bulbs, which emit most of their light in the visible range (and consequently do not get as hot). A typical 60-watt incandescent bulb emits only 6 watts of power as visible light. The rest is wasted as heat.

> Follows a chronological order; tells how the bulb works, not how to operate the bulb; uses specific measurements and technical vocabulary to explain the process accurately and precisely

Sample Technical Process Description: How an Incandescent Lightbulb Works

Source: Frank B. Meyers, University of California, Berkley

FOCUS

Focus on Informative Reports

Use the questions to encourage students to read the sample closely.

ASSESS

What If?

Use the questions to discuss how the sample would be different if the situation or audience changed.

Go to www.cengage.com/school/bcomm/techwtg for more detailed responses to these questions.

Writing@Work

Courtesy of Paige Heller

Paige Heller is a physical therapist at an outpatient orthopedic clinic in Sedona, Arizona. She treats patients daily and provides written documentation for each visit, including daily evaluation notes, periodic progress reports, and discharge summaries.

Paige's writing must be clear and concise, yet thorough and rich in detail. "A good physical therapy document needs to be readable by a varied audience that includes the patient, other physicians, and employers. These reports may also be used for legal purposes, so they must include large amounts of information in a small amount of writing."

To write a report that is brief and that contains all necessary information, Paige follows the "SOAP" formula for writing bulleted clinical notes. Each letter stands for its own bulleted item in the note:

- S stands for *subjective*—the first bullet states what the patient reports.
- O stands for *objective*—the second bullet states what the therapist observes and tests.
- A stands for *assessment*—the third bullet is an analysis of the S and O points.
- P stands for *plan*—the last bullet is a future/intended course of treatment.

Just as Paige writes her reports so they are useful for other practicing therapists and physicians, she must read others' reports in order to provide the most advanced and tested treatment possible. "Physical therapy is an evidence-based practice, which means we dictate our treatments according to the results of research and studies in the field. I frequently access online medical journals to review such reports. I also read physician reports of surgeries or diagnostics to better understand a patient's condition or injury." In other words, Paige's technical writing proficiency depends in part on her technical reading skills. In turn, other physical therapy professionals rely on Paige's technical writing ability, which is why accurate documentation is so important.

Think Critically

1. Why are the S and O bullets critical in Paige's physical therapy reports?

2. Why is the A bullet needed? Why is it important to assess the first two bullets?

Printed with permission of Paige Heller

GETTING STARTED ON INFORMATIVE REPORTS

Professionals in business and industry use specialized reports to convey information about their work. This chapter presents the most frequently used informative reports: summaries and abstracts, mechanism descriptions, progress and periodic reports, and news releases. These specialized reports use standard forms. Once you learn how to use them, you can develop reports using information from jobs or personal experience.

SUMMARY AND ABSTRACT

A **summary** is a condensed version of a document. When writing an essay, you generate details to develop or support a thesis and topic sentences. Summaries require writers to do the opposite: keep only general information and the most important details.

Abstracts are more condensed than summaries, often reducing documents to a thesis. The length depends on the audience's needs and expectations.

Some summaries and abstracts stand alone; others begin a longer technical document. By condensing the report's highlights before the audience reads the details, summaries save coworkers time. People at upper levels of an organization may choose to read only the summary sections of longer reports. They do so because their interest is in the big picture or health of the organization rather than the details or technical aspects of day-to-day operations.

Some employees use summaries to stay on top of the latest research and developments in their fields. These employees summarize publications in the career field as they emerge and file them for future reference.

Figure 8.1 on the next page is an article that an employee reads so that the employee can summarize it for his or her supervisor and files and for future reference. Figure 8.2 on page 191 contains two summaries and an abstract of the article in Figure 8.1.

To write a summary or an abstract:

1. When an oral presentation is given, take notes during the presentation or soon afterward. Thus, you are less likely to forget what the speaker said.

2. With a written document, read the document twice—or as many times as necessary to fully understand the content. As you read the second time, highlight the main ideas or cross out everything (all details) except the main ideas. Paraphrase main ideas. For longer summaries, choose a few important details to include. For abstracts, condense the paraphrased material.

3. In the summary's first sentence, include the thesis or main point of the document using your own words and sentence structure.

Warm Up

Recall the last movie or play you watched. How would you respond if a friend asked, "What was the show about?" Using what you remember about the show, write the answer you would give to your friend.

TYPICAL READER

Any person, whether manager, technician, or client/customer, who wants access to an overview of more detailed information, whether a company report, a journal article, a book, or another document.

WRITER'S FOCUS

Clearly presenting major ideas and, when needed, essential supporting information in a readable manner to enable users to understand the central points of a longer document.

ENRICH

Abstracts and summaries provide a valuable opportunity for students to write across the curriculum. Ask instructors to provide articles or have students select chapters or articles from other classes to summarize.

Have students think of uses for summaries. Some possibilities: a discussion with friends about what happened at last night's game, a television anchor's report of the news, a qualification statement in a resume, the body of a letter of application, a book report, and an answer to a discussion question.

RETEACH

Point out that an effective summary covers all of the major ideas in a document. Summarizing only a few major ideas is not adequate. Remind students that the details in a summary depend on the audience's expectations.

FOCUS

Figure 8.1

Encourage students to read the article as if it were a textbook reading assignment. Even if the student is not interested in agronomy, he or she can read actively and learn from the process of summarizing.

A Faster Way to Clean Roots

Agronomists, plant pathologists, and botanists—to name a few—are interested in the effects of soil and crop management practices on crop root systems. But before they can begin their studies, scientists usually have to spend time and energy cleaning soil off the roots. A new invention by the Agricultural Research Service (ARS) may help.

Soil scientist Joseph G. Benjamin, of ARS's Central Great Plains Research Station in Akron, Colorado, has created a root washer with a rotary design to automate and speed up the process. Other devices require more attention from the operator. The new device can clean up to 24 samples at a time, more than previous washers.

The washing cycle starts when a technician places a sample of soil and roots in the machine's chambers. As the sample rotates within the machine, it is dipped into and sprayed with water to remove the soil. Mud exits from the back of the machine. The cycle takes about 90 minutes, and the roots, which are not damaged by the machine, are then ready for study. "The root washer works well to easily and quickly separate plant roots and other organic materials from the soil," Benjamin says. He also points out that compared to other washers, his device can wash larger samples.

Once the roots are clean, a flatbed scanner is used to digitize their images for scientists to analyze with computer software. Through mathematical equations, Benjamin is able to determine the surface area of the roots contained in the sample. As Benjamin points out, "The human eye is still the best discriminator at determining what materials are roots and what are not." Benjamin's root washer is an enlarged version of a weed-seed washer invented by weed scientist Lori J. Wiles and others in ARS's Water Management Unit at Fort Collins, Colorado. Before her invention, nothing was available commercially to quickly wash soil from seeds.

Figure 8.1 Article to Be Summarized

Source: Elstein, David. United States. Dept. of Agriculture. "A Faster Way to Clean Roots." *Agricultural Research:* 2004 (52.1). Web. 10 Dec. 2009.

LONG SUMMARY OF "A FASTER WAY TO CLEAN ROOTS"

In "A Faster Way to Clean Roots," David Elstein announces a technological breakthrough for people who study plants and crop management. While scientists normally use considerable time cleaning dirt from plant roots by hand before the plants can be studied, a machine created by soil scientist Joseph G. Benjamin offers help.

Benjamin developed a device to rotate and clean 24 plants at once, decreasing the need for scientists to handle the plants and speeding the process. During washing, the machine dunks and shoots water at the roots but does not harm or change the root system. The water takes the mud with it when it drains from the machine.

When the clean roots are removed from the new machine, Benjamin's device uses a flatbed scanner, computer software, and mathematical equations to calculate the surface area of the roots. However, the inventor notes that the machine is not as effective as the human eye at distinguishing roots from other materials.

Benjamin based the design of his invention on a weed-seed washer invented by scientist Lori J. Wiles and colleagues at the ARS Water Management Research Unit in Fort Collins, Colorado.

SHORT SUMMARY OF "A FASTER WAY TO CLEAN ROOTS"

In "A Faster Way to Clean Roots," David Elstein announces a technological breakthrough for people who study plants and crop management. Before soil scientist Joseph G. Benjamin's creation of a machine to clean soil and organic matter from plant roots, scientists had to painstakingly remove the dirt from the root system of plants they wanted to study. Benjamin's invention does not damage the roots, and it mechanizes and speeds the preparation. Compared to other machines, Benjamin's rotary-design wash cycle prepares 24 samples for study faster and with less handling. When the plants are clean, Benjamin's device uses a flatbed scanner, computer software, and mathematical equations to calculate the roots' surface area.

ABSTRACT OF "A FASTER WAY TO CLEAN ROOTS"

In "A Faster Way to Clean Roots," David Elstein announces a technological breakthrough for people who study plants and crop management: soil scientist Joseph G. Benjamin's creation of a machine to clean soil and organic matter from plant roots without damaging the roots.

Figure 8.2 Examples of Summaries and Abstract

Figure 8.2

Compare the summaries and the abstract with the original. Note that more information is included in the summaries but that both have the same main idea. Help students see how writers identify main ideas. Remind students that a main idea is the same as a thesis statement or a topic sentence.

RETEACH

Remind students that a summary is often the first part of a long report. Sometimes summaries stand alone.

ENRICH

Students should know the difference between general and specific information. For practice, give them lists of words: *car, Toyota, red, vehicle,* and *sunroof.* Ask students to order the words from general to specific (*vehicle, car, Toyota, red Toyota, red Toyota with sunroof*). Students also can practice finding topic sentences in their textbooks.

Reproduce paragraphs on transparencies. Ask students to cross out the details. Then ask them what is left—the main ideas.

4. Make clear what you are summarizing. With an article, introduce the source in the first sentence by including the title and author's name. For a speech or meeting, credit the speaker in the opening sentence.

5. Decide whether your audience needs a few details or only main ideas. For long summaries, include only details that are especially important. For short summaries, leave out details. For abstracts, include only the most important general ideas. Be concise. Reduce the original document to the main idea in a few sentences.

6. Keep your summary information proportional to the original. If the author spent four paragraphs on one topic and two paragraphs on another, your summary should give proportional time and emphasis. For example, in your summary or abstract, do not include more information from the two-paragraph topic than from the four-paragraph topic.

7. Write in present tense.

8. Paraphrase; do not copy word for word.

9. Quote sparingly, if at all, and use quotation marks correctly.

10. Provide transitions to keep the summary from sounding choppy.

Do *not* give your opinion. A summary or an abstract should be objective.

 STOP AND THINK

If a summary includes three of an article's five main points, is it effective? Why or why not?

MECHANISM DESCRIPTION

A **mechanism description** describes the main parts of a device or machine. It explains what the purpose of the mechanism and overall design is, what the parts are, what they look like, and what their function is.

Mechanism descriptions are used in catalogs, instruction manuals, and employee training. Examples of mechanisms in the workplace include car parts, furniture, kitchen tools, doorstops, pencil sharpeners, and more sophisticated machines such as an engine and a DVD player. Mechanism descriptions are often included with instructions in product packaging.

Consumers can find a mechanism description in a manual that comes with new equipment, such as a computer or can opener. This description tells what the parts are, how they fit together, and what their functions are. Technicians and operators use the description to become familiar with the characteristics of the machine and to troubleshoot problems. New employees use a mechanism description to learn job responsibilities and safety procedures. Decision makers use mechanism descriptions to reach informed decisions, perhaps comparing current equipment with equipment proposed for purchase.

Figure 8.3 on the following page is a mechanism description that a community college electronics student produced to demonstrate his understanding of an everyday object that people use. The audience for the report was the instructor, other electronics students, and anyone curious about how things work.

To write a mechanism description,

1. Take notes, describing every part in detail. Assume that you are on the telephone. You must describe a mechanism that the listener has not seen.

2. Use **spatial order.** That is, explain the parts from left to right, right to left, top to bottom, bottom to top, or whatever pattern is logical.

3. Open with an overall physical description of the mechanism, a statement that identifies its general purpose (what it is designed to do), and a preview of its parts.

4. Divide the mechanism into its parts and discuss each part under a separate heading. Use proper names of the parts. Place headings in the same order you used in the preview list.

5. Provide a precise physical description of the parts. Include size, color, location, and material (what the mechanism is made of).

6. Include the purpose or function of each part.

7. Provide a graphic of the mechanism. Include exploded (enlarged) views of parts that are too small to be easily seen. Add callouts to label each part.

8. Use active voice whenever possible.

Do *not* explain how to operate the mechanism. Instead, describe what it does, what it looks like, what its parts are, and what they look like and do.

Blend Images/JupiterImages

FOCUS

Figure 8.3

The introduction to this
mechanism description
describes the purpose and
function of the machine, refers
readers to the graphic, and
previews parts to be discussed
in detail.

ONGOING ASSESSMENT

Stop and Think

The writer should use *1/2" in
diameter* because it is more
precise. Being precise and clear
is essential when writing effective
mechanism descriptions. Spatial
order is used in mechanism
descriptions.

Introduction: a general overview of the bulb, its purpose, the diagram, and the parts, which become headings for the remainder of the report

Basic parts identified in callouts in the diagram

Parts described in detail using precise measurements and numerical specifications

Incandescent Lightbulb

The 60-watt bulb in your kitchen fixture is a glass enclosure that illuminates a small area—roughly an 8' x 8' area—with 960 lumens (photometric units of light output) when an electric current passes through the filament. Figure 1 shows a 60-watt incandescent lightbulb that consists of four parts: glass bulb, inert gas, filament, and base.

Filament — Glass bulb

Inert gas —

Figure 1. 60-watt incandescent lightbulb

Bulb

The pear-shaped bulb is 2.5" in diameter at the thickest part and tapers to 1.0" in diameter at the smallest part near the base. The inside of the glass is coated with a diffusing material made of phosphor to give the glass its white appearance and to soften light, thereby reducing shadows. The wattage (60 watts) and voltage (120V) are stamped on top of the bulb in black print.

Gas

Inside the bulb, an inert gas (e.g., argon) replaces most of the air. The inert gas slows the evaporation of the filament, thus prolonging the life of the lamp.

Filament

The filament is made of tungsten, which is drawn into a fine wire only 0.001" in diameter. The tungsten wire is a meter or more of wire coiled or double-wound into a 2 cm or smaller coil. The filament is welded to the power leads in the base of the bulb that are embedded in a 1" x 1/8" cylindrical glass structure fused to the glass bulb. The tungsten filament heats to over 2500°C (4500°F) and produces the light.

Base

The base contains two electrical contacts and insulation. The base is a 1" threaded aluminum circular screw thread (resembling a wood screw) that can be screwed into the light socket of a fixture without falling out. Two contacts running up either side of the glass mount hold the filament. An electrical foot contact that looks like a 1/8" nail head is at the center of the base on the bottom. The metal contact conducts the electrical current into the bulb, activating the tungsten filament.

Figure 8.3 Example of a Mechanism Description

⬡ **STOP AND THINK**

In a mechanism description, should a writer describe a metal disk as (a) about the size of a penny or (b) 1/2" in diameter? What organizational pattern is used in mechanism descriptions?

PERIODIC REPORTS

Periodic reports explain accomplishments for all projects of a work group or of an entire organization over a specified time period. For instance, when you listened to your governor make a State of the State address or the President make a State of the Union address, you heard a periodic report. These speeches explore the many ongoing projects of the state or nation for the year. Periodic reports may cover different periods: a week (weekly), a month (monthly), three months (quarterly), or six months (semiannually).

Businesses and nonprofit organizations use periodic reports to inform shareholders, clients, vendors, donors, and employees of the organization's accomplishments and challenges. Figure 8.4 on the following two pages is an example of a periodic report prepared by a student intern.

To write periodic reports,

1. Consider all activities and accomplishments of the organization for the specified time period. Begin by noting the time period. Are you sharing information about the last two weeks, the past month, or the fiscal year? (A **fiscal year** is the operating year, such as the academic year, which often runs from July 1 through June 30.)

2. Meet your audience's needs. What are the audience's concerns, history with the writer and the project or organization, and roles?

3. Organize tasks so you can report them logically. Once lists are complete, categories of tasks become subheadings under a major heading. Organize so the reader can find important information easily.

4. Format for the audience. Many longer periodic reports are manuscript-formatted, appearing like an essay or a book with a title. These reports offer formality and distance appropriate for a diverse audience. When written for an internal reader, a short periodic report may be formatted as a memo. For an external reader, the report may be formatted as a letter.

5. For the introduction, develop an overview that briefly presents the highlights of the report. Mention each idea included in a major heading. Also state the reporting period, the time for which the document describes activities or progress.

6. For the body, compose a section for each activity category or type of work undertaken during the reporting period, with section headings and sometimes subheadings organized from most important to least important. For instance, the monthly activity report of a U.S. Navy recruiter might include the following work areas (and headings): Job Fairs, School-Based Meetings, Office Conferences, and Public Speaking Events. Under each heading, the recruiter describes, from most to least important, accomplishments during the reporting period. In the rest of the report, the recruiter may note problems encountered.

7. In the conclusion, highlight any key ideas and refer to the next report.

FOCUS

Figure 8.4

Use the report to review its elements: an introduction that provides an overview, body sections that cover all of the work areas of the organization and are identified by headings and subheadings, and a conclusion that previews the coming report.

Gives highlights of entire report

Provides as many specifics as possible; is organized from most important information to least important information

Memorandum

To:	Miss Helen Wooten, Adviser
From:	Ove Jensen, Student Intern *OJ*
Date:	March 5, 20—
Subject:	Job Shadowing a Radiologic Technologist at Grove Park Hospital

February has been a productive period in my second month of job-shadowing Ms. Laticia Garcia, radiologic technologist at Grove Park Hospital. The month was filled with action and variety. I observed work in the Neonatal Intensive Care Unit, the MRI (Magnetic Resonance Imaging) section, and the Radiology Lab. In addition, I completed one of the three research papers required for earning academic credit.

Neonatal Intensive Care Unit

During my first session with Ms. Garcia last month, which took place in the Neonatal Intensive Care Unit, I watched radiologists work with medically fragile premature and newborn babies. Ms. Garcia used an ultrasound machine to obtain images of the brains of two patients.

I further observed Ms. Garcia use a portable X-ray device to take film of the chest and abdomen of another young patient. Some of the infants in this unit weigh as little as 1 pound and are connected to many pieces of support equipment, such as respirators and heart monitors. These patients present unique challenges to radiologic technologists.

MRI Section

Because Ms. Garcia is a rotation supervisor, I was able to observe the operation of the MRI machine while she worked in that area. This room-sized piece of imaging equipment serves a variety of purposes in diagnosing patients' problems. During the four hours I shadowed Ms. Garcia in the MRI section, she worked with the following patients:

- An 82-year-old stroke patient

- A 14-year-old automobile crash victim with head trauma

- A quarterback for the university football team with a knee injury

- A 36-year-old woman suffering back pain

Figure 8.4 Periodic Report

ENRICH

Collect annual reports from nonprofit and for-profit organizations to share with students as examples of periodic reports. Check with taxpayer-supported hospitals, utilities, and schools. You also can request annual reports from corporations (or stockholders). Determine how the reports meet the audience's needs for information. For example, the annual report of a for-profit organization begins by answering the reader's first question: How is my investment doing?

8. Check for accuracy, particularly in statistics and names.

9. Use lists, numbered or set in columns, whenever possible to ensure easier reading.

10. Divide long discussions into paragraphs to reflect groups of ideas.

Periodic report writers should *not* include their opinions, instead providing facts and allowing readers to draw their own conclusions.

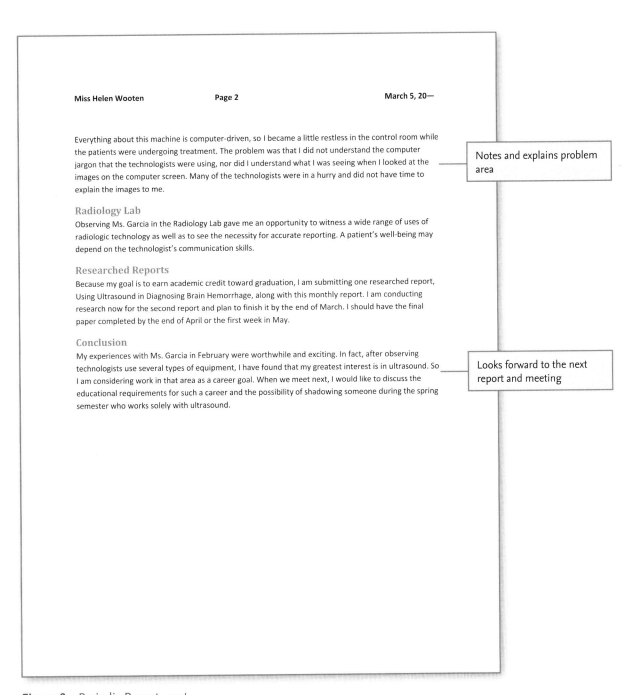

Everything about this machine is computer-driven, so I became a little restless in the control room while the patients were undergoing treatment. The problem was that I did not understand the computer jargon that the technologists were using, nor did I understand what I was seeing when I looked at the images on the computer screen. Many of the technologists were in a hurry and did not have time to explain the images to me.

Notes and explains problem area

Radiology Lab

Observing Ms. Garcia in the Radiology Lab gave me an opportunity to witness a wide range of uses of radiologic technology as well as to see the necessity for accurate reporting. A patient's well-being may depend on the technologist's communication skills.

Researched Reports

Because my goal is to earn academic credit toward graduation, I am submitting one researched report, Using Ultrasound in Diagnosing Brain Hemorrhage, along with this monthly report. I am conducting research now for the second report and plan to finish it by the end of March. I should have the final paper completed by the end of April or the first week in May.

Conclusion

My experiences with Ms. Garcia in February were worthwhile and exciting. In fact, after observing technologists use several types of equipment, I have found that my greatest interest is in ultrasound. So I am considering work in that area as a career goal. When we meet next, I would like to discuss the educational requirements for such a career and the possibility of shadowing someone during the spring semester who works solely with ultrasound.

Looks forward to the next report and meeting

Figure 8.4 Periodic Report, *cont.*

 **STOP AND THINK**

What three types of information are usually included in the introduction of a periodic report?

FOCUS

Warm Up

Use the Warm Up to introduce progress reports as one type. The sender is the school (provides grades and academic credits), and the receiver is the student (earns the grades). Students in elementary school receive separate marks for behavior and penmanship, while college students' grades may not be influenced by their behavior.

PROGRESS REPORTS

Like periodic reports, **progress reports** are documents that report progress for a period of time. Unlike periodic reports, which cover all of an organization's work, a progress report describes what has been done during a specified time on only one project, such as work on the construction of a building. A progress report covers in detail all achievements as well as plans for the upcoming reporting period toward completing one project.

Anyone in an organization may need to report progress made on a project. Readers may use information in a progress report to make decisions, to take actions, or to file for future reference. Figure 8.5 shows a progress report.

To write a progress report:

1. Organize a progress report to answer the readers' most important questions first. Use the following outline to plan for progress reports. Under each heading, the writer may add subheadings if several ideas will be covered in that section.

HEADING IN REPORT	WHAT THAT SECTION COVERS
Introduction	Report topic, purpose, and reporting period
Work Completed	What has been done
Work Scheduled	What needs to be done
Problems/Projections	What has gone wrong and when the work will be finished

2. In the opening or introductory section of the progress report,

   ■ Name the project.

   ■ Indicate the **reporting period,** which is the time the report covers.

   ■ State the purpose of the report (to tell readers the status of the project).

3. Use *I* or *we*—first person—where appropriate. You take responsibility for your actions and opinions by using *I*. Using *I or we* is not only acceptable, but also encouraged.

4. In the Work Completed section,

   ■ Note again the time period you cover. (This is optional; if it is included, it usually appears beside the heading or in the opening sentence of the section.)

   ■ Use past tense verbs.

   ■ Use subheadings (to separate tasks) or bulleted lists. When three or more tasks or topics are included in this section, subheadings are necessary. When only one or two tasks are included, subheadings are optional.

TYPICAL READER

Anyone inside or outside the writer's organization needing information on progress toward completion of a task.

WRITER'S FOCUS

Clearly describing achievements and plans toward completing a task in a standard organizational plan.

TEACH

Progress reports typically include the following topics or headings: Work Completed, Work Scheduled, and Problems/ Projections.

To: Yearbook Staff Members

From: Yearbook Staff Trip Committee

Date: February 1, 20—

Subject: Progress Report 3: Planning for Trip to Disney World

Because our yearbook staff trip to Disney World is less than two months away, we are working hard to make an enjoyable adventure possible. This report outlines the accomplishments, the work remaining, and one problem encountered during January.

WORK COMPLETED (January 1–February 1, 20—)

We are marking a few things off the to-do list. With our current level of enthusiasm, we will get there.

Finances and Reservations

The staff sponsored two doughnut sales to add $350 to the travel fund.

Three buses from the White Goose Line costing $800 each have been reserved. In addition, reservations have been made for three nights at the Disney Dunes Hotel and a deposit of $500 paid to the hotel.

Equipment

Because university policy requires insurance for the school-owned cameras and computers we will need, we have purchased a replacement value policy from Lunden Insurance to cover the time of our trip.

WORK SCHEDULED

The remaining responsibilities are earning the rest of the money and making additional reservations.

Finances

The fund balance now contains $9,675 of the $11,000 we need for the trip. Five other fund-raising projects have been scheduled. However, if the future projects are as successful as the last two, we may raise the remaining $1,325 after only three projects have been completed.

Reservations

We will order two-day passes for Disney World and one-day tickets for Sea World next week. Also, Mr. Zhao will make reservations for the Yearbook Banquet at Waterside Restaurant in Orlando.

PROBLEMS/PROJECTIONS

The University Board has agreed to consider our request to be excused from classes early on the day we leave. Otherwise, we cannot reach Orlando before three o'clock in the morning. If we arrive in the middle of the night, we will probably spend the day planned for Disney World catching up on sleep. We might think of changing the schedule if the board denies our request. Other plans are proceeding as expected, and we should have all work for the trip completed by March 16, two weeks before departure.

Figure 8.5 Internal Progress Report

Indicates that this is the third progress report on this project; notes the report topic

Describes the project being reported on, gives the reporting period, and states the purpose of the report

Covers what has been done on the project; includes the reporting period

Includes subheadings if the work accomplished falls under two or more categories

Covers work yet to be done

Explains any difficulties that may affect the project; gives a revised completion date if problems have caused delay

FOCUS

Figure 8.5

Use the figure to discuss memo format for internal readers; optional introduction; headings and subheadings; standard organizational plan; statement of reporting period with Work Completed; and Problems/ Projections section.

Communication Dilemma

James Berry, a pediatric occupational therapist, is tempted to give a parent a glowing report even though the 3-year-old patient is not making significant improvement in therapy sessions. Mr. Berry likes the parent and does not want to add to the parent's stress.

Think Critically

What are possible effects of misinformation in Mr. Berry's reports?

The U.S. Food and Drug Administration (FDA) publishes a website that contains links to press releases of the past decade. You will find everything from food and drug research to biologics and radiation protection.

Go to the NET Bookmark for Chapter 8. Find a news release that interests you and print it. Write several paragraphs to explain if and how it uses the guidelines for effective news releases.

www.cengage.com/school/bcomm/techwtg

■ Provide sufficient details and explanations about each job completed. Because your reader is probably most concerned about what you have done on the project, ensure that this section is clear and accurate. Place your most important ideas first. After all, this is your opportunity to tell what you have achieved.

5. In the Work Scheduled section,

■ Tell your audience what work needs to be done in the next reporting period.

■ Use future tense verbs.

■ Separate and emphasize each major task or job with subheadings, as you did in the Work Completed section. Remember to use subheadings when you have three or more tasks. Otherwise, subheadings are optional.

6. In the Problems section,

■ Describe any obstacles to completing the job. Inform the reader of anything that has affected the quality or quantity of work.

■ Either list and number or describe these problems in paragraphs.

■ Be honest and direct.

■ Report just the facts unless you need to assign responsibility for problems. Remember that finger-pointing can be counterproductive.

7. In the Projections section, give readers a new completion date if problems have stalled the project so that the original date cannot be met.

● STOP AND THINK

While both periodic and progress reports are issued periodically or in set increments of time, what is the difference between the two reports?

NEWS RELEASES

News releases, also called press releases, are reports of events or facts prepared for the **media,** which are systems or means of mass communication. The goal of the release is to inform the public of, for example, an employee promotion or a company expansion.

One type of press release is the public service announcement (PSA). **PSAs** differ from other news releases in that they present facts beneficial to the public. PSAs, for example, announce Red Cross blood drives, city council meetings, fund-raisers, and other public events. People and organizations send news releases to the media to share information with the public.

In many large organizations, **public relations,** the communication between a company and the outside world, is handled by departments that write news releases to help the company maintain a positive image. For instance, if a company executive is involved in a scandal, the public relations staff may prepare a news release to present the company's view and restore public confidence.

In smaller organizations without public relations departments, any employee may write a news release. The maintenance director might write a release describing the company's recycling efforts, a retail manager might cover the store's planned expansion, and a volunteer group's administrative assistant might outline the organization's upcoming fund-raising project.

Because the writer sends the release to select news agencies, the first readers are editors and news directors. They decide whether the news release will run. If the information is newsworthy and the release is well written so that little editing is required, the chance that it will be published increases. Other influential factors include space and time constraints.

If the release is published, the second audience is the public. The public is anyone who reads a newspaper or magazine, watches television, uses the Internet, or listens to the radio. Specialized media agencies receive news releases targeting a particular audience, so the second audience might also be a select group.

For instance, you are probably familiar with television stations that target specific people: MTV targets music lovers; TNN attracts country music fans; CNN focuses on people interested in world, economic, and political news; and the Disney Channel targets children. Audiences are looking for the same thing—timely and interesting information.

On the next page, Figure 8.6 shows a news release with a triangle indicating the part of the release an editor chose to publish. The last two paragraphs, which contained the least important information, were cut.

To write a news release,

1. Begin by analyzing the audience. Consider the editor or news director as well as the public.

2. Answer the classic Reporter's Questions: Who? What? When? Where? Why? and How? With answers to those questions, you have the most important information to include in the news release.

TEACH

Remind students to check their prewriting notes for accurate figures, including dates, to make sure numbers are not transposed.

FOCUS

Figure 8.6

This document clearly shows the importance of careful organization. Depending on how much space (for print media) or time (for audio and video media) the editor has, he or she might cut any or all of the last three paragraphs. The editor might use only the first paragraph, which contains the essential news. A poorly written or poorly organized release might not be used at all.

Use the figure to discuss organization and to show that editors do not always publish the entire release. Therefore, the writer needs to place the most important ideas near the beginning of the release, where they are less likely to be cut.

ENRICH

After brainstorming current events in school, the community, or the world, ask students to select one event. Have them write a news release opening about that event, including a hook and answers to the Reporter's Questions. Compare students' responses. Encourage positive responses by selecting the best elements from each release. Then ask the class to use the best elements in one draft they create together.

Complete the *Reorganizing an Ineffective News Release* worksheet available at www.cengage.com/school/bcomm/techwtg. Click the link for Chapter 8; then click Data Files.

STERLING
Public Information Office

City of Sterling
Office of the Mayor
1156 West McGill Street
Sterling, IL 61081-1908
Phone: 815-555-0197
Fax: 815-555-0177

NEWS RELEASE

Contact: Adam Riggs, Mayor's Office
815.555.0197
ariggs@city_of_sterling_il.gov

August 23, 20—

For Immediate Release

ROLLER ART DONATES SKATE PARK TO CITY

STERLING, IL — Roller Art has donated $100,000 to Sterling for the development of a park especially designed for in-line and roller-skating enthusiasts. The park will feature two oval tracks for straightforward skating and another area with five ramps for trick skating.

The 2.45-acre park site is located three blocks west of the city office quad. Roller Art deeded this undeveloped land to the city two years ago.

Construction on the property is expected to begin within the month, and Mayor Manuella Huerta says that the park, to be named Roller Royale, will be open by early summer.

Robert Nowicki, spokesperson for Roller Art, said that his company is happy to be able to give back to the community that has helped Roller Art become successful. Roller Art employs 48 people who design and manufacture roller skates.

Roller Art has a history of giving to Sterling. In its nine years of doing business in the community, the company has donated a total of $425,000 to the city and an equal amount to local nonprofit groups.

The local company has the top-selling in-line skates on the market, Rold World. Rold World, developed after years of research, combines speed with the maximum in directional control.

-30-

Figure 8.6 Model News Release Cut by Editor

Figure 8.7 shows an illustration of this idea-packed opening for a news release. Notice where the Reporter's Questions are addressed.

3. Beyond the Reporter's Questions, ask yourself these questions: (a) What will interest my audience? (b) What will grab their attention? (c) What would they ask if they could?

4. Plan for accuracy. Check your prewriting notes for accuracy in the following:

   ■ Facts

   ■ Numbers and statistics

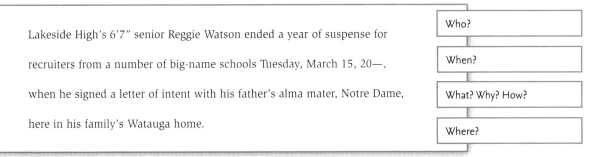

Lakeside High's 6'7" senior Reggie Watson ended a year of suspense for recruiters from a number of big-name schools Tuesday, March 15, 20—, when he signed a letter of intent with his father's alma mater, Notre Dame, here in his family's Watauga home.

| Who? |
| When? |
| What? Why? How? |
| Where? |

Figure 8.7 Reporter's Questions in News Release Opening

- Names
- Locations
- Quotations
- Completeness ("the whole truth")

With correct text, releases will have a greater chance of being published.

5. Plan for credibility. Exaggerations are overstatements or additions beyond the truth that can ruin a person's credibility. Instead, use information that can be verified. Avoid superlatives such as *the best, the fastest,* and *the worst* unless you can document or prove the statement. If your release opens with "R. J. Birch, the fastest 10K runner in the state," make sure you have her race times or other proof of your statement.

6. Compose the headline carefully because it will be read first. Include an active verb. Use present tense for current events, past tense for events already concluded, and future tense for scheduled activities. For example, the headline HALIFAX ACADEMY TO HOST STAR TREK CONVENTION uses an active verb that indicates future time (*to host*) because the event has not yet occurred. Be aware that your news release will compete with others for space or airtime (time to deliver a news story). Thus, the headline is your chance to make a positive first impression on the reader.

7. Open the body of the release with a **hook**—catchy wording or an idea that attracts attention. Dynamic wording or an intriguing idea seizes the audience's attention. Below are hooks used to open news releases.

- The nets are still hanging in Memorial Coliseum after last night's City League upset, but only because the Knights expect to return for them during the playoffs.

- When 600 first-year students show up for orientation at Schantz College on Saturday, they will receive something besides their dorm assignments.

- The Easter Bunny Brought What?

Those opening sentences attract attention so readers or listeners will want to know more.

©Zoriah/The Image Works

8. Order ideas from most important to least important and begin with the important answers to the Reporter's Questions. Organizing from most to least important achieves several purposes:

   ■ You make editors' work easier and the story's publication more likely.

   ■ You help readers find the most important information quickly and easily—even if they do not read the entire article.

   ■ Making cuts is easier, and you have more control of how they are made.

   If a news director has 20 seconds of airtime and your news release is 30 seconds, the news director must cut 10 seconds or choose not to use it. Likewise, print editors sometimes must cut inches to fit releases into the space available.

9. Format news releases so information the reader needs stands out, editors can make changes easily, and news anchors (who might read the text on the air) can easily follow the document. For illustrative purposes, the release is divided into three units: the top of the page or introductory information, the body or story, and pagination cues. Refer to Figure 8.8.

10. Properly format introductory information. Many large companies create letterhead for news releases. It is printed with the company name, postal and web addresses, telephone number, logo, and the words *NEWS RELEASE*. If your organization does not have special letterhead, use plain 8 1/2" × 11" paper. Use the following guidelines for introductory format:

    ■ Begin with the words *NEWS RELEASE* in all capital letters. Key the source of the document in initial caps if letterhead is not used.

FOCUS

Figure 8.8
Use the figure to point out
correct formatting, especially
the typical elements found at
the top and bottom of a news
release.

NEWS RELEASE from Halifax Academy   Contact: Cheyenne RedWing

January 14, 20—   Headmaster
                                                         602-555-0153

Release Date: Monday, January 15, 20—
                     Please embargo story until 1 p.m.

HALIFAX ACADEMY TO HOST STAR TREK CONVENTION

NEWTOWN, AZ — Alien life forms will invade Halifax Academy on Wednesday, January 17, 20—. Over
500 "Trekkies" plan to spend two days studying language, dress, technology, and relationships as
revealed in the television and motion picture series *Star Trek*. Memorabilia and collectors' booths set up
in Dravies Hall will be open to the public free of charge. Viewers, buyers, sellers, and traders are
welcome. The hours are 9 a.m. until 5 p.m. Wednesday and Thursday.

-30-

Figure 8.8 News Release Format

- Key *Contact* and a colon flush right across from *NEWS RELEASE*. After the colon, enter the name of the person responsible for the release as well as the person's job title and phone number.

- Record the date the document was written beneath *NEWS RELEASE*.

- Use *For Immediate Release* or place *Release Date* and a colon at the left margin under the date. After the colon, key the date and the specific time the information should be made public.

- Writers occasionally request a release to be held for a period of time before publication. If you want a story to be held, beneath or

Focus on Ethics

Isaac Nonn is a campaign worker for a candidate running for the state legislature. Isaac's candidate is slipping in the polls, and the opposition is gaining in popularity. Isaac recently received a packet in the mail from an anonymous sender, indicating that the opposition candidate was expelled from college for cheating before she transferred to the university from which she ultimately graduated. Isaac is thinking about forwarding the materials to local media outlets—perhaps anonymously.

Think Critically

How should Isaac handle the situation?

beside the release date, key *Please hold until [desired release time]* or *Please embargo story until [desired release time].* **Embargo** means "to withhold or delay publication."

■ Give the news agency a suggested headline in all capital letters.

11. To format the body of a release, preface it with a **dateline,** which identifies the location of the story. Key the dateline in all capital letters. In Figure 8.8, NEWTOWN, AZ is where the story takes place. After the location, (a) leave a space, (b) key a dash, and (c) leave another space.

12. Use pagination cues, a special code to help readers follow the text and read from one page to another. To use these cues,

■ Key the word *-more-* centered at the bottom of the page when the release will be continued on the next page.

■ End news releases with *-30-* or *###* centered after the last line.

Do not promote a product or a service in your release. If you are tempted to do so, remind yourself that news is who did what, where, when, why, and how, while advertisements are how new, improved, or cost-effective something might be. Editors rarely publish releases that read like sales literature.

 STOP AND THINK

Before a news release is published, what reader or readers must approve it?

CHAPTER 8
REVIEW

SUMMARY

1. Summaries and abstracts are condensed versions of longer documents. In a summary, the writer clearly and logically presents only main ideas. The length of the original and the writer's purpose determine the length. Abstracts are shorter than summaries and cover the main idea of the original.

2. A mechanism description describes the main parts of a device or mechanism and explains the purpose of the mechanism and overall design, the various parts, they way they look, and their functions.

3. Periodic reports describe the progress of all ongoing projects in an organization or organization division during a specified time period.

4. Progress reports describe the status of one project for a specified period. Progress and periodic reports require writers to consider the interests of the audience and the schedule of the project or the organization.

5. News or press releases are reports of events or facts prepared by employees to send to the media. The goal of the release is to have the media outlets publish the story and inform the public.

Checklist

- Have I designed, organized, and written the document with the audience in mind?

- Have I analyzed my audience(s) and determined what readers need?

- Is my format appropriate for the audience and the situation?

- Have I included relevant background information?

- Have I used a logical and appropriate organizational plan?

- Are the ideas under each heading organized appropriately?

- Is the information complete and accurate?

- Have I used lists where appropriate for ease of reading?

- Have I made my document easy to read by using descriptive headings? Do the headings follow parallel structure?

- Do I present accurate, specific details?

- Have I remained objective throughout the document?

- Have I presented problems as facts, not accusations?

CLOSE

Summary

Use the summary to review the various informative reports covered in the chapter. Encourage students to use the summary to become familiar with the types of report and their functions.

Stress the importance of accuracy, precision, and credibility with these informative reports.

Another way you can use the summary is to ask students to close their books and write five (or whatever number you think is appropriate) important ideas they learned in this chapter. Then ask students to compare their lists with the summary.

CLOSE

Checklist

Suggest that students refer to the checklist when editing and revising reports. Some students may want to use the checklist in the drafting process.

Also remind students to add items to the checklist based on their own needs. For example, if a student has problems with spelling, he or she should add that item to the checklist.

REVIEW

For a review of the key terms in the chapter, provide students with the *Key Terms* worksheet available as a supplemental activity on the IRCD.

You can find these fairy tales at www.cengage.com/school/bcomm/techwtg. Click the link for Chapter 8; then click Web Links.

Build Your Foundation

1. Write a one-sentence summary of one of the following well-known fairy tales: "Little Red Riding Hood," "Cinderella," "Sleeping Beauty," "Goldilocks and the Three Bears," or "The Three Little Pigs." Compare your summary with those of your classmates. If you read the story rather than working from memory, remember to use your own words.

2. The statements listed in items a–j will go into a progress report. Identify each statement as Work Completed, Work Scheduled, or Problems/Projections.

   a. We have purchased a site license from NetBright for our network.
   b. The CD-ROM, which was delivered last Friday, was damaged in shipping so that it is inoperable.
   c. We installed screen savers on all computers.
   d. If all work scheduled is completed as we expect, the network will be ready for the team orientation on September 23.
   e. This week the system director will order the serial cable we need.
   f. The hardware security system we requested was $300 over budget.
   g. Each computer will be named so that users can easily identify it.
   h. A system administrator must be trained before we can operate fully.
   i. We connected the laser printer to the network and tested it.
   j. We forgot to order a surge protector for the computer attached to the LCD projection panel, so we cannot use this equipment until the order arrives next week.

3. Some of the following sentences are vague, and some include the writer's opinions. Revise each sentence to make it specific and factual. Invent details as needed.

   a. The calibrator is several minutes off schedule.
   b. The phenomenal response to our new computer safety education program shows that this new program will benefit employees.
   c. To get to the warehouse, go down the hall a bit and turn left.
   d. The line was down for a while last Friday because of a lecture on safety.
   e. We can assemble the original air purifier in 45 minutes, but the fancy case of the new model results in a much longer assembly time than we planned.

4. Evaluate your progress on a hobby or collection. For instance, if you build sound systems, explain the pieces of equipment (for example, speakers and receivers) you have acquired and describe the equipment you will add. If you collect baseball cards or comic books, note the cards or books you own now and the items you want to trade or buy. Make notes about your progress. Then share those notes with your classmates.

Your Turn

5. Write a long summary, a short summary, and an abstract on one of the following: a magazine or journal article, a textbook chapter, a sporting event, a meeting, a TV show, a movie, a classroom lecture, or a speech. The material you use for the summaries and abstract might relate to your chosen career field, a recent news event, or a topic suggested by your instructor.

6. List five mechanisms you know well. These may be mechanisms you use at work, at home, or at school. Consider using simple devices or a single mechanism within a larger, more complex machine. Write a mechanism description for one of the items. In your report, include a diagram of the mechanism.

7. Write a periodic report using the following information.

   As the Drafting Club chair, you receive organization funds from the Student Government Association (SGA). You report to the SGA twice a semester to tell them what the club is doing. Your next report is due January 6, 20—. In this report, you will discuss Professional Pursuits, Service, and Membership. The club is more active than ever. Over the holidays, five members attended the American Institute of Building Design meeting in Pensacola and brought back information to share with other members. The club began the school year with 21 members, and two students joined during the second semester. This year's service project is to plan the city's first Habitat for Humanity house. Club members have completed the exterior drawings and submitted them for approval. They will finish the interior drawings before the school year ends. All 23 members of the club have participated in this service project.

8. Think of groups to which you belong: a family, a club, a neighborhood, a school. With one group and a particular time period in mind, plan and write a periodic report for a specific audience. Describe the ongoing activities for your group or for your unit of the larger organization.

9. Consider any project you are working on at home, school, or work as a topic for a progress report. Your audience will be a person or group of people who have an interest in or make decisions about the project. Use the appropriate format and organization for the topic and audience.

10. If you are seeking a summer or part-time job, applying for admission to a school, or working on a project, write a progress report to the appropriate person about how you are accomplishing your goals.

11. Contact several businesses or governmental agencies to request a copy of the organization's annual report, a periodic report outlining the status of the organization that is presented annually to shareholders, employees, vendors, and others. Analyze these reports to determine whether they fit the guidelines for periodic reports in this chapter.

Community Connection

12. Visit a nonprofit organization in your area. Learn about the mission and needs of the organization. Then locate a journal or newspaper article that is relevant to the nonprofit—an article you think might help with the organization's mission or goals. Write a one- to three-paragraph summary of the article. After submitting the article and your summary to your instructor for review, present the article and your revised and edited summary to the nonprofit's personnel.

13. Write a news release for your school or another organization with which you are affiliated to announce an upcoming event, an accomplishment, or other newsworthy information. Submit the release to your instructor and class. If appropriate after careful revision and editing, submit it to a local news agency for publication.

Investigative Reports

Goals

- Develop a trip report that meets the needs of the audience
- Compose an effective incident report
- Compose science reports
- Compose forensic reports

Terms

- conclusion, p. 218
- deductive reasoning, p. 217
- forensic reports, p. 221
- incident reports, p. 213
- inductive reasoning, p. 217
- objectivity, p. 218
- passive voice, p. 218
- result, p. 218
- scientific method, p. 217
- trip reports, p. 215

WRITE TO LEARN

Consider an investigation you made recently. Perhaps you had a problem with a piece of equipment and had to investigate what caused the problem. Or maybe you attended a workshop, a seminar, or an off-campus lecture or looked for a new apartment and needed to tell others what you learned. Or perhaps you tried a new recipe for your family or took part in a clinical trial. Think about your impressions of what is required to effectively report on an investigation. Write a paragraph describing the audience that needs to learn about this situation. List three to five pieces or types of information your audience may need. Write your impression of how your audience will use the information.

Focus on Investigative Reports

Read the sample incident report on the next page and answer these questions:

- When did the incident occur?
- Where is the date of the incident mentioned?
- What is the main idea? In other words, what was the incident?
- What kind of information is contained in the Outcomes section?

What If?

- The information was intended for only one reader—an administrator at the hospital?
- The person who improperly installed the probe was not known?

Hope Hospital

www.hopehospital.org

4200 Hillcrest Road • Bath, ME 04530-5990

Phone: 207.555.0169 • Fax: 207.555.0170

Report on Incident in Clinical Laboratory

Summary

On Wednesday, July 7, 20—, a technician improperly installed the sampling probe on the Olympus Chemistry Analyzer, causing the probe to bend and rendering the machine inoperable. After the vice president granted approval for the $1,206 replacement probe, it was purchased and installed on Friday, July 9, 20—. The technician has been cleared through drug testing, and the incident was declared Operator Error Without Prejudice (according to the Hope Hospital Employee Policy Manual). Clinical Laboratory managers designed in-service training and proper installation posters to prevent this incident from recurring.

Description

On Wednesday, July 7, 20—, during the regular daily maintenance on all instrumentation, Todd Ely, Laboratory Technician II, improperly installed the Olympus Chemistry Analyzer's sampling probe. Because it was improperly placed, the probe hit the side of the specimen sampling cup, causing the probe to bend. As a result, the bent probe could not aspirate samples.

Outcomes

Without the Olympus Chemistry Analyzer, one of three machines in the lab used for testing blood, urine, and other bodily fluids, the hospital experienced delayed turnaround times for critical patient test results. Some tests were delayed as much as four hours.

Approval to purchase a new probe was requested through the executive level because the cost of $1,206 placed the purchase in the Nonbudgeted Capital Equipment category. Approval was granted on Thursday, July 8, 20—, and the probe was ordered and shipped overnight. It arrived at 10:30 a.m. on Friday, July 9, 20—, and was installed immediately. The machine then worked properly.

Todd Ely was drug-tested as standard operating procedure dictates. Because his test was negative, he is continuing with his duties. The vice president declared the incident Operator Error Without Prejudice.

Conclusion

As a result of this incident, all technicians participated in an in-service on proper installation of sampling probes on the Olympus and the other two machines. In addition, a visual showing proper placement is now posted beside all three machines to remind technicians how to install sampling probes correctly.

Sample Incident Report

FOCUS

Focus on Investigative Reports

Use the questions to encourage students to read the sample closely.

ASSESS

What If?

Use the questions to discuss how the sample would be different if the situation or audience changed.

Go to www.cengage.com/school/bcomm/techwtg for more detailed responses to these questions.

Writing@Work

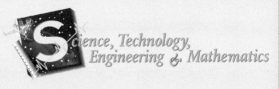

Anna Linnenberger works for a small Colorado-based optics research company called Boulder Nonlinear Systems (BNS). BNS builds spatial light modulators, which are essentially programmable lenses that can be used, for example, for satellite laser communications, data encryption, and optical tweezers for biological research.

At BNS, Anna is responsible for developing software, overseeing customer support, testing new products, writing proposals and reports, and running funded projects that are under way. According to Anna, "Writing skills are surprisingly underemphasized in engineering classes. Although I have a BS in computer engineering and am working toward a doctorate in electrical engineering, I learned most of my writing skills on the job from senior engineers."

Even with expert help, Anna finds proposals difficult to write well: "Not only are you often writing about a subtopic that you are not an expert on, but your audience is a proposal reviewer who probably isn't an expert either. So it can be challenging to propose an idea persuasively and clearly to your target audience."

For Anna, reporting on research projects that are under way is much easier than writing proposals. "Each research project requires progress reports and final reports that are written according to a predefined formula or outline. You are writing to the funding agency's technical point person for your project. They basically want to know that their money is being spent to develop the technology you proposed and that things are moving forward at a reasonable pace."

The writing style for Anna's engineering reports is minimalist: "Write clearly and get to the point quickly. You don't want to be wordy, and you never use first-person point of view such as 'I did this' or 'we did that.' All technical terms need to be defined the first time you use them." Anna hopes that her reports and proposals are used to "further optics research in new directions."

Think Critically

1. Go to BNS's website. Has the company explained its mission so that a nontechnical person can understand it? Does BNS need to explain its mission? Why or why not?

2. Why do you think writing skills are underemphasized in engineering classes? Do you think most engineers write as much as Anna does? Explain.

Printed with permission of Anna Linnenberger

APPLY

Writing @ Work

Think Critically

1. BNS explains its mission on the About Us page; however, the technical terminology may be difficult for a general audience to understand. Every organization should be able to define its mission, and readers are likely to be technical experts who will understand the terminology.

2. In the past, writing skills may have been underemphasized in engineering classes. Now, however, most people understand that communication is critical for engineers and other technical professionals. Yes, engineers write a great deal. Writing and speaking skills are essential.

INCIDENT REPORT

Incident reports, also called accident reports, describe an unusual incident or occurrence. The incident could be an accident, a surprise inspection, the outburst of an angry employee or customer, or a near-accident. When police write the details of a fender bender, they are writing an incident report. When an instructor "writes up" a student for missing class, he or she is writing an incident report.

The report must be carefully written to reflect what really happened, for it can become legal evidence used in court. It also must be written to accommodate the needs of a variety of readers. These readers may be heads of companies, managers, oversight organizations such as the FDA, insurance companies, and criminal justice personnel. Incident reports are used by many professionals. Anyone who is responsible for overseeing the safety of personnel, the public, operations, and equipment; for preventing accidents; or for dealing with the aftermath of accidents might read an incident report.

Incident reports communicate a precise description of what happened and provide a file for later reference. They also are written to help employees and organizations see what is occurring so they can formulate plans to prevent the incident from occurring again.

Figure 9.1 on the next page recounts an incident at a food production plant. The most likely readers are supervisors, managers, company heads, and food safety inspectors. Other possible readers are consumer groups, news agencies, representatives of insurance companies, criminal proceedings personnel, and union representatives. Because of the potential for many different readers and some distant from the writer, the report is formal, using an appropriate manuscript format.

To write an incident report:

1. Begin with a brief summary of what happened.

2. Add *Background* as a heading if information about events leading up to the incident would be helpful to your readers. Some incident reports combine the summary and background and do not use a separate heading for this part if it is short.

3. Under *Description,* tell exactly what happened in chronological order. Make sure you cover the Reporter's Questions: Who? What? When? Where? Why? and How?

4. Be honest and objective.

5. Use the Outcome section to provide the observable incident results.

6. Use the Conclusion section to tell what was learned from the incident and how to prevent it from happening again.

To get started, carefully note any evidence. Interview people separately who witnessed or who know about the incident. Do *not* include information you cannot verify.

Warm Up

Imagine a familiar scene: Children are playing together when something is broken. When an adult arrives, he or she asks, "What happened?" What responses do the children provide? Will all of the children give the same account? Will some responses be more useful to the questioner than others? If so, how and why? Describe similar situations from your work or academic life.

FOCUS

Warm Up

Humor is likely as students recall childhood pranks. Without a focus, reporters may include unimportant information. Some reporters will be more interested in placing blame than in discovering what happened. Clear, logical reports presented without emotion are most useful.

TEACH

Incident reports do not need to be about something dangerous; they can be about someone dropping a lunch tray or running out of gas.

Assign an incident report about a literary event, such as when the king and duke were tarred and feathered in *Huck Finn.*

TYPICAL READER

Anyone who is responsible for safety or who must handle a situation after an accident or incident.

WRITER'S FOCUS

Writing precise, detailed, and objective information that answers the audience's questions and is organized to be easily read and used.

INCIDENT OF CONTAMINATION, MIXING OPERATIONS

Summary

On January 31, 20—, between 8:00 a.m. and 10:15 a.m., Number 4 flour bin was contaminated by water leaking through a small hole in an overhead steam exhaust pipe, but no permanent damage was done to the facility or equipment. The contamination was isolated to the one bin, and the contents were discarded. After thorough testing, production resumed after ten hours. The report of contamination and all test results were filed in the plant office for regulatory review.

Description

On January 31, 20—, Alexine Blanc and Julio de Mola were preparing a batch of Double Devilish Chocolate Brownie mix. At 10:15 a.m., Blanc noticed clumps in the Number 4 flour bin. Because all dry ingredients supplied to Grandma's have anti-caking additives, Blanc and de Mola knew something was wrong.

As procedure dictates, Blanc informed Val Witt, Director of Mixing Operations. Witt stopped mixing operations and requested an emergency shut-off in Packaging. Nonessential personnel were dismissed. Witt directed a complete investigation. Ten 4-ounce samples from clumps in Bin 4 were sent to the laboratory for testing. Witt also tested five 4-ounce samples from each of the remaining bins.

After Witt talked with Jason Jarvis, Manager of Packaging, Jarvis ordered samples from 5 percent of the products packaged that day.

At 11:30 a.m., the lab tests indicated that the substance causing clumping in the flour contained water and metal rust particles. No foreign substances were found in the samples from the other six bins, nor did the tests show any problems with the samples from packaged goods.

The information about the foreign materials in Bin 4 led investigators to look for leaks over the bin. A piping company, Adair Contractors, located and repaired a 1/16-inch diameter hole in the juncture where two exhaust pipes meet.

Outcome

All materials in Number 4 flour bin were discarded. The empty bin was thoroughly sanitized before use. Once cleared by the laboratory, other bins were placed back in operation. Production was off-line for ten hours on January 31, 20—. None of the contaminated materials were packaged or shipped to consumers. No one was injured or sickened because of the incident.

Conclusion

In the future, bin covers will be closed tightly until batch mixing begins. Because the piping contractor has guaranteed the repair work for one year, I do not anticipate more leaking from this area. However, I do recommend a thorough inspection of the entire exhaust pipe system. In addition, I believe systematic testing of all ingredients would further ensure our promise of quality products.

Callout annotations (left margin):

- Summarizes what happened
- Provides a more detailed narrative of the incident; covers the incident from beginning to end; answers the major questions Who? What? When? Where? Why? and How?
- Tells what happened as a result of the incident; may repeat some information stated in the Description
- Explains what has been learned as a result of this experience and what will help prevent a similar incident

Figure 9.1 Example of Incident Report

⬢ **STOP AND THINK**

The Reporter's Questions should be answered in the Description section of an incident report. What are the questions?

TRIP REPORT

Trip reports tell supervisors and coworkers what was gained from a business trip. Trip reports are a condensed narrative. Often the report does not include everything about the trip, only those parts that are most useful to the organization. In this way, the trip report is similar to a summary because the writer includes only the essential details about the trip.

Businesses often send workers to conferences to learn the latest developments in their field. Sometimes associates visit other businesses to negotiate deals or to learn about operations. A trip is an investigation, a research mission from which the findings must be shared with others. Typically, trip reports provide managers with critical information resulting from a trip. In addition, coworkers may use information from trip reports to do their jobs.

Figure 9.2 on the next page is a trip report from Lily Lang detailing her findings from a business trip to China. While in China, she met with current and potential vendors for her company—a manufacturer and a wholesaler of hammocks, rugs, and other household and outdoor furnishings.

To write a trip report:

1. Report information your audience will find most useful. You do not need to include all of the details of the trip, only what your audience requires.

2. Preview the report in your introduction.

3. Cover the Reporter's Questions as you write the report: Who? What? When? Where? Why? and How? Write a section for each major concept or activity to be reported.

4. Include a heading for each section (major concept or activity) in the report body.

5. Use bulleted lists for important events or knowledge gained.

6. Decide whether your report needs Conclusions and/or Recommendations sections. Some trip reports require both, others neither, and some only one.

   ■ Use Conclusions to summarize the trip benefits or findings.

   ■ Use Recommendations to suggest further action(s).

7. Choose chronological order or order of importance.

8. Use active voice and first person—*I* or *we*—to make the report sound natural.

Do *not* try to retell every element of a trip. In addition, do *not* include information that has no relevance to your audience, such as the chance meeting of a childhood friend or the fabulous Indian restaurant you discovered.

Prepare for writing a trip report before you leave. Find out what the purpose of the trip is and what your organization expects you to learn. Investigate these concerns during your trip and address them in the report.

Warm Up

Suppose you are planning a vacation to a place from which someone you know just returned. What questions would you ask that person? Do you think that person's experience might enhance your trip in some way? If so, how?

FOCUS

Warm Up

Students can benefit from another person's experience (what to do, what to avoid, and what to expect) just as organizations benefit from the experiences of business travelers.

TYPICAL READER

Managers and administrators (and sometimes coworkers and clients/customers) who need information acquired during a trip to make decisions and plans.

WRITER'S FOCUS

Creating clear, well-organized, and focused information and constantly considering the audience's needs and roles.

TEACH

Introduce the trip report as investigative reporting.

Students do not need to include everything that took place, only what their readers (supervisors and coworkers) will find most useful.

To see a longer version of the trip report shown on the next page, go to www.cengage.com/school/bcomm/techwtg. Click the link for Chapter 9; then click Sample Documents.

MEMO TO: Cristina Santana, Vice President, Operations

FROM: Lily Lang, Pan Asian Liaison   *LL*

DATE: 5 November 20—

SUBJECT: Vendor Investigation Trip to China, 1–12 October 2010

My mission in China was to visit potential fabric suppliers to determine their capability to provide fabrics for our company's hammocks and outdoor furniture.

Lixin Textile Enterprises, Fabric Supplier in Beijing   **3 October 2010**

After meeting with Mr. Guo, the business owner, and Mr. Guo's sales manager, Sally, and touring the facilities, I realized that Lifestyle Fabulous should not pursue a relationship with this organization. Although this supplier had an impressive office building, display room, and website, I discovered that the company is a trading company that owns no factories.

> *Previews the rest of the report*

Hongyue Textile Co., Ltd., Fabric Supplier in Beijing   **4 October 2010**

Hongyue Textiles should be considered as a supplier. This company was not a scheduled visit. Mr. Guo and Sally took me to this fabric factory. During the visit, I discovered that the factory owner, Mr. Wang, is willing to do business with me directly or through Mr. Guo's company. Mr. Wang owns a weaving factory and a printing factory with a total of 300 employees. Mr. Wang has a reputation for being an honest person. His price is better than that of the Taiwanese fabric supplier with whom we currently contract, and his minimal order quantity also is more desirable. (See details in Attachment A.) For paper-printing polyester fabrics, solid olefin fabrics, and jacquard olefin fabrics, Hongyue Textiles has potential as a supplier to us for the following reasons:

- UV stability rate for both solid and jacquard olefin fabrics satisfies our requirements for outdoor furniture. (See Attachment B for colorfastness testing report.)
- Production lead time is 35 days after receiving purchase order.
- Sample lead time is five to seven days after receiving artwork.
- Minimum order quantity is 10,000 meters with up to eight colors per design.

Conclusion

The trip was successful. After meeting with potential fabric vendors, I learned a great deal about the complicated network of fabric customers and vendors. I also learned that many who represent themselves as factory owners or direct sellers are agents who would only increase our costs without adding value.

> *Sums up Lang's assessment of the trip*

Recommendation

I recommend that we negotiate a contract with Hongyue Textiles directly rather than use Mr. Guo as an intermediary.

> *Suggests what should be done with the information gained from the trip*

Figure 9.2 Example of Trip Report

FOCUS

Figure 9.2
Discuss the audience and the decisions made to meet the audience's needs, such as organization and details.

ONGOING ASSESSMENT

Stop and Think
Employees should discuss trip objectives with their supervisors before departure and include only information that is beneficial to the audience.

● STOP AND THINK
How do writers decide what to cover in a trip report?

SCIENCE LAB REPORTS

The best science is born of a curiosity about the world along with the creative thinking to figure things out. Scientific findings, however, add little to people's collective knowledge unless someone records what was done and what happened in a science report. In the classroom, lab reports become the vehicles for testing knowledge of concepts and procedures. In professional disciplines, lab reports become the basis of science articles submitted to major journals such as *Analytical Chemistry* and *Journal of Forensic Sciences*.

The steps of the **scientific method** dictate the structure of science reports. The scientific method uses both inductive and deductive reasoning. Reasoning from a particular observation (I sneeze every time I am around a rose) to a general conclusion (Therefore, I think roses make me sneeze) is called **inductive reasoning.** Reasoning from a general conclusion (I think roses make me sneeze) to a particular situation (I probably won't sneeze if I give my mother candy instead of roses) is called **deductive reasoning.** Using inductive reasoning, scientists arrive at a tentative hypothesis, then use deductive reasoning to test that hypothesis for validity. The science report is the written record of this process.

While some differences exist in the structure of a science report among various disciplines—names for a heading or the addition of a section—a science report always answers these questions: What was the purpose of the lab? What materials were used? What procedure was followed? What were the results? What were the conclusions?

Organize

As you review the notes taken during your experiment or procedure, organize your information into these sections:

- **Introduction:** Tells the purpose or the objective of the lab (what the lab is expected to prove) and can provide background of the situation under investigation, tells under whose authority the lab was conducted, and provides relevant dates. The introduction does not always have a separate heading in shorter reports.

- **Materials and Method** (also called *Experimental Section, Methodology,* or *Procedures*): Lists materials, items, evidence, and/or instruments used. This section describes the procedure and includes relevant calculations. Materials can be presented in a separate heading from *Methodology* if the report is long.

- **Results and Discussion** (or just *Results*): Presents test results with relevant calculations, including any accompanying graphics such as tables or graphs. This section presents the results and explains why things happened. Results can be presented in a separate heading from *Discussion* if the report is long.

- **Conclusion(s):** Includes a brief summary that tells how the test results, findings, and analyses meet the objectives of the lab. This section tells what was learned or gained from the experiment.

Warm Up

How do your science classes differ from your other classes (such as English, history, business, or physical education)? Explain why you think these differences exist.

FOCUS

Warm Up

Science: empirical data; observable results; proof; precise, technical details; focus on how/why things work; regularly updated information.

Other disciplines: less precise; study of human nature/creativity—literature, psychology, history, communication, and philosophy.

TEACH

Use the Inductive and Deductive Reasoning Teaching Master on the IRCD to show the difference between inductive and deductive reasoning.

TEACH

Use the Outline of a Typical Lab Report Teaching Master on the IRCD to show a typical outline of a lab report. Headings can change depending on the company, purpose, and discipline.

TYPICAL READER

- A scientist or professional interested in learning and critiquing the latest research in the field.

- An educator testing students' knowledge of a concept or process.

Both readers respect, understand, and follow the scientific method.

WRITER'S FOCUS

Setting up sound research design, recording results methodically, analyzing data, and drawing logical conclusions. Presenting research objectively, following the principles of the scientific method.

COMMUNICATION TECHNOLOGIES

New technologies have made modern scientific research possible. The developments of advanced instrumentation and experimental techniques have provided researchers the means to collect many forms of qualitative and quantitative data. Computer programs such as molecular modeling programs, *Ab Initio* quantum chemistry software, Mathcad, and Maple help process and analyze huge amounts of data.

Think Critically

Research one of these programs and explain how this program helps researchers make new discoveries in science.

Write

After organizing your data, you are ready to write. In most cases, you will be writing to an expert in the field. (An exception is forensics, which may require explanations for the lay reader too.) So you will most likely use the scientific jargon of the field. When writing, remember to:

1. Use precision when describing procedures or offering numerical calculations.

✓ Precise	✗ Approximate
The tadpole measured 3.15 cm long.	The tadpole measured about 3 cm long.

2. Use **passive voice** (the verb *to be* + the past participle of the verb) when describing the methodology or procedures. Passive voice focuses on the process and keeps the report objective.

✓ Passive Voice	✗ Active Voice
Tiny shifts in blood flow to parts of the brain were detected with functional MRI.	Using functional MRI, we detected tiny shifts in blood flow to parts of the brain.

3. Maintain **objectivity** by describing observable results without letting personal bias or emotions influence your observations.

✓ Objectivity	✗ Personal Bias or Emotions
The client fidgeted, her eyes darted around the room, and she pursed her lips tightly.	The client was clearly angry.

4. Separate observable results (the facts) in the Results section from conclusions drawn (what the facts mean) in the Conclusions section. A result is not the same as a conclusion. A **result** is simply what happened. A **conclusion** goes beyond what happened and requires the researcher to draw an inference and interpret the data.

✓ Results	✗ Conclusion
The patient's temperature remained stable, ranging from 97.5° to 98.1° over the last 48 hours.	The patient is no longer contagious.

5. Document any sources that were used and provide a list of references.

6. When required by the discipline and length of the lab, consider adding:

   - A Theory section if the lab relies on extensive theory.

   - An Instrumentation section if the lab tests equipment.

   - A Calculations section if the lab uses lengthy mathematical computations.

- A Recommendation section if future research is warranted.

- An Appendix (a separate section at the end of the report) if complex data such as tables and graphs would otherwise disrupt the flow of the report.

7. Use the straightforward language of the science report.

- ***To* Verb +** ***What*** **Phrases:** *To determine the differences* between several aquatic ecosystems, samples were taken in November from three sites in Georgia.

- **Lists:** A survey was sent to 150 students, 25 instructors, and 50 parents.

- **Description of Processes:** The *blood was drawn* from the patient's finger and placed on the slide. The *sample was examined* under a microscope.

- **Cause-to-Effect Reasoning:** The *data* from the table *suggests that* the resolution is highest with the pH 7/45% meOH buffer solution (alpha = 3.35).

Do not include results in the Conclusions section or conclusions in the Results section. Do not allow your personal bias to influence the conclusions you draw. Finally, do not leave out any relevant data. Record results exactly as they happen. On the next page, Figure 9.3 shows a science lab report.

The FDA publishes a website that contains links to press releases of the past decade. You will find everything from food and drug research to biologics and radiation protection.

Go to the NET Bookmark for Chapter 9. What key topics are in the FDA's news? What news is in the spotlight? Read one article and share five facts from the article with your classmates.

www.cengage.com/school/bcomm/techwtg

NET BOOKMARK

Ask students to visit the website. What information is currently featured? The site is credible because it is based on scientific evidence and sponsored by government research.

FOCUS ON ETHICS

It can be difficult to make decisions based on conflicting data. Jacob should look for more evidence before he manufactures the vaccine.

Focus on Ethics

Clinical trials are research studies that test the effectiveness of new drugs, vaccines, and medical procedures. Many of these trials are funded by private companies. Usually, these companies want to sell the medicines related to the study.

Changing or "fudging" data can be tempting for funding organizations when results of a lab experiment are unexpected or difficult to understand. Ideally, clinical trials and tests from several sources would show similar results. If that is the case, the results are considered to be true, or valid. Sometimes, though, studies show conflicting results.

Jacob Krishner is the president of AM Pharmaceuticals. His company sponsored a clinical trial for a vaccine to protect against malaria. Three other trials had already indicated the effectiveness of the vaccine. The most recent study, done on a relatively small sample and conducted by his newest research scientist, shows that the drug might have a serious side effect. The company has sunk a great deal of money into this project, and company profits are down.

Think Critically

What should Jacob do? Does he accept the latest test results? Does he manufacture the vaccine based on the other three studies? What should he consider as he makes his decision?

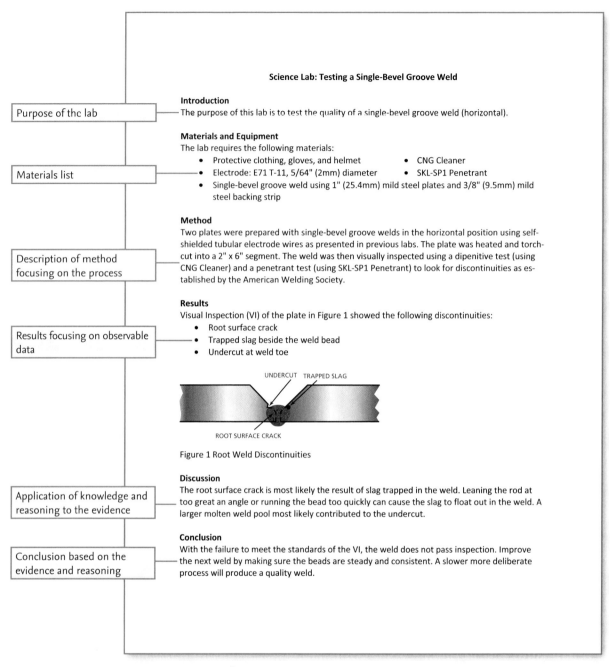

Figure 9.3 Science Lab Report

FOCUS

Figure 9.3
Use the model to illustrate the structure, precision, and tone of a science lab report.

ONGOING ASSESSMENT

Stop and Think
Results: observable outcomes; conclusions: inferences drawn based on the results. Passive voice keeps the reader focused on the process and maintains objectivity.

 STOP AND THINK

What is the difference between results and conclusions? Why do writers of science lab reports use passive voice?

FORENSIC REPORTS

Forensic reports are investigative reports that analyze evidence for legal purposes. From the Latin *forensic* ("of the forum," or "public"), forensics is the branch of science that uses scientific principles and methodology to evaluate various kinds of evidence. Forensic science includes a variety of specialties, including the study of handwriting, fingerprinting, blood, ballistics, tire treads, and computer hard drives. While television shows such as *NCIS* have made forensic work in a crime lab popular, noncriminal investigations use forensic science as well. Highly trained in their respective fields, forensic experts write reports and often testify in legal proceedings.

As a specialized type of science lab, forensic reports strictly adhere to the scientific method—similar to the science lab reports discussed in the preceding section. Attention to detail, reliance on test procedures, objective analysis, documented research, careful reporting, and observations based on evidence are all important. Ethical considerations are vital as the forensic specialist strives to present evidence without making unnecessary assumptions or unproven interpretations. The facts must speak for themselves. On the following page, Figure 9.4 shows a forensic report.

To write a forensic report:

1. Identify the credentials of the expert (name, title, education, and sometimes years of experience). This information can be included at the beginning or end of a report. As part of court testimony, the credentials are subject to careful scrutiny by the prosecuting and defense attorneys.

2. Identify the specimens under investigation, usually by number. These specimens may become exhibits in a case.

© Edw 2009/Used under license from Shutterstock.com

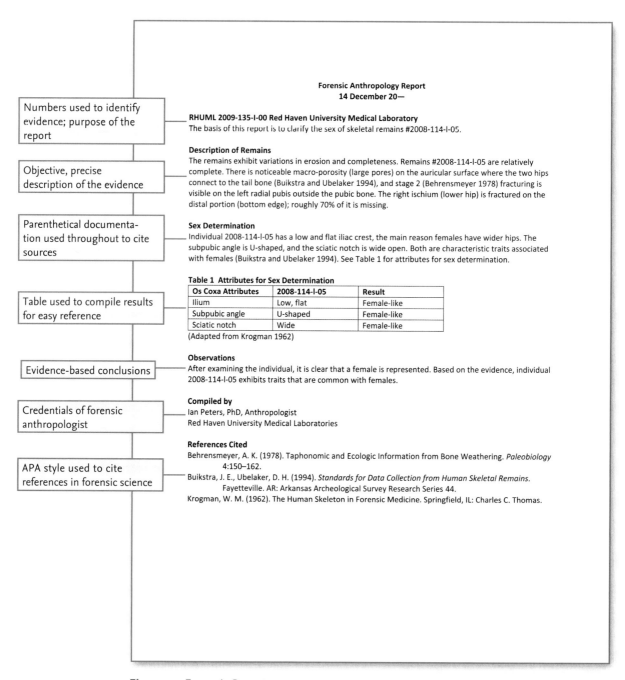

Numbers used to identify evidence; purpose of the report

Objective, precise description of the evidence

Parenthetical documentation used throughout to cite sources

Table used to compile results for easy reference

Evidence-based conclusions

Credentials of forensic anthropologist

APA style used to cite references in forensic science

Forensic Anthropology Report
14 December 20—

RHUML 2009-135-I-00 Red Haven University Medical Laboratory
The basis of this report is to clarify the sex of skeletal remains #2008-114-I-05.

Description of Remains
The remains exhibit variations in erosion and completeness. Remains #2008-114-I-05 are relatively complete. There is noticeable macro-porosity (large pores) on the auricular surface where the two hips connect to the tail bone (Buikstra and Ubelaker 1994), and stage 2 (Behrensmeyer 1978) fracturing is visible on the left radial pubis outside the pubic bone. The right ischium (lower hip) is fractured on the distal portion (bottom edge); roughly 70% of it is missing.

Sex Determination
Individual 2008-114-I-05 has a low and flat iliac crest, the main reason females have wider hips. The subpubic angle is U-shaped, and the sciatic notch is wide open. Both are characteristic traits associated with females (Buikstra and Ubelaker 1994). See Table 1 for attributes for sex determination.

Table 1 Attributes for Sex Determination

Os Coxa Attributes	2008-114-I-05	Result
Ilium	Low, flat	Female-like
Subpubic angle	U-shaped	Female-like
Sciatic notch	Wide	Female-like

(Adapted from Krogman 1962)

Observations
After examining the individual, it is clear that a female is represented. Based on the evidence, individual 2008-114-I-05 exhibits traits that are common with females.

Compiled by
Ian Peters, PhD, Anthropologist
Red Haven University Medical Laboratories

References Cited
Behrensmeyer, A. K. (1978). Taphonomic and Ecologic Information from Bone Weathering. *Paleobiology* 4:150–162.
Buikstra, J. E., Ubelaker, D. H. (1994). *Standards for Data Collection from Human Skeletal Remains.* Fayetteville. AR: Arkansas Archeological Survey Research Series 44.
Krogman, W. M. (1962). The Human Skeleton in Forensic Medicine. Springfield, IL: Charles C. Thomas.

Figure 9.4 Forensic Report

FOCUS

Figure 9.4
Use the report to illustrate the structure, precision, and tone of a forensic report.

TEACH
Both lab and forensic reports use the scientific method.

Akira Mehrs, the director of Spalding Photography Studio, must write an incident report about an altercation that occurred between an employee whom she respects a great deal and a customer. Darrell French, a photography aide, was accepting payment from Dawn Morton for a packet of her daughter's portraits. When Ms. Morton's credit card was declined, she became agitated, demanding that Mr. French run the card again and exclaiming that he must be doing something wrong. Mr. French walked away, leaving Ms. Mehrs to handle the situation. When Ms. Mehrs sits down to write the incident report, she considers omitting the fact that Mr. French walked away from his station because she realizes that that fact will detract from his service record.

Think Critically

Should Ms. Mehrs omit details from the report to protect her employee? Why or why not?

3. Organize the report according to the principles of the basic forensic report, as follows:

- **Evidence:** A description of the evidence collected.

- **Method:** A description of the method or procedure used to test the evidence, using charts, graphs, photos, and/or diagrams as necessary.

- **Observation** (sometimes called *Interpretation*, *Results*, or *Conclusion*): The conclusions that can be reasonably drawn from the evidence. The report also notes if the evidence is not conclusive or if evidence is missing.

© The Image Bank/Getty Images

ONGOING ASSESSMENT

Stop and Think

Because forensic specialists testify in court proceedings, their credentials help establish their credibility.

4. Write descriptions, discussion, and observations using the basic principles of scientific and technical communication: Use specific and precise measurements and vocabulary. Remain objective and focus on the process and the data.

5. Use strategies for communicating unfamiliar information to a lay audience. Explain terms as you write, provide quick definitions (in parentheses or in the next sentence), explain scientific concepts using common analogies, and break down complex processes step-by-step.

6. Provide headings and subheadings as necessary. For example, if you are asked to determine the number, sex, age, and condition of a set of bones, the report might include these headings: *Number, Sex, Age,* and *Condition of Remains.*

7. Provide references as they are used. You can cite references with parenthetical citations and a list of references at the end.

Do not allow prejudice or bias to influence your findings. Rely on evidence, not conjecture. Do not draw inferences if the evidence is incomplete. Simply point out that the evidence is insufficient.

 STOP AND THINK

Why is it important for forensic specialists to include their credentials in a forensic report?

CHAPTER 9
REVIEW

SUMMARY

1. Trip reports tell supervisors and coworkers what was gained from a business trip. The report includes only those details of the trip that are most helpful for the audience.

2. Incident reports, also called accident reports, describe an accident or an unusual incident or occurrence.

3. Lab reports answer these questions: What was the purpose of the lab? What materials were used? What was the procedure? What were the results? What are the conclusions?

4. Forensic reports give the credentials of the examiner, describe evidence, describe the method used to examine the evidence, and make observations.

Checklist

- Have I analyzed my audience(s) and determined what readers need to know?

- Have I designed, organized, and written the document with the audience in mind?

- Is my format appropriate for the audience and the situation?

- Have I included relevant background information?

- Are the data under each heading organized appropriately?

- Is the information complete and accurate?

- Have I presented problems as facts, not accusations?

1. a. subjective—is personal opinion in that not everyone would agree; b. objective—can be measured and proven; c. subjective—makes an unproved assumption about the reason for the patient's behavior; d. objective—can be measured and all can agree

2. Responses will vary. a. 23 minutes off; b. the 88% approval rating; c. go down the hall about 30 yards and turn left at the first intersection; d. 42 minutes

3. a. no; b. yes; c. no; d. yes; e. yes

4. a. math formula; b. algebra formula; c. flowchart; d. schematic

5. a. How large was the bear? Was it male or female? How many times did it drink? Exactly what time of day did it drink? b. How many decibels were tested? What levels were tested? How long was the testing? c. How many eggs? How long did the robin sit on the eggs? d. Exactly how much do the CPU and the monitor cost? How much is shipping and handling? What brands and models are the items?

6. a. Materials and Methods; b. Conclusions; c. Results/Discussion

Build Your Foundation

1. Are these statements subjective or objective? Explain.

   a. This is the best English class I have ever taken.
   b. This class covers the basic style and formatting of technical writing.
   c. The patient seemed angry, probably because of something that happened on the way to the office.
   d. The temperature is in the mid-80s with little chance of rain.

2. Some of the sentences below are vague, and some include the writer's opinions. Revise each sentence to make it specific and factual. Invent details as needed.

   a. The calibrator is several minutes off schedule.
   b. The phenomenal response to our new computer safety education program shows that this new program will benefit employees.
   c. To get to the warehouse, go down the hall a bit and turn left.
   d. The line was down for a while on Friday because of some lecture on safety.

3. Are the statements listed below observable results? Respond *yes* or *no*.

   a. The manager plans to review safety standards with all employees.
   b. The olive trees have lost 80 percent of their leaves.
   c. Mr. Domingues regrets his decision to close the recapping unit.
   d. After the robbery, the Gallery Movie Theater closed.
   e. The front line operator failed to read the Caution statement.

4. What type of graphics do these statements call for? Consider calculations, figures, and tables.

   a. The experiments were designed to demonstrate the properties of inverse functions. We experimented with several types of functions, including transcendental functions and polynomial expressions.
   b. The area of the platinum disk was found using simple algebra.
   c. An energy flow diagram (see Figure 2) was developed illustrating the energy flow and the student's position on the food web.
   d. The circuit in Figure 3 uses an op-amp as a multiplier.

5. Which part of the following statements could be more precise?

   a. The bear drank from the water hole several times in the afternoon.
   b. The decibels were tested at levels too low for human ears.
   c. The robin sat on a few eggs in its nest for a couple of weeks.
   d. The CPU costs around $500, the monitor costs about $350, and the printer costs $398.99 plus shipping and handling.

6. Where do these sentences belong in a lab report—under *Introduction, Materials and Method, Results, Discussion,* or *Conclusions?*

   a. For this activity, four potatoes, four pieces of wood, four cans, and a flame were used to determine evidence of carbon.
   b. The larger the food supply, the larger the guppy population.
   c. The data for absorbencies in Table 1 show excellent correlation and a strong linear relationship (R = 1.00) for Plot 1.

7. To practice explaining complex information to a lay audience, find a way to explain these laws of physics to a 6-year-old.

   a. Conservation of Matter: Matter is neither created nor destroyed.
   b. Third Law of Motion: For every action, there is an equal and opposite reaction.
   c. First Law of Motion: A body persists in its state of rest or of uniform motion unless acted upon by an external unbalanced force.

8. Think of ways to explain these complex processes so that a lay reader can easily understand the process. Look for a common occurrence or description to use as an analogy:

   a. How the subconscious affects a person's behavior
   b. How the human eye sees
   c. How lightning is formed

Your Turn

9. Think of a time when something went wrong—perhaps a problem at school or work. After identifying and analyzing your audience, write an incident report describing the incident and what you learned.

10. Visit a place of interest—perhaps a college, a business, a museum, or a sporting event. Think of questions to ask during your trip. Write a trip report to a real or fictional supervisor, answering the questions.

11. Conduct a science experiment at home. Get ideas from books, a science instructor, or online sources (Steve Spangler Science or ScienceBob). Take notes and write a lab report for English class.

12. Think of something about which you would like to know more—when your car gets better gas mileage or whether some brand of sunscreen works better than another. Ask a science instructor to help you design an experiment. Perform the experiment and write a lab report.

Community Connection

13. Volunteer at a daycare center, for a reading program, or for another activity. Write an incident report based on an event you witnessed or learned of. Address the report to the leader of the organization.

14. If you have a chance to travel to a conference, a seminar, a workshop, or another event, provide a trip report to the sponsors of the trip. Ask your classmates and/or instructor to help edit and revise the report.

15. Interview someone who performs experiments, conducts labs or medical tests, or examines evidence (a police officer or a medical examiner, for example). Ask how reports are written, how evidence is handled, and how the scientific method is used. Discuss the difficulty of remaining objective. Share a short written or oral report with your class.

16. Attend a court proceeding for a criminal case and take notes. How do forensic specialists provide expert testimony? Interview a lawyer and ask about the importance of forensic testimony and the procedure for admitting it into evidence. Tell your classmates how your findings compare with the chapter's information about forensic reports.

7. Answers will vary, but explanations should be simple and clear. Students might want to read their explanations to a 6-year-old to see if he or she understands the information.

8. a. compare the subconscious to a submerged iceberg or to tree roots; b. compare the human eye to a camera; c. compare lightning to static electricity

ASSESS

Your Turn

9–10. Make sure students adhere to the guidelines of the incident and trip reports. Remind students to use the appropriate checklist.

11–12. Make sure students adhere to the structure of the lab report. Remind students to use the checklist.

ASSESS

Community Connection

13–16. Relate the reports to the technical writing principles introduced in the chapter.

Instructions

Goals

- Analyze your audience's expectations and the steps required for instructions
- Determine an appropriate format for instructions
- Prepare a clear, concise set of instructions

Terms

- cautions, p. 233
- concurrent testing, p. 241
- explanation, p. 239
- field-test, p. 241
- imperative mood, p. 237
- instructions, p. 231
- online instructions, p. 243
- retrospective testing, p. 242
- step, p. 237
- warnings, p. 233

WRITE TO LEARN

Think of the last time you followed instructions. Maybe the instructions were from an instructor, your parent or guardian, your employer, a textbook, or an online help manual. In a short journal entry, answer these questions: Under what circumstances did you read the instructions? Were the instructions easy or difficult to follow? Explain. How did you handle any problems that resulted from poorly written instructions? If graphics were included, what kind were they? Were they helpful? Why or why not?

Focus on Instructions

Read the sample instructions on the next page and answer these questions:

- How does the writer make it clear what to do first, second, and so on?
- How many actions does each step represent?
- How does each step begin?
- Under "Charge the Battery," besides telling the reader what to do, what other information is included?
- What is the purpose of the two boxed notes, the graphics, and the two headings?

What If?

- The user had previously owned a BlackBerry® phone?
- The user had never owned a cell phone?
- The user was not a strong native speaker of English?
- The instructions were spoken rather than written?

Welcome to BlackBerry®

Get ready to experience the freedom and connectivity of your all-in-one mobile solution. Setting up your BlackBerry® Storm™ smartphone is easy. To begin your setup, verify that your SIM card and battery are inserted in your device and charge the battery.

> CAUTION: Read all user guidelines carefully before using your new BlackBerry® smartphone.

Insert the SIM Card and Battery

Your SIM card is a small rectangular plastic card that stores important information about your wireless service. Your SIM card might already be inserted in your BlackBerry® device.

1. Slide up the release buttons for the battery cover and lift off the battery cover. See Figure 1.
2. If the battery is inserted, remove the battery.
3. If your SIM card is already inserted, proceed to step 8.
4. Remove the SIM card from any packaging.
5. Hold the SIM card so that the metal contacts on the SIM card face down and the cutoff corner of the SIM card points toward the bottom-left corner of your device.
6. Slide the SIM card into the SIM card holder until it stops. See Figure 2.
7. Insert the battery so that the metal contacts on the battery align with the metal contacts on your device. See Figure 3.
8. Slide the metal notches at the top of the battery cover into the slots at the top of the device.
9. Push down the battery cover so that it clicks into place. See Figure 4.
   a. If the battery is charged, the device turns on.
   b. If the device does not turn on, charge the battery.

| Figure 1. Remove the battery cover | Figure 2. Insert the SIM card | Figure 3. Insert the battery | Figure 4. Replace the battery cover |

Charge the Battery

If your device did not turn on, follow these steps to charge your battery.

1. Connect the small end of the travel charger cable to the micro-USB port on the side of your BlackBerry® device. See Figure 5.
2. If necessary, perform one of the following actions:
   - Insert the plug blade attachment into the power adapter.
   - Fold down the plug blades on the power adapter. See Figure 6.
3. Plug the power adapter into a power outlet.
4. Charge the battery to full power.

Figure 5. Connect the travel charger cable to your device

Figure 6. Insert the plug blade attachment or fold down the plug blades

> TIP: You can use the micro-USB cable that came with your device to connect your device to your computer for charging. For more information, see the "About using your device with a computer" topic

Sample Instructions

Adapted from BlackBerry® User Guide. Reprinted with permission of BlackBerry®.

ASSESS

What If?

Use the questions to discuss how the sample would be different if the situation or audience changed.

Go to www.cengage.com/school/bcomm/techwtg for more detailed responses to these questions.

Courtesy of Stephen Freas

Writing@Work

Information Technology

Aaron Wartner is an application and database administrator for Accenture, an IT consulting firm in Cincinnati, Ohio. In his role, he is responsible for maintaining a digital planning system used by Accenture's customers.

Aaron's job creates a link between customers who use Accenture's technology and the technology itself. He has the tricky task of communicating with both his "techy" colleagues and with clients. "Much of my time is spent e-mailing information to or requesting action from my coworkers. I also write instructions for customers' scheduled maintenance activities that describe how to perform the work, how to coordinate with other teams, and the timing for each action."

Writing technical instructions that are easy to follow is not an easy task. "Instructions must be interpreted the same way by every reader to be successful," says Aaron. "So they must be understandable, and the intent must be clear. Consistency in describing objects and activities and careful use of technical jargon are a few ways I try to meet these goals."

Aaron begins writing a set of instructions for a certain task by doing that task himself. "I start by walking through the process to understand the flow of steps and to make sure that what I am doing will work. I identify and record each basic step as I go, preserving the order of steps. Once I have all of the steps, I create an outline of the process. Finally, I word the instructions for each step based on who the intended audience is."

After Aaron finishes a set of instructions, he follows them in his company's test system to make sure they work. "Having a test system allows us to fix errors in our instructions before they reach customers."

Think Critically

1. Do you think Aaron expected to do so much writing on his job? Explain.

2. Convert Aaron's description of the process he follows (paragraphs 4 and 5) into a simple set of instructions.

Printed with permission of Aaron Wartner

GETTING STARTED ON INSTRUCTIONS

Imagine you just purchased a new cabinet for your home theater system. You want to assemble the cabinet before your friends arrive to watch a movie. You have two hours to put the cabinet together. Because you are on a tight schedule, you begin to assemble the furniture without looking at the instructions. "It can't be that hard," you mumble under your breath. You are certain that reading the instructions will slow you down. An hour and a half later, you are still trying to connect the pieces. You are frantic because your guests will be knocking on your door in 30 minutes—and the cabinet is still in pieces on the floor. Finally, you look at the **instructions,** the sequence of steps explaining how to complete a task.

Who Reads Instructions?

People who read instructions need to perform a task or understand how someone else performs that task. The server being asked to close a restaurant needs to know the procedure for doing so. The surveyor measuring a road for underground pipes needs to know how to determine traffic patterns. You, assembling your newly purchased home theater cabinet, need to know how to set it up as quickly as possible.

You can empathize with a reader trying to follow a set of instructions. Instructions, with their graphics and technical language, can be intimidating. Consequently, some readers read instructions carefully, paying close attention to every word.

On the other hand, many readers, similar to you in the situation above, are impatient, trying to go through the steps without reading them first. Some readers, thinking they are familiar with the procedure, read only a few steps and think they know what to do. Other readers rely more on the graphics than the words for information.

Fancy (RF)/Jupiter Images

Warm Up

Do you usually read instructions before you attempt a procedure? Why or why not?

You can view sample instructions at www.cengage. com/school/bcomm/techwtg. Click the link for Chapter 10; then click Sample Documents.

FOCUS

Warm Up
Some students will say that they read instructions carefully; others will say that they do not. Use this question to help students understand how unpredictable readers can be. As writers, students must encourage readers to read the steps.

TEACH
If you have examples of poorly written instructions, share them with the class.

To understand how your audience affects the way you write instructions, see *Instructions for a Preschooler and a Teenager* at www.cengage.com/school/bcomm/techwtg. Click the link for Chapter 10; then click Sample Documents.

Whatever their approach, readers trust the writer to give them accurate, precise information in the proper sequence. Some instructions—electrical installation and medical procedures, for example—can be matters of life or death. For example, the instructions for installing a new light fixture can put a do-it-yourself home owner in danger of electric shock if the instructions fail to say "Before installing the fixture, turn off all electrical power running to the light outlet." In those cases, readers trust writers with their lives and with the lives of others.

Because your reader trusts you, you must make sure that your instructions are accurate and thorough. The amount of detail depends on how much knowledge your audience has about the process. A beginner, for example, needs more detail than someone with experience. Good instructions keep readers motivated to read carefully.

Planning Instructions

Before writing your own instructions, you must understand the procedure about which you are writing. If you understand the procedure, you will be better able to explain it to someone else. If you do not understand the procedure, your readers probably will not understand it either. When possible, work through the process yourself to see where your readers may get tripped up.

Use the following suggestions to analyze the process and to better understand the steps, the series of actions required to complete the process:

1. Create a flowchart with steps to the process. Write what someone should do first, second, third, and so on. Do not to skip any steps. Add and remove steps as needed.

2. In your mind, work the process backward. What is the purpose of the procedure? What is done last, next to last, third to last, and so on?

3. Watch a member of your target audience performing the task for the first time. Take notes. What is the very first step? What is the most difficult step? Which steps does the person misunderstand? Would additional information make things clearer? Interview this person after he or she has completed the procedure. Ask for suggestions to help you write a clear set of instructions.

⬤ STOP AND THINK

What would you tell a 4-year-old about making a peanut butter and jelly sandwich that you would not tell a person your age?

ORGANIZING AND FORMATTING INSTRUCTIONS

Now that you have analyzed the steps for your instructions, organize your information into sections for your reader. Then place that information into a sequence of chronological steps and an easy-to-read format.

Organizing Instructions

All instructions include steps of procedures and appropriate explanations along with additional details to clarify the procedure. However, instructions often contain other parts as well. Whether to include these parts depends on the audience and the purpose of the instructions.

Different writing situations require different organizational strategies. Although most instructions begin with an introduction, some do not. For example, the manual for a new car may contain an introduction at the beginning, but not for each major section. Furthermore, not all instructions require a list of materials. For example, telling someone how to use a blender would require only familiarity with the appliance, not a list of materials. But telling someone how to make pancakes would require a list of materials and ingredients.

Some instructions might require **cautions,** statements to indicate which actions might harm the mechanism. Others might require stronger **warnings,** statements to indicate which actions might cause injury or

How do you prefer to receive a set of instructions? Do you want to read written steps or to be told how to do something? Do you prefer watching someone perform a procedure or looking at pictures or a drawing of what to do?

FOCUS

Warm Up

Helping students voice how they read instructions can make them more aware of their own learning styles and how their readers might prefer to follow instructions.

TEACH

Make sure students understand the importance of safety. Written warnings and cautions are important to the safety of people and the maintenance of equipment.

FOCUS

Table 10.1

Point out the differences between the headings Less Explanation and More Explanation. The document changes when the writing situation and the needs of the audience change. Make sure students understand why one set of instructions may require all of the headings and another set may require only two headings.

ENRICH

Ask students to form groups and think of instructions that need cautions, a list of definitions, graphics, a list of materials (tools or ingredients), and warnings.

TEACH

Ask several students to write simple instructions in class—how to solve a math problem, how to get from one part of campus to another, or some other process.

ENRICH

Ask two students to come to the front of the class. One of them should be wearing shoes that lace up and tie. Tell one student to untie the shoes. Ask the other student to teach the first student how to tie the shoes. Tell the student tying the shoe to follow the directions precisely with no variation. See what happens. The entertaining results illustrate the difficulty of giving clear instructions.

harm to someone trying to follow the instructions. When you delete a file from your computer, a caution appears to ask whether you really want to send the file to the recycle bin. The instructions telling you how to administer flea and tick protection to your cat warn about the danger of the product coming in contact with your skin. Even your bag of popcorn has a warning: "HANDLE CAREFULLY—CONTAINS HOT AIR AND STEAM." You, too, are responsible for including proper cautions and warnings with any instructions you write.

Use Table 10.1 to determine what elements to add to instructions.

INCLUDE	IF
Cautions	Your reader could damage equipment by doing a step incorrectly. Insert cautions in your text before readers are likely to do anything harmful. Often a symbol or graphic accompanies the caution.
Definitions	Your reader must learn new terms to perform the procedure. Define six or more terms in a separate list or glossary. Define fewer than six terms when you first use the term.
Less Explanation	Your reader has performed the process before or the process is an emergency procedure in which reading explanations would prevent the reader from acting quickly.
More Explanation	Your reader is performing the process for the first time, the procedure is complicated, or the reader needs to know more to perform the procedure correctly.
Graphics	A picture, diagram, or flowchart would make the instructions easier to follow. Place a graphic as close as possible to the step it illustrates—above, below, or beside. Avoid placing the graphic on another page or at the end of the instructions.
Introduction	Your reader would benefit from any or all of the following information: background, purpose (what readers will be able to do when they finish), intended audience, scope (what the instructions do and do not cover), organization, best way to read the instructions, assumptions about readers' knowledge or abilities, and/or motivation to read the instructions carefully. An introduction appears at the beginning of the document.
Materials/ Tools	Your reader should gather materials, tools, or ingredients before following your instructions. Place this list before the steps.
Notes/ Tips	Additional but not essential information would aid your reader's understanding. Include a note immediately after the step to which it pertains.
Warnings	Your reader could get hurt by overlooking a step or not doing a step correctly. Place warnings before the reader is likely to do anything dangerous. Often a symbol or graphic that represents danger accompanies the warning.

Table 10.1

Formatting Instructions

Because readers are likely to be different and are often impatient, the format of your instructions should be easy to read. Use plenty of white space to make instructions look accessible. Number your steps using Arabic numerals (1, 2, 3, and so on) and align the steps in a list.

Another effective way to make instructions easy to use is to incorporate graphics such as flowcharts and diagrams. Graphics simplify a process and are useful for an intermediate reader who has performed the process before and needs only a quick refresher. Graphics aid the beginner as well, who will rely on both graphics and text to follow the procedure correctly. Sometimes different parts of a mechanism are shown at different times in the steps. Refer to your graphics with an explanatory statement such as "Refer to Figure 1 to see the location of buttons on the DVD player." You may add callouts that point to specific parts of your diagram to help readers find the parts you are discussing. Instructions that include referral statements cue the reader to look at the graphic at the appropriate time.

Formats may vary. For example, simple instructions may include only a one-sentence introduction and a list of numbered steps. Some instructions may contain only pictures. More complex instructions require several sections and graphics. A numbered list is preferred to define steps that must be completed in a certain order, although some instructions use letters or bullets to indicate steps. Figure 10.1 below and Figure 10.2 on the next page illustrate two simple formats for instructions.

FOCUS

Figure 10.2
Use the figure to show an alternative way to present instructions.

ENRICH
Try the "gossip" game by whispering instructions in one student's ear. Ask the student to whisper the instructions to the next person, continuing around the room. The students can say the instructions only once. No one can take notes or ask questions. See what happens to the instructions by the time they have reached the last student.

Make up your own instructions for the game or use one of these: (1) When you leave this classroom, turn left, walk eight steps, wait five seconds, and turn completely around. (2) Take a sheet of notebook paper, fold it in half lengthwise, draw a half moon on it, and pass it to the person behind you. Ask students what would help them remember the original instructions. They may say that writing down the instructions, taking notes, asking questions, or repeating the instructions would be helpful.

Figure 10.1 Instructions Using Pictures Only

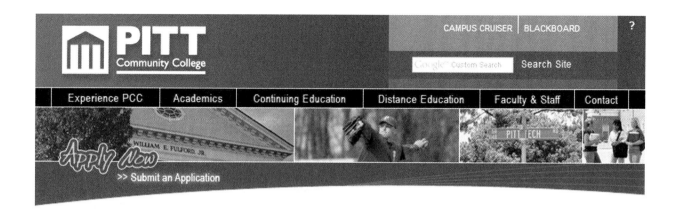

Print this page

Driving Directions

Physical Address:

1986 Pitt Tech Rd
Winterville, NC 28590
(252) 493-7200

From the North or South via I-95:

1. Take I-95 to Wilson.
2. Take Exit 119-A to US-264 E (toward Wilson, Goldsboro, or Raleigh).
3. Merge onto US-264 E. DO NOT take Exit 73B to Washington. When you approach Greenville city limits, US-264 E becomes Stantonsburg Rd.
4. Continue on Statonsburg Rd.
5. Turn right onto W. Arlington Blvd.
6. Turn right onto S Memorial Dr/NC-11 S.
7. Follow Memorial Dr/NC-11 S approximately 3 miles.
8. Turn right onto Tice Rd.
9. Take the first left onto Pitt Tech Rd. Pitt Community College will be on your right.

From East on HWY 264:

1. Take HWY 264 W toward Greenville.
2. Turn left onto S Memorial Dr/NC-11 S.
3. Follow Memorial Dr/NC-11 S approximately 3 miles.
4. Turn right onto Tice Rd.
5. Take the first left onto Pitt Tech Road. Pitt Community College will be on your right.

Figure 10.2 Simple Instructions with a List of Steps

ONGOING ASSESSMENT

Stop and Think

The organization for instructions varies because the subject and requirements of the instructions change. Some instructions call for a list of materials, some call for cautions, and others call for definitions.

Numbered steps and white space help readers follow the sequence.

Diagrams and flowcharts help readers see the process.

⬤ STOP AND THINK

Why does the organization of a set of instructions change from one set to another? How can page layout help someone read and follow instructions more effectively? What are some graphics that help readers better understand instructions?

COMPOSING INSTRUCTIONS

Organization, format, and graphics may vary, but all instructions require chronological steps. Except for instructions written for experienced readers, most instructions require explanations to accompany the steps.

Steps

A **step** is the action that a reader performs—what the reader actually does. Steps have a consistent and unique structure. Use the following guidelines for writing steps:

1. Make sure steps proceed *forward in time*—numbered, or in some cases lettered—with no backtracking to pick up a step that was forgotten.

✓ **Forward in Time**

a. Buckle your seat belt.

b. Insert the key into the ignition switch.

c. Turn the key forward until the engine starts.

✗ **Backtracking**

a. Insert the key into the ignition switch.

b. Turn the key forward until the engine starts.

c. Buckle your seat belt before you turn the key forward.

2. Begin each step with an active-voice verb in the **imperative mood** (a command: verb + object) and use second person (stated or understood "you" as the subject).

✓ **Action Verb to Start**

Trim the tip of the dog's nail.*

✗ **No Verb to Start**

The tip of the dog's nails should be trimmed.

*You can begin with a modifying word or phrase, as in "Carefully trim the tip of the dog's nail" or "To ensure a pain-free procedure, trim the tip of the dog's nail."

3. Use short sentences, which keep your reader focused on one step at a time. An overly complex or compound-complex sentence can create confusion.

✓ **Short Sentences**

Install a smoke detector inside each bedroom in which an occupant sleeps with the door closed. Smoke blocked by the door might not sound an alarm in the hallway. Also, the sleeper might not hear an alarm coming from another area of the house.

✗ **Long Sentence**

Install a smoke detector inside each bedroom in which an occupant sleeps with the door closed because smoke blocked by the door might not sound the alarm in the hallway and the sleeper might not hear an alarm coming from another area of the house.

Warm Up

Look at the sample instructions on page 229. Find the sentences that actually tell the reader to do something. What do you notice about the wording of these sentences? What do the other sentences tell the reader?

FOCUS

Warm Up

The sentences provide steps (actions) and explanations of steps. Have students describe what the explanatory sentences actually explain about the steps.

TEACH

Discuss how the examples under "Steps" illustrate the guidelines.

RETEACH

Use the Steps Teaching Master to review guidelines for writing steps.

4. Write only one instruction (one action) for each step.

   Exception: If two steps are closely tied to each other in time, reading them in the same step might be easier for the reader: "Release the clutch. At the same time, press the accelerator."

✓ **One Instruction per Step**	✗ **More Than One Instruction per Step**
a. Place your chin on the chin rest.	Place your chin on the chin rest and look at the light.
b. Look at the light.	

5. Make sure each step is truly a step—an action, something to do. A description implies action, but it does not direct the reader to actually do something.

✓ **An Action**	✗ **A Description**
Grasp the rope when it comes back to you.	The rope will come back to you.

6. Keep the natural articles *a, an,* and *the.*

✓ **With Articles**	✗ **Without Articles**
Send the electrician a notice to connect power to the house.	Send electrician notice to connect power to house.

7. Include precise, specific details (measurements, sizes, locations, time, parts, and restatement in more familiar language) to show your reader exactly what to do.

✓ **Sufficient Details**	✗ **Not Sufficient Details**
Loosen the chain to provide 3/8" of movement, or "give," between the front and rear sprockets.	Loosen the chain to provide some movement, or "give," in the chain.

8. Place any necessary explanations after the step. Placing the step first keeps the reader on task.

✓ **Explanation After Step**	✗ **Explanation Before Step**
Touch the number pad to enter the weight of the food to be defrosted. Make sure you enter the weight in pounds and tenths of pounds.	Make* sure you enter the weight in pounds and tenths of pounds. Touch the number pad to enter the weight of the food to be defrosted.

   *Although *Make* is a verb, it does not indicate a step, but explains how to enter the weight.

9. Use substeps when a major step is too broad to be clearly understood by your reader.

✓ **Use of Substeps**	✗ **Overgeneralized Step***
Play a G major chord.	Play a G major chord.

a. Place your third finger on the third fret of the bottom string.

b. Place your second finger on the second fret of the fifth string.

c. Place your third finger on the third fret of the first string.

*Whether to use substeps depends on your audience's knowledge and experience with the procedure.

Explanations

An **explanation** is an extension of the step it explains. An explanation uses the same number as the step it follows and is written immediately after the step.

1. Write the step. Then write the explanation if it is needed.

2. Write another step. Then write the explanation if it is needed.

3. Write another step. Then write the explanation if it is needed.

The number and type of explanations depend on your reader's previous experience. Not every step requires an explanation, but well-placed explanations guide and motivate your reader. Often explanations are written as a note following the step. Typical explanations include the following:

■ What not to do and why

  Darken the appropriate oval with a No. 2 pencil. Do not place stray pencil marks on the answer sheet. The computerized scanner may read the stray mark as an error

  Note: Warnings and cautions are important enough to include before the step that may cause a problem if it is not completed correctly.

■ Why a step is important

  Rinse the boiled egg with cold water as soon as you remove it from boiling water. The cold water will cause the egg to contract from the shell, making the egg easier to peel.

■ What happens when the reader does something

  (1) Press PROGRAM on the remote control. The MENU will appear on the TV screen. (2) To autoscan for a channel, press CHANNEL SCAN once on the remote control. The tuner scans the channels stored in the tuner's memory, stopping on each channel for about two seconds.

NETBookmark

The Plain Language Action and Information Network (PLAIN) is a government initiative mandating the use of plain, clear language in government documents. The site offers writing tips for making procedures easy to follow.

Go to the NET Bookmark for Chapter 10. Do a search for the No Gobbledygook Award and read about it. Print an example of a document written by a winner of this award. How does the document exemplify the use of plain language?

www.cengage.com/school/bcomm/techwtg

- How to perform the action—more detail

  Tighten the axle nuts. Make sure they are tight. There must not be any space between the inner nut, the wheel slip, and the axle nuts. If there is space, tighten the axle nuts more securely.

- What terms to define

  Beat the eggs until frothy, or until they look like sea foam. *or* A digital signal transmits electrical data using binary code, or "off" and "on" pulses.

  Note: If you have a number of definitions (approximately six or more), consider adding a separate section labeled "Definitions" or "Glossary." If you have fewer than six, define them as you write or place them in the introduction.

- How to make a decision

  Wrap a small section of hair around the curling iron. If you want curls to flip up, wrap the hair backward (away from the shoulders). If you want curls to curve under, wrap the hair down (toward the shoulders).

  Note: Branching the two methods into substeps is another possibility:

  1. Wrap a small section of hair around the curling iron.

     a. If you want curls to flip up, wrap the hair backward.

     b. If you want curls to curve under, wrap the hair downward.

Because some readers need more details, you must think carefully about how much explanation to add. Consider the answers to the questions that follow.

- What should readers not do? Why?

- Would readers be more likely to perform the steps correctly if they knew the significance of the action, the reason for performing the step, or more about the process?

- Would pointing out what should happen when readers execute a step help them? (The first time you performed the process, how did you know you had performed a step correctly?)

- Does the reader need help making a decision? Should some steps be subdivided into if/then scenarios? Refer to the curling iron example at the top of the page.

- Would the reader benefit from a brief definition?

- What questions will readers have?

- What are the most crucial steps, those steps that *must* be done correctly?

Finally, think back to the first time you performed the procedure and how awkward it felt to be a beginner.

- What did you do wrong the first time you performed the process?

- What questions did you have the first time you performed the process?

Field Tests

Always **field-test** your instructions by asking several people to try them before you send your final copy. Your field testers can provide you with valuable feedback by noting wording that is not clear, steps that are out of sequence, or steps that have been left out altogether. To administer a field test, also called a usability test, you must select a test method, design the test, select test subjects, and make revisions based on the data.

Concurrent testing and retrospective testing, discussed next, are two field tests that evaluate how effectively users can perform your instructions.

Concurrent Testing

Concurrent testing evaluates a product while it is being used or an activity while it is being performed. In a concurrent test, you observe your subjects reading and performing your instructions. You measure such things as their accuracy, speed, recall, and attitude.

Rhonda adapted an informal method of concurrent testing to evaluate instructions she wrote. Her instructions told AmeriCorps volunteers how to find the campsite for their training retreat. To make sure all 50 volunteers would find the site, she asked three classmates to follow her directions using a map she had drawn. Two classmates did not arrive at the campsite because they turned onto Riverside Road instead of Riverview Road. As a result, Rhonda knew that she needed to revise her instructions to emphasize the name of the correct road and to caution drivers against making the wrong turn. Because of the information Rhonda learned, all AmeriCorps volunteers found their way.

Focus on Ethics

When you pick up a prescription from the pharmacy, you receive an insert that gives you information about the drug—instructions for use, proper doses, and risks. By giving patients and doctors more information on which to base judgments about good health, drug companies accept an ethical responsibility to protect their consumers. Warnings appear on the inserts in order of risk severity:

- Contraindications
- Warnings
- Precautions
- Adverse reactions

In addition to these four risk categories, the FDA requires another category for selected drugs to indicate special problems that may lead to serious injury or death. These problems are displayed prominently in a box as a warning to consumers and physicians. Based on clinical data, the black box warning alerts physicians to carefully monitor the health of patients taking these drugs.

Think Critically

Why are the warnings given to both consumers and physicians?

Practice conducting a field test using the *Field Test Activity* worksheet available at www.cengage.com/school/bcomm/techwtg. Click the link for Chapter 10; then click Data Files.

TEACH

Field testing helps ensure that instructions are clear. However, where the field test shows a problem with instructions, it does not always reveal an obvious solution. Tell students that they may make many attempts before they implement a solution that works.

FOCUS ON ETHICS

Talk about the ethical responsibilities that pharmaceutical companies have to their customers. Bring an insert to class to show how this information is presented. Warnings are given to consumers and physicians because both have a right to know the possible side effects Also, warnings to both provide a check-and-balance system.

TEACH

Stress to students that concurrent testing observes someone performing the instructions and that retrospective testing asks for feedback after someone has performed the instructions. Writers of questionnaires should remain neutral, not leading participants to say or write something they would not think of on their own. You can refer students to Chapter 3 for a review of writing neutral surveys (questionnaires).

Concurrent testing for longer instructions involves a more formal procedure. For example, Arturo, the service manager for Satellite Dish Subsidiaries, wants to make sure that his instructions for installing a satellite dish for TV and Internet service are clear. He selects five test subjects in a rural community who range in age from 21 to 41 because these are the types of people who will likely be installing the dish. He then watches each person install the dish, taking notes about their errors, comments, questions, and frustrations. After watching the five subjects perform the installation, Arturo knows that two of them had difficulty mounting the dish in the correct location at the proper angle. He realizes that his steps about placement are confusing because each step contains too much information. So he makes the steps shorter and adds a roof diagram to show suggested areas for placement.

To design a useful concurrent study, decide whether your subjects should complete the whole procedure or just selected tasks. Rhonda and Arturo asked their subjects to perform the entire task. On the other hand, a usability study focuses only on selected tasks. One usability study of a website advertising cars asked users to perform these specific tasks: find the "sale of the day," descriptions of used models, and information about warranties.

As you observe your test subjects, ask yourself these questions:

- Were the subjects able to do what the instructions told them to do?

- How long did the subjects take to complete the task?

- How many mistakes did the subjects make?

- What steps were most difficult? least difficult?

- Were the subjects frustrated at any time? If so, explain.

- What did the subjects remember about the task 15 minutes after completing it?

- What did the subjects remember about the task 24 hours after completing it?

You also can ask subjects to think aloud, reading the instructions aloud and saying whatever comes to mind. Through this window to subjects' thoughts, you see how they are reacting to each step. You may want to record their performance so you can review it more closely later.

Retrospective Testing

A second way to test instructions is through the use of **retrospective testing**—asking subjects to complete a questionnaire or to answer questions about a task *after* they have performed it. Many field tests use a concurrent test along with a retrospective test. This way testers gain additional insights into the behavior of test subjects.

Surveys often are used for retrospective testing. Remember that a survey can include different types of questions. On the next page, Figure 10.3 shows

```
+---------------------------------------------------------------+
|                  Retrospective Test Questions                  |
|                                                                |
|  Question Types    Questions                                   |
|                                                                |
|  Multiple Choice   Was the introduction informative? Yes___  No___ |
|                                                                |
|                    After filling in the applicant's name, address, Social Security |
|                    number, and telephone number (steps 1–4), the next step |
|                    was to                                      |
|                    a. Enter the amount of money requested.     |
|                    b. Include the value of the car.            |
|                    c. Enter the current interest rate.         |
|                                                                |
|  Likert Scale      Rank on a scale of 1–10 (with 10 being most satisfied and 1 |
|                    being least satisfied) your satisfaction with the completeness* |
|                    of this document.                           |
|                                                                |
|                    1   2   3   4   5   6   7   8   9   10       |
|  Short Answer      Describe the first step you performed.      |
|                                                                |
|                    After reading step 6 (perhaps a critical step such as entering |
|                    gross income), what did you think you were supposed to do? |
|  Open              What suggestions do you have for improvement? |
|                                                                |
|                    What was the most difficult section? Why?   |
|  *Kelsey could ask about clarity of the wording or usefulness of the graphics. |
+---------------------------------------------------------------+
```

Figure 10.3 Survey Questions for a Retrospective Field Test

questions that Kelsey plans to ask his loan officers after they have field-tested his procedures for completing a car loan application.

Regardless of the test method you use, select a reasonable sample of subjects. To ask senior accountants to test instructions for using a machine lathe is not practical because they would not use the instructions. You would ask senior accountants to test instructions for new accounting software. Some experts recommend using at least five testers, but others do not believe that five testers is enough—especially for a longer document such as a manual or for interactive media such as a website. After completing your field test, you should compile your data, list problems from most frequent to least frequent, and devise solutions.

Online Instructions

No doubt you have used **online instructions,** or computer-based instructions, to order concert tickets, to track a UPS delivery, to set up e-mail and instant messenger accounts, or to complete a job application. Online instructions allow users to find out something, to get something, or to learn something quickly.

Online instructions include help menus, CD-ROMs, and web-based instructions. Help menus are one of the most popular types of online instructions. Most computer programs feature a help menu, typically in the upper right corner of the screen, or balloon help, the explanation that appears when you scroll over a menu item. Think about your educational career. You may recall using tutorials on a website or a CD-ROM to teach yourself grammar, keyboarding, or a foreign language.

Discuss how computer media are different from print media and how these differences can affect online instructions: With print media, pages can be flipped through, shuffled, and left in piles on a desk. Portions can be highlighted and underlined. Computer screens are one-dimensional and cannot be easily moved. However, the document can be printed.

TEACH
Specialized software aids in the creation of computer-based instructions. The help menus that students used were probably created using RoboHelp® software. This software is used to create help systems for desktop and web-based applications. ToolBook is used to create interactive instructions (e.g., taking a patient's blood pressure or injecting radioactive dye).

RETEACH
Show the Checklist for Online Instructions Teaching Master available on the IRCD.

COMMUNICATION DILEMMA

Employees all over the world read online instructions, so this dilemma is common in the workplace. For nonnative speakers of English, instructions should be visual. However, students must keep in mind that graphics have different meanings in different cultures. The color red does not mean "stop" in many countries. Likewise, the color green does not always mean "go." Some hand gestures that are not offensive in the United States are offensive in other parts of the world. In addition, some cultures read from right to left, rather than left to right. Emphasize that students should find out as much as they can about an international audience and design their instructions accordingly. One guideline is to conduct a field test with the target audience to ensure that instructions are clear.

ONGOING ASSESSMENT

Stop and Think

Steps proceed forward in time; use active-voice verbs and imperative mood; use short sentences; include only one instruction per step; show action; use the articles *a*, *an*, and *the*; include specific details; and include a needed explanation after the step.

Explanations tell what not to do, explain why something is important, tell how to make a decision, describe what happens when a step is done, and provide quick definitions.

Specific details make information easier to follow.

Field testing ensures accuracy.

Writers can use concurrent or retrospective testing.

Limit each unit of instruction to one screen size, use consistent design, provide a tree or map of the site, and insert navigational aids.

Communication Dilemma

You have just landed a job as a trainer for an international company that makes engines for fighter planes. Your job is to train new engineers, line managers, and other employees to assemble specific engine parts. This coming Monday you will conduct your first training session online, and your job is to prepare the training materials for the session.

On Friday afternoon before the scheduled training, your manager tells you that many employees taking the training are not from the United States. Participants live in Russia, Taiwan, Germany, and Japan. In addition, your boss explains that many of the trainees do not speak English.

Think Critically

How do you revise your training materials so that international employees will understand them?

To write online instructions, keep in mind the strategies presented in this chapter for writing and explaining steps, using white space and graphics, and providing cautions and warnings. In addition to the guidelines for writing paper-based instructions, online instructions should:

- Limit each unit of instruction to one screen size so it is not necessary for the user to scroll down the page.

- Use consistent design—font, font sizes, colors, graphics, and headers—so the reader learns to anticipate the organization and feels comfortable navigating.

- Provide a tree or map of the site and topics so readers can see the site at a glance.

- Insert navigational aids such as a link to the home page and to other important pages.

- Use keyword searches with several synonyms for the same action.

- Evaluate the usefulness of the instructions with a field test, revising the instructions if necessary.

Also, if you are teaching users to perform tasks on a screen, configure instructions so they do not take up the entire screen. By configuring your instructions this way, you allow users to work on the screen while they read the instructions.

⬤ STOP AND THINK

How are steps written? What kind of information do explanations contain? What kind of information makes instructions precise? Why is field testing important? How can a writer field-test instructions? What strategies should you keep in mind when writing online instructions?

CHAPTER 10 REVIEW

SUMMARY

1. Readers of instructions can be in a hurry, so writers must learn to compensate with carefully planned writing. Readers trust writers to be accurate and safety-conscious and to provide adequate explanation in their instructions.

2. All instructions contain itemized steps. Most instructions contain an introduction and graphics. The process and the audience determine whether a list of materials, warnings, cautions, notes, or definitions should be included.

3. Instructions are written in short chronological sentences using active voice and imperative mood. Each step must show an action. Explanations follow steps and tell what not to do, why a step is performed, what the results of a step are, and how to complete a step. Explanations should provide enough details to enable the reader to perform the step correctly and safely. When creating online instructions, the writer should limit each unit of instruction to one screen, use a consistent design (font, colors, and graphics), provide a tree or map of the site and topics, insert navigational aids on the home page, and configure instructions so that users performing tasks on the screen can see them while working.

CLOSE

Summary

Ask students to evaluate a set of online instructions using the summary points.

CLOSE

Checklist

Use the checklist during a peer review session. After students create their own instructions, either online or on paper, have each student exchange his or her instructions with another student and use the checklist for review.

REVIEW

For a review of the key terms in the chapter, provide students with the *Key Terms* worksheet available as a supplemental activity on the IRCD.

Checklist

- Do I thoroughly understand the procedure about which I am writing?

- Did I consider using graphics?

- Did I consider using an introduction, a list of materials, cautions, warnings, and notes?

- Have I written steps that move forward in time? Do my steps begin with a verb that commands? Have I used short sentences that include only one action per step? Are my steps truly steps, things to do? Have I kept the articles *a, an,* and *the*?

- Have I considered including explanations that tell what not to do and why? that include significant details to help the reader understand why a step is important? that tell the reader how to make a decision? that include descriptions of what will happen when the reader does something? that give enough details on how something should be done?

- Have I included enough precise details (for example, distances, sizes, places, or time)?

- Have I considered whether online instructions would be appropriate for my audience? Have I followed the additional guidelines for online instructions?

- Did I field-test my instructions with my target audience?

Build Your Foundation

1. Examine each step below. What kind of information would make each instruction more specific?

   a. Rotate the tool several times around the wire, leaving the spring closed.
   b. Draw part of an oval for the head.
   c. If the fitting has a tub spout, make a hole in the wall.
   d. Clean your room before you leave.
   e. Beat the meringue until stiff peaks form.
   f. Place the selvages of the material together.

2. Break up each sentence into shorter sentences that reflect one step per sentence.

   a. Remove the cover from the mic; press the transmit button on the mic; and by using a small screwdriver with a plastic or wooden handle, adjust the transmitting frequency.
   b. Take the two upper sections of the handle and using the shortest bolt with the nut provided, fasten them together as shown in the illustration in Figure 1.
   c. Read the passage and locate all nouns, underlining them with a single line.

3. Rewrite these steps so that each one begins with a verb in active voice and imperative mood. (The "you" can be understood.)

   a. The cook should touch the AUTO DEFROST pad to begin the defrosting process.
   b. When you want to play, you should press the START button.
   c. The aquarium floor requires a layer of gravel that, sloping from back to front, is about 6 to 8 centimeters deep at the front wall.
   d. We want you to come to the front of the room and use the available podium.

4. Label each of the following as steps, explanations, cautions, or warnings.

   a. When paddling, keep the canoe in line with the current.
   b. Make sure the supply voltage matches the voltage specified on the rating plate.
   c. Separate dark clothes from light clothes to prevent colors from running.
   d. Do not overload your dryer. For efficient drying, clothes need to tumble freely.
   e. When you have recorded your message, press the pound key.
   f. When the virus protection window appears, click OK immediately to decontaminate your drive. Failure to heed the virus warnings may cause you to lose data and contaminate other machines.
   g. To determine how tight the fasteners need to be, see the Torque Range chart in the back of this book.

5. Which of these guidelines for writing instructions apply to all instructions (print and online)? Which apply only to online instructions?

   a. Make sure each step represents only one action unless the actions are so closely related that they need to be in the same step.

b. Limit each unit of instruction to one screen size.

c. Evaluate the usefulness of your instructions with a field test.

d. Use a consistent design for each screen.

e. Provide a tree or map of your site and topics.

f. Do not omit *a, an,* and *the.*

g. Eliminate your reader's need to scroll down the page.

h. Insert navigational aids such as links to important pages.

i. Include appropriate cautions, warnings, and notes.

j. Use active-voice verbs in imperative mood for steps.

6. For a beginner using a word processing program such as WordPerfect® or Microsoft® Word, list help topics that this person would most likely use.

7. Visit WebMD.com to see online instructions for preventing the common cold. Are the instructions clear? Explain.

Your Turn

8. In small groups, write instructions for any of the following processes (or other process with which you are familiar). Analyze your audience, follow the guidelines for composing instructions and provide ample explanations.

making a bed	cleaning a room	changing the oil/tires
setting up a tent	using a calculator	playing a video game
setting up an aquarium	lifting weights	constructing a craft
brushing your teeth	mowing the lawn	changing a diaper
administering first aid	creating artwork	doing a yoga move

9. You have been asked to write online help instructions for a word processing program you know well. Write your instructions for one of these processes:

a. Changing the font type for an entire document

b. Underlining a word

c. Changing the margins

d. Copying and pasting a paragraph

e. Cutting and pasting a paragraph

f. Wrapping text around a photograph

Community Connection

10. Based on your experience and interviews with other students, write instructions for new students that explain how to register for classes or for a particular program. Although your school probably has registration instructions, the document you develop should be an "insider's guide" of insights that you and other students have gained about more direct methods, pitfalls, situations to avoid, and classes to take together and classes to avoid taking in the same term. For the new students, define unfamiliar terms and give precise locations and descriptions.

11. Visit a nonprofit organization in your community and learn about the procedures and processes used there. Ask if you can help by developing written instructions for a task or procedure, such as steps for closing the facility at the end of the day, making an enlargement on the copier, orienting a volunteer, or answering an office telephone.

6. Answers will vary, but possible help topics include how to save, how to change fonts, how to insert a graphic, how to create a table, how to insert clip art, and how to make a bulleted or numbered list.

7. Use examples to illustrate online instructions.

ASSESS

Your Turn

7. Make sure students have completed the prewriting by writing the steps beforehand, analyzing their audience, and using the checklist.

8. Ask students to go through the procedure several times and take notes. Then tell them to write the instructions, following the guidelines in the chapter. Ask them to format the instructions for a help menu. More ambitious students might provide screen shots of the instructions.

ASSESS

Community Connection

9. Follow the guidelines for writing instructions. Note that the audience is made up of new students.

10. Follow the guidelines for writing instructions.

Chapter 111

Employment Communication

Goals

- Plan employment communication
- Format and organize a resume
- Choose a type of resume
- Compose a resume
- Compose employment letters

Terms

- chronological resume, p. 257
- cover letter, p. 251
- electronic resume, p. 259
- follow-up letter, p. 251
- functional resume, p. 257
- keywords, p. 261
- online resume, p. 262
- parallel structure, p. 265
- priority order, p. 257
- resignation letter, p. 251
- resume, p. 251
- reverse chronological order, p. 257
- scannable resumes, p. 261
- solicited letter, p. 267
- text file, p. 261
- unsolicited letter, p. 267

TEACHING RESOURCES FOR CHAPTER 11

Instructor's Resource CD
Data Files
Data File Solutions
Lesson Plans
Teaching Masters
PowerPoint Slides
Chapter Tests with Solutions
Additional Chapter Activities
*Exam*View

Website
www.cengage.com/school/bcomm/techwtg
Crossword Puzzle
Data Files
Data File Solutions
Flashcards
Glossary
NET Bookmark
Sample Documents
Web Links

WRITE TO LEARN
Discuss goals. Tell students that strong communication skills (along with hard work and an education) can help them get a good job.

WRITE TO LEARN

Place yourself in the future, ten years from now. Write a one-page description of your life. Where do you live? What talents and interests have you pursued? What kind of job do you have? Are you happy with your job? How much money do you make? How did you create this life? In other words, how did you get here?

Focus on Employment Communication

Read the sample resume on the next page and answer these questions:

- Glance at the resume for ten seconds and then look away. What do you remember? In other words, what stands out?
- Does the resume look balanced and attractive? Explain.
- What information is included in each major section?
- How does Matt's work experience relate to his job objective?
- What impression does his earning some of his college expenses make? What kind of impression does his volunteer work make?

What If?

- Matt had 15 years experience in the computer industry? 10 years in the restaurant business? 5 years of military experience?
- Matt had won an academic scholarship or an award for web design?
- Matt were applying for a faculty position or a graphic arts position?

Matt R. Abboud
mabboud@comm.mcc.edu

Temporary
67B Whistle Run Apartments
Albuquerque, New Mexico 87103-4737
505.555.0173

Permanent
803 Princeton Road
Albuquerque, New Mexico 87118-1190
505.555.0149

OBJECTIVE	Computer programmer in an industrial environment
QUALIFICATIONS	<ul><li>3 years' experience in networking and computer support</li><li>AAS degree in Computer Programming</li><li>Experience in C ++, Microsoft SQL Server, Visual Basic 2008, and Windows Server 2008</li><li>Proficient in all Microsoft Office (2000/XP) products</li></ul>
EDUCATION	Maddox Community College, Albuquerque, New Mexico AAS, anticipated graduation May 2010 Major: Computer Programming, GPA 3.9/4.0

Major Courses

Advanced C++	Visual Basic 2008	Internet Programming
Java Programming	Database Concepts	Systems Analysis/Design
UNIX Fundamentals	Database Management	International Business
Windows Server Admin	Interpersonal Communication	Technical Writing

CO-OP EXPERIENCE	**Wadell Computer Industries**	**January 2010–Present**
	Albuquerque, New Mexico	

- Design and develop test specifications for software systems
- Evaluate existing computerized systems to improve efficiency
- Serve on Quality Assurance Team in IT department

	Landcaster Microsystems	**July 2009–December 2009**
	Santa Fe, New Mexico	

- Set up and maintained clients using Windows NT/Server 2008
- Maintained SQL server database
- Answered help desk calls

OTHER EXPERIENCE	**Earned half of college expenses working part-time**	**2005–2009**
	Auto Express, Santa Fe, New Mexico, Salesclerk	
	AG Shirt Factory, Santa Fe, New Mexico, Production Line Worker	
VOLUNTEER WORK	Special Olympics—Santa Fe, New Mexico	**2007**
	Big Brothers Big Sisters—Santa Fe, New Mexico	**2006–2008**

Sample Resume

FOCUS

Focus on Employment Communication

Use the questions to encourage students to read the sample closely.

ASSESS

What If?

Use the questions to discuss how the sample would be different if the situation or audience changed.

Go to www.cengage.com/school/bcomm/techwtg for more detailed responses to these questions.

Writing@Work

Courtesy of Kate Houck

Kate Houck manages the Implementation Team for Employment Law Training, a San Francisco–based company that provides employers with online compliance training. In addition to a BA in political science, she has extensive experience evaluating job applicants, interviewing, and hiring employees for companies ranging from Internet startups to Fortune 500s.

"The biggest challenge in reviewing a stack of resumes is culling the wheat from the chaff," explains Kate. "I look for a resume that has a good layout and concise, engaging statements about relevant experience and accomplishments. It should also demonstrate passion for or expertise in something. You can usually teach someone to do a job, but it is harder to teach someone to be an employee who cares."

The most glaring mistakes to avoid in a resume or cover letter are the easiest ones to prevent. Kate emphasizes that these documents "should have no typos or spelling errors. If you mess this up, you are just being careless." She also recommends that job candidates google themselves to eliminate undesirable public listings: "It may not be fair, but your online presence serves as a sort of reference in today's electronic age. So if there is anything posted that you don't want an employer to see, make sure it is under a pseudonym or restricted access; otherwise, it's fair game."

Having seen so many resumes has taught Kate precisely what makes a great resume and how to make her own resume float to the top of the pile: "The top two things I try to convey in my resume are competence and excellence. I not only highlight what I have done at each job, but also provide evidence that shows how I surpassed the objectives for that position. I don't want to be just a performer on my resume or at work; I want to be a star."

Think Critically

1. Does your resume meet Kate's standards for "good layout and concise, engaging statements about relevant experience and accomplishments"? Why or why not?

2. Would Kate see that you have "passion for or expertise in something?" How can you change your resume so that someone like Kate puts it at the top of the stack?

Printed with permission of Kate Houck

GETTING STARTED ON EMPLOYMENT COMMUNICATION

The job you seek may be a long-awaited dream job or a part-time job to help you through school. Whatever the job, you will need attractive and well-crafted employment communication to highlight your strengths for the job market. You will use your technical writing skills to analyze your audience's needs and then persuade your audience that you can fulfill those needs.

Employment communication includes a **resume** (a one- or two-page summary of your qualifications), a **cover letter** (to accompany the resume), a **follow-up letter** (to thank the employer for the interview and to summarize your qualifications), and possibly a **resignation letter** (to announce your intention to resign). Resumes and the accompanying letters are important because they:

- Create a professional, favorable impression.

- Allow you to control the presentation of your skills on paper.

- Encourage an employer to call you to arrange an interview.

- Give employers something to look at before you fill out any applications they may require.

- Maintain goodwill between you and your employer.

To get started on employment communication, assess your strengths, learn what you can about a prospective employer, and choose your references. Then consider the employer's perspective and expectations.

Assess Your Strengths

Good employment communication begins with self-assessment. Consider your skills, aptitudes, education, interests, and experience. Use the following questions to help you determine your strengths as an employee:

- **Education:** What is your grade point average (GPA)? What special classes have prepared you for a particular job? What degrees do you hold? Where did you go to school, and when did you graduate?

- **Employment:** What jobs have you held? Write the job title, city and state, and dates for each job you now have or have previously held. Describe your duties and special projects on the job. Be specific.

- **Accomplishments:** List your accomplishments (scholastic, job-related, extracurricular, or community) over the last several years. Include any honors or awards you received. What skills do these accomplishments and honors illustrate? Would these skills be useful in the workplace?

- **Skills:** What are your special talents? What can you do well? Are you a good problem solver, creative thinker, good communicator? Do you have special skill sets—with computers, machinery, sales? Make a list, even if it overlaps with something you have already written.

- **Character or personality traits:** Are you dependable, honest, and flexible? Are you outgoing, calm, and optimistic? Do you have a good sense of humor?

Warm Up

If you were the chief executive officer of a successful corporation, what kinds of employees would you hire? What would you want to see on a resume?

FOCUS

Warm Up

Use the Warm Up to help students think about employment from the employer's perspective.

TEACH

Writing employment communication is a complex task that requires much thought and research.

Ask students what technical writing skills they will use to write resumes and letters. Skills include audience analysis, persuasion, page design, organization, concise style, and specific language—all characteristics of technical writing.

Use the questions on the *Assess Your Strengths* worksheet and the *Research Your Employer* worksheet to help students find the information they will use to write a resume and a letter of application. Make sure they determine the most important information, for there may not be room to include all information in the resume.

When you finish your assessment, consider which responses would impress a prospective employer. Now you should have a better idea of what makes you valuable as an employee.

Research Your Prospective Employer

Learn all you can about your prospective employer, the company, and the job. Call the human resources office and find out about the company's hiring practices. Do you know anyone who works for or used to work for this company? You also can find information about major American companies in *Hoover's 500: Profiles of America's Largest Business Enterprises*. See if you can find the answers to the following questions:

- Who will be responsible for making the decision to hire you—an individual or a committee? If it is an individual, what position does that person hold? What skills is he or she looking for in an employee?

- What can you find out about the company—its mission statement, its current projects, its organization, its openings, or its past record?

- What can you learn about the position for which you are applying? What would you be expected to do, and with whom would you work?

Ideally, you will be applying for a specific job with a particular company—a Social Worker II position at the Richmond Department of Social Services, for example. In reality, though, you also may send out a number of resumes to different organizations for a certain kind of job. In these cases, you may not have time to research the jobs in depth, but you still want to find out what you can about the positions and the organizations to which you are applying.

Choose Your References

A reference is a person who knows you well enough to vouch for your skills and your character. This person should feel comfortable making positive statements about your work performance, giving examples of your accomplishments, and answering specific questions from a prospective employer.

technotr/iStockphoto.com

Choose three to five people to include as references. Work references—people for whom you have actually worked—make the best references. After all, your employer is interested in knowing how well you perform on the job. Educational references such as instructors, advisers, and guidance counselors also can attest to your abilities. Including one personal reference, someone (not a relative) who knows you well outside the workplace, is acceptable as long as you also include strong work references.

Before you list someone as a reference, ask the person to agree to be a reference for you. If this person hesitates or says no, ask someone else.

The trend today is not to include references on the resume, but to have a list prepared in case you are asked to provide them. Then if you are granted an interview, you can offer your list at that time.

ENRICH

Ask students to look up their dream job in *What Color Is Your Parachute?* or some other guide. Many career books (*Knock 'em Dead 2009* is a recent one) and websites are devoted to helping people find jobs. The advice is more exhaustive than what can be provided in this chapter.

Students can summarize an occupation's salary, qualifications, and employment potential from one of these sources.

Who Reads Employment Communication?

To write the best employment communication possible, you must understand your audience by considering the employer's perspective and expectations.

Employer's Perspective

Generally, employers seek someone whose credentials meet their company's needs, whose personality fits with their current staff, and whose career plan complements their goals. Employers are interested in an applicant's education, experience, skills, and work habits. Employers also want employees who have personal and professional integrity.

Your resume and cover letter show employers that you have the skills they need. At this stage, the resume and letter are the only means employers have of knowing who you are and what you can do for them. Therefore, you want to create a good first impression with your communication.

If you have done a good job of writing, you may be asked to interview for the job. In the interview, you have an opportunity to convince the employer that you are the candidate for whom he or she is looking. Thus, the goal of a resume and a cover letter is to create enough interest to be granted an interview. The goal of the interview is to persuade an employer to hire you.

Audience awareness is especially important when you are writing a resume and a cover letter. Focusing on the reader of the resume may be difficult because the resume is primarily about the writer. Nonetheless, because the reader is the person who does the hiring, his or her needs are most important. Let the keywords in the job announcement guide your writing and put yourself in the shoes of the individual doing the hiring.

Employer's Expectations

Your prospective employer expects your communication to conform to standard employment protocol. Employment communication must:

- Contain no errors. Resumes with misspellings, typos, and punctuation errors are routinely cast aside during initial screenings.

- Look neat and professional. For example, a resume with smeared ink or one whose print is too light makes the writer look careless. To look professional, resumes should be printed in letter-quality print on bonded (heavy, stiff) paper.

- Follow an accepted format. A resume that is too long, for example, or one that is printed on colored paper or uses an eccentric design looks as though the writer did not know how to format a resume properly.

- Emphasize your best qualities (even if you think you may be bragging).

TYPICAL READER

A busy manager scanning employment documents for key information.

WRITER'S FOCUS

Capturing the manager's attention by placing the most important qualifications in carefully designed and error-free employment documents.

ONGOING ASSESSMENT

Stop and Think

Students need to make sure their references know their career goals so the references will understand how to respond. Resumes may be discarded because applicants are not qualified or because omissions or errors reflect poorly on the applicant. Employers must hire qualified, responsible people.

⬤ STOP AND THINK

Choose three people who might agree to be references for you. What do you think these people would say about you? Are they familiar with your career goals? Why do employers discard some resumes initially? Why do employers read selected employment communication carefully?

Warm Up

Congratulations! You have been voted Most Likely to Succeed from your graduating class. A short article appears about you in your yearbook. What does the article say? Why are you most likely to succeed?

FOCUS

Warm Up

Help students think about their strengths, talents, and interests as others see them. You might ask students to work in pairs to answer the questions about each other.

FORMATTING AND ORGANIZING RESUMES

Because employers may spend no more than 15 to 45 seconds looking at your resume during the initial screening, you must make the resume memorable. Here you have the opportunity to show off your skills with page design using special features, appropriate headings, and organizational schemes.

Making Your Resume Stand Out

Have you ever noticed how some words in a newspaper or magazine ad jump out at you—those words in large bold type surrounded by white space? The ad is designed to create an immediate impression in a small amount of space.

Like a newspaper ad, the resume must impress a reader in little space. After all, you are designing an ad and selling yourself, your skills, and your expertise to a prospective employer. You want your most impressive qualifications to jump out at the employer during his or her first glance at your resume. For a high school student or a newly graduated college student, the resume should be only one page long. For people with several years of impressive work experience, a two-page resume is acceptable. Electronic resumes may be longer because they are generally scanned by a computer program for the initial screening and not by human eyes.

Part of the design strategy, then, is to consider how the resume looks. White space allowing ample margins results in a resume that is uncluttered and easy to read. Special features such as **boldfacing**, <u>underlining</u>, *italicizing*, CAPITALIZING, bullets (•), or asterisks (*) make important information stand out. But too many special features can make your resume appear cluttered and busy. The resume should look symmetric and balanced. Your name should stand out in a larger boldfaced type. Headings should be easy to spot. The font should be easy to read—Times New Roman, Calibri, or Arial, for example, in 10- to 12-point type.

Consider setting up your resume as a table (hide the grid lines) with information in columns and rows. You can place side headings in the first column and different sections in rows. Because side headings take up more space, if you have additional information, you may want to center or left-justify your headings.

Look at versions of resumes in this chapter as well as resumes on the Web and in career books. Choose a layout that works for the amount of information and the headings you decide to use. Your goal is to make your resume stand out.

Deciding Which Headings to Include

Making decisions about which headings to include is like making decisions about your daily wardrobe. You must put on certain clothes—jeans, shirts, shoes, socks—whatever your basic wardrobe consists of. However, you can choose accessories—jewelry, caps, scarves, belts—to express your individuality, those things that set you apart from others. Similarly, a resume must include basic information. However, optional headings, like accessories, highlight your strengths, minimize your weaknesses, and set your resume apart from others.

Basic Information
Basic information consists of your identification, education, and work experience.

- **Identification:** Include your name, complete address, telephone number(s), and e-mail address. You may include a permanent and temporary address.

- **Education:** Include the name, city, and state of the school from which you graduated; your dates of attendance and graduation or expected date of graduation; and your major or course of study. Sometimes it is helpful to include specific courses you took, as well as academic honors, your overall GPA or the GPA in your major classes (particularly if the GPA is good), and any extracurricular activities. If you already have a postsecondary degree, it is not necessary to list your high school degree.

- **Work Experience:** Include the name, city, and state of the company and the position or title and description of duties if it is related to the job for which you are applying. You also may include promotions, special accomplishments, and skills.

RETEACH

Help students understand that resumes are designed to stand out for the reader—to be seen and understood at a glance.

Ask students what they think should stand out in their resumes.

Have students complete the *Chart for Analyzing Resumes* worksheet available as a supplemental activity on the IRCD.

TEACH

Ask students to consider what optional headings they would include and why.

Tell students that if they have more than three jobs, they can list the three most current jobs unless there is something special about earlier ones. Another strategy to use when several jobs stretch over a long time span is to include the jobs from the last ten years.

Point out that many things could be considered special accomplishments even though no award was given—solving a problem or working on a committee, for example.

If students have no experience related to the job for which they are applying, they still should describe their responsibilities in unrelated jobs to show that they are dependable and possess a work ethic.

Ask students to observe Matt's and Juanita's resumes closely and talk about similarities and differences they see.

TEACH

Make sure students understand that they do not need to mention their high school degree in a resume when they have a postsecondary degree. Employers know that the high school degree is required for entrance into a postsecondary school.

TEACH

There is disagreement about
whether an Interest/Hobby
section should be on a resume.
Some employers are interested
only in job skills and consider
interests as "fluff." Others think
that an Interests section helps
them know an applicant better.
If students are new to the job
market and their resume is
short, if the interests are related
to the job, or if the interests are
noteworthy (e.g., a triathlete or an
accomplished artist), they might
include them—as long as the
resume fits neatly on one page.

Optional Headings

Many different names for headings can appear on resumes. All of them give your prospective employer a better idea of what you can do. Table 11.1 suggests some optional headings and offers a rationale for using each one.

POSSIBLE HEADINGS	PURPOSE	RATIONALE FOR USE
Job Objective Objective Career Objective Professional Objective	To identify the job or position for which you are applying	*Use if* the employer must determine what particular job or category of jobs in which to place you.
Skills/Abilities Professional Skills Leadership Skills Technical Skills Computer Skills	To highlight skills in a chronological presentation or in place of a chrono-logical presentation	*Use if* you want to show special skill sets, especially those skills that are not reflected in other sections. Here is an opportunity to highlight those skills that were listed in the vacancy announcement.
Military Experience Military Service ROTC	To summarize military experience	*Definitely use if* you have military experience. Military personnel are reputed to be dependable and hard-working. Some companies give preference to veterans.
Work Experience Other Work Experience Related Experience Computer Experience Volunteer Work	To include experience not directly related to the job or to differentiate between different kinds of appli-cable work experience	*Use if* the experience shows a consistent work history or *if* the experi-ence is remarkable in some way. Experience not directly related to the job listing shows your dependability and ability to learn and work with others.
Accomplishments Honors Awards Achievements	To enhance your re-sume with your unique accomplishments	*Use if* you want to draw at-tention to special awards, recognitions, and honors that complement educa-tional and work-related descriptions but do not seem to fit under either.
Summary Major Qualifications Summary of Skills	To summarize your qualifications in three to five bullets or in a short description	*Use if* you want to spe-cifically relate your qualifica-tions to the qualifications in the job listing.

Table 11.1

Organizational Strategies

Two organizational strategies govern the writing of all resumes: reverse chronological order and priority order.

Reverse Chronological Order

Some parts of the resume are presented in **reverse chronological order** (backward through time). The priority here is time; that is, what is most recent is considered to be most important. In particular, past jobs and schools attended should be listed in reverse chronological order. For example, when presenting your work experience, list your most recent job first, your second most recent job second, your third most recent job third, and so on.

Priority Order

Major sections are presented in **priority order**—from most important to least important. Whatever you present as most important should be the information that is most important to the prospective employer. When you have impressive work experience, that experience may be more important to your employer than education. If so, place work experience before education.

If you are a recent graduate without much work experience, you may want to include education first as the most important qualification. If you use a skills summary, you should place it early in the resume. That way, employers who quickly skim your resume can focus on your major qualifications even if they do not read further.

Within each section, lists of skills, duties, awards, and accomplishments also are organized from most important to least important.

⬛ **STOP AND THINK**

Which optional headings would you include in your resume? Why would you use them?

TYPES OF RESUMES

There are two fundamental types of resumes: the chronological resume and the functional resume. The **chronological resume** organizes information in reverse chronological order—or backward in time through a person's education and employment record—with the most recent information presented first. Instead of organizing information around time, the **functional resume** organizes information around a person's unique skills, giving an applicant the opportunity to highlight his or her special abilities or experience. This resume may have a section devoted to technical skills, sales abilities, or leadership skills. Some resumes are a combination of chronological and functional resumes, highlighting special skills in one area and using a chronological presentation for the work history.

ONGOING ASSESSMENT

Stop and Think

Employment Objective, Qualifications, Skills, Activities, and Achievements and Honors are examples of optional headings. They offer flexibility in that a person can choose one to highlight his or her unique qualifications.

FOCUS

Warm Up

Use the Warm Up to show students that depending on the content and purpose, subjects organize information differently. History is usually organized chronologically, and math is organized around skills.

Warm Up

Consider the different ways information can be organized. For example, when you study history, how is the information organized? When you study math, how is the information organized?

NET BOOKMARK
You might ask students to share with the class the pros and cons of one of the careers they chose.

TEACH
A chronological resume uses an accepted, familiar format; reads quickly; and shows a steady work history. However, it can be too long, can lack flexibility, and may appear unoriginal. A functional resume matches skills to the job, offers flexibility and an original format, and can cover up gaps in time.

Show the Advantages and Disadvantages of Chronological and Functional Resumes Teaching Master on the IRCD.

Show students the different resumes available as sample documents on the IRCD.

Chronological Resume

A chronological resume offers an approach that most employers recognize and accept. This resume:

- Provides a history of employment (regardless of the job) and education in reverse chronological order.

- Accounts for every year the applicant is out of school, with no gaps in time.

- Tends to emphasize dates in the resume's design.

- Uses predictable headings.

- Places education and work experience early in the resume.

The chronological resume offers several advantages. First, it is familiar to and readily accepted by employers. Second, it can be read quickly. Third, it draws attention to a steady and impressive work history.

Although the chronological resume is widely used, it is not ideal for everyone. First, a lengthy work history may make the resume too long. Second, the format is so structured that it may limit someone whose qualifications do not fit into its framework. For example, it may not be flexible enough for someone with little or no work experience. Third, it may be so similar to other resumes that it does not stand out and may get lost in the sameness of other chronological resumes.

Matt's resume on page 249 is an example of a chronological resume. Matt is applying for a job that is related directly to his degree. With only two years of related work experience, he believes that his degree is his strongest asset and that his related work experience (co-op) is his next strongest asset. The dates, separated from the main text of the resume, stand out. He lists his other work experience last because it is not as impressive as his related work experience. Notice that he does not describe his other work experience because it is not related to his job objective. Most employers would understand what these part-time jobs entail and would note them only because they show that Matt has a strong work ethic.

Functional Resume

Resumes organized according to function or purpose are more flexible than chronological resumes. Tailored to suit the requirements of a particular job, a functional resume:

- Summarizes the most important qualifications for the job.

- May not account for every year out of school.

- Emphasizes skills, accomplishments, and job titles regardless of time frame.

- Uses less predictable headings designed for the job.

- May present education and work experience later in the resume.

The functional resume offers several advantages. First, it helps the employer judge what skills and accomplishments are useful for the job. Second, the functional resume can be used in a variety of circumstances. For example, functional resumes are useful when you have plenty of work experience and skills that would take up too much space on a chronological resume. Functional resumes also are useful when applying for a job for which you have no formal education but for which you have marketable skills. For example, you may have learned carpentry skills from your father but do not have a degree.

The structure of a functional resume is flexible enough that you can minimize time lapses in education or job experience. If you have time lapses in your employment history, be prepared to account for them in an interview. Explain the lapse quickly and discuss the constructive things you did while out of work, such as taking classes or volunteering. Do not complain about being laid off or about problems you may have had with your former supervisor.

Juanita's resume in Figure 11.1 on the next page is a functional resume. Juanita's circumstances are different from Matt's, and a functional resume meets her needs. Juanita is not applying for her first full-time job upon graduating from college; she is applying for her first part-time job while she is in high school. Because she does not have a degree yet, her job skills are more important than her education. She has little work experience, so she capitalizes on her club and volunteer work to show that she can handle office responsibilities.

Electronic Resume

Technology has changed the way people look for and apply for jobs. Today the Internet and e-mail offer electronic ways to send and post resumes. An **electronic resume** is a chronological or functional resume that has been reformatted so that it can be sent electronically. It may take one of the following forms:

- **E-mail resume:** Sent as a formatted attachment to an e-mail or as part of an e-mail message

- **ASCII Text resume:** Sent with special text formatting as an attachment to or part of an e-mail

- **Scannable resume:** Sent as an attachment to an e-mail, part of an e-mail message, or mailed (but eventually scanned by an optical reader)

- **Online resume:** Posted on a company's or job search website or posted on an applicant's website

E-mail Resume

When sending an e-mail resume, whenever possible, you should send it as an attachment that saves your formatting. Let your employer know what software program and version you used to create the document. When possible, ask whether another program is preferred. If the company to which you are applying has the same word processing program you used to create the resume, sending an attachment is the best option. This way, there is little difference in the actual appearance of the electronic resume and the print resume. The only difference is how the resume is sent.

ENRICH

Ask students to use www. monster.com to compile a list of ten tips (from most to least important) for writing resumes, composing letters of application, or taking part in an interview.

Ask students to do an online search using the word *resume* to find other tips for writing resumes. Add their findings, with samples, to a bulletin board.

TEACH

Tell students that electronic resumes are increasingly popular as more companies search for applicants online.

Ask students to think of advantages of the electronic resume. Some answers include the fact that it is inexpensive to send, easy to send long distances, and flexible.

Ask students to note the similarities and differences between the text resume and the scannable resume.

TEACH

Let students correct formatting errors by having them complete the *Editing Faison's Resume* worksheet available as a supplemental activity on the IRCD.

Juanita Vargas
2117 Cypress Grove Drive
Weston, Florida 33331-7520
(954) 555-0185
jvargas@emailnow.net

Job Objective
Part-time position as an administrative assistant

Office Skills
- Office procedures
- Interpersonal skills
- Customer service
- Business correspondence
- Records management

Computer Skills
- Microsoft Office Professional 2007
- QuickBooks Pro 2009
- Microsoft Publisher 2007
- FileMaker Pro 10

Office Experience
ROYAL PALM FLOWERS, July 2007–Present
Part-time assistant in family-owned business: Answer phone, process orders, assist customers, order supplies, encode data using QuickBooks

BETA CLUB, October 2007–2008
Treasurer: Maintained account ledger, created annual budget, balanced budget, wrote checks

JUNIOR MAGAZINE SALES, January 2008–March 2008
Cochair: Directed sales staff, planned advertising campaign, sold magazines

Education
Davie High School, Weston, Florida. Anticipated date of graduation, June 2011
Office Technology Curriculum
Courses in Accounting, Office Management, Computer Technologies, Microsoft Office Professional 2007, and Business Writing

Activities
Future Business Leaders of America, Vice President, August 2009–June 2010
Soccer, Track, Softball, August 2006–present
Volunteer Reader for the Blind, August 2007–present

Honors and Achievements
Winner, Advertising Competition, FBLA, 2008
Runner-up, Sunrise Spelling Bee, 2009

Figure 11.1 Functional Resume

On the other hand, if the company does not have the same program you used to create the resume or if you are not sure about the program your employer uses, you need to explore other options.

ASCII Text File

One option is to send the document as part of the e-mail message. In this case, the employer receives the resume, but it may look jumbled with strange characters when the employer opens the e-mail.

To prevent the resume from looking jumbled, key the resume as an ASCII (American Standard Code for Information Interchange, pronounced *ask-ee*) text file. A **text file** can be opened regardless of the word processing program used. Most word processing programs allow you to save a document as a text (.txt) file, often referred to as a plain text file because of its simple, plain appearance. The disadvantage of a text file is the loss of formatting in a carefully designed print resume.

For instance, a resume written using an older version of WordPerfect® but saved as a text file should open on a personal computer that uses a current version of Microsoft® Word. Using the text file, you ensure that anyone can open your file. In addition, you can format to a limited degree by using the following suggestions:

- Use plain fonts (for example, large, open, "no tails" fonts such as Arial or Calibri) or consider Courier, a fixed font with each character taking up the same amount of space.

- Use 10- to 14-point font size.

- Use one column, flush with the left margin; do not use side headings or tables.

- Use capital letters for heading titles and other important information.

- Avoid boldface, italics, underlining, and other characters not on the keyboard.

- Use the space bar instead of tab keys.

- Use asterisks, dashes, or hyphens instead of regular bullets.

- Use wide margins set for 60 characters (1" left, 2.5" right).

- Use commas to indicate small breaks, semicolons to indicate breaks in a longer list, colons to set up a list, and periods to end sections.

Figure 11.2 on the next page shows Barbara's chronological resume formatted as an ASCII text file.

Scannable Resume

Scannable resumes are mailed as a print document, sent as an e-mail, or posted online to be scanned electronically for **keywords**, significant words that are included in the job announcement. A keyword search compares qualifications on the resume to qualifications the employer needs and determines whether the resume has enough matches to warrant a closer reading. If you are unsure whether a potential employer can read your word processing program, send the file as a text file. If you are confident that the employer will be able to read your word processing program, submit your resume as a word processing document and format your resume for an optical scanner.

COMMUNICATION TECHNOLOGIES

Many people looking for a job use social networking sites to connect with friends and professionals who might assist in the job hunt. One website, LinkedIn, helps people stay in touch with other professionals. You can create a profile that highlights your skills the way a resume does, and you can search for jobs. Employers can use LinkedIn to view an applicant's qualifications. The site also provides a way to get to know other people in your area of expertise while you are employed. You need to use good judgment about what you post on the site: do not divulge inappropriate personal or incriminating information—including photos and links.

Think Critically

Why is it important to use good judgment with regard to the information you post on a site such as LinkedIn?

BARBARA NORMANDY
607 Winnow Road, Apt. 307
Fort Collins, CO 80521-0452
(970) 555-0104

SUMMARY
Versatile background in retail, banking, and travel industries. Strong people skills. Ability to work well under pressure. Ability to organize tasks and people. Ability to learn new skills.

EXPERIENCE
K.W. Flooring and Windows, Loveland, CO, 8/05 to Present
Retail Manager: Sell carpet, flooring, storm windows; manage sales staff, order supplies and inventory; screen resumes; key documents; operate office machines; coordinate appointments; answer, screen, and route telephone calls.

Northeast American Bank, Central Islip, NY, 8/00 to 6/05
District Specialist: Acted as a liaison between regional and branch offices, worked on special projects, solved customer problems, gathered data, prepared reports, handled ten-line telephone with heavy traffic, keyed notes and correspondence, entered information into database, scheduled appointments.
Customer Service Representative: Opened new accounts; issued travelers checks, U.S. Savings Bonds, certificates of deposit, foreign drafts and currency; maintained vault supplies, processed collections, screened mail.
Teller: Balanced transactions, handled large sums of money, assisted in routine customer transactions.

Rothgar Travel Agency, Patchogue, NY, 1/91 to 5/00
Travel Agent: Handled in person and by telephone all travel arrangements for individuals and tour groups. Supervised bus tours and traveled.

EDUCATION
Sonheim Community College, Lincoln, NY, 1997, AAS Accounting
Mountain Range Junior College, Fort Collins, CO, 2006, 42 credits toward AAS Business Administration

VOLUNTEER WORK
Fort Collins Public Schools, Classroom volunteer 2005–2009
Relay for Life, Organized fund-raiser and teams 2001–2004
Options for Domestic Violence, Organized fund-raiser 2000
Angel Tree Ministry, Organized gift giving for 150 children 1997–2002

KEYWORDS
administrative assistant, retail, banking representative, teller, customer service representative, travel agent, manager, supervisor, specialist, volunteer, fund-raiser, organizer, team player, problem solver, people skills, liaison

Figure 11.2 Electronic Resume as ACCII Text File

Use the suggestions for formatting an ASCII text resume with these differences:

- You may use boldfacing, but avoid italics and underlining.

- If you print the resume, use dark black ink on white paper.

- If you mail the resume, do not staple or fold pages and use a large envelope so the resume lies flat.

Online Resume

An **online resume** is posted on a website. Typically, it is one you create, one your company or school hosts, or one sponsored by a web-based job-hunting service such as Monster Career Tools or CareerOneStop. Online job-hunting services provide instructions for posting web-based resumes.

Another option is to design your own website from which you post your resume and set up links to your portfolio, references, or professional organizations. Be aware, however, that employers are not likely to visit your personal website for initial screening. Send your resume—print, e-mail, or scannable—and note that you have a website with additional information.

Many job hunters post their resumes on websites that contain not only their resume, but also links to work samples. These websites are sometimes known as electronic portfolios. Employers can view your resume and work samples quickly and do not need to wait for you to send them. Most word processing software allows you to create such portfolios by converting your text to HTML, the language used to create web pages.

 STOP AND THINK

Describe the different ways to send an electronic resume. Under what circumstances would you convert a resume to a text file?

COMPOSING RESUMES

After you have analyzed your audience and assessed your strengths as an employee, you are ready to compose the parts of your resume. Writing a resume means working through drafts until you have written a professional document with *no errors*.

Word Choice

When writing a resume, you want to present information in as few words as possible. The word choice in a resume may be unlike anything you have written before. A resume has its own grammar rules: Sentences and paragraphs are not used because they take too long to read. Instead, resumes are written in fragments, lists, descriptive phrases, and verbs. Resume language is both general and specific, with carefully chosen details.

Nouns or Nouns + Descriptive Phrases

For naming *Activities, Honors, Achievements,* and *Awards,* use a list of nouns or nouns + descriptive phrases.

ACTIVITIES: Key Club treasurer, Girl Scout leader, member Lions Club

AFFILIATIONS: Key Club, Girl Scouts, Lions Club

SKILLS:

- Knowledge of both Windows and Macintosh environments
- Ability to program in a variety of languages, including Lotus Notes, C++, and Java
- Experience installing and configuring networks

ONGOING ASSESSMENT

Stop and Think

E-mail resumes are sent as attachments or as part of an e-mail. ACSII text resumes are sent when the applicant is unsure of the company's word processing program or are sent as part of an e-mail message. Scannable resumes are used when a company scans resumes with an optical reader. Online resumes are posted to a website.

Warm Up

Have you ever written a perfect paper—an essay, a letter, a short report? Is it possible to write something with no errors? Explain.

FOCUS

Warm Up

Use the Warm Up to discuss how difficult it is to write a "perfect" essay, especially one that is several pages long. There is much to consider: style, content, organization, grammar, and format. Despite the impossibility of reaching perfection, employment communication should be well-written and contain no errors.

COMMUNICATION DILEMMA

Grant should be honest. Some sources suggest that he answer the question honestly on the application and write a letter briefly explaining what happened and point out that he has been a law-abiding citizen for the past seven years and served honorably in the Army. He can explain that he was young, made a mistake, paid for it, and has worked hard since then to make a good life for himself and his family. His chances of getting the job by telling the truth are probably better than average. If during an interview he is asked to explain, he should look the interviewer in the eye; explain honestly and briefly; and say that he was wrong, he learned his lesson, and he now has a good record. Under these circumstances, D & J may be willing to take a chance on him. If Grant does not tell the truth and the crime is discovered, he will have lied to the firm and could be fired.

TEACH

Ask students to work in pairs to use *verb + what* phrases to describe activities they engage in at work or school.

Duplicate the resumes in the chapter or those in the sample documents on the IRCD. Ask students to work in groups, using a highlighter to indicate the verbs in the resumes. Ask students to mark the objects of the verbs (the "what") with a different colored highlighter. Finally, ask them to list all of the verbs used in the resumes.

Communication Dilemma

Grant, age 28, spent two years in the state penitentiary for shoplifting when he was 19 years old. Since that time, he attended classes, obtaining an associate degree in accounting, and spent three years in the U.S. Army. He now has a family and is an involved and respected member of his community.

Grant is applying for a job with D & J Accounting. The application asks if he has ever been convicted of a crime. Since his shoplifting offense, Grant has been a law-abiding citizen.

Think Critically

What are the possible consequences if Grant does not reveal the shoplifting incident? What are the possible consequences if he does? What should he do?

Verb + What

Verb + what is a quick, effective phrase to describe skills, qualifications, and work experience. Use action verbs to stress what you can do for an employer. Performance is more impressive than qualifications. The greater the variety of verbs, the more dynamic and effective the resume. Add details to the phrase to show more specific information.

Make sure the lists are consistent in tense: present tense for jobs you currently hold and past tense for jobs you no longer hold. If you have (or had) a title, include the title before your list of duties followed by a colon. Also organize your list of duties in order of importance.

Present Tense Verbs Describes Jobs You Currently Hold

encode data	install equipment	wait tables
provide child care	refurbish equipment	manage office staff

Past Tense Verbs Describes Jobs You No Longer Hold

sold merchandise	analyzed data	assisted customers
stocked groceries	filed reports	evaluated procedures

Job Titles Before Duties

Cashier: Operated register, greeted customers, and took orders
Shift Manager: Supervised 15 workers, enforced safety measures, and handled payroll

Table 11.2 shows other action verbs you may want to consider.

accomplished	coordinated	generated	reduced
achieved	counseled	identified	revised
administered	designed	increased	saved
attained	developed	investigated	solved
budgeted	devised	maintained	streamlined
built	established	mentored	strengthened
calculated	evaluated	organized	taught
completed	formulated	planned	trained
contributed	fulfilled	promoted	wrote

Table 11.2

FOCUS

Table 11.2

Talk about the traits that each verb emphasizes. For example, *coordinated* emphasizes teamwork and organization.

Specific Language

Think of your resume as the first piece of evidence a potential employer sees regarding your unique skills. As evidence, it should come with sufficient proof of your credentials and accomplishments. The proof comes in those specific, quantifiable bits of information you choose to use on your resume. What you choose to include in these roughly 160 to 350 words (for a one-page resume) proves your qualifications and tailors your resume to the skills your employer needs.

✓ Specific Language	✗ Vague Language
Objective: To work as a loan officer in a local credit union (expresses a particular position in a particular banking institution)	Objective: To work as a professional in a modern banking environment
Objective: To work part-time as a historical tour guide for a seventeenth-century governor's palace (responds specifically to the job announcement)	Objective: To obtain a summer part-time position
Ensured compliance with EPA and OSHA regulations (responds to query for experience with EPA and OSHA)	Enforced safety regulations
Met all 10 performance standards from 2001–2010 (specifies how many and when)	Consistently met performance standards

Parallel Structure

When setting up headings, providing information, or creating lists for resumes, use **parallel structure** (use of the grammatical structure already in place). Parallel structure provides consistency, enabling your reader to anticipate your structure.

This means if you begin your employment history with a job title, you list the job title first with every job. If you begin your employment history with the name of the company and the job title second, you list the company name first and the job title second for each job.

Descriptions also should be written in parallel structure.

✓ **Parallel**	✗ **Nonparallel**
Answered calls from field technicians, created service bulletins, analyzed warranty claims, authorized warranty repairs and modifications, communicated with design engineers.	I answered calls from field technicians. Was responsible for service bulletins. Duties included warranty claims analysis and warranty authorization numbers for specific repairs and modifications. Close communication with design engineers is ongoing.

Keywords for Scannable Resumes

When selecting keywords for a scannable resume, the rules of resume writing change. The print resume relies on verbs to demonstrate skills performed. The scannable resume, on the other hand, relies on nouns that list skills, qualifications, and job titles in a separate heading, *Keywords*. Following are some examples of keywords.

Skills: C++ programming, graphic design, marketing, statistical analysis, training, database management, communication, problem solving, management, organization, attention to detail

Job titles: Computer specialist, manager, supervisor, director, administrative assistant, chair, facilitator, nurse's aid, machinist, research assistant

Qualifications: Membership in professional organizations, licenses, certifications, degrees, awards

Using several synonyms for one word increases the chances that your keywords will match those of your employer. For example, because the words *hair stylist* and *cosmetologist* are synonyms, you should include both terms when your resume will be scanned. The scanning programs are very literal, though. For example, if the company asks for experience with Microsoft Office Suite, do not write "proficient in Word, Excel, and PowerPoint." Those terms may not match.

A machine can scan a three-page resume as quickly as a one-page resume. Thus, when in doubt, include more rather than less information when preparing a scannable resume. Print resumes save time for the reader by restricting length and using concise wording. Scannable resumes are thorough.

Punctuation

Because resumes do not contain complete sentences, applying traditional punctuation rules is difficult. If one piece of information ends naturally on a single line, you may choose not to put an end mark there. For other marks of punctuation:

- Use periods to break up large blocks of text or to indicate a change in information.

- Use colons to introduce lists.

- Use commas to separate simple lists of three or more items.

- Use semicolons to separate complex lists (lists that already contain commas) of three or more items.

Refer to the models in this chapter to see how the resumes are punctuated. Whatever system you adopt, use consistent punctuation throughout your resume.

 STOP AND THINK

What is the hardest part of writing a resume? Why? How does the wording of an essay differ from that of a resume? How does a traditional print resume differ from a scannable resume? What are the advantages of an electronic resume?

COMPOSING EMPLOYMENT LETTERS

Employment letters give you another opportunity to present your skills. Unlike the resume, these letters are written in traditional paragraphs and complete sentences, also showing the employer how well you write. Three types of employment letters are (1) cover letters to accompany the resume and to highlight the applicant's strengths; (2) follow-up letters to thank the employer for the interview; (3) and in some cases, resignation letters to announce a person's decision to leave a company. On occasion, e-mail correspondence takes the place of an employment letter.

Cover Letter

A cover letter is a sales letter. It is a persuasive letter that sells you as the product or service. As stated in Chapter 5, sales letters are composed of the hook, the sell, and the motivation to action. A cover letter is composed of an opening (an attention-getter or a hook), a summary of qualifications (the proof or sell), and a request for an interview (motivation to action).

Opening

The first paragraph should grab the reader's attention by:

1. Stating your interest in the job.

2. Describing your qualifications in a way that sets you apart from other applicants.

3. Explaining how you found out about the job.

4. Quickly summarizing your major qualifications for the job.

Most cover letters are **solicited**; that is, they are requested or advertised. With solicited positions, refer to the advertisement in the opening sentence.

Sometimes, however, you may submit an **unsolicited letter**. In this case, you are looking for employment with an organization that has not solicited or advertised a vacancy. Not all companies advertise their jobs, and you do not know whether there is an opening unless you ask. Your skills may be in such demand that a company creates a position for you. Writing an opening to an unsolicited letter is more of a challenge; you must generate interest immediately. Name-dropping may stimulate interest, or a dynamic opening can emphasize your advantages.

ONGOING ASSESSMENT

Stop and Think

Use students' responses to discuss the writing process.

Essay: sentences and paragraphs; resume: fragments, phrases, clauses, and lists

Print resume: carefully designed (e.g., font size, boldface, white space, multiple columns); scannable resume: single columns, fewer formatting features, list of keywords, sometimes longer; electronic resume: versatile, inexpensive method of delivery

Warm Up

Look closely at the cover letter in Figure 11.3 (page 270) that Matt wrote to accompany his resume. How is this cover letter like a sales letter?

FOCUS

Warm Up

Use the Warm Up to ask students to preview the structure of Matt's letter and to build on what they learned about sales letters.

ENRICH

Have students practice varying their sentence structure by completing the *Editing Kyle's Letter* worksheet available as a supplemental activity on the IRCD.

TEACH

In general, a cover letter should accompany a resume. A company interested only in a resume posted on its website may not have a place for the letter, but an e-mail or a message can include basically the same information—only in fewer words. E-mail resumes and scannable resumes should be accompanied by cover letters.

**Solicited Letter Opening
(refers to advertisement in the
opening sentence)**

A radiography degree and three
years' experience at Unity
Systems Health Care qualify
me for the radiography position
you advertised recently on Tri-
Point Hospital's web page of job
openings.

**Unsolicited Letter Opening
(generates interest with name
dropping and a unique background)**

Dr. Yu Zeng suggested that I contact
you about an opening in your
radiology department.

With degrees and certifications in
medical sonography, radiography,
echocardiography, and computed
tomography/magnetic resonance
imaging, think how valuable my
services would be to a small rural
hospital with a limited staff. My
bedside manner is impressive, and
I am available for employment.

Summary of Qualifications

The second and third paragraphs justify your claim that you can work for the
company by proving your credentials. The letter is not meant to be a copy of
your resume. The letter should emphasize qualifications but not repeat the
resume word for word. To provide proof that you can perform the job:

1. Describe your education.

2. Describe appropriate work experience.

3. Describe related skills.

4. Explain some of your abilities that you do not mention in your resume.

If you are a recent graduate, your education paragraph will come immediately
after your opening paragraph. It will specify your degree and major course of
study. It may include relevant courses, accomplishments, and areas of expertise.
If you have been in the work force for several years, your work experience

sjlocke/iStockphoto.com

Recently, the city manager of a small town was fired because he listed a degree in city planning on his resume that he did not actually have. Being two classes short of a college degree, he decided that that was as good as the degree—except that it was not. It was a lie.

Many people have "skeletons in their closets": a court conviction, a substance abuse problem, or an unfinished degree. It is true that on paper, someone with a conviction does not look as good as the person with a sterling record. Someone without the proper degree does not look as good as the person with the degree. However, the truth is better than any lie conceived to cover up the "skeleton." If a person cannot be trusted to complete employment data honestly, then he or she is not a good risk for a company.

The bottom line is this: Falsifying employment data carries serious consequences, such as immediate termination or prosecution. Some events in the distant past may have little bearing on the job hunt and need not be disclosed. However, if you are asked about something, do not lie.

Think Critically

What are the consequences for the city manager and the citizens of the town?

FOCUS ON ETHICS
Make sure students understand the importance of honesty. A person can be fired, even prosecuted, for falsifying records.

ENRICH
Share with students both the Common Interview Questions Teaching Master and the Questions Employers Should Not Ask Teaching Master on the IRCD. Hold mock interviews using these lists. Have students interview each other. Video-record the interviews and play them back. Tell students that most interviewers are trying to encourage the interviewee to talk. However, candidates should not be long-winded. They should answer the question, enunciating carefully and using correct grammar. Questions about people skills are important because industry wants people who can work well as part of a team.

will come immediately after the opening paragraph and describe relevant jobs and major work-related accomplishments. In the letter, you also have the opportunity to add information about your character, your work habits, your people skills, and any other information you believe is relevant to the job.

Request for Interview

The last paragraph in the cover letter motivates the reader to action by asking for an interview and making it convenient to contact you. Make sure you:

1. Refer to the enclosed resume.

2. Ask for an interview.

3. Tell how and when you can be reached by including your phone number(s) and/or e-mail address.

When composing your cover letter, vary your sentence structure. Although it is easy to begin every sentence with *I* when writing about yourself, try to begin some sentences with other words. For variety, consider beginning sentences with prepositional phrases, introductory clauses, and transitional words.

On the next page, Figure 11.3 shows a cover letter that Matt wrote to Hailey O'Dell, personnel director at Monarch Electronic Industries. Matt's letter gets his reader's attention by expressing interest in the job opening and stating his desire to move back to Arkansas. Then Matt uses two paragraphs to tell how his education and work experience make him a good match for Monarch. In the last two paragraphs, Matt reveals special knowledge of and interest in the company and asks for an interview. Note the variety of sentences in Matt's letter.

FOCUS

Figure 11.3
Show how the cover letter
follows the guidelines given.

ENRICH

Have students list questions they
can ask during an interview.
Explain to them the importance
of showing an interest in the
company during the interview.

Ask students to interview
employers to find out how they
expect applicants to dress for
an interview. Students probably
will find that most employers
expect applicants to dress up
(a conservative suit and tie for
a man; a conservative suit or
dress for a woman). For some
jobs, however, dressing up is
inappropriate. A construction
job, for example, requires casual
(but neat and clean) clothing.

Invite people from the
community to conduct mock
interviews with students,
share information about the
job market, or talk about
employment communication.

67B Whistle Run Apartments
Albuquerque, NM 87103-4737
June 15, 20—

Ms. Hailey O'Dell
Monarch Electronic Industries
3902 West Bennington Street
Charleston, AK 72933-5220

Dear Ms. O'Dell

Because of my desire to relocate to my home state of Arkansas, I would like to be considered for the programming position advertised in the *Daily Register* last week. With co-op experience at a company similar to Monarch's, I have first-hand knowledge of the challenges of working in an industrial setting.

I earned an AAS degree in Computer Programming from Maddox Community College. At Madddox's Unix-based computing lab, I learned to program in HTML, Visual Basic 2008, and C++ languages. In addition, I gained valuable experience with Microsoft Office (2003/2007), as many of our class assignments were completed using an application in the Office suite. My instructors praised the detail with which I wrote programming specifications. Furthermore, Maddox's up-to-date facility has given me the skills and confidence to adapt to any computer environment.

In addition to my education, I have experience meeting the computing needs of business and industry. At Jupiter Computer Industries, I used C++ and Visual Basic 2008 to design and develop test specifications for its software systems. Just before I graduated, I served on a quality assurance team to set up help desk protocols and improve user satisfaction. At Lancaster Microsystems, I installed and configured operating systems including Windows XP/Professional and Windows Server 2008. Other responsibilities included maintaining an SQL server database and taking turns at the help desk. My supervisor gave me superior evaluations, ranking me high in problem-solving skills and customer service.

Last year I attended a conference sponsored by Web Accessibility Initiative and am familiar with Web Content Accessibility Guidelines. Monarch's track record as a leader in making the Web accessible for people with disabilities is well documented. I would welcome an opportunity to help in this initiative.

My resume is enclosed for your consideration. I would be happy to schedule an interview to discuss my qualifications. You can reach me at (505) 555-0173 after 3 p.m., or feel free to e-mail me at mabboud@comm.mcc.edu.

Sincerely

Matt Abboud

Matt Abboud

Enclosure

Figure 11.3 Cover Letter

E-mail Cover Message

If you are sending an electronic resume (as an attachment or as part of the e-mail), you need a brief message to accompany the resume. Similar to the cover letter, the e-mail message is briefer.

1. Declare your intention to apply for a particular job.

2. Tell how you are sending the resume and, if applicable, what program you used to encode the resume.

3. Summarize your major qualifications in either a short paragraph or a list.

4. Ask for a meeting or an interview.

Follow-Up Letter

You send a follow-up letter, sometimes known as a thank-you letter, immediately after a job interview. The follow-up letter should:

1. Thank the employer for the interview.

2. Remind the employer of something positive that was said or that took place during the interview.

3. Explain why you are the best candidate for the job.

4. Express continuing interest in the job.

Sending a follow-up letter lets prospective employers know that you are still interested and reminds them of your qualifications. It also is permissible to send the follow-up message in an e-mail. With e-mail, make sure you use an appropriate, specific subject line (for example, *Follow-up to Interview*). On the next page, Figure 11.4 shows a follow-up letter that Matt wrote to Ms. O'Dell after his interview.

Resignation Letter

Whatever your reason for leaving a job, writing a letter of resignation to inform your current employer of your plans is a professional courtesy.

Your former employer may be contacted for a job reference. A well-written letter of resignation that gives reasonable notice helps ensure goodwill with your current employer. Later, when asked to provide a reference for you, your employer will likely say positive things. To maintain the goodwill of your employer, follow these guidelines:

- Find out the company procedure and chain of command. Normally, you write the letter to your immediate supervisor, who would, in turn, pass the letter up the chain of command. In a small work unit made up of people with whom you work closely, use the supervisor's first name, as you would in memos. In larger work units with a more formal structure, use the supervisor's last name.

- Announce your intention to leave the company. Be clear that you are writing a letter of resignation.

- State the last day you will work. Make sure that date provides enough notice according to company policy and your knowledge of company operations.

- Use courteous language. Use your manners (*please* and *thank you*) and qualifying words (*might, probably, most likely,* and *seems*) if necessary.

- Compliment your employer and the company. Thank your supervisor for any opportunities or special help he or she provided. If you are leaving because you are dissatisfied with the work environment, find something positive to say about the organization, even if it is brief.

- Offer to help the company prepare for your absence. You can offer to train your replacement or complete work projects in advance.

- Volunteer a reason for leaving only if you feel comfortable doing so. If the employer/employee relationship is strained, you may omit the reason

RETEACH

Emphasize that letters of resignation should be tactful and courteous. The person to whom an employee is writing the letter may one day provide a reference. Leaving on good terms is important. The person who is leaving should ask this employer if he or she will act as a reference.

TEACH

Tell students that even though a letter is the preferred method of communicating when an employee is resigning his or her position, e-mail may be suitable in some situations—when the employee is some distance away from his or her place of employment, timing is critical, or the employee has a close relationship with his or her employer. The e-mail can state that a more formal letter is coming in the mail.

FOCUS

Figure 11.4

Point out that the letter shows appreciation and keeps the memory of Matt fresh in the employer's mind.

67B Whistle Run Apartments
Albuquerque, NM 87103-4737
August 29, 20—

Ms. Hailey O'Dell, Personnel Director
Monarch Electronic Industries
3902 West Bennington Street
Charleston, AK 72933-5220

Dear Ms. O'Dell

Thank you for considering me for the position of computer programmer with your company. I enjoyed touring your facility and discussing ways to improve the SQL server database. As you may remember, I have two years' experience installing and configuring operating systems, specifically with Windows 2008. I would welcome the opportunity to put my knowledge to work for your company. My preference is to return to my home in Arkansas, and I am willing to relocate to any of your subsidiaries in the state.

I look forward to hearing from you soon. If you have additional questions about my qualifications, please call me at (505) 555-0173 or e-mail me at mabboud@comm.mcc.edu.

Sincerely

Matt Abboud

Matt Abboud

Figure 11.4 Follow-up Letter

or provide a simple one, such as the desire to pursue other interests. When there is a real problem at work, such as sexual harassment or discrimination, think carefully about explaining the reason.

■ Close with something positive. Thank your employer once more or say something positive about your upcoming plans.

Montel wrote the letter in Figure 11.5 to Donald Shappel, the director of Charter Disability Services, resigning the position he has held for nine years. Montel has enjoyed a close working relationship with his supervisor.

1080 Oak Trace Road
Atlanta, GA 30317-6690
November 30, 20—

Donald Shappel, Director
Charter Disability Services
503 North Chester Street
Atlanta, GA 30322-1005

Dear Donald

Please accept this letter of resignation, effective two months from now. January 30, 20—, will officially be my last day as interpreter for the hearing impaired for Charter Disability Services. My wife has accepted an administrative position at Dare Regional Hospital in Hopewell, Virginia. After much discussion, we believe it is in our best interest to move to her job location.

I have enjoyed the nine years working as lead interpreter. Your guidance, in particular, has enabled me to learn new skills and grow professionally. I am proud to have been a part of the Charter team and to have contributed to its fine work as an advocate for disability services.

Before I leave, I will complete the annual evaluations of my clients. Furthermore, I will be happy to spend my last week training my replacement. After I leave, I will be available by phone to answer any questions.

Again, thank you for the opportunity to work for Charter Disability Services. My wife and I will miss you and the staff, but we look forward to new opportunities in Virginia.

Sincerely

Montel Newsome

Montel Newsome

Figure 11.5 Letter of Resignation

STOP AND THINK

What is the purpose of a cover letter and a follow-up letter? Why should you give as much notice as possible in a letter of resignation?

CLOSE

Summary

Use the summary to make
sure students understand the
important concepts.

Ask students to discuss the
summary statements in groups,
recalling how the chapter
elaborated on each one.

Ask students to state which
summary statements they
understand best and which ones
they understand least. Students
can review chapter information
for those statements that are not
clear.

CLOSE

Checklist

Ask students to refer to the
checklist while writing resumes
and letters and to review the
checklist when revising. Students
could exchange papers in a
peer review exercise and use
the checklist to make comments
on each other's resumes and
letters.

REVIEW

For a review of the key terms in
the chapter, provide students
with the *Key Terms* worksheet
available as a supplemental
activity on the IRCD.

SUMMARY

1. You get started on employment communication by assessing your strengths, researching the prospective employer, choosing your references, and understanding your audience.

2. For a resume to stand out, it should look symmetrical, include ample white space, and use an easy-to-read font. Basic headings include Identification, Education, and Work Experience. Optional headings enhance the resume and tailor it to the job description. Information is organized in reverse chronological order and priority order.

3. Resumes are organized as chronological resumes or functional resumes. They also may be formatted as electronic resumes.

4. Resumes are written using parallel phrases and lists. Sentences and paragraphs are not used because they take too long to read.

5. Three types of letters and employment-related e-mail are cover letters/messages, follow-up letters/messages, and resignation letters.

Checklist

- Are all documents (resume, cover letter, follow-up letter, and e-mail) free from grammar, spelling, and punctuation errors?

- Are all documents reader-centered rather than writer-centered?

- Have I addressed the job qualifications (either the qualifications listed in an employment ad or the qualifications I think the job requires)?

- Have I chosen the most effective resume for my situation: chronological, functional, or electronic?

- Is my writing organized to reflect my strengths?

- Does the first sentence in my cover letter/message grab the reader's attention?

- Does my cover letter/message explain how I possess the necessary skills for the job and refer to any skills mentioned in the ad or job description?

- Did I give enough information so that I could be reached easily?

- Is the tone in my cover letter/message and follow-up letter/message positive and polite?

- Have I addressed my communication to the proper person?

- Have I complimented the supervisor and the company in my letter of resignation?

Build Your Foundation

1. What kind of information is left out of each of the following resume excerpts?

a. Identification	**c. Education**
Maria Valencia	Danville Technical College
589 Mohican Avenue	Associate in Applied Science
Providence, RI	GPA: 3.5/4.0

b. Experience	**d. Major Resume Headings**
Denton's Sport Shop, York, NE	Work Experience
Ordered inventory	Skills
Kept business ledger	Volunteer Work
Calculated payroll	Professional Affiliations

2. For each situation, decide whether a chronological or functional resume is appropriate. Suggest possible sections/headings for each situation.

   a. Boota worked for eight years as a dental hygienist. She stopped work for ten years while her children were small. She worked part-time in a day care center for three of those years and volunteered at her children's schools. She also kept the accounting ledger for her husband's restaurant. Now at 38, she has just completed an associate degree in accounting with a GPA of 3.9.

   b. Marcine just graduated with a degree in occupational therapy. Before she went to school, she worked as a carpenter's helper.

   c. Lyle retired from the Air Force two years ago and has taken a few marketing courses. As a teenager and young adult, he worked in his father's printing company. He is applying to be a sales representative for a publishing company.

3. For Francisco's resume, write the Work Experience section for the following three jobs. They span approximately five years. Make up any information that is missing.

   a. Francisco worked at Oleander Juice Bar. He took orders for and prepared juice drinks. He also operated the cash register and balanced the register each night. He became the crew manager after six months.

   b. Francisco worked for Complete Lawn Care. He mowed lawns for several businesses and residences. Part of his job included trimming bushes and raking leaves. He learned how to plant flowers and bushes and to apply insecticides and fertilizer.

   c. Working for Lucky Horse Stables, he groomed horses; cleaned out the stalls; fed, walked, and trained horses; and provided them with basic medical care.

4. Help the following individuals word their job objective statements.

   a. Lara wants to work as a nurse practitioner. She likes children and has experience working in a children's hospital.

   b. Henri has credentials in electronics and theater and is currently enrolled in an audio engineer program. He wants to work the sound system for musical groups.

   c. Molly's goal is to work with children with autism. She is applying to a highly renowned educational center.

5. a. Answers will vary. Note parallel structure, conciseness, and priority order. a. HVAC Technician: Installed air conditioning systems, ran duct work and gas lines, connected electrical and gas lines, replaced insulation in hurricane-damaged homes. b. Recording Engineer: Operate PA and computerized lighting systems, edit and master recordings in CD-R media, design CD package and labels, produce and sell CDs. c. Music Director: Directed choir rehearsals and performances; selected choral music; ordered music; assembled cantatas for special occasions; played the organ, piano, and handbells; sang for weddings.
6. Answers will vary. Encourage students to be thorough.
7. Answers will vary. Encourage descriptions that are concise and parallel and are in priority order.
8. No, the letter omits references to "high-energy, detail-oriented team player."
9. a. What kind of computers? How much education? What program languages? b. What kind of knowledge? c. What specific skills?

5. Revise the following descriptions of work history to reduce the number of words. Make sure you use parallel structure.

   a. HVAC Technician: I installed air conditioning systems, including running the duct work and running and connecting electrical and gas supply lines. Assisted in construction of company storage facility. We were offered contracts to replace insulation on hurricane-damaged homes.
   b. Recording Engineer: To edit and master recordings in CD-R media. Work to design package and labeling CDs. Produce and sell CDs at public concerts. Operated PA and computerized lighting systems for Little Theater Productions.
   c. Music Director: I directed choir during rehearsals and performances and selected music for weekly performances for the choir. Also, I ordered music from companies. When there was a special occasion, I put together a cantata of musical selections. The organ and piano—I played them, too, and sometimes handbells. Oh, and I sang for weddings.

6. Analyze your strengths as an employee. Select a partner in your class with whom to share employee strengths. How do your strengths differ? Give each other suggestions for which strengths to highlight in a resume or cover letter.

7. In groups of four, write a Work Experience section for the entire group using the strategies in the chapter. Include at least one job each member has held—whether full- or part-time.

8. Below is an ad for an administrative assistant. Following the ad is a draft of a cover letter for the position. Decide whether the excerpt addresses every qualification in the advertisement. What, if anything, is left out?

   ADMINISTRATIVE ASSISTANT High-energy, detail-oriented team player for our Greenville office to learn many office responsibilities. Prefer knowledge of Microsoft Office. Send resume to . . .

   As a graduate of Taggart Technical Institute, I have gained skills in word processing. In particular, I have worked extensively with all aspects of Microsoft® Office.

   I also am familiar with the most up-to-date office management systems. A part-time job with Apex Industries gave me the opportunity to work in an office with an efficient office manager. From the office manager, I learned important tips about filing, turning out timely correspondence, and scheduling appointments.

9. The following sentences from cover letters do not provide the details that prove the skill or qualification listed. What information should be added?

   a. I have educational experience with personal computers and basic programming.
   b. I have worked in my family's construction business for the past seven years, so I have extensive knowledge of how a building should be put together. I have worked on every phase of a job.
   c. I am a 2010 graduate of Vancouver Community College with an associate degree in medical office technology. Throughout my college career, I gained many skills.

10. Zeno is preparing to apply for a construction job. On his worksheet, he has listed the following seven people as possible references. Read the descriptions and help him decide which references to use.

- Jack Garriet: Zeno's high school drafting teacher

- Rosie Montero: Zeno's neighbor and an administrative assistant at the high school

- Dr. Gretchen Walker: head of local Habitat for Humanity, for which Zeno has volunteered (Habitat for Humanity helps build and finance houses for people who could not otherwise afford them.)

- Rochelle Currier: Zeno's neighbor and an architect; she supervised a high school construction project on which Zeno worked

- Roy Janak: manager of Kemp Building Supplies; sold supplies to Zeno

- Meredith McDougan: Zeno's 12th-grade English teacher

- Chevron Tucker: Zeno's uncle and a member of the clergy

11. Interview a parent or friend who has a job that he or she likes. Find out what kind of resume this person wrote, what process was used by the hiring company, and what the interview was like. Has resume writing changed since this person was hired? Share your findings with the class.

Your Turn

12. Pretend you have just completed the degree (with a high GPA) you have always wanted. Create a resume and cover letter to apply for your dream job.

13. Write a functional resume highlighting your skills for a job in your field. Use Juanita's resume as a model. Write a cover letter to accompany it.

14. Rewrite the resume you wrote for item 12 or 13 as an electronic resume. Choose between a text file resume or a scannable resume.

15. Write a letter of resignation for a job you have had for five years.

16. Write a resume and cover letter for someone who has been in the work force at least five years. Take notes to assess this person's strengths using the questions at the beginning of the chapter. Ask the employee to give you a description of a job he or she would like to have along with a job objective. Does this person need a chronological or a functional resume?

Community Connection

17. Visit your local Employment Security Commission to learn about the local job market and how applicants find and apply for jobs. What jobs are available? How does an applicant apply for a job? What is the unemployment rate? What suggestions do the case workers have for applicants? Prepare a short report for the class about what you learn.

18. Visit or call your college's placement center or a head-hunting agency. Find out what services are offered and how to register for them. Is there a fee? Do services come with a guarantee? Is there an online job site? Share what you learn with the class in a short oral report.

10. Students may give valid reasons for most references, but Rosie Montero and Roy Janak are least important.

11. Answers will vary. A parent's or friend's personal experience can provide valuable information. Some of those experiences will be supported by information in the chapter, but some may show that people find jobs in other ways.

ASSESS
Your Turn
12. Review the section about resumes and cover letters.
13. Review the section about resumes and cover letters.
14. Review the section about electronic resumes.
15. Review the section about resignation letters.
16. Review the section about resumes and cover letters.

ASSESS
Community Connection
17. Relate information in the reports to strategies covered in the chapter.
18. Information that students share with the class can be used to help locate jobs upon graduation.

Presentations

Goals

- Understand audience and formality
- Plan for audience, topic, graphic aids, location, time, and stage fright
- Determine how to organize and compose presentations
- Prepare outline, notes, and appearance
- Rehearse for a presentation
- Present with confidence
- Organize a group presentation

Terms

- adrenaline, p. 287
- anecdote, p. 288
- auditory, p. 294
- direct approach, p. 287
- external audiences, p. 281
- feedback, p. 294
- formal presentations, p. 281
- indirect approach, p. 288
- informal presentations, p. 281
- internal audiences, p. 281
- rhetorical question, p. 288

WRITE TO LEARN

Recall speakers whose performances you have enjoyed. For instance, you may have had an instructor who held your attention from the moment you entered the classroom. Perhaps you appreciated a speaker at a club meeting or special event. What made these speakers effective communicators? List the qualities and actions that helped these speakers to be effective. For instance, consider these questions: What did the speaker do to get your attention at the beginning? What did the speaker provide as visual support so you could better understand the message?

Focus on Presentations

Read the sample presentation slide on the next page and answer these questions:

- Who is the intended audience?
- What does the title contribute to the slide?
- Why is the information in the notes not covered in the slide?
- Does the slide need animation? Why or why not?

What If?

- The writer had intended to deliver the presentation only online?
- Readers were unfamiliar with America's economic situation?
- All audience members were experts in accounting?

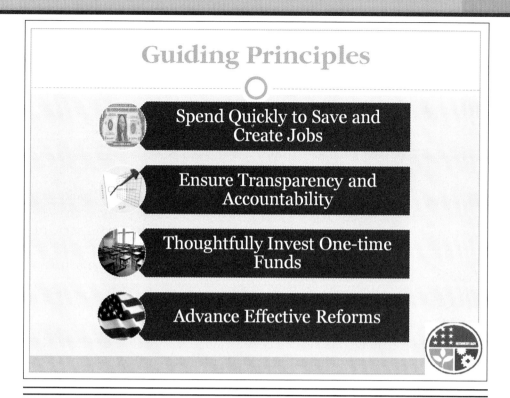

Guiding Principles

The overall goals for stimulating the economy in the short term and for investing wisely; funds are used to improve schools, raise achievement, drive reforms, and produce better results for children and young people for the long-term health of our nation

Four principles guide the distribution and use of ARRA funds:

Spend funds quickly to save and create jobs. ARRA funds will be distributed quickly to states, local educational agencies, and other entities to avert layoffs, create and save jobs, and improve student achievement. In turn, states and LEAs are urged to move rapidly to develop plans for using funds that are consistent with the law's reporting and accountability requirements and to begin spending funds promptly to help drive the nation's economic recovery.

Ensure transparency, reporting, and accountability. To prevent fraud and abuse, support the most effective uses of ARRA funds, and measure and track results accurately, recipients must publicly report how funds are used. Due to the unprecedented scope and importance of this investment, ARRA funds are subject to additional and more rigorous reporting requirements than what normally apply to grant recipients.

Invest one-time ARRA funds thoughtfully to minimize the "funding cliff." ARRA represents a historic infusion of funds that is expected to be temporary. Depending on the program, these funds are available for only two to three years. These funds should be invested in ways that do not result in unsustainable continuing commitments after the funding expires.

Enhance student achievement through school improvement and reform. Used this way, these funds close the achievement gap and help students from all backgrounds achieve high standards.

Sample Presentation Graphics

From *The American Recovery and Reinvestment Act: Saving and Creating Jobs and Reforming Education,* United States. Dept. of Education. Web. 3 Apr. 2009.

FOCUS

Focus on Presentations

Use the questions to encourage students to read the sample closely.

ASSESS

What If?

Use the questions to discuss how the sample would be different if the situation or audience changed.

Go to www.cengage.com/school/bcomm/techwtg for more detailed responses to these questions.

Writing@Work

Courtesy of Elizabeth Tripodi

Elizabeth K. Tripodi is an attorney in Washington, D.C. She represents primarily shareholders of publicly traded companies in lawsuits against the company when there has been fraud.

For Elizabeth, a successful presentation is multifaceted: "A good presentation immediately provides an overview of where the presentation is going. It involves some sort of visual aid as well so that a listener is engaged both aurally and visually. Finally, I think anecdotes always make a presentation more interesting."

When preparing a presentation, Elizabeth meticulously researches and outlines her material. "Research is such a key element, especially when preparing for a hearing before a judge. You need to be prepared to address any and all of the judge's concerns. After researching, I outline my presentation. Following an outline ensures that I'm clear, concise, and that my audience can follow my reasoning."

"After outlining, it's practice, practice, practice," says Elizabeth. "I like to start rehearsing in a room by myself, getting comfortable with the material and my arguments. It also helps me to hear my own voice," she notes. "I often ask other attorneys to pretend they are the judge hearing my case so that I can practice performing well under pressure and reacting to various scenarios."

Elizabeth knows that delivering a great presentation depends in part on connecting with your audience. "If I know what the audience expects, I will tailor my presentation to them. In addition, I think eye contact with your audience is essential. Be comfortable with your material and try not to read from a script. Finally, make sure your presentation style suits your personality. For me, it's about seeming professional, friendly, and intelligent."

Think Critically

1. Who are Elizabeth's audiences in the courtroom?

2. What can Elizabeth learn by practicing in front of someone who role-plays the judge? What does she risk if she does not practice this way?

Printed with permission of Elizabeth Tripodi

GETTING STARTED ON PRESENTATIONS

The success with which you handle oral reporting may determine whether you are successful in your profession. You may have the best new product idea for your company. However, for your idea to become a reality, you must communicate it to the management team and convince the team members to try the product. This chapter explains how to plan, organize, compose, prepare, rehearse, and present oral reports effectively.

The higher up the corporate ladder you move, the more likely you are to give oral presentations. The audience, formality, and purpose may vary. For instance, you may give presentations to **internal audiences** (listeners in the presenter's organization). Your audience may be colleagues above or below you in the organizational hierarchy—or both. You also may give presentations to **external audiences** (listeners outside the speaker's organization), such as suppliers, vendors, and customers.

Some oral presentations will be as informal as an impromptu gathering where you answer questions. These spontaneous **informal presentations** occur without preparation or rehearsal. Instead, you use your experience and knowledge to provide insight. Listeners will expect thought and clarity, but they will not expect you to recall precise details. Other presentations will be elaborate and carefully prepared sessions. These **formal presentations,** planned in advance and rehearsed, are usually scheduled for an office, an auditorium, or a conference room. These locations may include tools for the presenter's use—ranging from a podium and microphone, to a whiteboard, to more high-tech aids such as SMART Board™ interactive whiteboards and LCD projectors. Formal presentations often include printed material for distribution, posters, product samples or models, and multimedia slides.

During your career, you may be asked to present solutions to problems; results of investigations; policies or procedures; progress on projects; benefits of ideas, products, or services; or training seminars.

Warm Up

What presentations or public speaking do you expect to do in your career?

FOCUS

Warm Up

Use the Warm Up to reinforce the importance of presentation skills, not only for students' academic careers, but also for their professional careers.

COMMUNICATION DILEMMA

Jody should demand that the "borrowed" material be removed unless Shelton gets permission from the other company and gives credit for the material.

TYPICAL READER/LISTENER

Any person or employee needing information delivered verbally, often with graphic aids to enhance the message.

WRITER'S FOCUS

Providing clear information targeted to the audience's needs and delivered appropriately for the situation.

Communication Dilemma

Shelton Corbett and Jody Kolema were assigned to make a presentation before their company's board of directors on new licensing guidelines. Because of other projects taking longer than expected, Shelton and Jody are behind schedule in planning their presentation. As they begin rehearsing with slides, Jody realizes that Shelton has incorporated complete passages as well as a visual aid from another company's website.

Think Critically

What action, if any, should Jody take?

PLANNING

The planning stage is essential in the creation of presentations. This is the stage in which you analyze your audience, develop a topic, create effective graphic aids, assess the location, plan your time, and anticipate stage fright.

Audience

Analyzing your audience is as important in oral reports as it is in written reports. You need to know your listeners in order to connect with them.

Begin your audience analysis by asking why you are making the presentation and what you want to achieve. You must understand the goal if you want to reach it. For instance, Will's manager asked him to comment on a new pillow display. Will explained at length how he thought the pillows were too soft when, in fact, all the manager wanted to know was whether the display was sturdy and safe. If Will had understood that his manager was asking about the staging of the display, Will could have answered appropriately.

Once your purpose is clear, try answering the following questions:

- Who is the audience—customers? clients? technical experts? managers? sales staff? product developers?

- What is the audience's role? How will the audience use the information?

- Will the audience be a single person, a small group, or a large group?

- If the audience is a group, is that group made up of the same types or roles (all engineers or all sales staff) or is it diverse?

- Is the audience more comfortable with words or with numbers and statistics?

- What impresses the audience?

- What are the audience's expectations?

- Will the audience use the information themselves or pass it along to others?

- How much, if anything, does the audience already know about the topic?

- Is the audience familiar with the jargon related to this topic? Or will you need to define and explain technical aspects of the presentation?

- How comfortable is the audience with technology? Does the audience expect multimedia in the presentation?

- What history does the audience have with this topic? Is the audience likely to come with an approving, neutral, or hostile attitude?

The better you know your audience, the more effective you can be in meeting the audience's needs and achieving your purpose.

Topic

Sometimes speakers choose their own topics. However, when asked to speak at work (and in school), you often are assigned a topic. In business, managers often ask employees to prepare a written document such as a progress report, a solution to a problem, or an incident report. After submitting the written report, the employee may be asked to make an oral presentation. For example, Edith Frost, a machinist at Tarboro Machine Corporation, wrote a report that suggested three new safety measures for all machine operators. She submitted the report to the plant safety officer and the vice president. Edith's supervisor then asked her to present her plan at the next managers' meeting.

Graphic Aids

Research suggests that an audience takes in less than 25 percent of what a speaker says. One way to increase your audience's comprehension is by using graphic aids. Graphic aids clarify ideas and highlight important information, allowing audiences to both see and hear the message.

Guidelines for Choosing What to Illustrate

When you think of adding graphic aids, you must decide what to illustrate. Use these questions to help you:

- What information is most important?

- What data is most complex or most difficult to understand?

- What concepts, statistics, or figures are particularly important?

A general guide for preparing graphic aids is to create letters that are 1" high for each 10' of distance between the viewers and the graphic. So if audience members at the back of the room are 20' from the marker board, letters should be 2" or taller to ensure easy viewing.

When preparing slides or transparencies, use 24-point or larger type.

Because about one out of every ten people cannot distinguish between red and green, these colors should not be used together in graphs or charts.

Items in a bulleted list should use parallel structure.

Once you answer those questions, you will have selected the ideas your audience needs to understand and, as a result, determined what ideas to illustrate. The next question is how best to illustrate a particular idea.

Types of Graphic Aids

Graphic aids can include photographs, line drawings, charts, tables, objects, or multimedia. For instance, a presenter discussing environmental hazards might use a flip chart to diagram the amount of chemicals found in groundwater. A student speaking to her classmates about erroneous ideas associated with cerebral palsy brought her brother, a police detective with cerebral palsy, to class as a graphic aid.

The various types of graphic aids—flip charts, transparencies, slides, multimedia, dry erase boards, handouts, physical objects, and more—range from simple and inexpensive to complex and costly. The time and cost of development must be considered along with effectiveness when choosing graphic aids. You do not want to spend a great deal of time or money to create a working prototype of a new product when no action or decision is expected. The time and expense could not be justified for a simple informational presentation. However, the investment might be reasonable if production decisions were to be made.

Photodisc/Getty Images

In addition to time and cost, the location (room or space) and audience size are factors in determining the types of graphics to use. For example, flip charts and posters are appropriate for small audiences in close spaces. Objects, demonstrations, marker boards, and transparencies may work well with a medium-sized group as long as everyone can see the graphic easily. In large meeting facilities, multimedia presentations and films provide images that are large enough for everyone to see.

Other factors to consider are artistic talent (yours or your company's) and equipment. If your organization has a graphic arts department that can produce quality graphs, charts, photographs, films, or electronic aids, your only challenge may be selecting the ideas you want illustrated and choosing from your options. On the other hand, you may have to rely on your own skills and talent. When professionals are not available, you may need to choose a simple graphic aid because you can prepare it easily. That is, you might create a simple slide presentation instead of planning, developing, and editing a film that includes sound and captions.

Guidelines for Creating Graphic Aids

When you develop graphics, keep your audience's needs in mind. The following guidelines will help you:

- Make the graphic large enough for everyone to see easily—even people sitting in the back or the corners of the room.

- Do not crowd numbers or images on a graphic aid.

- Remember that although attractive design counts, the message is more important.

- Consider handouts for the audience, which they can refer to later.

The following tips are for use with presentation software such as PowerPoint®:

- Select landscape layout for your slides. It gives you longer lines for your text.

- Give each slide a title or heading.

- Select a font that the audience can easily read from a distance, such as **Times New Roman Bold** or **Arial Black**.

- Use serif fonts to improve readability. Because sans serif fonts present a cleaner, crisper image, use these fonts for titles of slides.

- Choose a font size that is readable and that suggests the importance of elements on the slide. Generally, these sizes are appropriate:

  - Titles: 24–36 points

  - Other text: 18–24 points

  - Source notes: 14–16 points

- Capitalize the first letter of important words in titles of slides. Words that are in all uppercase letters are difficult to read.

- In bulleted lists, capitalize only the initial letter of the first word (and, of course, proper nouns and proper adjectives).

- Use the Notes section as a reminder of your next point; specific facts, figures, or quotations; cues when someone else will be advancing the slide; or reminders such as "Make eye contact."

- If you have clip art or an image that supports the text on a slide, place it in the lower right corner.

- Keep slides simple and uncluttered. Use phrases and keywords and limit the number of lines on a slide to six or fewer.

- If you use transition effects between slides, make the effect meaningful.

- On your speaker's notes pages, number the slides so you can quickly move to a particular slide when someone asks a question.

- Do not preset timings in your slides. If you advance the slides manually, you can pace yourself rather than force your speech to fit the predetermined increment of time for each slide.

TEACH

Sans means "without" in French.

Letters in a 72-point font are 1" tall.

Tell students to consider the effect of colors in designing graphic aids. For example, blue is a conservative color that adds formality, while yellow is brighter and less formal. Red, orange, and yellow encourage movement and anxiety, while blue and green are calming.

Tell students to think of associations their audience may have with certain colors. Because red depicts "stop," danger, blood, or financial loss, it is not a good choice for a pie chart showing budget projections.

Advise students that if they plan to prepare a handout for the audience, they should add a header or footer with the presentation title, date, name(s) of the speaker(s), and name of the organization. Some speakers include a telephone number, an e-mail address, or a postal address.

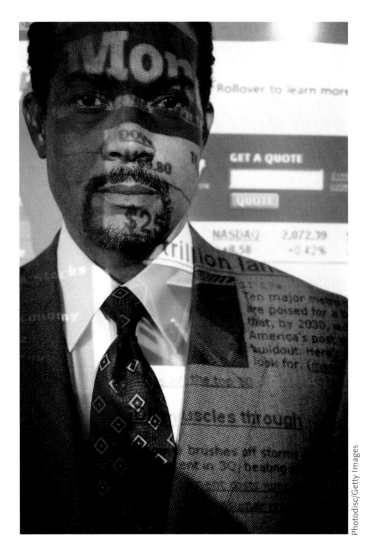

Photodisc/Getty Images

Location

Presenters also should plan for the presentation's location, which can be very important. For example, if you will be making a union presentation to a construction crew at an outdoor job site, using a projector and screen probably is not an option. If you are using a small conference room to make a presentation about new soccer league rules, demonstrating an illegal shot block could be difficult.

In addition to their own needs regarding location, presenters should plan for the audience's needs as well. Answer the following questions about the location to prepare for your presentation.

Speaker's Considerations

■ Is a speaker's podium available? Is a table or space available for handouts and demonstration tools?

■ Will you be standing directly in front of the audience, or will you be sitting in front of or with the audience?

■ Is the stage elevated, or are you on the same level as the audience?

■ How much space does the room encompass? How well does sound carry? How loudly will you need to speak in order to be heard?

■ If a microphone is needed, is it a wireless, podium, or handheld mic?

■ Is audiovisual equipment installed, or must you bring your own?

■ Is available equipment compatible with your software and hardware?

■ Will you need passwords, keys, or codes to access the equipment, software, or Internet?

■ How much space do you have for moving around during your presentation?

■ Are people available to help you with equipment or to distribute handouts?

■ Will someone introduce you, or will you introduce yourself?

Audience's Considerations

■ Is the location difficult to find or reach? Are directions available?

■ Is the location accessible for people with disabilities?

■ If needed, are restrooms and refreshments available? Where?

■ Will all members of the audience be able to see and hear?

- Is the location appropriate and comfortable (design, lighting, temperature) for the type of presentation?
- Will the audience be seated or standing?
- Are the seats arranged appropriately for the group in attendance?

Time

Presenters should plan to meet the time expectations of the audience. If you are invited to present, the person who invites you should let you know how much time you have to speak. If the host does not give you a time, ask. Speakers who ignore audience expectations often lose the audience's attention. For example, when you go to class, you expect the class to be conducted within the typical time period. How would students respond if their instructor kept the class 30 minutes beyond the usual time? Listeners often respond by fidgeting, focusing on distractions, and sometimes even walking out. Keep listeners' attention by complying with the time frame you are given.

Also plan for the proper rate of speaking. Speak slowly when you share difficult or complex ideas and pause after each major section or idea. Nervous speakers tend to talk too fast and may frustrate the audience. To avoid this problem, be aware of your pacing.

Stage Fright

You may think it odd that a textbook tells you to plan for stage fright when most people want to avoid it. Yet stage fright is not something to eliminate; it is energy you should use. Many professional speakers will tell you that you cannot eliminate nervous reactions when speaking. Those reactions, they say, are natural responses to stress. Instead of trying to suppress stage fright, let it work for you. To harness this energy, you should:

- Recognize and plan for how your body responds to anxiety.
- Anticipate excess **adrenaline** (a stimulant that excites and creates extra energy) to give your introduction and important points extra emphasis.

⬤ STOP AND THINK

Would an audience of your classmates be more interested in how school policy affects taxpayers or how school policy affects students? Explain.

ORGANIZING AND COMPOSING

When you are making a presentation, listeners cannot refer to a previous page if they find your ideas unclear or confusing. Therefore, you should organize and compose your oral presentations for the listeners' situation and needs.

Selecting an Organizational Plan

For most presentations, you will probably use the **direct approach.** With the direct approach, you state the main idea first and then explain and support

Warm Up

Think of messages you have prepared to give orally, such as planning to ask someone for a date or a favor. Under what circumstances would it be better to communicate an important message in writing? Under what circumstances would it be better to communicate an important message in a formal oral presentation? In a brief journal entry, explain the differences and similarities between oral and written composition.

As you discuss composing introductions, give students an opportunity to practice formulating introductions. Give them a presentation topic and ask them to write only an introduction.

To test the statement that listeners remember the first and last points they hear, call out 10 to 15 random words. Then ask students to write down the words they remember. Results will probably prove that listeners do remember the first and last items more easily.

TEACH

Remind students to be careful with humor. A joke or humorous story can create rapport between the speaker and the audience. When exaggerated, though, listeners may perceive the topic as insignificant.

In an introduction, speakers may explain the situation that caused the need for the report or identify the person who requested the information.

Tell students that if they have conclusions or recommendations, they should present them in the introduction so listeners will understand data in the body of the report.

RETEACH

Remind students that choosing an effective organizational plan for the body is especially important because listeners depend on it and the preview to help them understand the report's message.

TEACH

Speakers might consider these organizational strategies: spatial order (e.g., top to bottom, east to west, or left to right), chronological order (e.g., 1950 to the present or from the beginning to the end of a work shift), most-important-to-least-important order, least-important-to-most-important order, and problem-solution order.

that idea with details. Stating the main idea first lets your listeners know what your subject is, what points you will make, and how you will proceed.

On the other hand, if you know that your audience opposes the point that you support or if you want to be especially persuasive, consider using the **indirect approach.** With an indirect approach, you gradually build your evidence, convincing the audience of your point, which you state at the end of your presentation.

Previewing Organization

Regardless of organizational strategy, give the audience a preview so they know what plan you are following. The preview is like a map showing a driver where to turn and how far to go. Your preview explains the order of your ideas. Here are two examples of typical preview statements:

- This recommendation contains four major parts: review, staffing, operational policy, and production.

- The SOP for student interns involves completing treatment plans, writing care instructions, and recording patient progress.

Composing the Introduction

Listeners typically recall the first and last points they hear. Therefore, plan for a strong introduction and conclusion. If you are uncertain how to introduce your presentation, think as your audience might. What would get your attention? You would want to know the topic; the points the speaker will support; and how this issue affects you, the listener. Your introduction should announce the topic and points you will make. In addition, you want to give the listeners something to which they can relate—some connection. For example, an address by a woman to her town's commissioners began this way: "My friend Marquita died last month. She should not have been in the path of a car going 45 miles per hour, nor should any of your children, grandchildren, or neighbors. Our town must protect its citizens by providing bicycle paths and enforcing helmet laws."

Depending on your audience and purpose, try one of several introductions:

- A direct quotation, usually from a well-known source

- A **rhetorical question**—a question designed to provoke thought; a question for which the speaker expects no answer

- A startling fact or statistic to grab a listener's attention

- A statement you then disprove

- An **anecdote,** a humorous story

For example, if you were making a class presentation on the advantages of modern medicine, you might begin this way:

> If you were born in the United States in 1990, you had a life expectancy of 75.4 years. On the other hand, people born in 1970 were expected to live only 70.8 years. According to these statistics, you will outlive your mother and father by 4.6 years. (United States: National Center for Health Statistics)

The startling fact that the audience's generation is expected to live 4.6 years longer than their parents' should grab the listeners' attention, particularly because these statistics relate to the audience's mortality.

Composing the Body

These guidelines will help you compose the body of an oral presentation:

- Address people. Include the words *you* and *your* early and often.

- Use words your audience will know. Define unfamiliar terms.

- Use simpler sentences than you use when writing.

- Give listeners information they want or need and fully explain its relevance.

- Emphasize main points. Because listeners take in only a small percentage of what they hear, repeat or restate essential ideas.

- Announce transitions so the audience will not miss the connection from one point to the next.

- Answer questions you think your audience is likely to ask.

- Stay within your time limit, meeting the audience's expectations.

Composing the Conclusion

Conclusions are important because they are the last point or topic the audience will hear. Therefore, they require as much planning as introductions do. An effective conclusion should hold the audience's attention, summarize key points, and call for action if requested.

⬢ **STOP AND THINK**

John wants to persuade his parents, who do not allow him to drive long distances alone, to let him drive 55 miles to a basketball tournament. The ideas that John plans to share with his parents are that (a) driving is the least expensive and safest way to get to the tournament, (b) he has behaved responsibly when given other opportunities, and (c) the bus does not travel to the location. Place these ideas in the most effective order for John to present to his parents.

PREPARING

After you complete the planning process, you need to prepare notes and your image. Doing so will help ensure that you deliver an effective presentation. Risks are huge if you neglect your preparation. Without notes, you are left with only your memory, which sometimes fails under stress. Without personal preparation, you may become preoccupied with your clothing or hair, feeling greater frustration and losing ground with the audience.

TEACH

Speakers can appropriately say "In conclusion . . ." as they begin their conclusions. This statement is a signal for listeners to pay attention. Audiences expect key information at this point.

ONGOING ASSESSMENT

Stop and Think

Assign the Stop and Think as a critical-thinking exercise. This activity also gives students an opportunity to practice organization. The audience is opposed to the main idea, so the indirect approach should be used. Possible answer: c, b, a

FOCUS

Warm Up

Use the Warm Up to stress the importance of using notes or outlines to give polished presentations. Answers may vary, but someone will probably talk about a speech given without adequate preparation and the ensuing embarrassment. The problems might include talking too long, going off the topic, forgetting important points, or giving inaccurate information.

Warm Up

Think about your experiences speaking both with and without notes. If possible, discuss these experiences in small groups. Review the benefits of using notes and problems you have had with them.

Outlines and Notes

A practiced performance with an outline or notes yields an informal, conversational style. Speakers may generate an outline using presentation software such as Microsoft® PowerPoint® or develop an outline using a word processor or a pen. With an outline or notes on index cards or paper, you will be able to talk to your audience, not read to them.

To reach this point, you must organize your ideas effectively. If you were writing a report, your next step would be to compose sentences, build paragraphs, and create a document. For an oral presentation, however, you should avoid extended writing. A complete paper with sentences and dense paragraphs might encourage you to read the text rather than interact with your audience. Or fearing that you might lose your place in all of that text, you might avoid the text entirely and try to speak from memory.

An outline or notes should show each main point in your presentation. Under each main point, list facts, figures, or quotations that support the point. For precision and accuracy, do not trust your memory for such specific information in front of an audience. For example, the outline in Figure 12.1 shows one section of a report on progress for upgrading warehouse computers.

For the first point of an outline or a note card, write a word or phrase that will trigger your memory. Then go on to the next point of your speech.

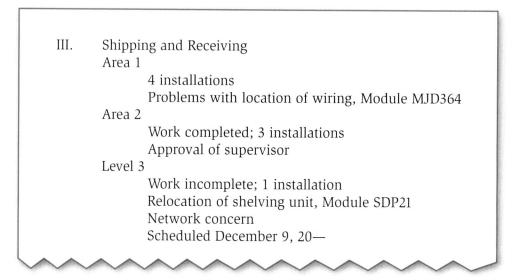

III.   Shipping and Receiving
        Area 1
                4 installations
                Problems with location of wiring, Module MJD364
        Area 2
                Work completed; 3 installations
                Approval of supervisor
        Level 3
                Work incomplete; 1 installation
                Relocation of shelving unit, Module SDP21
                Network concern
                Scheduled December 9, 20—

Figure 12.1 Excerpt from a Presentation Outline

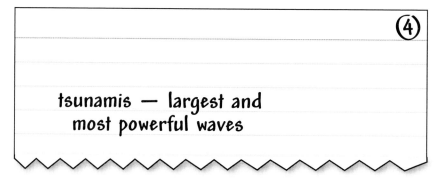

④

tsunamis — largest and
most powerful waves

Figure 12.2 Note Card for Oral Presentation

For each idea, prepare a point in an outline or on a note card similar to the one in Figure 12.2. This card reminds the speaker that this section of the talk is about tsunamis, the huge destructive waves that often occur in the Pacific Ocean, striking places such as Sri Lanka, Japan, and Indonesia.

If you are developing computer slides for a presentation, most software allows you to add notes. These notes reinforce the logical flow of the discussion and highlight details such as statistics, quotations, and important facts. For instance, PowerPoint® allows you to print handouts with two, three, four, six, or nine slides per page, including space for notes.

Figure 12.3 on the following page shows a PowerPoint® handout. You can use it to add notes for yourself, or you can give it to the audience so they can write notes as you talk.

When preparing outlines or notes, remember these important points:

- Do not write notes as complete sentences or long phrases. Even experienced speakers would be tempted to read these.

- Prepare neat notes that are surrounded by adequate white space. Use large print so you can read the notes easily.

- Structure notes uniformly: use numbered lists, bulleted lists, or outline form.

- If you are using cards, write only one idea on each card. If you are using printed notes or outlines, use a large, easy-to-read serif font.

- Number notes or cards from beginning to end. On note cards, place the card number in the upper right corner, as shown in Figure 12.2. Should the cards become disorganized, you can sort them quickly.

- Use outlines and notes to spark your memory. By glancing at the words, you will be able to look at your audience and deliver a portion of your speech. Thus, you can converse with the audience using a polished approach.

Personal Appearance

In addition to note cards and graphic aids, image has a big impact on the way listeners receive a speaker's message. You probably know how appearance can affect communication in everyday situations. For example, think about the way a salesperson might treat you if you are wearing worn jeans and an old T-shirt. If you have not experienced this treatment yourself, you likely have seen other people treated differently because of their clothing or grooming.

When you select clothing for a presentation, consider the audience's expectations and the situation in which you will be speaking. For instance, someone addressing city council would probably dress as formally as its members do (in business attire). On the other hand, a speaker addressing children at a youth center would dress more casually. Whatever you wear, make sure you are comfortable in the outfit. If you feel good about the way you look, you will speak with confidence.

If you have done everything you can to prepare for success, you are ready to move to the rehearsal phase.

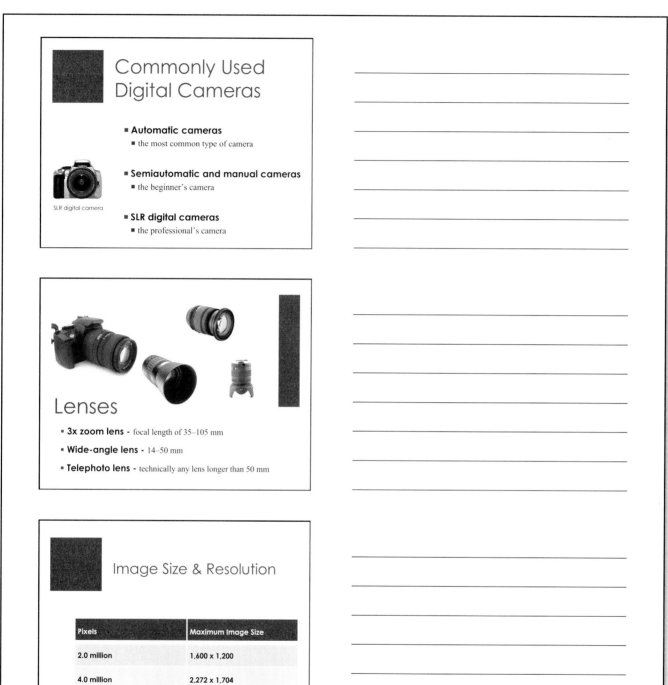

Figure 12.3 PowerPoint® Handout with Space for Notes

Permission by Kassie Bryan

ONGOING ASSESSMENT
Stop and Think
For a presentation about running or athletic training at a gym or fitness center, the presenter might wear running shorts as a graphic aid.

 STOP AND THINK
Would running shorts ever be appropriate dress for a presentation? Explain.

REHEARSING

Expert presenters—even professional speakers—will say that you must rehearse if you want to give a successful presentation. Practicing helps you develop a conversational style. In fact, good speeches are a conversation between speaker and audience, only slightly more polished than the conversations you have with friends. Practice provides experience—experience that soothes nerves and builds confidence. After several rehearsals (with adjustments each time), you will have a presentation with which you are pleased and you can trust that your presentation will go well.

Using your note cards and graphic aids, you should practice your speech. When you first deliver the talk, you can identify parts you like and dislike. Delivering the speech a second time, you can change what you do not like. When you are comfortable with your delivery, you have rehearsed enough. You have reached a conversational style.

Speakers practice their speeches in different ways, including using an audio recorder, a mirror, a video camera, or a live audience. With experience, you will decide which methods work best for you.

Using an Audio Recorder

After recording your presentation, take a break. Later, with the benefit of time and a fresh perspective, listen to your recording for the following:

- Rate (how fast you talked)

- Volume (how loudly or softly you talked)

- Pronunciation (how distinct your words were)

- Inflections (what your changes in pitch and tone were)

- Time (how much time you took to present your ideas)

If you find that you are talking too rapidly, something that often occurs when people are nervous, adjust your pacing. Change your volume so everyone can hear you but will not think you are yelling. Listen and correct pronunciation, particularly of unfamiliar or challenging words. Avoid speaking in monotone by varying your pitch and tone appropriately for the message. Finally, check the length of your rehearsed presentation to ensure that you are within your time limit.

Using a Mirror

Watch yourself in a mirror as you practice your presentation. Put yourself in the role of the audience. What do you see that will enhance or detract from the message? Check for:

- Appropriate facial expressions. For example, do not grin when delivering sad news such as suicide rates. Likewise, do not finish your presentation without having changed expressions.

- Effective use of your body and hands. (Do your hand movements emphasize major points, or do they tend to distract your listener from the topic?)

ONGOING ASSESSMENT
Stop and Think
After students discuss the question in small groups, ask them to share their answers with the class. Answers will vary, but students should note that a tape recorder provides only auditory feedback. It does not disclose facial expressions, body language, or other concerns.

FOCUS
Warm Up
Use the Warm Up to generate discussion about the positives of public speaking.

Using a Video Camera

Do not review the presentation immediately. Wait until you have more perspective—perhaps in an hour or the next day. When you do view the recording, pretend to be your audience. Look for strengths as well as weaknesses. With this **auditory** (sound) and visual information, check for the following:

- How you sound
- Whether your pacing works
- How you look
- What message you deliver

Using a Live Audience

Ask a friend or family member to listen to you practice your presentation. After delivering the speech, invite **feedback**—comments and suggestions to help you improve. Try some of these questions:

- What was my speech topic?
- What point did I try to prove?
- Did I make eye contact?
- Did I speak loudly enough?
- Did I tend to use verbal tics such as *and, uh, um,* or *like*?
- Was my conclusion effective?
- Did I pronounce words correctly?

 STOP AND THINK

While an audio recorder provides useful feedback when you are rehearsing a speech, what does it *not* tell you? In small groups, discuss your answers.

Warm Up

Discuss these questions with your classmates: Can oral presentations be fun? How can you make presenting fun?

PRESENTING

Once you have thoroughly prepared, check the environment to ensure the best situation and present with confidence.

Checking the Room

Arrive early for your presentation. During that time, make sure listeners will be comfortable and can see clearly and hear well. Consider seating, lighting, temperature, equipment, and graphic aids.

Seating

Check the arrangement of chairs. Are they arranged so that you can communicate effectively? For example, if you want group discussion, the chairs should be placed so that people can see each other. Also, everyone in the room should be able to see you (and any other presenters) easily.

Lighting

Make sure your audience will have enough light to see and take notes. Correct any glaring and overly bright spots. In a room that is lighted properly, your audience can concentrate on your message.

Temperature

Check the temperature controls. People who are uncomfortably hot or uncomfortably cold will not be good listeners.

Equipment and Graphic Aids

Check all equipment to make sure it is working properly and prepare for problems. Remember Murphy's Law: If something can go wrong, it will! Make sure you have an extra bulb for the projector, markers, and anything else you might need.

Before the event, determine how you will post or display your materials. Consider visibility and access when arranging your graphic aids. Graphics need to be located so that:

- Everyone in the room can easily see them.
- You can point to the graphics as you talk.
- You can reach equipment to make adjustments, such as turning up the volume.
- The equipment has a power supply.

Delivering the Message

Having prepared for the presentation, you are ready to enjoy talking with your audience. Use the following pointers to help you deliver an effective message:

- Use appropriate facial expressions.
- Maintain eye contact, which shows your interest and concern.
- Explain every graphic. Tell people exactly what you want them to understand.
- Post or distribute handouts only when you want the audience to use or read them. You may ask someone to distribute them for you.
- Consult your notes, but do not read from them.
- Continue to talk even when something goes wrong. Recover as best you can, but go on. Do not call attention to a mistake by apologizing.
- Remember that your audience wants you to succeed. Your audience's desire for an effective presentation, along with the self-confidence you gained from being fully prepared, will ensure a positive experience.
- Give your audience an opportunity to ask questions if the program and time allow. If you cannot answer a question, respond in a positive way: "I'm sorry that I don't have the answer to your question, but I'll be happy to check my sources and get back to you later this week."

● STOP AND THINK

Should you display your poster before you begin to speak? Is eye contact with your audience desirable? Explain.

TEACH

Speakers may prepare the room 30 minutes or several days before a presentation. If it is the latter, the speaker should check the room immediately before the presentation to ensure that nothing has been disturbed.

Ask students to think of situations that could go wrong and ways to handle those situations.

TEACH

Tell students that speakers who complete their presentation despite problems (e.g., equipment malfunctions or dropped notes) usually earn the respect and admiration of the audience.

A speaker who is presenting with slides should use the feature for blacking out or whiting out the screen when answering a question that does not relate to the current slide. That way the audience can focus on the discussion instead of the slide.

ONGOING ASSESSMENT

Stop and Think

You should display your poster before you speak only when you want the audience to refer to it at the beginning of the presentation. Otherwise, display the visual when you discuss its content.

Yes, eye contact is essential.

ORGANIZING A GROUP PRESENTATION

Presenting with others requires special consideration. Collaboration provides many opportunities to share diverse perspectives and expertise. However, group presentations require careful planning if they are to be effective. Collaborators must act as a team and plan for developing a topic, setting time limits, moving between speakers, providing graphic aids and handouts, answering questions, and managing the presentation.

Dividing the Topic

When collaborating on a presentation, speakers must plan roles and responsibilities. One important issue to discuss is who will be responsible for presenting what information. For example, three employees making a planning proposal might divide the discussion this way: Speaker 1—introduction of speakers, their qualifications, and the problem prompting the proposal; Speaker 2—the proposed solution and the budget; Speaker 3—the conclusion and the requested action. Therefore, the division of topics may dictate the order of presenters.

Focus on Ethics

You live in an age when a great deal of business is being conducted globally. That means that at some point in your career, you may have an opportunity to attend a meeting in Japan, give a presentation in Australia, or create and present a training course via a videoconference in Brazil.

Because more business is being conducted globally, knowing the proper methods for presentations across cultures is extremely important. Beginning with the presentation planning stage, you must be aware of how cultural practices and expectations of the audience are different from your own. Research the audience's culture and plan for differences to ensure that your presentation is well received.

For example, while presenting to an international audience, you should be aware of gestures that are not universal. In Greece, nodding your head up and down means "no," not "yes." In Australia, a "thumbs-up" gesture is considered inappropriate.

You also should research the formality of the culture. Jokes are not appropriate for some audiences. Dressing formally makes other audiences uncomfortable.

No matter what cultural differences you face, the most important rule to remember is to respect those differences.

Think Critically

What are some cultural differences evident in your community? How does being aware of them give you the opportunity to be a more effective communicator?

In addition, sometimes a speaker's expertise will require that he or she deal with a particular aspect, such as an accountant explaining a budget. If speakers are equally qualified to present the material, the group must define other reasons for assigning roles.

Setting Time Limits

The same way individual speakers must stay within a time limit when making a presentation, group presenters also have an obligation to stay within a time frame. After the group determines the length of the entire presentation, the members should decide the time allotted each member, keeping in mind the material each member will cover and its relative significance. Given a 30-minute slot in the agenda, the team members presenting the planning proposal might divide their time this way:

Speaker 1	Introduction of speakers and their qualifications; problem prompting the proposal	10 minutes
Speaker 2	Proposed solution and budget	15 minutes
Speaker 3	Conclusion and requested action	5 minutes

Speaker 2 is allotted the most time because explaining the proposed plan and justifying its budget are critical. If the audience does not understand this information, the proposal may not be approved. In addition, Speaker 2 must prove that a significant problem exists. Speaker 3 needs less time, not because concluding is unimportant, but because conclusions should be direct and brief, giving the audience time to ask questions.

Members of groups should be even more careful than individual speakers to stay within their time limit. If one speaker exceeds his or her time limit, another presenter is left with less time.

Transitioning Between Speakers

Audiences expect to be introduced to speakers. In a group presentation, the speakers may choose to have another person introduce them or to introduce themselves at the beginning of the session. Another option is for each presenter to be introduced right before he or she begins to speak.

When various speakers are answering questions, listeners prefer to be reminded of the responding speaker's name. Often a moderator will name the presenter as the moderator asks him or her to address a question, such as "Dr. Quan, would you like to answer the question on profiling?"

Providing Graphic Aids and Handouts

Group presenters should discuss the use of graphic aids and handouts when planning their presentation. Coordinating the appearance of slides,

COMMUNICATION TECHNOLOGIES

In today's age of global communications, many presentation teams are made up of members from across the globe. Therefore, presenters must have a way to keep track of presentation documents and ideas. They also must have a quick way to distribute the most current documents and keep team members up to date. That is where virtual office space comes into play. This space can be on the Web or on their company's intranet. It allows the storage of shared files as well as space for discussion groups. Members also can use virtual bulletin boards to post the latest updates.

Think Critically

What are advantages and disadvantages of having office space on the Web? on an organization's intranet?

COMMUNICATION TECHNOLOGIES

Having office space on the Web is convenient because everyone has access, but it also may be accessible to people outside the organization, a vulnerability in the case of to sensitive information. On the other hand, the organization's intranet may be more secure but less accessible to clients or others outside the organization.

Use the *Oral Report Evaluation Form* worksheet on the website when you practice oral presentations. Go to www.cengage.com/school/bcomm/techwtg. Click the link for Chapter 12; then click Data Files. The worksheet gives you the opportunity to learn from the evaluation and from advice provided by the listeners.

NET BOOKMARK

Use the NET Bookmark to engage students' critical-thinking skills. Many students may believe that presentation software has no downside. Tufte's perspective is that people rely too much on the software, resulting in dreadful presentations.

ONGOING ASSESSMENT

Stop and Think

The order may be decided by the portion of the topic each speaker presents. For example, the speaker whose area of expertise logically should be discussed first will be the opening presenter.

Although a chairperson is not necessary, groups are likely to function more effectively when someone manages the process.

transparencies, and handouts adds to the professionalism of a group presentation. For example, members could agree to use one slide template; a certain color, scheme, or typeface; or the same headers and footers. Members should decide when to distribute handouts. Will all handouts be provided to listeners at one time, or will each presenter be responsible for distributing his or her own handouts? Because some speakers do not want the audience reading handouts while they speak, they may prefer to distribute all handouts at the end of the presentation. Other speakers may want the audience to have copies of materials so they can take notes during the discussion. Speakers should discuss and agree on a plan before the presentation.

Speakers also must decide what equipment they will need. For instance, when two speakers plan to use overhead transparencies and the third speaker wants an LCD projector, they should agree on where to place the equipment and whether any equipment must be moved between presentations. Presenters using the same multimedia equipment should know their software needs and make sure the equipment is compatible.

Answering Questions

Group presenters should anticipate questions and plan how to answer them. In some presentations, the group may allow each speaker to take questions when the speaker ends his or her portion. Other groups will answer questions only after all presenters have completed their speeches. Presenters also should know whether a moderator will assign each question to a particular presenter or whether the presenters will select questions. Speakers are wise to plan answers for questions they expect to be asked. Therefore, collaborators might divide the topic areas so that each presenter can prepare for questions in a certain area.

Groups may perform more effectively with leadership. Thus, many groups have a lead presenter, a chairperson, or someone who manages the process. The lead presenter often represents the group in discussions with meeting planners and acts as liaison, then corresponds with group members to keep them informed. The lead presenter sometimes speaks first, previewing the presentation or stating objectives, or last, summarizing key points and moderating questions. The lead presenter may have other responsibilities, including:

- Keeping speakers on schedule; calling time for those who talk too long.

- Keeping questions moving; preventing arguments and the monopolization of discussions.

- Responding to requests for more information; mailing materials.

An effective leader will ensure that all group members' talents are used and that all opinions are heard.

 STOP AND THINK

In a collaborative presentation, how do speakers determine who will speak when? Do groups need a lead presenter or chairperson? Why or why not?

CHAPTER 12 REVIEW

SUMMARY

1. Your ability to effectively present your ideas orally to others will affect your success in the workplace.

2. Plan for your audience, topic, graphic aids, location, and stage fright.

3. Use audience analysis to organize as well as to compose the presentation's introduction, body, and conclusion.

4. Preparing involves creating an outline or notes and making adjustments to your image.

5. After planning, organizing, composing, and preparing, rehearse using a variety of methods to polish your presentation.

6. Check the seating, lighting, temperature, equipment, and graphic aids to create the best possible listening environment.

7. When presenting as part of a team, think about how the team will divide the topic among presenters; what amount of time to allot each speaker; how to move between speakers; how to handle graphics, handouts, and questions; and who will manage the presentation process.

Checklist

- Have I carefully analyzed my audience and clearly defined and focused the topic?

- Have I planned how I can effectively use my response to stage fright?

- Have I composed a strong and effective introduction? body? conclusion?

- Will my outline or notes allow me to deliver a conversational performance instead of reading a speech or speaking without aid?

- What type of graphic will be most effective for enhancing critical or complex ideas and for speaking to a group?

- Have I prepared for an appropriate and professional appearance?

- Have I rehearsed and gathered feedback for improvement?

- Have I checked the room for seating, lighting, temperature, equipment, and graphics?

- Have I effectively delivered the message using facial expressions, eye contact, graphics and handouts, notes, confidence, and questions?

- For a collaborative presentation, have my team and I divided the topic among speakers, established time limits, planned transitions, coordinated graphics and handouts, planned for questions, and considered the selection of a team leader or chairperson?

CLOSE

Summary

Use the summary to review the various strategies covered in the chapter.

Stress the importance of audience analysis, planning, and rehearsing.

Another use of the summary is to ask students to close their books and write five (or whatever number you think is appropriate) important ideas they learned in the chapter. Then ask students to write quiz or discussion questions to share with the class.

CLOSE

Checklist

Suggest that students refer to the checklist when developing presentations.

Also remind students to add items to the checklist based on their own needs. For example, if a student has problems with pronunciation, he or she should add that item to the checklist.

REVIEW

For a review of the key terms in the chapter, provide students with the *Key Terms* worksheet available as a supplemental activity on the IRCD.

ASSESS

Build Your Foundation

1. A technical writer should consider audience first. The speaker should consider what will grab the fifth-graders' attention. They may not be accustomed to 50 minutes of lecture, but they might respond enthusiastically to 15 minutes of lecture containing a five- to ten-minute slide presentation and a tortilla-making demonstration.

2. Because giving instructions on how to complete a form is a lecture, the arrangement of desks in rows facing the front of the room would work well. Students also may discuss the types of graphics they would use (e.g., an overhead projector or a computer with an LCD projection panel).

3. The introduction should grab the listener's attention, establish a connection, announce the topic, and preview the main points of the discussion to come.

4. To develop a plan for preparing for the presentation, students will need to review each step in the process presented in this chapter. You also can refer students to the checklist at the end of the chapter.

5. In the Planning section of the chapter, students should review the guidelines for choosing what information to illustrate; in the Presenting section, they should review the information about equipment and graphic aids.

ASSESS

Your Turn

6. Encourage students to be honest about their strengths and weaknesses. They can build on their strengths while improving weak aspects of their presentations.

Build Your Foundation

1. You have been asked to speak to your nephew's fifth-grade social studies class about Mexico and your work there as a Habitat for Humanity volunteer. The social studies class lasts 50 minutes. If the instructor tells you to talk as long as you like, what factors might you consider when deciding on length?

2. Mrs. Nicoletti, a counselor, has asked you to explain to a group of 35 first-year students how to complete their registration cards. The entire process involves using decisions the students have made previously and entering data on a preprinted form. Choose a room in your school with which you are familiar and imagine this location. What would be the most effective way to arrange chairs for this presentation? Consider graphics you might use. Consider how much, if at all, you want the students consulting with each other. Other factors could be the room's size and the location of permanent features such as built-in cabinets. Write a description of how you would arrange the room or draw the layout you think would be best.

3. Using one of the topics below or a topic your instructor supplies, develop an idea for an effective attention-getting introduction for your peers, other students in your school. Remember to state your topic and to preview the points you will make in order to connect with your audience.

cost of prescription drugs	the Internet and entertainment	mass transit in rural or urban United States
globalization	teen employment	local pollution concerns

4. Fast-forward your life several years and imagine a time when your supervisor first says to you, "Great job on this report! Now you can present the report at the _____ meeting." (Fill in the blank with managers', stockholders', team, committee, or some other group.) Suppose you have six weeks before the date of the presentation. Develop a timeline with the tasks you will undertake to prepare for an effective oral presentation. The plan should identify what you will do and when you will do it during the six weeks. Remember that you already have a written report, but you need to develop an oral presentation appropriate for a different audience. Also remember that this is your first professional presentation, so you want adequate rehearsal time to build your confidence level.

5. Select or create a graphic aid that you can use in a two-minute presentation to clarify or emphasize an idea. For example, you might bring a tool to class and demonstrate how to use it. Or you could draw a graph or chart and explain the process or statistics it illustrates. You also could show a photograph, poster, or painting and explain the idea or concept it supports.

Your Turn

6. Review an oral report you presented recently—in school or elsewhere, formal or informal. List some changes you would make to improve your effectiveness if you were to present it again.

7. Attend a presentation at school, in the community, or at work. If a live presentation is not possible, watch a video of a speaker, perhaps

a politician, an editorial commentator, or an infomercial promoter. As you view the presentation, make two lists: (1) positive elements that make the speech work and (2) negative elements, things that detract from the presentation's effectiveness.

8. Choose a written report you completed recently or find a model in a textbook. Write an essay about decisions and changes you would make to present the written information in an oral report.

9. Research a career you are considering. Look for information on employers, salaries, working conditions, educational requirements, and hiring rates. You could go to the library, talk with a counselor, visit someone working in the field, or talk with an instructor in the curriculum area. When you have as much data as you need, think about making an oral presentation to classmates who might be interested in the same career.

   a. Write a brief analysis of your audience.
   b. Decide on the main idea for your presentation. Write it in one complete sentence.
   c. List at least two ideas for information that could be enhanced with a graphic aid.
   d. Create at least one of the graphic aids listed in item c.
   e. Prepare the outline or notes you would use for this presentation.

10. Plan a speech that you could deliver to your graduating class. Consider audience and purpose when planning the speech. Will you need graphic aids? If so, what kind of graphic aids would be appropriate? Share your topic and notes with other students to gain feedback. Finally, deliver the speech to your peers and ask for additional feedback.

Community Connection

11. Visit a senior center or a child care center in your area. Interview people to determine topics of interest for the seniors or children. After doing research (if needed) and collecting information, develop and deliver a presentation at the center. Remember that you will probably need the staff's permission and help to arrange a time and setting. Also consider the attention span of your audience.

12. Choose a cause for which you are concerned or passionate, such as recycling, a soup kitchen, or proper hand washing. Develop and deliver a presentation. The audience might be your class, a club, or another group.

13. As a representative of your school, offer to make a presentation at a local library or community center on a topic of interest to the public. You might choose a topic related to your school and its activities, such as academic or athletic programs, clubs and other activities, the arts (a planned theater production), diversity among students, or contributing factors for your school's excellence. Or you could suggest a topic that interests you and that you think would interest others. Plan and prepare for the presentation, rehearsing in front of your classmates. Using their feedback, adjust your graphic aids and delivery. If you can get permission from a person in authority, deliver the presentation at the library or community center. Otherwise, deliver the presentation to your classmates.

Recommendation Reports

Goals

- Determine how a recommendation report is used and adjust the structure to accommodate the reader
- Devise criteria for evaluation after determining the problem and possible solutions
- Organize a recommendation report using the appropriate format
- Compose a recommendation report by evaluating criteria and drawing conclusions using a point-by-point analysis

Terms

- appendixes, p. 317
- criteria, p. 308
- persuasive writing, p. 309
- point-by-point organization, p. 316
- rank, p. 318
- receptive audience, p. 309
- recommendation report, p. 308
- solicited, p. 308
- standard, p. 318
- subcriteria, p. 312
- unreceptive audience, p. 309
- unsolicited, p. 308

TEACHING RESOURCES FOR CHAPTER 13

Instructor's Resource CD

Data Files
Data File Solutions
Lesson Plans
Teaching Masters
PowerPoint Slides
Chapter Tests with Solutions
Additional Chapter Activities

Exam *View*

Website

www.cengage.com/school/
bcomm/techwtg

Crossword Puzzle
Data Files
Data File Solutions
Flashcards
Glossary
NET Bookmark
Sample Documents
Web Links

WRITE TO LEARN

Show students that they have experience with persuasive reporting that recommends a solution after the evaluation of a common set of criteria.

WRITE TO LEARN

Think of the last time you had to choose between two things. Maybe you had to decide between two classes or two restaurants. In a one-page journal entry, describe the process you used to make your decision, including your comparisons and evaluations.

Focus on Recommendation Reports

Read the sample recommendation report on pages 303–306 and answer these questions:

- What two items are being compared?
- On what factors (also known as criteria) is the recommendation based?
- Why is this report presented in memo format?

What If?

- The writers were not concerned about the environment?
- The audience (decision maker) was opposed to the idea of purchasing a car for courier service?

TO:	Roberta Boyles
FROM:	Lorraine Nevelle and Rodrigo Reyes *LN* RR
DATE:	July 15, 20—
SUBJECT:	Purchase Recommendation for Courier Service Vehicle

INTRODUCTION

The purpose of this report is to recommend which new vehicle the courier service for Interstate Development (doing business as Urban Girl Clothing) should purchase. The vehicle currently used to circulate documents and product among the six downtown retail stores, a 2006 Dynasty XL7, poses a safety hazard to the drivers and pedestrians because of brake and transmission problems. It also does not present a positive image for the company because four wrecks have left it dented and rusty. We have narrowed our choices to two hybrid cars: 2011 Dynasty Freedom Hybrid and 2011 BLAU Pronto Hybrid. To determine which vehicle to recommend, we developed the following criteria:

1. Safety

2. Function

3. Cost

4. Efficiency and Environmental Impact

RECOMMENDATION

We recommend that the Courier Service purchase the 2011 Dynasty Freedom Hybrid. First, both vehicles have been proven safe, but the Freedom Hybrid is likely to earn the same safety awards as its 2010 model. Second, this car offers a great deal of trunk space for transporting goods, considerably more than the competition. Third, the cost of the Dynasty Freedom Hybrid is within the allocated budget and is likely to be less (including rebates and discounts) than that of the Pronto Hybrid. Fourth, the Freedom, with an electric motor that can reach speeds of up to 47 miles per hour, seldom engages the gas engine in city driving, achieving 41 miles per gallon. Yet its 191 horsepower engine (electric and gas) provides all the power that drivers need.

Sample Recommendation Report

FOCUS

Focus on Recommendation Reports

Use the questions to encourage students to read the sample closely.

ASSESS

What If?

Use the questions to discuss how the sample would be different if the situation or audience changed.

Go to www.cengage.com/school/bcomm/ techwtg for more detailed responses to these questions.

SCOPE

Interstate Development's directors have suggested that we rank safety as the first criterion. The well-being of our employees and the public is our first priority.

Function is our second criterion. The car we purchase must be able to transport bulky, heavy loads of product and display items as well as personnel up to 11 miles between each of our six stores.

To make sure we stay within budget, we have ranked our third criterion as cost. The directors have allocated $26,500 for a new Courier Service vehicle.

Efficiency and environmental impact is our fourth criterion. The directors have set the goal of reducing our carbon footprint by 20 percent over the next five years. We would like the new vehicle to contribute to that effort.

The remainder of this report will compare both cars to the four criteria.

DISCUSSION

Safety

A new vehicle must include:

- Driver, front side, and passenger side airbags.

- Antilock brake system.

- Vehicle stability control system.

2011 Dynasty Freedom Hybrid. According to the Dynasty website and sales brochures from a local dealership, the Freedom Hybrid has all three airbags as standard equipment. The Freedom also includes antilock brakes and stability control as well as a rearview camera and LiNC to allow hands-free operation of phones and music systems.

An innovative feature available on the Freedom is the No Blind Spot System with Crossing Alert, which warns of the approach of hidden traffic. This safety feature could be valuable in preventing accidents that have occurred with Courier Service cars in the past. Another important note is that the 2010 Freedom was the Insurance Institute's Top Safety Pick Award winner, and the government gave it a 5-star rating, the highest possible, for safety. Therefore, we expect the 2011 model to be rated highly as well.

Sample Recommendation Report, cont.

FOCUS

Use the sample recommendation report to review the methodical way in which these reports prove their point.

Have students read the report. Note its features. The headings/subheadings help readers predict and comprehend the message and help writers maintain organization and focus.

The graphic aids make comparing simple.

The critical message of the report is in the recommendation section.

The scope section defines and describes criteria.

Roberta Boyles
Page 3
July 15, 20—

2011 BLAU Pronto Hybrid. The BLAU Pronto's standard equipment includes the three airbags, antilock brakes, and stability control.

Conclusion. While both vehicles meet the subcriteria for safety, the Freedom Hybrid is likely to have a higher safety rating from the government and the Insurance Institute because of the 2010 design features.

Function

The new vehicle will be driven almost entirely inside the city to deliver documents, boxes or single items of clothing, display materials, and occasionally personnel. Thus, the car needs to be large enough to accommodate packages as well as people comfortably and safely.

2011 Dynasty Freedom Hybrid. The Freedom seats five and has front legroom of 42.3 inches and rear legroom of 36.7 inches. It has a trunk volume of 16.5 square feet.

2011 BLAU Pronto Hybrid. The Pronto seats five and has front legroom of 41.7 inches and rear legroom of 38.3 inches. It has a trunk volume of 10.6 square feet.

Conclusion. Both vehicles are designed to seat five people and have similar space for occupants. However, the Dynasty Freedom has a considerably larger trunk volume for transporting boxes and display elements such as mannequins.

Cost

Because the directors allocated $26,500, the cost of the vehicle must not exceed that amount.

2011 Dynasty Freedom Hybrid. The price range for the Freedom Hybrid is $19,270–$26,150. Dynasty has a $725 destination fee.

2011 BLAU Pronto Hybrid. The price range for the BLAU Pronto is $26,150–$29,045. BLAU has a $750 destination fee.

Conclusion. Both vehicles could meet the third criterion. The price ranges listed are MSRP (manufacturer suggested retail price) and do not include rebates or tax incentives for purchasing hybrid/fuel-efficient cars.

Sample Recommendation Report, cont.

FOCUS
Point out that the discussion section is where the writers again name each criterion and then compare the potential solutions based on the criteria.

Roberta Boyles
Page 4
July 15, 20—

Efficiency and Environmental Impact

The new vehicle must be efficient and environmentally friendly. Interstate Development's directors suggest the following features:

- Hybrid or all electric engine

- Fuel economy

- Low environmental impact

Table 1 depicts a comparison of subcriteria for both vehicles.

FEATURES	DYNASTY Freedom Hybrid	BLAU Pronto Hybrid
Engine	2.5L Atkinson-Cycle I4 gas 191 horsepower	2.4L CVT 187 horsepower
MPG	41 city/34 highway	33 city/34 highway
Transition, electric to gas	electric up to 47 mph	electric up to 45 mph

Table 1. Comparison of Efficiency Features

2011 Dynasty Freedom Hybrid. The Freedom Hybrid boasts 41 miles per gallon in the city, where its electric motor can be used up to speeds of 47 miles per hour. Because the car can reach speeds of up to 47 miles per hour on its electric motor, it rarely needs to use the gas engine in city driving. A bonus is that its eco-friendly cloth seats are made of recycled fabric.

2011 BLAU Pronto Hybrid. Although the Pronto Hybrid meets the subcriteria, its statistics are similar to but do not match those of the Freedom.

Conclusion. The Dynasty Freedom Hybrid meets and exceeds our subcriteria for efficiency and low environmental impact.

Sample Recommendation Report, cont.

Writing@Work

Courtesy of Anne Nickel

Anne Nickel is a brand engagement consultant in London, England, for a global brand-building company called The Brand Union. Her job requires a combination of marketing and management skills. She advises clients about what they need to change inside their organization to fit and promote their brand.

In her role, Anne writes recommendation reports to help clients learn how to strategically adjust their marketing campaigns, business practices, communication methods, and reward policies. According to Anne, these reports combine information gathered through other kinds of writing. "In order to write a recommendation report, one also has to write interview questions, interview notes, an implementation plan, and briefs for the design team that tell them what to produce for the client. So it requires a diverse writing skill set."

She believes that persuasive documents like these need to do many things at once in order to have the desired effect on their audience. "Recommendation reports require both rational and emotional persuasion. Case studies and statistics can be used as evidence for rational persuasion. Visuals, like graphics and video, help emotional persuasion by bringing life to ideas beyond the words used to enunciate them."

Anne emphasizes that brilliant evidence and graphics will not do anything for your report if you fail to address the correct audience. "It is important to direct your recommendation to a person who will be open to your ideas and support them. Sometimes this person is the top decision maker and in control of the budget, but other times it is someone who has the connections or authority to be a cheerleader for your ideas and pitch them to the powers that be."

Think Critically

1. Think of a brand that you use regularly. Why do you continue to choose it over other brands? Is it style, prestige, price, value, habit, loyalty, convenience, or something else? How much of your choice is rational (that is, based on the actual qualities of the product)?

2. What recommendations do you have for the brand? Think about ways the manufacturer could sell more of the product, add features that consumers like you would pay more for, reduce its environmental impact, and so on.

Printed with permission of Anne Nickel

Look at the sample
recommendation report
that introduces this chapter.
Where is the actual
recommendation made? Is
this a logical place for the
recommendation? Why or
why not?

FOCUS

Warm Up

Use the Warm Up to examine
the sample report, focusing on
where the recommendation
section is and what it says. It is
after the introduction because
it states the point the rest of the
report explains and justifies. It
appears early in the report for
those who want to read only the
main idea.

TYPICAL READER

Someone who must make a choice between
several options; a decision maker who is
seeking accurate, specific information focused
on prioritized factors for each option.

WRITER'S FOCUS

Meeting the reader's needs by addressing the
reader's prioritized factors for each option
in a clear, detailed, accurate manner and
by organizing the information logically and
presenting it in the standard organizational
plan for recommendation reports.

ENRICH

Tell students about a choice
you made for the school year
that affected them. Describe
the thinking process you went
through to make your decision.

RETEACH

Writers of persuasive documents
need to analyze their audiences
carefully. Explain that solicited
reports do not need a detailed
explanation of the problem but
that unsolicited reports may
need more explanation.

WHAT IS A RECOMMENDATION REPORT?

The **recommendation report** is a problem-and-solution report, a written answer to a need that arises in the workplace. Most problems, however, have more than one solution. The recommendation report suggests the best solution to a problem or need. It helps readers make a choice. Employees write recommendation reports to help decision makers choose the best solution. Recommendation reports help people solve large and small problems, from constructing a building to selecting a new computer.

Sometimes the recommendation is the purchase of equipment. In the sample at the beginning of the chapter, Lorraine Nevelle and Rodrigo Reyes examine two vehicles and recommend the 2011 Dynasty Freedom Hybrid for Interstate Development's courier service. Throughout this chapter, you will look more closely at some of the decisions Lorraine and Rodrigo made while writing their report.

Sometimes a recommendation report proposes a course of action. For example, Hennepin Logging has decided to expand and has narrowed the location of its new plant to three towns in Virginia. The report compares and contrasts the three sites against the **criteria**—factors on which a decision is based—the company thinks are important and recommends a location. You will see how the writer gathers data and plans the report.

The last time you bought school supplies, you chose from among several alternatives. Knowing that you needed a three-ring binder, you probably examined several different three-ring notebooks. The choice you made depended on factors you considered important and may have included cost, special features such as clipboards or zippered pencil pouches, durability, and color. Companies go through the same thinking process when they make choices.

Decision makers who have the power to implement your recommendations read recommendation reports. Sometimes one person reads the report, and a committee or board often votes on recommendations. The report is usually written to a supervisor, but sometimes recommendations are made to coworkers.

The report can be **solicited** (asked for) or **unsolicited** (not asked for). In solicited reports, your reader asks you to analyze several alternatives. This reader understands the need and will be more receptive to your suggestions.

In an unsolicited report, your audience is not expecting your recommendations. You may have difficulty gauging this reader's reaction. Your reader may be receptive and appreciate your initiative in helping to make decisions. On the other hand, your audience may be unwilling to accept your recommendations for a variety of reasons. For example, Kamelia, a production supervisor at a large wholesale nursery, was asked by her manager to help select the walkie-talkies to be issued to all employees. Because Kamelia's supervisor was already committed to purchasing the walkie-talkies, he was receptive to her recommendation.

Communication Dilemma

Blaine Schroeder is an accountant for Gildstein's Business Managers. He has the difficult job of recommending to his supervisor which construction company should construct a small office building: Wilmore Construction Company Inc. or Galloway Builders. Wilmore is a larger company and has a better reputation for finishing tasks on schedule.

Bids from both companies fall within Gildstein's budget, but the office building must be completed in time for holiday sales. Galloway Builders is owned by Schroeder's brother-in-law, Ethan Galloway. The Galloways have a child with a serious medical condition and really need the money they would earn from this contract. Schroeder's wife wants him to recommend her brother's company for the job. She claims that families should look out for one another.

Think Critically

What should Blaine Schroeder do?

COMMUNICATION DILEMMA

Divide students into groups and have them list the pros and cons of each choice. Then have a class discussion about students' choices.

TEACH

Show the Strategy for Receptive and Unreceptive Audiences Teaching Master on the IRCD. Use it to note the different placements of the recommendation section for a receptive audience and for an unreceptive audience.

TEACH

Discuss scenarios in which decision makers might be receptive as well as unreceptive, perhaps even strongly opposed. Remind students that writers of recommendation reports should be diligent in their audience analysis, learning about any history or prejudices that might affect the way the audience receives the recommendations. For example, an electrical contractor who was forced to spend time and money removing installed equipment from a job site because the company had a large recall might not want to buy that brand again.

However, Troy received a different reaction from his supervisor. Troy, a landscape maintenance technician, took the initiative to develop a recommendation report in which he suggested buying a golf cart. Troy believed the golf cart would be helpful in carrying chemicals for spraying, moving new plants, and getting around the grounds to inspect for pests. However, his employer, who had not requested the recommendation report, did not agree that a golf cart was necessary or would improve the quality of work. Troy's audience was not receptive to his recommendation.

An analysis of your audience's attitude may affect how you organize your report. A **receptive audience,** readers who are open to ideas or suggestions, will be ready to read the recommendation early in the report (as is presented in the sample at the beginning of this chapter). An **unreceptive audience,** readers who are not open to ideas or suggestions, will require more careful research and supporting information up front, with the recommendation coming last. You need to lead this reader carefully to your recommendation. Table 13.1 shows the strategies for accommodating receptive and unreceptive audiences.

Recommendation reports are persuasive. **Persuasive writing,** writing to convince others, requires that you analyze audiences carefully, for your job

RECEPTIVE AUDIENCE	UNRECEPTIVE AUDIENCE
Introduction	Introduction
Recommendation	Scope
Scope	Discussion with more details
Discussion with limited details	Recommendation

Table 13.1

ONGOING ASSESSMENT

Stop and Think

Place the recommendation section at the end of the report, after the discussion section.

Readers are more likely to be persuaded when they believe the report has answered all of their questions and met all of their requirements. To be convincing, writers must know their audiences well.

FOCUS

Warm Up

Discuss the importance of a clearly defined problem. For instance, consumers who do not understand the dangers of using the same cutting board for raw meats and other foods would not see the need for disposable cutting sheets. The company not only had to tout the convenience of throwing away a messy cutting surface, but also had to explain the health aspect—avoiding cross contamination of food preparation areas.

Warm Up

Some television commercials help viewers define a problem. Some commercials are problems about which people already know. Other commercials are problems that listeners may not have considered before.
List some problems that commercials define. For example, an ad selling mouthwash may make people wonder whether they have bad breath.

is to convince your reader to act on your recommendation. Researched facts, opinions of authorities, and logical thinking are the tools you need to be convincing. Learn what information your reader expects in the final report and how detailed the research should be. For example, in the earlier situation, Kamelia knew that her audience approved of purchasing the new equipment but had not chosen the brand or model. As a result, she could focus her report on comparing the types of walkie-talkies.

Troy, on the other hand, did not have his audience's support from the beginning. He was concerned not only with comparing the different golf carts, but also with convincing the decision maker that golf carts were needed. Further, if Troy had analyzed the audience, he would have learned that three years earlier employees inside the planting sheds had ordered two golf carts to move flats of seedlings from area to area. But the carts were removed when employees were found to be playing with and abusing them. If Troy had been aware of the previous incident, he could have prepared his report to account for this history and explain how it would not be repeated.

⬤ STOP AND THINK

If the reader of the vehicle recommendation had been unreceptive, where would you have placed the recommendation section? Why must writers of persuasive reports analyze audiences carefully?

STARTING A RECOMMENDATION REPORT

After you have analyzed your audience, you must define your problem, brainstorm solutions, and devise criteria.

Define Your Problem

In a solicited report, the person or group who requested the recommendation report has identified the problem. The problem is usually evident, but put it into words anyway. In the opening sample report, Lorraine and Rodrigo stated the problem: "The vehicle currently used to circulate documents and product among the six downtown retail stores, a 2006 Dynasty XL7, poses a safety hazard to the drivers and pedestrians because of brake and transmission problems. It also does not present a positive image for the company because four accidents have left it dented and rusty."

In an unsolicited report, the problem may need more explanation. Unlike the solicited report, the unsolicited report is not requested. No one except the report writer has noticed the problem or considered solutions. Therefore, you must make certain that readers see the problem and its importance clearly. If the problem needs more explanation than one or two sentences, consider placing the explanation in a separate paragraph or paragraphs in the introduction.

State the problem as specifically and precisely as possible. For example, "The roof of Roosevelt Farms Bed and Breakfast leaked during the October 2, 2009, hurricane and stained the dining room ceiling" is a better problem statement than "Roosevelt Farms Bed and Breakfast had a leak."

Brainstorm Solutions

Now brainstorm solutions to the problem. You may need others to help you generate possible solutions. Explain the problem to your colleagues and tell them you would like their ideas. Tell them that the focus is creative problem solving and that the time for criticism will come later.

Take notes as ideas emerge. You could act as moderator to keep the group on track and stop any criticism that creeps in. Narrow the choices to two or three. You may use others' advice to help narrow the choices.

When Lorraine and Rodrigo brainstormed solutions to the vehicle problem, they generated a list of six vehicles. They narrowed the list to two when they decided that an all-electric vehicle cost too much.

The search for solutions also may require research. Professional journals and newsletters, LISTSERVs, government documents, and company reports may reveal findings that influence your recommendations. Seek as much information as you need to brainstorm solutions.

Devise Criteria

As you narrow your solution choices, decide what criteria to use. Interview people about what is important to consider when making your choice. Ask all concerned—administration, workers, people who have used one of the solutions. Getting opinions is important so that the solution you recommend works for everyone.

Roneika West was asked to write a report for Hennepin Logging to recommend a town in Virginia for the construction of a new plant. After several meetings, three sites were selected as possible locations. Roneika consulted with others to help her devise criteria. Table 13.2 shows some of the preliminary information she gathered by consulting Hennepin's management, the workers who will relocate, and a furniture manufacturer who buys wood from the company.

FROM	TOWN SHOULD HAVE
Administration	10-acre plot of land Available workforce Adequate power supply
Workers who will relocate	Effective, successful schools Affordable housing
Local furniture manufacturer	Safe roads Consistent, adequate water supply

Table 13.2

Use the feature to explore the issue of fair representation. Report writers should ask themselves whether they are treating all other stakeholders as they themselves would like to be treated.

Stakeholders who were excluded might become antagonistic or disenfranchised and disengaged.

Focus on Ethics

Writers, especially writers of recommendation reports, should consider the interests of all stakeholders or all parties and people involved in an issue. Because the decisions made based on the information and analysis in the recommendation report could affect the stakeholders, a report that represents the views of only one person or a few people is unfair. This report could even be detrimental to the health of an organization or a company.

Highway construction is an example in which many opinions and perspectives result in the best recommendation. Building a new road affects many people. The highway can improve or destroy businesses, increase or decrease property values, bypass or relocate homes, and change the character of communities.

Public hearings, city council meetings, and other gatherings are usually held for people to review the choice of plans and to hear other people's ideas. The process takes a great deal of time, possibly five or ten years or more. However, the process is vital to the fairness of all stakeholders.

Imagine a system in which roads and highways or schools are built with no opportunity for citizens to provide input. If only one person or group is represented in the decision making, many unanticipated problems could result.

Think Critically

Think of some decisions that excluded certain stakeholders. How might these situations have affected stakeholders who were not excluded?

From this preliminary list, Roneika was able to classify like items under larger categories. The categories—resources, utilities, and living conditions—became the criteria for her first draft. The smaller units under each category that help to define each criterion (singular of *criteria*) became the **subcriteria,** or more specific categories of criteria, as follows:

Resources	Utilities	Living Conditions
land	power	schools
workforce	water	housing
roads		

Next, Roneika worked to further define each of the subcriteria. Again, she went back to her colleagues and asked these questions: What is a fair price for the land? How many people are needed in the workforce? What kind of labor is needed, skilled or unskilled?

If your list of criteria is longer than four or five items, reevaluate their importance to limit your list to no more than five. Working with more than five criteria might overwhelm your readers.

FORMATTING AND ORGANIZING RECOMMENDATION REPORTS

The recommendation report is a highly structured report that uses a consistent outline and a comparison/contrast discussion. You may have seen such reports written as multipage paper documents. However, the best format for a recommendation report may not be a multipage paper document. In fact, you have many formatting choices for these types of reports.

If you are submitting a report to a prospective client, you might send it as an e-mail attachment, post it to a website, create and send a CD-ROM, or provide hyperlinks in a Microsoft® Word document. As with other decisions, you should base your choice of format on the audience's needs.

For instance, an audience that frequently uses the Internet would appreciate the ease and speed of having access to an online report. In contrast, some readers are more comfortable with a traditional print document; so the writer could submit a paper copy or send the document as an e-mail attachment. Whatever the format, recommendation reports follow the same basic outline.

Outline

The recommendation report consists of introductory material, a recommendation (summary of discussion), scope (what the report covers and why), and discussion (analysis of criteria—the factors used in making the decision).

Introduction

The introductory section:

- States the purpose of the report.

- Briefly explains the problem.

- Narrows the choice to two or three items.

- Gives a criteria list.

- Previews the rest of the report.

- May include the investigation method.

The model introduction in Figure 13.1 on the next page orients the readers to the information in the body of the report—the site recommendation for a real estate license review course. This

FOCUS

Figure 13.1

The complete version of the recommendation report is available as a sample document on the IRCD.

TO:	Marcia Yates, President, Realtors Association
FROM:	Reggie Thaxton, Site Coordinator _RST_
DATE:	November 22, 20—
SUBJECT:	Site Recommendation for March 20— License Review Course

At the June 20— Realtors Association meeting, the board agreed to sponsor a review course to be held in March before the spring licensing exam. Board members believed that a six-hour review course held before the state licensing exam would increase the pass rate, helping members to move from salesperson to broker. You asked that I send you my site recommendation by the end of November so that you could include the announcement, prices, and registration information in the December newsletter.

This recommendation report suggests the site that I believe will meet our needs. After consulting with the Visitors Bureau and other meeting planners as well as examining sales brochures from meeting facilities, I narrowed the options to two locations: the Paradise Hilton and the Narona Garden Club. Each meeting space has been evaluated using the criteria listed below, from most important to least important element, suggested by board members:

1. Location
2. Cost of meeting rooms
3. Equipment
4. Food service

Figure 13.1 Sample Introduction

---

model introduction explains the history and the problem, the recommended solution, the criteria, and the investigation method.

Recommendation

The recommendation section of the report:

- Makes the recommendation.

- Uses criteria to summarize reasons for the recommendation.

Because readers want the important information first, the recommendation section appears early in the report unless the report is unsolicited. As Figure 13.2 shows, this section may be brief. In longer reports describing more complex situations, the section could be several paragraphs. If you offer multiple recommendations, number and list them.

Recommendation

I recommend that the March 20— review course be held in the meeting room of the Paradise Hilton. This venue offers a central location, a reasonable cost for use of the facilities (when the hotel caters the luncheon), access to requested electronics with on-site technicians for service, and hot and cold menus.

Figure 13.2 Sample Recommendation

Scope

The scope section:

- Lists criteria, in descending order from most important to least important, that were given in the introduction.

- Explains why the criteria were chosen and why they are ranked as they are.

This discussion assures writers and readers that they agree on important factors in the decision. This section also explains how information is analyzed, as shown in Figure 13.3 in the description of criteria and explanation of why each criterion was chosen.

Discussion

The discussion section:

- Analyzes each of the criteria thoroughly.

- Draws conclusions about which item is better for each criterion.

Organize the discussion section of the report by criteria, starting with the most important and moving to the least important. Give each criterion a major heading. Each criterion is introduced with an explanation of essential elements or features. Then each item being considered is compared to the ideal set in the introduction. Finally, a conclusion shows the results of the comparison for the criterion. Figure 13.4 presents one part of a discussion section.

TEACH
Remind students to check that criteria appear in the same order in the scope and discussion sections.

SCOPE

Board members noted that location is critical because most of our members who are registered to take the exam are already employed in the business and will not want to be away from work any longer than necessary. Therefore, the driving time to this review session should be as short as possible. Location is the first criterion.

Because the cost of meeting rooms for the course must be passed on to participants through registration fees, the price for use of the facility must be reasonable. Thus, charges for the use of rooms are the second criterion. Presenters who will teach the review courses have requested an overhead projector with a screen and a computer with a projection system. To be certain the electronics work in the meeting rooms, I prefer that the facility provide them so that we do not need to rent them or ask presenters to bring their own equipment. Availability of equipment, therefore, is the third criterion.

To fit six hours of training into a one-day drive-in format, board members suggested that the program and its pricing include a meal and refreshments for two breaks. For that reason, in-house food service is the fourth criterion. The recommendation report will compare the Paradise Hilton and the Narona Garden Club to these criteria:

1. Location

2. Charges for the use of rooms

3. Availability of equipment

4. In-house food service

Figure 13.3 Sample Scope Section

DISCUSSION

Location

The site for the review course should be within a one-hour drive for all members in our region. The location should be easily accessible from a major highway and well marked on the city bypass.

Paradise Hilton. The Paradise Hilton, in the historic district in the city center, is five minutes from Interstate A1 and within 45–50 minutes of all members. The hotel has many billboards advertising its location on major highways outside and within the city. In addition, the state highway signs direct travelers from the bypasses to this hotel and two other hotels in the historic area. Visitors say that the Paradise Hilton is easy to find.

Narona Garden Club. The Narona Garden Club is located in a residential neighborhood just south of the capitol and southwest of the historic area. It is within an hour's drive for our members. While many signs in the city point to its location, no signs on the highway and only one on each bypass make this location difficult for out-of-town visitors to find.

Conclusion. While both locations meet the criteria, the Paradise Hilton is most central and is easier to find because of better signage.

Figure 13.4 Discussion Section

Remember, receptive readers are interested primarily in the recommendation, which is why it appears early in the report. Unreceptive readers, however, are more likely to be persuaded if the recommendation is placed last, after the discussion.

Comparison/Contrast Discussion

Most recommendation reports follow an organizational plan called *point by point,* as in the sample report at the beginning of the chapter.

Point-by-point organization zigzags from one item to the next, comparing or contrasting some aspect of one item to the same aspect of another item. Under the safety heading in the opening sample report, the writers compare the safety features of the two cars. Both vehicles are collected under one point, or criterion—in this case, safety. Figure 13.5 shows the zigzag from one item to another.

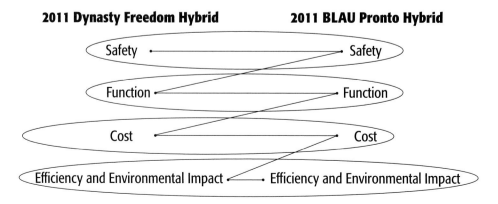

Figure 13.5 Point-by-Point Organization

Table 13.3 links a general outline for this section (left column) to the headings in the discussion section (right column) in the model report.

Appendixes

Appendixes are another component of some recommendation reports. **Appendixes,** the plural of *appendix,* are supplementary materials that appear at the end of a document. Report writers may decide to attach information, documents, or supporting materials they believe will aid the audience in understanding the report.

Each document or supplementary item is entered and labeled as a separate appendix. Usually, elements that become appendixes are not directly involved in the report but are closely aligned to information presented.

For instance, a recommendation report suggesting the hiring of four part-time salesclerks rather than one full-time employee could include a company salary scale as Appendix A and a chart of employee shifts and positions as Appendix B. Some information drawn from these documents would probably be used in the report, but the entire documents might be too distracting to include. So they would appear at the end of the document as appendixes, where readers may refer to them.

TEACH

Show the Point-by-Point Organization in Recommendation Report Model Teaching Master on the IRCD. Help students see the connection between the organization in Figure 13.5 and the organization of the discussion section in the opening sample document.

Complete the *Point-by-Point Organization* worksheet available at www.cengage.com/school/bcomm/techwtg. Click the link for Chapter 13; then click Data Files.

CRITERION 1	SAFETY
Item 1: Explain everything about item 1.	2011 Dynasty Freedom Hybrid
Item 2: Explain everything about item 2.	2011 BLAU Pronto Hybrid
Conclusion: Which item is better and why?	Conclusion
CRITERION 2	FUNCTION
Item 1: Explain everything about item 1.	2011 Dynasty Freedom Hybrid
Item 2: Explain everything about item 2.	2011 BLAU Pronto Hybrid
Conclusion: Which item is better and why?	Conclusion
CRITERION 3	COST
Item 1: Explain everything about item 1.	2011 Dynasty Freedom Hybrid
Item 2: Explain everything about item 2.	2011 BLAU Pronto Hybrid
Conclusion: Which item is better and why?	Conclusion
CRITERION 4	EFFICIENCY AND ENVIRONMENTAL IMPACT
Item 1: Explain everything about item 1.	2011 Dynasty Freedom Hybrid
Item 2: Explain everything about item 2.	2011 BLAU Pronto Hybrid
Conclusion: Which item is better and why?	Conclusion

Table 13.3

ONGOING ASSESSMENT

Stop and Think

Use the Stop and Think to review concepts and to encourage students to think ahead.

The introduction contains the most diverse information,

Alvaro likes contact sports (football, soccer, and boxing), Italian food, country music, and horror films. In small groups, design an ideal Saturday for Alvaro. Why did you choose these activities for Alvaro? Now design an ideal Saturday for your group.

including the purpose of the report, the problem, the choices under consideration, the criteria, and a preview. The preview is like a thesis. It predicts the development of the document. It helps prepare the reader for the rest of the content. Students often have the most difficulty writing the scope section.

FOCUS

Warm Up

Use the Warm Up to discuss criteria. Alvaro's criteria for an ideal Saturday deal with the general categories of sports, food, music, and film. The standards are partially set when students learn that Alvaro likes contact sports, Italian food, country music, and horror films. In your classroom, students' criteria may be different. Ask students to speculate why Alvaro's Saturday and their Saturdays are different.

 STOP AND THINK

What heading of a recommendation report contains the most diverse information? What does it mean to "provide a preview of the rest of the report"? Which part of the report will be most difficult for you to write? Why?

COMPOSING RECOMMENDATION REPORTS

While decisions about formatting and organizing a recommendation report are likely to have an impact on readers' perceptions, those elements are secondary to decisions made in composing: setting criteria, evaluating criteria, and researching criteria.

Setting Criteria

Criteria, the factors on which you base a decision, play an important role in the recommendation report. Table 13.4 shows where and how criteria are used.

The criteria you choose depend on what you, your audience, and your colleagues think is important. Safety, function, cost, and efficiency and environmental impact are important factors in the choice of a new car for Interstate Development, as noted in the introduction of the report at the beginning of this chapter. After you select criteria, you must present them in a logical, consistent way.

All criteria must be presented with a name, a **rank** (the relative importance of one criterion to another), and a **standard** (a means of defining and limiting a criterion). Choose a simple name, usually a noun that is parallel to the other criteria. Some reports use questions such as *What is the cost?* and *How safe is this option?*

Give each criterion a rank to show its relative importance to the other criteria. Which is the most important criterion? the second most important? the third most important? List them in descending order, from most to least important. The rank of criteria may change depending on the circumstances.

For example, younger workers with families moving with the Hennepin Logging operations to Virginia might rank the criteria for an acceptable town as schools (first), family entertainment (second), and medical facilities

CRITERIA ARE		
Introduced	in the	Introduction
Summarized	in the	Recommendation
Explained and ranked (Why chosen and ranked?)	in the	Scope
Evaluated (one by one)	in the	Discussion

Table 13.4

(third). Older workers might rank the criteria as medical facilities (first), family entertainment (second), and schools (third).

Finally, determine the standards of (or limits to) the criteria. For example, if Interstate Development will not pay more than $26,500 for a vehicle, then that amount, $26,500, sets the standard for cost. If families moving with Hennepin Logging to Virginia expect a class A trauma center to be within a half hour's drive of the town, an accredited trauma center with a class A certification within a 25-mile radius could be the standard for medical facilities.

You may need help refining your criteria. In the opening sample report, the vehicle had to meet several subcriteria under safety. Seek ideas and opinions from as many stakeholders as possible. In your report, list subcriteria when you get to the appropriate criterion section. Like criteria, subcriteria should be listed in descending order of importance.

In the opening sample report, the vehicle had to meet several subcriteria under safety. Because the decision makers consider safety to be of primary concern, it is ranked as the first criterion. The standard is security for passengers and cargo. And subcriteria include driver, front side, and passenger airbags; an antilock braking system; and a stability control system. The recommendation is based on findings related to the criteria and subcriteria. Table 13.5 summarizes how to develop the criteria in your report.

Evaluating Criteria

Evaluating criteria is a step-by-step process. Jacob is comparing the safety features of two swing sets for his daycare center: Play Time Gym Set and Kiddie Swing Set. Consider the three subheadings—Play Time Gym Set, Kiddie Swing Set, and Conclusion—under the criterion *Safety* in a recommendation report comparing playground equipment for a daycare center. Under *Play Time Gym Set,* the writers discuss the safety subcriteria for one set of swings. Under *Kiddie Swing Set,* the writers discuss the same safety subcriteria for another set of swings. On the following page, Table 13.6 shows how, through discussion, the writers check off the subcriteria one by one.

The checklist shows at a glance that the Play Time Gym Set more completely meets the preschool's needs for safety. The Play Time Gym Set meets four out of four needs; the Kiddie Swing Set meets one out of four needs. A simple count shows that the Play Time Gym Set wins in the safety category. After the comparison is made, the results are easy to summarize in the conclusion, which follows the discussion of each item.

COMMUNICATION TECHNOLOGIES

Some recommendation reports are long, formal, and directed to a large and diverse audience. In such cases, these reports are often published online instead of or in addition to being published in print. Do an online search for one such recommendation by the New Jersey Teen Driver Study Commission.

Think Critically

After reviewing the report, make a list of similarities and differences between the New Jersey report and the sample recommendation report beginning on page 303.

COMMUNICATION TECHNOLOGIES

Both reports explore and evaluate options to make recommendations. However, the New Jersey report is more in-depth, has a broader scope, and makes more recommendations than the sample recommendation report does.

Students can find the New Jersey report by searching on the keywords *New Jersey Teen Driver Study Commission.*

NAME	A noun, noun phrase, or question
RANK	Criteria listed from most important to least important
STANDARD	A limit that clarifies each criterion (cost, size, quantity, and so on)
SUBCRITERIA	A list of more detailed criteria that fall under one criterion heading

Table 13.5

THE PLAY TIME GYM SET MEETS THE SUBCRITERIA EASILY.		
Smooth edges	✓	It has plastic seats with rounded edges.
Secure cap covers	✓	Fewer caps are needed because of the round edges.
Slide under 10 feet	✓	Slide is 6 feet long.
Inability to absorb heat	✓	Slide is plastic and will not absorb heat.
THE KIDDIE SWING SET DOES NOT MEET ALL OF THE SUBCRITERIA.		
Smooth edges	✗	It has galvanized frames with few rounded edges.
Secure cap covers	✗	More cap covers are needed.
Slide under 10 feet	✓	Slide is 6 feet long.
Inability to absorb heat	✗	Slide is metal and will absorb heat from the sun.

Table 13.6

Suppose the Kiddie Swing Set had met only the special features and cost criteria and the Play Time Gym Set had met only the safety criteria. Then you would make a judgment call. Safety is ranked as the first concern, more important than special features and cost. Therefore, you would recommend the Play Time Gym Set.

Suppose, however, that both items meet the criteria. Then you should look for some deciding factor. Maybe the cost of one item is lower. Maybe the delivery is quicker or the guarantee is better. In those rare cases where there is no real difference between the two items, you are free to recommend either one—or you may want to set other criteria.

nidda/iStockphoto.com

Researching Criteria

Research data for a recommendation report can come from a variety of places. Much of the research you conduct for a recommendation report will be field research in which you use surveys, interviews, and visits. Websites, manuals, and catalogs can provide product information. Print media in the library can be useful too. *Consumer Reports,* government publications, business indexes, professional journals, and the many ways to research electronically also can provide data you need.

Roneika West, in her recommendation report to Hennepin Logging, used several sources. She interviewed coworkers and workers at another logging operation. She surveyed the employees who would move to the new site. Roneika visited the three towns in Virginia and interviewed town officials. She reviewed government tax base documents on the Internet. Sometimes personnel, sales brochures, a visit to a store, or sales representatives provide all of the information the writers need.

Riser/Getty Images

Be alert to opportunities to present research data in graphics. The opening sample report uses tables of features. Other possibilities for graphics are pictures or diagrams of equipment, pie graphs of survey results, and bar graphs to compare items.

⬣ STOP AND THINK

Name the sources you might use to research the following recommendation report topics: bass fishing boats, novels, and uniforms for nurses.

ONGOING ASSESSMENT

Stop and Think

Bass fishing boats: boat dealer, sales brochures, others who have used this type of boat, Coast Guard, *Consumer Reports*

Novels: instructors, *The New York Times Book Review,* other book reviews, scholarly critiques of the works, others who have read the books, reputable websites

Uniforms for nurses: clothing companies, sales catalogs, other nurses who have worn the uniforms, other nurses who will wear the uniforms, those who determine dress codes for hospital, cleaners

CLOSE

Summary

Review major points from the chapter using the summary. Ask students to close their textbooks and write a journal entry in which they summarize what they believe to be essential ideas from the chapter. Then have students work in small groups to compare each other's responses and the summary.

CLOSE

Checklist

Review the checklist with students to be sure they understand concepts and terminology. Encourage them to use the checklist for editing and revising their own and others' recommendation reports.

Tells students that they should add particular items to the checklist that they want to remember when editing and revising. For instance, students who make errors in pronoun reference might add that to their list.

REVIEW

For a review of the key terms in the chapter, provide students with the *Key Terms* worksheet available as a supplemental activity on the IRCD.

CHAPTER 13 REVIEW

SUMMARY

1. Decision makers read recommendation reports. Reports can be solicited (asked for) or unsolicited (not asked for). For receptive audiences, place the recommendation section early in the report. For unreceptive audiences, place the recommendation section later in the report.

2. Writers get started on a recommendation report by defining the problem, generating possible solutions, and devising criteria. They interview colleagues and others to help with the prewriting process.

3. The recommendation report follows a tight structure using a consistent outline and a comparison/contrast discussion. The major sections include an introduction, the recommendation, the scope, a thorough discussion, and appendixes. The comparison/contrast organization follows a point-by-point pattern that discusses all solutions under one heading or criterion. The recommendation report may be presented in one of many different formats based on the audience's needs.

4. Criteria are presented in the introduction, summarized in the recommendation, explained in the scope, and thoroughly analyzed in the discussion.

Checklist

- Have I devised a reasonable set of criteria by which to judge the items under analysis?

- Have I further defined the criteria by setting standards and including appropriate subcriteria?

- Does my introduction give the purpose of the report, define the problem, narrow choices, and introduce criteria in order of importance?

- Have I considered whether my audience is receptive or unreceptive? If the audience is unreceptive, did I make the necessary adjustments to accommodate an unreceptive audience?

- Does the scope explain why the criteria were chosen and why they were ranked as they were?

- Is the organization of the discussion clear? Does it follow a point-by-point organizational pattern?

- Have I used graphics appropriately? Is the document attractive?

- Have I considered the appropriate format for my audience and the appendixes that would help the audience make an informed decision?

Build Your Foundation

1. Using the Internet, research one of the products listed below. Then determine an audience, a person or group that might use the product. Using the information you gather on different types or models and different manufacturers' products, devise a reasonable set of criteria by which to judge the items under analysis. Name and describe the audience and list the criteria in order of importance. Also explain each criterion and why it was selected.

    a. Golf clubs
    b. Smartphone
    c. DVD player/recorder
    d. Digital camera
    e. Cosmetics (for men or women)
    f. Backpack

2. Suppose you work for a real estate management company. In one of the office buildings your company manages, the heating and air conditioning unit stopped working today. The technician assigned to repair the equipment says that the unit cannot be fixed and should be replaced. The tenant cannot run her business without adequate heating, so she expects immediate action. The technician suggests TempPro heating units as well as Environease machines. He says that both are good products, each with a five-year warranty.

    a. Other than warranty, what criteria might the real estate management company establish?
    b. Suggest a standard for one of the criteria.
    c. Write a problem statement for a recommendation report using this situation. Add specific information as needed.
    d. What graphics might be useful in the recommendation report developed in this case?

3. Sunee's doctor has told her to eat a nutritious diet low in fat, cholesterol, and salt and high in complex carbohydrates. Help her evaluate the butter substitutes listed below in the two columns on the right based on the criteria on the left. What conclusion can you draw from your evaluation?

Substitute	Margarine (1 tbsp)	Table spread (1 tbsp)
#1 Low in fat	17% fat	11% fat
#2 Low in cholesterol	0% cholesterol	0% cholesterol
#3 Low in salt	4% salt	5% salt
#4 High in complex carbohydrates	0% complex carbohydrates	0% complex carbohydrates

4. Revise the following recommendations section:

    After thoroughly studying the options, I recommend the following actions: closing the drive-through payment window, reducing the day-shift staff by one employee, encouraging more use of the computerized self-serve stations in the office, and using student interns

ASSESS

Build Your Foundation

1. Encourage students to analyze the audience they select, carefully considering what elements the audience would find important when making a purchasing decision.

2. a. Criteria may include cost, timing of installation, operational efficiency (cost to run), availability of parts, and noise levels during operation.
   b. Cost could be $5,000. (If the company sets the standard or limit at $5,000, then the recommended machine should cost $5,000 or less.)
   c. One possible response: The heating and air conditioning unit at 1432 Albemarle Place cannot be repaired and must be replaced as quickly as possible so the client can keep her business open. d. Tables or graphs could compare operating costs of the two machines, photos or drawings could show the two units, schematics could compare installations, and tables could provide various parts of warranty coverage for each product.

3. Students can use this activity to evaluate criteria and brainstorm the research needed. Table spread meets the subcriteria better than margarine. Compared to margarine, table spread has 6 percent less fat and equal levels of cholesterol and carbohydrates. Even though the table spread has more salt, the difference is small. Because low fat was rated as the first subcriterion, it is most important.

4. One possible solution: After reviewing the options, I recommend the following actions: (a) Reduce the day-shift staff by one position. (b) Encourage more use of computerized self-serve stations. (c) Train student interns to instruct patrons on the convenient, easy-to-use online options.

ASSESS

Your Turn

5–9. Make sure students include all necessary information and consider audience when organizing and formatting. Remind students to use the checklist when they edit and revise.

10. In this activity, students can see the effects of poor preparation, poor audience analysis, and poor writing. In some cases, recommendations are not accepted for reasons beyond the writer's control (e.g., lack of funds).

to teach patrons how convenient and easy the online options are to use. Otherwise, I suggest we do nothing at this time and study our operations for other possible solutions.

Your Turn

In small groups, use one of the following scenarios to answer items 5–9. You do not need to use the same scenario for all five questions.

a. You are on the Entertainment Committee to decide which band to hire for the annual Holiday Ball. According to the survey you sent, employees are evenly divided on which of three groups to choose: Newton Jazz Ensemble, Midnight City Rock Band, or Down and Dusty Country Band.

b. You are on the Hampton Scholarship Committee. Hampton Company gives a $1,000 scholarship to a deserving student every year. The guidance counselor has chosen Dario Mesa and Allison Jurevicius as the top two contenders for the scholarship. You and the committee must select one of these students.

c. As a member of Ammsco Chemical's Quality Circle, you must decide what microwave to buy for the new employee lounge. You have narrowed your choice to two: the Trimstyle Model 1400 and the Even Cook Model 550. You, along with the members of your Quality Circle team, must choose the new microwave.

5. Write an introduction to a recommendation report for item a, b, or c. Add details if necessary. Look at the model and at the outline under "Formatting and Organizing Recommendation Reports" in this chapter. You may begin your introduction with "The purpose of this report is to. . . ."

6. For any two of the preceding scenarios, brainstorm a list of criteria. Narrow your list to the top three or four. Rank them in order from most important to least important.

7. Choose one of the lists of criteria from item 5. Apply a standard, or limit, to each of the criteria. Devise subcriteria for one of the criteria.

8. In an oral or written scope section, tell your classmates why you chose your criteria and why you ranked them the way you did.

9. Generate an outline for two of the scenarios. Follow the format shown below. For now, make your best guess for the conclusion under each criterion.

Criterion 1	Criterion 2	Criterion 3
Item 1	Item 1	Item 1
Item 2	Item 2	Item 2
Conclusion	Conclusion	Conclusion

10. Request from your school or district administration a copy of a recommendation report that failed. Review the report using the guidelines in this chapter. Write an explanation of why you believe the report is ineffective and what you would do to improve it.

Community Connection

11. List some problems or opportunities in your community. Focus for a moment on the one you care about most. Could two or three courses of action solve this problem? Write a report to your city official recommending a course of action. Research your courses of action using the library or other resources.

12. Ask several local businesses for examples of recommendation reports they have used. Review the reports and compare them to the guidelines covered in this chapter. Choose one report to critique. Discuss its strengths and weaknesses and share your findings with the class.

13. Identify a faculty or staff member at your school who is preparing to make a decision, perhaps what to purchase (such as a new microscope for the science lab) or which selection to make (such as the speaker for graduation or a band for Homecoming). Ask the decision maker for the opportunity to prepare a recommendation report based on the situation. With permission to proceed, complete the following tasks:

    a. Interview the stakeholders. Using your interview notes, create a document that defines what each stakeholder seeks in a solution.
    b. Use the information gathered from stakeholders to devise criteria.
    c. Brainstorm potential solutions and research the two that look to be most promising.
    d. Develop your recommendation report comparing the two solutions to the criteria.
    e. Seek constructive criticism from your classmates and instructor.
    f. Revise the report.
    g. Submit the revised recommendation report to the decision maker and to your instructor.

14. Check with your schools' clubs and organizations to learn about any products or services they are considering. For example, if one of the clubs or organizations is planning a dance or performance, perhaps the group will be searching for a band, a DJ, a karaoke machine, or stage sets. Ask if you can do the research and write a recommendation report. Remember that you will need to interview some of the organization's leaders to establish criteria. After developing the report, submit it to your instructor and/or classmates for their review. Revise, edit, and then submit it to the organization. Ask for the group's feedback and final decision.

15. Local governments are likely to use recommendation reports to make decisions about many things, from purchasing vans and buses to contracting with paint companies. For that reason, arrange an appointment to interview someone in city government who writes recommendation reports. During the interview, ask about the research, the writing process, and the final document. If possible, get a copy of a report and have the interviewee explain its development. Focus on skills that will help you become a better report writer. Write a summary of the important information you gained during the interview.

16. With a partner, write a recommendation report to a local agency in which you suggest an action or a decision that will improve circumstances for a group of people or all citizens of the community.

11. Consider using this writing task as a group assignment. Assign the task to two or three students and ask them to collaborate to generate one report. Encourage peer editing using the checklist.

ASSESS

Community Connection

12. Form groups of three or four students. Remind students to write thank-you letters to the businesses that helped them. The exercise gives students an opportunity to use their letter writing skills (good news message) covered in Chapter 5.

13. This is an excellent real-world writing assignment. Students will likely learn a great deal from the critiques of their peers as well as those of leaders of the organization.

14–15. Students may complete these activities alone or in groups. Students not only gain knowledge about recommendation reports (and may collect samples), but also can practice their interview (Chapter 11) and summary writing (Chapter 8) skills.

16. Students may consult the local Chamber of Commerce or newspaper for a listing of agencies working in the community. Remind students to follow the writing process, especially when seeking feedback and editing/revising.

Chapter 14

Proposals

Goals

- Define proposals and determine their purpose
- Plan to write proposals
- Compose information proposals
- Compose formal proposals

Terms

- appendix, p. 342
- executive summary, p. 330
- letter of transmittal, p. 342
- limitations, p. 335
- memo of transmittal, p. 342
- pagination, p. 343
- prefatory material, p. 345
- proposal, p. 329
- RFP, p. 331
- scope, p. 335
- solicited proposal, p. 330
- unsolicited proposal, p. 331

WRITE TO LEARN

Think of a time when you had a successful sales experience. Perhaps you persuaded a person or a group to buy a product or service or to agree to an idea such as a fund-raiser or a community or family project. In a journal entry, write a narrative about that experience. Include ways in which you prepared to make the sale as well as a description of your audience.

Focus on Proposals

Read the sample proposal on the next page and answer these questions:

- Who might the head custodian have consulted about the proposed solution?
- What are some alternative solutions the group may have considered?
- Do you agree with the recommendation to hire a new custodian? Why or why not?
- What would you include in a list of the positive and negative supporting ideas for one alternative solution that you choose?

What If?

- Most of the events requiring special setup were scheduled in the summer when school was not in session?
- The school had a hiring freeze?
- The current custodians' hours and wages had been reduced because of budget problems?

TO:	Dr. Martin Svoboda, Principal
FROM:	Emmett Yackley, Head Custodian
DATE:	July 14, 20—
SUBJECT:	Proposal for Additional Night Custodian

Problem

The custodians who work the evening shift cannot complete all of the special setups required for meetings *and* clean the rooms efficiently. Hiring an additional custodian to work the midnight shift would help ensure that all of the work gets done.

Background

The workload for the night shift consists of cleaning the classrooms and offices, the halls, and the restrooms. When setups are required, custodians must move tables and assemble rows of chairs. In addition, the cleaning of these areas still must be done. The number of special setups has been increasing, as the following data shows.

	January	February	March	April	May	June	Half-Year Total
2008	7	12	18	21	21	19	98
2009	9	12	21	23	24	19	108
2010	11	17	24	26	31	25	134

Teachers, students, and visitors often comment that the building sometimes looks clean and sometimes appears dirty. Unfortunately, a dirty building does not make for good public relations.

Solution

An additional custodian working the midnight shift could dismantle the setups. This person would free the regular night custodians to clean. When no special setups are required, this person could help clean, wash and polish floors, and vacuum offices. The estimated cost to fill the position of a night shift custodian is $22,500–$25,000 a year.

Benefits

If the midnight shift workload was shared by an additional custodian, the problems described would be eliminated.

Conclusion

Staffing this new position will be costly, but I believe the benefits far outweigh the financial considerations. I hope you will pursue the hiring of a custodian for the night shift.

Sample Proposal

FOCUS

Focus on Proposals

Use the questions to encourage students to read the sample closely.

ASSESS

What If?

Use the questions to discuss how the sample would be different if the situation or audience changed.

Go to www.cengage.com/school/bcomm/techwtg for more detailed responses to these questions.

Writing@Work

Courtesy of Meredith Beattie

Meredith Beattie is co-founder of The BEL Group, a company that works toward capacity building in the government and nonprofit sectors. She writes grant proposals for workforce development, public safety infrastructure, and K–12 educational and cultural programs.

"Competitive proposal development requires time up front to carefully consider the long-term effects of having a proposal accepted," says Meredith. "The difficulty is that an organization's staff may have little time to meet with you and want you to 'just write it.' This can lead to a proposal that wins the grant, but is not feasible for the organization to implement. Getting organizations to spend planning time with you translates into a better working team and a realistic proposal."

The writing process is a complex endeavor that requires methodical attention to detail. "A proposal has many moving parts, so the absolute first thing one should do when beginning to write is to read, tear apart, and 'become one' with the entire proposal structure," advises Meredith. "The sections of a proposal are interrelated. If you do not have a thorough grasp of the complete picture, you can create a proposal that is full of contradictions."

In Meredith's experience, collaboration with the organization's stakeholders is key to a realistic proposal. "Reaching agreement on the overall goal, the resources available to meet the goal, and the benchmarks the organization will meet provides a clear framework for the writer. An accepted proposal becomes the foundation of the contract with the funder. Reminding your stakeholders of this may help them articulate reasonable and achievable goals."

A major difficulty in writing a persuasive proposal is that the writer does not know who his or her audience or competitors are. "Your writing needs to be able to carry any reader—expert or neophyte—to the inevitable conclusion that the applicant is best positioned to fulfill the intent and requirements stated in the application," says Meredith. "Your proposal may be the 200th one the reviewer reads, so make it as easy as possible to digest, avoid colloquialisms, and be compelling without being sensational."

Think Critically

1. Why is it important that Meredith work with the organization to plan the proposal? What may happen if she does not get enough input?

2. How would a writer make a proposal "as easy as possible to digest"?

Printed with permission of Meredith Beattie

WHAT IS A PROPOSAL?

A **proposal** is a persuasive document that offers a solution to an identified problem or need. Proposals attempt to sell an idea, a product or service, or a new concept or plan. Proposals may be brief or long. A one-page request for a room change written to a club adviser and a 2,000-page multivolume document selling a new type of amphibious tank to the Department of Defense are examples of proposals.

Proposal comes from the base word *propose*. Have you ever proposed an idea for a party to your friends? Do you know anyone who has proposed marriage? If you are thinking of the meaning "to suggest" or "to make an offer," you are beginning to understand the purpose of a proposal.

A proposal can be a request for support. For instance, the local Boys and Girls Club may send a proposal to the United Way requesting money to resurface the club's tennis court. Another proposal might offer a customer goods or services. If a school organization sells candy to raise money, the project probably began with a proposal from the candy supplier.

The successful proposal persuades an audience to accept the solution offered and to invest in the idea, product, plan, or service. Employees can use proposals to respond to problems rather than merely complain about them. The proposal provides a professional means of presenting the employees' ideas for change, which can be empowering.

As Figure 14.1 illustrates, proposals can be categorized in several ways relating to the audience: (1) internal or external; (2) formal or informal; (3) solicited or unsolicited; or (4) sales, research, grant, or planning.

Warm Up

What physical projects took place at your school during the past year (for example, repainting, repairs, new walkways, or new landscaping)? As you read this part of the chapter, list the types of proposals likely to have been written before this work could have been done.

TYPICAL READER

Any person (owner, manager, director, technician, or client/customer) who makes decisions.

WRITER'S FOCUS

Clearly and persuasively presenting information the reader needs in order to make an informed decision, anticipating questions and arguments, using an organizational plan that is logical and convincing, and developing appropriate visual aids to enhance the message.

FOCUS

Warm Up

Most of these projects would have been initiated with an internal planning proposal if school personnel did the work. If an outside contractor was involved, external sales proposals would have been likely.

TEACH

Remind students that a single proposal might fall within several categories.

Proposal Category	Definition of Category
A. internal	within the organization
external	outside the organization
B. formal	contains parts used in formal reports
informal	omits elements of formal reports; is often briefer
C. solicited	is written in response to a request
unsolicited	is written independently without a request
D. sales	attempts to sell a product or service
research	seeks approval for a research study
grant	asks for funding for a project
planning	attempts to persuade the audience to take a certain action

Figure 14.1 Types of Proposals

Internal and External

Readers of some proposals will be internal—that is, inside the writer's organization. Other readers will be external, or outside the writer's organization. Internal proposals usually attempt to sell an idea or a plan, such as how providing on-site day care can reduce the absentee rate at work, how merit raise funds should be distributed, and how eliminating classes the day before finals can ease stress and improve scores. External proposals frequently try to sell goods or services as well as ideas.

Informal and Formal

A proposal is informal or formal based on the degree to which the conventions of formal report writing are followed and how "dressed up" the document looks. Formal proposals contain more parts than informal proposals. Writers decide how formal a document should be based primarily on the audience and its needs.

Because informal proposals often address an internal audience that understands why the document was written, these proposals are often brief, generally from one to ten pages. An informed audience eliminates the need for background information or an explanation of the problem. In addition, the report has a flexible organizational plan, uses less formal language, and is frequently presented as a letter or memo. Occasionally, however, a brief informal proposal may be written to an external audience when the subject matter and proposed solution are simple and require little explanation.

A proposal going to someone close (in the ranks of the organization) to the writer is usually informal. Likewise, a problem and solution that can be explained in a simple manner are presented in an informal report. The proposal writer would not invest the often lengthy preparation time involved in a formal proposal to suggest something as simple, for example, as changing lunch schedules to allow for a company-wide meeting.

Formal proposals, on the other hand, usually address an external and often unfamiliar audience. They are organized according to standard elements of formal researched reports, with a cover page, a letter of transmittal, a title page, a table of contents, a list of illustrations, an **executive summary** (a summary of the key information in each section of the proposal), body discussion divided by headings and subheadings, appendixes, a glossary of key terms, and a bibliography. (Not all formal reports will have all of these sections.)

Solicited and Unsolicited

A proposal is solicited or unsolicited depending on the audience's role in its initiation. A **solicited proposal** is a proposal that the reader asked the writer to prepare. A request may come from a manager at work who sees a problem. The manager asks an individual or a team to study solutions to the problem and present recommendations in a proposal. The request might also appear in an **RFP,** or request for proposal. The RFP states exactly what the customer seeks. Proposal writers then prepare their documents to address the needs stated in the RFP. An **unsolicited proposal** begins when the writer discovers a problem, such as an inefficient production line or a lack of water fountains for employees who use wheelchairs. The writer independently identifies a problem, explains it, and offers solutions.

Sales, Research, Grant, and Planning Proposals

Based on function, or what the writer wants the audience to agree to do, proposals fall into one of four categories: sales, research, grant, and planning. Each category is explained below.

- The sales proposal tries to sell a product or service.

- The research proposal asks for approval to begin a study or an investigation. A marine biologist at a university, for instance, might request approval (and perhaps funding) to study the effect of acid rain on a particular fish species.

- The grant proposal seeks money from a government agency, foundation, or other funding source for a specified project, such as developing a horseback riding program for children with cerebral palsy.

- The planning proposal attempts to persuade an audience to take a particular action, as in a plan to improve food service at a restaurant's drive-through window by rearranging preparation tables for efficiency.

A single proposal may combine several of the categories mentioned here. As you read proposals, you may discover that all four categories apply to one document.

Formatting

The best format for a proposal is determined by the needs of the audience and the function or type of proposal. Writers who are submitting a formal proposal to a prospective client might want to prepare a bound booklike document for decision makers to read and review. The writers of an informal proposal that suggests ways to improve recycling efforts in a printing company could send their proposal to the manager as an e-mail attachment.

A company that installs fiber-optic cable in public buildings could post a proposal to a website for viewers' access. Some proposal writers take advantage of images and hyperlinks to persuade the audience by sending a CD or DVD with sound and video and links to useful sites.

Decision makers throughout business and industry read proposals. Most of these people read only a portion of the proposal. They read those sections that deal with their area of interest and expertise. Thus, readers evaluate the proposal based on the data presented in the section or sections they review, passing their acceptance or rejection to the person or group making the final decision.

TEACH

Review the opening sample proposal with students. Discuss the research and problem solving involved in writing it. Use the Informal Proposal for an Internal Audience Teaching Master to point out that the problem and solution are clearly outlined in the informal proposal model and that the solution seems to be a reasonable answer to the problem.

ENRICH

If you invite professionals to speak to your class, ask them to discuss specifically the power and effect that proposals have in their work environment.

● **STOP AND THINK**

Why would a single proposal be categorized in more than one way?

GETTING STARTED ON PROPOSALS

Now that you know about the different types of proposals, you are ready to plan for writing one. The proposal begins with a problem or need. The problem may be one that you discovered or one that someone pointed out to you, as in an RFP or in a memo or letter from another professional.

A problem-solving strategy such as the one listed below can make your work as a proposal writer easier and can help you focus on the problem.

- Determine whether you have a problem or need.

- If you do, define the problem or need and your purpose.

- Conduct preliminary research.

- Determine the scope and limitations of your study.

- Identify the factors or subparts of the problem or need.

- Brainstorm possible solutions.

- Gather data to support the possible solutions.

- If possible, test and evaluate the solutions.

Once you have gone through the problem-solving process and are ready to write your proposal, you can use one of several strategies to help you appeal to your audience. Create a chart with a line drawn down the middle. On the left side of the chart, write everything you think the readers need or want from the solution. For instance, if you have an RFP, the criteria, as with a job advertisement, are probably noted there. If you do not have an RFP, make the list based on your research and insight into the problem and audience.

On the right side of the chart, list what your solution offers the reader in fulfilling his or her wants or needs. In other words, for every want or need in the left column, explain how your plan will satisfy that want or need. Thus, you will have persuasive tools ready to begin composing your proposal. Table 14.1 relates to a sales proposal for football helmets.

CRITERIA	RESPONSE
Protects players	• 1" of solid tempered plastic covered with fiberglass for resistance • 34" foam padding from ear to ear • Adjustable liner for greater protection
Is economical	• $29.90 per unit, 10% less than the average football helmet • 10-year warranty/automatic replacements

Table 14.1

Focus on Ethics

Monina Dagsaan is a new administrative assistant at a company that produces exercise videos and infomercials. One of her first assignments is to read proposals from a dozen catering companies to provide food for the cast and crew on the days they shoot. Her boss, Hank Phelps, gives her the RFP to which the catering companies are responding. He also gives her an internal document about current catering costs, issues with the current caterer, and the amount the company hopes to save with a new caterer. Monina's job is to sort through the proposals and give Hank the top three or four proposals.

Monina notices that one of the proposals stands out from the others in how closely it meets the needs of her company. It addresses the problems with the current caterer, which were not listed in the RFP, and the cost it proposes matches the exact amount her company wants to spend. Monina thinks that the person who wrote this proposal must have seen her company's internal document.

Think Critically
What should Monina do?

Another technique that some proposal writers use when analyzing their audience is to imagine how the readers think and feel. Anticipating the readers' questions and concerns may help you understand the readers' points of view and anticipate their needs. You also can gather audience information relating to the issues in the proposal, as shown in Table 14.2.

You can add other questions to this audience analysis as you consider the problem, solution, and benefits of the solution.

 STOP AND THINK
Why should proposal writers define or state the problem?

Problem	• Is the reader aware of the problem? • How much does the reader know about the problem? • What factors about the problem most concern the reader?
Solution	• What do the criteria (perhaps in an RFP) established by the audience tell you about the audience? • How would you prioritize the decision maker's concerns: personnel, money, time, production, public image, and ethics? • How open-minded or how critical will your audience be?

Table 14.2

FOCUS

Warm Up

Allow time for students to work in groups to discuss the Warm Up. In describing what traits, characteristics, or actions give persuasive people credibility, students will identify qualities they too can develop and use. Possible solutions: a personal history of integrity and reliability; a demonstrated knowledge of the subject area; and the ability to speak, write, and listen well.

TEACH

Display the Outline for Informal Proposals Teaching Master as you explain the organizational strategies for informal proposals.

COMPOSING INFORMAL PROPOSALS

The organizational strategy of the informal proposal, like that of many technical reports, is designed for the busy decision maker. The proposal usually opens with the most important information. So writers give information about the problem and solution at the beginning of the report. The organization of the rest of the proposal is flexible to fit the different situations that writers are likely to encounter in their work. No matter how you organize your proposals, you must remember your audience throughout the writing process and ask yourself if you are responding to all of their questions and doubts.

Informal proposals begin with an executive summary, or abstract. Following the summary information, the proposals contain the same parts as any other written document: an introduction, a body, and a conclusion. The summary, or abstract, is a condensed version of the proposal. The introduction presents the problem and solution and whatever background information the reader needs. The body of the proposal is the main section. It covers the facts—the specific evidence to convince the reader that the plan is worthwhile.

The last section, the conclusion, wraps up the report and spurs the reader to action.

The specific information contained—and thus the headings used (with the exception of the Executive Summary, or Abstract)—in each section may vary. Depending on the problem and solution being proposed, the writer decides which subsections to include and which to omit. Possible headings used in each section are listed in Table 14.3.

SECTION	POSSIBLE HEADINGS
Introduction	Introduction Problem Addressed and Solution (could be two headings) Objectives of Proposed Plan Background Data Sources Scope and Limitations
Body	Methods Scheduling Capabilities and Qualifications of Personnel Materials and Equipment Expected Results Plan for Evaluating Results Feasibility Budget (usually in tabular form) Justification of Budget Items (where necessary)
Conclusion	Conclusion Summary of Key Points Request for Action

Table 14.3

Drafting the Summary

The summary, or abstract, is designed with the busy decision maker in mind. In a short informal proposal, this section may appear on the title page or, typically, as the first paragraph in the report. It provides a brief overview of the essential ideas presented in the proposal. The summary should include a problem statement, the proposed work objectives, the project impact, and the work plan. Cost is not usually discussed in the summary because writers first want to present all of their evidence to persuade readers. They hope readers will not be "turned off" by the cost, but will be convinced by the proposal to justify the expense.

Drafting the Introduction

The introduction answers the "why" in the reader's mind. It explains why the proposal was written. You must identify the problem up front. Another important element of the introduction is your proposed solution to the problem. This statement should be clear but brief. Later, in the body, you will provide further details and justify your proposal.

Image Source/Getty Images

The introduction further explains your objectives, or what you hope to accomplish, and clarifies the value of the work and why it is worth the investment you seek. You also may need to include a brief background of the problem in this section.

For example, a proposal to college administrators that recommends doubling the number of bike racks on campus will be taken more seriously when the writer explains the problem leading to the proposal and the way the bike racks address the problem.

> Students' budgets are tighter than ever, and the cost of commuting adds to students' financial burden. The college raised the cost of a campus parking permit twice in the last two years, and the one-way fare on the most popular bus route to campus is currently $3.65. Secure bike racks placed around campus would encourage students to commute by bike.

An explanation of the background shows your reader that you have a grasp of the problem. In addition, the introduction may explain the need for a solution. Some readers may ask, "Why not simply leave things as they are?" For these readers, note the effects of ignoring the problem.

The introduction also explains how you or other personnel are qualified to solve the problem. In addition, you might describe where you will seek information to help you solve the problem. Data sources could be printed materials (for example, books, reports, or brochures), interviews, observations, or experiments. The introduction also might define the **scope,** or the extent to which you will search for solutions, as well as any **limitations,** or boundaries, of the project (for example, restrictions on time, space, equipment, money, or staff).

Explain that proposal writers
write only the sections of the
body for which they have
collected information or only
the sections the reader needs.
For example, if the proposal
required no materials or
equipment, the writer would not
include that section.

Writers usually choose to write
a feasibility section when the
audience is likely to think the
proposed idea is improbable,
that is, when the audience may
doubt the reasonableness of the
proposal.

Any items in the budget that are
or may seem excessive should
be explained in a justification
section.

TEACH

Use the Informal Proposal for
an External Audience Teaching
Master when you discuss the
section "Explore the Composing
Strategies with a Model."

Drafting the Body

After you have described the problem and solution in the introduction, you use the body of the informal proposal to become more specific about your plan. The specific details—facts, figures, statistics, dates, locations, and costs—are the materials you use to persuade your audience. For this section, you address *only* the topics in Table 14.4 that you and your readers need.

Methods	Explain your methodology—what your approach to the problem will be, what criteria (perhaps from the RFP) you will meet, and what outcome or product you will deliver at the date you specify. Justify your plan of work and any exceptions to the RFP as needed.
Scheduling	Present a calendar of the work planned and expected completion dates to assure your audience that you anticipate efficiency. Effectively illustrate scheduling as appropriate. Flowcharts or timelines are excellent for visual presentation of timetables. List numbers and qualifications of personnel. Describe facilities (both available and needed) to be used.
Capabilities	Assure your audience that you can deliver the work you propose by (1) noting the abilities of people involved and (2) describing your organization's successful track record.
Materials and Equipment	Review materials and equipment to be used. This section is particularly important in scientific projects and construction projects.
Expected Results	Explain what you think the result of your work will be.
Plan for Evaluating Results	Outline your plan for evaluating the success of the solution once it is implemented.
Feasibility	Explain how you find the solution reasonable to implement.
Budget	Present (typically in a table) the costs for the work, including salaries, equipment, materials, travel, communication, services, and other expenses.
Justification	Explain clearly and persuasively the reason for any expenses your audience may question.

Table 14.4

Drafting the Conclusion

The conclusion should be straightforward and brief. It might include a summary of key points, such as those noted in the summary section, and it should call for the audience to take action. Make the call to action specific and clear, including dates, deadlines, and amounts.

Explore the Composing Strategies with a Model

Consider a sample problem to illustrate the composing process: Chaya Sotelo, a graduate of Martinique College, has noticed that the online newsletter, *The Martinique,* contains little information about the careers and lives of alumni. Occasionally, the newsletter carries a brief report about a former student who has gone on to be quite successful, but she would like to see stories about the careers of "everyday" alumni too. You will follow Chaya through the process of writing a short informal proposal to the editor, in which she suggests a solution. Chaya decides to write the summary last, pulling ideas for the summary from the proposal.

To help the editor understand the problem, Chaya considers the "why" question. She writes a clear statement of the problem: **Except for occasional brief reports, no news about the careers and lives of Martinique College alumni appears in the online newsletter *The Martinique*.** Then she lists her goals, as follows:

- Include specific features on alumni and their chosen careers.

- Include general news about alumni.

- Report on alumni who deserve attention for their career achievements.

- Provide a forum for alumni.

- Encourage more alumni to read the website.

Chaya brainstorms several solutions to meet these goals: (1) Develop a link on the website for alumni to submit personal and career information, (2) request that alumni be given space for contributions, and (3) ask *The Martinique* to cover alumni news in a more comprehensive manner.

Chaya moves from brainstorming to analysis. For each solution she developed, she lists positives and negatives. For example, for the first solution, developing links on the website, she lists the following:

Positive	Negative
Alumni would be able to highlight positive aspects of graduating from Martinique.	Would enough alumni be interested?
Alumni and students would be able to network.	Would alumni be willing to participate?
Alumni would read and support their website.	Would alumni read the website and support its sponsors?

Chaya realizes that her proposal is directed to an editor, Gina Hollinger, who is interested in the effects of Chaya's proposed action on Ms. Hollinger's work: profits, personnel, schedule, and image. Chaya knows that a solid plan with accurate facts and figures is necessary to convince her reader. After choosing the plan with the most "positives" and the least "negatives," she again brainstorms ideas to include in the body of her proposal.

Chaya decides that the best solution is to include an article in the quarterly online newsletter *The Martinique*. She must assure Ms. Hollinger of a sound plan for implementing this idea. Chaya explains the specifics of her idea and proposes how the work will be done. To make the work process clear, she develops a chart that shows each step in the development of the feature. The chart identifies who or what is responsible for each phase. Chaya uses this chart to check for steps she might have overlooked.

Chaya prepares to write her conclusion by reviewing her strongest selling points. She knows that her closing should include a summary of key points and make a call to action. Chaya presents the benefits of including a new alumni-generated column in *The Martinique* and asks Ms. Hollinger to consider adding the new feature to the quarterly online newsletter. Chaya also offers to volunteer if the proposal is accepted. In addition, she provides her contact with information that makes it easier for Ms. Hollinger to respond to the proposal. Read Chaya's final two-page draft in Figure 14.2.

P.O. Box 1423
Davenport, IA 52809-2128
October 23, 20—

Ms. Gina Hollinger, Editor
The Martinique
113 South Sperry Road
Room 101
Davenport, IA 52802-3108

Dear Ms. Hollinger:

As an alumni of Martinique College who has pursued a career in commercial art, I read your online newsletter regularly. I have been impressed with the innovative design and attractive page layout of your publication, and I admire its distinctive look. However, I have noticed one element that could be improved.

Problem

The problem is lack of news about alumni who have graduated from Martinique College. Your reporters cover the events of Martinique College very well, yet little mention is made of the lives and careers of alumni. I believe that current students would be interested in learning what former students have been doing since graduating and that alumni would be interested in reading about former classmates. With the tough economic times, it also would be a way for alumni to share helpful information about the job market, careers, job openings, and specific job skills.

Solution

News about alumni could be obtained at no expense to *The Martinique*. Your webmaster could create an online questionnaire as a way for alumni to submit their personal and professional information. Using one of your top-notch editors to compile and edit the material, you could include an article about one alumnus or alumna in each quarterly newsletter. Of particular interest to readers would be "life after graduation"—travels, career moves, suggestions for soon-to-be graduates, and any personal information alumni would care to share. Readers also might be interested in knowing in what part of the country the alumni live and whether they have lived or are currently living overseas.

Objectives

Including news about alumni may have several positive effects. More students and alumni are likely to read the newsletter, and they may benefit by doing so. *The Martinique* will benefit by developing more readers, who, in turn, will support its sponsors. In fact, alumni may choose to advertise their businesses in the newsletter, benefiting themselves as well as *The Martinique*.

Figure 14.2 Informal Proposal for an External Audience

Ms. Gina Hollinger
Page 2
October 23, 20—

Methods and Scheduling

If you accept this proposal, your webmaster could likely create an online questionnaire in no more than one month. During that time, you could "spread the word" about the upcoming change to the newsletter, ask students and alumni to submit suggestions for the name of the article, and determine guidelines and responsibilities of your staff. In fact, I would be willing to volunteer my time in whatever capacity you need, as I live within a short drive of Martinque's campus.

The workflow, as illustrated in Figure 1 below, is designed so that all work will be done well and on time. Your in-house editorial board will review story ideas, select the best, assign writers and photographers, help with editing, and submit the final article to you for publication. The editorial board will approve all work before it is submitted to you.

Figure 1: Workflow Process for Substituting Articles

Maintaining the Article

During summer break and school holidays, the article could be suspended. On the other hand, you could retain readers by continuing the article or perhaps reprinting a particularly popular article.

Conclusion

An alumni-generated article in *The Martinique* will be beneficial in many ways. It will create new readers and keep readers informed of alumni's successes after they leave college. It will not cost you any more in time or wages. It will bring alumni and students closer and allow them to network. Please consider making these things happen by allowing space for an alumni article in Martinique College's online newsletter. In addition, please call me at 555-0112 if you would like to accept my offer to serve as a volunteer for the newsletter.

Sincerely,

Chaya Sotelo

Chaya Sotelo

Figure 14.2 Informal Proposal for an External Audience, cont.

ONGOING ASSESSMENT

Stop and Think

CEOs are likely to read the summary first and then other sections related to the general operations of the company, such as the budget. Of all of the readers, CEOs are most likely to read the entire report.

Technical experts are interested in the sections in the body of the proposal that contain technical descriptions and details, such as Methods, Materials and Equipment, Expected Results, and Plan for Evaluating Results.

Financial officers want to review the budget and its justification.

● STOP AND THINK

In a large organization, different people are likely to read only the sections of a proposal relating to their area of expertise. Name the sections the following employees might read: a chief executive officer (CEO), a technical expert, and a comptroller (financial officer).

FOCUS

Warm Up

Begin a discussion of the elements of a formal proposal. Also compare the elements that students find in textbooks with the list of the parts of formal proposals in this section. You also can compare parts of a formal and informal proposal. Make sure students review the sample of the formal proposal at the beginning of the chapter.

RETEACH

Remind students of the value of prewriting by asking them how important planning is to their ability to present a convincing argument. They should realize that planning is crucial. Remind them that a writer might develop a marvelous solution, but if the solution does not meet the criteria set forth by the readers, it will not convince them.

COMPOSING FORMAL PROPOSALS

The preceding section of this chapter presented information about informal proposals. Informal and formal proposals are similar. Both are persuasive documents that offer the writers' answers to the readers' problems or needs. In both proposals, writers choose from the same optional subsections in the same order under the headings *Introduction, Body,* and *Conclusion.*

Formal proposals may differ from informal proposals in the following ways:

- Tone, such as the detached, professional voice writers might use with a high-level official

- Additional parts of the report, such as the glossary, appendixes, and transmittal correspondence

- Complexity of the outcome, such as the construction of a new building or the $2 billion purchase of jet airliners

Although formal proposals are not used as frequently as informal proposals, they are called for in many circumstances. The following examples are typical:

- A marine biologist, disturbed by the fish kills in a local estuarine system, wants to study the effect of municipal wastewater dumping on the fish. The biologist seeks funds from the State Department of Fish and Wildlife for a five-year project.

- The owner of a Montessori preschool receives an RFP from a local assisted-living center to open a branch of the preschool at the center.

- A mechanic in a ball-bearing plant is inspired to improve the precision of a robotic welding machine after studying similar machines at another facility. Having decided on the adjustments needed and the cost in work hours and materials, the mechanic requests approval from her manager.

As you read about formal proposals, look at the sample formal proposal in Figure 14.3, starting on page 346.

Prewriting

Prewriting techniques should help you plan to write a formal proposal. During the prewriting phase, you collect and organize data and determine your objectives. Because a formal proposal is often longer and more involved than other technical reports, prewriting is especially important.

Planning for Persuasion

The readers of formal proposals need to be convinced, as a salesperson convinces a customer. If you are to be a successful proposal writer, you must address your audience effectively and prevent any skepticism. Here are some guidelines for convincing your audience.

- Collect as many facts as you can to support your proposed plan.

- Be accurate. Plan to check your data. If your reader discovers a discrepancy, an exaggeration, or a mistake, you lose credibility.

Communication Dilemma

A team of employees at Blue Vale Packing worked for two months on a sales proposal to a major national mail-order company. The proposal offered to supply all foam packaging materials for the business. Because this proposal could represent a major portion of Blue Vale's business, the team worked diligently to develop and present the best plan possible. However, a serious problem arose that the team had not anticipated. Most sales proposals must be approved and signed by someone in an executive position in the organization. The team scheduled time for researching, prewriting, composing, and editing before the submission deadline. What they did not anticipate was that the president of Blue Vale was leaving on a four-week business trip ten days before the due date. Therefore, the president would not be available to approve or sign the proposal in time to meet the submission deadline.

Think Critically

What could the team do? Could they salvage the situation and meet the submission deadline? If so, how?

- Study your audience and the situation so you understand the reader's point of view. Planning with an understanding of the reader allows you to write a more convincing proposal.

- Be realistic in your planning. Do not propose to do a job in two weeks to make a sale when you honestly believe the work will take a month. You may suffer the consequences later because your proposal becomes a legal document when it is accepted.

Planning for Integration

Another goal of prewriting the formal proposal is planning for integration. The entire document must come together as a logical whole. The description of the problem, for example, will affect how the reader views the effectiveness of the solution. When different writers are composing different sections, a primary writer or editor should plan and edit the entire report for consistency.

Planning for Graphics, Definitions, and Supplemental Materials

As you gather data, consider whether a graphic would help your audience understand the information. Then decide what type of graphic aid will most clearly depict the idea (for example, a pie graph, a diagram, or a bar graph).

Plan what terms you will use and whether your readers will need definitions for them. If the proposal needs definitions, decide whether you serve your audience better by placing the definitions in the report or in a glossary at the end of the report. If you need to provide only a few definitions, it may be easier for you to include definitions in the text. (Your reader will probably find that arrangement easier to use as well.) However, proposals that require numerous definitions should probably contain a glossary after the body of the report.

In addition to graphics and definitions, think about materials you might like your readers to have access to but do not want to include in the body of the proposal. Consider placing relevant but not essential materials in an **appendix** (material that you want readers to have access to but that is not a primary part of the proposal). For example, if you used the results of a questionnaire in your proposal, you may want to show interested readers how you gathered data by including the questionnaire as an appendix. You can read more about appendixes on page 345.

Parts of Formal Proposals

The format of formal proposals is designed to aid the readers. Each formal proposal follows the same basic plan so that readers and writers know what to expect and where to find the information they seek. Remember, many expert readers review only one or two sections of a formal proposal.

The parts listed below make up the formal proposal. Those parts with an asterisk (*) are used in informal proposals as well.

Letter or Memo of Transmittal	Body (or Discussion)*
Title Page	Conclusion (or Summary)*
Table of Contents	Glossary
List of Illustrations	Appendixes
Executive Summary (or Abstract)*	Works Cited
Introduction*	

Letter or Memo of Transmittal

The **letter** or **memo of transmittal** is similar to the cover letter that is mailed with a resume. It is an official greeting and an introduction of the document to the reader. Write a letter to accompany a proposal when you are addressing an external audience and a memo when you are addressing an internal audience. Key the letter or memo using acceptable formatting guidelines.

Because the message is usually good news for the audience, this letter or memo uses the direct strategy, as follows:

1. Begin with the purpose, the fact that you are submitting a proposal. Name the proposal topic and explain whether you are responding to an RFP, responding to a request, or initiating the proposal on your own.

2. Note areas of special interest to the reader.

3. Thank the audience for reviewing the proposal. You may offer to provide more information or answer questions.

The letter or memo of transmittal is usually written last, after the proposal.

Title Page

The title page of a formal proposal, like a book cover, gives the reader important information about the document. In designing the title page, use white space to make the page attractive. Be clear, accurate, complete, and precise in composing the title page. Provide the following:

- A descriptive title of the proposal

- The name of the company or companies involved

- The names of the writers
- The date the proposal is being submitted

As part of the title page, some internal proposals have a routing list of readers who will review the document.

Note that a precise title such as *Proposal to Develop a Policy Governing Substitute Staffing for Absentee Technicians in the Fiber Twist Area* or *Proposal to Purchase and Install the Evermorr Secure 3120 Security System in Glynndale Condominiums* is useful because it gives readers more information than a vague title such as *Proposal to Deal with Absent Workers* or *Proposal to Improve Security in Glynndale Condominiums.*

Table of Contents

The table of contents should be designed so that it is attractive, easy to read, and clear. The table of contents may appear alone on a page or on the same page with the list of illustrations, which appears at the bottom. The words *Table of Contents* in all capital letters should be boldfaced and centered at the top of the page. The list of contents should start at the left margin under the title and visually demonstrate relationships between ideas. Typically, section headings are flush with the left margin and subheadings are indented underneath.

Enter headings and subheadings on the left side of the page, **pagination** (the arrangement of page numbers) on the right side of the page, and leaders (periods) between each heading and its page number.

List of Illustrations Begin with the words *List of Illustrations* (using initial caps and bold-faced type) at the left margin under the last entry in the table of contents. Under the title, provide the label, number, and descriptive title of the graphic on the left and the page on which the illustration is located on the right.

Executive Summary (or Abstract)

Centered at the top of the page, key the words *Executive Summary* or *Abstract* (in all capital letters and boldfaced type). The executive summary is usually two to four paragraphs on a page by itself.

Write the executive summary after you finish the rest of the report. Keep the reader in mind while you compose it. This section, as the title *Executive Summary* implies, is designed with the administrator in mind. Busy executives want the story quickly and want only the essential information: the problem, the solution, and the benefits of the solution. Because these readers are concerned with the big picture, the overall health of the organization, they may not read the specific information in the body of the proposal, only the summary. However, proposal writers should plan the summary for all readers, not just executives.

COMMUNICATION TECHNOLOGIES

Word processing software has features to aid in creating a formal proposal, such as a feature to create a table of contents and styles for each section of the proposal. If you are working on a group proposal, you can create a master document as the template for the proposal. Drafts can be circulated among the team members, with editorial changes and comments marked in the drafts.

Think Critically

Create a document with heading styles (or add headings to an existing document) and generate a table of contents. Explore different ways to format the table of contents.

Introduction, Body of Discussion, and Conclusion

In long reports (perhaps 20 pages or more), each major section heading may begin a new, separate part of the formal proposal. Each section starts on a new page with the heading name, such as *Introduction,* in all capital letters and boldfaced type centered at the top of the page. In shorter reports, the entire body may flow from one section to another without page breaks.

The Introduction The introduction is the framework that prepares readers for the body of the proposal. The introduction answers the questions *what* and *why.* No matter which subparts of the introduction you include in your document, clearly state for your readers the problem and a solution or alternative solutions. If you determine that the readers need background information, summarize the situation and the proposer's qualifications. Include information about your company and personnel that will enhance the credibility of your proposal, such as the number of years in business, staff and equipment resources, previous clients, and success with similar projects. Because any reader may read the introductory material, remember to communicate in a way that administrators, managers, technical experts, and financial managers can understand. Introductions should be strong and clear, in which case people are likely to read them. In addition, by coming at the beginning of the proposal, introductions make an important first impression.

The Body of Discussion If the introduction sets the framework of ideas, the body of a formal proposal is the crux of the argument, the specifics of persuasion. In the body, you explain how the technical data prove that your idea (solution) will work. Describe methods for carrying out the project, specific tasks, time schedules, personnel, facilities, and equipment. You could include an organizational chart of people working on the project so the reader will know who is responsible for particular areas. In addition to outlining what you will do, these specific details convince the reader that your approach is best for the situation. The project's budget should clearly show and perhaps justify the costs. The graphics you have planned should enhance the text of your proposal, not take the place of the text.

Furthermore, keep in mind that the body of the proposal is most often read by technical experts, who have the skills and ability to understand the detailed technical information. These readers expect precise, accurate, and up-to-date information.

The Conclusion Be concise and direct when you write the conclusion of your formal proposal. You have already provided the information to sway your audience to your point of view. This is not the time to add to a sales pitch—or *any* new information that belongs in the body of the proposal. Instead, summarize your most convincing points regarding the importance of the project and the benefits of the solution. Then suggest a course of action.

Glossary

If you include a glossary, design it to be easy to read. In the text of the proposal, designate words appearing in the glossary using asterisks, italics, or another highlighting technique. Include a footnote or parenthetical note beside the first entry telling readers they can find definitions in the glossary.

Complete the *Revising Glossary Entries* worksheet available at www.cengage.com/school/bcomm/techwtg. Click the link for Chapter 14; then click Data Files.

At the top of the glossary page, center the title *Glossary* (in all capital letters and boldfaced type). Make the entry word—the word being defined—stand out by using boldface or columns. When using columns, place the entry words on the left and definitions on the right. Alphabetize all words, acronyms, and symbols, as dictionaries do.

Consider the needs of your readers when you choose the words to define and determine the extent of the definitions. Do not define words the audience already understands. At the same time, if several people will read your proposal, define a term even if you think that only one reader will need the definition. Avoid overly technical definitions (unless you are writing a highly technical proposal for an audience that is familiar with the vocabulary used in the proposal). Use language the readers will understand and consider including graphic aids if they will help readers understand the proposal.

Works Cited

If your proposal uses ideas or text from a source you need to credit, prepare works cited or documentation pages according to the guidelines of the style manual you are using. Consult the style manual your organization or the RFP requires and follow it precisely.

Appendixes

An appendix is material you want readers to have access to but that is not a primary part of the proposal. In the body of the proposal, where the topic an appendix supports is mentioned, refer readers to the appendix, as in "See Appendix C." Each appendix is labeled with the word *Appendix* and given a letter or number and a descriptive title, similar to the system for identifying graphics. Put every document in a separate appendix.

Page Numbers

Assigning page numbers for formal proposals works the same as pagination in books. **Prefatory material,** or material placed before the actual report begins, is numbered with lowercase Roman numerals. Prefatory material includes a letter or memo of transmittal, a title page, and a table of contents.

The first two pages, the letter or memo of transmittal and the title page, are not numbered. The table of contents, the third prefatory page, is numbered iii. The first page, which usually begins with the Executive Summary, is not numbered. Place an Arabic number 2 on the next page. (In other words, 2 is the first Arabic page number because the first page of the body is not numbered.) Number the rest of the document with Arabic numerals in sequence. Center page numbers at the bottom or in the upper right corner of the page.

⬣ **STOP AND THINK**

Who reads the executive summary, or abstract, of a formal proposal? Where should terms be defined in a formal proposal?

ONGOING ASSESSMENT

Stop and Think

Use the Stop and Think to review the elements of a formal proposal.

Executive summaries provide essential information—an overview of the proposal—for executives concerned with the big picture, not the details. However, any member of the audience may choose to read this section as a preview or an orientation.

Definition of terms and their placement should be guided by the audience's needs. Definitions may be placed within the text; for example, *Grading, or the sloping of soil for proper drainage, is necessary for site preparation. Grading, the sloping of soil for proper drainage, is necessary for site preparation. Grading (the sloping of soil for proper drainage) is necessary for site preparation.* Another option is to place terms and definitions in a glossary after the text and before the works cited and the appendix(es).

TO: Barkley Wolfe, Manager
Eastbrook Shopping Center

FROM: Delores Ondecko, Chief of Operations *DO*

DATE: November 23, 20—

SUBJECT: Proposal for Improving Exterior Lighting at Eastbrook

I am submitting for your review my department's proposal to upgrade the exterior lighting system at Eastbrook Shopping Center. This document responds to our October 15, 20—, tenants' meeting and subsequent discussions with you regarding safety on the property.

Of special note are the following sections addressing questions you or our tenants brought up:

Customer attitudes (in Figure 1) 2
Standard illumination levels (Methods) 3
Cost estimate 5

Thank you for reviewing our data and suggestions. We look forward to your response. If you decide to accept our proposal, we are eager to implement the needed changes.

Figure 14.3 Formal Proposal

TEACH
The memo or letter of transmittal is the official "handing over" of the proposal.

PROPOSAL FOR IMPROVED EXTERIOR LIGHTING
AT EASTBROOK SHOPPING CENTER

Prepared for
Barkley Wolfe, Manager
Eastbrook Shopping Center

Prepared by
Delores Ondecko, Chief of Operations

November 23, 20—

Figure 14.3 Formal Proposal, cont.

TABLE OF CONTENTS

List of Illustrations

Figure 14.3 Formal Proposal, cont.

TEACH
Remind students that careful proofreading,
especially of a table of contents, is important so
that readers do not become frustrated.

EXECUTIVE SUMMARY

Evidence from our security office, police records, and customer attitude survey proves that Eastbrook Shopping Center has a problem with inadequate lighting outside the building at night.

To improve the lighting so that it meets recommendations of the Illuminating Engineering Society and other experts, we need to exchange our current 150-watt bulbs for 400-watt bulbs and install five new pole lights and six new wall-mount lamps.

The recommended changes will cost less than $1,700 and will improve our security level, liability rating, and public image, along with decreasing our energy costs.

Figure 14.3 Formal Proposal, cont.

TEACH

Although the abstract, or executive summary, is usually brief, it is very important because it may be the only element of the proposal that some readers see.

INTRODUCTION

Problem

Inadequate illumination in Eastbrook Shopping Center's parking areas is a serious concern. As good corporate citizens, we have a responsibility to the community to maintain a safe environment. As merchants, we recognize that shoppers and employees expect and have a right to a safe environment. We risk losing customers if Eastbrook does not maintain a secure, peaceful image. We also must watch expenses. However, it is evident from our research that as a result of poor lighting, safety on our grounds is not ensured.

Solution

Problems with lighting can be eliminated if we upgrade our exterior lighting system to meet recommendations of local law enforcement and utilities personnel and Illuminating Engineering Society (IES)* guidelines. (Terms designated by an asterisk are defined in the glossary on page 6.) To increase illumination sufficiently in all areas outside the building, we must exchange our 150-watt mercury vapor* bulbs for HPS* bulbs as well as add six wall-mount lights and five new poles in the parking areas.

Objectives

The purpose of this proposal is to improve the quality of exterior lighting at Eastbrook Shopping Center so that customers, employees, and staff feel safe walking to and from the building and their vehicles and so that our parking area does not become the site of illegal activities.

Background

Our records for the last six months prove that we do, indeed, have a problem:

8 incidents of shoplifting (unresolved)	3 purse snatchings
1 assault and battery	1 kidnapping

Further, the police department rates the relative safety of Eastbrook to be low compared to other shopping centers. (See Appendix A.)

In addition, the survey our marketing agency conducted last month showed that more than 50% of the 400 respondents feel some concern for their safety in entering or exiting our building after dark. Refer to Table 1 for the breakdown of the responses.

Figure 14.3 Formal Proposal, cont.

Table 1. Attitudes Regarding Eastbrook's Exterior Environment at Night (by percentage)

Respondents by Age	Extremely Comfortable	Slightly Comfortable	Comfortable	Slightly Uncomfortable	Uncomfortable
18–20	5	31	15	42	7
21–35	15	19	39	15	12
36–50	5	14	22	23	36
over 50	1	9	13	28	49
TOTAL	26	73	89	108	104
PERCENT	7	18	22	27	26

If this unsafe image continues in the public mind, we will begin to lose valuable customers and eventually will lose business occupants of our shopping center. Note particularly the high rate (49%) of people over 50 who are uncomfortable. With the "graying of America," this group includes a large number of customers we cannot afford to lose. Businesses will move to a location where they and their customers feel safe. Moreover, we risk a lawsuit if incidents occur that we could have prevented.

Data Sources

The data used to create this proposal came from our security records, interviews with Edison Electric public safety directors at other shopping centers, a customer survey we commissioned, data and recommendations from law enforcement and the Illuminating Engineering Society*, and an experiment conducted by our staff.

Scope and Limitations

In seeking solutions, we wanted to increase safety without creating the image of an armed fortress. The solution must appeal to the public and our business occupants. In addition, any changes we make should be visually attractive and not unpleasant for our commercial and residential neighbors. We also have considered cost and energy consumption.

DISCUSSION

Methods

To determine the amount of light currently being produced, we used a footcandle meter* at the base of each pole. An Edison Electric representative recommended an average of one footcandle* per square foot (Smith). Research revealed that *IES Lighting Handbook* supports increasing the typical roadway lighting level by 50% for mall parking lots, suggesting 0.25 to 0.50 or more footcandles (Rea 22.22–23).

Figure 14.3 Formal Proposal, cont.

Our results indicated that Eastbrook's lights are generally lower than the suggested illumination. The readings ranged from a high of 1.8 to a low of 0.1, as you can see in Figure 1 below.

Figure 1. Exterior Light Intensity and Proposed Fixture Additions

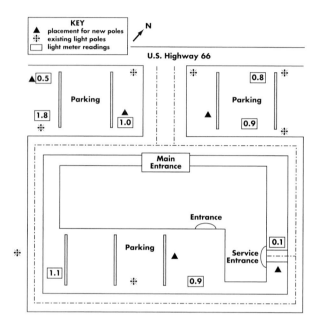

In addition, a video-recorded experiment revealed that in landscaped sections of our parking lots, a person could stand undetected beside a tree or large shrub until the observer was as close as 2 feet. Our research shows that almost all parking and pedestrian walkway areas need increased lighting.

Given the video-recorded experiment and the footcandle meter readings we collected, an engineer at Edison Electric recommended placement of five new lighting poles outside our building, as indicated on the map in Figure 1 above. Along with the new pole lights, the engineer said that six wall-mount lights installed on the building should bring illumination up to the standard recommendation levels. The six lights will be mounted as follows: one on each side of the main entrance and one on each side of the back entrance, with the remaining two placed on the northeast and the southwest walls (Smith).

Figure 14.3 Formal Proposal, cont.

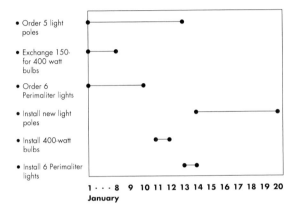

Scheduling

We would like to make the suggested improvements as soon as possible. Once equipment has been ordered and received, the project should take less than two weeks, as you can see in Figure 2.

Figure 2. Schedule for Improving Eastbrook's Exterior Lighting

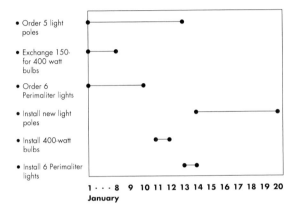

The installation of the five new poles according to IES guidelines will require an outside contractor. Edison Electric has the special equipment needed and can install the poles in one week. Because we do not have the cherry picker required to do this job, the utilities company also will need to replace our 150-watt bulbs with the new 400-watt bulbs. This task should take no more than one day. Three members of our maintenance staff can install the six wall-mount lights in less than one day. The entire project should be complete and lighting improved within a month.

Materials and Equipment

We can purchase the 400-watt bulbs from our current supplier, Witherspoon Inc., for only $10 per unit more than we are paying now for the 150-watt bulbs. Moreover, Witherspoon will exchange our current stock of 150-watt bulbs for 400-watt bulbs.

Edison Electric will order the materials and erect the five new poles we need. We should contract with Edison to service the pole lights because we do not own the equipment to do so ourselves.

Figure 14.3 Formal Proposal, cont.

Cost

The adjustments necessary to upgrade exterior lighting and implement IES guidelines will cost $1,688.75. The following budget details the expenses for this project.

Five 40-foot metal poles	5 @ $211.95	$1,059.75
Six Perimaliter lights	6 @ $70.00	420.00
Shipping charges for exchanging bulbs		34.00
Edison Electric service fee		175.00
		$1,688.75

In addition to the one-time installation costs, service costs will affect our budget. Operating costs will decrease if this proposal is implemented. Two reasons for the decrease are the longer life and the lower energy consumption of HPS lamps. Mercury vapor lamps have an average rated life of 18,000–24,000 hours (Kaufman 8–102), while HPS lamps are likely to be good for 24,000 hours or more (Sorcar 57). In addition, Edison Electric experts suggest that we will see an 8–10% reduction in energy use with the HPS lamps, even taking into account the increased wattage (Smith).

CONCLUSION

If Eastbrook's exterior lighting is not improved, future problems are likely to occur. We might face a decrease in the number of customers willing to shop with us during the evening and an increase in our insurance rates as a result of liability suits. This proposal is a corrective as well as preventive measure that increases the safety level for everyone on the property at night. Eastbrook will benefit from a stable environment both night and day.

We recommend that $1,688.75 be allocated in this quarter's operating budget for the installation of five new 40-foot metal light poles and six new wall-mount fixtures along with the replacement of all 150-watt mercury vapor bulbs with 400-watt HPS lamps. These changes will enhance our security and our image at a reasonable cost.

Figure 14.3 Formal Proposal, cont.

GLOSSARY

bulb   A synthetic light source operated with electricity.

footcandle   A unit of illuminance.

footcandle meter   A meter that indicates the amount of light one candle will produce in one foot of space.

HPS   high-pressure sodium. A bulb whose light is derived mainly from sodium vapor.

IES   Illuminating Engineering Society of North America, a professional organization founded in 1906 and dedicated to the theory and practice of illuminating engineering.

lamp   A synthetic light source operated with electricity.

mercury vapor   A bulb whose "light is mainly produced by radiation from mercury vapor" (Sorcar 333).

Figure 14.3 Formal Proposal, cont.

WORKS CITED

Abbott, Marvin, Chief of Security, Golden Crossing Mall. Personal Interview. 5 Nov. 20—.

Kaufman, John E. *IES Lighting Handbook: The Standard Lighting Guide.* 5th ed. New York: The

Illuminating Engineering Society, 1972. Print.

Rea, Mark S., ed. *IESNA Lighting Handbook: Reference and Applications.* New York: Illuminating

Engineering Society of North America, 2000, Print.

Smith, Jason, Chief Engineer, Edison Electric. Personal Interview. 1 Nov. 20—.

Sorcar, Prafulla C. *Energy Saving Lighting Systems.* New York: Van Norstrand Reinhold, 1982. Print.

Figure 14.3 Formal Proposal, cont.

APPENDIX A
Police Security Ranking for
Shopping Centers and Malls

Metropolitan Police Quarterly Report
June 20— Security Ranking—Shopping Centers and Malls

1 = Most Secure Environment   5 = Least Secure Environment

Rankings are based on a formula including reported incidents, severity of crime, victims, and cost.

Monrovian Heights	1	Wrightly Way Mall	3
Riggan's Place	1	Anandana Plaza	3
Crossroads Mall	2	Caruso's Crossing	4
South Dunbury Center	2	Eastbrook Shopping Center	4
Newtown Shopping Center	2	Benton Shopping Center	5
Village Mall	2	Bargain Hunter's Way	5

Figure 14.3 Formal Proposal, cont.

CLOSE

Summary

Use the summary to review key elements of the chapter. Also offer students an opportunity to ask questions to clear up any confusion they may have.

CLOSE

Checklist

Encourage students to use the checklist for editing and revising as well as for reviewing chapter information.

REVIEW

For a review of the key terms in the chapter, provide students with the *Key Terms* worksheet available as a supplemental activity on the IRCD.

CHAPTER 14
REVIEW

SUMMARY

1. Proposals are persuasive documents that suggest a solution to a problem or a change.

2. Proposals are defined and categorized according to the audience and their needs: internal or external; informal or formal; solicited or unsolicited; sales, research, planning, or grant.

3. Proposals are in memo, letter, or manuscript format, the choice determined by the audience and the complexity of the proposal.

4. The introduction identifies the problem and offers a solution, along with any background information the audience might find helpful. The body uses facts, figures, statistics, graphics, and other evidence to convince readers to accept the solution or change. The conclusion restates key points and calls on the audience to take action.

5. Formal proposals contain many special parts that have unique formatting guidelines. These parts may include a letter or memo of transmittal, a title page, a table of contents, a list of illustrations, an executive summary (or abstract), an introduction, a body (or discussion), a conclusion (or summary), a glossary, appendixes, and a works cited section or bibliography.

Checklist

- Have I identified the problem I want to see resolved?

- Have I analyzed my audience and then listed the audience's needs?

- Have I brainstormed alternate solutions? Have I listed positives and negatives for each solution on my list?

- Have I thought about and listed my goals?

- Have I explained the problem clearly in the introduction?

- Does the body give readers enough information to make a decision?

- Have I provided enough evidence, such as facts, figures, and testimony?

- Does my conclusion contain the most important ideas from the proposal? Does it call for action from the readers?

- Have I made information easy to use with headings and subheadings?

- If I am writing a formal proposal, have I included all of the parts that are needed?

Build Your Foundation

1. Interview an employee about a particular problem as well as the solution for which he or she was responsible. Write a description of the problem, the methods the employee used to solve the problem, the effectiveness of the solution, and the employee's (and employer's) satisfaction with the work.

2. Use library research to learn more about a great problem solver or innovator (for example, Thomas Edison, Mother Theresa, Albert Einstein, Eleanor Roosevelt, or Jonas Salk). Find out as much as you can about the methods the person used in seeking solutions. Give an oral presentation of your findings to your class.

3. Interview a proposal writer to find out how his or her company uses formal proposals, who else in the writer's organization writes proposals, and how successful the proposals have been. Ask what this writer thinks is essential in preparing an effective formal proposal.

4. Use the Internet, regional or state newspapers, or professional journals to search for requests for proposals.

   a. Copy the RFPs and bring them to class for discussion.
   b. From a careful reading of one RFP, identify the problem or need.
   c. Identify the audience the proposal writer needs to address.
   d. Brainstorm a list of ideas to include in the proposal's introduction.

5. Prepare a list of glossary terms for the RFP you read in item 4. If the RFP has a glossary, evaluate it for completeness. Identify any terms the writer omitted that are unfamiliar to you. Research and define the terms.

6. Choose two problems for which you would consider proposing a solution. Write one or two paragraphs describing the problem and the decision maker (audience) for each problem.

7. For item 6, list possible solutions to each problem or need you identified.

8. Using a problem whose solution has already been implemented, re-create the thinking process that the proposal writers might have used by:

   a. Developing a list of positive and negative aspects of the solution.
   b. Creating a list showing how the solution meets the needs of the audience or solves the problem.

9. Read or listen to the international news for one week. Pick an issue and write a statement of the problem. Brainstorm at least four solutions and list the positives and negatives of the two most realistic solutions.

10. Critique a proposal from business or industry. Analyze how the writers met (or did not meet) the needs of the audience. Review the proposal's formatting features. Determine its organizational patterns. Share the results of your critique orally or in an essay.

11. Have you heard the saying "Every problem used to be a solution"? Everyone involved in the U.S. health care debate acknowledges that the current employer-based insurance system has its problems. Research the origins of the current system and put yourself in the shoes of those decision makers from long ago. Use your imagination to list several alternatives they may have brainstormed. Then make a list of what you think they considered to be the positives and negatives of the system

Build Your Foundation

1. The process students write about in their descriptions will help them as they learn more about proposals.
2. Students learn about the many different ways problems can be solved.
3. Students see how proposals are used in a work setting.
4. Answers will vary depending on the RFPs students find. This step-by-step approach should help students see the connection between the RFP (the statement of the problem as perceived by the audience) and the solution the proposal suggests.
5–11. These activities help students prepare for writing proposals on their own. Answers will vary.

ASSESS

Your Turn

12. Refer students to the chapter checklist as well as the problem-solving strategies found in "Getting Started on Proposals."

13. Although responses will vary, students should be aware that item a is the solution and item b is the methodology (or the type of information that appears in the body of a proposal). Also, this activity helps students realize the importance of audience analysis, especially because they will be working with an audience with which they are familiar.

14. With students working as a class or in small groups, identify a problem. Ask each group of students to prepare a proposal offering the decision maker the best solution(s). Remind students to assign responsibilities for researching, identifying and analyzing audience, creating graphics, writing and revising, and editing. This group activity will result in a variety of experiences and learning opportunities. You can serve as group leader, or a student can be elected to manage the project.

15. Tell students to refer to the checklist in this chapter. One possible response is available as a teaching master on the IRCD.

they eventually chose. Make sure you analyze the situation from the earlier point of view, when the current employer-based health insurance system was selected as the best choice.

Your Turn

12. Write a proposal convincing your parents or guardians to take you (or to allow you to go with friends) on the vacation of your dreams. Identify the problem, explain the solution, convince them of the reasonableness of your plan, and justify the cost by preparing a budget.

13. Imagine that you asked your parents or guardians for a car. They said, "Yes, but. . . ." Your responsibility will be to pay for insurance, gas, and maintenance if they buy this car for you. In an informal proposal:

a. Explain the type of car you want and why you want it.
b. Describe how you will pay for the car's expenses if you do not have money and your parents or guardians do not want you to work more than ten hours a week, as would be required at a restaurant, grocery store, or department store. Identify your problem and consider alternative solutions. Be creative. Think of ways you can earn money other than by holding a regular job. List as many options as you can.
c. Write the solution you would propose to your parents or guardians.

14. With a group of classmates who share your interests, write a formal proposal to solve a specific problem. Identify a problem at school, at work, or in the community that must be dealt with by decision makers distant from you on the organizational ladder (for example, a superintendent, president, dean, or member of the board of trustees). Your proposal should require some research. Your internal formal proposal should include the following:

a. Transmittal letter or memorandum
b. Executive summary
c. Introduction
d. Body, including sufficient details for an informed decision, timeline or schedule, appropriate visuals, and a budget if costs are involved
e. Conclusion, including a specific call to action

Here are examples of problems to solve.

School	Work	Community
new or improved equipment	equipment or work space	sidewalks and bike paths
access to the computer lab	wages or department budget	zoning or use of land
snack bar	improved working conditions	street/traffic signs
new club or sport	sponsorship of team sports	access for people with disabilities to neighborhood stores
needed programs	insurance and benefits	street and park lighting

15. Write an informal sales proposal to Karyn Grissom, owner of Mason Office Center. As owner of Green Thumb Planting, an indoor plant service, you are asking Ms. Grissom to become a new client. After visiting the office complex, you determine that the building could use 31 large and 14 medium-sized low-light plants. Your service provides plants and

pots, weekly maintenance, and monthly replacement of sickly plants. If Ms. Grissom accepts your proposal, you can install the plantings within one week. For your service, she will pay a $350 installation fee and a $35 maintenance fee each month thereafter. Your proposal should persuade her to sign a service contract. Create and use any additional details or graphics you need to prepare an effective document.

Community Connection

ASSESS

Community Connection

16–19. These assignments provide students the opportunity to fine-tune their understanding of proposal development and to practice their skills.

16. Visit a nonprofit organization in your community to learn about the procedures and processes used there. Explain to your contact at the nonprofit that you are studying proposals for this class and ask if he or she can help you practice some of the prewriting steps for a proposal. Ask your contact to select an issue that he or she would like to apply for grant money to solve. Following the process that Chaya Sotelo used to prepare her proposal, starting on page 336, do the following:

   a. List the goals for the proposal (the things the organization would like to have happen as a result of getting the grant).
   b. Brainstorm different ways to meet these goals.
   c. Analyze each possible solution by listing its positives and negatives.

   Offer to share your document with the organization and make sure you thank everyone with whom you worked for his or her time—while you are there and afterwards—by sending a written thank-you note.

17. Identify a local government agency whose work involves proposals. For example, your town or city government's Public Works Department might publish RFPs or RFBs (requests for bids) seeking proposals or bids for pending construction projects. Or the Health Department might issue RFPs to select the best contractor for providing substance abuse counseling in the community. Ask for copies of RFPs and, if possible, interview the writer(s).

   a. Write a brief narrative after your interview with the RFP writer(s) to explain to your instructor and classmates how the professional(s) develop RFPs. Explain who contributes information and how the final document is approved for publication.
   b. Share the RFPs with your class. Use them to identify criteria requested by the issuing agency in the proposal. In other words, what factors does the agency want to see covered in the proposals to solve the problem or fill the need?

18. Schedule an appointment to meet with a professional grant writer, perhaps at school or at a local nonprofit organization. Ask for permission to review a recently funded or approved grant. Using the guidelines in this chapter, explain in a brief essay the factors that led to the grant's success.

19. In teams of three to five class members, identify a local organization that could have a stronger presence on your campus. Perhaps a local ice cream shop could open a kiosk. Or a smoking cessation group might run a semester-long program. Develop a proposal addressed to the appropriate decision maker at your school in which you attempt to persuade him or her to approve your plan. Remember to analyze your audience carefully, considering any reservations or negative history he or she might have regarding the plan.

Chapter 15

Ethics in the Workplace

Goals

- Explain what it means to act ethically
- Describe a culture of ethics
- Develop a plan for resolving an ethical dilemma
- Understand the barriers to ethical behavior

Terms

- code of ethics, p. 369
- corporate code of ethics, p. 369
- dignity, p. 375
- ethics, p. 365
- personal code of ethics, p. 370
- principles, p. 365
- rights, p. 375
- utility, p. 375
- values, p. 365
- whistle-blower, p. 377

WRITE TO LEARN

Think of someone you admire and respect, someone you want to be like—a parent, friend, teacher, or political or entertainment figure. What, in particular, has this person done to earn your respect? If you were to ask this person what values—for example, honesty, hard work, and courage—are important, what would he or she say? Write a journal entry describing this person and naming some of his or her accomplishments. Summarize by identifying which values are important to this individual.

Focus on the Ethics in the Workplace

Read the ethical principles on the next page and answer these questions:

- Why does the Society for Technical Communication (STC) list the six core values in this order?
- What are five things technical communicators can do to practice honesty?
- How can technical communicators maintain professionalism?
- Why do the principles include confidentiality?

What If?

- The principles were being explained to students considering a career as a technical communicator?
- Technical communicators needed STC guidelines for writing blogs and text for web pages?
- A banking or finance industry wanted to use similar principles?

Ethical Principles for Technical Communicators

As technical communicators, we observe the following ethical principles in our professional activities.

Legality
We observe the laws and regulations governing our profession. We meet the terms of contracts we undertake. We ensure that all terms are consistent with laws and regulations locally and globally, as applicable, and with STC ethical principles.

Honesty
We seek to promote the public good in our activities. To the best of our ability, we provide truthful and accurate communications. We also dedicate ourselves to conciseness, clarity, coherence, and creativity, striving to meet the needs of those who use our products and services. We alert our clients and employers when we believe that material is ambiguous. Before using another person's work, we obtain permission. We attribute authorship of material and ideas only to those who make an original and substantive contribution. We do not perform work outside our job scope during hours compensated by clients or employers, except with their permission; nor do we use their facilities, equipment, or supplies without their approval. When we advertise our services, we do so truthfully.

Confidentiality
We respect the confidentiality of our clients, employers, and professional organizations. We disclose business-sensitive information only with their consent or when legally required to do so. We obtain releases from clients and employers before including any business-sensitive materials in our portfolios or commercial demonstrations or before using such materials for another client or employer.

Quality
We endeavor to produce excellence in our communication products. We negotiate realistic agreements with clients and employers on schedules, budgets, and deliverables during project planning. Then we strive to fulfill our obligations in a timely, responsible manner.

Fairness
We respect cultural variety and other aspects of diversity in our clients, employers, development teams, and audiences. We serve the business interests of our clients and employers as long as they are consistent with the public good. Whenever possible, we avoid conflicts of interest in fulfilling our professional responsibilities and activities. If we discern a conflict of interests, we disclose it to those concerned and obtain their approval before proceeding.

Professionalism
We evaluate communication products and services constructively and tactfully, and seek definitive assessments of our own professional performance. We advance technical communication through our integrity and excellence in performing each task we undertake. Additionally, we assist other persons in our profession through mentoring, networking, and instruction. We also pursue professional self-improvement, especially through courses and conferences.

Adopted by the STC Board of Directors
September, 1998

Ethical Principles for Technical Communicators
Reprinted with permission of STC

FOCUS
Focus on Ethics in the Workplace
Use the questions to encourage students to read the sample closely.

ASSESS
What If?
Use the questions to discuss how the sample would be different if the situation or audience changed.

Go to www.cengage.com/bcomm/school/techwtg for more detailed responses to these questions.

Courtesy of Rick Leuner

Writing@Work

Transportation, Distribution & Logistics

Rick Leuner is a sales associate for NAI Realvest, a commercial real estate brokerage firm in Orlando, Florida. He helps companies find and purchase or lease large facilities to serve as offices, stores, and warehouses. He also looks for buyers or lessees for commercial spaces that are being built or have been vacated in his territory.

In general, Rick is bound by real estate ethics codes implemented at local, state, and national levels. "Members of the National Association of Realtors (NAR) are required to periodically pass a test on the NAR Code of Ethics, a document that spells out the ethical practices one must use with other realtors, clients, and the public. I also follow regulations and legal requirements set by Florida state regulators. These rules have the force of law for any person practicing real estate in Florida."

In Rick's field—and many others—ethical behavior draws more business opportunities. Therefore, it is beneficial to observe proper business decorum. "Our industry relies greatly on networking with fellow professionals to close deals. Referrals are an important source of business, and brokers frequently refer clients to their most respected colleagues when they know that all parties will benefit. This process of referral creates a web of goodwill between peers and encourages brokers to earn a positive reputation and share their business in the future."

In addition to helping his colleagues, Rick protects his clients' confidential information. "I need to understand their detailed business requirements to provide the best real estate service and advice," explains Rick. "Businesspeople do not readily reveal this proprietary information to outsiders, so I must earn my clients' trust and respect their desire for confidentiality. Whether this is guaranteed through nondisclosure agreements or with a handshake, the promise is the foundation for a respectful, successful business relationship."

Think Critically

1. In Rick's field, why does ethical behavior draw more business opportunities?

2. Think about two career fields with which you are familiar. Is networking as important in these fields as it is in commercial real estate? What are some of the confidentiality issues in these fields?

Printed with permission of Rick Leuner

WHAT IS ETHICS?

The principles and values that help people resolve questions of right and wrong make up their **ethics.** A system of ethics, or morality, is based on **values,** the ideals that govern a person's actions. Many people have similar values—believing in honesty, justice, hard work, and equality, for example. Values help people set rules, or **principles,** to guide their behavior. When you make a decision to return a $10 bill to a stranger who unknowingly dropped it, you are making an ethical decision. Your honesty motivates you to return the money to its owner rather than keep it for yourself.

People's ethics come initially from their families and culture, where they may have learned the Golden Rule: Do unto others as you would have them do unto you. Also, the world's great religions contain moral systems of conduct by which people are encouraged to live: do not kill, do not steal, and do not lie. As people mature, many of them reassess the moral code passed down to them, revising it according to their experiences. For example, a youngster taught not to kill may reassess that lesson if, as a young adult, this person is asked to defend his or her country.

Benefits of Ethical Decisions

Living ethically allows people to reap the consequences of their behavior—such as gaining the respect of others and having access to the privileges of society. Responsible and ethical people get to vote, borrow money, serve in public office, and travel freely. Acting ethically:

- Helps a person live amicably and responsibly with other human beings.

- Keeps an individual's conscience clear and provides peace of mind.

- Defines a person's character, showing what kind of person he or she is.

Mitch is a pharmacy technician at Fullterton's. As he was organizing prescriptions for pickup, he saw one for Antabuse, a medication that helps alcoholics control the compulsion to drink. The prescription was for the high school principal, who suspended Mitch several years ago when, according to Mitch, he did not deserve it. Mitch is tempted to tell his wife about the prescription. He knows she can keep a secret.

Mitch decided not to say anything to his wife that evening. And coincidentally, the next day he happened to run into the principal. Although Mitch felt somewhat self-conscious, he greeted the man with a clear conscience. That afternoon Mitch went to work, feeling good about himself. He was not the type of person who had to spread a juicy story to get attention from others.

Warm Up

What kinds of quick ethical decisions must you make as you go through your day?

Photographer's Choice/Getty Images

Diego Cervo, 2009/Used under license from Shutterstock.com

Consequences of Unethical Behavior

When people do not behave ethically, they are subject to the pitfalls that are the result of their poor judgment—possible convictions, questionable reputations, and guilt. Unethical behavior affects not only an individual personally, but also family members and members of society who must deal with the consequences.

At work one afternoon, Mitch thought through the consequences of telling his wife about the principal's prescription. First, he liked his job and knew he could be fired for a breach of confidentiality. Second, he considered the consequences if prescriptions of other customers were revealed. Mitch's sister, who takes an antidepressant, would be terribly embarrassed if anyone except her family knew. Third, he realized his motive—revenge against someone he thought had done him an injustice—was immature. If only more people like Mitch would stop to think through the consequences of their actions and examine their motives!

In the highly publicized 2001 Enron scandal, investors lost huge sums of money, thousands of workers lost their jobs and retirement money, the former chief financial officer Andrew Fastow faced a prison sentence, and the public lost confidence in big business. What was the motive for falsifying financial records on such a large scale? In retrospect, what would the leaders of Enron say now that they have seen the full consequences of their actions?

Like Mitch, everyone faces the temptation to do wrong, to take the easy way out, or to give in to a malicious impulse. Unlike Mitch, not everyone takes the time to reason through the implications of a choice. The Enron incident illustrates that consequences of unethical behavior can be far reaching and long lasting. The recent economic downturn of 2009 was due in large part to the practice of some financial institutions loaning money for overvalued houses to people who could not repay the loans and to consumers who lived beyond their means. The consequences of those choices will affect people's lives for years to come.

 STOP AND THINK

Define *ethics*. What are the benefits of living an ethical life? What are the consequences of making poor ethical decisions?

CREATING A CULTURE OF ETHICS

The Ethical Resource Center's 2007 *National Business Ethics Survey* provides some disturbing news. Over half of the employees questioned saw someone involved in an ethical violation, and most hesitated to report a violation because of fear of reprisals (Harned).

To encourage their employees to act ethically, companies can create a culture of ethics, a climate that supports integrity, mutual respect, and fair-mindedness. In such a climate, everyone knows that values matter. To create such an ethical culture, leaders must set the example and actively promote ethical behavior.

Ethical Leaders

In 1982, when Tylenol represented 15 percent of Johnson & Johnson's profits, someone found a way to lace Tylenol with cyanide. As a result of the tampering, seven people died. Even though the company did not cause the deaths, the public stopped purchasing Tylenol. As a result, Johnson & Johnson's market share lost $1 billion (Baker).

In 1986, Johnson & Johnson faced a similar threat of tampering. This time the company wasted no time in removing Tylenol from store shelves. The company decided not to make Tylenol available to consumers until it solved the packaging problem by producing a tamper-free cap. As a result, the public learned it that could trust Johnson & Johnson to do the right thing. Within five months, the company had recovered most of its market share.

Johnson & Johnson is a good example of a company that acted ethically. One reason the company quickly chose to do what was best for its customers was its culture of ethics. When the question was posed—Do we recall our product?—there was no doubt the recall was the right thing to do. On the next page, Figure 15.1 shows Johnson & Johnson's Credo of Values. Written in 1943, it made a commitment to the company's customers. Chairman James Burke's leadership during the Tylenol crisis reestablished that commitment.

The experience at Johnson & Johnson underscores one of the principal findings of the Ethics Resource Center's 2000 *National Business Ethics Survey*: Leaders who model positive ethical behavior affect the ethical climates of the institutions they run. Managers, supervisors, and coworkers who set good examples mean that other employees are more likely to make appropriate moral choices. Employees who perceive their leaders as moral beings:

- Feel less pressure to compromise ethical standards.

- Observe less misconduct on the job.

- Are more satisfied with their organization overall.

- Feel more valued as employees.

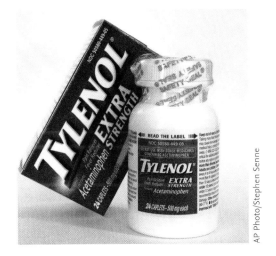

AP Photo/Stephen Senne

Warm Up

Name an organization to which you belong—a club, your family, or a religious institution—that upholds strong ethical principles. What are those principles? How do you feel when you participate in this organization?

FOCUS

Warm Up

Give students a chance to talk about organizations such as Boy Scouts and Girl Scouts, youth groups, and ROTC that have strong ethical creeds that value honesty, courage, and equality, among others.

Ask students to describe a culture of ethics. People feel respected. They are free to tell the truth and admit mistakes, proud to work in the environment, and not worried about management hiding things or twisting facts.

ENRICH

Ask students what products they or their family members use that Johnson & Johnson makes. A few include Acuvue® contact lenses, Listerine®, Neutrogena®, Splenda®, baby lotions and powders, Rolaids®, Sudafed®, and Benadryl®.

TEACH

Point out the importance of ethical leaders who set an example for their companies to follow.

For more information on the Tylenol crisis, go to www.cengage.com/school/bcomm/techwtg. Click the link for Chapter 15; then click Web Links.

Our Credo

We believe our first responsibility is to the doctors, nurses and patients,
to mothers and fathers and all others who use our products and services.
In meeting their needs everything we do must be of high quality.
We must constantly strive to reduce our costs
in order to maintain reasonable prices.
Customers' orders must be serviced promptly and accurately.
Our suppliers and distributors must have an opportunity
to make a fair profit.

We are responsible to our employees,
the men and women who work with us throughout the world.
Everyone must be considered as an individual.
We must respect their dignity and recognize their merit.
They must have a sense of security in their jobs.
Compensation must be fair and adequate,
and working conditions clean, orderly and safe.
We must be mindful of ways to help our employees fulfill
their family responsibilities.
Employees must feel free to make suggestions and complaints.
There must be equal opportunity for employment, development
and advancement for those qualified.
We must provide competent management,
and their actions must be just and ethical.

We are responsible to the communities in which we live and work
and to the world community as well.
We must be good citizens—support good works and charities
and bear our fair share of taxes.
We must encourage civic improvements and better health and education.
We must maintain in good order
the property we are privileged to use,
protecting the environment and natural resources.

Our final responsibility is to our stockholders.
Business must make a sound profit.
We must experiment with new ideas.
Research must be carried on, innovative problems developed
and mistakes paid for.
New equipment must be purchased, new facilities provided
and new products launched.
Reserves must be created to provide for adverse times.
When we operate according to these principles,
the stockholders should realize a fair return.

Figure 15.1 Johnson & Johnson's Credo of Values
Reprinted with permission of Johnson & Johnson

FOCUS

Figure 15.1

Try this activity with Johnson & Johnson's Credo. Ask students to read it to themselves and pick out one or two phrases they like. When you give the go ahead, ask students to simultaneously repeat the phrase three times with meaning. Then ask a few students to tell why they like the phrase or phrases they chose.

Digital Vision/Getty Images

Culture of Ethics

Responsible leadership sets the stage for a creating a culture of ethics in the workplace. To create an ethical climate at work, one that fosters responsible behavior from employees and their leaders, the Ethics Resource Center encourages companies to hire ethics officers and set up ethical oversight committees. In addition, companies should commit publicly to ethical behavior. Leaders should evaluate and reward employees' ethical conduct, keep communication lines open, and—and most importantly—"walk the talk." A good place to begin is with a published **code of ethics,** a written pledge to make responsible, moral decisions.

A **corporate code of ethics** states a company's commitment to ethical behavior. Generally, organizational codes express similar core values that are important to the company's operation—integrity, fairness, and respect for others. Most corporate codes also include rules that are specific to their discipline (for example, checking and double-checking sources in news reporting and maintaining confidentiality in counseling).

A corporate code aims to protect the public rather than the members of the organization. Ideally, the code is enforceable and includes penalties— reprimands, probation, termination, legal action, or extended leave without pay. For instance, a doctor who harms patients not only can be prosecuted, but also can lose his or her license to practice.

Writing a Code of Ethics

In companies for which no code of ethics exists, you may be asked to help write one. Or you may start your own business, one that could benefit from a written code. Writing a code of ethics requires you to think about your personal values and to reflect on the values you want your employees to exhibit.

TEACH
Remind students of the various ways companies can create a culture of ethics—having an ethics officer and/or ethics committee, publishing a code of ethics, and "walking the talk."

ENRICH
You can review the Enron scandal at www.chron.com/news/specials/enron. You will find Enron's Code of Ethics at www.thesmokinggun.com/enron/enronethics1.html. The introductory memo on page 2 shows that Ken Lay signed off on the code of ethics, but just because a company has a code does not mean it is followed.

If you have written a personal code of ethics, share it with your students. If not, consider writing one—together with the students—and sharing it. You could explain the thought process you used to come up with ideas. You are then taking part in the assignment, and students will be motivated by your efforts.

FOCUS

Figure 15.2

Ask someone to read the Personal Philosophy aloud. Ask students what is important to this nurse.

ENRICH

Talk about different periods of history and how each generation's values are influenced by the times: Depression era children who dealt with poverty tend to be thrifty. WWII children lived with uncertainty and worried about loved ones in danger; they value financial security. Children from the sixties may have been affluent and lived with the threat of nuclear war and Vietnam; they live for today and tend to be idealistic. Ask students to look up these generations to see what influenced them: builders, boomers, Gen Xers, and Millennials.

To raise your awareness of your personal code of ethics, complete the *Code of Ethics Inventory* worksheet available at www.cengage.com/school/bcomm/techwtg. Click the link for Chapter 15.

Personal Code

The process begins with your **personal code of ethics**, a statement of your values and standards. You can begin by taking a hard look at your own sense of values and ethical conduct.

Consider writing a personal creed or personal philosophy, as one nurse did in Figure 15.2. A presenter at a workshop asked participants to pretend they were flies on the wall at their own wake or funeral, listening to the stories people told about them after they had passed away.[1] What were they hoping to hear? After reflecting on this question, the nurse wrote down ideas that eventually made their way into this code. His code hangs on his office wall so he can refer to it when he has a difficult decision to make.

You might begin a similar process of writing a creed that expresses your core values and conveys what is important to you. Find a quiet place where you can think without interruption and consider these questions:

- **What are your core values?** List values that are important to you, such as compassion, courage, and honor. Narrow your list to between three and five items that really speak to you.

- **What are you passionate about?** Think about your career goals or your hobbies. What do they tell you about your life's purpose or direction? For example, if you like taking care of animals, perhaps you see yourself working as a zoologist or a veterinarian.

- **What lessons have you learned?** What lessons have you learned from the situations you have encountered? If you have recovered from a serious illness or accident, you may now appreciate the importance of family or of finding beauty in each day.

Personal Philosophy

I am here to help others. So important is this belief to me that I became a nurse—to help others heal so they can live healthy, productive, and happy lives. While I will use my skills and knowledge to promote good health practices, I accept that death comes to all. When the time comes, I will respect my patients' last wishes and let go, honored to be witness to this sacred passage.

"To be rather than to seem" sums up my approach to life. I will stay true to myself and not obsess over what others think.

I will adapt to changing circumstances, but will not sacrifice my integrity. I value truth, even when it is unpleasant.

I consciously and willfully choose to see the good in people and circumstances. "People, not things" is my motto. The pursuit of things will never come at the expense of people.

I will remember the wisdom of my grandmother whose 97 years were a testament to common sense, resourcefulness, simple values, and fundamental decency.

Figure 15.2 Personal Code of Ethics

[1]See Stephen Covey's *The 7 Habits of Highly Effective People* for similar exercises and other aids to writing personal mission statements.

Now that you have some ideas for your personal code, organize those ideas and express them in complete sentences. Choose a title; then put the draft aside. Come back a few days later to revise and finalize your draft. When you are finished, you may want to frame it and keep it close at hand. From time to time, you can revise it as circumstances influence your values.

Corporate Code

A corporate code is likely to be a collaborative effort involving several team members. The following suggestions may help you come up with ideas for your code:

- **What are the company's values?** Start with a discussion of personal values. If your team members have written personal codes, share them. Look for similarities in your values. Brainstorm values that are important to your organization. Look for overlapping personal and corporate values to see which ones are most critical.

- **What kinds of ethical conflicts are typical of your organization?** You want statements that deal with the underlying ethics behind those conflicts. Do the conflicts revolve around personnel problems, pay issues, discrimination, customer fairness, plagiarism, or malpractice? What ethics underlie those issues—fairness, equality, honesty? In other words, when an ethical dilemma arises, what values drive the resolution of the conflicts?

- **How does the company want to treat others—its employees as well as its customers or clients?** Consider asking for feedback from members of your organization—members other than the writing team. Perhaps you can conduct a focus group, a small meeting in which members respond to prompts and someone in the meeting writes down the comments. Now might be a good time to review the codes of other companies in your field to see how they are organized.

After putting your ideas together, rank your information in order of importance to your organization, employees, and clients. Ask one person in the group to write a draft of a code based on the input thus far. The group can read the draft and make suggestions. After putting the code aside for a while, come back to it for final revising and editing. Ask for approval from the governing body of the organization before you publish the code.

When the company's philosophy is written down where employees can easily see it, it becomes more real. In times of crisis, the words can inspire and guide employees' decision-making processes.

Some corporate codes are long and include sections such as a Preamble, Responsibilities, and Consequences. Some are short, such as the Ethical Principles for Technical Communicators on page 363 and the Firefighter Code of Ethics in Figure 15.3 on the next page. Notice how the Firefighter Code addresses the specific concerns of the firefighter: "to safeguard . . . life and property against the elements of fire and disaster . . . and maintain proficiency in the art and science of fire engineering."

TEACH

Point out that writing a corporate code of ethics is similar to writing a personal code. However, the writing is usually a collaborative effort and is tailored to the needs of the organization.

FOCUS

Figure 15.3

Ask students if any of them have family members who are firefighters or emergency personnel. If so, ask him or her to read the Firefighter Code aloud.

ASSESS

Stop and Think

A culture of ethics is created by modeling ethical behavior, hiring ethics officers, taking advantage of ethics committees, writing and publishing a code, and rewarding ethical behavior. Johnson & Johnson's story is one of a big company doing the right thing despite suffering a huge financial loss. Writing a personal code begins in a quiet place to reflect on one's values, decisions, and goals. An organizational code begins by exploring the company's values, looking at behavior specific to the field, collaborating with other employees, and taking notes.

FOCUS

Warm Up

Ask students to write the answer to this question before you ask a few volunteers to share theirs. You might share a dilemma you faced and tell what you did, why you did it, and what the outcome was.

Warm Up

Think of the most difficult ethical decision you ever made. What standards did you use to make your decision? Are you happy with the choice you made? Would you do something different today? Explain.

Code of Ethics

As a firefighter and member of the International Association of Fire Fighters, my fundamental duty is to serve humanity; to safeguard and preserve life and property against the elements of fire and disaster; and maintain a proficiency in the art and science of fire engineering.

I will uphold the standards of my profession, continually search for new and improved methods and disseminate and share my knowledge and skills with my contemporaries and descendants.

I will never allow personal feelings, nor danger to self to deter me from my responsibilities as a firefighter.

I will at all times, respect the property and rights of all men, the laws of my community and my country, and the chosen way of life of my fellow citizens.

I recognize the badge of my office as a symbol of public faith, and I accept it as a public trust to be held so long as I am true to the ethics of the fire service. I will constantly strive to achieve these objectives and ideals, dedicating myself before God to my chosen profession—saving of life, fire prevention and fire suppression.

As a member of the International Association of Fire Fighters, I accept this self-imposed and self-enforced obligation as my responsibility.

Figure 15.3 Firefighter Code of Ethics
Reprinted with permission of IAFF

 STOP AND THINK

What are some ways to create a culture of ethics? Tell the story of Johnson & Johnson and the Tylenol scare. How might you get started on a personal code of ethics? How might you get started on a corporate code of ethics?

WHAT DO YOU DO WHEN FACED WITH AN ETHICAL DILEMMA?

The best approach is to prevent an ethical conflict in the first place by acting above board, talking about decisions with people you trust, following your personal values, and knowing and following the values held by your company. Sometimes the first indication that you are facing an ethical dilemma is a feeling of discomfort. Self-reflection may help clarify your feelings. More analysis may be required when you are not sure what to do.

Clarify Your Position

You may need to clarify your position before you decide whether you have an ethical dilemma and what, if anything, you should do about it. On the following page, read about the dilemma Pilar faced at work.

Pilar's manager has asked her not to report the latest investment totals until next month, after the auditors have left. But Pilar knows that the company is legally bound to report them by the 25th of each month. She could wait, as her supervisor requested, but reporting the figures late would not be legal. She feels conflicted. After all, her supervisor hired her and even covered for her when her child was in the hospital last month. Pilar values loyalty, yet she also values honesty and a work ethic of doing what she is supposed to do when she is supposed to do it. She has been at this job only a short time and is not sure what to do.

Pilar used the following questions to help clarify her position regarding the dilemma and to reach a solution.

Would my actions be legal? If you are not sure, ask a lawyer or read your company's code of ethics. If the answer is no, you risk engaging in unethical behavior.	Postponing the latest investment figures is clearly not legal, but Pilar wonders who would be responsible—she or her manager? Pilar is not sure how to handle the request, but she knows that breaking the law is not an option.
Have I thought through the possible consequences of my actions? If not, you need to think about where this action will lead and what will happen if you do nothing.	Pilar knows that failing to report the totals on time could cause her to lose her job if someone discovers what she did. There also is the problem of using the company as a reference for future jobs. And what would she say when asked why she left the company? To complicate things even more, there is a chance that she could be prosecuted. If she does nothing, her manager could still report the figures inaccurately. Pilar does not like the direction her thoughts are taking.
How uncomfortable am I? Will you be able to sleep tonight? How would you feel if the situation was published in the newspaper? If you cannot sleep and would be embarrassed if others knew, your action may be the wrong one.	Yes, Pilar is waking up in the middle of the night with her manager's request on her mind. Pilar pictures her coworkers in the lounge discussing her unflattering mug shot in the local newspaper. She shudders, feeling extremely uncomfortable.
What central conflict am I facing? Continue to think about your dilemma until it is clear to you which values are in conflict.	Pilar's central conflict is whether to be loyal to her manager or to do what she knows is right.
Is there an obvious solution? Sometimes human beings overcomplicate matters when there may be a simple and direct way to handle things.	After a few days of worrying, Pilar decides to tell her manager that she is not comfortable altering the dates on the report. Pilar points out the risk to both of them of not complying with the law. When Pilar finishes the conversation, she sees that her manager feels conflicted too. Together they figure out the best way to present the data and point out that next quarter's figures—after fall sales are in—are likely to be better. Pilar's solution actually improves her relationship with her manager.

Ethics in the Workplace | 373

Analyze Your Ethical Dilemma

Some situations may require more analysis—especially if a course of action does not present itself early in your thought process. Read Wilma Kwon's ethical dilemma and follow her line of thinking as she analyzes the dilemma and comes up with alternatives.

TEACH

Ask a student to read Wilma Kwon's dilemma aloud while the other students note what is important for her to consider.

Ask students to read the steps and Wilma's responses to them beginning on this page. Have students work in small groups to discuss Wilma's thinking process. Is there anything to add? Do students agree with her solution? Why or why not?

Apply the steps to this situation: Luisa overhears her boss talking about dumping some barrels of toxic waste into the creek behind the plant. Mercury is one of the contaminants that would be dumped.

> Wilma Kwon is chair of the selection committee for the position of vice president of production for Valli Shirt Factory. One applicant, 57-year-old David Zeltzer, has 23 years of experience, looks impressive on paper, has good references, and does well in the interview. When Wilma recommends him for the job, the president hesitates, wanting to hire a younger man instead—someone just out of college with no work experience. Wilma protests, but the president is firm. Wilma is angry. Her committee screened 32 applicants and conducted four interviews in good faith that the president would accept its recommendation. She found a good candidate. The president's decision looks like age discrimination to her. Wilma is worried about the legal ramifications if David decides to sue.

Take time to think about what is happening. You have heard it before: Count to 10. Do not react impulsively.	Wilma decides to take the weekend to think things over and to calm down.
Examine the facts. Ask questions. Play detective. Rumor, innuendo, and excessive drama are not the same as facts. What really has happened?	On Monday, Wilma reviews the selection committee's minutes and determines that her committee followed all company policies and broke no laws. She examines the company's records on hiring and finds a troubling trend toward hiring younger candidates over well-qualified older ones. She recalls her conversation with the president and takes some notes.
Clarify your short-term and long-term goals. Sometimes it is important to meet a short-term goal. However, after weighing the consequences of a short-term goal against a long-term goal, you may find that pursuing a long-term goal is a wiser, more stable option.	Wilma's short-term goal is to hire someone as quickly as possible. The company is going through some tough economic times and needs a person with experience and talent. Her long-term goal is to find someone who will bring innovation to the company so it is still thriving in 15 years.
Talk to someone you can trust. Maybe you can talk to an employee who has been with the firm a long time. Or you could talk to a friend, relative, minister, or counselor.	Wilma shares her concerns with a committee member who has been with the company since it began. He reminds Wilma that the founder of the company was an older gentleman and encourages her to keep looking for a solution. Wilma also consults the human resources director, who says to gather more evidence and see if she can convince the president to hire David.
Review your company's code of ethics. Sometimes a review of your company's code of ethics will provide the answer you seek.	Wilma reviews the company's creed and finds the statement: "Valli Shirt Factory is an equal opportunity employer committed to diversity." She is reminded of the importance of diversity—for herself as a woman, as well as for others.

Talk to legal counsel. It never hurts to find out just where you and the company stand legally.	Wilma talks to the company's lawyer, who says it is difficult to prove discrimination. But if the two candidates' qualifications are that different—and with a prior record of hiring younger employees over older ones—the company could have a problem proving that it did not discriminate.
Listen to your conscience. Review your personal code of ethics to tune in with your values. What does your inner voice tell you to do?	Wilma recalls the statement in her own code about having the courage to stand up for what is right. Wilma believes that David is the best candidate for the job, and she is not comfortable with any form of discrimination. She now feels compelled to speak out on his behalf.
Explore alternatives. Brainstorm alternatives. List the advantages and disadvantages of each.	Hiring the younger candidate would be the easiest thing to do now, but what happens to the company if he cannot perform the job successfully? In addition, if David decides to sue, a lawsuit would be stressful, time-consuming, and expensive. Trying to convince the president to hire David also would take time and might strain Wilma's relationship with him. On the other hand, if Wilma can convince him to hire David, the company could hire a good employee and avoid a lawsuit.
Choose an alternative. After weighing the pros and cons, it is time to act on the alternative that is both ethical and logical.	Wilma makes an appointment with the president to present her findings. She asks the human resources director to join them. If the president still insists on hiring the younger candidate, at least he will be aware of the consequences.

TEACH

Ask students to work with a partner to come up with situations that require people to think of rights, justice, utility, care, empathy, consistency, values and principles, universal consequences, and/or extenuating circumstances.

Ask students to pick out the three criteria they use most often when deciding how to handle an ethical dilemma. Which criteria do they not consider as often?

Choose a Responsible Course of Action

Over the centuries, philosophers and religious leaders have given advice on how to select a responsible course of action. The following criteria are often touted as a way to judge the "right" thing to do:

- **Rights:** Will my actions infringe on the **rights** (personal freedoms) and **dignity** (self-respect) of others? If I drink and drive, I am taking away someone else's right to drive on a safe roadway. If I neglect to wash my nursing home patient's hair, I am depriving her of her dignity.

- **Justice:** Are my actions just or fair? Are the good or bad consequences to be uniformly divided among all members of the group? Deciding that all of my employees except my friend Cecelia must work on a holiday does not provide justice for all. Equality is when the same opportunities and consequences apply to everyone.

- **Utility:** Will my actions affect most people in the best way possible? In other words, **utility** is based on what action will do the most good and the least harm. If I vote for a tax increase for the middle class and do not vote to tax the upper class proportionately, I may be voting to tax the group that is least able to bear the burden financially. This practice fails to affect most people in the best way possible.

Communication Dilemma

Nereza, a research assistant, taps lightly on her supervisor's door before walking into his office—as she has done many times before. Richard is sitting with a male employee. They are looking out the window and laughing. Richard calls Nereza over and makes a joke about Claire, an overweight coworker who is getting out of a car. Nereza says, "I like Claire. She does a good job. Besides, we all have our physical challenges" (as she looks at Richard's receding hairline). Nereza shoots Richard a "you should know better" look and leaves.

Think Critically

What do you think about Nereza's reaction?

- **Care:** Do my actions show that I care about and am considerate of others? If I have an opportunity to show care and compassion for the machinist on my staff whose house just burned down and I do not act, I have failed not only my employee, but also my community.

- **Empathy:** Do I have empathy for other people? Have I asked myself what it would feel like to be in another person's shoes? Before I decide whether to let an employee go because of poor sales or lay the person off, I could ask myself how I would like to be treated. I could give the person as much notice as possible, provide some kind of severance pay, or offer to rehire him or her when business improves.

- **Consistency:** Is my decision consistent with my other policies? If my policy is to allow makeup tests for students who have legitimate reasons to miss a test and I do not allow Nora to make up a presentation she missed, I am not being consistent.

- **Values and principles:** Is my action consistent with the values and principles I follow? If I value honesty but I do not let the grocer know that he undercharged me $15 for the steaks I ordered, I am not honoring my values of honesty and integrity.

  - **Universal consequences:** To envision universal consequences, think about what would happen if everyone did the same action. If everyone threw their soda cans onto the highway, what would happen?

  - **Extenuating circumstances:** Do extenuating circumstances need to be taken into account? My instructor does not accept late papers, but if I am in an accident on my way to class, perhaps she would change her rule based on my unusual circumstances.

With any ethical dilemma, after you have chosen an alternative, evaluate what you did. Do you need to change something? Would you do things differently the next time? Your reevaluation may cause you to adjust your behavior the next time you have a similar moral dilemma.

The Ethics Resource Center conducts independent research and publishes articles for institutions interested in maintaining high standards of ethics.

Go to the NET Bookmark for Chapter 15 and browse the Center's resources. Read one resource carefully and find three important pieces of information to share with your classmates.

www.cengage.com/school/bcomm/techwtg

AP Photo/Ron Edmonds

When Do You Blow the Whistle?

In 1994, Dr. Jeffrey Wigland, the former vice president of tobacco giant Brown & Williamson, appeared before Congress and the Food and Drug Administration. He testified that the corporation had strong evidence of the addictive nature of nicotine and had used additives to deliver the nicotine more readily. Dr. Wigland was fired in 1993 after questioning the use of one additive in particular. As a result, he suffered financial loss, death threats, divorce, and litigation. When asked if he wishes he had not blown the whistle, Dr. Wigland says, "I do think it's worth it. In the end, people see the truth."

A **whistle-blower** is a person who publicly alleges an organization's wrongful practices. Dr. Wigland is a good example, but there are many others—Enron's Sherron Watkins and Firestone's Thomas A. Robertson. As you can see from Dr. Wigland's example, whistle-blowing takes courage and conviction. And although some companies welcome reports of misdeeds so they can correct them, many want only to continue business as usual.

Laws have been enacted to protect whistle-blowers from retribution from their employers, but fighting for that protection can be a long, messy, and stressful process. Dr. Wigland was subjected to a smear campaign. Karen Silkwood, a chemical technician who was investigating safety violations at the power plant for which she worked, died under suspicious circumstances.

Whistle-blowing can be risky. However, consider the example of Firestone. The lives saved as a result of learning that Firestone tires were defective

ASSESS

Stop and Think

Questions for clarifying an ethical dilemma: Is the action legal? What are the consequences? How uncomfortable am I? What is the central conflict? Is there an obvious solution? Criteria for analyzing a dilemma: Think about what is happening, examine the facts, clarify your goals, talk to someone you can trust, review your company's code of ethics, talk to a lawyer, listen to your conscience, explore alternatives, and choose an alternative. You choose a responsible course of action by considering rights, justice, utility, care, empathy, consistency, values and principles, universal consequences, and extenuating circumstances.

Warm Up

Why do some people have a difficult time doing the right thing? What are the obstacles to making good ethical choices?

FOCUS

Warm Up

Introduce the barriers to ethical behavior. Possible answers: People do not want to get into trouble, they do not know what to do, they do not think through a situation, and they value loyalty to a person over loyalty to the right course of action.

TEACH

Point out the conditions under which illegal activities tend to occur.

benefits anyone who travels the roadways. How do you decide whether to blow the whistle? For most people, whistle-blowing is a matter of strong conscience, something to be used as a last resort.

If you are thinking about blowing the whistle on an organization, carefully consider the consequences. Try to find a way to work out your differences by talking to someone. If negotiation is not an option, most authorities suggest that you thoroughly document the infractions and keep your notes in a safe place. Maintain good relationships with as many people in the company as you can and talk over the situation with someone you trust. Most importantly, *seek the advice of an attorney who specializes in whistle-blowing in your field.*

⬢ STOP AND THINK

What questions can help you clarify an ethical dilemma? What criteria help you analyze a dilemma? How do you choose a responsible course of action?

WHY IS IT SO DIFFICULT TO BEHAVE ETHICALLY?

In the South during the 1940s, Sallie Mae Knight, a social worker, was a heroine to her clients. A white woman, she stood up for African-American children—all by her 5'2" self—and faced down a white male bureaucracy.

Standing up for the welfare of children, as Ms. Knight did, is the right thing to do. But people do not always do the right thing. If asked, many people could think of a time when they caved under peer pressure. Good people often allow their values to be compromised. Why? Ethics are more easily compromised under certain conditions, and people use defense mechanisms to avoid facing uncomfortable feelings of guilt.

Conditions

According to M. S. Baucus and J. P. Near, illegal activities are more likely to occur in larger companies than in smaller companies and when resources abound rather than when they are lacking. Illegal activities also take place during times of change and growth— before a company has a chance to examine its ethics—and in certain industries in which wrongdoing seems to create a climate of complicity. For instance, politics

Digital Vision/Getty Images

gets a bad rap because people think it does not matter how a politician behaves as long as he or she gets elected.

Another problem is the legal system. While several hundred laws respond to ethical concerns, most laws actually lag behind current debates on ethics. In other words, *legal* is not the same as *ethical*. It might not be illegal to talk about your boss behind his back, but it is unethical. At one time, it was legal but not ethical to own slaves. When enlightened and passionate people stand up for just causes, laws catch up to the ethics.

Defense Mechanisms

Finally, because people like to see themselves in the best light possible, they often refuse to see their bad behavior for what it is. Perhaps you will recognize the common defense mechanisms listed next.

- **Bandwagon approach:** When one company sees other companies behaving unethically, the company can easily justify the practice: Everyone is doing it. If they can do it, so can we.

- **Denial:** People deny that anything is wrong. The situation is not that bad, they say, or they look the other way because it is easier to do that than to deal with the problem. Denial usually makes matters worse, not better.

- **Rationalization:** People invent excuses for their behavior. A person may think, I have to look out for myself, or this is what I have to do right now. I'll do better—later. Rationalization is generally a way to avoid looking at the real issues.

- **False sense of security:** Who is going to know? People reason that no one will find out, but if someone does, their supervisor will be able to cover for them. Experience shows that the errors of a person's ways are eventually discovered. Besides, that person knows what he or she has done and must live with the consequences.

- **Stress:** Stress clouds people's judgment. The pressure to make a sale, bring in money, or meet a deadline can push people to the edge. It may be best to deal with the stress and the moral dilemma separately, as they are two different issues.

- **Revenge:** People want payback. Someone may justify that because the government tax code is unfair, he or she will fight back by not claiming income from a part-time job. However, two wrongs do not make a right.

- **Blame:** People believe that because they did not create a situation, they do not have to correct it. A wise person understands that it is best to deal with the situation at hand—regardless of who caused it.

Doing the right thing requires self-knowledge and courage. When individuals improve their ethical behavior, society reaps the rewards.

⬤ **STOP AND THINK**
Why do people behave unethically?

TEACH
Ask students if they have ever used one of the defense mechanisms listed. Share a defense mechanism you have used.

ASSESS
Stop and Think
Unethical behavior can be the result of working conditions, a lack of a strong ethical culture, and defense mechanisms.

SUMMARY

1. Ethics are the principles and values that help people resolve questions of right and wrong. Responsible ethical decisions provide peace of mind and allow people to live together amicably. Irresponsible choices bring negative consequences such as convictions, sullied reputations, and guilt.

2. Creating a culture of ethics in the workplace supports responsible decision making. Leaders must actively promote values. Personal and corporate codes provide guidelines for proper behavior.

3. Working through an ethical dilemma requires careful thought to clarify and analyze the dilemma before selecting a responsible course of action. Whistle-blowing may be an option as a last resort.

4. Conditions in the workplace and defense mechanisms can contribute to unethical behavior.

Checklist

- Do I know the benefits of ethical choices and the consequences of unethical choices?

- Can I provide suggestions for creating a culture of ethics?

- Have I made a list of my core values?

- Have I determined my life's purpose?

- Have I determined how I want to treat others?

- Do I use questions to help clarify my ethical position and come up with an alternative?

- Do I use questions to help analyze an ethical dilemma and select an alternative?

- Do I use criteria to help choose a responsible course of action?

- Am I aware of the defense mechanisms that I and others use to make poor ethical choices?

Build Your Foundation

1. Rank the values below from 1 through 15 in order of their importance to you, with 1 being most important and 15 being least important. Then work with a few classmates to compare your rankings. Add the numbers for each value to see which values are important to the group. Discuss why people ranked the values as they did.

honesty	recognition	peace	freedom
justice	altruism	nature	family
equality	self-sufficiency	friendship	health
compassion	community	success	

2. What value is implied by each of the following well-known sayings? For instance, the proverb "Give a man a fish and you feed him for a day; teach a man to fish and he'll eat forever" advocates the value of education.

   Different strokes for different folks.

   A penny saved is a penny earned.

   Where there's a will, there's a way.

   What goes around comes around.

   Stop and smell the roses.

   Haste makes waste.

   Look before you leap.

   Pretty is as pretty does.

3. Discuss the values implied by these sayings from other cultures.[2]

   Even a sheet of paper has two sides. (Japanese)

   Bury the hatchet beneath the root of the tree. (Native American)

   One does evil enough when one does nothing good. (German)

   Shrouds are made without pockets. (Yiddish)

   Unjustly got wealth is snow sprinkled with hot water. (Chinese)

   One head cannot hold all wisdom. (Maasai)

4. Bring in examples of current ethical dilemmas from news sources such as newspapers, television, or the Internet. Discuss the examples in terms of the criteria under "Choose a Responsible Course of Action" beginning on page 375.

5. Reruns of older television shows and movies present moral dilemmas that earlier generations faced. Share with the class an episode or a movie that presents a moral dilemma and explain different sides of the controversy. Or explain two sides of an ethical dilemma you have faced.

6. Read through the tobacco timeline at http://www.tobacco.org/resources/history/tobacco_history.html. Discuss possible ethics violations in the tobacco industry.

7. Which of the defense mechanisms on page 379 have you or someone you know used? Share one example with your classmates.

ASSESS
Build Your Foundation

1. Answers should spark lively discussion about different value systems.

2. Answer will vary, but may include acceptance of people's differences, thrift, strong will and hard work, justice, enjoyment of simple pleasures, importance of planning before acting, importance of thinking before acting, and behavior over looks.

3. Answers will vary. Responses may include open-mindedness, forgiveness, goodness, generosity, fairness, and collaboration. Point out that every culture has sayings. Perhaps individual students can share some from their culture.

4. This activity gives you the opportunity to discuss current ethical dilemmas. News is likely to cover environmental issues, political intrigue, Hollywood lifestyles, and health issues, to name a few. Use the criteria for making responsible decisions in your discussion.

5. It is interesting to see the dilemmas presented in older TV shows (e.g., Leave It to Beaver, The Brady Bunch, and 7th Heaven) compared to current shows.

6. This website provides incriminating evidence about the tobacco companies' attempt to keep the truth about nicotine from the public.

7. Answers will vary, but students should see that everyone uses defense mechanisms. By being aware of the mechanisms, people can prevent them from influencing their decisions.

[2]See http://wiseoldsayings.com for these and other aphorisms.

8. Codes will vary. Encourage students to take pride in their codes of ethics. Ask students who are willing to share their creeds to read them aloud. Then find a place to post or publish them.

9. Codes will vary. You will find many examples at http://ethics/iit.edu. Search on the keywords *codes of ethics.*

10. Codes will vary. They should reflect behavior for an educational setting.

11. Answers will vary. Students may note the following: a. a soldier's patriotism; b. an employee who wants to be honest but is sneaky; c. a coworker's ambition and Norm's loyalty to his coworker; d. Olga's expression of fairness and equality.

12. Answers may vary. a. Jayden's and Becca's denial and Becca's stress and false sense of security. Jayden examines the facts, considers where his actions may lead, and confronts Becca. He considers rights, utility, care, empathy (for sick people), values and principles, and universal consequences (the dangers of unsafe drugs). b. Susan considers the long term, examines the facts, and consults with others; she might worry, place blame, or deny the situation. She considers rights, utility, justice, care, empathy, and values and principles.

Your Turn

8. Write a personal creed. Find a quiet place and take notes about your values and their importance to you. Think about ethical decisions you have made. What do those decisions say about you? Write your code as an essay, a poem, a letter, or a list.

9. Write an ethics statement for the career you plan to enter. Then look up a code of ethics from a company in your field. The Center for the Study of Ethics in the Professions (http://ethics.iit.edu) publishes codes from different fields. How does your code compare to the company's?

10. In a small group or as a class project, write a code of ethics for your class. Consider such things as values that promote proper classroom behavior and optimal learning. Post your code on the classroom bulletin board.

11. What value(s) or belief(s) motivate the people in the following scenarios? Are the people acting ethically? Explain.

   a. An amputee who served in Iraq said that despite his disability, he wants to return to Iraq to serve his country.
   b. An employee takes $25 from the petty cash fund to pay for a movie. The employee returns the money the next day.
   c. Norm shares an idea for an advertising slogan with another employee, who then passes it along to the supervisor as her own. Norm never reveals that the idea was his originally and lets his coworker take the credit.
   d. Olga, a middle-aged mother of three, supervises a young crew of help desk personnel, five men and two women. When the men's jokes become a little racy, Olga simply but firmly reminds them, "Gentlemen, this is not a bar and ladies are present. Keep the language G-rated." The conversation then tends to become more respectful.

12. Analyze the following ethical dilemmas using relevant questions and criteria from in the chapter. What advice do you have for Jayden and Susan? Discuss possible solutions and test them using the criteria beginning on page 375 under "Choose a Responsible Course of Action."

   a. Jayden is a chemist at a pharmaceutical plant. Part of quality control is to check samples of each drug for purity and potency. Jayden notices that the person in charge of pulling the samples, Becca, does not test every drug, turning her attention to other tasks instead. When Jayden asks Becca about it, she replies, "What's your problem? I've got too much to do to keep up with all of them. We've never found a bad sample anyway." To complicate the matter, Jayden used to date Becca, having recently broken up with her. "Maybe Becca's right," he thinks. "We're all pretty careful." What should Jayden do?
   b. It is December 10, and Susan Petrov has a big decision to make. She is the chief executive officer of Chesterson Refrigeration, a small company with U.S. and overseas locations that makes refrigerators and freezers. Because sales have dropped, the plant, which employs 786 workers, must lay off 240 employees if it is to remain open. Some employees are near retirement, a large number have worked for the company for ten years or more, some are college students, and some are legal immigrants. Susan is hoping that sales will pick up next summer. Limited funds are available to use as severance pay, and a

13. Answers may vary. a. Gil's denial, blaming, and rationalizing; he could get expelled. He could tell Tazim no and sit on the other side of the room. b. Cisco's denial; consequences include possible harm to patients and a drug addiction for Val.

14. Encourage students to find out how organizations create a culture of ethics.

15. Students will discover that different generations prioritize values differently.

few scholarships are available for retraining. How should Susan handle the situation? What is the most ethical way to decide who gets laid off? When should the layoffs begin? Is there anything Susan can do to make the situation better? When and how should she announce the layoffs?

13. Look for possible defense mechanisms at work in the following dilemmas. What are the central conflicts in each case? What might happen if Gil and Cisco do nothing? Suggest possible solutions. Test those solutions using the criteria beginning on page 375 under "Choose a Responsible Course of Action."

   a. Gil is a freshman at North Central State. He has been helping Tazim, a classmate who has been struggling in their calculus class. Tazim wants to sit next to Gil during the final exam so Tazim can check his answers against Gil's. Gil is not concerned, thinking that he is not the one who is cheating; he is just taking the exam. What are the consequences if Gil lets Tazim check a few answers? What should Gil do?

   b. Cisco and Val are medical assistants at Tremont Hospital. Cisco has noticed that Val is often late to work. She also calls in sick more than she used to. She has a new boyfriend who has a reputation for drinking and drugging. Cisco notices that Val has lost weight, and she is not her usual bubbly self. One day Cisco sees her nervously eyeing the medicine cart. He decides then that her problems are not his concern. Maybe she is just working too hard. What might be going on? What should Cisco do?

Community Connection

14. Visit a local business, charity, hospital, or wellness center. Ask someone in a position of authority to describe the ethical climate there. Write a short informative report on what you found. If the organization has a written creed or mission statement, ask if you can have a copy.

15. Ask five senior citizens to rank their values using the list in item 1 of "Build Your Foundation" on page 381. Ask them to explain their rankings. Then ask five people under the age of 20 to rank and explain their values. What differences do you see in the values the two generations provided? Prepare a short written report to present to your class.

Works Cited

Baker, Mallen. "Companies in Crisis—What To Do When It All Goes Wrong." *Mallenbaker.net Corporate Social Responsibility, n.d.* Web. 5 May 2009.

Baucus, Melissa S. and Janet P. Near. "Can Illegal Corporate Behavior Be Predicated? An Event History Analysis." *Academy of Management Journal* 34.1, (1991): 9–36. Print.

ERC. *2000 National Business Ethics Survey*. Ethics Resource Center. 2000. Web. 6 June 2009.

—. "Ten Things You Can Do to Avoid Being the Next Enron." *Ethics Resource Center*. 29 May 2009. Web. 13 Dec. 2009.

Harned, Patricia J. "Letter." *2007 National Business Ethics Survey*. 2007. Web. 5 May 2009.

Wigland, Jeffrey. Interview. *60 Minutes*. CBS. New York. 4 Feb. 1996. Television.

Technical Reading

Goals

- Explain the difference between technical reading and literary reading
- Preview and anticipate material before you read
- Use strategies for reading technical passages

Terms

- acronyms, p. 395
- annotating, p. 391
- anticipate, p. 387
- background knowledge, p. 387
- formal outline, p. 392
- graphic organizers, p. 393
- informal outline, p. 392
- literary reading, p. 387
- pace, p. 391
- previewing, p. 387
- technical reading, p. 387
- technical vocabulary, p. 394

WRITE TO LEARN

How does a science or computer textbook differ from a literature textbook? Do you read scientific or technical material differently from the way you read literature? If so, how? Do you like to read? Why or why not? How often do you read scientific or technical information? How do you remember what you read? Write a journal entry addressing these questions.

Focus on Technical Reading

Read the sample of technical reading on the next page and answer these questions:

- What features of technical writing do you recognize in the passage?
- What has the reader done to interact with and understand this passage?
- What kind of information has the reader noted?

What If?

- The passage included more technical vocabulary?
- The information in the passage was part of a presentation on satellites?
- The passage included a couple of graphics?

Satellites Have Become Important Tools in Ocean Exploration   *How?*

The National Aeronautics and Space Administration (NASA), organized in 1958, has become an important institutional contributor to marine science. For 4 months in 1978, NASA's *Seasat*, the first oceanographic satellite, beamed oceanographic data to Earth. More recent contributions have been made by satellites beaming radar signals off the sea surface to determine wave height, variations in sea-surface contour and temperature, and other information that interests marine scientists.

Satellites IMPT in marine research

①
TOPEX

The first of a new generation of oceanographic satellites was launched in 1992 as a joint effort between NASA and the Centre National d'Études Spatiales (the French space agency).The centerpiece of **TOPEX/Poseidon**, as the project is known, is a satellite orbiting 1,336 kilometers (835 miles) above Earth in an orbit that allows coverage of 95% of the ice-free ocean every 10 days. The satellite's TOPography Experiment uses a positioning device that allows researchers to determine its position to within 1 centimeter ($\frac{1}{2}$ inch) of Earth's center! The radars aboard the satellite can then determine the height of the sea surface with unprecedented accuracy. Other experiments in this 5-year program include sensing water vapor over the ocean, determining the precise location of ocean currents, and determining wind speed and direction.

History of research

②
JASON

Jason-1, NASA's ambitious follow-on to *TOPEX/Poseidon*, launched in December 2001. Now flying 1 minute and 370 kilometers (230 miles) ahead of *TOPEX/Poseidon* on an identical ground track, *Jason-1's* primary task is to monitor global climate interactions between the sea and the atmosphere. Its 5-year mission has been extended.

③
SEASTAR

SEASTAR, launched by NASA in 1997, carries a color scanner called SeaWiFS (sea-viewing wide-field-of-view sensor). This device measures the chlorophyll distribution at the ocean surface, a measure of marine productivity.

measures how?

④
AQUA

NASA launched **AQUA,** one of four of NASA's next generation of Earth-observing satellites, into polar orbit on 4 May 2002. It is the centerpiece of a project named for the large amount of information that will be collected about Earth's water cycle, including evaporation from the oceans; water vapor in the atmosphere; phytoplankton and dissolved organic matter in the oceans; and air, land, and water temperatures. AQUA flies in formation with sister satellites TERRA, AURA (Figure 2.28), PARASOL, and *CloudSat* to monitor Earth and air.

⑤
GPS

A satellite system you can use every day? The US. Department of Defense has built the GPS **(Global Positioning System),** a "constellation" of 24 satellites (21 active and 3 spare) in orbit 17,000 kilometers (10,600) above Earth. The satellites are spaced so that at least 4 of them are above the horizon from any point on Earth. Each satellite contains a computer, an atomic clock, and a radio transmitter. On the ground, every GPS receiver contains a computer that calculates its own geographical position using information from at least 3 of the satellites. The longitude and latitude it reports are accurate to less than 1meter (39.37 inches) depending on the type of equipment used. Handheld GPS receivers can be purchased for less than US$70. The use of the GPS in marine navigation and positioning has revolutionized data collection at sea.

Other uses?

Sample of Technical Reading

From *Essentials of Oceanography* by Garrison, 2009. Reprinted with permission of Brooks/Cole, Cengage Learning.

FOCUS	ASSESS
Focus on Technical Reading	**What If?**
Use the questions to encourage students to read the sample closely.	Use the questions to discuss how the sample would be different if the situation or audience changed.
	Go to www.cengage.com/school/bcomm/techwtg for more detailed responses to these questions.

Courtesy of Stephen Freas

Writing@Work

Architecture & Construction

Stephen Freas is a construction subcontractor in Winston Salem, North Carolina. He is a supervisor on job sites and manages small crews to build projects based on drawings provided by the general contractor. He writes contracts, e-mails with clients, and often consults manuals and building codes.

The contracts Stephen writes are more than just fine print to be skimmed and signed. "A contract lets the client know exactly what we're going to do—what materials and processes will be necessary, what those will cost, and what the potential risks are," says Stephen. "A detailed contract also prevents us from doing costly work for free."

Stephen's job requires him to do a great deal of technical reading. "Reading construction plans and technical manuals requires a physical engagement with the writing," he says. "In these texts, an action usually follows each sentence or image. This makes for slow but 'action-packed' reading that helps you accomplish something you had no idea how to do previously."

Stephen often combines information gleaned from several different pieces of technical writing in order to make proper decisions. For example: "Once, we built a handicap ramp to the specifications written by the contractor. Upon inspection, the city told us that the ramp did not meet its building code standards. I refused to rebuild the ramp until I read the city code myself. The code listed specifics such as ramp thickness; railing height; and, most important, ramp slope. I calculated that in order to meet city code specifications, the ramp needed to be three times longer than the contractor's original plan and, coincidentally, the same slope as the existing sidewalk."

Stephen credits his technical reading dexterity to countless hours of following instruction manuals for his car, photography, climbing, and other hobbies.

Think Critically

1. Why does Stephen consider construction plans and technical manuals to be "action-packed"?

2. Think about the completed handicap ramp from the point of view of Stephen, the general contractor, and the building inspector. What solution would work for everyone?

Printed with permission of Stephen Freas

TECHNICAL READING VS. LITERARY READING

Technical reading is distinguished by technical subject matter, an emphasis on precision, specialized vocabulary, use of graphics, and descriptions of mechanisms and processes. Reading a technical text is different from reading literature. **Literary reading** requires the reader to draw inferences—to read between the lines and interpret symbolic language. Technical documents, though, require you to grasp the logic of text packed with detailed and precise information. Those who digest technical information quickly can stay on top of the latest developments in their field. To aid in understanding, proficient readers familiarize themselves with the text before they read and interact with the text as they read.

b019821/iStockphoto.com

BEFORE YOU READ

Fortunately, there are things you can do before you read to aid your comprehension of the passage.

Preview the Material

Previewing warms up the mind for reading, just as stretching warms up the body for exercise. After previewing, you read with greater efficiency and retention because you know what to expect.

When previewing, skim the introduction to determine the subject. Turn headings into questions, **anticipate** and foresee the information to follow, and notice where information is placed. In a manual, for example, thumb through the pages to see where the schematics and descriptions of parts are located. Use the preview to activate your **background knowledge,** what you already know about the subject, to gain more meaning from the passage.

The example on the next page shows how one student previewed the sample passage on page 385 by anticipating the subject and turning the headings into questions.

Warm Up

Why do people read literature? Why do people read technical documents?

FOCUS

Warm Up

Use the Warm Up to discuss technical documents used in various fields.

ENRICH

Look through Thoreau's *Walden* for examples of literary and technical reading (how he measured the pond or his description of the bean field).

TEACH

Spending two minutes previewing will save time later. Practice previewing chapters in this book or other textbooks the students have.

Use the Strategies for Technical Reading Teaching Master on the IRCD as a preview to the chapter.

FOCUS

Warm Up

Use the Warm Up to discuss the different kinds of technical documents students may read on the job.

Warm Up

What kinds of technical documents will you read in your chosen trade or profession?

Subject: The title "Satellites Have Become Important Tools in Ocean Exploration" and the first sentence suggest that the passage will discuss how satellites are used to study the ocean.

Questions: How are satellites used to study the oceans?
What kind of data do satellites provide?
How useful is this data?

Anticipate the Line of Reasoning

Knowing the typical reasoning of technical passages will help you anticipate and mentally prepare for the reasoning. Most technical passages focus on:

- A process or procedure (steps; how something works).

- A cause/effect relationship (what makes something happen).

- A mechanism (what something looks like and what it is supposed to do).

Figure 16.1 shows a process description of air flow in coastal regions. This process description, however, also includes several cause/effect relationships. One action causes another action. As a result, this chain reaction also is responsible for the process.

Land breezes and sea breezes are small, daily mini-monsoons. Morning sunlight falls on land and adjacent sea, warming both. The temperature of the water doesn't rise as much as the temperature of the land, however. The warmer inland rocks transfer heat to the air, which expands and rises, creating a zone of low atmospheric pressure over the land. Cooler air from over the sea then moves toward land; this is the **sea breeze** (Figure 7.15a). The situation reverses after sunset with land losing heat to space and falling rapidly in temperature. After a while, the air over the still-warm ocean will be warmer than the air over the cooling land. This air will then rise, and the breeze direction will reverse, becoming a **land breeze** (Figure 7.15b). Land breezes and sea breezes are common and welcome occurrences in coastal areas.

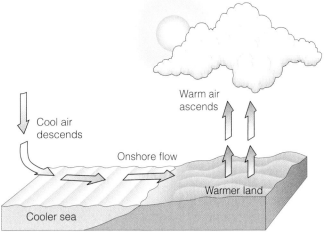

(a) In the afternoon, the land is warmer than the ocean surface, and warm air rising from the land is replaced by an onshore sea breeze.

(b) At night, as the land cools, the air over the ocean is now warmer than the air over the land. The ocean air rises. Air flows offshore to replace it, generating an offshore flow (a land breeze).

Figure 7.15 The flow of air in coastal regions during stable weather conditions

Figure 16.1 Process Description

Source: Tom Garrison, *Essentials of Oceanography*, 5th ed., 2009, 157. Reprinted by permission of Brooks/Cole Cengage Learning.

Communication Dilemma

Discriminating readers use their critical-thinking skills to look out for information that is inaccurate, biased, sensationalized, or lacking in pertinent details.

When you use data from your reading, you have an ethical obligation to double-check that data, looking for other sources that report the same findings. Publications that must be produced quickly—such as newspapers, magazines, and books on the latest technology—are subject to errors. Information published with few, if any, editorial guidelines—for example, some articles on the Internet and stories in tabloids—are subject to unscrupulous uses.

The next time you find an Internet article that promises the fountain of youth or hands you a get-rich-quick scheme, be skeptical and remember that you cannot believe everything you read.

Think Critically

What might motivate people to publish articles that are not completely factual?

Figure 16.2 shows another process: instructions for scanning an image. The reasoning here is linear—a chronologically organized sequence of events.

It is recommended that when scanning printed images, you do the following:

1. Scan the image at twice the resolution as you normally would to capture more information.

2. Use the despeckle filter (Filter > Noise > Despeckle) in Photoshop to minimize the dotted texture.

3. Use the Gaussian blur filter (Filter > Blur > Gaussian Blur). Adjust 0.1–0.9 to "soften" or blur the image and minimize the Moiré pattern.

Figure 16.2 Step-by-Step Process

From *An Introduction to Web Design + Programming* by Wang and Katila, 2004

Figure 16.3 shows cause-to-effect reasoning as the text explains how humans contribute to the extinction of species. Notice the use of words such as *cause, because,* and *as a result* to pinpoint the causes and effects.

Humans cause habitat loss, degradation of habitat, and habitat fragmentation, all of which can endanger a species. Humans also directly reduce populations and endanger species by overharvesting. Species introductions also cause declines of native species. In most cases, a species becomes endangered because of multiple factors. Sometimes, a decline in one species as a result of human activity leads to decline of another species.

Figure 16.3 Cause-to-Effect Relationships

From *Ecology and Behavior* by Starr et al., 2009

Technical writing uses cause-to-effect reasoning and a description of processes and mechanisms.

Tell students that by anticipating the line of reasoning, they can read more efficiently.

Ask students to select statements in the figures that deal with processes, cause-to-effect reasoning, and descriptions of mechanisms.

Use the Common Technical Transitions Teaching Master on the IRCD to show important transitions for processes and cause-to-effect reasoning.

FOCUS

Figure 16.4
Point out the graphic and the use of description to show the parts of a light switch.

Figure 16.4 shows a mechanism description that describes the function of each part of a light switch.

Figure 2-38 shows the parts of a basic single-pole switch. The main parts include the following:

- Switch toggle: Used to place the switch in the ON or OFF position when moved up or down.

- Screw terminals: Used to attach the lighting circuit wiring to the switch. On a single-pole switch, the two terminal screws are the same color, usually bronze.

- Grounding screw terminal: Used to attach the circuit-grounding conductor to the switch. It is green in color.

- Mounting ears: Used to secure the switch in a device box with two 6-32 size screws.

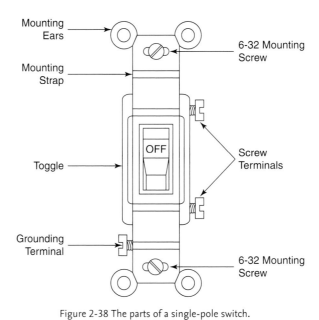

Figure 2-38 The parts of a single-pole switch.

Figure 16.4 Mechanism Description

Source: Fletcher, Gregory. *Residential Construction Academy: House Wiring*, 2nd ed. 2008, Delmar/Cengage Learning, 52. Used with permission of Delmar/Cengage Learning.

 STOP AND THINK
How do you preview a reading passage? What kind of reasoning processes are typical of technical passages?

AS YOU READ

Because technical reading is different from other kinds of reading, you must approach technical reading with a plan. Good readers pace themselves and interact with the text by annotating the passage, repeating information aloud, understanding the vocabulary, paying attention to numbers, and studying graphics.

Pace Yourself

Runners **pace** themselves, proceeding slowly and regularly, to expend their energy evenly throughout a race. You, too, should pace yourself when you read by following these suggestions:

- Read slowly. Technical reading is packed with details. Make sure you take them all in.

- Read small amounts of information for short periods of time (perhaps 10 to 15 minutes). Then take a break, summarizing information and taking notes.

- Read the selection twice. During the second reading, you can see what you missed the first time. Also, a second reading allows you to see the transitions that denote how the parts of the passage fit together.

Activate Your Background Knowledge

The more you read in a technical subject, the better reader you will become in that area. For example, if you regularly read auto mechanics magazines, you will comprehend a new article about a hybrid car better than someone who regularly reads computer magazines.

Knowledge of the subject and familiarity with vocabulary used in the area gives you background knowledge on which to build a new understanding. You activate this knowledge when a concept or an example reminds you of something you already know.

As you read, allow your mind to form associations with knowledge you have already stored. When Adrienne read a discussion of synthetic elements in the periodic table, she already knew that *synthetic* means "man-made." Therefore, she could identify synthetic elements as having been made in a lab.

Annotate the Reading Passage

Writing about what you read is important for retaining information. As you write, you activate more areas of the brain and, therefore, understand and retain more information. In this way, annotating jump-starts your learning.

Annotating a passage means taking your own notes and interacting with the text. When annotating a passage, use abbreviations, note what is significant, outline the passage, use graphic organizers, and/or answer questions.

COMMUNICATION TECHNOLOGIES

Electronic readers such as Amazon's Kindle™ and Sony's Reader Digital Book are changing the way people read. Users can download books, magazines, and newspapers into an eReader in a matter of seconds. The hand-held devices are thin and fit easily into a pocket or purse. The eReader allows users to annotate reading passages on the screen. Prices range from between $200 and $700. The next generation of eReaders will use Electrofluidic Display Technology (EFD) to create the visual brilliance of the printed page.

Thinking Critically
What are the advantages and disadvantages of using an eReader?

Tell students to work on refining their own system of note taking and abbreviating.

Inform students that no two sets of notes will be the same. Even the sample notes in Figures 16.5, 16.6, and 16.7 differ slightly. However, details should relate to the main idea. The main idea should not vary greatly from one set of notes to another.

To practice annotating a text, complete the activity *Technical Reading: Passage 1* **worksheet available at www.cengage.com/school/ bcomm/techwtg. Click the link for Chapter 16; then click Data Files.**

TEACH
In high school, students are not able to write in their books, but college students will find the system of note taking used in the worksheet helpful.

FOCUS
Figure 16.5
Use the formal outline to show one way of outlining a passage.

Use Abbreviations

To help you write about what you read, devise or borrow a system of abbreviations for marking information. Here are a few examples:

IMPT or !	important information
EX or ex	example
∴	math symbol for therefore
b/c	because
?	questions; don't understand
① ② ③	items in a sequence

Note What Is Significant

Take notes on a technical passage by summarizing sections and writing the main ideas in your own words. Also note any specialized vocabulary, answers to questions you posed during the preview, descriptions of processes, and cause-and-effect reasoning. Mark segments you do not understand so you can reread, ask questions, and seek clarification.

If you own the book or article, you can mark important information with annotations, your handwritten notes, in the margins. If you prefer to take notes in a notebook, write the same information there. The opening sample on page 385 shows a technical passage with a student's annotations. Notice how the student uses symbols and abbreviations.

Consider an Outline

Figure 16.5 shows a **formal outline,** which is set with Roman numerals, numbers, and a system of letters, for the oceanography passage. Figure 16.6 shows an **informal outline,** a less structured system, for the same material. Both outlines help the reader see major divisions in the passage and serve as effective summaries.

Satellites Have Become Important Tools in Ocean Exploration

I. Major NASA satellites in ocean exploration
  A. TOPEX/Poseidon 1992
    1. Accuracy to within 1 cm of Earth's center
    2. Data on sea height, water vapor, ocean currents, winds
  B. Jason-1 2001
  C. SEASTAR 1997
  D. AQUA 2002
    1. Flies with sister satellites
    2. Measures Earth's water cycle

Figure 16.5 Formal Outline

FOCUS

Figure 16.6
Use the informal outline to show a less formal way of organizing ideas in a passage.

Figure 16.7
Use the graphic organizers to show visual/spatial ways to take notes on a reading passage.

Ask students to note what is different about the way the organizers are set up. The first one is a top-down organization, using rectangles, with the main idea at the top. The second one is a more central system, using ovals, with the main idea in the middle.

**Satellites Have Become Important Tools
in Ocean Exploration**

NASA Satellites
TOPEX/Poseidon 1992
   – Satellite positioning within 1 cm of Earth's center
   – Data—height of sear surface, water vapor, oceans currents, winds
Jason-1 2001
SEASTAR 1997
   – Data—chlorophyll and marine productivity
AQUA-2002
   – 1 of 4 satellites
   – DATA—Earth's water cycle

Figure 16.6 Informal Outline

Consider Graphic Organizers

Some students draw **graphic organizers** to map the relationships among ideas by using circles, blocks, and lines. A circle or block represents the central idea. Lines between circles or blocks show how other parts of the topic relate to the central idea. Figure 16.7 illustrates two organizers.

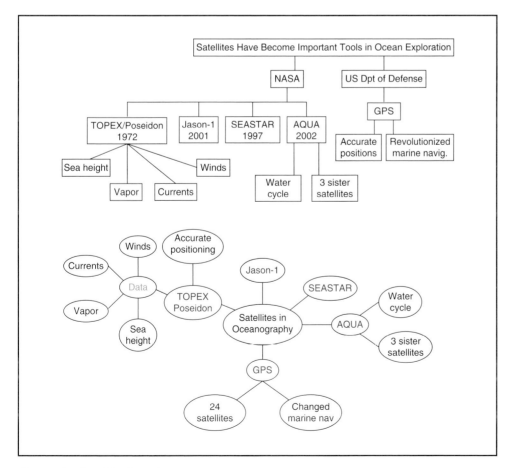

Figure 16.7 Graphic Organizers

FOCUS

Figure 16.8

Use the figure to show that questioning is an effective reading tool.

TEACH

Stress the importance of using more than one sense when learning. Many people talk to themselves while they are studying.

Answer Questions

Answering questions also can be a helpful note-taking tool. The questions can be your own or your instructor's, or they can be from end-of-chapter exercises.

Figure 16.8 shows written answers to questions. One student answers the questions posed during the preview and then moves to the end-of-chapter questions.

Answers to questions in preview:

1. *Satellites beam radar signals off the surface of the ocean. SEASTAR uses a color scanner (SeaWiFS) to measure the distribution of chlorophyll.*

2. *Satellites provide information about ocean currents, water vapor, marine productivity, wind direction and speed, and sea height. GPS satellites provide information about location and position.*

Answer to an end-of-chapter question:

How does the GPS work? Satellites (21 active; 3 spare) orbit 10,600 miles above Earth. At least 4 are above the horizon at any time from any place on Earth—each with a computer, an atomic clock, and a radio transmitter. Each GPS receiver on Earth has a computer to calculate its position (accurate to within 1 meter) from 3 satellites in longitude and latitude.

Figure 16.8 Answers to Questions

Repeat More Difficult Notes Aloud

Hearing what you have written and read in silence may help you retain difficult information. Try repeating the following notes aloud:

Freud divided the personality into the id, the pleasure principle; the ego, the reality principle; and the superego, the morality principle. Freud divided the personality into the id, the pleasure principle; the ego, the reality principle; and the superego, the morality principle. Freud divided the personality into . . .

jhorrocks/iStockphoto.com

After reading this passage, a student probably could name the three parts of the personality and describe each one.

Understand the Vocabulary

Sometimes you can figure out **technical vocabulary,** specialized terms, from the context—from a description or an example. Other times the term is defined in the text— after a linking verb, in parentheses, or in an appositive.

Figure 16.9 shows examples of several terms defined in a text. Note that some words, such as *alley* and *husband,* do not mean the same thing for the production specialist or conservationist as they do for you. Even terms that are familiar may be used in different ways for the technical reader. Also notice the use of **acronyms** (letters that stand for a long or complicated term or series of terms).

FOCUS

Figure 16.9
Use the sentences to illustrate the importance of knowing the vocabulary. Point out that sometimes the vocabulary may be a familiar word used in an unfamiliar way (*alley,* for example).

FOCUS

Figure 16.10
Use this excerpt to illustrate the use of an extended definition. Point out how the examples, descriptions, and additional data further expand the understanding of the word *deserts.* Ask students what would make the definition even clearer—a photo, for example.

A parasite lives in or on another living organism called its host, feeding on the host without killing or benefiting the host.

A market is a group of buyers and sellers interested in transacting business over a particular good or service. A competitive market is a market with sufficient buyers and sellers so that the market price is not significantly impacted.

The alley, or space between two columns of text, is too wide.

Environmentally conscious citizens are careful to husband our natural resources and protect those resources for future generations.

Childhood vaccines include the MMR (measles-mumps-rubella) vaccine and IPV (inactivated polio vaccine).

Figure 16.9 Vocabulary Defined in a Text

When you cannot determine the vocabulary from the context, use a dictionary or a glossary provided in the document to look up the term. Another option is to ask an expert to define a word for you.

Some definitions need more than a phrase or a sentence and extend to a paragraph or more. Figure 16.10 illustrates an extended definition of the term *desert.* The examples and description help the reader gain a more complete understanding of the term.

Deserts are regions that receive an average of less than 10 centimeters (4 inches) of rain per year. Most are located at about 30° north and south latitude, where air depleted of moisture sinks. In these regions, the low humidity allows much sunlight to reach the soil surface, so the ground heats fast during the day. Low humidity also causes the ground to cool fast at night. Soils are typically nutrient poor and somewhat salty. Despite these forbidding conditions, some plants and animals survive, especially in areas where moisture is available in more than one season.

The driest of all deserts may be Chile's cool Atacama Desert, which lies in a rain shadow behind the Andes.

Figure 16.10 Extended Definition

From *Ecology and Behavior* by Starr et al., 2009

Learn to Read Graphics

Be prepared to think visually when you begin to read a technical passage. Draw a picture of what you are reading—on paper or in your mind. To read graphics included in the text, make sure you understand the purpose of each type of graphic. Then closely study the graphic as well as the author's explanation of it. How does the graphic support the author's message? What does the author want you to notice about the graphic?

Understand the Purpose of the Graphic

Become familiar with the purpose of each type of graphic. When you see a diagram, for example, know that the purpose is to help you see what an object looks like. You can then read the graphic with that purpose in mind. Recall the following graphics and their purpose:

- Tables organize numerical and verbal data in rows and columns.
- Pie graphs show how the whole is divided into parts.
- Bar graphs contrast sets of data.
- Line graphs show trends over time or relationships among data.
- Flowcharts present various processes, including decision-making processes, or the hierarchy of an organization.
- Gantt charts present a timeline for a project.
- Diagrams and photos show what something looks like.

Read the Graphic Closely

After you have finished noting what kind of graphic you are reading and what its purpose is, read the graphic closely, noticing everything about it.

The Internet is a seemingly never-ending supply of technical information. Many sites let you download entire technical articles and books. Onlinenewspapers. com provides links to many newspapers, journals, and specialty publications from all over the world.

Go to the NET Bookmark for Chapter 16. Locate a newspaper from another state or country. Then find an article that you find interesting and read it. Share highlights of the article with your class.

www.cengagelearning.com/school/bcomm/techwtg

- Read the title to determine the subject matter of the graphic.
- Look for keys or legends to see what each part presents.
- Read the callouts to identify parts.
- Read the x-axis and the y-axis to see the relationship among the sets of data.

Next, relate the information in the graphic to the author's discussion of the graphic. What does the author want you to notice about the graphic? If you are asked to remember a diagram, you may want to draw the diagram yourself.

A number of the technical reading passages in this chapter illustrate the importance of graphics. Figure 16.1 uses a picture and arrows to represent the creation of land and sea breezes. Figure 16.4 includes a diagram of a light switch to make the description easy to follow. Each graphic presents technical information efficiently and clarifies the explanation provided in words.

Focus on Ethics

You are a chemist at a pharmaceutical company who has been given the task of determining the effects of a controversial medicine on humans. You have not been given much time and money to complete your research, however. Because you do not have time to spare and because your company wants to be able to claim that the medicine is safe, you find only two articles from the same journal and use information from them in your report. You would like to check other articles in case the information you found has been discredited, but the findings could prevent your company from marketing the medicine. You submit the report, which states that the medicine is safe for humans. Over the next couple of months, your study is discredited because of the negative side effects that many consumers experienced when they took the medicine.

Think Critically

What would be the effects of this discovery—for you and for your company?

Pay Attention to Numerical Data

Resist the temptation to read too quickly through discussions that contain numbers. Note that the number $1,231.49, while only six digits long, actually stands for nine words—one thousand two hundred thirty-one dollars and forty-nine cents. Even though digits save space on the page, you need to take time to process the digits mentally as words.

 **STOP AND THINK**
What are the technical reading strategies?

FOCUS ON ETHICS
Students should understand that if they publish something without checking accurate and reliable sources, they and their company could suffer legal consequences, not to mention the harm that inaccurate information causes people who act on the information.

Think Critically
As a chemist, you could be fired or sued and would suffer the guilt of knowing that you may have caused harm to people who took the drug. Your company could be sued as well, resulting in possible financial problems and loss of reputation.

TEACH
Tell students not to ignore numerical data, but to read the data as if the numbers were words.

ONGOING ASSESSMENT
Stop and Think
Reading strategies include previewing the material, anticipating the line of reasoning, pacing oneself, activating background knowledge (reading more in the subject area), taking notes, repeating difficult notes aloud, understanding the vocabulary, learning how to read graphics, and paying attention to numerical data.

CLOSE

Summary

Use the summary to review the strategies for reading technical documents.

CLOSE

Checklist

Tell students to review the checklist the next time they have a technical reading assignment. The checklist may aid them in studying a technical or scientific subject.

REVIEW

For a review of the key terms in the chapter, provide students with the *Key Terms* worksheet available as a supplemental activity on the IRCD.

CHAPTER 16
REVIEW

SUMMARY

1. Technical reading is different from literary reading in its subject matter and its emphasis on precision, specialized vocabulary, use of graphics, and descriptions of mechanisms and processes.

2. Before you read technical documents, preview the material and anticipate the line of reasoning.

3. As you read technical documents, pace yourself, activate your background knowledge, annotate the passage, repeat difficult notes aloud, make sure you understand the vocabulary, read the graphics, and pay attention to numerical data.

Checklist

- Have I previewed the material I am preparing to read?
- Have I anticipated the line of reasoning? Is the reasoning a process or procedure, a cause-and-effect relationship, or a mechanism?
- Have I paced myself?
- Have I activated my background knowledge?
- Have I annotated the reading passage with notes, an outline, a graphic organizer, and/or answers to questions?
- Have I considered repeating difficult notes aloud?
- Do I understand the vocabulary?
- Have I read the graphics?
- Have I paid close attention to numerical data?

Build Your Foundation

1. How did you read technical passages before you read this chapter? Will you change anything about how you read technical passages now? Explain.

2. Compile a list of three terms in a technical field with which you are familiar. Ask your classmates if they understand the vocabulary.

3. Conduct a poll of 20 people to find out which kind of reading each person prefers—technical or literary. What kind of technical articles do they read? Which kind of reading do you prefer? What kind of technical articles do you read?

4. Analyze your textbooks or technical magazines. Isolate one chapter or one article. How much of the vocabulary is new to you? How much technical vocabulary is in the passage? How many graphic aids are there? Do some of the passages use numbers? If so, how? Which parts would be clearer if you repeated them aloud? How would you organize this information if you had to learn it for a test?

5. Locate the technical word and the part of the sentence that defines that word in these sentences from *A+ Guide to Hardware* by Jean Andrews.

   a. "A short circuit, or a short, occurs when uncontrolled electricity flows from the hot line to the neutral line or from the hot line to ground . . ." (103).
   b. "A rectifier is a device that converts alternating current to direct current" (102).
   c. Voltage regulators "provide a degree of protection against swells or spikes (temporary voltage surges) and raise the voltage when it drops during brownouts or sags (temporary voltage reductions)" (109).
   d. "Registers are small holding areas on the processor chip that work much as RAM does outside the processor" (131).
   e. "Called flash ROM, the software stored on these chips can be overwritten by new software that remains on the chip until it is overwritten" (27).
   f. "A ground bracelet, also called an antistatic strap or ESD bracelet, is a strap you wear around your wrist" (51).
   g. "Fiber-optic cables transmit signals as pulses of light over glass strands inside protected tubing . . ." (450).
   h. VoIP (Voice over Internet Protocol), also called Internet telephony, was once a novelty on the Internet . . ." (461).

Your Turn

6. Read the excerpt on the next page from *Principles of Economics*. Pick out the technical reading elements.

   a. Do you see a description of a process? If so, where?
   b. Do you see cause-and-effect reasoning? If so, where?
   c. Do you see specialized vocabulary of the discipline? If so, which terms? Are the terms defined in the text so that you understand what they mean?
   d. Look at the graphic closely. Interpret the graphic and explain how you read it.

DEMAND

To an economist, the term *demand*—whether the demand for tickets or the demand for roses—has a very specific meaning. **Demand** is a relationship between two economic variables: (1) *the price of a particular good* and (2) *the quantity of that good that consumers are willing to buy at that price during a specific time period,* all other things being equal. For short, we call the first variable the **price** and the second variable the **quantity demanded.** The phrase *all other things being equal,* or *ceteris paribus,* is appended to the definition of demand because the quantity that consumers are willing to buy depends on many other things besides the price of the good; we want to hold these other things constant, or equal, while we examine the relationship between price and quantity demanded.

Demand can be represented by a numerical table or by a graph. In either case, demand describes how much of a good consumers will purchase at each price. Consider the demand for bicycles in a particular country, as presented in Table 1. Of course, there are many kind of bicycles—mountain bikes, racing bikes, children's bikes, and inexpensive one-speed bikes with cruiser brakes—so you need to simplify and think about this table as describing demand for an average, or typical, bike.

PRICE	QUANTITY DEMANDED	PRICE	QUANTITY DEMANDED
$140	18	$240	5
$160	14	$260	3
$180	11	$280	2
$200	9	$300	1
$200	7		

Table 1 Demand Schedule for Bicycles (millions of bicycles per year)

Observe that as the price rises, the quantity demanded by consumers goes down. If the price goes up from $180 to $200 per bicycle, for example, the quantity demanded goes down from 11 million to 9 million bicycles. On the other hand, if the price goes down, the quantity demanded goes up. If the price falls from $180 to $160, for example, the quantity demanded rises from 11 million to 14 million bicycles.

. . . The **law of demand** says that the higher the price, the lower the quantity demanded in the market; and the lower the price, the higher the quantity demanded in the market.

Source: Taylor and Weerapana, *Principles of Economics*, 2010, 53–54. Used with permission of Cengage Learning.

7. Take notes from the passage below using suggestions from the chapter.

a. Preview the passage, making annotations. Either photocopy the passage and write on it or take notes on a separate sheet of paper.

b. Outline the passage (formally or informally) or draw a graphic organizer.

c. Answer the questions posed during your preview and read them aloud.

7. Students gain practice and learn which strategies work best for them.

ASSESS

Community Connection

8. This assignment makes students aware of technical reading in different fields.

9. This assignment gives students the chance to practice technical reading strategies and perform a service.

Invention, Innovation, and Diffusion. Technological change occurs when new ideas are developed into new products that increase production, such as the steel plow, the harvester, the combine, the automobile, radar, the telephone, the computer, the airplane, lasers, and fiber-optic cable. Economists distinguish between an **invention**, which is the discovery of new knowledge or a new principle, such as electricity, and **innovation**, in which the new knowledge is brought into application with a new product, such as the electric lightbulb. Economists also distinguish between the innovation itself and the **diffusion** of the innovation throughout the economy, a process that involves advertising, marketing, and spreading the innovation to new uses, such as the use of the electric lightbulb to create night shifts in factories.

The sewing machine is a good illustration of invention, innovation, and diffusion. By 1847, inventors had built 17 different machines capable of mechanically forming a stitch. But only one of these, Elias Howe's sewing machine, developed into a commercially successful innovation. As Howe tried to sell his invention to consumers, he found out how to modify it to make it more useful and attractive. Soon the invention turned into a popular innovation that was used widely. Wide diffusion of the innovation occurred as others produced household versions of the sewing machine, like the one marketed by the Singer company. This story also illustrates that innovation and diffusion require the work of an entrepreneur who recognizes the potential of the invention.

Technology depends in part on scientific knowledge, and many people feel that science will become more and more important in driving the future technological change. But technology is much more than scientific knowledge. The discovery of DNA did not improve technology until it was applied to genetic engineering. The knowledge of mathematics made the invention and development of computers possible, a technology that has obviously improved productivity.

Source: Taylor and Weerapana, *Principles of Economics*, 2010, 606–607. Used with permission of Cengage Learning.

Community Connection

8. Interview two people who work in technical fields. Find out how much they read on the job and what strategies help them understand and remember the information they read. Write your interview in question-and-answer format.

9. Find an article to read to a shut-in, a visually impaired person, or a group of school children. Annotate your text and become familiar with the vocabulary beforehand. Write a short trip report to summarize your experience.

YOU ATTITUDE

TEACH
Remind students that everyone appreciates attention and respect. Thus, a reader-centered attitude will improve all communication.

With the exception of the science lab report, most technical writing should be reader-centered rather than writer-centered. A reader-centered approach, or *you* attitude, attempts to look at situations from the reader's perspective instead of the writer's perspective. The *you* attitude points out advantages to the reader and makes him or her more likely to accept what the writer says.

Use the *you* attitude to persuade your audience to think or act in a certain way. For example, you might send an e-mail to your supervisor asking for time off, a letter to a newspaper editor opposing a proposed city curfew, or a letter to a dry cleaner asking for a reduction in your bill because your clothes were not clean when you picked them up.

Notice the difference between the *I* or *we* attitude and the *you* attitude in the following example. The *you* attitude sounds friendlier and more positive. The *you* attitude stresses how a customer can benefit from buying a home from Mountain View Homes. Using the *you* approach is psychologically smart as a motivator, and it makes a good sales pitch.

Manufactured Home Dealer

I or *we* attitude:

Do we, at Mountain View Homes, have deals! Our 14 x 70 single-wides have been marked down 20%. And our 14 x 80s can be purchased with a rebate of $1,000!

You attitude:

You can find a real deal at Mountain View Homes. You can purchase our 14 x 70 single-wides at 20% off the regular price. And you can receive a rebate of $1,000 on a brand new 14 x 80.

To use the *you* attitude, simply consider the situation from your reader's viewpoint. What is the advantage to him or her? Then, where appropriate, add more *you*'s and *your*'s to your message and take out some of the *I*'s, *we*'s, or company names. Point out the benefit of your message to your reader.

The Inside Track: Your Turn

1. Rewrite these sentences to reflect a stronger you attitude. Remember, you cannot eliminate uses of *I*, *we*, and company names, but you can slant the writing to be more reader-centered. Add any information that will help the reader see the advantages.

   a. We will ship the rest of your order next week.

   b. Powell Insurance Company is reliable. We have been in business at the same location for more than 50 years.

   c. I want you to take the conversational Spanish classes for several reasons.

   d. Your overdue account must be paid within 30 days. Otherwise, we will give you a poor credit rating and stop taking your orders.

   e. We do not have your order in stock. We will notify you when we do.

   f. I expect you to be in the office by 8 A.M. for several reasons.

   g. I do not think you should choose clothes that are difficult and time-consuming to take care of.

   h. We want all students to stay on school grounds during lunch so they will not be late for class.

   i. We have marked down all furniture for our moving sale. We would rather sell the furniture than move it. Everything must go!

   j. You are required to take 30 semester hours of general college courses.

2. Rewrite the following announcements to reflect a stronger you attitude.

   a. Our Volunteer Club has many items for sale. Members are selling tapes, CDs, and club T-shirts that have never been worn. One member is bringing boxes of science fiction novels. We are selling game cartridges and earrings. The earrings are handcrafted by one of our members. We have a set of golf clubs, a black-and-white TV, and a chest of drawers. These items and many more can be seen at 2323 East Third Street on Saturday morning at 6 A.M. We hope to raise enough money to help victims of the recent flood in our area.

   b. Mama's Kitchen, a hip new home-cooking restaurant, is proud to announce its grand opening at 2349 Michelin Circle on Saturday, January 31, 20—. Renowned chef and owner Daria O'Doole, says that her restaurant will offer the best blue plate specials in town, and she wants everyone to come in and try her meatloaf, which is made from a recipe handed down to her and originating with her great-grandmother. Ms. O'Doole wants to keep her blue plate specials under $10 because she says her mother taught her to be frugal.

ASSESS

(continued)

fiction novels. For golfers, we have a set of golf clubs. A small black-and-white TV and chest of drawers are perfect for a college dorm. Come see these and many more items. Know that your dollars will help the recent flood victims.

TEACH

Discuss how proper tone can help create goodwill.

TONE

Tone refers to the emotional overtones that words emit. Words not only provide information, but also convey emotions. Because human beings are both rational and emotional creatures, tone can affect the way readers react to words.

Unlike the objective tone in technical reports, letters give writers an opportunity to show a range of emotions—from apathy to warmth, from enthusiasm to anger. While some unanswered complaint letters may appropriately display anger, most letters you write should convey a positive, upbeat, and reader-centered tone.

Read the following passage. Describe the tone. Which words contribute to that tone?

Chemical Processing Division Members:

Do not be late for the hazmat training on Tuesday, September 8. The session is scheduled for 8 to 11 A.M. The trainer has another appointment after our training. Arrive promptly at 8 A.M. or earlier. If you are not seated by 8 A.M. in Room TR2045, you will find the session closed to you. Then you will be required to earn your certification at a later session.

Here you see that the short, terse style creates a negative tone. The words *Arrive promptly* and *If you are not seated by 8 A.M.* may spark anger in some employees who perceive that they are being treated like children. The following version is improved.

Chemical Processing Division Members:

We are pleased you have registered for hazmat training on Tuesday, September 8, 8–11 A.M.

Please plan to arrive in Room TR2045 no later than 8 A.M. Our instructor must conduct the session on schedule so he can begin his afternoon training on time.

Thank you for your cooperation. If you have any questions, please contact . . .

A positive tone makes people more likely to cooperate. You can create a positive tone by using the following suggestions:

- **Avoid Negative Words.** A number of words carry such negative messages that you should try to avoid them. Words such as *never, failed, cannot,* and *regret* often can be replaced with more positive words.

- **Use Tact.** Choose your words carefully. Be sensitive to their impact. Instead of saying that you do not like a particular sweater, try saying that the sweater shows personality.

- **Accentuate the Positive.** Be optimistic. Most people prefer to do what is right and best for all concerned. Remember that you can think of the cup being half full (accentuating the positive) instead of half empty (accentuating the negative).

- **Remember Your Manners.** Say *please* and *thank you.*

Note the differences in the following examples. What did the writer do to change a negative tone in the first column to a more positive tone in the second column?

Do not sign the evaluations.	Please keep the evaluations anonymous.
If you fail to sign the form, your return will be late.	Please sign the form to avoid unnecessary delays.
We insist that you include a deposit.	Please enclose a deposit.
We received your fax in which you claim that we sent you damaged goods.	Your faxed letter of July 5 indicates that you received damaged goods.
If you decide to visit our museum . . .	When you visit our museum . . .
Your essay is disorganized.	Concentrate on organizing your ideas.

The Inside Track: Your Turn

Make the following statements more user-friendly by rephrasing them to sound more positive.

1. Your outfit is too loud for the commercial. Mr. Carlson will not like it. It will clash with the background.

2. We told you to be at work by 8 A.M. sharp!

3. You claim to have had a flat tire on the way to the Springfield warehouse.

4. We cannot allow you to make inappropriate comments.

5. You have had more than enough time to pay the small amount shown on the enclosed bill.

6. If you cannot attend the rehearsals on time, you cannot speak with the product development team.

7. Our sweatshirts will not shrink.

8. You will not encounter any problems with our software.

9. Do not walk on the grass. Stay on the sidewalks!

10. If you do not contact us before November 17, we will not have time to process your request.

11. You are working too fast to be accurate. You are making careless errors.

12. Our stores are never closed.

13. If you decide to contribute to the children's fund, your money will never be spent unwisely.

ASSESS

Your Turn

1. Mr. Carlson thinks more conservative colors will blend better with the chosen background for the commercial.

2. We'll see you tomorrow at 8 a.m.

3. We understand that you had a flat tire on the way to the Springfield warehouse.

4. We are looking forward to hearing any appropriate comments.

5. Please include payment by return mail.

6. Your promptness for all practices will help ensure our success with the product development team.

7. Our sweatshirts are preshrunk to ensure continued proper fit.

8. Our software is user-friendly. *or* Our software runs smoothly and efficiently.

9. Please walk on the sidewalks.

10. Contact us before November 17 so we have time to process your request.

11. Please work carefully and accurately. *or* Work at a steady pace to ensure accuracy.

12. Our stores are open 24 hours a day for your convenience.

13. When you contribute to the children's fund, your money is used wisely.

PARALLELISM

TEACH
Remind students of the importance of parallelism in all writing, not just technical writing.

When the grammatical terms ("English teacher language") are troublesome for students, they still may be able to hear and recognize the elements that do not fit or are not parallel even when they do not understand the grammar.

In writing, two sets of words are parallel because they use the same grammatical structure. Your ability to recognize parallel structure depends on your ear and your knowledge of grammar. Words, phrases, and clauses joined by coordinating conjunctions and used in lists should be parallel.

Parallel Words, Phrases, and Clauses

Can you hear that these sets of words are not parallel?

1. I like running, biking, and to paint.

2. He told us to wash the developer pan and that we must sweep the floor.

3. I like to inventory the stock, list the overruns, and to read orders reports.

The grammatical structure of these sentences may help you see where the break in parallel structure occurs:

    S V   Gerund Gerund   Infinitive

1. I like running, biking, and to paint.

In Sentence 1, the infinitive breaks the parallelism because the list started with *-ing* words, gerunds.

    S   V Indirect object Infinitive phrase   Dependent clause

2. He told us to wash the developer pan and that we must sweep the floor.

In Sentence 2, the dependent clause breaks the parallelism because the list started with an infinitive phrase.

    S V   *to* + verb/object   verb + object   *to* + verb/object

3. I like to inventory the stock, list the overruns, and to read orders reports.

In Sentence 3, *to* was not repeated in each part of the series; so the parallelism was broken.

Here are improved versions of the above sentences:

1. I like running, biking, and painting.
   I like to run, bike, and paint.

2. He told us to wash the developer pan and to sweep the floor.
   He told us to wash the developer pan and sweep the floor.
   He told us that we must wash the developer pan and sweep the floor.

3. I like to inventory the stock, to list the overruns, and to read orders reports.
   I like to inventory the stock, list the overruns, and read orders reports.

Parallel Lists

The itemized list below is not parallel. Which parts of the list are more alike than other parts?

> At the next Spanish Club meeting, we will discuss these items:
>
> - Next year's budget
> - Which person to nominate for chair
> - Implementing our attendance policy
> - Whether to donate money to the senior class project
> - Elections

The above list is not parallel because one item is a noun preceded by an adjective, two are listed as questions, one starts with an *-ing* word, and one is a simple noun. To make the list parallel, begin each part of the list the same way. Use all *-ing* beginnings, all questions, all nouns, or all nouns preceded by adjectives.

The following list makes the entire group parallel with the first item by repeating the adjective(s) + noun structure.

> - Next year's budget
> - Chair nominations
> - Attendance policy
> - Senior class project donations
> - Upcoming elections

Parallel Order

Using the same order of information also makes parts of a resume parallel.

For example, if you present the employment experience of Position 1 as Name (of business), City/State (of business), Dates (of work), and Job Title, you must present the experience of Position 2 in the same order. Do not put dates first, name second, address third, and so on.

The following example shows three job descriptions that use correct parallel order.

> Taylor Computer Manufacturing; Erie, PA; July 2009–Present; Project Manager
>
> Hix Landscaping Service; Pittsburgh, PA; May 2008–June 2009; Assistant Landscape Technician
>
> BookWorld Publishing Services and Discount Books; Pittsburgh, PA; October 2005–March 2008; Salesclerk

TEACH
Explain that parallel structure makes writing easy to understand because it repeats a structure the reader has already seen.

Understanding parallel structure is critical for creating effective resumes. Refer students to sample resumes in Chapter 11, beginning on page xxx.

1. What to include in next year's budget; which person to nominate for chair; how to implement our attendance policy; whether to donate money to the senior class project; when to hold elections. *or* Students could write complete questions from the list. *or* Students could begin each listing with an *-ing* word, such as *Planning next year's budget.*

2. This activity personalizes the concept of parallel order.

3. Chairperson of Booster Club; Delivery person for Meals on Wheels; United Way volunteer; Recorder for Debate Team *or* Students could begin with past tense verbs: *Chaired, Delivered, Accepted, Recorded.*

4. Possible solutions: a. The fitness instructor ran a marathon, participated in a triathlon, and won a weight-lifting contest. b. Leo Vasquez, Chief of Operations; Carla Willoughby, Quality Assurance Director; and Lucy Alva, Human Resources Department Manager, are all receiving computer upgrades this year. c. Shoe repairers liked stiletto heels because the tips needed frequent repair, doctors warned against stiletto heels because they caused sprained or broken ankles, and the heels were banned from airplanes because they could pierce the floors.

5. a. The letter directed us to preview, sign, and return the contracts promptly. b. The rules were fair but not enforceable. c. Margarita and Jerome were told to be at the office at 2 p.m. and to refill the rental car with gasoline. d. She had trouble explaining her position and making a decision. e. The new product line is noted for its durability, attractiveness, and reliability.

6. Answers will vary. Students should select one model and make other entries parallel to it.

The Inside Track: Your Turn

1. Refer to the unparallel list at the top of the previous page. Make the list parallel to the second item, "Which person to nominate for chair." Then make the list parallel to the third item, "Implementing our attendance policy." Which of those two lists do you prefer? Why?

2. Make a list of your morning routine. Set up your list with this statement: *Every morning I follow the same routine.*

3. Make the activities in the following list parallel:

   - Chairperson of Booster Club
   - Delivered Meals On Wheels to shut-ins
   - United Way: accepted pledges
   - Recorder for Debate Team

4. Make each of the following sentences parallel by filling in the blank with an appropriate word or phrase.

   a. The fitness instructor ran a marathon, _____, and won a weight-lifting contest.

   b. The following people will be receiving computer upgrades this year: Leo Vasquez, Chief of Operations; Carla Willoughby, Quality Assurance Director; and Lucy Alva, _____.

   c. Shoe repairers liked stiletto heels because the tips needed frequent repair, doctors warned against stiletto heels because they caused sprained or broken ankles, and _____.

5. Correct these sentences for faulty parallelism.

   a. The letter directed us to preview the contracts, sign them, and to return them promptly.

   b. The rules were fair but that they could not be enforced.

   c. Margarita and Jerome were told to be at the office at 2 P.M. and that they had to refill the rental car with gasoline.

   d. She had trouble explaining her position and which decision to make.

   e. The new product line is noted for its durability, its attractiveness, and it is reliable.

6. Make the following sets of job descriptions parallel in structure.

   a. Baylor Industries, Huntington, WV. June 2007 to February 2010—. Sales Representative: called on customers and kept accounts.

   b. Sales Director. January 1999 to August 2009. United Sales Corporation, Beckley, West Virginia. Duties included supervising sales personnel, training new personnel, and calling on customers.

   c. Cookeville, TN, May 2002 to September 2008 Murphy's Art Supply, Salesclerk, ordered art supplies, created company newsletter, arranged displays, and wrote proposal to acquire funds to open a coffee shop in the store.

   d. Branyon Fine Arts Group, taught piano and voice lessons, Cookeville, TN, October 2006 to present, served as music teacher.

ECONOMY

Good technical writing is economical. As good food is rich in nutrition and low in fat and sugar, good technical documents are rich in meaning and low in unneeded words and phrases. Technical writers who think of their readers try to write clearly and concisely so that documents take less time and trouble to read. As a writer, you also save production time and costs when your writing is economical. The following tips will help you cut unnecessary words and phrases:

TEACH
Stress the benefits of economical writing. It is more efficient, clearer, and easier to read.

- *Avoid* There Is/There Are *and* It *Sentence Openings*. Revise sentences starting with *There is* or *There are* to give the sentence a subject at the beginning, where it will get more attention, followed by an action verb. *There is* and *There are* sentences are not wrong, but they are weak sentences that waste words. Getting directly to the point of the sentence is better. Look at the following examples:

WEAK:	There are 10 units of amoxicillin stored in the warehouse.
IMPROVED:	Ten units of amoxicillin are stored in the warehouse. (passive voice)
	The warehouse stores 10 units of amoxicillin. (active voice)
WEAK:	There is a direct relationship between the consumption of animal fats and cholesterol levels.
IMPROVED:	The consumption of animal fats relates directly to cholesterol levels. (active voice)

The technique for revising these sentences is as follows: (1) Cross out the *There is* or *There are* opening. (2) Move the subject of the sentence to the opening position. (3) Create an action verb, sometimes from a word that follows the subject.

Likewise, sentences should not start with *it* unless the *it* refers to a specific person, place, or thing already mentioned. When you see that *it* in a sentence is incorrectly used, omit the *it*. Revise the sentence to give a stronger meaning without the unneeded word. Refer to the following examples:

WEAK:	It gives me great pleasure to introduce our new quality assurance officer, Rebecca Beckett.
IMPROVED:	I am pleased to introduce our new quality assurance officer, Rebecca Beckett.
WEAK:	It is the thermostat that received an electrical surge.
IMPROVED:	The thermostat received an electrical surge.

- **Delete Unnecessary Modifiers.** In the following examples, you can see that the modifier placed before each word is unnecessary. These words do not need modification. For instance, can something be very essential? No, something is either essential or not essential. Here are other common examples of unnecessary modifiers:

highly satisfactory	extremely competent
very rare	slightly expensive
barely visible	perfectly clear

Strategies for economical writing are meant to be used in editing and revising, not for generating ideas and drafting.

Suggest that students select one or two strategies to add to their checklists for editing and revising. Once those strategies become a natural part of the student's writing process, students might add one or two other strategies to the checklist.

■ **Avoid Redundancy.** Redundancy is needless repetition. Redundancy adds words but does not add meaning. Omit unnecessary repetition. You can probably think of other redundant expressions to add to the list below.

refer back	advance warning	cancel out
blue in color	large in size	the state of Nevada
the month of June	basic fundamentals	3 A.M. in the morning

■ **Reduce Needless Phrases, Clichés, and Overused Expressions.** Writers sometimes pad their writing, intentionally or unintentionally, with unnecessary phrases. Do not use an entire phrase when a single word will do. Each phrase listed below would be better replaced by its single-word equivalent after the equal sign.

due to the fact that = because	prior to = before
in the event that = if	at a later date = later
be aware of the fact that = know	at a rapid rate = rapidly
in this modern day and age = today	in many cases = often, frequently

Many of the overused expressions listed below may sound familiar to you because you have read or heard them often. Although these clichés may be easy to write because they jump from your memory, they are not exciting to read. Each of the following clichés is followed by a possible replacement.

every effort will be made—we will try	attached herewith is—attached
as per your request—as you asked	upon receipt of—having received
as a general rule—generally	under separate cover—separately
I will be most grateful if—Please	afford an opportunity—allow
for the reason that—because	based on the fact that—because of

■ **Replace *-ion* Nouns with Stronger Action Verbs.** Use of *-ion* nouns often adds words without advancing meaning. These nouns can usually be omitted, making the sentence shorter and stronger.

Notice in the improved sentences that the *-ion* nouns have been turned into action verbs.

WEAK:	The Food and Drug Administration, under public pressure, took into consideration the adoption of several new Alzheimer's medications.
IMPROVED:	The Food and Drug Administration, under public pressure, considered adopting several new Alzheimer's medications.
WEAK:	Heidi came to the conclusion that the report was a summation of court procedure.
IMPROVED:	Heidi concluded that the report summarized court procedure.

- **Avoid Strings of Prepositional Phrases.** Some prepositional phrases may be necessary to join ideas, but too many of them can be distracting. Whenever possible, revise sentences to remove excessive prepositional phrases.

WEAK:	The drop in deposits by students in their accounts at the bank is of great concern for management.
IMPROVED:	Decreasing student bank deposits concerns management.
WEAK:	The EPA office in Anchorage plans to send out warnings to residents about possible contamination from lead in the water.
IMPROVED:	The Anchorage EPA office will warn residents about possible lead-contaminated water.

- **Remove Unneeded *That*.** In many sentences with a relative clause beginning with *that*, writers can omit *that* without changing the meaning.

WITH *THAT*:	The camera operator thought **that** the set was too dark.
WITHOUT *THAT*:	The camera operator thought the set was too dark.

Read the sentence aloud without *that*. If the sentence makes sense and the meaning does not change, you can omit *that*.

The Inside Track: Your Turn

1. Revise the following sentences to omit the *There is/There are* and *It* openings.

    a. There are ten cases of welding rods on order.

    b. It is certain that the cable to connect the CD-ROM to the computer is missing.

    c. There is a solution that strips the silver from the film to create the photographic contrast.

    d. It is phosphate that encourages growth of algae in the river.

    e. It gives me great anxiety knowing that the federal inspectors may come any day.

2. Revise the following sentences to eliminate unnecessary modifiers, redundancies, and needless phrases.

    a. The new packaging, which is oval in shape, has proven quite satisfactory in tests in the northeast market.

    b. The CAD software is 5% faster than it was prior to the upgrade.

    c. Designers should be aware of the fact that hidden cameras record their production process.

    d. In this modern day and age, we expect almost all jobs to involve computer use.

    e. As a general rule, the attorney general ensures victims that every effort will be made to protect their privacy.

TEACH
Remind students that some prepositional phrases are appropriate. The problem exists only when a number of them are run together.

ASSESS
Your Turn
1. a. Ten cases of welding rods have been ordered. b. The cable to connect the CD-ROM to the computer is missing. c. A solution strips the silver from the film to create the photographic contrast. *or* A solution that strips the silver from the film creates the photographic contrast. d. Phosphate encourages growth of algae in the river. e. I worry the federal inspectors may come any day.
2. a. The new oval packaging has proven satisfactory in northeast market tests. b. The CAD software is 5% faster than before the upgrade. c. Designers should know that hidden cameras record their work. d. Today we expect most jobs to involve computers. e. Generally, the attorney general ensures victims that he or she will try to protect their privacy.

ASSESS

Your Turn

3. a. The bulletin describes a closed electrical circuit.
b. The committee considered our amendment. c. Naoko's project will continue if UpStart provides financial support. d. The Research Division recommended that all toxic wastes be disposed of through Standard Corporation. e. The synthetic fibers act like natural filament.

4. a. As you requested, I am sending the antenna to fit your AS302 model. b. The fragrance combinations seem to sell well in large U.S. metropolitan areas. c. The LaserWriter toner cartridge needs to be replaced carefully. d. The photographer precisely and swiftly loaded the film into the camera. e. Please allow me to interview for the vacant accounting position.

5. Answers will vary. The revision of the following paragraph is an example of a solution:

Good Heart Inc. is recalling more than 2,600 automatic external defibrillators. The U.S. Food and Drug Administration (FDA) has received reports of electrical problems with the machine's electrode pads, which are placed on the patient's chest. Although rare, this problem could make using the device dangerous.

3. Revise these sentences to replace the *-ion* nouns with stronger action verbs.

   a. The bulletin provides a description of a closed electrical circuit.

   b. The committee took our amendment into consideration.

   c. The continuation of Naoko's project depends on the financial support of UpStart.

   d. The Research Division presented a recommendation that all toxic wastes be disposed of through Standard Corporation.

   e. The synthetic fibers make an action like natural filament.

4. Revise the following sentences to omit clichés and unnecessary prepositional phrases.

   a. As per your request, I am sending the antenna to fit your AS302 model.

   b. The combinations of fragrance seem to sell well in areas of large metropolitan population in the United States.

   c. The toner cartridge for the LaserWriter needs to be replaced with care.

   d. With precision and swiftness, the photographer loaded the film into the camera.

   e. I will be most grateful if you can afford me an opportunity to interview for the vacant position in your accounting area.

5. Revise the following paragraphs, using the skills you learned in this section to make the writing economical and easier to comprehend.

   a. There are more than 2,600 automatic external defibrillators being recalled by Good Heart Inc. It has been learned that the United States Food and Drug Administration (FDA) has received reports of electrical problems of the machine in the electrode pads for placement on the chest. Although very rare, this problem could make the use of the device dangerous.

   b. Defibrillators are used by emergency responders, amateur and professional, to treat sudden, unexpected, and unforeseen cardiac arrest. Good Heart Inc. representatives said every effort will be made to locate customers and replace defective units. Purchasers may refer back to their invoices; if the model number is BC 4039–BC 5011, in many cases, these machines are included in the recall. These units were manufactured from January in the year of 2010 through August in the year of 2011.

   c. While the recall is voluntary, the FDA is considering further investigation and a mandatory recall at a later date. It is not known how many people have been adversely affected by malfunctions of automatic external defibrillators from Good Heart Inc.

USING NUMBERS

The following rules are generally accepted as guidelines to help you decide when to write numbers as figures and when to write numbers as words in technical documents.

1. Generally, use figures for numbers 10 and above. Use words for numbers one through nine.

> Oleander Community College presented 22 partial scholarships and 15 full scholarships to first-year students.
>
> Two computers and four of the operators were relocated to Operations.

2. Use figures when a series contains numbers above and below 10.

> The client's estate included 498 acres of land, 173 paintings, 3 mansions, and 15 thoroughbreds.

3. Use figures when several numbers (including fractions) are presented in a single sentence or in several related sentences.

> The delivery is lacking 2 metric tons of steel I-beams, 3/4 case of stainless steel bolts, 1/8 of the paint needed, and 1 spool of electrical wire.

4. Use figures for units of measurement. Note that the unit of measurement may be expressed as a word, an abbreviation, or a symbol.

18 meters	5 1/3 cups	4.25 liters	55 mph
5.5 centimeters	66 2/3 feet	75 MHz	35 mm film
0.05 margin of error	14.4 K baud	32"	8" x 10"

5. Use figures for fractions and decimals presented with whole numbers.

5 1/3   66 2/3   72.6   10.25

6. Use figures to express exact amounts of money.

$181.95   8¢ $0.95

7. Use figures for data presented in tables and illustrations.

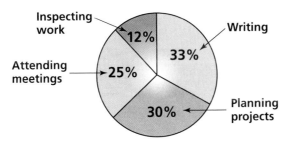

Figure 1 Time Spent on Tasks

8. Use figures for addresses and dates.

    Route 5 Box 182   103 East Maple Street   January 3, 1865

9. Use figures to express age.

    3 years old   a man in his 20s   an 18-year-old woman

10. Use figures for identification numbers.

> The correct number is 378-18-3555.
>
> The engine number is JEMH00347WE99678.

11. Use figures for one of two numbers written next to each other.

    two 42-cent stamps   16 two-liter bottles

12. Use figures to indicate time not expressed with o'clock.

    8 A.M.   12:10 P.M.

13. Use figures for statistics and scores.

> The odds were 3 to 1 in the district attorney's favor.
>
> The Cavaliers won the game, 96–89.

14. Use figures for page and volume numbers.

> Turn to page 45 in volume 2 of your manual.

15. Use figures and words for very large numbers (over 6 digits).

    $6 trillion   4 million people   5.3 billion years

16. Use words at the beginning of a sentence. Rewrite awkward sentences so that the numbers are written as figures within the sentence.

> Nine thousand seven hundred and sixty-six citizens signed the petition.
>
> The petition contained 9,766 signatures.

17. Use words for indefinite or approximate numbers.

> More than one hundred scientists attended the symposium.
>
> Approximately 50 frogs were examined for the parasite.

18. Use words for fractions not connected to whole numbers.

> Approximately three-fourths of the nurses have been vaccinated.

19. Use words for ordinals below 10. Use figures and last letters for ordinals over 10.

third base   ninth inning   10th person   21st birthday

The Inside Track: Your Turn

1. In each pair of sentences [(a) and (b), (c) and (d), and so on], choose the sentence that illustrates the best use of numbers and figures.

    a. The credit union is offering 8.25% interest for CDs.
    b. The credit union is offering eight and a quarter percent interest for CDs.

    c. AG Goldsmiths reported the theft of eighteen diamonds over two carats each.
    d. AG Goldsmiths reported the theft of 18 diamonds over two carats each.

    e. 5,031 people reside within the city limits.
    f. Five thousand thirty-one people reside within the city limits.

    g. The bus departs at three in the afternoon.
    h. The bus departs at 3 p.m.

    i. Over 1/2 of the laboratory rats were infected.
    j. Over one-half of the laboratory rats were infected.

2. Using the guidelines from this section, rewrite the following passages to use numbers and figures appropriately.

    a. Penguin is the common name for fifteen species of flightless marine birds. They live on four continents in the Southern Hemisphere. One penguin, the Galapagos, lives within six degrees of the equator. Penguins can swim through the water at speeds of up to twenty-five miles per hour. The largest species, the emperor penguin, ranges from three to four feet tall. The smallest, the Adelie, stands about two feet tall.

    b. On the twenty-third of February in the year two thousand and seven, one hundred forty-two mallards were tagged off the coast of Florida. For five years, researchers tracked approximately seventy of the mallards over three hundred and ninety-seven miles. The ducks survived in temperatures as low as minus ten degrees Celsius. A report was distributed to twenty-seven agencies in seven states. The research cost six thousand forty five dollars and fifty-six cents. It is estimated that seven and one half million mallards inhabit the southeastern area of the United States. Biologists estimate that ninety percent of the mallards follow predictable patterns of migration.

CLARITY

TEACH

Make sure students understand the importance of clarity.

Good technical writing is clear. To make your writing clear, follow these suggestions:

1. Use traditional *S-V-MODIFERS, S-V-OBJECT*, or *S-V-COMPLEMENT* word order.

   ■ *Incorrect:* Behind Tray 2 and beside Bin 3 is where the blockage occurred.

   ■ *Correct:* The blockage occurred behind Tray 2 and beside Bin 3.

   ■ *Incorrect:* The production order she wrote.

   ■ *Correct:* She wrote the production order.

   ■ *Incorrect:* Hectic was the ambassador's schedule.

   ■ *Correct:* The ambassador's schedule was hectic.

2. Write moderately short sentences (12–24 words).

   ■ *Incorrect:* The registration procedure begins with the student making an appointment with his or her adviser, at which time the adviser and student will discuss the student's career goals, placement test scores, and transcripts to determine a schedule of classes that the adviser will enter into the computer and that the student will pay for before the registration period ends—that is, unless the computers are down, in which case the student must come back another time.

   ■ *Correct:* The registration procedure begins with the student making an appointment with his or her adviser. At this time, the adviser and student will discuss career goals, placement test scores, and transcripts to determine a schedule of classes. Next, the adviser will enter the schedule into the computer. The student will pay for the classes by the end of the registration period. If the computers are down, the student must come back.

3. Place the main idea (the subject or topic) first.

   ■ *Incorrect:* The board of directors agreed to open three new staff positions as well as fill five vacant slots. The board also voted last week to invest the money awarded in the lawsuit in facility upgrades. Now the board is considering a motion to halt dividends for the next two years. The board of directors favors company growth over dividends.

   ■ *Correct:* The board of directors favors company growth over dividends. The board also voted last week to invest the money awarded in the lawsuit in facility upgrades. The board of directors agreed to open three new staff positions as well as fill five vacant slots. Now the board is considering a motion to halt dividends for the next two years.

4. Use active voice—unless you have a good reason to use passive voice.

   ■ *Incorrect:* The new computers were purchased by the school board.

   ■ *Correct:* The school board purchased the new computers.

(Also see The Inside Track: Active Voice and Passive Voice on pages 418–420.)

5. Use parallel structure.

- *Incorrect:* Orientation consisted of the following activities:
  - Meeting our adviser
  - Tour the campus
  - Placement tests

- *Correct:* Orientation consisted of the following activities:
  - Meeting our adviser
  - Touring the campus
  - Taking placement tests

(Also see The Inside Track: Parallelism on pages 406–408.)

6. Use first person *(I or we)* whenever possible.

- *Incorrect:* The defective parts were returned to the AM Machining Company.

- *Correct:* We returned the defective parts to the AM Machining Company.

7. Choose precise nouns and verbs.

- *Incorrect:* Last night the security guard sounded an alarm.

- *Correct:* On Wednesday, October 16, 20—, at 8:53 P.M., Juwan Minnifield, the security guard on duty at the southeast entrance of Whitley Laboratory reported smoke coming from under the Electronic Control Room door.

The Inside Track: Your Turn

1. The following sentences lack clarity. Revise these sentences to make the meaning clearer.

   a. The speed limit is somewhere between 50 and 60 mph.

   b. The tickets are to be distributed sometime next week by the committee.

   c. In came my father to tell me the good news.

   d. Maintain good health by exercising regularly, eating a balanced diet, and for goodness sake, keep a positive attitude.

2. Using the suggestions from this section, rewrite the following paragraph to make the sentences and the message clearer.

   First, he hoed a small area until the dirt was broken up. Then he raked out the clumps of grass, pulling up those stubborn weeds. The fertilizer was applied lightly and worked into the ground with a hoe. Next, plastic stuff was placed all over the plot of land and stuck to the ground at intervals of 3 feet to keep the grass from growing and to allow the rain to drain through and bring needed moisture to the roots. Then holes were cut in the plastic stuff, not too far apart. François planted some flowers through the plastic stuff into the ground. Then over the plastic stuff and around the plants pebble rocks were placed to hold down the plastic and so the area would look neat. François made planting a garden look easy.

ACTIVE AND PASSIVE VOICE

TEACH

Discuss with students situations when active voice is more effective than passive voice and when passive voice should be used.

Which of these sentences do you prefer? Why?

Active Voice:	Mariah hit the ball during Saturday's game.
Passive Voice:	The ball was hit during Saturday's game by Mariah.

Most people prefer the first sentence because it is direct, clear, and interesting. As a result, it is easier to read than the second sentence.

Look at the verbs in each sentence. The active voice sentence uses only one verb. The passive voice sentence uses two verbs: the verb *to be* + the past participle of another verb. (The verb *to be* includes *is, am, are, was, were, to be, been,* and *being*.) The past participle is simply the past tense form of the verb that uses a helping verb.

Look at the subject in each sentence. In the active voice sentence, the subject is the doer of the action. In other words, Mariah performs the action: she hits the ball. In the passive voice sentence, the subject is being acted upon. In other words, the ball was acted upon (was hit) by Mariah.

Use active voice when you want to emphasize an action. Because active voice sentences are more direct, you should write in active voice unless you have a good reason for writing in passive voice. Sometimes there are good reasons to use passive voice, as the following rules explain.

1. If you do not know the doer of the action, passive voice gives you the opportunity to leave out the doer.

Passive:	The money was taken.
Active:	The thief took the money.

ASSESS

Your Turn

1. a. Passive voice verb: *is submitted*. Active voice: The manufacturing engineer submits the accident report. b. Passive voice verb: *were lost*. Active voice: The computer lost the minutes for Wednesday's meeting. c. Passive voice verb: *has been deactivated*. Active voice: The security chief deactivated the computerized key to my office. d. Passive voice verb: *is being sponsored*. Active voice: The Alpha Deltas will sponsor the Area VI Tennis Classic in May. e. Passive voice verb: *were ordered*. Active voice: My assistant, who is managing the landscaping project, ordered the blueberry bushes.

2. Maybe you know who the doer is, but do not want to say. Sometimes passive voice can help you be diplomatic or polite.

Passive:	Your blueprints have been delayed.
Active:	We lost the blueprints.
Passive:	The microscope was broken.
Active:	You broke the microscope.

3. Scientific writing calls for an objective tone, which is hampered when the doer of the action is included in the sentence. Scientific writing focuses on the process, not the person.

Passive:	The fluid volume was increased 20% with the addition of sodium.
Active:	The fluid volume increased 20% with the addition of sodium.
Active:	The researcher increased the fluid volume 20% by adding sodium.

4. Sometimes the receiver of the action is more important than the doer. You can emphasize the receiver by using passive voice. Ads, in particular, like to stress *you* as the receiver of services that companies can offer.

Passive: Ted Kennedy was elected to the U.S. Senate for nine terms.

Active: The people of Massachusetts elected Ted Kennedy senator for nine terms.

Passive: You are kept up-to-date with *Newsweek*.

Active: *Newsweek* keeps you up to date.

- **Changing Voice: Passive to Active.** Look for two-word passive voice verbs—the verb *to be* and the past participle. If you see that a report contains too many passive voice sentences, convert the passive verbs to one-word active verbs by (1) placing the doer as the subject of the sentence, (2) adding a doer that is not included in the sentence, or (3) turning the simple subject of the verb into a direct object.

Passive: The car was repaired by the mechanic.

Active: The mechanic repaired the car.

Passive: The window was replaced last month.

Active: Calvin replaced the window last month.

- **Changing Voice: Active to Passive.** If your science report calls for more passive voice construction, decide what process, material, or mechanism you want to emphasize and place that item in the subject position. Make sure your verb includes *to be* + the past participle. Or if you would prefer not to point an accusing finger at a particular person, focus the sentence on the object that received the action.

Try changing the direct object of the verb into the simple subject of the passive voice verb.

Active: The scientist added a cooling agent to the compound.

Passive: A cooling agent was added to the compound.

Active: Phillipa completed the company's annual report yesterday.

Passive: The company's annual report was completed yesterday.

The Inside Track: Your Turn

1. Find the passive voice verbs in the following sentences. Then change these passive voice sentences to active voice.

    a. The accident report is submitted by the manufacturing engineer.

    b. The minutes for Wednesday's meeting were lost on the computer.

    c. The computerized key to my office has been deactivated.

    d. The Area VI Tennis Classic is being sponsored by the Alpha Deltas in May.

    e. The blueberry bushes were ordered by my assistant, who is managing the landscaping project.

quality assurance staff.
j. Active voice verb: *finished*. Passive voice: The wedding cake was finished two hours before the ceremony.

3. The artwork you requested for the Employee Appreciation display will not be ready for the November 15, 20—, deadline [may use passive voice: "Artwork has been delayed"]. Although the graphics professionals usually are aware of scheduling, this time my assistant, Frank Stanwych, overlooked two other major projects [is inappropriate because it sounds accusing; can omit this sentence or say something like "Schedules have been revised. . . ."].

Despite our problems, some of your requests will be completed on schedule [is inappropriate; should use active voice to emphasize and sound positive]. The two lighted stars can be hung from the skylight [is inappropriate; should use active voice for emphasis]. The posters covered with employees' photographs may be printed [should use active voice for emphasis]. In addition, Erin Taft and Vinnie Delgado will produce the traditional Employees of the Year Awards booklet [active is appropriate for emphasis]. The booklet will be available to visitors and staff beginning December 1 [use active, as in *Visitors and staff can have copies on December 1* to end on a positive note].

TEACH

Warn students of the negative connotations sometimes attached to *Madam*.

f. According to our parents, my brother and I are needed to run errands for the family business this Saturday.

g. Jerry McGinty has been placed on inactive status by the coach.

h. All plastics are required to be placed in recycling bins by order of the City Council.

i. Thanksgiving dinner is being served at the shelter on Wednesday.

j. With six weeks of consecutive shopping orders, coupons for free gas are offered by Lambert Food Stores.

2. Find the active voice verbs. Then change these active voice sentences to passive voice.

a. John Hinkley shot President Reagan.

b. The chemist introduced sulfuric acid to the mixture.

c. Shelly Malone, your teacher's aide, sent three difficult students to the office last week.

d. An unknown person robbed Mr. Miller's convenient mart last Thursday evening.

e. Onyx Computer provides you with complete support.

f. You waste fuel when you idle your car at stop signs.

g. Balducci's invites you to shop the big sale.

h. The technician in framing spilled glue on your portrait.

i. Jensen Furniture's quality assurance staff thoroughly tested the lounge chair's durability.

j. Helen finished the wedding cake two hours before the ceremony began.

3. Read the following memo. Consider the content and identify the audience. Decide which verbs should be active and which should be passive and revise accordingly.

TO:	Salvadore Alvarez, Public Relations Director
FROM:	Elenore Lucia, Crew Chief, Graphics
DATE:	October 31, 20—
SUBJECT:	Production Delay for Employee Appreciation Project

The artwork you requested for the Employee Appreciation display will not be ready for the November 15, 20—, deadline. While the graphics professionals usually are aware of scheduling, this time my assistant, Frank Stanwych, overlooked two other major projects.

Despite our problems, some of your requests will be completed on schedule. The two lighted stars can be hung from the skylight. The posters covered with employees' photographs may be printed. In addition, Erin Taft and Vince Delgado will produce the traditional Employees of the Year Awards booklet. The booklet will be available to visitors and staff beginning December 1.

GENDER-UNBIASED LANGUAGE

Technical writers should be sensitive to diversity in the workplace. One way to begin is to use gender-unbiased language.

TEACH

Use the Effective Transitions Teaching Master to teach techniques for making effective transitions in writing.

1. Avoid biased language by choosing words that include both genders.

USE	RATHER THAN	USE	RATHER THAN
representative	Congressman	synthetic	manmade
firefighter	fireman	polite	ladylike
police officer	policeman	doctor	woman doctor
mail carrier	mailman or postman	nurse	male nurse
chair/presiding officer	chairman	people/humanity/ human beings	mankind
supervisor/manager	foreman	synthetic	manmade

2. Avoid biased language by using pronoun references that include both genders.

The following sentence implies that all scientists are men:

> Each scientist files his laboratory's OSHA report after completing his quarterly review.

Two ways to solve this problem are to (1) reword the sentence to omit any reference to gender and (2) include both genders.

a. Each scientist files the laboratory OSHA report after completing the quarterly review.

b. All scientists file their laboratories' OSHA reports after completing their quarterly review.

c. Each scientist files his or her laboratory's OSHA report after completing the quarterly review. (Using *his or her* can be awkward when it is repeated in a number of sentences.)

3. Avoid biased language by referring to men and women in the same way when using courtesy titles in similar situations. The preferred title for women (unless you know the woman's preference) is *Ms.*

USE THIS	NOT THIS
Darnell Griggs and Erica Stokes	Darnell Griggs and Erica
Mr. Barnes and Ms. Pedroza	Peter Barnes and Ms. Pedroza
Austin and Kara Peterson	Mr. and Mrs. Austin Peterson
Caroline and Anthony Russo	Caroline Russo and her husband

1. a.   d.   f.

2. a. All of the paratroopers were trained to their maximum ability. b. Miss Maxine Faulkner, Mr. Faustino Diaz, and Mr. Kha'n Vu are listed as having senior security clearance. c. The doctor should begin her letter to the Swiss hospital administrator with *Dear Administrator"* because she does not know the administrator. d. All businesspeople need to be aware of their educational options. e. Nurses must record their observations in the patients' charts. f. All people are responsible for making the earth a cleaner, safer place to live. g. First Lady Michelle Obama, Supreme Court Justice Sonia Sotomayor, and former Vice President Al Gore appeared in the photograph. h. The supervisors (or managers) will file their reports with the CPD director each Friday. i. Did you ever want to be a firefighter or a police officer when you were young?

3. Answers will vary. One possible solution follows. Retirement Planning Committee: Dr. Patrice Harbaugh has been an excellent dentist for more than 20 years. Her colleagues send their best wishes, and patients at Mirabelle Center will miss her. Her team members—Benny Castillo, Alice Lazar, Theo Baines, and Melinda Baines—offer congratulations on her retirement.

4. Avoid biased language in letter salutations by including both sexes. Of course, you should use the receiver's name if at all possible. When you cannot determine the receiver's name, these options may be used:

   a. Use a job title such as Dear Personnel Officer.

   b. Omit the salutation and complimentary close (simplified letter style).

   c. As a last choice, use either of the following: Dear Sir or Madam or Dear Madam or Sir (alphabetical).

The Inside Track: Your Turn

1. In each pair of sentences [(a) and (b), (c) and (d), and (e) and (f)], select the sentence that uses gender most appropriately.

   a. The Human Resources Officer is responsible for notifying candidates of their interview day and time.
   b. The man in charge of the Human Resources Department is responsible for notifying each candidate of his interview day and time.

   c. The mailman is late, and I'm hoping for a response from Lucas Marthey and Julianna.
   d. The mail carrier is late, and I'm hoping for a response from Lucas and Julianna Marthey.

   e. A female pastor conducted the funeral service.
   f. An Episcopal pastor conducted the funeral service.

2. Revise the following sentences to eliminate biased language.

   a. Each of the paratroopers was trained to his maximum ability.

   b. Miss Maxine Faulkner, Fausto Diaz, and Kha'n Vu are listed as having senior security clearance.

   c. The woman doctor should begin her letter to the Swiss hospital administrator with *Dear Sir* because she does not know the administrator.

   d. Any businessman needs to be aware of his educational options.

   e. The nurse must record her observations on the patients' charts.

   f. All mankind is responsible for making the earth a cleaner, safer place to live.

   g. Mrs. Michelle Obama, Supreme Court Justice Sonia Sotomayor, and Al Gore appeared in the photograph.

   h. The foremen will file their reports with the CPD director each Friday.

   i. Did you ever want to be a fireman or a policeman when you were young?

3. Revise the following paragraph to avoid gender-biased language.

   To Whom It May Concern: Dr. Patrice Harbaugh has been an excellent female dentist for more than 20 years. Each of her colleagues sends his best wishes, and patients at Mirabelle Center will miss her. Her team members—Dr. Castillo, Miss Alice Lazar, and Theo and Melinda Baines—offer congratulations on her retirement.

EFFECTIVE TRANSITIONS

Like any good writing, technical documents need logical connections between ideas. These connections make writing smooth and improve readers' comprehension. The following four techniques help a writer achieve these logical relationships between ideas and between sentences and paragraphs:

- Repeated keywords
- Pronouns
- Parallel structures
- Transitional terms

TEACH
Use the Transitional Terms Teaching Master and suggest that students refer to this list and practice incorporating some of the terms they do not use often.

Repeated Keywords

Repeated keywords often refer to the topic or important information in a document. They remind readers of what is significant in the discussion or what the document is trying to achieve. For example, if you were writing about lumber cut for housing construction, you might begin with the word *lumber* and later repeat that word or use synonyms such as *boards, logs, planks*, or *timber*.

Pronouns

While repeating keywords can improve coherence, using the same word over and over can become boring. Therefore, writers also use pronouns to tie ideas together. Read the partial instructions below to see how the pronouns connect ideas and improve coherence.

> When you are planning to paddle down a river, get an accurate large-scale map and mark the rapids on it. Study it and keep it handy. Rapids are caused by a drop in the riverbed, so remember that you might not see them when you approach.

The pronoun *it* refers to map, and the pronoun *them* refers to rapids. The difference in the singular *it* (*map* is singular) and the plural *them* (*rapids* is plural) keeps readers from becoming confused.

Parallel Structures

Writers also use parallel structures to link content within and between sentences. Like parallel lines, parallel structures in writing are aligned, meaning that words, phrases, and sentences are grammatically similar, as shown in the next pair of examples.

> Survey respondents preferred ice fishing, skiing, snowboarding, and skating.
>
> *not*
>
> Survey respondents preferred ice fishing, skiing, snowboarding, and to skate.

> As a parent, I care about the safety of my children. As a police officer, I care about the rights of individuals. And as a citizen, I care about getting criminals off the streets.
>
> *not*
>
> As a parent, I care about the safety of my children. The rights of individuals is important to me in my role as a police officer. Because I am a concerned citizen, I want to get criminals off the streets.

The repeated grammatical structure helps to connect ideas.

Transitional Terms

Transitional terms (or transitions), the fourth technique for improving coherence, are words or phrases that highlight the relationships between ideas.

Below is a list of some transitional terms you might use. The column on the left indicates the relationship the term implies in its connection.

MEANING	TRANSITIONAL TERMS
Addition	*also, in addition, moreover, furthermore, and, as well as, besides*
Contrast	*but, however, yet, nevertheless, on the contrary, on the other hand*
Time	*before, after, currently, afterward, during, later, now, recently, then, meanwhile, while, at the same time*
Emphasis	*in fact, of course, indeed, truly*
Example	*for instance, for example, to illustrate*
Sequence	*first, second, third,* and so on; *next; finally; last*
Cause and effect	*therefore, consequently, thus*
Similarity	*likewise, similarly, also, in the same way*

The following paragraph shows how transitional terms can be used to improve coherence.

> This past summer I had guests from Sweden who told me about cooking in bed. <u>At first</u>, I thought my friend sat in bed while preparing vegetables. <u>No</u>, she told me that she literally cooks her food in bed <u>while she goes to the beach</u>. <u>For example</u>, she starts potatoes on the stove and <u>once the water is boiling</u>, removes the pot from the stove, places it in the bed, and surrounds it with blankets. The potatoes are done <u>when she returns a few hours later</u>. <u>However</u>, I would be concerned about bacteria growing during this kind of low-temperature slow cooking.

ASSESS

Your Turn

1. a. A thunderstorm is a process. *It* begins with warm air rising. *The storm then* feeds on moisture and heat. *As* the rising air becomes cooler, water drops form from the condensing vapor. A picture of the air currents inside a *thunderhead* could look like a nest of writhing

The Inside Track: Your Turn

1. Identify transitional elements in the following passages.

   a. A thunderstorm is a process. It begins with warm air rising. The storm then feeds on moisture and heat. As the rising air becomes cooler, water drops form from the condensing vapor. A picture of the air currents inside a thunderhead could look like a nest of writhing snakes.

   b. In 1940, Comity's hired its first female employee. In 1948, Comity's made that employee the company president.

   c. The PTO shaft was slightly bent in the crash. Consequently, I cannot operate the conveyor belt.

2. Revise the following sentences to create parallel structure.

   a. With the new Najik, enjoy scanning that is faster, works more precisely, and that can be more economical than ever before.

   b. First is the group that reacts to the trend by selling every energy stock in the portfolio. As a result of the trend, the second group responds with a threat to sell every energy stock in the portfolio.

   c. First, select a single or double mat for the print, and then the picture will need a frame, and finally you must choose whether to use nonglare or plain glass.

   d. Security officers will be stationed in the following locations:

   - In the entrance foyer
   - The computing center
   - The president's office will be heavily guarded
   - Two officers will be on the roof of the manufacturing building.

   e. According to some users, the Turbo 040 is the superior product; others say the best machine is the ChipStar.

3. Combine each of the following groups of short, choppy sentences into a single sentence by using transition strategies.

   a. The veterinarian prescribed an anesthetic. The anesthetic was for the dog. The pharmacy could not fill the prescription.

   b. Sound waves that hit a plain wall bounce back to distort the sound. Sonex-covered walls absorb sound waves that hit the walls. Absorbing these waves enhances the sound.

   c. The problem with the collating machine is worn gears. The mirrors on the collating machine are scratched and are part of the problem. The collating machine's levers, which are bent, are a problem.

   d. To apply for the position, job candidates must fill out an application form. They must fill out the form completely. The candidates must submit a resume. They must supply a list of three references.

Glossary

A

abstracts short, concise versions of longer pieces of communication; include only the most important general information

academic writing the expository and persuasive writing done in academic circles; examples include personal essays, research papers, analyses, and arguments

accommodate to adjust; to change circumstances so that others will be more comfortable or more at ease

acronyms letters that stand for a long or complicated term or series of terms

adrenaline a stimulant; something that excites and creates extra energy

ambiguous more than one interpretation is possible; describes writing that means different things to different people

anecdote a humorous story

animation text or graphics that move

annotations handwritten notes, often placed in the margins of a document being read

anticipate to guess or predict before actually reading a passage what kind of reasoning it might present

appendix (plural, *appendixes*) usually the last element or special part of a formal report; a place to include documents, data, or graphics not necessary to the discussion in the report but perhaps helpful or interesting to the audience

archives collections or repositories of documents

auditory related to the sense of hearing or perceived through the sense of hearing

B

background knowledge knowledge and vocabulary that a reader has already learned and then calls upon to better understand new information

bar graph a graph using a horizontal axis and a vertical axis to compare numerical data presented in rectangular bars

block letter style the letter style that aligns the return address, dateline, and closing at the left margin

blog a website with periodic news or commentary posted in reverse chronological order; short for *weblog*

buffer something positive written to soften bad news to come

C

callouts names of specific parts of a diagram that are connected to the diagram or drawing with lines

cautions statements designed to keep a person from harming the mechanism with which he or she is working

chart a drawing with boxes, words, and lines to show a process or an organizational structure

chronological resume a traditional resume that provides a history of employment and education in reverse chronological order

citations written indications of the sources for borrowed materials

close-ended questions questions that restrict the number of possible answers

code of ethics a written pledge to make responsible, moral decisions

collaborative writing writing with others in a group

conclusion the logical, inductive leap made after all of the details of an experiment are considered; what is learned from an experiment

concurrent testing determining the usefulness of a product or an activity by observing someone's performance while he or she is using the product or engaging in the activity

copyediting proofreading a document for correctness in spelling, grammar, and mechanics

corporate code of ethics a document stating a company's commitment to ethical behavior; includes core values, rules specific to the industry, and often penalties for violations

cover letter a letter accompanying a resume that highlights the applicant's strengths

criteria the plural form of *criterion;* the factors on which a decision is made; things to consider when making a decision

culture the special beliefs, customs, or values that are specific to a particular group of people or a particular region

D

dateline the feature of a press release that identifies the location of a story

decision flowchart a type of flowchart that uses symbols to indicate the critical steps in making a decision

deductive reasoning reasoning from the general to the particular

demographics defining characteristics of an audience; information about a group such as the age, sex, income, and educational level of its members

design elements considerations in writing a document that affect page layout; the way a document looks

diagram a line drawing

dignity a person's sense of self-respect

direct approach a presentation strategy in which the main idea is stated first, then the idea is explained and supported with details

direct quotation the use of borrowed ideas, words, phrases, and sentences exactly as they appear in the original source

discussion forum a website where users can discuss items of interest or get specific questions answered

documentation a system of giving credit for borrowed ideas and words

draft an early version of a document that is subject to change

drafting the stage after planning when the writer actually writes a first, second, or third (or later) version of the document

E

electronic resume a chronological or functional resume that is formatted so that it can be sent electronically as an e-mail resume, an ASCII Text resume, a scannable resume, or an online resume

embargo to withhold or delay publication of a story

ethics a system of moral standards and rules that guides human behavior

executive summary a short synopsis of the content of a proposal that is written to meet the needs of a busy decision maker; it is located after the table of contents in a formal proposal

explanation information coming after a step that provides additional data to clarify the step

exploding pie graph pie graph that separates, or "explodes,"one wedge from the graph, drawing attention to that piece of the pie

expository writing writing to explain or inform

expressive writing writing to express or portray personal observation or feeling

external audience receivers outside the sender's organization; listeners outside an organization

F

FAQ an acronym for *Frequently Asked Questions;* a document posted on the Internet containing answers to common questions about a topic

feedback the verbal and nonverbal response to a communication process or product

field research research done in the field, especially through surveys and interviews

field-test to check instructions with a small sample of people to see whether the instructions are clear

fiscal year an organization's operating year

flowchart a drawing with lines and arrows to show a process or series of steps

follow-up letter a letter thanking a prospective employer for an interview

forensic reports investigative reports that analyze evidence for legal purposes

formal outline a listing of main ideas and subtopics arranged in a traditional format of Roman numerals, capital letters, numbers, and lowercase letters

formal presentations presentations that are planned in advance, carefully prepared and rehearsed, and often accompanied by visual aids

formal table numerical information set up in rows and columns and drawn with rules; used to present figures

format the details of a document's arrangement: the type of document, its length, the preferred style manual, and its organization; the layout of a publication; standard elements of a document's presentation

freewriting writing freely to discover an idea; can be open (no topic yet), focused (on a topic), or looping (stopping, summarizing, and continuing)

functional resume a nontraditional resume that organizes information around a person's unique skills in order to highlight his or her special abilities or experience

G

Gantt chart a type of bar graph used to schedule the major tasks of a complex project; it uses bars to depict the length of time needed to complete each task

goodwill a feeling of friendship; the value of doing things that create mutual admiration and respect

graphic organizers the use of circles, rectangles, and connecting lines in notes to show the relative importance of one piece of information to another

graphics information presented in a visual form, such as tables, graphs, and diagrams

groupthink the tendency of group members to conform to the wishes of the group without thinking through an issue individually

H

hierarchical order the order in which names are listed from the top to the bottom of an organizational chart

home page the first page of a website

hooks in a news story, opening elements whose purpose is to engage the reader, grab his or her attention, and lead into the subject; attention-getters; words or sentences designed to engage the reader or to create interest in an idea

hyperlink a word, phrase, or graphic used to allow readers of a web page to move easily to another page; also called a *link*

I

icon a simple, easily recognizable picture or drawing that represents an idea or a concept; often used as a signal for recurring ideas or themes in a document

imaginative writing writing such as novels, short stories, drama, and poetry whose situations grow out of fantasy or imagination; events and people are fictional although the themes may reveal universal truths

imperative mood the form of a verb that signals a command or an instruction; the subject is "you" or understood "you"

incident reports reports that objectively relate the details of unusual events, such as accidents or equipment malfunctions

indirect approach a presentation strategy in which the main idea is not presented up front; the speaker builds evidence to convince the audience of his or her point

inductive reasoning reasoning from the particular to the general

inferences judgments about a reading that the author does not make for the reader

informal outline a listing of main ideas and subtopics arranged in a less traditional format of single headings and indented notes

informal presentations presentations that occur without preparation or rehearsal

informal table a graphic that uses rows and columns drawn without rules or stubs

instructions a sequence of steps explaining how to complete a task

interactive refers to any document, such as a website, that responds to user input

internal audience receivers inside the sender's organization; listeners within an organization

Internet a global system of networks connecting computers through the World Wide Web, e-mail, instant messaging, and other protocols

J

jargon the highly specialized language of a discipline or technical field

K

keywords important words, especially nouns, that indicate subject areas in a web document; words in a scannable resume that match the employer's list of key qualifications

L

letter of transmittal a letter formally or officially conveying a formal report from the writers to the external audience

limitations factors or situations that prevent problem solving

line graph a graph using a horizontal axis and a vertical axis to show a trend or relationship among numbers

literary reading reading literature such as short stories, essays, poetry, and novels

M

mechanism description a description of the main parts of a device or machine; includes the purpose of the device and an overall description, a description of the parts, and the function of each part

media systems or means of mass communication

medium a means by which information is conveyed, such as a newspaper article, a television commercial, or a speech before a live audience

memo of transmittal a memo formally or officially conveying a formal report from the writers to the internal audience

modified block letter style the letter style in which the dateline and closing begin at the center of the page

multiple audience an audience that includes readers whose points of view differ

multiple bar graph a graph using horizontal and vertical axes to compare data, drawn with more than one bar for each measurement

multiple line graph a graph using more than one line to compare data

O

objectivity an attitude signifying that no personal bias or opinion has distorted or slanted a researcher's thinking

online instructions instructions using computer technology as the medium; include help menus, CD-ROMs, and web-based instructions

online resume a type of electronic resume posted on a website

open-ended questions questions that encourage the respondent to provide any answer he or she likes; the questions give no suggested answers

organizational chart a drawing with boxes, words, and lines to show how an organization is structured

P

pace to read efficiently; to read at a rate that is slow enough to allow the mind to absorb information but fast enough to complete the reading assignment

pagination the assignment of sequential page numbers within a document

parallel structure use of the same grammatical structure of a phrase or sentence

paraphrase to present someone else's ideas in your own words, phrases, and sentence structure

passive voice the verb *to be* plus the past participle of the verb; used in scientific writing to focus on the process instead of the performer

periodic reports reports that explain the accomplishments for all projects of a work group or of an entire organization during the reporting period

periodicals materials published at specified intervals of time, such as magazines, journals, newsletters, and newspapers

personal code of ethics a personal creed or philosophy that expresses an individual's core values

persuasive writing writing to convince others

pictograph a type of bar graph that uses pictures instead of bars to represent data

pie graph a circular graph showing how parts relate to the whole, which equals 100 percent

plagiarism the act of using another person's words and/or ideas without properly documenting their source or giving credit

planning the first stage of the writing process, during which a writer thinks of an idea and plans how to develop and research it

point-by-point organization a comparison/contrast structure that covers two or three items under one criterion

population the group from whom you want to gather data

prefatory material parts or elements of a report (letter or memo of transmittal, title page, and table of contents) that come before the main text

previewing looking over a reading assignment before reading it; determining the subject matter and any questions about the material before reading it

primary audience the readers or listeners to whom you are responsible first; often the readers(s) who requested or authorized the document

primary sources direct or firsthand reports of facts or observations, such as an eyewitness account or a diary

principles rules that guide behavior

priority order the organization of a resume that presents information from most important to least important

progress reports reports that describe the work that has been completed during a specified time on only one project

proposal a persuasive document that offers a solution to an identified problem or need

PSAs an acronym for *public service announcements;* news published for the benefit of the public

public relations plans or actions taken by an individual or an organization to create a positive relationship with the public

publishing sending a document to the person who requested it

purpose a specific end or outcome to be obtained; what you want your reader to do after reading your document

R

rank the relative importance of one criterion to another; usually ranked from most important to least important

receptive audience readers who are open to ideas or suggestions in a recommendation report

recommendation report a report that responds to a need that arises in the workplace; it suggests the best solution to a problem or need, helping the readers to make a choice

recursive a circular or back-and-forth motion; describes the movement of the writing process back and forth between predictable stages

reliable data data that provide results that can be duplicated under similar circumstances

reporting period the time span covered by a report

resignation letter a letter written to an employer or a supervisor stating the writer's intention to resign his or her position with the company

respondents people chosen to answer questions

result an observable effect of an experiment

resume a one- or two-page summary of a person's job qualifications; uses elements of page design to highlight the applicant's most impressive qualifications

retrospective testing checking the usefulness of a product or an activity after someone has used the product or performed the activity

reverse chronological order the organization of a resume that presents information backward in time

revising reading a document and making changes in content, organization, and word choice

RFPs an acronym for *request for proposal;* an advertisement seeking proposals to solve a problem or fill a need and often listing criteria for the solution

rhetorical question a question designed to provoke thought; a question for which the speaker expects no answer

rights personal freedoms that must be respected

role the function or job someone performs at work

RSS an acronym for *Really Simple Syndication;* standardized web feed formats that allow blog posts to be sent directly to readers

S

sample a subgroup with the same characteristics as the entire population

scannable refers to text for the Web that allows readers to locate important words and phrases quickly, using short paragraphs and sentences, headings, lists, and keywords

scannable resumes resumes written to be scanned for keywords by an optical scanner

scientific method the use of both inductive and deductive reasoning and a system of controls to objectively explore natural phenomena

scope the extent of treatment, activity, or influence; what is included and what is not included; what you examine in your efforts to solve a particular problem

secondary audience the reader(s) to whom you are responsible after you have met the needs of the primary audience

secondary sources indirect or secondhand reports of information, such as the description of an event the writer or speaker did not witness

shaping a step early in the writing process during which a writer narrows a topic, determines a direction for a topic, generates subtopics, and organizes the subtopics

solicited refers to a document, such as a report, in which readers ask for several alternatives

solicited letter a letter of application written for an advertised position

solicited proposal a proposal that is written in response to an RFP or upon the request of a supervisor or manager

spatial order refers to mechanism descriptions that explain the parts from left to right, right to left, top to bottom, or bottom to top or in another logical pattern

specific audience a single person or group whose point of view is the same

standard a means of defining and limiting a criterion

step one action in a set of instructions

style the way an author uses words and sentences

subcriteria smaller categories under a category that help to define each criterion

summarize to condense longer material, keeping essential or main ideas and omitting unnecessary parts such as examples and illustrations

summary a condensed version of a piece of communication; includes general information and may include a few important details

T

target audience the audience for which a message is written; the audience with whom the writer seeks to communicate

technical communication communication done in the workplace; the subject is usually technical; the purpose and audience are specific; the approach is straightforward

technical reading reading science, business, or technology publications

technical vocabulary specialized words used in specific ways unique to a particular discipline

technical writing writing done in the workplace; the subject is usually technical, written carefully for a specific audience; the organization is predictable and apparent; the style is concise; the tone is objective and businesslike; special features include visual elements

tentative outline an informal, changeable plan for organizing topics and subtopics

testimonials personal stories or people's statements (often from famous people) that endorse a product or service

text file an ASCII plain text file that can be opened by most word processing programs

tone emotional overtones; the way words make readers feel

trip reports reports that tell what was accomplished during a trip and what was learned from the trip

U

unreceptive audience readers who are not open to ideas or suggestions

unsolicited refers to a document, such as a report, that has not been asked for; the audience is not expecting the recommendations

unsolicited letter a letter of application written for an unadvertised position

unsolicited proposal a proposal in which the writer identifies a problem or need that he or she discovered, explains it, and offers solutions

usability the ease with which an audience can access and use a website

utility a means of evaluating actions based on what will do the most good and the least harm

V

valid data data that provide an accurate measurement of what an individual intends to measure

values ideals that govern a person's or an organization's actions

verbal tables tables that use words instead of numbers and the information is given in rows and columns

W

warnings statements designed to keep a person from being harmed

Web Accessibility Initiative (WAI) a program intended to make web content available to users with a wide range of disabilities; websites should follow the program's Web Content Accessibility Guidelines 2.0

whistle-blower a person who publicly alleges an organization's wrongful practices

wiki a website that allows users to author web pages collaboratively

World Wide Web a collection of online resources such as websites

writing process the stages a writer goes through to write a document; includes planning (prewriting, shaping, researching), drafting and revising, and copyediting

BBC (British Broadcasting Corporation), 24
Beattie, Meredith, 328
BEL Group, The, 328
Bias
  avoiding, 218
  in commercial websites, 59
  critical thinking to identify, 389
  in language, 31
Bibliographies
  in documentation, 54–55
  in tables, 148
  working, 43
Big Brothers, 101
BlackBerry handheld device, 128
BlackBerry User Guide, 229
Black box warning, for drugs, 241
Blackwell, Christopher, 22
Blaming, ethics *versus,* 379
Blind Copy, in e-mail, 112
Block letter style, 121
Blogs, 179–180
Body, of document, 87
Body of discussion, for proposals, 344, 351–353
Body language, 97
Boldface, to highlight, 139, 255, 261
BookShelved.com, 181
Borders, 173
Boulder Nonlinear Systems (BNS), 212
Brainstorming, 311
Brand Union, The, 307
Breadcrumb trail, for web pages, 171
Brief correspondence. *See* Correspondence
British Broadcasting Corporation (BBC), 24
Britton, W. Earl, 16
Brown & Williamson Tobacco, 377
Budget, for proposals, 336
Buffer, in bad new correspondence, 124–125
Build Your Foundation feature
  audience and purpose, 40
  correspondence, 132
  design of documents, 162
  ethics, 380–381
  informative reports, 208
  instructions, 247–248
  investigative reports, 225–226
  presentations, 300
  proposals, 359–360
  recommendation reports, 323–324
  resumes, 275–277
  technical reading, 399
  technical research, 74

technical writing overview, 18
  Web, writing for, 183–184
  writing process, 100
Bulleted lists
  in correspondence, 108, 112
  in discussion forums, 182
  for emphasis, 139, 255
  guidelines for, 285
  as special feature, 14
  in trip reports, 215
Bulletin boards, electronic, 182
Bureau of Labor Statistics, U.S. Department of
    Labor, 16
Burke, James, 367
Business letters, 8, 121. *See also* Resumes
Business Management and Administration, 250

C

Callouts, in diagrams, 159, 193
Capital letters, 138–139, 255, 285
Care, ethics and, 376
CareerOneStop website, 262
Careers. *See* Resumes; Writing at Work feature
Case studies, 307
Catalog of U.S. Government Publications, 51
Cause-to-effect order, as organization, 84–85,
    219, 389
Cautions, in instructions, 233–234
CDs (compact disks), 35
Character, on resumes, 251
Charts, 142, 155–158
Chicago Manual of Style, The, 37, 53
Chronological order, as organization, 84, 256–257
Chronological resumes, 257–258
Citations, 44, 55–57
Clarity, 6
Classifying, as organization, 84
Clichés, avoiding, 176
Clinical trials, 219
Clip art, 14
Close-ended questions, 67
Cluster mapping, 83
Clusty.com, 50
CNN television, 201
Code of Ethics, 369–372
Collaborative writing, 79, 93–98
  advantages of, 93–94
  disadvantages of, 94–95
  organizing, 95–97
  wikis for, 181
  work habits for, 97–98

Microsoft PowerPoint software for, 134, 290, 298
organization of, 287–288
outlines and notes for, 290–292
overview, 281
personal appearance in, 291
rehearsing, 293–294
room check for, 294–295
stage fright and, 287
summarizing, 189
time expectations for, 287
topics for, 283
website, 60
Write to Learn feature, 278
Writing at Work feature, 280
Your Turn feature, 300–301
Press releases, 201–206
Previewing technical reading, 387
Prewriting, 110–114, 340–342
Primary audiences, 30
Primary sources, 64–72
definition of, 46
example of, 44
experimentation, 71–72
interviews, 68–70
observation, 70–71
surveys, 64–68
Principles, ethical, 365, 376
Print form, 47–48
Priority order, as organization, 257
Privacy, 112, 114, 179
Problem and solution, as organization, 84–85
Problem-solving strategy, for proposals, 332–333
Procedures, 32
Processes, description of, 219
Production artists, technical writers as, 14
Professional appearance, 107
Professions, writing in, 7. *See also* Writing at Work feature
Progress reports, 198–201
Project management, 105
Proportions, in graphs, 158
Proposals, 9, 326–361
Build Your Foundation feature, 359–360
Community Connection feature, 361
description of, 329–331
example of, 327
Focus feature, 326
formal, 340–357
example of, 346–357
parts of, 342–345
prewriting, 340–342
informal, 334–339

primary audiences for, 31
problem-solving strategy for, 332–333
Write to Learn feature, 326
Writing at Work feature, 328
Your Turn feature, 360–361
ProQuest databases, 49
PSAs (public service announcements), 201
Psychology Today, 24
Publication dates, 57
Publication Manual of the American Psychological Association, 37, 53
Public Broadcasting System (PBS), 52
Public domain, 53
Public relations, 201
Publishing, 53, 91–92
Pulitzer Prize, 52
Punctuation, 121, 261, 266–267
Purpose
of design, 141–142
of document, 33–34, 38, 40–41
on home page, 178
of website, 60
in writing for Web, 168
See also Audiences for technical writing

Q

Quantitative scales, for graphs, 158
QuarkXPress software, 12
Questionnaires, 243
Questions
for interviews, 69
in notetaking, 394
in presentations, 298
for revising, 89
rhetorical, 288
to shape ideas, 83
for surveys, 66–67
Quotations
citations for, 55
for informative reports, 192
in notetaking, 63–64
to support topic, 87

R

Ragged right text, 138
Ranking criteria, 318
Rationalization, ethics *versus,* 379
Readability, 89, 145, 166, 285
Readers. *See* Audiences for technical writing
Reading. *See* Technical reading
Reasoning, 217, 388
Receptive audiences, 309